Reading & Language

INSIDE

LANGUAGE · LITERACY · CONTENT

PROGRAM AUTHORS

David W. Moore

Deborah J. Short

Michael W. Smith

Alfred W. Tatum

Josefina Villamil Tinajero

Acknowledgments

Grateful acknowledgment is given to the authors, artists, photographers, museums, publishers, and agents for permission to reprint copyrighted material. Every effort has been made to secure the appropriate permission. If any omissions have been made or if corrections are required, please contact the Publisher.

Photographic Credits

Cover (front): Squirrel Treefrog in Hibiscus Flower, JH Pete Carmichael. Photograph © JH Pete Carmichael/Riser/Getty Images.
Cover (back): Hibiscus Flower, Bali, Indonesia, Loeiza Jacq. Photograph © Loeiza Jacq/Gamma-Rapho via Getty Images.

Acknowledgments continue on page 670.

For product information and technology asistance, contact us at
Cengage Learning Customer & Sales Support, 1-800-354-9706

For permission to use material from this text or product, submit all requests online at **www.cengage.com/permissions**
Further permissions questions can be emailed to
permissionrequest@cengage.com

National Geographic Learning | Cengage Learning
1 Lower Ragsdale Drive
Building 1, Suite 200
Monterey, CA 93940

Cengage Learning is a leading provider of customized learning solutions with office locations around the globe, including Singapore, the United Kingdom, Australia, Mexico, Brazil, and Japan. Locate your local office at **www.cengage.com/global**.

Visit National Geographic Learning online at **ngl.cengage.com**
Visit our corporate website at **www.cengage.com**

Printer: RR Donnelley, Willard, OH

ISBN: 978-12854-37125

Printed in the United States of America

13 14 15 16 17 18 19 20 21 22

10 9 8 7 6 5 4 3 2 1

Contents at a Glance

Reviewers

We gratefully acknowledge the many contributions of the following dedicated educators in creating a research-based program that is appealing to and motivating for middle school students. In addition to the contributors listed below, we also thank the many teachers, students, and administrators whose feedback over the last several years helped shape the original program and this updated program.

Dr. René Saldaña, Jr., Ph.D.
Texas Tech University

Dr. Saldaña teaches English and education and is a widely published trade book writer. His books include *The Jumping Tree* and *Finding Our Way: Stories*. His stories have also appeared in anthologies such as such as *Guys Write for GUYS Read, Face Relations, Every Man for Himself* and in magazines like *Boy's Life* and *READ*.

Teacher Reviewers

Idalia Apodaca
English Language Development Teacher
Shaw Middle School
Spokane, WA

Pat E. Baggett-Hopkins
Area Reading Coach
Chicago Public Schools
Chicago, IL

Judy Chin
ESOL Teacher
Arvida Middle School
Miami, FL

Sonia Flores
Teacher Supporter
Los Angeles Unified School District
Los Angeles, CA

Brenda Garcia
ESL Teacher
Crockett Middle School
Irving, TX

Margaret Jan Graham
Montford Middle School
Tallahassee, FL

Susan Harris
Department Head Language Arts
Cobb Middle School
District - Leon
Tallahassee, FL

Kristine Hoffman
Teacher on Special Assignment
Newport-Mesa Unified School District
Costa Mesa, CA

Patricia James
Reading Specialist
Brevard County
Melbourne Beach, FL

Dr. Margaret R. Keefe
ELL Contact and Secondary Advocate
Martin County School District
Stuart, FL

Julianne Kosareff
Curriculum Specialist
Paramount Unified School District
Paramount, CA

Lore Levene
Coordinator of Language Arts
Community Consolidated School
District 59
Arlington Heights, IL

Kathleen Malloy
9th Grade Coordinator and Reading Coach
Godby High School
Tallahassee, FL

Natalie M. Mangini
Teacher/ELD Coordinator
Serrano Intermediate School
Lake Forest, CA

Laurie Manikowski
Teacher/Trainer
Lee Mathson Middle School
San Jose, CA

Patsy Mills
Supervisor, Bilingual-ESL
Houston Independent School District
Houston, TX

Juliane M. Prager-Nored
High Point Expert
Los Angeles Unified School District
Los Angeles, CA

Patricia Previdi
ESOL Teacher
Patapsco Middle School
Ellicott City, MD

Dr. Louisa Rogers
Middle School Team Leader
Broward County Public Schools
Fort Lauderdale, FL

Rebecca Varner
ESL Teacher
Copley-Fairlawn Middle School
Copley, OH

Hailey F. Wade
ESL Teacher/Instructional Specialist
Lake Highlands Junior High
Richardson, TX

Cassandra Yorke
ESOL Coordinator
Palm Beach School District
West Palm Beach, FL

Program Authors

David W. Moore, Ph.D. Arizona State University

Dr. Moore taught high school in Arizona public schools before becoming a professor of education. He co-chaired the International Reading Association's Commission on Adolescent Literacy and has published research reports, articles, book chapters, and complete books including *Developing Readers and Writers in the Content Areas, Teaching Adolescents Who Struggle with Reading*, and *Principled Practices for Adolescent Literacy*.

Deborah J. Short, Ph.D. Center for Applied Linguistics

Dr. Short is a co-developer of the research-validated SIOP Model for sheltered instruction. She has directed scores of studies on English Language Learners and published scholarly articles in *TESOL Quarterly, The Journal of Educational Research, Language Teaching Research*, and many others. Dr. Short also co-wrote a policy report: *Double the Work: Challenges and Solutions to Acquiring Language and Academic Literacy for Adolescent English Language Learners*.

Michael W. Smith, Ph.D. Temple University

Dr. Michael Smith has won awards for his teaching both at the high school and college level. He contributed to the Common Core State Standards initiative by serving on the Aspects of Text Complexity working group. His books include *"Reading Don't Fix No Chevys": Literacy in the Lives of Young Men, Fresh Takes on Teaching Literary Elements: How to Teach What Really Matters About Character, Setting, Point of View, and Theme*, and *Oh, Yeah?! Putting Argument to Work Both in School and Out*.

Alfred W. Tatum, Ph.D. University of Illinois at Chicago

Dr. Tatum began his career as an eighth-grade teacher and reading specialist. He conducts research on the power of texts and literacy to reshape the life outcomes of striving readers. Dr. Tatum's books include *Reading for Their Life: Re-Building the Textual Lineages of African American Adolescent Males* and *Teaching Reading to Black Adolescent Males: Closing the Achievement Gap*.

Josefina Villamil Tinajero, Ph.D. University of Texas at El Paso

Dr. Tinajero consults with school districts to design ESL, bilingual, literacy, and biliteracy programs. She has served on state and national advisory committees for standards development, including English as a New Language Advisory Panel of the National Board of Professional Teaching Standards. Dr. Tinajero has served as president of the National Association of Bilingual Education and the Texas Association of Bilingual Education.

DECISION
Point

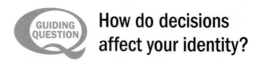
How do decisions
affect your identity?

Writing ✏

▶ **Paragraph**
Problem-and-Solution, Chronological Order, Spatial-Order, Compare-and-Contrast
▶ **Personal Narrative**

Pages 1W–65W

STAND
OR
FALL

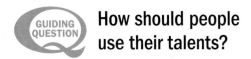
How should people use their talents?

Writing ✏

▶ **Summary Paragraph**
▶ **Modern Fairy Tale**

Pages 66W–107W

MAKING A
DIFFERENCE

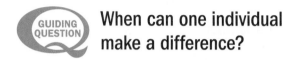 **When can one individual make a difference?**

Writing ✎
▶ **Problem-Solution Paragraph**
▶ **Problem-and-Solution Essay**

Pages 108W–147W

At Home in the
World

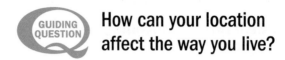

GUIDING QUESTION How can your location affect the way you live?

Writing ✎
▶ **Research Report**

Pages 148W–225W

OUR PRECIOUS WORLD

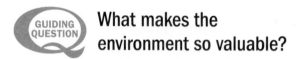 **What makes the environment so valuable?**

Writing ✎
▶ **Narrative Poem**
▶ **Business Letter**
▶ **Friendly Letter**

Pages 226W–261W

CONFLICT AND
RESOLUTION

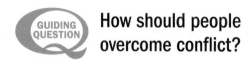 How should people overcome conflict?

FAIR IS FAIR

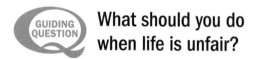

GUIDING QUESTION What should you do when life is unfair?

INSIDE

Writing ✎

▶ **Cause-and-Effect Paragraph**
▶ **Cause-and-Effect Essay**

Pages 304W–345W

Food for Thought

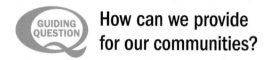

GUIDING QUESTION How can we provide for our communities?

Unit 8

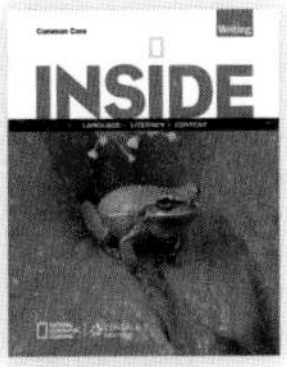

Writing
▶ **Public Service Announcement**
▶ **Persuasive Essay**

Pages 346W–385W

Genres at a Glance

DECISION
Point

GUIDING
QUESTION
Q

How do decisions affect your identity?

READ MORE!

Content Library
Making Healthy Choices
by Carolyn Newton

Leveled Library
Stuck in Neutral
by Terry Trueman
Facing the Lion
by Joseph Lemasolai Lekuton
and Herman Viola
Surviving Hitler
by Andrea Waren

Web Links
myNGconnect.com

◀ Indian immigrants attend a religious festival in
Barcelona, Spain.

Focus on Reading

Reading Strategies

Reading strategies are thinking tools that help you understand texts. Use reading strategies before, during, and after reading.

Plan: How It Works

To plan, first **preview** what you will read. Study headings, visuals, and boldface words to find out what the text is about. Then **set a purpose**. Decide what you intend to gain from the text. Finally, **predict** what you will read in the text. Form an opinion about what will happen next, then check, or confirm, your prediction as you read.

A Special Game

Last Saturday, my friends and family saw me play my first soccer game. A couple of minutes into the game, the ball was suddenly at my feet. I thought about Coach's advice to make quick decisions on the field. I passed the ball to Marco, who was near the goal. He kicked the ball and scored! I definitely made a good decision.

Monitor: How It Works

As you read, monitor your understanding of the text. If something is unclear or confusing, stop and reread or read on to clarify ideas and vocabulary. Change your reading pace. Read slowly when something is confusing or difficult. Read more quickly if you understand things well.

Plan: Practice Together

Preview and set a **purpose** for reading "A Special Game." Then, as you read, predict what will happen next. Confirm your predictions during and after reading.

Monitor: Practice Together

Reread "A Special Game." Tell a partner where you stopped to reread or read on. Explain how you figured out new words or ideas.

▶ **Plan**

Preview, set a **purpose**, and predict what you will find in the text before reading it more carefully.

▶ **Monitor**

Notice confusing parts in the text, then reread or read on to make them clear.

Strategy in Action

" The title tells me this text is about a special game. I expect to learn what made the game special. Yes, the first sentence mentions that this was the writer's first game. "

Strategy in Action

" As I read on, I discover that the narrator made a good decision that made the game special. "

Academic Vocabulary

• **purpose** (**pur**-pus) *noun*
A **purpose** is a reason for doing something.

Ask Questions: How It Works

As you read, stop and ask yourself questions to learn new information and to clarify words or ideas. Use a question word, such as *Who, What, When, Where, Why,* or *How.* Use the text to answer your questions.

Sometimes you might need to reread to find the answer. If the answer is not "right there," use the "think and search" strategy. Look all through the text and put together the information you find to answer the question.

▶ **Ask Questions**
Think actively by asking and answering questions about the text.

A Little Help

Sam's day began in the ordinary way. The usual kids were waiting at the bus stop. But today, a really big new kid was there, too. Sam saw him yank Juan's backpack off and start digging through it. Sam made a decision. He turned around and ran back home.

Five minutes later, Sam and his dad pulled up to the bus stop. Sam's dad soon sent the bully on his way. Sam was proud he made a choice that helped keep his friends safe.

Strategy in Action

" I wonder why Sam ran away from the bus stop. Why didn't he stay to help his friends?"

Strategy in Action

" I remember a story I read about a bully. I understand Sam's feelings."

Make Connections: How It Works

To make connections, think about how information in the text reminds you of experiences from your life, other texts you have read, or what you know about the world.

▶ **Make Connections**
Combine your knowledge and experiences with the author's ideas and information.

Ask Questions: Practice Together

Read "A Little Help." Pause when you read and ask a question. Reread to find an answer to your question.

Make Connections: Practice Together

Reread "A Little Help." Think about what you know or have read about young people making smart decisions to keep themselves and others safe. Make connections. Tell a partner about the connections and how they helped you understand the text.

Focus on Reading

Visualize: How It Works

Creating mental pictures while you read can help you better understand and remember information. Look for words that tell you how things look, sound, smell, taste, and feel. Picture the scene in your mind.

▶ **Visualize**
Imagine the sights, sounds, smells, tastes, and touch of what the author is describing.

Visualize: Practice Together

Read "A Pitcher's Choice" As you read, stop and create mental pictures in your mind. After you read, discuss what you visualized with a partner. Explain how your imagination helped you understand the text.

A Pitcher's Choice

On October 6, 1965, nearly 48,000 people gathered at Metropolitan Stadium in Minneapolis, Minnesota. It was the first game of the World Series between the Los Angeles Dodgers and the Minnesota Twins.

The familiar ballpark smells of popcorn and hotdogs filled the air. Excited fans proudly displayed their team colors. Loud cheering and good-natured arguing combined with peppy music as the teams warmed up.

As the game began, rowdy fans grew quiet. No doubt many of them mourned the fact that one of baseball's greatest pictures, the Dodgers' Sandy Koufax, would not be pitching.

You see, October 6, 1965, was Yom Kippur. This is the holiest of Jewish holy days. Koufax, a Jewish man, had decided he would not pitch on this day. The lefty was without a doubt the Dodgers' best pitcher. Many Dodgers fans refused to believe that he would not be there for the first game of the World Series. Koufax was more than a pitcher, however. He was a man of faith and a man of his word.

The Dodgers lost the opening game, but they won the Series. Who pitched the final game on October 14, 1965? Sandy Koufax, of course!

Strategy in Action

" I imagine the smell and taste of the ballpark food. I see and hear the excitement in the stadium."

Strategy in Action

" I was angry when my parents made me go visit a relative and miss a big concert. I infer that some fans were mad at Koufax for not pitching an important game."

Make Inferences: How It Works

Authors don't always state information directly. They give clues, and then you must "read between the lines" to make inferences. You also add your own knowledge and experiences to the author's clues so that you can better understand the text.

I read "This is the holiest of Jewish holy days. Koufax, a Jewish man, had decided he would not pitch on this day." **+**

I know that many people believe it is wrong to work on certain holy days. **=**

And so Pitching is Koufax's job, so he believes it is wrong to work on Yom Kippur.

▶ **Make Inferences**

When the author does not say something directly, use what you know to figure out what the author means.

Determine Importance: How It Works

When you determine importance, you look for and **identify** the main idea and the details that are necessary to understand the main idea. Use just the main idea and the most important details to summarize the text.

The main idea is...	The important details include...
Sandy Koufax did not pitch in the first game of the World Series.	• Koufax was one of baseball's greatest pitchers.

▶ **Determine Importance**

Focus your attention on the author's most significant ideas and information.

Make Inferences: Practice Together

Read "A Pitcher's Choice" again. As you read, look for other details in the text that are not fully explained. Use your own knowledge and experiences, along with the author's clues, to make inferences.

Determine Importance: Practice Together

Reread "A Pitcher's Choice." Look for and **identify** the main idea and supporting details, and also for details that mean something to you. Record what you find. After reading, summarize the main idea and share your summary with a partner.

Academic Vocabulary
- **identify** (ī-den-tu-fī) *verb*
  When you **identify** something, you name it or tell what it is.

Focus on Reading

Synthesize: How It Works

To synthesize, combine various ideas to come up with a new understanding of ideas in a text. You may draw conclusions by combining ideas to form clear statements of your understanding. You may form generalizations by combining your personal knowledge with ideas in the text to make a statement that applies to many situations.

▶ **Synthesize**

Combine ideas from the text and blend them into a new understanding.

Synthesize: Practice Together

Read "Dining Dilemma." Use text evidence from the selection and your own thoughts to draw conclusions and make generalizations.

Dining Dilemma

Every year on my birthday, I get to choose the restaurant where my family will go to celebrate. When I was little, the choice was pretty simple for me. I wanted to go to a place that served pizza and had a game room.

In recent years, however, I have agonized over the choice for weeks. The difficulty is that I really love all types of food now that I am older. Plus, we live in a big city with lots of different kinds of restaurants. How can I decide if I want Thai or Mexican, Indian or German, Italian or … well, you get the idea!

So, when I found out recently about a new restaurant in my neighborhood, my decision was easy. The restaurant is called The Tropic of Cancer. The menu includes foods from countries in a part of the globe called the Tropic of Cancer!

At The Tropic of Cancer, everyone in my family found a new favorite food. That was the best birthday present ever!

Strategy in Action

" The text tells a lot about restaurants in the narrator's city. I conclude that the narrator pays close attention to what is happening around him or her."

Try It!

Read "Skating into the Future." Use the reading strategies you've been practicing before, during, and after reading to help you understand the selection.

Skating into the Future

When do you know that it's time to make a big change in your life? How do you decide to let go of one thing and reach for another? Read about one young athlete's decision to try for a more well-rounded lifestyle.

Lena glided across the ice, stepped out of the rink, and sat down on a bench. It was the same bench she had sat on nearly every day during the past six years before and after practice. She also sat there during competitions while awaiting her scores.

Lena's duffel bag was in its usual place on the ground beside her. She reached in and grabbed her blade guards. As she snapped them into place, she fought back her tears. Was this really her last day with Coach Natalia? Was she really going to leave this bench, this skating rink behind her?

Lena had started ice-skating lessons when she was just 5 years old. She had loved skating so much that her parents had been willing to spend lots of money on her lessons, uniforms, and travel to competitions. They were proud of her skating, and they never complained about having to get up early to get her to the rink. Natalia and Lena had an hour of ice time before school every day. On Saturdays and Sundays, Lena's early morning lessons lasted three hours.

Now all that was ending. Lena had made the decision that other things in life were more important to her now than ice-skating. Besides, she could see that she had reached the peak of her abilities. She accepted the fact that she would never be on the Olympic skating team. Now it was time for a different kind of life.

She would miss the feeling of nailing a perfect jump or ending a twirl with a flourish, but she wanted to share a more typical teenage experience. She wanted to go to slumber parties and hang out with her friends on the weekends.

She was making the right decision, wasn't she? Lost in thought, she heard Natalia's soft voice behind her.

"Lena, I will miss you. You have been a wonderful student."

Lena turned, blinking her eyes to hold back the tears. She swallowed hard and smiled at her coach. "Natalia, I'll come and see you often. I will miss you too!"

"It is good, what you are doing, Lena. You are a young woman now. You should have a full life, enjoying everything. Remember what I taught you about jumping? You cannot learn a jump if you don't risk trying it. Sometimes you have to fall many times until you get it right."

Lena gave Natalia a big hug. "I remember. I will always remember all of your lessons."

As Lena walked outside, she focused on her future. She had a lot of plans to make. She was ready to keep her feet on the ground instead of on the ice. And yes, she was ready to try a few risky jumps.

Focus on Vocabulary

Use Word Parts

A **suffix** is a word part added to the end of a base word. The suffix changes the part of speech and the meaning of the word.

The suffix –*ful* means "full of." Add it to the noun *fear* and you change the noun into an adjective. The new word *fearful* means "full of fear."

EXAMPLE

base word	suffix

fear + ful = fearful

How the Strategy Works

When you read, you may come to a word you don't know. **Analyze** the meanings of the word parts to understand the whole word.

EXAMPLE   You cannot go to the store **shoeless**.

1. Look closely at the word to see if you know any of the parts.
2. If the word has a suffix, cover it up.   **shoeless**
3. Think about the meaning of the base word.
4. Uncover the suffix and determine its meaning.
5. Put the meanings of the word parts together to define the whole word. Be sure the meaning makes sense in the passage.

Follow the Strategy in Action to figure out the meaning of *wonderful*.

Who are you really? What makes you who you are? Is it your body? Is it your brain?

New discoveries have given us more knowledge about how our wonderful brains work. Even as babies, we already seem ready to learn. What we learn and when we learn it shapes how we continue to learn.

Strategy in Action

" I see the suffix -*ful* in this word. I'll cover it. There is the base word *wonder*. I know -*ful* means 'full of.' So *wonder* + *ful* means 'full of wonder.' "

☑ **REMEMBER** You can use the meanings of word parts to figure out the meanings of unknown words.

Academic Vocabulary
- **analyze** (a-nu-līz) *verb*
  When you **analyze**, you separate something into parts and examine, or study, it.

Practice Together

Read this passage aloud. Look at each underlined word. Find the word parts. Put their meanings together to figure out the meaning of each underlined word.

Suffix	Meaning
-ful	"full of"
-able, -ible	"can be" or "can do"
-ion, -tion	"act of"
-less	"without"

YOUR BRAIN
The Mind-Body Connection

You know that you use your brain to make decisions. You also know that your brain is part of your body. The connection between the brain and the rest of the body is one that scientists study carefully.

Your brain is a powerful organ. Your brain helps you make decisions about what to do with your body. For example, suppose you choose to stay up late. Then you skip breakfast.

The next morning your mind may not be as sharp as usual. You might feel dizzy and act careless.

Rest, food, exercise, stress, and even the air around you affect your brain. The understanding that taking care of your body takes care of your brain can be remarkable. Those choices may affect how well you make other decisions.

Try It!

Read this passage aloud. What is the meaning of each underlined word? How do you know?

The Decision

I have an important decision to make. Should I stay on the volleyball team or join the speech and debate team? I don't know what to do. I feel helpless and can't make a decision. I love playing volleyball and don't want to give it up. It's one of the most enjoyable sports to play. I want to join the speech and debate team to improve my speaking skills. I think the experience will be useful for me. The only problem is that they both have weekly practice at the same time. I can't do both at the same time. Which selection should I make? Do I try something new, or should I stick with what I do best?

American Names

by Tony Johnston

Diversity, 2005, Elizabeth Rosen. Acrylic on chipboard, collection of the artist.

SELECTION 1 OVERVIEW

▶ **Build Background**

▶ **Language & Grammar**
Ask and Answer Questions
Use Complete Sentences

▶ **Prepare to Read**
Learn Key Vocabulary
Plan, Monitor, Ask Questions

▶ **Read and Write**
Introduce the Genre
Realistic Fiction
Focus on Reading
Plan, Monitor, Ask Questions
Critical Thinking
Reading Fluency
Read with Intonation
Vocabulary Review
Write About the Guiding Question

▶ **Connect Across the Curriculum**
Vocabulary Study
Use Compound Words
Research/Speaking
Research Healthy Food
Language and Grammar
Ask and Answer Questions
Writing and Grammar
Write About Your Name

Build Background

What's in a Name?

Digital Library

myNGconnect.com
◐ View the video.

▲ Our names tell people who we are.

Connect

Anticipation Guide Think about your name and what it means to you. Then tell whether you agree or disagree with these statements.

	Agree	Disagree
1. Your name is an important part of who you are.	_____	_____
2. All names have a special meaning.	_____	_____
3. People judge others based on their names.	_____	_____

Anticipation Guide

Language & Grammar

Ask and Answer Questions

CD

Look at the photos and listen to the interview. Then ask your partner a question about himself or herself. Answer your partner's question.

PICTURE PROMPT and INTERVIEW

Who Are You?

Sheila: Madu, where are you from?

Madu: I am from Egypt.

Sheila: What does your name mean?

Madu: My name means "of the people."

Sheila: What do you like to do?

Madu: I ride my bike! I love my bike. It gives me freedom.

Madu

Sheila: Eva, what is something special about you?

Eva: I love music. I can play four instruments. Guitar is my favorite.

Sheila: How do you spend your free time?

Eva: I practice my music. I also babysit a lot.

Sheila: What are your goals for the future?

Eva: I want to be a music teacher. I want to teach children to play music.

Eva

1 TRY OUT LANGUAGE
2 LEARN GRAMMAR
3 APPLY ON YOUR OWN

Use Complete Sentences

A complete sentence has two parts: the **subject** and the **predicate**. The **subject** tells whom or what the sentence is about. The **predicate** often tells what the subject does.

Subject	Predicate
My mother	named me.

To find the parts in most sentences, ask yourself:

1. Whom or what is the sentence about? Your answer is the **subject**.
2. What does the subject do? Your answer is the **predicate**.

Sentence	Whom or What?	What Does the Subject Do?
My father named me.	My father	named me
My name comes from Swahili.	My name	comes from Swahili

In a command, the subject is understood. You do not usually say the subject when you give the command.

Four Kinds of Sentences

1. A **statement** tells something.
   My name is special.
2. A **question** asks something.
   What is your name?
3. An **exclamation** expresses a strong feeling.
   That is a cool name!
4. A **command** tells someone what to do.
   Tell me your name.

Practice Together

Match each subject to a predicate. Say the new sentence.

1. My brother	**a.** shares his name with my father.
2. His name	**b.** calls my brother by his real name.
3. His teachers	**c.** comes from an African word.
4. His friends	**d.** use his nickname.
5. My father	**e.** use his real name.

Try It!

Match each subject to a predicate. Use your own information. Say the new sentence.

6. My name	**a.** use my full name.
7. My friend	**b.** prefers my nickname.
8. My _____	**c.** use nicknames.
9. My teachers	**d.** comes from _____.
10. My friends	**e.** named me.

▲ Their names unite them.

Interview a Friend

ASK AND ANSWER QUESTIONS

Many things make each person special. Find out more about a friend by asking questions.

Work with a partner to write six questions, one for each question word. Think about what you want to learn.

Question Word	Asks About	Example Question
Who?	a person	Who is your best friend?
What?	a thing	What are your hobbies?
Where?	a place	Where were you born?
When?	a time	When is your birthday?
Why?	a reason	Why is your name special?
How?	an explanation	How do you go to school?

Take turns asking and answering the questions with your partner. Then share what you found out about your partner with the whole group.

HOW TO ASK AND ANSWER QUESTIONS

1. When you want information, you ask questions. Start your questions with *Who, What, Where, When, Why,* or *How.*
2. Give information in your answer. Use complete sentences.

> Where does your name come from?

> My name comes from an African Swahili word. It means *king.*

USE COMPLETE SENTENCES

Use complete sentences when you answer your partner's questions. Make sure each sentence has a **subject** and a **predicate**.

Question: Why is your name special?

Answer: **My dad** **shares my name**.

Prepare to Read

Learn Key Vocabulary

Study the Words Use the steps below.

1. Pronounce the word. Say it aloud several times. Spell it.
2. Rate your word knowledge.
3. Study the example. Tell more about the word.
4. Practice it. Make the word your own.

Key Words

culture (kul-chur) *noun*
▶ page 24

A **culture** is a set of beliefs and customs that a group of people share. Dancing is a custom found in many **cultures**.

disfavor (dis-fā-vor) *noun*
▶ page 20

When you show **disfavor**, you show that you don't like something. A thumbs down is one way to show **disfavor** about something.
Base Word: **favor**

doubt (dowt) *noun*
▶ page 22

When you feel **doubt**, you are not sure. The girl had **doubts** about the food.

erase (e-rās) *verb*
▶ page 19

When you **erase** something, you make it go away. We can **erase** mistakes when we write.
Synonyms: **delete, remove**
Antonym: **add**

excessive (ik-ses-iv)
adjective ▶ page 19

When something is **excessive**, it is too much. That is an **excessive** number of pancakes for one person.

pact (pakt) *noun*
▶ page 26

A **pact** is a promise between people. Friends might make a **pact** to always help each other.

scrape (skrāp) *verb*
▶ page 22

When you **scrape** something, you damage it. Did you **scrape** your knee when you fell?

shame (shām) *noun*
▶ page 22

When you feel **shame**, you feel badly about something you did. She felt **shame** about the mistake she made.
Antonym: **pride**

Practice the Words Complete a Vocabulary Example Chart. Connect your own experiences with each Key Word.

Word	Definition	Example from My Life
doubt	a feeling of not being sure	I have doubts about how I did on my math test.

Vocabulary Example Chart

Plan, Monitor, and Ask Questions

Plan Look over the text before you start to read. Predict what might happen or what you might learn about. Set a purpose for reading the text.

Monitor When you don't understand something, **reread** the text or **read on** to clarify ideas.

Ask Questions Stop and ask questions to check your understanding.

Look Into the Text

Plan: I think this story will be about Los Angeles.

Three years ago our family came up from Mexico to L.A. From stories they'd heard, my parents were worried for our safety in "that hard-as-a-fist Los Angeles." But Papi needed better work.

Monitor: I don't know what "hard-as-a-fist" means.

" When I reread the sentence, I can see that *hard-as-a-fist* means unsafe. "

Question	Answer
Why did the family move to L.A.?	L.A. had better jobs for Papi.

Question-Answer Chart

Practice Together

Begin a Reading Strategies Log Use a Reading Strategies Log to show how the strategies help you understand text. The first row shows how one strategy helped one reader. Reread the passage and add to the Log.

Text I read	Strategy I used	How I used the strategy
Page: 18 **Text:** Our family came... to L.A.	☑ **Plan** ❑ **Monitor** ❑ **Ask Questions** ❑ _____	To plan, I predicted that the story will be about LA.

Realistic Fiction

Realistic fiction is about people, relationships, and problems like those in real life. These types of stories can be easy to relate to your own life.

When you preview realistic fiction, look for words that are **emphasized**. They can help you set a **purpose** for reading and make predictions.

> My parents hate that I'm Arthur. I mean, totally H-A-T-E. I can tell because when I break this news, my mother starts cooking excessively. Her way of organizing the world. My father goes carefully quiet.

As you read, monitor your understanding by rereading or reading on to clear up any confusions. Ask and answer questions to clarify why the characters act or feel the way they do.

American Names

by Tony Johnston

Diversity, 2005, Elizabeth Rosen. Acrylic on chipboard, collection of the artist.

△ **Critical Viewing: Effect** Study the faces in the image. What ideas do you think the image expresses about people?

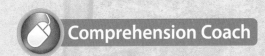

How does the narrator feel about American names?

My name's Arturo, "Turo" for short. For my father, and my grandfather, and *his* father, **back and back**. Arturos— like stacks of strong adobe bricks, forever, my grandmother says.

Really, my name *was* Arturo. Here's why: Three years ago our family came up from Mexico to L.A. From stories they'd heard, my parents were worried for our safety in "that **hard-as-a-fist** Los Angeles." But Papi needed better work.

Rosa, my little sister, wailed, "'Nighted States, no! Too dark!" My brother, Luis, and I pretty much **clammed up**. I guess **numbed** by the thought of leaving our home, and a little scared, too, about the tough **barrio**.

Los Angeles, 2002, Jose Ramirez. Mixed media on canvas, private collection.

Critical Viewing: Design What impression is created by the artist's choice of details and colors in this painting of Los Angeles?

In Other Words
back and back the same name passed down from father to son
hard-as-a-fist big tough city
clammed up stayed quiet
numbed still upset
barrio neighborhood

Like some random, windblown weeds, we landed in L.A., home to movie stars and crazies and crazy movie stars.

Luckily, I had some English when I got here. "It is good to have Eeenglish in your pocket," my parents pressed us always, "*por las cochinas dudas*." For the dirty doubts, that is. Just in case. So, for the dirty doubts, we've all got a little English.

In school, I get Miss Pringle. Miss Pringle's okay, I guess. She's always kind of floating where she goes, and talking in a bright and airy way. My friend Raúl says she's got **excessive** sparkle." Raúl loves weird words.

ANYWAY, first day of school, Miss Pringle, all chipper and bearing a rubbery-dolphin smile, says, "Class, this is Arthur Rodriguez." Probably to make things easier on herself. Without asking. *Ya estuvo*. Like a used-up word on the chalkboard, Arturo's **erased**.

Who cares? Not me. With such a name as Arthur, I'll fit in at this school real well. Like a pair of chewed-up Nikes. Not stiff and stumblingly new. American names are cool. Frank. Mike. Jake. They sound sharp as nails shot from guns.

I'm not the only one who's **been gringo-ized**. There's Jaime and Alicia and Raúl. Presto change-o! With one breath of teacher-magic, they're James and Alice and Ralph. (Our friend Lloyd, alias Rat Nose, is already a gringo, so his name's untouchable.)

When we're together, we joke about our new names.

"So, *'mano*," Raúl says with **bravura** (another one of his words), "how's it feel to be Arthur, like a Round Table guy?"

"*Muy* cool." I slip into full *pocho*, an English-Spanish mix.

"Hey, Alice," I say.

"Yeah?"

"Seen Alicia?"

She scans the hall. Digs in her backpack. "No, man. She's *gone*."

We all laugh. But I notice Alicia's eyes, like two dark and hurting bruises. I fluff it off, easy as dandruff flakes in a TV ad.

My parents hate that I'm Arthur. I mean, totally H-A-T-E. I can tell because when

> **I'll fit in at this school real well.**

Key Vocabulary
excessive *adj.*, too much
erase *v.*, to remove

In Other Words
Ya estuvo. That was it. (in Spanish)
been gringo-ized become American
'mano brother (short for *hermano* in Spanish)
bravura courage (in Spanish)
Muy Very (in Spanish)

Literary Background
According to legend, or a traditional tale, King Arthur ruled England around 500 C.E. It is believed that he formed the **Round Table**, a group of brave knights, to protect England.

El Lonche, 1993, Simon Silva. Oil on canvas, private collection.

I break this news, my mother starts cooking excessively. Her way of organizing the world. My father goes carefully quiet.

Most parents I know would spit out choice curses if their children chose names that hurt their ears. Maybe even smack them. Not mine. Mami and Papi are like two soft doves. They **work on a policy of gentleness**. They've never touched us in anger. Never **talked severely**. So their silent **disfavor** hits harder than the sting of slaps. Tough tortillas. I'm going gringo.

Key Vocabulary
disfavor *n.*, dislike, disapproval

In Other Words
work on a policy of gentleness try to be nice always
talked severely yelled at us

Look Into the Text

1. **Confirm Prediction** Was your prediction correct? How does Arturo react to his new American name?

2. **Compare** Did Arturo's parents have the same reaction? Explain.

3. **Character's Viewpoint** How does Alicia feel about her American name? How can you tell?

The one who hates my name most is my *abuelita*. Grandmother always dresses in cricket-black, in ***luto*** for my grandfather, who died. She's eighty-something. So old, her skin looks like it's woven from brown cobwebs. She's got two braids wound so high on her head, they must have been growing during her whole life. Unlike my parents, Abuelita's no dove. Like a little fighting rooster, she's got *bravura* to spare.

Even though she's **feisty**, God guides her life. She closes most conversation with an after-breath of "*Dios mediante*," God willing.

Since Grandfather died, she lives with us. She came all the way from Aguascalientes, Mexico, on a Norteño bus, with only her prayer book, a photograph of Grandfather, and her *molcajete*.

A *molcajete's* a three-legged grinding stone, carved of lava spit from some old volcano. It's hollowed and pitted, like a cupped hand scarred with acne. Abuelita uses it to grind chilies. For salsa and stuff. Takes longer than forever. Jeez! She could do it with one *zzzzzip* of the blender switch! If that lava-lump was mine, I'd chuck it out.

"Theeesss name Arter—eeet burns in my earsss like poissson." Since my **Spanish's a little crippled from pouring the English on**, Abuelita hisses her English to be sure I can't escape her point. *Muele, muele, muele.* She grinds her disfavor into me at every chance. The heat of peppers fills her voice as she **pulverizes** chilies extra vigorously, for some tasty Mexican dish. If my new name were a chili pepper, she'd pulverize that, too.

In Other Words
luto mourning (in Spanish)
feisty full of courage
Spanish's a little crippled from pouring the English on Spanish is not very good because I speak English a lot
pulverizes crushes

Cultural Background
Aguascalientes is one of the fastest growing cities in Mexico. Its name means Hot Waters in English.

At every chance she turns "Arturo" on her tongue, like a pearl.

What does *she* know, this thin-as-an-eyelash old woman from Hot Waters, Mexico? Man, this is L.A. To get by, you need American names.

Apart from problems of names, here there are problems of gangs. Like those saber-toothed tigers in pits of tar, kids get sucked into them. For protection from invaders from other areas. Or to have a place to go, or something to do. Even some old guys, fathers with kids, are gang members.

My father's the kind of person who removes his hat in a restaurant and blesses his plate of tacos. Not prime gang material. I hope I'm not, either. Though the pull at school is pretty strong, I keep looking for something else to do.

My friends live on my block. All the time they come over to hang out in Abuelita's kitchen. They're there now, **dragged by their noses**. By the pure power of chili dust. And the tang of cilantro.

When they enter, she pinches their

If my new name were a chili pepper, she'd pulverize that, too.

cheeks and claims they are *"muchachos muy lindos"* and calls them by their true names: Jaime, Alicia, Raúl.

"Hola, Lloyd." She aims a dripping spoon straight for Rat Nose. "You love *menudo*? You taste."

Abuelita speaks with such excessive *bravura*, each name **scrapes** my mind like the *scritch-scritching* claws of a feisty rooster.

"Jeez!" I say to myself, cringing with **shame**. But my friends seem totally unfazed. Even pleased. Raúl's got a heart tattoo (not real, just inked on). It's so big, it blues his muscle. Grinning, he pumps his tattoo for Abuelita. *¡Caray!* Don't they remember? We peeled off those old names, like onion skins. Still, a worm of **doubt** squirms in my mind.

My friends slump themselves over the arms of chairs like overcooked noodles and chat easily with my grandmother. Alice's eyes—at the sound of her real name, they **flame up**, bright with excessive sparkle. *Por* please!

Look Into the Text

1. **Confirm Prediction** Was your prediction correct? How do the friends react when Abuelita uses their real names?
2. **Character's Point of View** Why does Arturo "cringe with **shame**"?
3. **Compare and Contrast** How are Arturo and Abuelita similar and different?

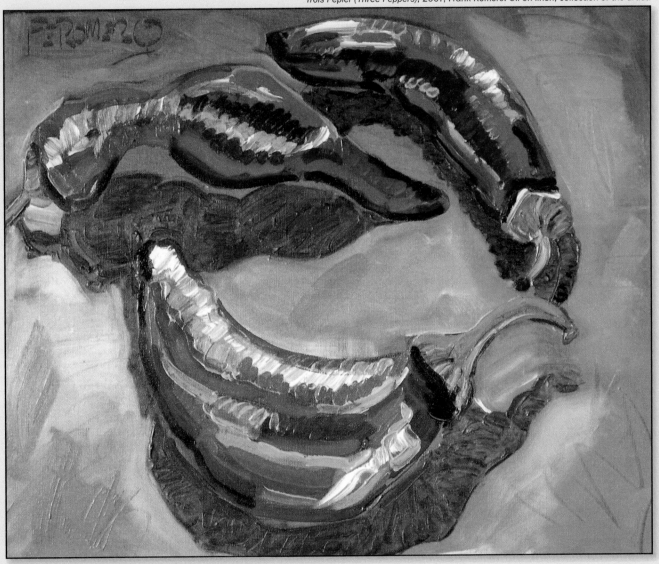

Trois Pepier (Three Peppers), 2007, Frank Romero. Oil on linen, collection of the artist.

▲ Critical Viewing: Design How does the artist's use of shadows and colors create energy?

One night I'm struggling with geography homework. Trying to map out where Marco Polo went. *Hijos*, did that guy get around! His route **looks like some bad knitter's tangled yarn**. Like my sister Rosa's when she's trying to learn.

Through the blinds, my room's banded with moon. Everything's quiet. Even the crickets are sleeping. Then I hear something. Mumbling. Coming from Abuelita's room. Our rooms are back to back. Like when you check your size against somebody else.

My room's painted white. But Abue's, it's totally Mexican pink, the color she believes the Mexican flag should be. Her walls dance with *calacas*, skeletons, of all sizes and materials—clay, wood, wire, papier-mâché. Abue **thumbs her nose at** Death.

Abuelita's talking to Grandfather, muttering to the ghost of his photograph, I bet.

"Arturo," she says, holding that word in her mouth gently, like a highly breakable egg. She speaks Spanish only.

"He's a good boy, our Turo. Just a little bit mixed up. One day, *Dios mediante*, he will recognize how good is your name. One day he will know what it means—Arturo. He is me. He is you. And all before. And all to come."

I hear a long, moist sigh then. Like the breath of a tired teakettle. I hear tears glaze her voice. I feel a blaze of embarrassment to be listening in on this private conversation.

My heart feels squeezed out. Abuelita has known all along what I should have known. It's okay to be Arturo. **What a *menso*-head I am.** *Un idiota de primera.* To give up my name. It's to give up my family. To let myself—all of us—be erased to chalkboard dust.

In this moment my history holds me. Like a warm ***sarape***. I feel tears come. In this moment I want to hug Abuelita.

I look out my window. At the half-moon. Like a perfectly broken button.

It's late. But I call my friends anyhow.

"*Por* please," I joke, "come over."

Key Vocabulary
culture *n.*, the beliefs and values of a group

In Other Words
looks like some bad knitter's tangled yarn is everywhere; is not direct
thumbs her nose at is not scared of
What a *menso*-head I am. I am so stupid.
sarape blanket (in Spanish)

"*¿Ahora?*"

"Now. *Ahoritita.*"

And they come—Ralph and Alice and James and Rat Nose—all expectant and wondering what in *diablos* is going on. Before any of them can **wedge a word in, I blurt**,

"We're taking back our names. **We don't, we're borrados.** Blotted out."

"You mean 'Rat Nose' is dead?" Ralph moans. "Such an *excelente* and rodential name?"

Untitled, 2001, Sandro Chia. Oil on canvas, private collection.

▲ **Critical Viewing: Theme** How does this painting relate to the theme of identity?

In Other Words
¿Ahora? Now? (in Spanish)
Ahoritita Right now. (in Spanish)
wedge a word in, I blurt say anything, I say quickly
We don't, we're borrados. If we don't, we're erased.

"Rat Nose lives. We'll call ourselves whatever we want, but those teachers can't make us into someone new. Those teachers, they must be *formal*."

They're pretty cool with that. Especially Alice. Little stars bloom in her eyes. Ralph's **already itching** for morning, he says, so he can **apprise** Miss Pringle. I itch to apprise my family, now snoring deeper than zombies. Especially Abuelita.

We make a **pact**. Right there in her chili-laden kitchen. On the most Mexican thing around—one by one we place our hands on Abuelita's *molcajete*, ugly as a pockmarked thug.

In solemn ceremony we retrieve our names. Ourselves. Into the bold night air we say with utmost bravura:

¡Raúl!

¡Alicia!

¡Jaime!

¡Lloyd!

¡Arturo!

When we apprise her of our stand on names, Miss Pringle's pretty surprised. But she limps along with it. (A result of "the incident" is that other kids go for their own "name-reclaimment.")

Not long after, they're selling T-shirts and plants and stuff at school. To raise funds for a computer. I buy a little cactus, **prickly** to touch and with one red bloom.

After school, I give it to Abuelita: "Ta-*ta!*" she laughs when I **spring** it from behind my back, and she hugs me with the gift between us, but somehow we don't get poked.

"¡*Ay, Arturo*, **mi pequeño** *cactus!*" Abuelita exclaims. Like I'm prickly sometimes, but **have a chance of flowers.**

Santa Fe Roadside Prickly Pear, 2007, Claudette Moe. Acrylic on canvas, collection of the artist.

Key Vocabulary

pact *n.*, a promise or agreement between people

In Other Words

already itching so excited
apprise tell
In solemn ceremony we retrieve our names. Very seriously, we take back our Spanish names.
prickly sharp

spring quickly take
mi pequeño my little (in Spanish)
have a chance of flowers mostly good

Abuelita's prickly but full of goodness. As far from gangbangers as Papi is. I wish I could be like her, getting people's names back for them—or something important like that. So far I'm just hanging out. Being like some weird L.A. weather report: prickly—with a chance of flowers. ❖

About the Author

Tony Johnston (1942–) grew up in California and spent fifteen years living in Mexico. She likes books that "come from the heart." When she was in sixth grade, her teacher had students keep journals of words they came across and loved or hated. "Ever since, I've been keeping lists of the wonderful words I bump into. Whenever I can, I toss them out like flowers, hoping that others will catch them and love them and hold onto them—and use them."

Look Into the Text

1. **Confirm Prediction** Was your prediction correct? How did family and **culture** affect Arturo's decision?

2. **Character and Plot** How did Arturo change from the beginning to the end of the story? What events caused the change?

Saying Yes

by Diana Chang

"Are you Chinese?"
"Yes."

"American?"
"Yes."

5   "Really Chinese?"
"No…not quite."

"Really American?"
"Well, actually, you
see…"

10 But I would rather say
yes

Not neither-nor,
not maybe,
but both, and not only

15 The homes I've had,
the ways I am

I'd rather say it
twice,
yes

Look Into the Text

1. **Paraphrase** Explain in your own words what the poet means by "both, and not only."

2. **Compare** How is the message in the poem similar to Arturo's experience in "American Names"?

Connect Reading and Writing

Vocabulary
culture
disfavor
doubt
erase
excessive
pact
scraped
shame

CRITICAL THINKING

1. **SUM IT UP** Review the Reading Strategies Log you created while reading. What was most important for you to understand in each part of the story? Include these ideas in a summary of the story.

Text I read	Strategy I used	How I used the strategy
Page: 18 Text: Our family came...to L.A.	☑ Plan ❑ Monitor ❑ Ask Questions ❑ _____	To plan, I predicted that the story will be about L.A.

Reading Strategies Log

2. **Interpret** Arturo says he is **erased** when Miss Pringle changes his name. What does he mean? How might he feel **shame**?

3. **Analyze** Look at the Anticipation Guide you filled out before you read the story. Do you want to change any of your answers now? Why or why not?

4. **Draw Conclusions** What does Arturo realize about his **culture**? How is this similar to or different from the message in "Saying Yes"? With a partner, share reasons that support your conclusions.

READING FLUENCY

Intonation Read the passage on page 624 to a partner. Assess your fluency.

1. My tone never/sometimes/always matched what I read.

2. What I did best was _____ .

READING STRATEGY

> What strategy helped you understand the selection? Tell a partner about it.

VOCABULARY REVIEW

Oral Review Read the paragraph aloud. Add the vocabulary words.

> If you move to another country, you experience a new _____ . You may enjoy some customs and show _____ toward others. You may have _____ about whether you fit in, or feel _____ that others may see you as different. Well, don't _____ who you are. Change is never easy. Sure, a few changes are good, but _____ changes make it seem as if your feelings were being _____ against stone. Make a _____ with family members to share the best of both countries.

Written Review Imagine you are a friend of Arturo's. Write an explanation of the **pact** you made. Use at least five vocabulary words.

 **WRITE ABOUT THE** GUIDING QUESTION

Explore Identity

How does **culture** affect a person's identity? Reread the selections to find examples that support your ideas. Then write your opinion.

Connect Across the Curriculum

Vocabulary Study

Use Compound Words

> **Academic Vocabulary**
> • **compound** (**kahm**-pownd) *adjective*
>   Something that is **compound** is made up of two
>   or more parts.

Sometimes two words combine to create a **compound** word. Often, the meaning of a **compound** word is closely related to its two base words:

birth + day = birthday

> *Birth* means
> when I was born. *Day*
> is time. Birthday
> must mean the day
> I was born.

Study Compound Words Work with a partner. Find the base words for each of these **compound** words from "American Names."

1. grandmother (p. 18)   3. backpack (p. 19)
2. windblown (p. 19)   4. something (p. 21)

Discuss the meanings of the two base words in the **compound** word. Then decide the meaning of the new word. Reread the sentence in the selection. Do you understand it differently now?

Write Sentences Write sentences that use each of these **compound** words. Trade sentences with your partner.

Research/Speaking

Research Healthy Foods

SOCIAL
SCIENCE

① **Research and Collect Data** Choose a food you don't know much about to research. Ask: Is this food healthy? Use the Internet and the library to learn more about your topic.

② **Narrow the Topic** Focus your topic by asking more specific questions.

③ **Support Your Research** Use two or three authoritative sources to support your topic. Authoritative sources contain trustworthy information that is relevant to your topic. For example, facts about a food's popularity are not relevant for judging whether or not it is healthy. Always support your reasoning with relevant evidence.

④ **Present Your Results** Describe your food to the class. Explain why it is or is not healthy. Remember to speak clearly and use formal language.

Ask and Answer Questions

Role-Play Work with a partner. Role-play an interview with a character from the story to learn about his or her ideas about culture. Ask questions that begin with *who, what, where, when, why,* and *how.* Trade roles. Answer your partner's questions with complete sentences.

> Why do you like the name Arturo?

> I share it with my father and grandfather and his father.

Write About Your Name

Study the Models An effective sentence is clear, interesting, and complete. A complete sentence has a subject and a predicate. When you use complete sentences, your writing is clear.

NOT OK

> Arturo and his friends get new names from their teacher. Their teacher didn't ask them first. Miss Pringle them new names. At first, like their gringo-ized names. Arturo's parents hate his new name. His grandmother it even more. One night, learns why.

The reader thinks: **"What did Miss Pringle do?"** The sentence isn't clear because it is not complete.

OK

> Arturo and his friends get new names from their teacher. Their teacher didn't ask them first. Miss Pringle assigned them new names. At first, they like their gringo-ized names. Arturo's parents hate his new name. His grandmother hates it even more. One night, Arturo learns why.

This writer uses complete sentences with a subject and predicate.

Add Sentences Think of two sentences to add to the OK model above. Be sure to use complete sentences.

WRITE ON YOUR OWN Write about the importance of your name. Is it important to always use your formal name? What if someone calls you something else? When is it OK to use a nickname—for example, Ed instead of Edward? Check your sentences to make sure they are complete.

▲ Friends often have nicknames for each other.

A complete sentence has both a subject and a predicate.

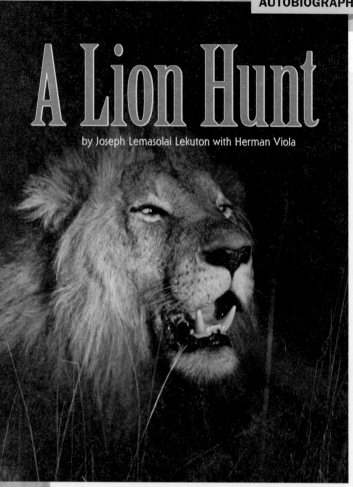

A Lion Hunt

by Joseph Lemasolai Lekuton with Herman Viola

SELECTION 2 OVERVIEW

▶ **Build Background**

▶ **Language & Grammar**
Give Information
Use Nouns in Sentences

▶ **Prepare to Read**
Learn Key Vocabulary
Make Inferences, Determine Importance, Synthesize

▶ **Read and Write**
Introduce the Genre
Autobiography
Focus on Reading
Make Inferences, Determine Importance, Synthesize
Critical Thinking
Reading Fluency
Read with Expression
Vocabulary Review
Write About the Guiding Question

▶ **Connect Across the Curriculum**
Vocabulary Study
Use Suffixes
Listening/Speaking
Discuss Different Viewpoints
Language and Grammar
Give Information
Writing and Grammar
Write About Bravery

Build Background

Connect

Group Discussion Sometimes we have to make big decisions that can change who we are. Is it always brave to decide to do something new? Discuss this question with your group. Give examples of when doing something new might be brave and when it might not be brave.

Learn About Bravery

Whether as a warrior or a teacher, Joseph Lemasolai Lekuton knows what it means to be brave. He had to be brave to leave his family and go to school.

Digital Library myNGconnect.com
↻ View the video.

▲ Joseph Lemasolai Lekuton

Language & Grammar

Give Information

CD

Listen to the chant and chime in.
Listen to the CD for more information.
What does it tell you about lions?

CHANT

The Lion

The lion is a great big cat.
It's as simple as that—
A lion is a great big cat,
With great big claws,
And great big teeth,
And a great big taste
For any kind of meat.
If you see a lion
Just tip your hat
And scat!

Use Nouns in Sentences

A **noun** names a person, place, thing, or idea.

A **lion** watches a **boy** in the **field**. **Danger** is near.

A **singular noun** names one person, place, thing, or idea.

A **plural noun** names more than one person, place, thing, or idea.

	More Nouns
Person	boy, brother, friend, hunter
Place	field, school, village
Thing	cloud, rock, shoe, stick
Idea	bravery, danger, silence

- To make most nouns plural, just add **-s**.

  hunter + -s = hunters   Two **hunters** track the lion.

- If the noun ends in **s**, **z**, **sh**, **ch**, or **x**, add **-es**.

  dish + -es = dishes   They take **dishes** to the camp.

- If the noun ends in **y**, look at the letter before the **y**.
  If it is a consonant, change the **y** to **i**. Then add **-es**.

  story + -es = stories   At the camp, they hear many **stories** about lions.

- If the letter before the **y** is a vowel, just add **-s**.

  boy + -s = boys   Many **boys** hunt the lion.

- Some nouns have special plural forms.

  man—**men**   **Men** cheer the hunters.

  foot—**feet**   The hunters' **feet** are sore.

Practice Together

Tell if the noun in the box names a person, place, thing, or idea. Say the plural form of the noun. Then say the sentence and add the plural noun.

1. | bush | At least two lions are in the _____.
2. | brother | The _____ walk slowly away.
3. | foot | Their _____ move silently.
4. | field | The _____ are suddenly empty.

Try It!

Tell if the noun in the box names a person, place, thing, or idea. Write the plural form of the noun on a card. Then say the sentence and add the plural noun.

5. | snake | Even the _____ move quickly away.
6. | fox | _____ hide fast.
7. | boy | The _____ yell for help.
8. | family | Their _____ are worried about them.

▲ **Danger is near.**

Tell About Your Favorite Animal

GIVE INFORMATION

Find a picture of your favorite animal. Use an encyclopedia book or an online encyclopedia to find information about the animal. Tell a partner about your animal.

> ### HOW TO GIVE INFORMATION
>
> **1.** Think about the information you want to include. What do you want to say?
> **2.** Use details and specific nouns to give precise information.

Lakes are good homes for bullfrogs.

To get started, draw pictures of your favorite animal. Show where it lives. Show what it eats. Show where it sleeps and how it behaves around people.

USE SPECIFIC NOUNS

When you tell about your animal, use many details that give information. Use nouns that give your partner a clear, precise picture of the people, animals, places, things, or ideas that you tell about. Which words on the scale below are the most precise?

NOT SPECIFIC ➝ **SPECIFIC**

person	scientist	▶ frog scientist	▶ herpetologist
animal	amphibian	▶ frog	▶ North American bullfrog
place	North America	▶ United States	▶ eastern United States
thing	lots of things	▶ frog food	▶ snakes, worms, and insects
idea	time	▶ lifespan	▶ 7 to 9 years

Not precise: The animal lives in water.
Someone wrote about bullfrogs' food.
Bullfrogs are native to North America.

Precise: The North American bullfrog lives in ponds.
A herpetologist wrote that North American bullfrogs eat snakes, worms, and insects.
North American bullfrogs are native to the eastern United States.

▲ Bullfrogs live in ponds.

Prepare to Read

Learn Key Vocabulary

Rate and Study the Words Use the steps below.

1. Pronounce the word. Say it aloud several times. Spell it.
2. Rate your word knowledge.
3. Study the example. Tell more about the word.
4. Practice it. Make the word your own.

Rating Scale

1 = I have never seen this word before.

2 = I am not sure of the word's meaning.

3 = I know this word and can teach the word's meaning to someone else.

Key Words

bravery (brā-vu-rē) *noun*
▶ page 40

Bravery means courage, or not being afraid. Firefighters show **bravery** when they put out fires.
Base Word: **brave**

brotherhood
(bruth-ur-hood) *noun* ▶ page 44

A **brotherhood** is a close group of people. A sports team can be a **brotherhood**.

decision (dē-si-zhun) *noun*
▶ page 44

A **decision** is a choice. You make a **decision** when you choose clothes to wear each day.
Base Word: **decide**

defend (dē-fend) *verb*
▶ page 40

When you **defend** something, you protect it. A mother animal **defends** her young.
Synonyms: **protect, guard**
Antonym: **attack**

pride (prīd) *noun*
▶ page 40

When you feel **pride**, you feel good about something you or someone else does. The boy felt **pride** when he graduated from high school.

society (so-sī-i-tē) *noun*
▶ page 49

A **society** is a group of people who share beliefs and goals. In American **society**, we value public discussions of key issues.

symbol (sim-bul) *noun*
▶ page 40

A **symbol** is an object that stands for something else. In the United States, the Bald Eagle is a **symbol** of power.

warrior (wor-ē-yur) *noun*
▶ page 40

A **warrior** is someone who protects his people. Some **warriors** hunt animals for food.
Synonyms: **hunter, fighter**

Practice the Words With a partner, make an Expanded Meaning Map for each Key Word.

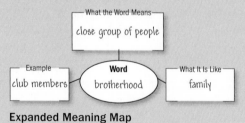

Expanded Meaning Map

Make Inferences, Determine Importance, Synthesize

Make Inferences Authors don't always give information directly. Put clues together with what you know from your experience to make sense of the text.

Determine Importance Look for main ideas and the most important details. Then use the most important details to summarize the text.

Synthesize As you read, your mind combines many bits of information to form a new understanding.

Make Inferences: It sounds like the author is very sure of himself. I don't think he knows what he's talking about because he's never chased a lion.

Synthesize: People in Kenya admire those who've killed lions. People I know admire actors or athletes.

Look Into the Text

... all the young warriors...told me, "Wow, you know yesterday we chased this lion" ... I always said, "Big deal!" What's the big deal about a lion? It's just another animal ... In northern Kenya, the lion is a symbol of bravery and pride ... If you kill a lion, you are respected by everyone.

" I think that every culture has certain people that others look up to because of something they do."

Determine Importance: I think it's important to know that the author lives in Kenya and how his culture feels about lions.

Practice Together

Begin a Reading Strategies Log Use the Reading Strategies Log to show how the strategies help you understand text. The first row shows how one strategy helped one reader. Reread the passage and add to the Log.

Text I read	Strategy I used	How I used the strategy
Page: 40 **Text:** What's the big deal about a lion?	☑ **Make Inferences** ❑ **Determine Importance** ❑ **Synthesize** ❑ _____	Making an inference about the author's attitude helps me understand the selection better.

Autobiography

An autobiography is narrative nonfiction in which an author tells the story of his or her own life.

Often the author wontt' tell you everything directly, but you can add what you know to make inferences about the person's experiences. Also while reading, decide which details are the most important. Knowing just the important ideas makes it easier to remember key events in a person's life.

Look Into the Text

> My brother said, "Yes, that's a good idea," and it was agreed. For the first time I felt like I was part of the brotherhood of warriors. I had just made a decision I was proud of.

Once you have a read a few lines or an entire page of text, decide how the information fits together. Synthesize what you've read and learned to come up with a new understanding.

A Lion Hunt

by Joseph Lemasolai Lekuton with Herman Viola

Set a Purpose

Find out what the narrator thinks about lions.

I'M GOING TO TELL YOU the lion story. Where I live in northern Kenya, the lion is a **symbol** of **bravery** and **pride**. Lions have a special presence. If you kill a lion, you are respected by everyone. Other **warriors** even make up songs about how brave you are. So it is every warrior's dream to kill a lion **at one point or another**. Growing up, I'd had a lot of interaction with wild animals—elephants, rhinos, cape buffalo, hyenas. But at the time of this story—when I was about 14—I'd never **come face-to-face with** a lion, ever. I'd heard stories from all the young warriors who told me, "Wow, you know yesterday we chased this lion—" bragging about it. And I always said, "**Big deal**." What's the big deal about a lion? It's just another animal. If I can **defend** myself against elephants or rhinos, I thought, why not a lion?

I was just back from school for vacation. It was December, and there was enough rain. It was green and beautiful everywhere. The cows were giving plenty of milk. In order to get them away from **ticks**, the cattle had been taken down to the lowlands. There's good grass there, though it's drier than in the high country, with some rocks here and there. There are no ticks, so you don't have to worry about the health of the cattle, but the area is known for its fierce lions. They roam freely there, as if they own the land.

Key Vocabulary

symbol *n.*, something that represents something else

bravery *n.*, having no fear

pride *n.*, self-respect

warrior *n.*, a hunter

defend *v.*, to protect from attack

In Other Words

at one point or another someday

come face-to-face with seen; been close to

Big deal. Why is it so important?

ticks small creatures that can spread disease

▲ Giraffes, impalas, zebras, and gazelles near Lake Nakuru. Lake Nakuru National Park, Kenya

I spent two days in the village with my mom, then my brother Ngoliong came home to have his hair braided and asked me to go to the cattle camp along with an elder who was on his way there. I'd say the cattle camp was 18 to 24 miles away, depending on the route, through some rocky areas and a lot of shrubs. My spear was broken, so I left it at home. I carried a small stick and a small club. I wore my *nanga*, which is a red cloth, tied around my waist.

Cultural Background

Here is Lekuton as a Maasai warrior, wearing some of his finest traditional beads.

It took us all day to get there, but at sunset we were walking through the gap in the **acacia-branch fence** that surrounded our camp. There were several cattle camps scattered over a five-mile **radius**. At night we could see fires in the distance, so we knew that we were not alone. As soon as we got there my brother Lmatarion told us that two lions had been terrorizing the camps. But lions are smart. Like thieves, they go somewhere, they look, they take, but they don't go back to the same place again.

Well, that was our unlucky day. That evening when the cows got back from **grazing**, we had a lot of milk to drink, so we were well fed. We sat together around the fire and sang songs—songs about our girlfriends, bravery songs. We **swapped** stories, and I told stories about school. The others were always curious to understand

▲ Maasai men and boys watching their cattle.

In Other Words

acacia-branch fence small trees
radius area
grazing eating grass
swapped shared, told

Cultural Background

The **Maasai** are a famous warrior tribe in Kenya whose lives center on herding cattle. The Maasai move frequently in search of water and good grazing lands. The success of the Maasai is measured by the number of cattle they have.

school. There were four families in the camp, but most of the older warriors were back at the village seeing their girlfriends and getting their hair braided. So there were only three experienced warriors who could fight a lion, plus the one elder who had come down with me. The rest of us were younger.

We went to bed around 11:30 or 12. We all slept out under the stars in the cattle camp—no bed, just a **cowhide** spread on bare soil. And at night it gets cold in those desert areas. For a cover I used the nanga that I had worn during the day. The piece of cloth barely covered my body, and I kept trying to make it longer and pull it close around me, but it wouldn't stretch. I curled myself underneath it trying to stay warm.

Everything was silent. The sky was clear. There **was no sign of** clouds. The fire was just out. The stars were like millions of diamonds in the sky. One by one everybody fell asleep. Although I was tired, I was the last to sleep. I was so excited about taking the cows out the following morning.

We all slept out under the stars.

During the middle of the night, I woke to this huge sound—like rain, but not really like rain. I looked up. The starlight was gone, clouds were everywhere, and there was a drizzle falling. But that wasn't the sound. The sound was all of the cows starting to pee. All of them, in every direction. And that is the sign of a lion. A hyena doesn't make them do that. An elephant doesn't make them do that. A person doesn't. Only the lion. We knew right away that a lion was about to attack us.

The other warriors started making a lot of noise, and I got up with them, but I couldn't find my shoes. I'd taken them off before I went to sleep, and now it was **pitch black**. Some warriors, when they know there's danger, sleep with their shoes in their hands and their spears right next to them. But I couldn't find my shoes, and I didn't even have a spear. Then the lion made just one noise: *bhwuuuu!* One huge roar. We started running toward the noise. Right then we heard a cow making a **rasping**, **guttural** sound, and we knew that the lion had her by the throat.

Look Into the Text

1. **Author's Point of View** What is the narrator's opinion about lions?
2. **Summarize** What events occurred the first night at the cattle camp?
3. **Inference** Were the **warriors** prepared to fight the lion? Why or why not?

COWS WERE EVERYWHERE. They ran into one another and into us, too. We could hear noises from all directions—people shouting, cows running—but we couldn't see a thing. My brother heard the lion right next to him and threw his spear. He missed the lion—and lucky for the rest of us, he missed us, too. Eventually, we began to get used to the darkness, but it was still difficult to tell a lion from a cow. My brother was the first to arrive where the cow had been killed.

The way we figured it was this: Two lions had attacked the camp. Lions are very intelligent. They had **split up**. One had stayed at the southern end of the camp where we were sleeping, while the other had gone to the northern end. The wind was blowing from south to north. The cows smelled the lion at the southern end and **stampeded** to the north—toward the other waiting lion.

When I asked my brother, "Hey, what's going on?" he said, "The lion killed Ngoneya."

Ngoneya was my mother's favorite cow and Ngoneya's family was the best one in the herd. My mother depended on her to produce more milk than any other cow. She loved Ngoneya, really. At night she would get up to pet her.

I was very angry. I said, "I wish to see this lion right now. He's going to **see a man he's never seen before**."

Just as we were talking, a second death cry came from the other end of the camp. Again we ran, but as we got closer, I told everyone to stop. "He's going to kill all the cows!" I told my brother. And I think this is where school thinking comes in. I told him, "Look. If we keep on chasing this lion, he's going to kill more and more. So why don't we let him eat what he has now, and tomorrow morning we will go hunting for him." My brother said, "Yes, that's a good idea," and it was agreed. For the first time I felt like I was part of the **brotherhood** of warriors. I had just made a **decision** I was proud of.

Key Vocabulary
  brotherhood *n.*, a close group of people
  decision *n.*, a choice someone makes

In Other Words
  The way we figured it was this We decided this is what happened
  split up hunted separately
  stampeded went together quickly
  see a man he's never seen before be afraid of me

It was muddy, it was dark, we were in **the middle of nowhere**, and right then we had cows that were miles away. They had stampeded in every direction, and we could not protect them. So we came back to camp and made a big fire. I looked for my shoes and I found them. By that time I was bruised all over from the cows banging into me, and my legs were bloody from the scratches I got from the acacia thorns. I hurt all over.

We started talking about how we were going to hunt the lion the next day. I could tell my brother was worried and wanted to get me out of danger. He said, "Listen, you're fast, you can run. Run and tell the people at the other camps to come and help. We only have three real warriors here; the rest of you are younger."

"**No way**," I said. "Are you **kidding** me? I'm a warrior. I'm just as brave as you, and I'm not going anywhere." At this point, I hadn't actually seen the lion, and I absolutely refused to leave.

▲ Nighttime on the Savannah, or grasslands of Kenya, offers little protection from lions.

In Other Words
the middle of nowhere a place far
   from everything else
No way No
kidding joking with

My brother said, "I'm going to ask you one more time, please go. Go get help. Go to the other camp and tell the warriors that we've found the two lions that have been terrorizing everyone, and we need to kill them today."

And I said, "No, I'm not going."

So he said, "Fine," and sent the youngest boy, who was only about eight.

When daylight came, I took the little boy's spear and walked out from the camp with the others. Barely 200 yards away were the two lions. One had its head right in the cow, eating from the inside. And one was just lying around: She was full. As we approached them, we sang a lion song: "We're going to get the lion, it's going to be a great day for all of us, all the warriors will be happy, we'll save all our cows."

As we got closer, the older man who was with us kept telling us to be careful. We should wait for help, he said. "This is dangerous. You have no idea what lions can do." But no one would listen to him.

The other guys were saying, "We can do

We came face-to-face with the lions.

it. Be brave, everyone." We were encouraging each other, **hyping ourselves up**.

My brother was so angry, so upset about our mother's favorite cow that he was crying. "You killed Ngoneya," he was saying. "You are going to **pay for it**."

Everyone was **in a trance**. I felt that something inside me was about to burst, that my heart was about to come out. I was ready. Then we came face-to-face with the lions. The female lion walked away, but the male stayed. We formed a little semicircle around the male, with our long spears raised. We didn't move. The lion had stopped eating and was now looking at us. It felt like he was looking right at me. He was big, really big. His tail was thumping the ground.

He gave one loud roar to warn us. Everything shook. The ground where I was standing started to tremble. I could see right into his throat, that's how close we were. His mouth was huge and full of gore from the cow. I could count his teeth. His face and mane were red with blood. Blood was everywhere.

In Other Words
hyping ourselves up making each
    other excited
pay for it be punished
in a trance focused

The lion slowly got up so he could show us his full **presence**. He roared again. The second roar almost broke my eardrums. The lion was now pacing up and down, walking in small circles. He was looking at our feet and then at our eyes. They say a lion can figure out who will be the first person to spear it.

I edged closer to my brother, being careful not to give any sign of lifting or throwing my spear, and I said, "Where's that other camp?"

My brother said to me, "Oh, you're going now?" He gave me a look—a look that seemed to say, You watch out because someone might think you are afraid.

But I said, "Just tell me where to go." He told me. I gave him my spear. "It will help you," I said, and then I **took off** in the direction of the other cattle camp. No warrior looked back to see where I was going. They were all concentrating on the lion.

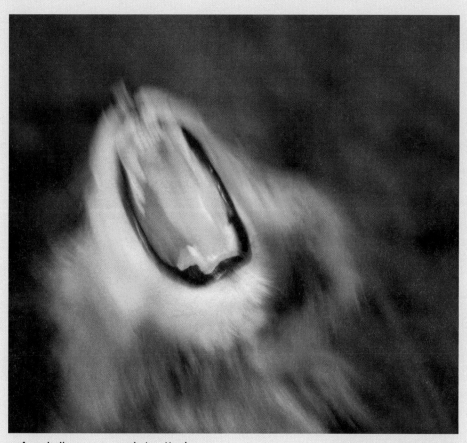

▲ A male lion roars, ready to attack.

Look Into the Text

1. **Summarize** How did the warriors plan to get the lions?
2. **Paraphrase** Tell in your own words what the narrator's brother wanted him to do.
3. **Confirm Prediction** What did the narrator do when he saw the lion? Was your prediction correct?

Find out what happens after the narrator runs away.

A S I RAN TOWARD THE NEXT CAMP I saw that the little boy had done his job well. Warriors were coming, lots of them, chanting songs, asking our warriors to wait for them. The lion **stood his ground** until he saw so many men coming down, warriors in red clothes. It must have seemed to him that the whole hillside was red in color. The

▲ The Maasai wear a lot of red clothing. The color red represents power and is sacred. The Maasai also use a red dye to draw on their skin. They make the dye by mixing clay with water or animal fat.

In Other Words
stood his ground was ready to fight

lion then started to look for a way out.

The warriors reasoned that the lion had eaten too much to run fast and that the muddy ground would slow him up. They thought they could run after him and kill him. They were wrong. As soon as they took their positions, the lion surged forward and took off running. The warriors were left behind. There was nothing they could do except pray that they would meet this lion again.

From that time on, I knew **the word in the village was** that I had run away from the lion. There was no way I could prevent it.

"You know the young Lekuton warrior?"

"Yeah."

"He was afraid of the lion."

My brother tried to support me, but in our **society**, once word like that gets out, that's it. So I knew that I'd have to prove myself, to prove that I'm not a coward. So from then on, every time I came home for vacation, I went to the cattle camp on my own. I'd get my spear, I'd get my shoes. Even if it was 30 miles from the village, I'd go on my own, through **thick and thin**, through the forest and deserts. When I got there I'd take the cattle out on my own. Always I hoped something would attack our cattle so I could protect them. ❖

About the Author

Joseph Lemasolai Lekuton wrote about his life experiences in the book *Facing the Lion: Growing up Maasai on the African Savanna*. In 2006, National Geographic named the author an Emerging Explorer for his many accomplishments. Today, Lekuton lives in Kenya and serves as a member of parliament in the Kenya National Assembly.

Key Vocabulary
society *n.*, group of people who share a common purpose

In Other Words
the word in the village was people were saying
thick and thin easy and difficult areas

Look Into the Text

1. **Summarize** What did people in the village think of the narrator after the lion hunt? How did the narrator react?
2. **Theme** How does this selection relate to the unit theme?

From Kenya to America and Back Again

◄ The family of Joseph Lemasolai Lekuton, who was born in northern Kenya, is part of a sub-group of the Maasai, called the Ariaal.

Joseph Lemasolai Lekuton was fourteen at the time the events in this narrative took place. He wanted to prove to his tribe that he was a brave warrior. As he grew up, Lekuton did prove himself in many ways.

Lekuton's soccer skills earned him a scholarship to an excellent high school in Kenya. Lekuton did so well in high school that he earned a full scholarship to an American college.

After graduating from college, Lekuton became a social studies teacher in Virginia. He strived to teach his students the benefits of both tribal life and a western education. He linked Kenyan and American cultures by organizing school trips to Kenya. "Cultures can learn so much from each other," he said. "We may be divided by bodies of water and masses of mountains but as human beings we all identify with the same fundamental things."

Lekuton continued to help Kenya. His work helped provide educational opportunities and clean water to villages there. For his service to the country, Lekuton became the youngest recipient of Kenya's Order of the Grand Warrior in June of 2001.

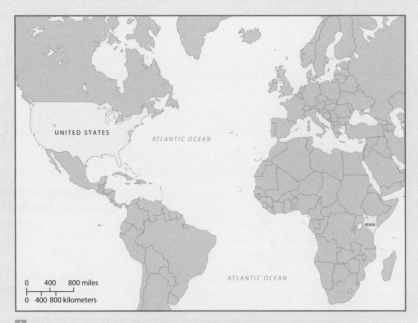

UNITED STATES

ATLANTIC OCEAN

KENYA

ATLANTIC OCEAN

0   400   800 miles
0   400 800 kilometers

▲ Interpret the Map How far away is the United States from Kenya?

Connect Reading and Writing

Vocabulary
bravery
brotherhood
decisions
defend
pride
societies
symbol
warriors

CRITICAL THINKING

1. SUM IT UP Review the Reading Strategies Log you created while reading. What do you find most useful about each of these strategies?

Text I read	Strategy I used	How I used the strategy
Page: 40 Text: What's the big deal about a lion?	☑ Make Inferences ❏ Determine Importance ❏ Synthesize ❏ _____	Making an inference about the author's attitude helps me understand the selection better.

Reading Strategies Log

2. Compare In "American Names" and "A Lion Hunt," both narrators make **decisions** that affect their identities. Explain how the decisions are alike and what the decisions are a **symbol** of.

3. Evaluate When the narrator sees the lion, he makes a **decision**. How might this action show fear or **bravery** in his **society**?

4. Explain Recall the group discussion you had about **bravery**. How have your ideas changed after reading the selection?

READING FLUENCY

Expression Read the passage on page 625 to a partner. Assess your fluency.

1. My voice never/sometimes/always matched what I read.

2. What I did best was _____ .

READING STRATEGY

What strategy helped you understand this selection? Tell a partner about it.

VOCABULARY REVIEW

Oral Review Read the paragraph aloud. Add the vocabulary words.

> Some _____ depend on _____ for survival. They hunt for food. They _____ people from attack. Together, they feel great _____ in their common _____ . Sometimes they hunt lions. Then they must show great _____ because lions are dangerous. They have to make quick _____ because lions are fast. Lions are also a _____ of strength.

Written Review Imagine that Lekuton made a different **decision**. Write a new ending for the selection. Use four vocabulary words.

WRITE ABOUT THE GUIDING QUESTION

Explore the Decision Point
Was Lekuton's **decision** an act of **bravery** or **pride**? How did it affect his identity? Find details from the selection that support your ideas.

Connect Across the Curriculum

Vocabulary Study

Use Suffixes

Suffix	Meaning
-ful	full of
-ness	quality or state of
-ous	full of
-ly	in the manner of

Academic Vocabulary
- **analyze** (a-nu-līz) *verb*
  When you **analyze**, you separate something into parts and examine, or study, it.

A **suffix** is a word part at the end of a base word. The suffix changes the meaning of the base word.

```
[ base word ]    [ suffix ]

   dread    +    -ful   =   dreadful
```

> *Dread means fear and –ful means full of. So dreadful must mean full of fear or dread.*

Use Base Words Work with a partner. Cover up the suffixes on these words from "A Lion Hunt." Find the base word and **analyze** its meaning. Uncover the suffix and determine its meaning. Put the meanings of the word parts together to define the whole word.

1. darkness   **2.** painful   **3.** slowly   **4.** dangerous

Write a sentence using each word. Trade sentences with a partner. Discuss how each suffix affects the meaning of the base word.

Listening/Speaking

Discuss Different Viewpoints

A viewpoint is a person's attitude toward a topic. Imagine that you and your group are people in Lekuton's village discussing his decision to run for help.

SOCIAL SCIENCE

1 **Choose a Viewpoint** Tell your viewpoint to the group.

2 **Share Your Ideas** Share your reasons for your viewpoint. Use relevant details from the text to support your viewpoint.

3 **Listen and Respond to Other Viewpoints** Listen carefully and respectfully to others to hear their viewpoints. Ask them to explain their viewpoints and the evidence they chose.

4 **Evaluate Reasoning and Evidence** Make notes about how others support their viewpoints. Do they have enough evidence? Is their evidence relevant to the topic of Lekuton's decision and actions?

5 **Tell What You Discovered** Summarize your discussion for the class.

Give Information

Group Share With a group, give information about the place you are from or the place where you live now. Think about what you want to say. Use specific nouns to give detailed, precise information.

> My city has a large natural habitat zoo. Its African exhibit has five miles of walkways.

Write About Bravery

Study the Models To make your writing interesting, use nouns that say exactly what you mean.

JUST OK

I read a <u>thing</u> about <u>lions</u>. A <u>boy</u> went on a hunt to a <u>place</u> with some <u>people</u>. The <u>boy</u> wanted to prove <u>something</u>. Then the lion killed some <u>cows</u>. The <u>boy</u> ran away. He was sorry and tried to prove his <u>bravery</u> later.

> These nouns are not specific. The reader thinks: "What 'thing' did the writer read? Where was the hunt?"

BETTER

I read a <u>story</u> about <u>lions</u>. A <u>teenager</u> went on a hunt in <u>Kenya</u> with <u>his brother</u> and <u>an elder</u> from his village. The <u>teenager</u> wanted to prove his <u>bravery</u>. Then the lion killed <u>his mother's favorite cows</u>. The <u>teenager</u> ran away. He was sorry and tried to prove his <u>bravery</u> later.

> The writer used specific nouns. The reader will have a better picture.

Add Sentences Think of two sentences to add to the BETTER model above. Be sure to use specific nouns.

✎ **WRITE ON YOUR OWN** Write about a time when you were brave. Use specific, precise nouns. Use a singular noun for "one" and a plural noun for "more than one."

REMEMBER

- To make most nouns plural, add **-s**.
- If the noun ends in **s, z, sh, ch,** or **x,** add **-es**.
- If the noun ends in **y** after a consonant, change the **y** to **i**. Then add **-es**.
- Some nouns have special forms.

▲ A warrior proves his bravery.

from The House on Mango Street
by Sandra Cisneros

illustrated by
Rafael Lopez

Build Background

Explore Homes and Houses

What does home mean to you? Discover what it means to others.

Connect

Quickwrite "Good things come to those who wait" is a common expression. But that may not always be true. Often, people must make decisions to follow their dreams. What is your biggest dream in life? What steps will you take to make it happen?

Digital Library

myNGconnect.com
🔄 View the images.

▲ People identify strongly with their homes.

Language & Grammar

1 TRY OUT LANGUAGE
2 LEARN GRAMMAR
3 APPLY ON YOUR OWN

Express Ideas and Opinions

CD

Study the painting and the quotation.
Listen to what others think.

Amy: A girl stands at a window. I think she's waiting for someone to visit her.

Andrew: I disagree. I see water and a boat. I think she wants to leave home and sail across the water.

Laura: In my opinion, she's daydreaming about what she will be when she is older.

Amy: Maybe you are right. The quotation makes me think she's dreaming about her future.

Andrew: In my opinion, the quotation is too simple. It takes more than a dream to reach your goals.

What do you see in the painting? What do you think?

PICTURE PROMPT

Young Girl at the Window, 1925, Salvador Dali. Oil on board.

"The future belongs to those who believe in the beauty of their dreams."

—Eleanor Roosevelt

Language and Grammar, continued

Use Action Verbs

- **Verbs** tell what a person *does*, *has*, or *is*. An action verb tells what a person does.

    EXAMPLE   Marie **writes** about her goal.

- A complete predicate in a sentence often tells what the subject does. The **verb** is the most important word in the predicate.

Sentence	Complete Predicate	Verb
Marie **writes** about her goal.	**writes** about her goal	**writes**
She **dreams** about traveling around the world.	**dreams** about traveling around the world	**dreams**

- The **verb** has to agree with, or match, the subject. Add **-s** to the verb if the subject tells about one place, one thing, or one other person.

    EXAMPLES   Marie **tells** her sister.
    The girls **tell** their mother.

Practice Together

Say each sentence with the correct verb.

1. Marie (read/reads) books about different countries.
2. She (plan/plans) many adventures.
3. Marie's sister (help/helps) her plan.
4. The sisters (eat/eats) at different kinds of restaurants.
5. The girls (learn/learns) about many cultures.

Try It!

Read each sentence. Write the correct verb on a card.
Then say the sentence with the correct verb.

6. The girls (discover/discovers) new ideas.
7. Their mother (help/helps) them make plans.
8. Marie (want/wants) to go far away.
9. Her sister (agree/agrees) with her.
10. Their friends (send/sends) them information, too.

▲ A reader discovers new ideas.

Tell a Partner

EXPRESS IDEAS AND OPINIONS

Everyone has ideas and opinions. How do you think this photo shows a dream or a goal? What's your opinion about it?

Gather your ideas and opinions in a chart.

My Ideas	My Opinions
That building is very tall.	In my opinion, the girl looks small next to the building.
It must be in a big city.	I think she might be moving there.

Then use your chart to tell a partner what you think. Trade roles.

HOW TO EXPRESS IDEAS AND OPINIONS

1. To express an idea, tell what you see.

2. To express an opinion, tell what you think or feel. Give reasons for your opinion.

> I think the girl wants to work in that building.

USE VERBS

Think about the **verbs** you will use when you express your ideas and opinions. The verbs you use need to agree with the subjects of your sentences.

Remember to add **-s** to the verb if the subject is singular.

Singular subject: The girl **stares** at the skyscraper. I think she has a goal.

Plural subject: Many people **work** in the building. I think it's in a big city.

Prepare to Read

Learn Key Vocabulary

Study the Words Use the steps below.

1. Pronounce the word. Say it aloud several times. Spell it.
2. Rate your word knowledge.
3. Study the example. Tell more about the word.
4. Practice it. Make the word your own.

Key Words

appreciate (u-prē-shē-āt)
verb ▶ page 66

When you **appreciate** something, you understand its importance. You **appreciate** an umbrella when it rains.

despite (di-**spīt**) *preposition*
▶ page 66

Despite means even though or without regard to. The man felt cold, **despite** his warm jacket.

disgusted (di-**skus**-tid)
adjective ▶ page 67

To be **disgusted** means that you dislike something. Some people are **disgusted** by frogs.

expectation
(eks-pek-**tā**-shun) *noun* ▶ page 62

An **expectation** is something you look forward to or have ideas about. We had great **expectations** about our project.
Base Word: **expect**

landlord (**land**-lawrd) *noun*
▶ page 62

A **landlord** is a person who owns land or buildings. My **landlord** always makes sure the building is clean.

rent (rent) *noun*
▶ page 62

When you pay **rent**, you pay money to the owner of a property to live there. The mother paid **rent** for the family's apartment every month.

strength (strength) *noun*
▶ page 66

Strength is the quality of being powerful. The **strength** of the storm destroyed many homes.

temporary (tem-pa-rair-ē)
adjective ▶ page 64

When something is **temporary**, it lasts only a short time. They had **temporary** housing and would soon move.

Practice the Words Make a Study Card for each Key Word. Then compare your cards with a partner.

> *expectation*
>
> **What it means:** something you look forward to or have ideas about
>
> **Example:** My expectation about the party was right—it was fun!
>
> **Not an example:** I had no idea how the book would end. I had no expectations.

Study Card

Make Connections, Visualize

Make Connections When you read a text, combine information from what you read with what you already know from other texts, your own life, or the world.

> ### Look Into the Text
>
> The house on Mango Street is ours, and we don't have to... share the yard with the people downstairs, or be careful not to make too much noise...

Make Connections: My family shares a yard with our neighbor. Sometimes noise from my band bothers our neighbors.

Visualize Picturing what you are reading about helps you better understand how things look, sound, smell, taste, or feel.

> ### Look Into the Text
>
> But the house on Mango Street is not the way they told it at all... Bricks are crumbling in places...

Visualize: I picture a house that is falling apart. It looks dirty and smells bad. The walls feel weak and rough.

Practice Together

Begin a Reading Strategies Log Use the Reading Strategies Log to show how the strategies help you understand text. The first row shows how one strategy helped one reader. Reread the passage and add to the Log.

Text I read	Strategy I used	How I used the strategy
Page: 62 **Text:** We don't have to...share the yard with the people downstairs, or be careful not to make too much noise...	☑ **Make Connections** ☐ **Visualize** ☐ _____ ☐ _____	Making connections to houses I know about helps me understand how the character and her family live.

Short Fiction

Short fiction tells a brief story about imaginary people, places, things, or events. The writer uses characters' words, feelings, and actions to describe events and move the plot along.

What do you see in your head when you read these lines? Do they remind you of anything you've read before?

Look Into the Text

> You live *there*? The way she said it made me feel like nothing. *There*. I lived *there*. I nodded.
>
> I knew then I had to have a house. A real house.

I see two people talking to each other. One has a mean look on her face, while the other looks embarrassed. I can make a connection to my own life, when I let a mean comment make me feel like nothing.

To better understand a story, try to visualize the characters and events. Also think about connections you can make to your own life or to other texts you've read.

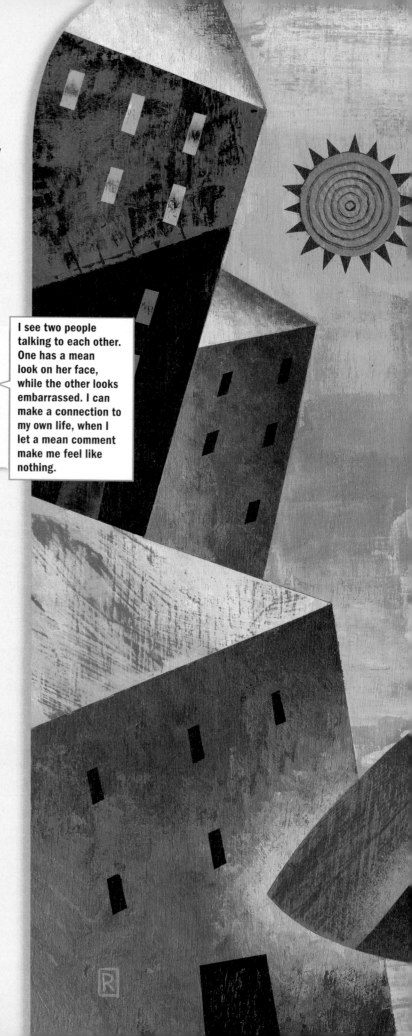

from The House on
Mango Street

by Sandra Cisneros

illustrated by
Rafael Lopez

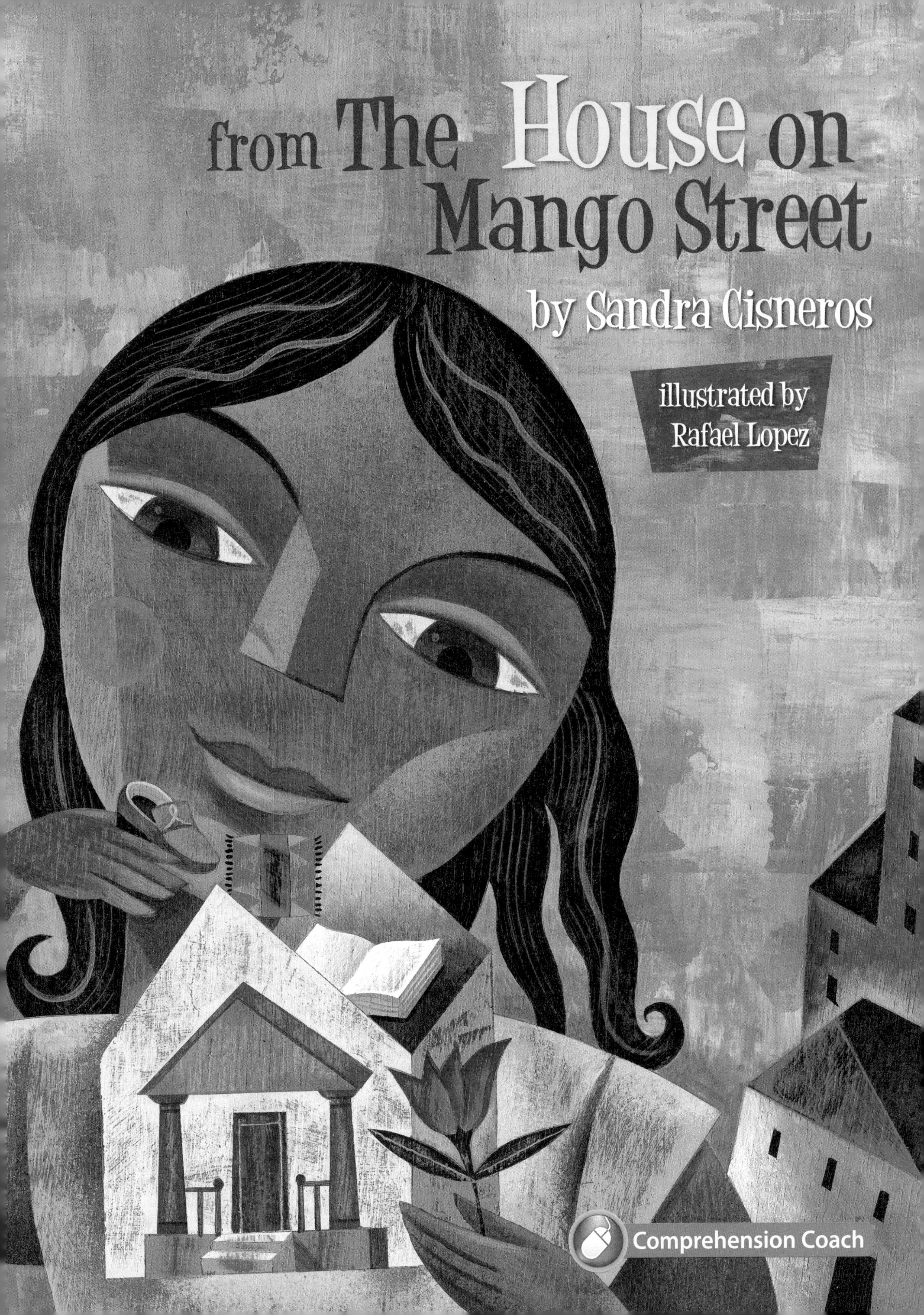

Comprehension Coach

The House on
Mango Street

We didn't always live on Mango Street. Before that we lived on Loomis on the third floor, and before that we lived on Keeler. Before Keeler it was Paulina, and before that I can't remember. But what I remember most is moving a lot. Each time it seemed there'd be one more of us. By the time we got to Mango Street we were six—Mama, Papa, Carlos, Kiki, my sister Nenny and me.

The house on Mango Street is ours, and we don't have to pay **rent** to anybody, or share the yard with the people downstairs, or be careful not to make too much noise, and there isn't a **landlord** banging on the ceiling with a broom. But even so, it's not the house we'd thought we'd get.

We had to leave the **flat** on Loomis quick. The water pipes broke and the landlord wouldn't fix them because the house was too old. We had to leave fast. We were using the washroom next door and carrying water over in empty milk gallons. That's why Mama and Papa looked for a house, and that's why we moved into the house on Mango Street, far away, on the other side of town.

They always told us that one day we would move into a house, a real house that would be ours for always so we wouldn't

Key Vocabulary

expectation *n.*, something that a person looks forward to

rent *n.*, money paid to live on an owner's property

landlord *n.*, a person who owns land or buildings

In Other Words

flat apartment

have to move each year. And our house would have running water and pipes that worked. And inside it would have real stairs, not **hallway stairs**, but stairs inside like the houses on TV. And we'd have a basement and at least three washrooms so when we took a bath we wouldn't have to tell everybody. Our house would be white with trees around it, a great big yard and grass growing without a fence. This was the house Papa talked about

In Other Words
hallway stairs stairs shared by everyone in the building

Language Background
Apartments and flats refer to the same type of housing, or style of buildings where people live. The term *apartment* is more commonly used in North America.

when he **held a lottery ticket** and this was the house Mama **dreamed up** in the stories she told us before we went to bed.

But the house on Mango Street is not the way they told it at all. It's small and red with **tight** steps in front and windows so small you'd think they were holding their breath. Bricks are crumbling in places, and the front door is **so swollen** you have to push hard to get in. There is no front yard, only four little elms the city planted by the curb. Out back is a small garage for the car we don't own yet and a small yard that looks smaller between the two buildings on either side. There are stairs in our house, but they're ordinary hallway stairs, and the house has only one washroom. Everybody has to share a bedroom—Mama and Papa, Carlos and Kiki, me and Nenny.

Once when we were living on Loomis, a nun from my school passed by and saw

You live there?

me playing out front. The laundromat downstairs had been boarded up because it had been robbed two days before and the owner had painted on the wood YES WE'RE OPEN so as not to lose **business**.

Where do you live? she asked.

There, I said pointing up to the third floor.

You live *there*?

There. I had to look to where she pointed—the third floor, the paint peeling, wooden bars Papa had nailed on the windows so we wouldn't fall out. You live *there*? The way she said it made me feel like nothing. *There.* I lived *there*. I nodded.

I knew then I had to have a house. A real house. One I could point to. But this isn't it. The house on Mango Street isn't it. For the time being, Mama says. **Temporary**, says Papa. But I know how **those things go**.

Key Vocabulary
temporary *adj.*, for a short time

In Other Words
held a lottery ticket dreamed of winning money
dreamed up thought about
tight small, narrow
so swollen too big for the frame so
business customers
those things go plans can change

Look Into the Text

1. **Narrator's Point of View** How do the girl's **expectations** of a real house compare to the house on Mango Street?

2. **Compare and Contrast** How is life on Mango Street like and unlike life on Loomis?

3. **Inference** Why does the girl "feel like nothing"? Explain.

▲ Critical Viewing: Effect How do you think the girl feels? How do the colors, shapes, and angles help create this mood?

Four Skinny Trees

They are the only ones who understand me. I am the only one who understands them. Four skinny trees with skinny necks and pointy elbows like mine. Four who do not belong here but are here. Four **raggedy excuses** planted by the city. From our room we can hear them, but Nenny just sleeps and doesn't **appreciate** these things.

Their **strength** is secret. They send ferocious roots beneath the ground. They grow up and they grow down and **grab the earth between their hairy toes and bite the sky with violent teeth** and never quit their anger. This is how they keep.

Let one forget his reason for being, they'd all droop like tulips in a glass, each with their arms around the other. Keep, keep, keep, trees say when I sleep. They teach.

When I am too sad and too skinny to keep keeping, when I am a tiny thing against so many bricks, then it is I look at trees. When there is nothing left to look at on this street. Four who grew **despite** concrete. Four who reach and do not forget to reach. Four whose only reason is to be and be.

Key Vocabulary

appreciate *v.*, to understand the value of something
strength *n.*, the quality of being powerful
despite *prep.*, even though

In Other Words

raggedy excuses worn and weak trees
grab the earth between their hairy toes and bite the sky with violent teeth use their roots and branches to hold on

A **Smart** Cookie

I could've **been somebody**, you know? my mother says and sighs. She has lived in this city her whole life. She can speak two languages. She can sing an opera. She knows how to fix a TV. But she doesn't know which subway train to take to get downtown. I hold her hand very tight while we wait for the right train to arrive.

She used to draw when she had time. Now she draws with a needle and thread, little knotted rosebuds, tulips made of silk thread. Someday she would like to go to the ballet. Someday she would like to see a play. She borrows opera records from the public library and sings with **velvety lungs** powerful as morning glories.

I could've been somebody, you know?

Today while cooking oatmeal she is Madame Butterfly until she sighs and points the wooden spoon at me. I could've been somebody, you know? Esperanza, you go to school. Study hard. That Madame Butterfly was a fool. She stirs the oatmeal. Look at my **comadres**. She means Izaura whose husband left and Yolanda whose husband is dead. Got to take care all your own, she says shaking her head.

Then out of nowhere: Shame is a bad thing, you know? It keeps you down. You want to know why I quit school? Because I didn't have nice clothes. No clothes, but I had brains.

Yup, she says **disgusted**, stirring again. I was a smart cookie then.

Key Vocabulary
disgusted *adj.*, feeling ashamed

In Other Words
been somebody become someone important
velvety lungs a beautiful voice
comadres godmothers (in Spanish)

Look Into the Text

1. **Interpret** Describe the trees. How are the trees a symbol of the narrator's life?
2. **Character** What details show that Esperanza's mother is smart, even though she did not finish school?

A **House** of My Own

Not a flat. Not an apartment in back. Not a man's house. Not a daddy's. A house all my own. With my porch and my pillow, my pretty purple **petunias**. My books and my stories. My two shoes waiting beside the bed. Nobody to **shake a stick at**. Nobody's garbage to pick up after.

Only a house quiet as snow, a space for myself to go, **clean as paper before the poem**.

◣ Critical Viewing: Setting What details do you see in this image? How do they relate to the text?

In Other Words
petunias flowers
shake a stick at get mad at
clean as paper before the poem
   a place that no one has lived
   in before

△ Critical Viewing: Plot Describe this image. How does it relate to the girl's experience in the text?

Mango Says
Goodbye Sometimes

I like to tell stories. I tell them inside my head. I tell them after the mailman says, Here's your mail. Here's your mail he said.

I make a story for my life, for each step my brown shoe takes. I say, "And so she trudged up the wooden stairs, her sad brown shoes taking her to the house she never liked."

I like to tell stories. I am going to tell you a story about a girl who didn't want to belong.

We didn't always live on Mango Street. Before that we lived on Loomis on the third floor, and before that we lived on Keeler. Before Keeler it was Paulina, but what I remember most is Mango Street, sad red house, the house I belong but do not belong to.

I **put it down on paper** and then the **ghost does not ache** so much. I write it down and Mango says goodbye sometimes. **She does not hold me with both arms.** She sets me free.

In Other Words
put it down on paper write
ghost does not ache memories do
   not hurt me
**She does not hold me with both
   arms.** My past does not stop me.

One day I will pack my bags of books and paper. One day I will say goodbye to Mango. I am too strong for her to keep me here forever. One day I will go away.

Friends and neighbors will say, What happened to that Esperanza?

Where did she go with all those books and paper? Why did she **march** so far away?

They will not know I have gone away to come back. For the ones I left behind. For the ones who **cannot out**. ❖

About the Author

Sandra Cisneros

Throughout her childhood, **Sandra Cisneros** (1954–) and her family moved many times. She read books to make a home in her imagination. There was a book called *The Little House* that she checked out of the library over and over again. The house in the story was her dream house. Soon Cisneros started writing her own stories. In 1984, she published *The House on Mango Street*. Now she lives in a house of her own in San Antonio, Texas.

In Other Words
march go
cannot out are not able to leave

Look Into the Text

1. **Character's Motive** Why does the girl write about the house on Mango Street?

2. **Check Prediction** The text doesn't give the answer, but it gives more evidence. What do you think now: Will the girl "say goodbye to Mango"? Why or why not?

Connect Reading and Writing

Vocabulary
appreciate
despite
disgust
expectations
landlord
rent
strengths
temporary

CRITICAL THINKING

1. **SUM IT UP** Review the Reading Strategies Log you created while reading. What was most important for you to understand in each part of the story? Include these ideas in a summary of the story.

Text I read	Strategy I used	How I used the strategy
Page: 62 **Text:** We don't have to...share the yard with the people downstairs, or be careful not to make too much noise...	☑ **Make Connections** ☐ **Visualize** ☐ _____ ☐ _____	Making connections to houses I know about helps me understand how the character and her family live.

Reading Strategies Log

2. **Draw Conclusions** Mama's life does not match her **expectations**. What does Esperanza learn from her?

3. **Compare** Esperanza doesn't want to have to pay **rent** to a **landlord**. How is her dream house different from the other places she has lived?

4. **Make Judgments** Think about all three selections. **Despite** mistakes, Arturo, Lekuton, and Esperanza all make important decisions. Whose decision do you think was the hardest? Explain.

READING FLUENCY

Phrasing Read the passage on page 626 to a partner. Assess your fluency.

1. I did not pause/sometimes paused/ always paused for punctuation.

2. What I did best was _____ .

READING STRATEGY

What strategy helped you understand this selection? Tell a partner about it.

VOCABULARY REVIEW

Oral Review Read the paragraph aloud. Add the vocabulary words.

People have different _____ about their homes. Some people pay _____ to a _____ . Some people want to own a home. Every kind of home has different _____ . Most people _____ their homes even if they are _____ . Sometimes people must put up with a home, _____ the _____ they might feel about it.

Written Review Draw a house for Esperanza. Write captions to explain why she would **appreciate** this home. Use at least four vocabulary words.

WRITE ABOUT THE GUIDING QUESTION

Explore Personal Decisions

Esperanza's **expectations** and disappointments lead her to make a decision about her future. Reread the selection. Then explain what she did and why.

Connect Across the Curriculum

Vocabulary Study

Suffix	Meaning
-ion	condition or action
-ful	full of

Use Word Parts

> **Academic Vocabulary**
> - **connection** (ku-**nek**-shun) *noun*
>   The **connection** between two things is something they have in common.

If you see a word with a **suffix** or a **compound word** that you do not know, analyze the base word. For a word with a suffix, cover the part of the word that is not the base word. Here you see that *protect* is the base word.

protection = protect + ion

In a compound word, the **connection** of two base words makes a new word.

bird + house = birdhouse

Find Base Words Work with a partner. Find the base words. Find the **connection** between the base word and the meaning of the whole word.

1. downstairs (p. 62)
2. washroom (p. 62)
3. expectation (p. 62)
4. hallway (p. 63)
5. everybody (p. 63)
6. powerful (p. 67)

Write a Description Use at least three of these words to write about your own home. Share your description with a partner.

Literary Analysis

Analyze Theme

> **Academic Vocabulary**
> - **analyze** (a-nu-līz) *verb*
>   When you **analyze**, you separate something into parts and examine, or study, it.

What Is the Story's Message? The title "The House on Mango Street" presents a topic. The topic is what the story is about. In this story, the main character wants a house of her own. A story also has a **theme**, or message, about the topic. To identify the theme of the story, pay attention to the thoughts, words, and actions of the characters.

Analyze Theme To analyze the author's message, notice how characters' thoughts, words, and actions change over the story. Notice what the characters learn. At the beginning of the story, the girl mentions moving a lot. How does this idea develop over the story? What does the girl learn and how does she change?

Express Ideas and Opinions

Pair Share With a partner, share your ideas and opinions about what you want to do when you are older. Give reasons for your opinions. Be sure the verbs you use agree with the subjects of your sentences.

> I want to be a chef. I think it's exciting to create new dishes.

Write with Colorful Action Words

Study the Models When you write, you want to catch your reader's interest. One way to do that is to use colorful action verbs. Many verbs tell what someone or something does—*eats, nibbles, munches, gobbles, gulps, devours*. These action verbs can be boring, like *eats*, or they can give a colorful, vivid picture, like *gobbles* or *devours*.

JUST OK

> Esperanza looks at the house on Mango Street. Four trees grow in the front near the street. Bricks on the house break slowly. The front door doesn't want to open.

The reader thinks: "This writing is plain."

BETTER

> Esperanza frowns at the house on Mango Street. Four trees grab the earth in the front near the street. Bricks on the house crumble slowly. The front door clings to the house. It doesn't want to open.

The reader thinks: "This is better. The verb 'frowns' helps me know that Esperanza doesn't like what she sees."

Add Sentences Think of two more sentences to add to the BETTER model above. Try to use colorful verbs from the chart.

Instead of . . .	Try a colorful verb like . . .
go	crawl, hobble, walk, hurry, race
look at	glance at, notice, observe, gaze, watch
laugh	grin, giggle, chuckle, cackle, howl
talk	chat, chatter, discuss, speak
write	jot down, scribble, record, compose

WRITE ON YOUR OWN Write about something you learned from Esperanza. Use colorful action verbs in your sentences. Use some action verbs from the chart or try a thesaurus. It can help you find more precise and colorful verbs.

REMEMBER

- Add **-s** to the action verb only when the subject is third-person, singular.

  One tree grow**s** in the backyard.

The Road Not Taken

by Robert Frost

Two roads **diverged** in a yellow wood,
And sorry I could not travel both
And be one traveler, long I stood
And looked down one as far as I could
5   To where it bent in the undergrowth;

Then took the other, as just as fair,
And having perhaps the better **claim**
Because it was grassy and wanted wear,
Though as for that the passing there
10   Had worn them really about the same,

And both that morning equally lay
In leaves no step had trodden black.
Oh, I marked the first for another day!
Yet knowing how way leads on to way
15   I doubted if I should ever come back.

I shall be telling this with a sigh
Somewhere ages and ages **hence**:
Two roads diverged in a wood, and I,
I took the one less traveled by,
20   And that has made all the difference.

In Other Words
diverged split
claim look
hence in the future

Compare Across Texts

Compare Universal Themes

"American Names, "A Lion Hunt," and "The Road Not Taken" tell about people who are faced with difficult decisions. What is the **connection** among their themes?

How It Works

Collect and Organize Ideas You can use a chart to help you compare ideas across these three texts. What questions might help you compare?

Title	Question: What situation does each narrator face?	Question: What decision does each narrator make?
"American Names"	Arturo is trying to fit in at school. His teacher calls him "Arthur."	Arturo decides to take back his name.
"A Lion Hunt"	Lekuton wants to appear brave and fight a lion.	
"The Road Not Taken"		

Comparison Chart

Practice Together

Study and Summarize Ideas Compare the answers for the first question, then summarize. Think about ways the texts are alike.

> The speakers of "American Names", "The Lion Hunt," and "The Road Not Taken" feel torn between different places. Arturo feels trapped between his Hispanic culture and his new American one. Lekuton attends school and feels caught between two different worlds. The poem's narrator does not know which path in the woods to take.

Try It!

Copy this chart to collect answers for the second question. Summarize them. You can use this frame to help you express your comparison.

The narrators all struggle with _____. Arturo feels torn between Hispanic and American identities. At first, he _____, but then _____. Lekuton feels caught because _____. To try and prove himself, he _____. The narrator of the poem can't decide _____. He finally chooses _____ and feels _____ about it.

Academic Vocabulary
- **connection** (ku-**nek**-shun) *noun*
  The connection between two things is something they have in common.

DECISION
Point

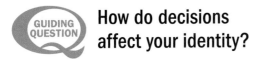

How do decisions affect your identity?

Content Library

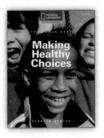

Leveled Library

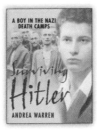

Reflect on Your Reading

Think back on your reading of the unit selections. Discuss what you did to understand what you read.

Reading Strategies

In this unit, you were introduced to eight different reading strategies and how they can be applied to text to make you a better reader. Choose a selection from this unit. Explain to a partner how you applied reading strategies to better understand the text. Tell about at least four different strategies. Then explain how you will plan to use each of the eight reading strategies in the future.

Explore the

Throughout this unit, you have been thinking about decisions and identity. Choose one of these ways to explore the Guiding Question:

- **Discuss** With a group, discuss the Guiding Question. Give examples from real life of decisions that affect who you are. Compare them to decisions in the selections.

- **Describe** Each selection describes a place that affects the main character's identity. Describe a place that is important to you. Give details to help listeners see it in their minds.

- **Write** Write a letter to one of the authors of these selections. Tell what you liked about the narrative.

Book Talk

Which Unit Library book did you choose? Explain to a partner what it taught you about decision making.

STAND OR FALL

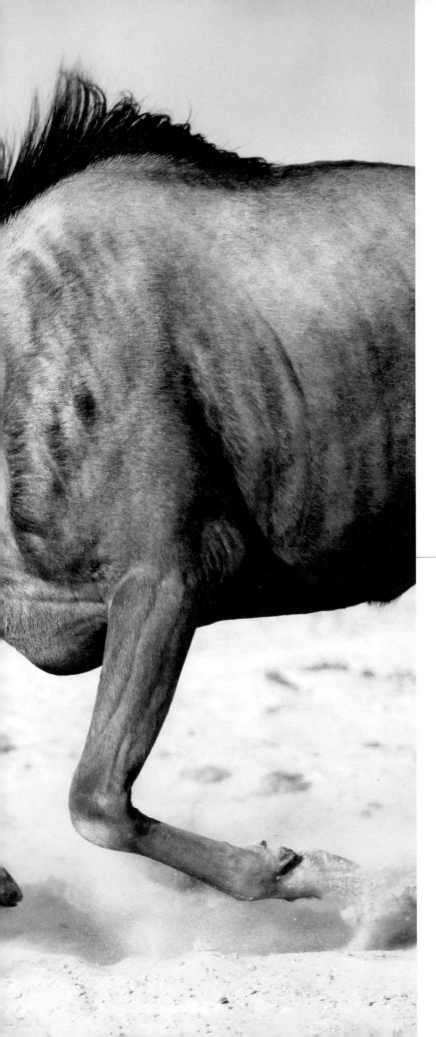

GUIDING QUESTION

What happens when people come face-to-face with a rival?

READ MORE!

Content Library
   Amazing Animals
   by Kate Boehm Nyquist

Leveled Library
   Romiette and Julio
   by Sharon M. Draper
   Speak
   by Laurie Halse Anderson
   The Dragon Prince
   by Suzanne Jurmain

Web Links
   myNGconnect.com

◀ Two male wildebeests lock horns
in a battle for territory.

Focus on Reading

Elements of Fiction

▶ **Plot**
▶ **Character**
▶ **Setting**

Every story has at least three parts, or **elements**—plot, characters, and setting. These **elements** of fiction work together to build a story.

Plot: How It Works

The **plot** is what happens in the story. It is what the characters experience.

- Plots are based on a **conflict**, or problem, that the main character faces.
- The plot develops during the **rising action** as complications occur and the characters try to solve the problem.
- The turning point in the plot is called the **climax**.
- **Falling action** leads from the climax to the **resolution**, the stage where the problem is solved at the end of the story.

Read "A Walk in the City" aloud to see the stages of the plot.

A Walk in the City

One afternoon a girl named Red walked into the city to take soup to her sick grandmother. She suddenly heard a barking sound behind her. Red turned around and saw a dog staring at her. She was scared of dogs so she started to walk faster. The dog followed her. "How am I going to get rid of this dog? What should I do?" Red wondered.

The dog kept following Red. Then he started to whine. Suddenly, she remembered the soup in her hands. She set down the soup, and the dog ate it up. After he finished, he came up to her. She stood still, not moving. Then he licked her foot and wagged his tail.

She realized he had been hungry and might be lost. She read his tag. The address was right next to her grandmother's apartment! So Red continued to her grandmother's, with the dog following her.

setting
character

conflict

rising action

climax

resolution

Academic Vocabulary

• **element** (el-u-munt) *noun*
   An **element** is one part of a whole.

Plot: Practice Together

Read "A Walk in the City" again. As you read, listen for events of the plot and tell where they go on this Plot Diagram.

Character: How It Works

Characters are the people or animals that take part in the plot.

- Each character's traits, actions, words, and decisions affect what happens in the plot.
- Writers tell readers about their characters by:
  - saying directly what the character is like
  - showing the characters' thoughts, words, and actions
  - telling what other characters think of him or her.
- These writing techniques are called **characterization**.

See these techniques in action as the writer characterizes Kit Fox below.

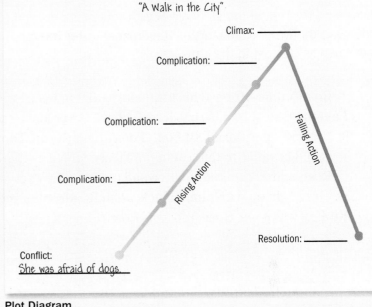

"A Walk in the City"

Climax: _____

Complication: _____

Complication: _____

Complication: _____

Rising Action

Falling Action

Resolution: _____

Conflict:
She was afraid of dogs.

Plot Diagram

A Foxy Challenge

The sun was setting as Kit Fox left her desert den. Hunting had not been good the night before, and she was hungry. She needed to find food, so she trotted off across the dry land hunting for food. Soon, Kit Fox saw Roadrunner with a fresh meal in his beak. Roadrunner looked up nervously. Foxes and birds are usually enemies in the desert.

Telling about the character directly

"Ah, I see that you have a yummy mouse for your evening meal," Kit Fox said. She eyed the bird's catch hungrily. "That must have been easy for you to catch. I've heard that you are very speedy."

Character's words and actions

Academic Vocabulary

- **characterization** (kair-ik-tur-iz-ā-shun) *noun*
  The way writers show their characters is called **characterization**.

Character: Practice Together

Now read the rest of the story aloud with your class. As you read, listen for the ways the writer characterizes Roadrunner. After you read, complete the activities listed next to the passage.

> Roadrunner dropped his meal and held it in his claws. "Oh, yes, I am the fastest bird in this desert. I have never lost a race!"
>
> "Never?" questioned Kit Fox. "I don't believe you. I am very fast myself. Let's race to that cactus. We'll see who gets there first."
>
> Roadrunner counted to three and raced to the cactus. Kit Fox never caught up with him. In fact, when Roadrunner returned, Kit Fox was gone. Gone, too, was Roadrunner's meal.

1. Make a Character Description Chart for both Kit Fox and Roadrunner. What new information about Kit Fox did you learn at the end of the story?
2. How would the plot change if Roadrunner were more clever than Kit Fox?

Character	What the Character Is Like	How I Know
Roadrunner	not clever	Roadrunner falls for the trick
Kit Fox	tricky	Kit Fox tricks Roadrunner

Character Description Chart

Setting: How It Works

Setting is the time and place where a story happens.

- Setting includes the customs and the way people think at that time and place. During the course of the story, the setting may change.
- The time and place affect how the characters think and act.
- Setting also affects the plot. For example, a story set in a hot desert would probably not include characters being caught in a hurricane.

See how one writer uses the **element** of setting.

> ### A Foxy Challenge
> The sun was setting as Kit Fox left her desert den. Hunting had not been good the night before, and she was hungry. She needed to find food, so she trotted off across the dry land hunting for food. Soon, Kit Fox saw Roadrunner with a fresh meal in his beak. Roadrunner looked up nervously. Foxes and birds are usually enemies in the desert.

The time and place

Customs of the time and place

Setting: Practice Together

Now read a different version of this story aloud with your class. As you read, listen for details about the setting. After you read, complete the activities next to the passage.

It was almost midnight when Kit Fox left her den in the alley behind the trash bin. Hunting had not been good the night before because of the storm and flooding, and she was hungry. She needed to find food, so she crept along the alley hunting for food. Soon, Kit Fox saw Roadrunner with a rain-soaked meal in his beak. Roadrunner looked up nervously. It was dangerous for a bird to be out this late, especially around strangers.

1. Describe the time and place and what the characters think.
2. Compare the different settings in these two versions of "A Foxy Challenge."
3. With a partner, predict how the plot of the second version would be different from the first plot as a result of the different setting.

Try It!

Read the following passage aloud and answer the questions about the **elements** of fiction. Tell how you know.

A Music Caper

"Who stole my new CD?" shouted Rudy from his room. He was getting ready for school.

One by one, Rudy approached his family members. He knocked on his sister's door. "Cara, give me back my CD," he said. She opened the door. "I don't have it Rudy," she replied. Rudy looked around. His CD was not there.

Then he went to his brother's room. "Andrew, where is my new CD?" "I don't have it, Rudy," he replied.

"Mom, Dad, have you seen my new CD?" Rudy said as he searched the kitchen. He looked everywhere but still couldn't find it. "I don't have it, Rudy," his mom said. "Rudy, you've asked each one of us, and you've searched every room. We don't have it," his dad said.

Rudy was not convinced. If his new CD was missing, someone must have taken it. He sat at the breakfast table sulking.

Later as Rudy sat on the bus to school, he reached into his backpack to get his science book. As he searched for the book, he felt a square shape. Rudy had found his new CD. It had been in his backpack all along!

That day after school, Rudy apologized to his family. Then they all sat down together to listen to his new CD.

1. What is the setting?
2. Who are the characters and what are they like?
3. What is the conflict?
4. How does the main character resolve the conflict?
5. How would the plot be different if the characters were fish and the setting was the ocean?

Focus on Vocabulary

Relate Words

Synonyms are words with similar meanings that describe the same concept. No two synonyms mean exactly the same thing. They have specific definitions and different shades of meaning. For example, one word might have a much stronger meaning than its synonym does.

EXAMPLE   Amber had to play hard to **beat** her opponent, but she was finally able to **vanquish** the other player.

Knowing the specific meaning of a synonym and how it **relates** to other words can help you better understand what you read. A Synonym Scale like the one below can help you sort out the shades of meaning of words that describe the same concept.

Synonym Scale

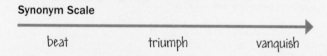

How the Strategy Works

The more words you know about a concept, the better you will be able to express your own thoughts and understand exactly what someone says.

1. Every time you read, take the opportunity to learn new words.
2. Put words into groups, or categories, to see how they **relate** to one another. This will help you understand their specific definitions.
3. Use a Synonym Scale to rank synonyms from weakest to strongest.

Use the strategy to figure out how the underlined words **relate** to each other.

> Our school tennis team won the city finals this year. My sister Jana is the team captain. People say Jana is the best player on the team. Everyone was <u>excited</u> about our victory. Jana was <u>thrilled</u> because she won every one of her games.

Strategy in Action

" *Excited* and *thrilled* both mean a shade of 'happy,' but I think a player would be happier to win than fans would be, so *thrilled* must be stronger than *excited*."

☑ **REMEMBER** Using shades of meanings and knowing how synonyms **relate** to one another can help you understand a word's specific meaning.

Academic Vocabulary
- **relate** (ri-lāt) *verb*
  When you **relate** things, you show how they are connected.

Read this passage aloud. Then, work with your class to make a Synonym Scale for the underlined words.

The Sound of Drums

Someone gave my upstairs neighbor a drum set for his birthday. He has been practicing on those drums ever since, and the sounds coming through the ceiling are driving me crazy!

At first, he spent hours tapping a simple beat with one drum stick. It was quiet, so I didn't mind too much.

Then he moved on to learning how to play the bass drum. He seems to enjoy thumping loudly on the bass. The sound coming through the ceiling is giving me a headache.

I have started pounding on the ceiling to get him to quiet down. It isn't working. He keeps practicing.

I am afraid that next I'll hear him clashing the cymbals. That will wake up the whole building!

Then all the neighbors will be knocking on his door complaining about the noise!

Try It!

Read the following passage and notice the underlined synonyms. Which year had the best tasting barbeque? How do you know?

It's All in the Family

Every August, brothers Joe and George compete to see who makes the best barbeque. They have had this cooking rivalry for years, and the family loves it. Relatives from around the country come to picnic and enjoy the brothers' food. Everyone votes to decide which barbeque is the best that year.

Two years ago, Joe's entry won the contest. People called it "tasty." Last year George won. Everyone declared that his special sauce made with cranberries was scrumptious. This year was different. Both men had experimented with strange ingredients. Neither brother's barbeque was even appetizing! The family voted against them both and decided they should work together from then on.

On the Menu

by Susan E. Goodman

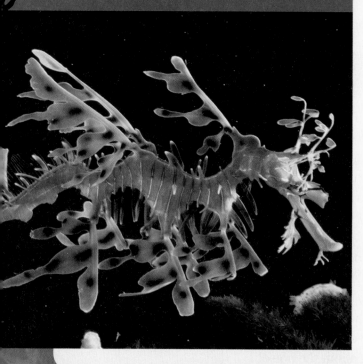

Build Background

Watch Animals in Nature

How does an animal survive in nature? Animals have different ways of protecting themselves. They may hide, run, or try to blend in with their environment.

Connect

Play a Game Make cards with pictures of animals on them. Show a card to a partner. Does this animal hunt other animals? Is this animal hunted by other animals? Put each card in a *Hunter* or *Hunted* pile. Do some cards belong in both piles?

Digital Library

myNGconnect.com
↻ View the video.

▲ This grasshopper blends into the grass so that other animals won't see it.

Language & Grammar

Define and Explain

CD

Study the photo. Read the labels.
Listen to the information.

PICTURE PROMPT

How Does an Octopus Disappear?

Octopuses have well-developed brains. They are smart animals.

head

Octopuses have very good eyesight. They have a large eye on either side of their heads.

eye

An octopus has eight arms called tentacles. They are attached to the octopus's head. Each tentacle has two rows of suckers on it.

tentacle

ink

An octopus squirts ink to protect itself. The ink forms a cloud. It looks like smoke. The octopus "disappears" in the ink.

1 TRY OUT LANGUAGE
2 LEARN GRAMMAR
3 APPLY ON YOUR OWN

Use Pronouns as Subjects

A **pronoun** refers to a noun. A **subject pronoun** is a pronoun that is the subject of a sentence.

Subject Pronoun	Example Sentence
• Use **I** to talk about yourself. • Use **we** to talk about another person and yourself.	• **I** study ocean animals. • Lisa and I read books about the ocean. **We** study the photos.
• Use **you** to talk to another person. • Use **you** also to talk to more than one person.	• **You** are a good photographer. • Class, **you** are all good photographers.
• Use **he** to talk about one man or boy. • Use **she** to talk about one woman or girl. • Use **it** to talk about one thing, place, or idea. • Use **they** to talk about more than one person, place, thing, or idea.	• The diver photographs an octopus. **He** uses an underwater camera. • Lisa studies octopus behavior. **She** is amazed by their ability to hide. • The octopus squirts ink. **It** escapes quickly. • Octopuses have eight arms. **They** also have good eyesight.

Practice Together

Say each sentence with the correct subject pronoun.

1. Mark and I study a photo of an octopus. (We/They) are curious.
2. The poison of some octopuses is dangerous. (He/It) can hurt people.
3. The scientist takes a picture of an octopus underwater. (She/They) swims away slowly.
4. Octopuses are not good swimmers. (He/They) use their arms to crawl on the ocean bottom.

Try It!

Write the correct subject pronoun on a card. Then say the sentence and add the pronoun.

5. Octopuses are very smart animals. (We/They) can change how they look.
6. Sometimes an octopus cannot trick its enemy. Then (they/it) uses ink to disappear.
7. A diver examines an octopus. (He/They) wears special gloves.
8. My sister and I want to learn more about octopuses. (We/You) do research on the Internet.

▲ A scientist examines the suckers on an octopus.

Tell About an Animal's Behavior

DEFINE AND EXPLAIN

Animals act in all kinds of ways that can surprise us. Which animal do you want to find out more about?

Work with a partner to research an animal. Find out how the animal behaves and what makes it special. Use books, the Internet, or other sources to find information about the animal you choose.

Download a photo or draw a picture of the animal. Label its body parts. Include interesting facts about the animal's behavior with your labels.

With your partner, show your picture to a group of classmates. Tell your classmates how your animal behaves. Explain the interesting facts you discovered.

▲ A good explanation includes details.

HOW TO DEFINE AND EXPLAIN

1. Explain the meaning of the word or topic.
2. Give details or examples.
3. Use visuals for explanations.

> Two rows of suckers are on each arm of the octopus. They are used for tasting things.

USE PRONOUNS AS SUBJECTS

Think about the pronouns you will use in your explanation.

First use a **noun** to tell about your animal. Then use a **subject pronoun** to refer to it. Remember, a subject pronoun can refer to a subject noun.

Subject noun: The **octopus** changes color to trick enemies.

Subject pronoun: **It** can blend into the background.

Prepare to Read

Learn Key Vocabulary

Study the Words Use the steps below.

1. Pronounce the word. Say it aloud several times. Spell it.
2. Rate your word knowledge.
3. Study the example. Tell more about the word.
4. Practice it. Make the word your own.

Key Words

adaptation (a-dap-**tā**-shun) *noun* ▸ page 101

An **adaptation** is a feature or behavior that helps animals survive. This cat's arched back is an **adaptation** that protects it.

advantage (ad-**van**-tij) *noun* ▸ page 97

When you have an **advantage**, you have a better chance to succeed than others. If you are stronger or faster, this is an **advantage**.

camouflage (kam-a-flazh) *noun* ▸ page 96

Camouflage is a color or pattern that helps people or animals hide. Lions use **camouflage** to help them hide when they hunt.

disguise (dis-gīz) *noun* ▸ page 94

When you wear a **disguise**, you try to look different from what you normally look like. A **disguise** can help people or animals hide.

predator (pre-du-tur) *noun* ▸ page 94

A **predator** is an animal that eats other animals for food. Lions and tigers are **predators**.
Antonym: **prey**

prey (prā) *noun* ▸ page 102

Prey is an animal that other animals eat. A mouse is **prey** for a snake.
Antonym: **predator**

survive (sur-vīv) *verb* ▸ page 96

When you **survive**, you stay alive. In cold weather, you need warm clothes to **survive**.

threat (thret) *noun* ▸ page 96

A **threat** is a danger. Clouds show the **threat** of a storm.
Synonym: danger

Practice the Words Make an Example Web for each Key Word. Work with a partner to think of examples.

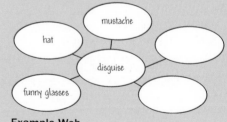

mustache

hat

disguise

funny glasses

Example Web

Relate Cause and Effect

How is writing organized? A cause-and-effect text **structure** shows what happens and why. A cause is why something happens. An effect is what happens because of the cause. Often there are several causes and effects in one selection.

As you read, take note of things that happen and why they happen.

Reading Strategies

- Plan
- **Monitor** Notice confusing parts in the text, then reread or read on to make them clear.
- Ask Questions
- Make Connections
- Visualize
- Make Inferences
- Determine Importance
- Synthesize

Look Into the Text

> When an armadillo spots a predator, it first tries to run away. A scared armadillo darts for the safety of its burrow. A burrow is an underground home.
>
> But that's just the beginning. If an armored armadillo cannot get away, it hides in its shell.

Practice Together

Begin a Cause-and-Effect Chart A Cause-and-Effect Chart can help you organize causes and effects. This Cause-and-Effect Chart shows a cause from the passage above. Can you find the effect? Each row shows a different cause and effect. Reread the passage above, and then fill in the second cause.

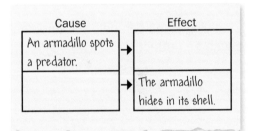

Academic Vocabulary

- **structure** (**struk**-chur) *noun*
  A **structure** is how parts are arranged or organized.

Science Article

A science article is nonfiction writing that tells about ideas and information in the natural world. It gives facts about animals, environments, discoveries, or other science topics.

Science articles sometimes use a cause-and-effect text structure. This structure tells what happens and why it happens.

Look Into the Text

The sea dragon is covered with — cause skin that looks like leaves, which helps the dragon look like a piece of seaweed. A hungry meat-eater — effect would stay away from anything that looks like seaweed.

Clarifying ideas can help you understand cause and effect.

On the **Menu**

by Susan E. Goodman

Is that seaweed? Look again. The sea dragon's disguise helps the sea dragon stay off another fish's menu. Hiding is one of many animal tricks for staying alive.

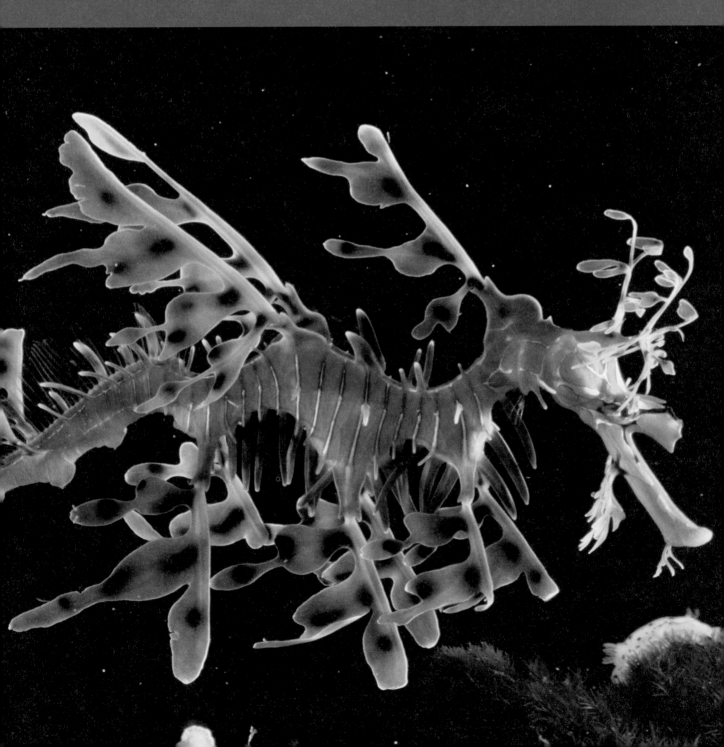

Staying Alive

Staying alive can be a big challenge for some animals, especially when other animals want to eat them. Read on to discover the **self-defense tricks** that animals use to stay alive.

Master of Disguise

Over time, animals have developed many ways to stay away from **predators**. A predator is an animal that hunts and eats other animals. Hiding is one of the best ways to stay alive.

Some animals hide by looking like the places where they live. To see how this works, let's look at the leafy sea dragon. You may never have heard of this sea creature, but it is **a master of disguise**.

The sea dragon is covered with skin that looks like leaves, which helps the dragon look like a piece of seaweed. A hungry **meat-eater** would stay away from anything that looks like seaweed.

Leaf-like skin is just one part of the sea dragon's disguise. Its fins make another part. They are small. They slowly push the dragon

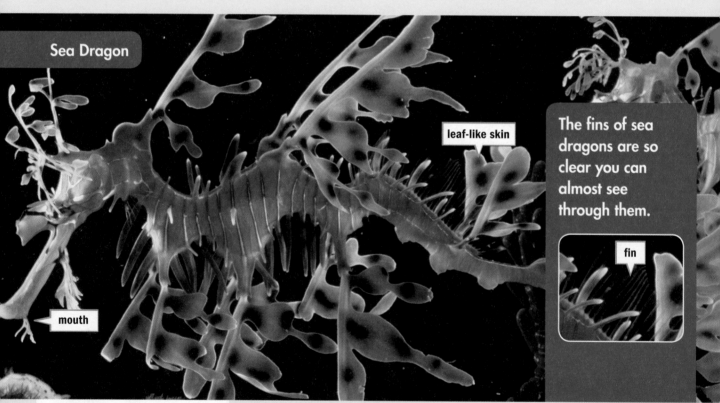

Sea Dragon

leaf-like skin

The fins of sea dragons are so clear you can almost see through them.

fin

mouth

Key Vocabulary
predator *n.*, an animal that eats other animals
disguise *n.*, a different look that keeps someone or something from being recognized

In Other Words
self-defense tricks ways to protect oneself
a master of very good at
meat-eater animal that eats other animals

through the water. So the dragon looks like it's floating—just like seaweed.

The sea dragon's mouth completes its disguise. The mouth looks like just another seaweed stem. There are even small "leaves" at the end! Yet it's actually a tube that works like a straw. That mouth is great for **slurping up** the dragon's favorite food—sea lice. Yum!

Show-Offs

The leafy sea dragon hides to stay safe, while other animals stay safe by showing their colors. They want other animals to see them.

Scientists call these bright colors warning colors because the colors tell predators to stay away.

You have probably seen animals that have warning colors. Think, for instance, of all those insects that buzz by you on warm days. When one flies by, you likely **swat it away**. But what happens when a yellow bug flies in your face? Do you swat it? Or do you jump away?

You guessed it. Yellow is a warning color. It tells you that the pesky pest might be a bumblebee or a yellow wasp, and you don't want to bug those insects.

Some grasshoppers show off their own bright colors. A few are even red and blue. Those colors don't just look **spiffy**, they also tell predators to stay away.

Of course, hungry predators sometimes ignore the warning. They still go after the grasshopper. If that happens, the grasshopper has **a backup defense**. It makes lots of foam, and the foam tastes so bad that the predator won't do it again.

▼ The bright colors of this South African grasshopper warn predators away.

In Other Words
slurping up eating
swat it away hit it with something
   to make it go away
spiffy nice, pretty
a backup defense another way
   to protect itself

Look Into the Text

1. **Details** What parts of the sea dragon give it a good **disguise**?
2. **Cause and Effect** Why do some animals hide and others show off their colors?

Blending In

Many animals use colors to match the place they live in. This is called **camouflage**. Some even change colors with the seasons.

The snowshoe hare has rusty brown fur in summer so it **blends in with** the colors of fields. In fall, the hare loses its brown fur and grows thick white fur. The new fur matches the snow in winter and keeps the hare warm.

On the Ball

Color doesn't offer enough protection for some other animals, so they have different defenses that help them **survive** in the wild.

The armadillo needs all the defenses it can get. It is only about two feet long and weighs 15 pounds. It has small teeth, so it cannot even bite to protect itself.

Instead the armadillo has **an armored** shell. The armor is made out of **bony plates**. Armor protects this animal from bumps and

Rolling, Rolling, Rolling. . .

1 At the first sign of a threat, an armadillo tries to run away. If that doesn't work, the armadillo stops.

2 Then, the armadillo begins to tuck itself into a ball. It folds its head and legs inside its shell.

Key Vocabulary
camouflage *n.*, colors that help animals hide
survive *v.*, to continue to live
threat *n.*, danger

In Other Words
blends in with matches
an armored a protective
bony plates a hard covering

bruises. Another **advantage** of the armor is that it makes it much harder for a predator to eat an armadillo.

An armadillo does not just rely on its armor, though. It has a couple of other tricks. When an armadillo spots a predator, it first tries to run away. A scared armadillo **darts for** the safety of its burrow. A burrow is an underground home.

But that's just the beginning. If an armored armadillo cannot get away, it hides in its shell. First it tucks in its legs and ears. Then it rolls its shell together. It turns itself into a living ball. It's an animal **roll-up**.

Most hungry hunters don't know how to eat an armadillo roll-up. They can **prod and poke** and toss the roll-up around, but they cannot find a tasty bite to eat.

3 Finally, the armadillo tucks its tail next to its head. Now the shell covers the animal's whole body.

4 After rolling itself into a ball, the armadillo is safe. Predators cannot find a tasty morsel to eat.

In Other Words
darts for runs to
roll-up that looks like a ball
prod and poke push and hit it

Look Into the Text

1. **Describe** Use the photos and details from the text to tell what an armadillo looks like.

2. **Cause and Effect** What does the armadillo do to protect itself against a **threat**?

Lying Lizard

Like the armadillo, the frilled lizard tries to run away when it **spots** a predator. It darts up a tree, or it hops on its back legs and dashes across the forest. But that doesn't always work.

Sometimes the lizard can't just run away.

When that happens, it tries to **bluff its way out of becoming a tasty treat**. It pretends to be bigger than it really is, and it also acts **tough**.

The lizard opens its mouth as wide as it can. The skin around its neck pops

Before

The frilled lizard looks harmless most of the time.

In Other Words

spots sees
bluff its way out of becoming a tasty treat look like something it isn't so that it won't get eaten
tough mean

Science Background

Frilled lizards live in northern Australia's hot, dry forests. They are appropriately named after their neck frill that opens when they want to scare off a predator. Their color allows them to hide because they match the land and the trees they live on.

out like an umbrella. The lizard hisses and whips its long tail around. This makes the lizard look bigger and scarier than usual.

These moves often work, and they scare some predators away. Other hungry hunters may not be scared exactly, but they go looking for other snacks. Few animals want to **mess with this crazy critter**.

Either way, the lizard wins. It lives to eat its own supper of delicious insects and spiders.

After

To scare a predator away, the lizard spreads its skin.

In Other Words
mess with this crazy critter bother this strange animal

Look Into the Text

1. **Explain** How does the lizard protect itself against a **predator**?
2. **Compare** How are a lizard's defenses like those of other animals?

School Safety

Many fish live in groups, or schools. That's because **there is safety in numbers**.

At the first sign of trouble, schooling fish swim as close together as they can get. Then the school makes lots of twists and turns. All that movement makes it hard for predators to make a meal out of just one fish.

Many other animals also stay safe by moving in groups. Predators cannot see individuals in a large group.

In Other Words

there is safety in numbers it is safer to swim with other fish than to swim alone

By swimming in schools, fish make themselves harder to catch.

Common Defenses

These are only a few of the ways that animals escape predators. They have other defenses, too.

Just look around. Cats arch their backs to look big and scary. Green grasshoppers blend into grass. Claws and teeth help animals fight.

These **adaptations**, or useful traits, are quite different. Yet they share one purpose. They all keep an animal from **landing on the menu**.

Key Vocabulary
adaptation *n.*, a feature or a behavior that lets an animal stay alive

In Other Words
landing on the menu getting eaten by another animal

Look Into the Text

1. **Paraphrase** Tell in your own words how moving in groups helps some animals **survive**.
2. **Problem and Solution** Name an animal from the article and tell how it defends itself against a **predator**.

Looking for Prey

Camouflage helps animals hide from hungry predators. Did you know that it also helps predators hide from their **prey**? Why would predators need to hide? Sometimes they need help finding—and catching—dinner.

Some predators are awfully slow, and they can't run as fast as their prey. Camouflage lets them **sneak up at their own pace**.

Other predators are quick but sneaky. Clever coloring helps them hide from view. They lie in wait, hoping a meal will wander by. Surprise! The predator snaps up its prey.

A Bump on a Log

One predator that uses camouflage is the crocodile. Have you ever noticed the shape of a crocodile's head or the appearance of its skin? These features **help the beast nab** its next meal.

A crocodile can stay underwater for hours. It lies perfectly still in a river or lake with only its eyes and nostrils showing above the surface. It looks around and watches for food.

The crocodile's skin is rough and bumpy. In **murky** water, it looks a lot like a floating log—except that this log can bite. When an animal comes near, the crocodile leaps forward and **snatches** its prey.

A crocodile hides as it waits for its prey.

Key Vocabulary
prey *n.*, an animal that is eaten by another animal

In Other Words
sneak up at their own pace quietly approach when they are ready
help the beast nab help the animal catch
murky dark
snatches takes, grabs

A death adder moves its tail from side-to-side to attract prey.

Trick or Treat

Death adders are sneaky snakes. Like crocodiles, they use tricks to **scare up** their food.

A death adder's coloring makes it hard to see. The snake is mostly brown. When it lies on brown ground, it blends right in. Death adders **just love hanging out** under leaves and grass—which makes them even harder to see.

But there's one thing a death adder leaves in plain view: its tail. Why does it do this? That's simple. The tip of its tail looks like a worm. When a small animal approaches for a snack—wham! The adder strikes. It's trick-or-treat, animal style. ❖

In Other Words
scare up find, catch
just love hanging out enjoy hiding

Look Into the Text

1. **Explain** How does the crocodile use **camouflage**?
2. **Paraphrase** Use your own words to tell how a death adder finds food.

Find the Adaptations

Animals have many adaptations that help protect them from predators. Some animals have colors that match the places they live. Some have shapes that make them hard to see. Figure out and explain these nature puzzles.

What to Do

1 Look closely at each photo.

2 Find the animal and describe its color and shape.

3 Explain how its color and shape help it survive.

Snowshoe Hare

Thorn Bug Insects

Lizard

Snake

Spider

Tree Frog

▲ Some animals use camouflage so well that you can look right at them and not see them.

Look Into the Text

1. **Viewing** Which two animals in these photos use their shapes to hide?

Connect Reading and Writing

Vocabulary
adaptations
advantage
camouflage
disguise
predators
prey
survive
threat

CRITICAL THINKING

1. **SUM IT UP** Use your Cause-and-Effect Chart to summarize in the science article.

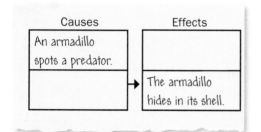

Causes	Effects
An armadillo spots a predator.	The armadillo hides in its shell.

Cause-and-Effect Chart

2. **Describe** Tell how **prey** protect themselves from **predators**.

3. **Interpret** The headings give clues about how animals **survive**. Choose two headings. Tell how each heading describes that animal's survival skills.

4. **Explain** What kinds of **threats** do animals in the selection face? What other animals do you know that face these **threats**?

READING FLUENCY

Phrasing Read the passage on page 627 to a partner. Assess your fluency.

1. I did not pause/sometimes paused/ always paused for punctuation.

2. What I did best in my reading was _____.

READING STRATEGY

What strategy helped you understand this selection? Tell a partner about it.

VOCABULARY REVIEW

Oral Review Read the paragraph aloud. Add the vocabulary words.

Every animal wants to _____, or stay alive. Some animals hunt other animals. They are _____. The animals they hunt are called _____. Animals use different _____ to stay safe. Sea dragons are protected by their _____. Armadillos roll into a ball if there is a _____. Animals also use adaptations to catch prey. Crocodiles use _____ to look like a log. This gives them an _____ over their prey.

Written Review Make picture cards for the animals from the selection. Write captions on the backs of the cards describing the animal and how it **survives**. Use four vocabulary words.

WRITE ABOUT THE GUIDING QUESTION

Explore What Happens When People Come Face-To-Face With a Rival
Which **adaptation** from the selection do you think is the most amazing? Reread the selection to find examples that support your opinion.

Connect Across the Curriculum

Relate Words: Synonyms

> **Academic Vocabulary**
> - **relate** (ri-lāt) *verb*
>   When you **relate** things, you show how they are connected.

Synonyms are words that mean about the same thing, but have different shades of meaning. You can see how words **relate** to one another in a thesaurus, a book that lists synonyms.

Revise Sentences Rewrite these sentences by replacing the underlined words with more specific synonyms. Use a thesaurus to find the synonyms.

1. The armadillo's hard shell makes it an <u>unpleasant</u> meal for predators.

2. To escape predators, the frilled lizard <u>moves</u> across the forest floor.

3. Some animals are so <u>little</u> that large predators can't find them.

4. Elephants and other <u>strong</u> animals have very few predators.

Relate Cause and Effect

An effect is what happens, and a cause shows why it happens. Relating causes and effects can help you understand a text.

One **cause** can have more than one **effect**. Read this passage from "On the Menu." Note that predators can have more than one reaction to the lizard looking big and scary. This means there is more than one effect.

> The lizard opens its mouth as wide as it can. The skin around its neck pops out like an umbrella. The lizard hisses and whips its long tail around. This makes the lizard look bigger and scarier than usual.
> These moves often work, and they scare some predators away. Other hungry hunters may not be scared exactly, but they go looking for other snacks. Few animals want to mess with this crazy critter.

Relate Multiple Causes and Effects Sometimes, one effect has more than one cause. Look back at the section of "On the Menu" that discusses how and why fish travel in schools. The effect is that traveling in schools makes it harder for predators to catch just one fish. What are the two causes?

Define and Explain

Pair Share With a partner, choose one animal from the story. Work together to talk about and explain the special features of this animal. Use correct subject pronouns.

> The armadillo has an armored shell. The armor is made of bony plates.

> The bony plates protect the armadillo. They also keep predators from eating the armadillo.

Write About an Animal

Study the Models The first time you name your animal, use a noun. After that, use a subject pronoun to talk about the same thing. Don't keep repeating the same noun. This will keep your reader's interest because you will have smooth sentences.

JUST OK

The leafy sea dragon is a true master of disguise. The leafy sea dragon has skin that looks like leaves. The leafy sea dragon has clear fins. The fins are so clear you can almost see through them! The fins propel the sea dragon slowly through the water. Another part of the sea dragon's disguise is its mouth. The mouth looks like a seaweed stem. The mouth even has small leaves at the end!

> The reader thinks: "All the sentences sound the same!" That's because the writer repeats the same noun.

BETTER

The leafy sea dragon is a true master of disguise. It has skin that looks like leaves and clear fins. The fins are so clear you can almost see through them! They propel the sea dragon slowly through the water. Another part of the sea dragon's disguise is its mouth. It looks like a seaweed stem and even has small leaves at the end!

> This mix of nouns and pronouns brings variety to the sentences.

Add Sentences Think of two more sentences to add to the BETTER model above. Be sure to use correct subject pronouns.

✏ **WRITE ON YOUR OWN** Write about a different animal in the selection. How does it protect itself? How does it trick predators? Use the animal's name in the first sentence. Then use the correct subject pronoun after that.

REMEMBER	
Use the correct subject pronoun.	
Singular (One)	**Plural (More than One)**
I	we
you	you
he, she, it	they

The Three Chicharrones

by Patricia Santos Marcantonio
illustrated by Bill Mayer

SELECTION 2 OVERVIEW

▷ **Build Background**

▷ **Language & Grammar**
Retell a Story
Use Forms of the Verbs *Be* and *Have*

▷ **Prepare to Read**
Learn Key Vocabulary
Learn a Reading Strategy
Analyze Modern Fiction

▷ **Read and Write**
Introduce the Genre
Modern Fairy Tale
Focus on Reading
Analyze Modern Fiction
Apply the
Focus Strategy
Monitor
Critical Thinking
Reading Fluency
Read with Intonation

Vocabulary Review
Write About the
Guiding Question

▷ **Connect Across the Curriculum**
Vocabulary Study
Relate Words: Cognates
Literary Analysis
Analyze Character Traits
Language and Grammar
Retell a Story
Writing and Grammar
Write About a Folk Tale

Build Background

Explore Creative Storytelling

What makes an old story new? Author Patricia Santos Marcantonio uses fresh ideas to retell an old favorite.

Connect

What If? How would the story of "The Three Little Pigs" be different if it happened in your town today? How would the story be different if it was on TV, in a movie, or in a graphic novel? Work with a partner to think of ideas. Share them with the class.

Digital Library

myNGconnect.com
↻ View the images.

▲ A scene from "The Three Little Pigs"

Language & Grammar

Retell a Story
CD

Listen to a Vietnamese folk tale about a rooster.
Then listen to this retelling of the folk tale.

FOLK TALE

The Rooster and the Jewel

There is a rooster who is all alone.
He is very hungry and weak.

He wanders around the countryside,
looking everywhere for food. He can't
find anything to eat.

Then the rooster finds a shiny
stone on the ground. He stares
at it for a long time.

Finally, he says, "People would fight
over this jewel. It would be valuable
to them. But to me, the jewel is
worthless because I cannot eat it.
Shiny stones will not keep me alive."
And the starving rooster continues
to look for food.

Use Forms of the Verbs *Be* and *Have*

The verbs *be* and *have* have special forms to tell about the present.

Present of *Be*

Forms of *Be*	Negative
I **am**	I'm **not**
you **are**	you **aren't**
he, she, or it **is**	he, she, or it **isn't**
we **are**	we **aren't**
they **are**	they **aren't**

Present of *Have*

Forms of *Have*	Negative
I **have**	I **don't have**
you **have**	you **don't have**
he, she, or it **has**	he, she, or it **doesn't have**
we **have**	we **don't have**
they **have**	they **don't have**

Use the correct form of the verb.

EXAMPLES **Forms of *be***

Present: The rabbit **is** more like a human in tales.

Negative: He **isn't** exactly like an animal.

EXAMPLES **Forms of *have***

Present: The rabbit **has** human traits in tales.

Negative: He **doesn't have** many animal traits.

Practice Together

Say each sentence. Then say it again and make the sentence negative.

1. I (am/are) interested in folk tales.
2. Most countries (have/has) folk tales.
3. Often, a folk tale (have/has) a lesson.
4. A hero (is/are) clever.

Try It!

Say each sentence. Write the negative form of the verb on a card. Then say the negative sentence.

5. The animals in folk tales (have/has) human traits.
6. The villains (is/are) evil.
7. Sometimes a folk tale (have/has) magic objects.
8. Usually, the stories (is/are) short.

▲ A coyote and a rabbit are characters in a Mayan folk tale.

Tell the Group a Folk Tale

RETELL A STORY

People enjoy listening to others tell stories. You may have heard stories or folk tales from your own family. Think of a tale you have heard.

Think about the story you will retell. Make a story map like the one below to remember what happens. List the important details you want to include.

Story Map

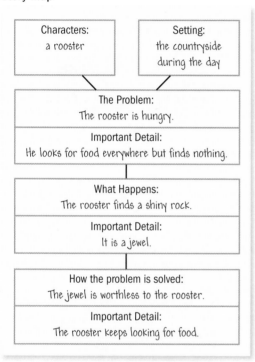

Now retell your story to a group of classmates.

HOW TO RETELL A STORY

1. Introduce the characters and setting.
2. Use details to tell about the problem.
3. Use more details to tell how the problem is solved.

> A rooster is all alone and very hungry. He looks everywhere for food.

USE CORRECT FORMS OF *BE* AND *HAVE*

When you retell your story, be sure to use the correct form of *be* and *have*.

In the Present: The rooster **is** hungry. He **has** no food.

In the Negative: He **isn't** happy. He **doesn't have** any food to eat.

Prepare to Read

Learn Key Vocabulary

Study the Words Use the steps below.

1. Pronounce the word. Say it aloud several times. Spell it.
2. Rate your word knowledge.
3. Study the example. Tell more about the word.
4. Practice it. Make the word your own.

Key Words

advice (ad-vīs) *noun*
▶ page 116

To give **advice** means to share wise words. Parents give **advice** to their children.

business (biz-nis) *noun*
▶ page 125

A **business** is where you do work for money. Some people's place of **business** is in an office.

cheat (chēt) *verb*
▶ page 122

When you **cheat**, you act unfairly. It is wrong to **cheat** on a test.

deal (dēl) *noun*
▶ page 118

A **deal** is an agreement. If you agree to mow your neighbor's lawn for money, you have made a **deal** with your neighbor.

deserve (di-zurv) *verb*
▶ page 122

When you **deserve** something it means you have worked hard to earn it. If you study hard for a test, you **deserve** a good grade.

fortune (for-chun) *noun*
▶ page 116

A **fortune** is a large amount of money or a lot of good things. The woman worked hard to earn her **fortune**.

frustration (frus-trā-shun) *noun* ▶ page 124

If you feel **frustration**, you feel angry that you can't do something. If you do not understand your homework, you may feel **frustration**.
Related Word: **frustrated**

property (prop-er-tē) *noun*
▶ page 118

Property is what someone owns, like a house or land. People can sell their **property** to someone else.

Practice the Words Make a Category Chart. List each Key Word under Noun or Verb. Work with a partner to think of sentences for each word.

Noun	Verb
advice	cheat

Category Chart

Analyze Modern Fiction

How Can You Analyze Modern Fiction? When you read a modern work of fiction, you may find that many things seem familiar. Ask yourself, "How is this similar to other stories I have read or heard?" Once you find a connection, compare the characters, setting, and plot of the new story to the one you know to find the differences.

Reading Strategies

· Plan

> **Monitor** Notice confusing parts in the text, then reread or read on to make them clear.

· Ask Questions
· Make Connections
· Visualize
· Make Inferences
· Determine Importance
· Synthesize

Look Into the Text

The next morning, the Chicharrones were ready to set out.

"Don't be greedy like a *cerdo*." Their father grunted his advice. "And this is the most important thing to remember: Watch for the wolf at the door. He will try to take all you have, but you won't know it until you have nothing left."

"What?" replied Pereza, who had only half listened, while Gordo recounted his money.

"*Gracias* for the useful words, *Papá*," Astuto said.

And so the brothers hugged and bade farewell to each other and their father. They got into their cars and drove off in three different directions.

> This story reminds me of the fairy tale about the three little pigs and the wolf.

> **"I notice that the Chicharrones have different names. They count their money and drive cars."**

Practice Together

Use a Venn Diagram A Venn Diagram can help you analyze a modern version of a story you know. Use the middle of a Venn Diagram to tell what is similar and the two outer circles to tell what is different. This Venn diagram shows a few things that are similar. Think about the story of "The Three Little Pigs." Then reread the passage and find details that are different, such as characters, setting, or plot. Add them to the Venn Diagram.

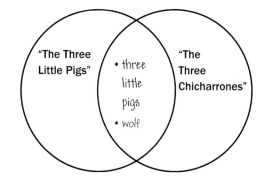

"The Three Little Pigs" | • three little pigs • wolf | "The Three Chicharrones"

Modern Fairy Tale

A fairy tale is a short, made-up story that has been told over the years. A modern fairy tale puts a new twist on an old story. As you read, look at how the plot, setting, and characters of this story are different from a traditional fairy tale. What is modern? What is like other stories you have read?

The **plot**, or events, of a fairy tale often tell about good and evil. The **setting** of most fairy tales is either a castle, the country, or a forest. The **characters** are usually simple and have one **character trait**, such as greedy or lazy.

Look Into the Text

Just then came a *rap-tap-tap* on the door. Pereza peered out his window. "Let me introduce myself. I'm Dinero Martínez. And I'm going to make you rich."

Monitor as you read to make sure you understand the key ideas.

The Three Chicharrones

by Patricia Santos Marcantonio
illustrated by Bill Mayer

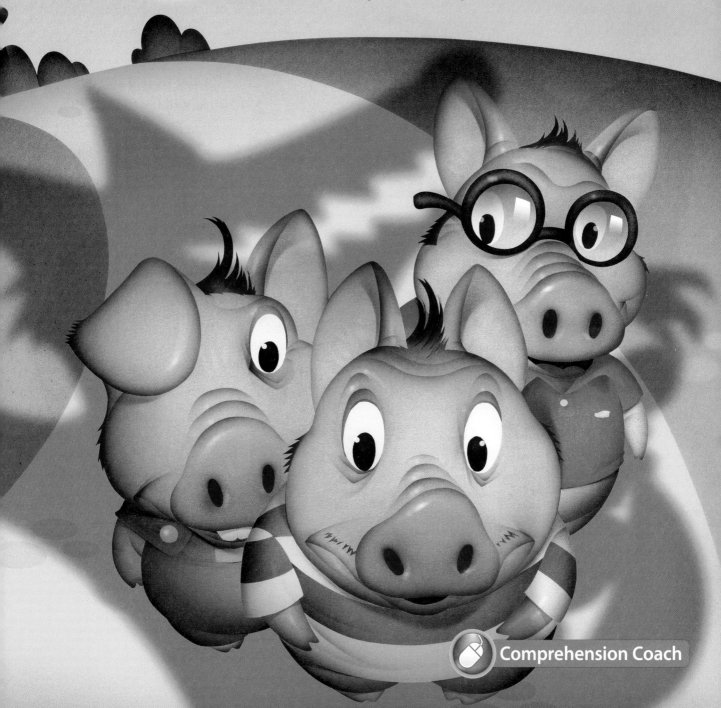

Papá Chicharrón smiled at his three sons. Each had curly black hair, small dark eyes, tiny ears, and round, round stomachs, just like their father.

"Pereza, Gordo, and Astuto, it's time for you to **go into the world** and make your **fortunes**."

He handed them each little bags. "You'll receive the same **number of *pesos*** I received from my *papá* when I was your age."

They opened their bags and found two hundred coins.

"Can't we stay here a little longer, *Papá*?" **drawled Pereza**, yawning, for he was lazy.

"This is impossible. How can we make our way in the world like this?" **whined** Gordo, who always looked for the quickest way to everything.

"I'll do my best, *Papá*," said Astuto, who always worked hard.

Watch for the wolf at the door.

"With two hundred *pesos* and a lot of work, I did well for myself." Their father spread his arms out, **indicating** his large house. "Now, get packed, *hijos*."

The next morning, the Chicharrones were ready to **set out**.

"Don't be greedy like a *cerdo*." Their father grunted his **advice**. "And this is the most important thing to remember: Watch for the wolf at the door. He will try to take all you have, but you won't know it until you have nothing left."

"What?" replied Pereza, who had only half listened, while Gordo recounted his money.

"*Gracias* for the useful words, *Papá*," Astuto said.

And so the brothers hugged and **bade farewell** to each other and their father. They got into their cars and drove off in three different directions.

Key Vocabulary	In Other Words	
fortune *n.*, a large amount of money	**go into the world** live by yourselves	*hijos* children (in Spanish)
advice *n.*, wise words	**number of *pesos*** amount of money	**set out** go on their journeys
	drawled Pereza said Pereza slowly	*cerdo* pig (in Spanish)
	whined complained	*Gracias* Thank you (in Spanish)
	indicating pointing to	**bade farewell** said goodbye

Pereza hadn't gone very far when he saw a small piece of land for sale at 120 *pesos*. On the land was a bale-mountain of straw. He said to himself, "A house of **paja** does seem foolish, but I can build it in no time and then take a nap."

He bought the land and built his house, which he called the **Casa de Paja**, and indeed, the work did not take long. Pereza slept for the rest of the day, too lazy to spend his other *pesos*.

Meanwhile, Gordo had traveled a little

In Other Words

paja straw (in Spanish)
Casa de Paja House of Straw
(in Spanish)

Language and Literary Background

Sometimes a writer gives a name to the characters to show what they are like. *Chicharrones* is Spanish for "pork rinds." The names of the three Chicharrones–Pereza, Gordo, and Astuto–are the Spanish words for laziness, fat, and astute (or smart).

farther down the road when he saw a parcel of land for sale at 150 *pesos*, which came with a gigantic pile of **piñon**-tree sticks.

"Sticks are a good start," he told himself. "With the rest of the money, I can gamble and make more money so I can have a big fine house. I can't wait too long to get rich."

Gordo closed the **deal** on the land and built his house of *piñon* sticks. As soon as he finished what he called **Palacio Piñon**, he got in his car and headed off to build the rest of his fortune at cards.

Astuto drove the farthest, stopping only when he spotted the exact land he wanted. The **property** had a nice view of the valley and included a tower

of adobe bricks. The land cost 220 *pesos*, so he sold his car to make up the difference.

Taking his time, Astuto built his house of adobe. He didn't mind the sweat and **toil** because he knew he would end up with a strong home. When he was finally done, Astuto searched for a job.

Meanwhile, at the *Casa de Paja*, Pereza had just finished taking another nap.

"Maybe **mañana** I'll start looking for work. But it's too nice of a day for that. I think I'll go fishing instead. I can sleep a little as I wait **for a bite**."

Just then came a *rap-tap-tap* on the door.

Pereza peered out his window.

"Let me introduce myself. I'm Dinero Martínez. And I'm going to make you rich."

Just then came a rap-tap-tap on the door.

Key Vocabulary
deal *n.*, agreement to purchase or do something
property *n.*, someone's house and land

In Other Words
piñon pine nut (in Spanish)
Palacio Piñon Pine Nut Palace (in Spanish)
toil hard work
mañana tomorrow (in Spanish)
for a bite to catch a fish

Look Into the Text

1. **Paraphrase** Use your own words to retell the father's **advice** to his sons as they left home.
2. **Compare and Contrast** What did each brother do after he left home? How were their actions similar and different?

Dinero Martínez was tall and skinny, with big ears and eyes that looked **not merely hungry to make a deal, but famished**. He wore a hairy gray suit and carried a big black briefcase. Parked out front was his *jalapeño*-green sports car.

Pereza opened the front door a little. "Do I have to do any work to get rich?"

"Not at all, young ***señor***. I'll give you top *peso* for your house and land—top *peso* I say, and you don't have to **lift a fingernail** except to sign." Dinero was smooth as his

In Other Words

not merely hungry to make a deal, but famished
   untrustworthy and evil
señor sir (in Spanish)
lift a fingernail do any work

Language and Literary Background

The name Dinero is the Spanish word for money. The author chose this name for the evil character to show his greed.

shiny car and offered double what Pereza had paid in the first place.

"***Bueno***." Pereza yawned.

The ink wasn't even dry on the papers when Dinero's eyes turned hard as rusty coins. "Chicharrón, you must leave. There's soon going to be a huff and a ***soplo***, and down goes your silly *casa*. Just look over there."

A bulldozer rumbled along.

Pereza was hardly out of his straw house before the machine chugged and churned and *Casa de Paja* was flat.

"Foolish Chicharrón, you would have gotten five times more for this land if you weren't so lazy. But I caught you napping." Dinero laughed and laughed as he tacked up a sign: FUTURE **SITE** OF A NEW HOTEL.

FUTURE SITE OF A
NEW HOTEL

In Other Words
"***Bueno***." "Good." (in Spanish)
The ink wasn't even dry on the papers when Right after signing
soplo puff (in Spanish)
site location

"No matter," Pereza said with a shrug. "I have money. But all this dealing has made me tired." He drove away, looking for a good place to take a nap.

A few days later, Gordo was busy planning a party for his gambling friends when he heard a knock.

Dinero Martínez was at the door.

"I'm going to make you rich," Dinero said.

Gordo's eyes became wide.

Dinero **did more of his smooth-talking**, and soon Gordo **was signing on the dotted line**. All the while, Gordo told himself that he would take the money and place larger bets to get rich even faster.

After Gordo sold the land, Dinero **bellowed**, "Bring on the bulldozer!"

Along came the machine, and down went the *Piñon Palacio* in a huff and a *soplo*.

I'm going to make you rich.

"Chicharrón, you could have gotten a lot more *pesos*. Now it's too late, so get off my land," Dinero ordered Gordo, who started packing his car.

"Gordo!" he heard someone call.

Up the road, Pereza was walking with a suitcase in hand.

"What happened to your car?" Gordo asked.

"Someone stole all my money when I fell asleep by the side of the road, and I had to sell my car to buy food," Pereza said, rubbing his feet.

"Ah, I see that you've met Dinero Martínez."

"He just showed up at my door," Gordo replied.

"Never mind, Brother. Get in my car. We'll go to the racetrack and win big, then we'll buy even more land."

The brothers turned for a last look and saw a sign go up where Gordo's house had once stood: COMING SOON: NEW CASINO.

In Other Words

did more of his smooth-talking told more lies
was signing on the dotted line agreed to sell his house
bellowed cried out loudly

Look Into the Text

1. **Confirm Predictions/Plot** Was your prediction correct? What happens to Pereza after he makes the **deal** with Dinero?
2. **Character/Opinion** Who is more foolish, Pereza or Gordo? Give reasons from the text.

ut Dinero Martínez wasn't through with the Chicharrones. A few days later, he showed up at the house of Astuto.

"***Buenas tardes***, young *señor*. I am ready to make you a great offer on your land and house." Dinero straightened his tie.

Astuto listened because he was polite. He also smiled because he knew what his land was worth.

"Thank you, Señor Martínez, but I am not interested in selling," Astuto said.

Dinero **upped** his offer.

Astuto felt **deep down in his pudgy stomach** that this Martínez in the hairy gray suit was trying to **cheat** him.

"Again, no thanks," the brother said.

Dinero's eyes became **red slits of anger**. "You are making a mistake, Chicharrón."

"That may be," Astuto replied, "but you are the one leaving **empty-handed**."

Dinero got in his sports car and zoomed away.

From the other direction came Pereza and Gordo, walking with their suitcases. They had lost all their money betting and had had to sell Gordo's car for food.

"***¡Hermanos!***" Astuto called out happily.

At supper, Gordo and Pereza told their brother how they had failed to listen to their father's advice and had lost their homes to a wolf who showed up at the door.

"I **deserved** what I got," Pereza said. "I was too lazy to keep my land or money."

"*Ay, yi, yi.*" Gordo slapped his head. "I wanted to take the fast road to a good life. I gambled and lost."

Then and there, Pereza promised to work hard and Gordo vowed never to make another wager.

"No, my brothers, you haven't lost everything. We have each other," Astuto said.

Key Vocabulary

cheat *v.*, to act unfairly
deserve *v.*, to get what you have earned

In Other Words

Buenas tardes Good afternoon (in Spanish)
upped increased
deep down in his pudgy stomach very sure

red slits of anger very small because he was angry
empty-handed with nothing
"***¡Hermanos!***" "Brothers!" (in Spanish)

"We will live together."

"But what about Dinero Martínez?" Gordo said.

"He doesn't look like the type to give up so easy," Pereza added.

Astuto grinned. "We are the Chicharrones, and we can handle him if we work together."

Gordo, Pereza, and Astuto laughed and settled down for a nice evening before the fire, snacking on pork rinds and salsa.

The next day, Dinero warned the brothers that Astuto's land was located in a **flood plain** and would be filled with water when it stormed.

Astuto wouldn't sell.

The next day, Dinero told the brothers that a freeway was going to be built right through their land. He would **take it off their hands** for more than the freeway department would ever pay.

"No, *gracias*," Astuto replied.

Dinero returned and advised the brothers that the house was in the path of several tornadoes known to hit at springtime, so they would be better off selling than being swirled away.

The brothers wouldn't budge.

"CHICHARRONES!" Dinero bellowed with **frustration**, because this was the first time in his **sleazy** career that he could not close a deal. "Someday my bulldozer *will* come with a huff and a *soplo*, and well, you know the rest…"

"How do we get rid of this pest?" Gordo asked that night at supper.

"I have a plan," Astuto said.

"Of course you do," Pereza replied. "That's why we love you."

The following morning, Gordo and Pereza were out working in the garden. They talked loud to each other because they knew Dinero was listening around the corner.

"I'm really looking forward to going to the *fiesta* in town tonight," Gordo said, picking corn.

"We're all going to have a good time," Pereza said, plucking tomatoes off the vine.

"Ah-ha!" Dinero said to himself. "I'll burn down the house while they are gone. Then they'll *have* to sell the land to me."

Wearing their best clothes, the brothers started walking toward town.

When they were out of sight, Dinero sneaked up to the adobe house. He lit a match and was ready to start the fire when a bright light shone in his face.

Dinero bellowed with frustration.

Key Vocabulary
frustration *n.*, a feeling of anger and confusion

In Other Words
flood plain valley
take it off their hands buy their land
sleazy dishonest
fiesta party (in Spanish)

"Hands up," a deep voice commanded. Dinero turned around to see the Chicharrones with County Sheriff Sánchez.

"You've been cheating folks long enough, Dinero Martínez," Sheriff Sánchez said. "I'm going to see to it that you lose your **license** to do **business**. You won't be able to sell a ***ratón*** to a ***gato***."

"Wait, let's talk," Dinero pleaded, **using his best salesman voice**. "I know about some great land in Florida."

Key Vocabulary
business *n.*, work someone does to earn money

In Other Words
license permission
ratón rat (in Spanish)
gato cat (in Spanish)
using his best salesman voice trying to get the sheriff to let him go by offering him something

The sheriff shook his head and led him away. "Say **adiós**."

Dinero knew he hadn't made a deal. "*Adiós*, Chicharrones."

"*Adiós*, Dinero." The Chicharrones waved goodbye.

After working hard and saving their *pesos*, the brothers decided to go into business for themselves. They started ***Residencias*** Chicharrones, which were homes for those just starting out in life. The houses they built weren't made of straw or *piñon* sticks, but of adobe bricks that were **sturdy** and would last. ❖

About the Author

As a little girl in Pueblo, Colorado, **Patricia Santos Marcantonio** loved to read fairy tales. She also enjoyed her parents' jokes and storytelling. Soon, she was writing stories of her own.

Marcantonio says she wanted the stories to honor her Mexican American heritage. So she decided to retell famous fairy tales in a creative new way. Her first book, *Red Ridin' in the Hood*, won the Américas Award.

In Other Words
adiós goodbye (in Spanish)
Residencias Homes, Residences (in Spanish)
sturdy strong

Look Into the Text

1. **Confirm Prediction** Did Dinero cheat Astuto? Was your prediction correct?

2. **Summarize** How do the brothers work together to fool Dinero?

3. **Opinion** What do you think of the way the story ends? Explain.

Connect Reading and Writing

Vocabulary
advice
business
cheat
deal
deserve
fortune
frustration
property

CRITICAL THINKING

1. SUM IT UP Use your Venn Diagram to compare the fairy tales.

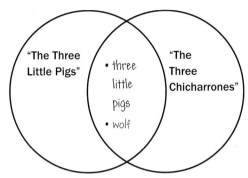

"The Three Little Pigs"

• three little pigs

• wolf

"The Three Chicharrones"

Venn Diagram

2. Make Judgments Do you think Astuto should have let his brothers live on his **property** with him? Why or why not?

3. Synthesize When Dinero tries to **cheat** the brothers, Astuto has a plan. Pereza says, "Of course you do" and "That's why we love you." Why does Pereza say this? Use details from the story to explain.

4. Compare Across Texts Which adaptations from "On the Menu" would have helped the pigs defend themselves against Dinero?

READING FLUENCY

Intonation Read the passage on page 628 to a partner. Assess your fluency.

1. My tone never/sometimes/always matched what I read.

2. What I did best in my reading was _____ .

READING STRATEGY

What strategy helped you understand this selection? Tell a partner about it.

VOCABULARY REVIEW

Oral Review Read the paragraph aloud. Add the vocabulary words.

To make a _____ , you have to work hard. For example, you could start a _____ . You could buy _____ and then sell it to make money. Follow this _____ . Never _____ or lie. If you make a _____ with someone, you must keep it. Even when you experience _____ , keep working. Hard workers _____ to do well.

Written Review How can the brothers use the lessons they learned in their new **business**? Write a journal entry about it. Use five vocabulary words.

WRITE ABOUT THE GUIDING QUESTION

Explore What Happens When People Come Face-To-Face With a Rival

What **advice** did the three Chicharrones follow to survive Dinero? Explain. Read the selection again. Support your answers with examples from the text.

Connect Across the Curriculum

Relate Words: Cognates

> **Academic Vocabulary**
> • **definition** (de-fu-**ni**-shun) *noun*
>   The meaning of a word is its **definition**.

What Are Cognates? A cognate is a word that looks similar in two different languages. For example, the Spanish word *artista* looks like the English word *artist*. Both mean "a person who creates art." False cognates look similar but have different definitions. The Spanish word *ropa* looks like the English word *rope*, but *ropa* means "clothing."

Use Cognates You can use cognates to better understand what you read. For example, the name *Astuto* is a cognate of the word *astute*. *Astuto* and *astute* mean "smart." The character *Astuto* is smart.

Spanish	English
familia	family
círculo	
danza	
acción	

Analyze Cognates With a partner, discuss what English words the Spanish words are like.

Analyze Character Traits

> **Academic Vocabulary**
> • **affect** (u-**fekt**) *verb*
>   When you **affect** something, you change it in some way.

The way characters act depends on their traits, or special qualities. These traits **affect** what happens in the story. Character traits cause things to happen and lead characters to make decisions.

Dinero Martínez is greedy. He wants to take the Chicharrones' land.

> Dinero . . . looked not merely hungry to make a deal, but famished. . . . Dinero's eyes turned hard as rusty coins.

What the other characters do in response to Dinero depends on their own character traits. Character traits can **affect**, or change, the plot.

Analyze How Actions Reveal Character Traits Choose a character from "The Three Chicharrones" and list his traits. Discuss what his actions reveal. Write what happens in the plot because of his traits.

Retell a Story

Group Talk With a group, make a plan for retelling "The Three Chicharrones." Decide which details to include and who will retell each part. Then do the retelling. Use correct forms of *be* and *have* in your story.

> Papá tells the three Chicharrones that it is time to go into the big world. Two of the pigs don't understand why they need to leave.

Write About a Folk Tale

Study the Models When you write about stories and folk tales you have read, write clear and complete sentences so your reader will understand what you have to say. Remember that a complete sentence has both a subject and a predicate that go together.

▲ Brer Rabbit is a character from folk tales.

NOT OK

> Folk tales are fictional stories that often have children and animals in them. The animals have human traits—they talk and act like humans. Some animals <u>is</u> evil like the wolf in "Little Red Riding Hood." Other animals are clever like the rabbit in the "Brer Rabbit" tales. No matter what the animals are like, each folk tale <u>have</u> a lesson to teach.

> The reader thinks: "This isn't very clear. Is it one animal or some animals?"

OK

> Folk tales are fictional stories that often have children and animals in them. The animals have human traits—they talk and act like humans. Some animals <u>are</u> evil like the wolf in "Little Red Riding Hood." Other animals are clever like the rabbit in the "Brer Rabbit" tales. No matter what the animals are like, each folk tale <u>has</u> a lesson to teach.

> The subjects and verbs go together. Now the sentences are clear.

Add Sentences Think of two sentences to add to the OK model above. Use complete sentences. Make subjects and verbs agree, or go together.

✎ **WRITE ON YOUR OWN** Write about a favorite folk tale or other story that you know. Use forms of *be* and *have* in some of your sentences. Check your subjects and verbs to be sure they agree.

REMEMBER

Use the form of the verb that goes with your subject.

Forms of *Be*	Forms of *Have*
I + am	he she + has it
he she + is it	I you we + have they
we you + are they	

Dragon, Dragon

by John Gardner
illustrated by Brandon Dorman

Build Background

Discover Dragons

Dragons are imaginary creatures, but they hold real interest for people in every culture. They appear in art and literature all over the world.

Connect

Take a Vote What does it take to win against a rival? Do you need strength, wisdom, courage, luck, or love? Vote for one and defend your vote.

Digital Library
myNGconnect.com
◉ View the video.

▲ Dragons are a popular subject in art.

Engage in Conversation

CD

Listen to the song.
Sing along with the chorus.

SONG

The King's Plan

(sung to the tune of "When the Saints Go Marching In")

Chorus (*townspeople*)
   The dragon roars
   And scares the knights
   The wizard has no spells to cast.
   The king is mad
   At the destruction
   Someone must do something fast!

Verse 1 (*queen sings*)
   My husband dear
   I want to know
   When does the dragon leave our land?
   His roar is loud
   No one is happy
   It is worse than a rock band!

Verse 2 (*king sings*)
   My dearest queen
   I have a plan
   We will have dancing and a feast.
   I will give
   Our precious daughter
   To the one who kills the beast.

Chorus (*townspeople*)

Use Indefinite Pronouns

Use an **indefinite pronoun** when you are not talking about a specific person or thing.

- Some **indefinite pronouns** are always singular. They always need a **singular verb** that ends in **-s**.

    EXAMPLES   **Everybody hates** the dragon.
                  Nobody likes the dragon.

Singular Indefinite Pronouns

another	each	everything	nothing
anybody	either	neither	somebody
anyone	everybody	nobody	someone
anything	everyone	no one	something

- Some **indefinite pronouns** are always plural. They always need a **plural verb**.

    EXAMPLE   **Many** of the townspeople **fear** the dragon.

Plural Indefinite Pronouns

both	many
few	several

Practice Together

Say each sentence. Use the correct form of the verb.

1. The king and queen are mad. Both (want/wants) the dragon dead.
2. No one (know/knows) how to kill the dragon.
3. Somebody (need/needs) to battle the beast.
4. Something (have/has) to be done about the monster.

Try It!

Read each sentence. Write the correct form of the verb on a card. Then say the sentence and add the correct form of the verb.

5. Each of the sons (try/tries) to kill the dragon.
6. Many of their ideas (sound/sounds) good.
7. Several of the townspeople (dream/dreams) of killing the dragon.
8. Nothing (seem/seems) to work.

▲ Everyone wants the dragon dead!

Talk with a Partner

ENGAGE IN CONVERSATION

Pretend you are a townsperson who wants to get rid of the dragon. With a partner, continue the conversation from the song.

Share your ideas and listen to your partner.

- Ask and answer questions.

EXAMPLE

Do you think the king's plan is a good idea?

Yes, but I would not want to be the princess!

- Use words to show you are listening.

EXAMPLE

Yes, I see. OK.

- Use gestures to show you are listening.

EXAMPLES   Nod your head. Smile at something funny. Make eye contact with your partner.

Now have a conversation with your partner about the dragon and the king's plan.

HOW TO ENGAGE IN CONVERSATION

1. Introduce a topic and comment on it.
2. Ask and answer questions about the topic.
3. Use words and gestures to show you are listening.

I like dragons. How do you feel about them?

I think dragons are scary. Don't you?

USE INDEFINITE PRONOUNS

Use **indefinite pronouns** when you talk about the other townspeople with your partner. Check your **verbs** to be sure they agree with your subjects.

Plural: **Many** of us **want** to kill the dragon.

Singular: **Everyone** **wonders** who will do it.

Prepare to Read

Learn Key Vocabulary

Study the Words Use the steps below.

1. Pronounce the word. Say it aloud several times. Spell it.
2. Rate your word knowledge.
3. Study the example. Tell more about the word.
4. Practice it. Make the word your own.

Key Words

bargain (**bar**-gen) *noun*
▶ page 142

A **bargain** is an agreement between people about what each person gives and receives. He made a **bargain** with the sales person for the car.

decent (**dē**-sent) *adjective*
▶ page 148

When you are **decent**, you are good and kind. A **decent** person welcomes a new neighbor.

kingdom (**king**-dum) *noun*
▶ page 138

A **kingdom** is a land or area ruled by a king or queen. The **kingdom** was made up of three countries.

nervous (**ner**-vus) *adjective*
▶ page 141

When you are **nervous**, you feel worried. The basketball player felt **nervous** before the game.

opinion (u-**pin**-yun) *noun*
▶ page 144

An **opinion** is a belief about something. Reporters ask people for their **opinions** about events in the news.

plague (**plāg**) *verb*
▶ page 138

When something really bothers you, it **plagues** you. The thought of the Monday morning math test **plagued** her all weekend.
Synonym: **bother**

quest (**kwest**) *noun*
▶ page 144

A **quest** is a journey or trip to find something. The knight is on a **quest** to find the dragon's cave.
Synonyms: **hunt, search**

recite (ri-**sīt**) *verb*
▶ page 144

When you **recite** something, you are speaking or reading something aloud in public. Every morning before class, we **recite** the Pledge of Allegiance.

Practice the Words Make a Study Card for each Key Word. Then compare your cards with a partner.

nervous

What it means: to feel scared or unsure

Example: I was <u>nervous</u> about giving my speech.

Not an example: I felt confident about the test.

Study Card

Analyze Plot

How Does a Plot Develop? Most stories begin with a conflict, or forces in the story that disagree and **affect** the character or characters. A character may disagree with another character or with an unfortunate event. A character might even have a conflict within himself or herself, such as not being able to decide what to do.

As the plot moves forward, the characters face complications, or events that make the conflict worse. Finally, the events reach a climax, or turning point. Events at the end of the story lead to the resolution, or end, of the conflict. As you read, identify the plot events, including the conflict, complications, climax, falling action, and resolution.

Reading Strategies

- Plan
- **Monitor** Notice confusing parts in the text, then reread or read on to make them clear.
- Ask Questions
- Make Connections
- Visualize
- Make Inferences
- Determine Importance
- Synthesize

Look Into the Text

There was once a king whose kingdom was plagued by a dragon. The king did not know which way to turn. The king's knights were all cowards. They hid under their beds whenever the dragon came into sight. They were of no use to the king at all.

> The dragon creates a conflict for the kingdom.

Practice Together

Begin a Plot Diagram A Plot Diagram can help you understand how a plot develops. This Plot Diagram shows the conflict at the beginning of the story. Reread the passage above, and add details about the complications. Add more details to the diagram as you read.

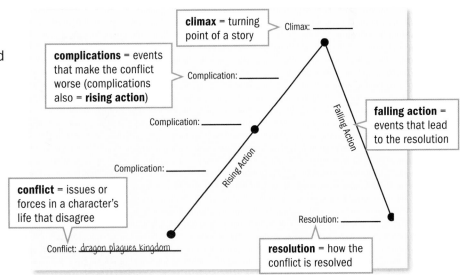

climax = turning point of a story

Climax: _____

complications = events that make the conflict worse (complications also = **rising action**)

Complication: _____

Complication: _____

Complication: _____

Rising Action

Falling Action

falling action = events that lead to the resolution

conflict = issues or forces in a character's life that disagree

Conflict: _dragon plagues kingdom_

Resolution: _____

resolution = how the conflict is resolved

Academic Vocabulary

- **affect** (u-**fekt**) *verb*
  When you **affect** something, you change it in some way.

Short Story

A short story is a brief, made-up narrative. Every story has a plot, setting, and characters.

Plots need conflict: issues or problems in a character's life. A conflict can be between characters, between a character and something else, or between a character and his or her own worries.

The first sentence of this story tells its main conflict. The plot will be about the conflict between the dragon and the kingdom.

Look Into the Text

> There was once a king whose kingdom was plagued by a dragon. The king's knights were all cowards. They hid under their beds . . .

Monitor as you read to make sure you understand important details in the story.

Dragon, Dragon

by John Gardner

illustrated by Brandon Dorman

There was once a king whose kingdom was **plagued** by a dragon. The king did not know **which way to turn**. The king's knights were all cowards. They hid under their beds whenever the dragon came in sight. They were of no use to the king at all. And the king's wizard could not help either because, being old, he had forgotten his magic spells. Nor could the wizard look up the spells that **had slipped his mind**. He had unfortunately misplaced his wizard's book many years before. The king **was at his wit's end**.

Every time there was a full moon the dragon came out of his **lair** and **ravaged** the countryside. He frightened maidens and stopped up chimneys. He broke store windows and set people's clocks back. He even made dogs bark until no one could hear himself think.

He tipped over fences and robbed graves and put frogs in people's drinking water and tore the last chapters out of novels.

He stole spark plugs out of people's cars and put firecrackers in people's cigars and stole the clappers from all the church bells. He sprung every bear trap for miles around so the bears could wander wherever they pleased.

And **to top it all off**, he changed around all the roads in the kingdom. People could not get anywhere except by starting out in the wrong direction.

"That," said the king in a fury, "is enough!" And he called a meeting of everyone in the kingdom.

Now it happened that there lived in the kingdom a wise old cobbler who had a wife and three sons. The cobbler and his family came to the king's meeting and stood way in back by the door. The cobbler had a feeling that since he was nobody important there had probably been some mistake. No doubt the king had intended the meeting for everyone in the kingdom except his family and him.

"Ladies and gentlemen," said the king when everyone was present, "I've **put up** with that dragon as long as I can. He has got to be stopped."

Key Vocabulary

kingdom *n.*, a land or area ruled by a king or queen

plague *v.*, to bother or make trouble again and again

In Other Words

which way to turn whom to ask for help
had slipped his mind he forgot
was at his wit's end did not know what to do
lair resting place; den
ravaged damaged, ruined
to top it all off even worse
put up been patient

All the people whispered amongst themselves. The king smiled, pleased with the impression he had made.

But the wise cobbler said gloomily, "It's all very well to talk about it—but how are you going to do it?"

And now all the people smiled and winked as if to say, "Well, King, he's **got you there**!"

The king frowned.

"It's not that His Majesty hasn't tried," the queen spoke up loyally.

"Yes," said the king. "I've told my knights again and again that they ought to slay that dragon. But I can't *force* them to go. I'm not a **tyrant**."

"Why doesn't the wizard say a magic spell?" asked the cobbler.

"He's done the best he can," said the king.

The wizard blushed and everyone looked embarrassed. "I used to do all sorts of spells and chants when I was younger," the wizard explained. "But I've lost my spell book. I begin to fear I'm losing my memory too. For **instance**, I've been trying for days to recall one spell I used to do. I forget,

just now, what the deuce it was for. It went something like—

> *Bimble,*
> *Wimble,*
> *Cha, Cha*
> CHOOMPF!

In Other Words
got you there made a good argument
tyrant cruel leader
instance example

Language Background
Among and **amongst** both mean "to be in a crowd" but each word is used in different areas of the world. **Among** is commonly used in American English while **amongst** is more often used in British English.

Suddenly, to everyone's surprise, the queen turned into a rosebush.

"Oh dear," said the wizard.

"Now you've done it," groaned the king.

"Poor Mother," said the princess.

"I don't know what can have happened," the wizard said **nervously**, "but don't worry, I'll have her changed back **in a jiffy**." He shut his eyes and **racked his brain for** a spell that would change her back.

But the king said quickly, "You'd better **leave well enough alone**. If you change her into a rattlesnake we'll have to chop off her head."

Meanwhile the cobbler stood with his hands in his pockets, sighing at the waste of time. "About the dragon…" he began.

"Oh yes," said the king. "I'll tell you what I'll do. I'll give the princess' hand in marriage to anyone who can make the dragon stop."

"It's not enough," said the cobbler. "She's a nice enough girl, you understand. But how would an ordinary person support her? Also, what about those of us that are already married?"

"In that case," said the king, "I'll offer the princess' hand or half the kingdom or both. Whichever is most convenient."

The cobbler scratched his chin and considered it. "It's not enough," he said at last. "It's a good enough kingdom, you understand, but it's too much responsibility."

"**Take it or leave it**," the king said.

"I'll leave it," said the cobbler. And he shrugged and went home.

But the cobbler's eldest son thought the **bargain** was a good one. The princess was very beautiful and he liked the idea of having half the kingdom to run as he pleased. So he said to he king, "I'll accept **those terms**, Your Majesty. By tomorrow morning the dragon will be slain."

"Bless you!" cried the king.

"Hooray, hooray, hooray!" cried all the people, throwing their hats in the air. The cobbler's eldest son **beamed with pride**, and the second eldest looked at him enviously. The youngest son said **timidly**,

Key Vocabulary
bargain *n.*, agreement, deal

In Other Words
Take it or leave it Either accept my offer or don't
those terms your offer
beamed with pride looked very proud
timidly with fear

"Excuse me, Your Majesty, but don't you think the queen looks a little unwell? If I were you, I think I'd water her."

"**Good heavens**," cried the king, glancing at the queen who had been changed into a rosebush, "I'm glad you mentioned it!"

In Other Words
Good heavens Oh, no

Look Into the Text

1. **Details** How does the dragon **plague** the kingdom?
2. **Problem and Solution** Why does the king call a town meeting? What does he hope it will accomplish?
3. **Character's Motive** Why does the oldest son decide to try slaying the dragon?

Now the cobbler's eldest son was very clever. He was known **far and wide** for how quickly he could multiply fractions in his head. He was perfectly sure he could slay the dragon by somehow or other playing a trick on him. He didn't feel that he needed his wise old father's advice. But he thought it was only polite to ask, and so he went to his father, who was working as usual at the cobbler's bench, and said, "Well, Father, I'm off to slay the dragon. Have you any advice to give me?"

The cobbler thought a moment and replied, "When and if you come to the dragon's lair, **recite** the following poem.

Dragon, dragon, how do you do?
I've come from the king to murder you.

Say it very loudly and firmly and the dragon will fall, God willing, at your feet."

"How curious!" said the eldest son.

And he thought to himself, "The old man is not as wise as I thought. If I say something like that to the dragon, he will eat me up in an instant. The way to kill a dragon is to **out-fox** him." And keeping his **opinion** to himself, the eldest son **set forth** on his **quest**.

When he came at last to the dragon's lair, which was a cave, the eldest son slyly disguised himself as a peddler. He knocked on the door and called out, "Hello there!"

"There's nobody home!" roared a voice.

The voice was as loud as an earthquake. The eldest son's knees knocked together in terror.

"I don't come to trouble you," the eldest son said meekly. "I merely thought you might be interested in looking at some of our brushes. Or if you'd prefer," he added quickly, "I could leave our catalogue with you and I could drop by again, say, early next week."

Have you any advice to give me?

Key Vocabulary
recite *v.*, to speak or read something aloud
opinion *n.*, a belief about something
quest *n.*, an adventurous journey

In Other Words
far and wide everywhere
out-fox be smarter than; trick
set forth went

"I don't want any brushes," the voice roared, "and I especially don't want any brushes next week."

"Oh," said the eldest son. By now his knees were knocking together so badly that he had to sit down.

Suddenly a great shadow fell over him. The eldest son looked up. It was the dragon.

The eldest son **drew** his sword, but the dragon lunged and swallowed him in a single gulp, sword and all. The eldest son found himself in the dark of the dragon's belly.

What a fool I was not to listen to my wise old father!" thought the eldest son. And he began to **weep bitterly**.

In Other Words
drew pulled out
weep bitterly get angry and cry

"Well," sighed the king the next morning, "I see the dragon has not been slain yet."

"I'm just as glad, personally," said the princess, sprinkling the queen. "I would have had to marry that eldest son, and he had warts."

Now the cobbler's middle son decided it was his turn to try. The middle son was very strong and was known far and wide for being able to lift up the corner of a church. He felt perfectly sure he could slay the dragon by simply **laying into him**. But he thought it would be only polite to ask his father's advice. So he went to his father and said to him, "Well, Father, I'm off to slay the dragon. Have you any advice for me?"

The cobbler told the middle son exactly what he'd told the eldest.

"When and if you come to the dragon's lair, recite the following poem.

Dragon, dragon, how do you do?
I've come from the king to murder you.

Say it very loudly and firmly, and the dragon will fall, God willing, at your feet."

"What an odd thing to say," thought the middle son. "The old man is not as wise as I thought. You have to **take these dragons by surprise**." But he kept his opinion to himself and set forth.

When he came in sight of the dragon's lair, the middle son **spurred his horse to a gallop**. He thundered into the entrance swinging his sword with all his **might**.

But the dragon had seen him while he was still a long way off. Being very clever, the dragon had crawled up on top of the door so that when the son came charging

In Other Words
laying into him using his strength
**take these dragons by
  surprise** surprise a dragon
spurred his horse to a gallop made
  his horse run
might strength

in he went under the dragon and on to the back of the cave and slammed into the wall. Then the dragon chuckled and got down off the door, taking his time. He strolled back to where the man and the horse lay unconscious from **the terrific blow**. Opening his mouth as if for a yawn, the dragon swallowed the middle son in a single gulp and put the horse in the freezer to eat another day.

"What a fool I was not to listen to my wise old father," thought the middle son when he **came to** in the dragon's belly. And he too began to weep bitterly.

Look Into the Text

1. **Confirm Prediction** What happened to the sons? Was your prediction correct?
2. **Character's Point of View** What **opinion** do the sons have of their wise father's advice? Why?
3. **Character** The middle son "felt perfectly sure he could slay the dragon." Why?

That night there was a full moon. The dragon ravaged the countryside so terribly that several families moved to another kingdom.

"Well," sighed the king in the morning, "still no luck **in this dragon business**, I see."

"I'm just as glad, myself," said the princess, moving her mother, pot and all, to the window where the sun could get at her. "The cobbler's middle son was a kind of humpback."

Now the cobbler's youngest son saw that his turn had come. He was very upset and nervous, and he wished he had never been born. He was not clever, like his eldest brother. He was not strong, like his second-eldest brother. He was a **decent**, honest boy who always **minded** his elders.

He borrowed a suit of armor from a friend of his who was a knight. When the youngest son put the armor on it was so heavy he could hardly walk. From another knight he borrowed a sword. It was so heavy that the only way the youngest son could get it to the dragon's lair was to drag it along behind his horse like a plow.

When everything was **in readiness**, the youngest son went for a last conversation with his father.

"Father, have you any advice to give me?" he asked.

"Only this," said the cobbler. "When and if you come to the dragon's lair, recite the following poem.

Dragon, dragon, how
do you do?
I've come from the king
to murder you.

Say it very loudly and firmly, and the dragon will fall, God willing, at your feet."

"Are you certain?" asked the youngest son uneasily.

"As certain as one can ever be in these

> He wished he had never been born.

Key Vocabulary	In Other Words
decent *adj.*, good and kind	**in this dragon business** slaying the dragon **minded** listened to **in readiness** ready

matters," said the wise old cobbler.

And so the youngest son set forth on his quest. He traveled **over hill and dale** and at last came to the dragon's cave.

The dragon, who had seen the cobbler's youngest son while he was still a long way off, was seated up above the door, inside the cave. He was waiting and smiling to himself. But minutes passed and no one came thundering in. The dragon frowned, puzzled, and was tempted to peek out. However, **reflecting that patience seldom goes unrewarded**, the dragon kept his head up out of sight and went on waiting.

In Other Words
over hill and dale for a long time
**reflecting that patience seldom
goes unrewarded** remembering that
patience is a good thing

At last, when he could **stand it no longer**, the dragon **craned his neck** and looked. There at the entrance of the cave stood a trembling young man in a suit of armor twice his size. He was struggling with a sword so heavy he could lift only one end of it at a time.

At sight of the dragon, the cobbler's youngest son began to tremble so violently that his armor rattled like a house caving in. He heaved with all his might at the sword and got the handle up level with his chest, but even now the point was down in the dirt. As loudly and firmly as he could manage, the youngest son cried—

> *Dragon, dragon, how*
> *do you do?*
> *I've come from the king*
> *to murder you!*

"What?" cried the dragon, **flabbergasted**.

"You? *You?* Murder *Me???*" All at once he began to laugh, pointing at the little cobbler's son. "*He he he ho ha!*" he

roared, shaking all over, and tears filled his eyes. "*He he he ho ho ho ha ha!*" laughed the dragon. He was laughing so hard he had to hang onto his sides. He fell off the door and landed on his back, still laughing, kicking his legs helplessly, rolling from side to side, laughing and laughing and laughing.

The cobbler's son was annoyed. "I *do* come from the king to murder you," he said. "A person doesn't like to be laughed at for a thing like that."

"*He he he!*" wailed the dragon, almost sobbing, gasping for breath. "Of course not, poor dear boy! But really, *he he*, the *idea* of it, *ha ha ha*! And that simply ridiculous *poem*!" Tears streamed from the dragon's eyes and he lay on his back perfectly helpless with laughter.

"It's a good poem," said the cobbler's youngest son loyally. "My father made it up." And growing angrier he shouted, "I want you to stop that laughing, or I'll—I'll—" But the dragon could not stop for

In Other Words
stand it no longer not wait anymore
craned his neck bent his neck down
flabbergasted surprised

the life of him. And suddenly, in a terrific rage, the cobbler's son began flopping the sword end over end in the direction of the dragon. Sweat ran off the youngest son's forehead, but he **labored on**, blistering mad. At last, with one **supreme heave**, he had the sword standing on its handle a foot from the dragon's throat. **Of its own weight** the sword fell, slicing the dragon's head off.

"*He he ho huk,*" went the dragon—and then he lay dead.

In Other Words
labored on kept trying to slay the dragon
supreme heave great push
Of its own weight Because it was so heavy

The two older brothers crawled out and thanked their younger brother for saving their lives. "We have learned our lesson," they said.

Then the three brothers gathered all the treasures from the dragon's cave and tied them to the back end of the youngest brother's horse. They tied the dragon's head on behind the treasures, and started home. "I'm glad I listened to my father," the youngest son thought. "Now I'll be the richest man in the kingdom."

There were hand-carved picture frames and silver spoons and boxes of jewels and chests of money and silver compasses and maps telling where there were more treasures buried when these ran out. There was also a curious old book with a picture of an owl on the cover. Inside the book were poems and odd sentences and recipes that seemed to make no sense.

When they reached the king's castle, the people all leaped for joy to see that the dragon was dead. The princess ran out and

kissed the youngest brother on the forehead, for secretly she had hoped it would be him.

"Well," said the king, "which half of the kingdom do you want?"

"My wizard's book!" exclaimed the wizard. "He's found my wizard's book!" He opened the book and **ran his fingers along under the words**. He then said in a loud voice, "Glmuzk, shkzmlp, blam!"

Instantly the queen stood before them **in her natural shape**. Except she was soaking wet from being sprinkled too often. She glared at the king.

"Oh, dear," said the king, hurrying toward the door. ❖

About the Author

John Gardner

John Gardner (1933–1982) grew up on a farm in Batavia, New York. He started writing stories when he was eight years old. His parents often read aloud Shakespeare's works to the family. This inspired him to write old-fashioned tales with a modern twist. Gardner's books on the craft of writing have had a strong influence on writers of all ages. *Dragon, Dragon and Other Tales* was named Outstanding Book of the Year by the *New York Times*.

In Other Words
ran his fingers along under the words started reading
in her natural shape and she was changed back into herself

Look Into the Text

1. **Confirm Predictions** Was your prediction correct? In what ways did the youngest son's actions surprise you?

2. **Compare and Contrast** How is the youngest son different from his brothers?

3. **Conclusion** What lesson do the two older brothers learn?

Leapin' Lizards!
Is That a **Real** Dragon?

How would you feel if you came face to face with a dragon? Lucky for you, dragons are only make-believe.

But, wait. Here is a Komodo dragon and as you can see, it's real. How can that be?

Despite its name and scary appearance, the Komodo dragon is actually a lizard. In fact, it's the world's biggest lizard. The average Komodo weighs more than 150 pounds and can grow almost 10 feet long. Most Komodos are found today on the islands of Indonesia.

Unlike storybook dragons, Komodos don't breathe fire, but they sure like to eat. A Komodo can eat up to 80 percent of its own weight in one meal!

It can also swim, race up a tree, and run faster than 15 miles per hour. Now that's one creature that's not draggin' its feet.

Komodo dragon ▶

Habitats in 2008

▲ Today, only 2,500–5,000 Komodos are left in the world, mostly in Indonesia.

Connect Reading and Writing

Vocabulary
bargain
decent
kingdoms
nervous
opinions
plague
quest
recite

CRITICAL THINKING

1. **SUM IT UP** Use your Plot Diagram to summarize the story.

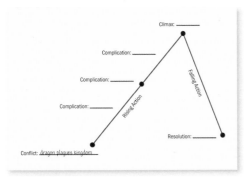

Plot Diagram

2. **Draw Conclusions** What is the cobbler's **opinion** of the king's offer? What does this show about the king? Support your reasons with examples.

3. **Compare** "Dragon, Dragon" and "Leapin' Lizards!" are about different kinds of "dragons." Explain how both animals could make people **nervous**.

4. **Analyze** Which son was able to slay the dragon? Why?

READING FLUENCY

Expression Read the passage on page 629 to a partner. Assess your fluency.

1. My voice never/sometimes/always matched what I read.

2. What I did best in my reading was _____.

READING STRATEGY

What strategy helped you understand this selection? Tell a partner about it.

VOCABULARY REVIEW

Oral Review Read the paragraph aloud. Add the vocabulary words.

When problems _____ kings and queens, they don't worry or feel _____. They just ask kind and _____ people to help them. Sometimes, rulers must go on a _____ all around their _____ to find wise people. They ask them to share their knowledge and _____. They may make a _____ to give gold for wise words. They may even _____ these wise words aloud to help them remember.

Written Review Imagine you are on a **quest** to find a dragon. What would you do? Write a journal entry about it. Use four vocabulary words.

WRITE ABOUT THE (GUIDING QUESTION)

Explore What Happens When People Come Face-To-Face With a Rival

Not all the sons had what it takes to win. Who did not? What should they have done differently? Support your opinion with examples from the text.

Connect Across the Curriculum

Relate Words: Use Synonyms and Antonyms

Academic Vocabulary

- **scale** (skāl) *noun*
  A **scale** is a graphic organizer that shows how a series of items are related.

Analyze Word Relationships A **scale** can show how words are related. *Beautiful* is a stronger word than its synonym, *pretty*.

This **scale** shows how the antonyms *polite* and *rude* relate.

Synonym-Antonym Scale

The words at opposite sides of the scale are antonyms.

Synonym Scale

As you move up the list, each word suggests more beauty.

Make Synonym-Antonym Scales Make a **scale** for each of these words from the selection. Use a thesaurus to help you collect words for the **scales**.

1. coward 2. wise 3. timid 4. clever 5. weep

Analyze Dialogue

Many stories include dialogue, or conversations between two or more characters. Dialogue can move a story forward by providing plot details. It can also provide clues about the characters and their traits.

Read this passage from "Dragon, Dragon." The conversation explains that the king and princess are still waiting for someone to slay the dragon. It also shows that the princess is not upset about the death of the eldest son.

> "Well," sighed the king the next morning. "I see the dragon has not been slain yet."
> "I'm just as glad, personally," said the princess, sprinkling the queen. "I would have had to marry that eldest son, and he had warts."

How Dialogue Reveals Character Traits Look back at "Dragon, Dragon" and analyze what the dialogue shows about the cobbler and his sons.

Engage in Conversation

Role-Play With a partner, role-play a conversation between one of the sons and the dragon. Use some indefinite pronouns like *somebody* or *nobody* in your conversation.

> I am here to stop you, Dragon!

> Nobody talks to me like that.

Write About a Character in the Story

Study the Models When you write about a character, you want your sentences to make sense and to be clear to your reader. To avoid confusing your reader, be sure the subjects and verbs go together.

NOT OK

> The dragon scares everyone in the kingdom. The people know the dragon causes a lot of destruction and confusion. Several of the people leaves the kingdom. No one feels safe. Everyone hope that someone will finally stop the dragon.

> **The reader thinks:** "How many people leave the kingdom?" It's hard to tell from this sentence.

OK

> The dragon scares everyone in the kingdom. The people know the dragon causes a lot of destruction and confusion. Several of the people leave the kingdom. No one feels safe. Everyone hopes that someone will finally stop the dragon.

> **The subjects and verbs now agree, and the meaning is clearer.**

Add Sentences Think of two sentences to add to the OK model above. Use at least one indefinite pronoun. Check that your subjects and verbs agree.

WRITE ON YOUR OWN Write about a character in the story. Is the character brave? Is the character helpful? Make sure your subjects and verbs agree.

REMEMBER

These indefinite pronouns use a singular verb:

another	everybody	no one
anybody	everyone	nothing
anyone	everything	somebody
anything	neither	someone
each	nobody	something
either		

These indefinite pronouns use a plural verb:

both	few	many	several

These indefinite pronouns use either a singular or a plural verb:

all	most	some
any	none	

from the Adventures of
TOM SAWYER

BY MARK TWAIN

Tom Sawyer ' "Well, I don't see why I oughtn't to like it." ' (Tom Sawyer Whitewashing the Fence by Norman Rockwell) The Adventures of Tom Sawyer; Twain, Mark; 1936

1   Tom began to think of the fun he had planned for this day, and his sorrows multiplied. Soon the free boys would come tripping along on all sorts of delicious expeditions, and they would make a world of fun of him for having to work—the very thought of it burnt him like fire. He got out his worldly wealth and examined it—bits of toys, marbles, and trash; enough to buy an exchange of work, maybe, but not half enough to buy so much as half an hour of pure freedom. So he returned his **straitened means** to his pocket, and gave up the idea of trying to buy the boys. At this dark and hopeless moment an inspiration burst upon him! Nothing less than a great, magnificent inspiration.

2   He took up his brush and went tranquilly to work. Ben Rogers hove in sight presently— the very boy, of all boys, whose ridicule he had been dreading. Ben's gait was the hop-skip-and-jump—proof enough that his heart was light and his anticipations high. He was eating an apple, and giving a long, melodious whoop, at intervals, followed by a deep-toned ding-dong-dong, ding-dong-dong, for he was personating a steamboat. As he drew near, he slackened speed, took the middle of the street, leaned far over to starboard and rounded to ponderously and with laborious pomp and circumstance—for he was personating the Big Missouri, and considered himself to be drawing nine feet of water.

3   Tom went on whitewashing—paid no attention to the steamboat. Ben stared a moment and then said:

4   "Hi-*yi! You're* **up a stump, ain't you?**"

5   No answer. Tom surveyed his last touch with the eye of an artist, then he gave his brush another gentle sweep and surveyed the result, as before. Ben ranged up alongside of him. Tom's mouth watered for the apple, but he stuck to his work. Ben said:

6   "Hello, old chap, you got to work, hey?"

7   Tom wheeled suddenly and said:

8   "Why, it's you, Ben! **I warn't noticing.**"

In Other Words
straitened means tiny amount of treasure
up a stump, ain't you in trouble, aren't you
I warn't noticing I didn't see you.

9 "Say—I'm going in a-swimming, I am. Don't you wish you could? But of course you'd **druther** *work*—wouldn't you? Course you would!"

10 Tom contemplated the boy a bit, and said:

11 "What do you call work?"

12 "Why, ain't *that* work?"

13 Tom resumed his whitewashing, and answered carelessly:

14 "Well, maybe it is, and maybe it ain't. All I know, is, it suits Tom Sawyer."

15 "Oh come, now, you don't mean to let on that you like it?"

16 The brush continued to move.

17 "Like it? Well, I don't see why I oughtn't to like it. Does a boy get a chance to whitewash a fence every day?"

18 **That put the thing in a new light.** Ben stopped nibbling his apple. Tom swept his brush daintily back and forth—stepped back to note the effect—added a touch here and there—criticized the effect again—Ben watching every move and getting more and more interested, more and more absorbed. Presently he said:

19 "Say, Tom, let me whitewash a little."

20 Tom considered, was about to consent; but he altered his mind:

21 "No—no—I reckon it wouldn't hardly do, Ben. You see, Aunt Polly's awful particular about this fence—right here on the street, you know—but if it was the back fence I wouldn't mind and she wouldn't. Yes, she's awful particular about this fence; it's got to be done very careful; I reckon there ain't one boy in a thousand, maybe two thousand, that can do it the way it's got to be done."

22 "Oh, shucks, I'll be just as careful. Now lemme try. Say—I'll give you the core of my apple."

23 "Well, here—No, Ben, now don't. I'm afeard—"

24 "I'll give you *all* of it!"

25 Tom gave up the brush with reluctance in his face, but **alacrity** in his heart. And while the late steamer Big Missouri worked and sweated in the sun, the retired artist sat on a barrel in the shade close by, dangled his legs, munched his apple, and planned the slaughter of more innocents. There was no lack of material; boys happened along every little while; they came to jeer, but remained to whitewash. And when the middle of the afternoon came, from being a poor poverty-stricken boy in the morning, Tom was literally rolling in wealth.

26 Tom said to himself that it was not such a hollow world, after all. He had discovered a great law of human action, without knowing it—namely, that in order to make a man or a boy covet a thing, it is only necessary to make the thing difficult to attain.

"What do you call work?"

Compare Across Texts

Compare Characters, Settings, and Problems

"The Three Chicharrones" and "Dragon, Dragon" are tales about outwitting a rival. Compare the characters, settings, and problems in the two stories.

How It Works

Collect and Organize Ideas To compare the main characters, make a Venn Diagram.

Venn Diagram

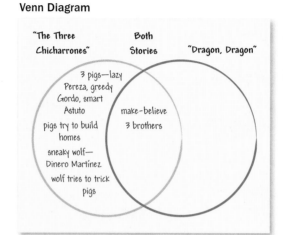

Practice Together

Make Comparisons and Summarize Complete the "Dragon, Dragon" side of the diagram. Add more things that are **similar** about the characters in the middle. Then summarize. Here is a comparison and contrast paragraph for the characters of the two stories.

Summary

> The characters in both "The Three Chicharrones" and "Dragon, Dragon" are make-believe. The three Chicharrones are three pig brothers who must deal with a sneaky wolf. The three brothers in "Dragon, Dragon" are people, but there is a talking dragon. Although the characters are fictional, they often act like real people. In both stories, the characters use their wits to trick their enemies.

Try It!

Make a diagram to compare the settings of the stories, and another to compare the conflicts. Summarize them. You can use a frame like this.

Both "The Three Chicharrones" and "Dragon, Dragon," are set in a world that is _____. The time of "The Three Chicharrones" is _____, while "Dragon, Dragon" seems to take place _____. "The Three Chicharrones" takes place _____, while "Dragon, Dragon" happens in _____.

Academic Vocabulary
- **similar** (si-mu-lur) *adjective*
  Things that are **similar** are almost the same.

STAND
OR
FALL

 What happens when people come face-to-face with a rival?

Content Library

Leveled Library

Reflect on Your Reading

Think back on your reading of the unit selections. Discuss what you did to understand what you read.

Focus on Reading **Elements of Fiction: Plot, Character, Setting**

In this unit, you learned about three elements of fiction: characters, setting, and plot. Choose either "The Three Chicharrones" or "Dragon, Dragon" and write a brief summary of the elements.

Focus Strategy **Monitor**

As you read the selections, you learned to monitor your reading. Explain to a partner how you will use this strategy in the future.

Explore the

Throughout this unit, you have been thinking about what happens when people come face-to-face with a rival. Choose one of these ways to explore the Guiding Question:

- **Discuss** In these selections, it is not always the strongest who succeed. In a group, discuss what it really takes to win. Share examples from your life, and listen to the experiences of others.
- **Ask Questions** On a slip of paper, write the name of a character in one of the selections. Don't tell which one you have chosen. Take turns asking a partner questions to guess which character it is.
- **Write and Draw** Draw a real or made-up creature that has what it takes to survive coming face-to-face with a rival. Add labels to identify and explain its special features.

Book Talk

Which Unit Library book did you choose? Explain to a partner what it taught you about how people come face-to-face with a rival.

MAKING A
DIFFERENCE

3

When can one individual make a difference?

READ MORE!

Content Library
The Emancipation Proclamation
by Marianne McComb

Leveled Library
The House of Dies Drear
by Virginia Hamilton
Finding Miracles
by Julia Alvarez
The Bronx Masquerade
by Nikki Grimes

Web Links
myNGconnect.com

◀ A group of civil rights demonstrators march from Selma to Montgomery in 1965.

Focus on Reading

Text Structure

▶ **Chronological Order**
▶ **Problem and Solution**

Writers **organize** information and ideas in different ways. You can better follow a writer's ideas and remember information if you see how it is **organized** .

How It Works

Before you read, preview the text to figure out the topic and see what kind of writing it is. Look for clues that tell you what the organization is.

Chronological Order A writer uses chronological, or time, order to help readers see how people, attitudes, and situations change over time. Study this example and look for **time words** .

Soccer for All

At an early age, Taylor Bell saw the need for more opportunities for disabled youth to play team sports. Taylor first researched soccer programs in other cities. Then, he scheduled a soccer camp to see how people would respond. Next, he trained coaches and found fields for the players. Finally, he created game schedules.

Time words help show the order of events. Some time words are:

before	after
next	soon
then	finally

Problem and Solution A writer who chooses **problem and solution** organization wants readers to learn about an issue, or problem, and how it could be solved. Study this passage to identify the **problem** and **solution** .

Soccer for All

Taylor Bell, an 18-year-old soccer player from Arkansas, saw a need for more activities for young people with disabilities. — **Problem**

Taylor decided to start a soccer program for disabled youth. He researched soccer programs in other cities and met with soccer organizations to learn how to set up a soccer camp. — **Solution**

Academic Vocabulary

● **organize** (or-gu-nīz) *verb*
To **organize** means to arrange things in a certain order.

Practice Together

Read the following passages aloud. As you read, listen for clues that show how each passage is organized. How does each organization affect the meaning of the passage?

Shaheen Mistri

While in college, Shaheen Mistri spent time with children in India's poorest areas. Shaheen learned that a major problem facing poor children was not having access to quality education. Shaheen wanted to help solve the problem. She gathered a group of her friends, and they began teaching children who lived in the slums. She later founded an organization that has expanded to help more than 4,500 children have access to quality education.

Shaheen Mistri

Shaheen Mistri was born in Mumbai, India. She lived in many places while growing up. Then, at the age of eighteen, she returned to Mumbai. She was surprised by the poor areas in the city. Soon Shaheen enrolled in college and worked with poor children to help them get a better education. In 1989, Shaheen founded an organization to provide better education to children. During the past fifteen years, the organization has helped thousands of children in India.

Try It!

Read the following passages aloud. How is each passage organized? How do you know? How does the organization affect the meaning of each?

Bring It On

Gangs and drugs were problems in teenager Geneva Johnson's New York neighborhood. Geneva decided to take action. She started "Bring It On!," an organization that offers young people a variety of volunteer activities. Geneva learned how to raise money and organize volunteers. Now her group organizes community projects that help kids practice leadership and make healthy choices.

Bring It On

To create her community service group "Bring It On!," teenager Geneva Johnson first learned how to raise money and set up a volunteer organization. Then, she found about 20 kids to become helpers. Next, the group worked on community service projects. Eventually, Geneva's organization helped more than 1,000 kids practice leadership and make healthy choices.

Focus on Vocabulary

Use Word Parts

Word parts include **base words**, **prefixes**, and **suffixes**. If you **focus** on word parts you already know, you can figure out the meanings of new words.

EXAMPLES

Word Parts			
Base Word **work** *verb* to make an effort at a task	**Prefix (*re-*)** **rework** *verb* to do something again	**Suffix (*-able*)** **workable** *adjective* something that is able to be done	**Prefix and Suffix** **unworkable** *adjective* something that is not able to be done

How the Strategy Works

When you read, you may come to a word you do not know. Check the word's parts to help you understand the word's meaning.

EXAMPLE The number of patients was **unmanageable** for one doctor.

1. Look closely at the word to see if you know any of the parts.
2. Cover any prefixes and suffixes. un**manage**able
3. Think about the meaning of the base word.
4. Uncover the prefixes and suffixes and determine their meanings.
5. Put the meanings of the word parts together to understand the whole word. Be sure the meaning makes sense in the passage.

Use the strategy to figure out the meaning of each underlined word.

Do you agree that one person can make a difference? Or do you <u>disagree</u>? Rosa Parks, an African American seamstress in Alabama, made a <u>remarkable</u> difference with one action. In 1955, she refused to give up her seat on the bus to a white person. At that time in Alabama, African Americans were required by law to give up their seats to white people.

Strategy in Action

" I see the prefix *dis-*. I'll cover it. There is the base word *agree*. I know *dis-* means 'the opposite of.' So *dis* + *agree* means the opposite of *agree*."

☑ REMEMBER You can figure out the meaning of an unknown word when you **focus** on the meanings of the word parts.

Academic Vocabulary
- **focus** (fō-kus) *verb*
  When you **focus** on something, you pay attention to it.

Practice Together

Read this passage aloud. Look at each underlined word. Focus on the word parts, and put their meanings together to figure out the word.

History
A Day at a Time

▲ Peoples' choices change history.

Most people think history is a <u>retelling</u> of big events and famous people. But history is actually a <u>review</u> of everything that happens. History is always being made because of the choices people make. Change is <u>unavoidable</u>. Sometimes people are <u>unaware</u> of how <u>powerful</u> their choices can be. For example, Rosa Parks probably never thought that refusing to give up her bus seat would become such an important event in United States history. Look around you. Perhaps a choice you or a friend makes will show you a <u>preview</u> of history to come.

Try It!

Read this passage aloud. What is the meaning of each underlined word? How do you know?

The 1960s: A Time of Change

The 1960s may seem like ancient times to you. Yet many people think the 1960s were the most amazing years in the United States. There were many changes during those years, and it was not a <u>peaceful</u> time. Four presidents held office in just ten years. The space program went from sending small rockets into space to sending men to the moon. Some people worked against <u>unjust</u> laws. Some tried to keep things the same.

Values changed, too. African Americans, young people, and women all became <u>forceful</u> voices for peace and against <u>unequal</u> treatment under the law. A war split the country into supporters and <u>antiwar</u> groups. New leaders arose. Some of them were killed in <u>unthinkable</u> acts of violence.

The challenges of the 1960s may seem far away today. Those years, though, prepared the way for the world you know today.

The Civil Rights Movement

by Kevin Supples

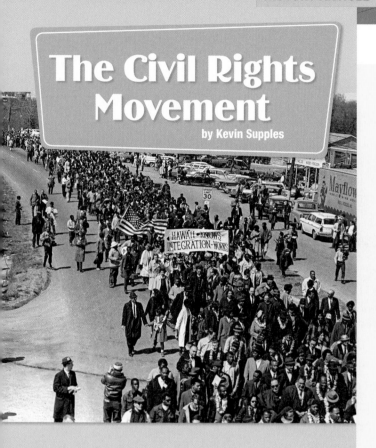

Build Background

Discover Civil Rights

"The Civil Rights Movement" shows how individuals worked together to achieve fairness for all. Now meet the people who made the difference.

Connect

Group Discussion Imagine that your school made a rule that divided people: Students whose names begin with vowels are not allowed to use the main entrance. What would that be like? Discuss your ideas with the class.

Digital Library

myNGconnect.com
◉ View the video.

▲ Rosa Parks acted on her beliefs.

Language & Grammar

1 TRY OUT LANGUAGE
2 LEARN GRAMMAR
3 APPLY ON YOUR OWN

Ask for and Give Information

CD

Look at the photograph and listen to questions and answers about the picture.

PICTURE PROMPT

From Selma to Montgomery

Student: What does this picture show?

Teacher: It shows people who participated in a march in the 1960s.

Student: Why did the people march?

Teacher: They marched to protest laws that made it hard for African Americans in Alabama to vote.

Use Present, Past, and Future Tense Verbs

The tense, or time, of a **verb** shows when an action happens.

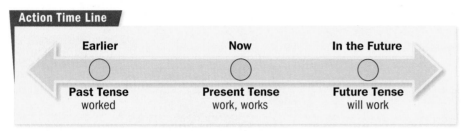

Action Time Line

Earlier	Now	In the Future
Past Tense	**Present Tense**	**Future Tense**
worked	work, works	will work

- The **present tense** tells about an action that happens now or often. Add **-s** to the verb to tell about one person, place, or thing.

    EXAMPLES   Today, laws **treat** all people fairly. (*happens now*)

                    The government **protects** our civil rights. (*happens often*)

- The **past tense** tells about an action that has already happened. Add **-ed** to most verbs when you talk about a past action.

    EXAMPLES   In the 1960s, Congress **passed** a voting rights law.

- The **future tense** tells about an action that will happen in the future. To show the future, add **will** before the verb.

    EXAMPLES   Tomorrow, we **will learn** about a civil rights march.

Practice Together

Say each sentence. Then say it again and change the <u>verb</u> to the past tense and the future tense. Say both new sentences.

1. Aunt Sally <u>works</u> as a lawyer.
2. She <u>protects</u> everyone's civil rights.
3. Aunt Sally <u>visits</u> our class
4. We <u>ask</u> her a lot of questions.

Try It!

Say each sentence. Write the past and the future tense form of the <u>verb</u> on a card. Then say both new sentences.

5. The people <u>gather</u> their signs.
6. The signs <u>show</u> their messages.
7. They <u>walk</u> peacefully down the street.
8. Each marcher <u>supports</u> equal rights.

▲ People marched for equal rights.

Learn About a Civil Rights March

ASK FOR AND GIVE INFORMATION

Look at the photograph of the March on Washington. This famous civil rights march took place on August 28, 1963. What does the photograph show? What information about the march can you tell others?

In a small group, complete a Question-Answer Chart about the photograph. Give facts or details in your answers.

▲ Marchers protested at the March on Washington on August 28, 1963, in Washington, DC.

Question-Answer Chart

Question	Answer
1. Where did the people march?	The people marched in Washington, DC.
2. What was one thing the people wanted?	
3.	

Trade questions with another group. Answer their questions by giving information. Then trade roles.

HOW TO ASK FOR AND GIVE INFORMATION

1. Ask a question that starts with *Who, What, When, Where, Why, How, Are, Were, Can, Do,* or *Did*.

2. To answer, give facts or details.

> Why did this march happen?

> The people marched because they wanted to show their support for the passage of fair laws.

USE PRESENT, PAST, AND FUTURE TENSE VERBS

When you give information, you may tell about something that happens now or often. If so, use a verb in the **present tense**. Or you may tell about something that already happened. If so, use a verb in the **past tense**. If you tell about something that will happen at a later time, use a verb in the **future tense**.

In the Present: Why **do** people march today?
People **march** today for what they believe in.

In the Past: Why **did** people march in 1963?
People **marched** in 1963 for equal rights.

In the Future: Why **will** people march in the future?
People **will march** in the future to support change.

Prepare to Read

Learn Key Vocabulary

Study the Words Use the steps below.

1. Pronounce the word. Say it aloud several times. Spell it.
2. Rate your word knowledge.
3. Study the example. Tell more about the word.
4. Practice it. Make the word your own.

Rating Scale

1 = I have never seen this word before.

2 = I am not sure of the word's meaning.

3 = I know this word and can teach the word's meaning to someone else.

Key Words

civil rights (siv-ul rīts) *noun*
▶ page 177

Your **civil rights** are the rights you have as a member of society. Many people marched to gain **civil rights** for all.

determined (dē-tur-mind) *adjective* ▶ page 177

When you are **determined** to do something, you work hard at it. The football team was **determined** to win.
Related Word: **determination**

equality (ē-kwal-i-tē) *noun*
▶ page 177

When you have the same rights as other people, you have **equality**. **Equality** is important within any group of people.
Related Words: **equal, equalize**

integrate (in-ti-grāt) *verb*
▶ page 180

When you **integrate** groups, you bring them together. Martin Luther King, Jr., worked to **integrate** schools.
Synonym: **combine**
Antonym: **segregate**

prejudice (prej-ū-dis) *noun*
▶ page 176

If you have **prejudice**, you judge things and people before you know about them. **Prejudice** is a form of ignorance.
Related Word: **judge**

protest (prō-test) *verb*
▶ page 187

To **protest** something means to show you are against it. Americans **protested** unfair treatment of African Americans.

Practice the Words Make a Study Card for each Key Word. Then compare your cards with a partner's.

> **determined**
>
> **What it means:** to work hard for something
>
> **Examples:** I was <u>determined</u> to get an A on the test, so I studied hard.
> She was <u>determined</u> to win the race.
>
> **Not examples:** I wanted an A, but I did not study.
> She didn't like to run races but thought she might win anyway.

Study Card

segregation
(seg-ri-gā-shun) *noun* ▶ page 176

Segregation is when people are kept apart. The **segregation** of African American people in the 1950s was wrong.
Antonym: **integrate**

separate (sep-u-rut) *adjective*
▶ page 179

If you are **separate** from other people, you are not with them. It is not fun to feel **separate** from the group.
Antonym: **together**

Text Structure: Chronological Order

How Is Writing Organized? Some writing is organized in time order. Chronological order shows events in the order they happened. Time words give readers clues to when events happened.

As you read, look for time words that can help you understand the chronological order of events.

Reading Strategies
- Plan
- Monitor
- **Ask Questions** Think actively by asking and answering questions about the text.
- Make Connections
- Visualize
- Make Inferences
- Determine Importance
- Synthesize

Look Into the Text

> Marshall was born in Maryland in 1908. He was raised in a proud middle-class family. Smart and hard working, he was a fine student. Marshall went to college and later attended law school at Howard University in Washington, DC. Marshall graduated in 1933, first in his class.

Practice Together

Start a Time Line Make a Time Line to show the chronological order of events. This Time Line shows the first event from the passage. Reread the passage and add another event to the Time Line.

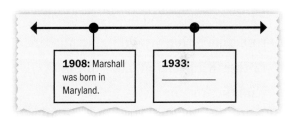

1908: Marshall was born in Maryland.

1933: _____

Academic Vocabulary

- **organize** (**or**-gu-nīz) *verb*
  To **organize** means to arrange things in a certain order.

History Article

A history article tells about real events that happened in the past.

History articles usually present information in chronological order so that readers can see how events developed through time. **Time words** signal when events happened.

Look Into the Text

While at Boston University finishing his studies to be a minister, King met Coretta Scott . . . . The two were married in 1953, and the following year, Reverend King became pastor of a church in Montgomery, Alabama. He quickly became known for his wisdom and powerful preaching. Then in December 1955, an event took place that would make Martin Luther King, Jr., a leader of the Civil Rights Movement.

As you read a history article, ask yourself questions to help you check your understanding of the events.

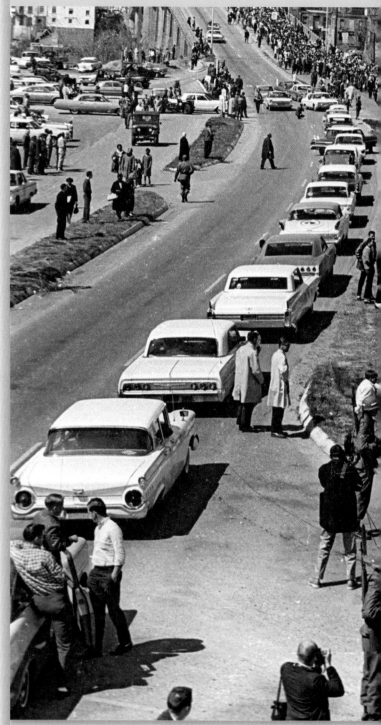

▲ On March 7, 1965, 600 people in Alabama began a march to demand civil rights. When they reached the State Capitol building in Birmingham on March 25, there were 25,000 people marching.

The Civil Rights Movement

by Kevin Supples

Comprehension Coach

America in 1950

A Divided Society

The 1950s were good years for many Americans. They had jobs that paid well, new homes **in the suburbs**, and good schools for their children. But African Americans were one group who did not **share fully in all this**. In the 1950s, **prejudice** against African Americans was **widespread** in the United States.

One of the worst results of this prejudice was **segregation**, the practice of keeping people apart based on race.

Segregation was different in different parts of the United States. The South was home to more than half of African Americans. In the South, segregation was **enforced** by Jim Crow laws. These laws

▲ A child uses a drinking fountain outside of a North Carolina courthouse. In the 1950s, segregation controlled the everyday lives of most African Americans.

Key Vocabulary

prejudice *n.*, unfair opinions about a person, group, or race

segregation *n.*, the division of people into groups based on race

In Other Words

in the suburbs outside the city
share fully in all this have all of this
widespread very common
enforced supported; made legal

had controlled the lives of Southern blacks since the late 1800s. Jim Crow laws said that blacks and whites must use different schools, restaurants, hotels, theaters, parks, sections of trains and buses, and so on. Even funeral homes and cemeteries were segregated! In the few places where blacks and whites shared public services—such as post offices and banks—African Americans had to wait for all whites to be served first.

In the North, segregation happened by **practice and custom**. Many African Americans moved to Northern cities during the 1940s, and whites responded by moving to the suburbs. African Americans **found themselves trapped** in city slums—poor neighborhoods where housing and schools were bad and where there were few jobs.

Both Northern and Southern segregation were wrong and both forms of segregation denied black people an **equality** that they had a right to as Americans. In the 1950s, some African Americans were **determined** to change things. They started the **Civil Rights** Movement. This **movement** brought together many people and for some, the struggle to win equality became their life's work.

▲ Many white people moved out of Northern cities when African Americans moved in. Neighborhoods like Harlem, New York (pictured), suffered because of a lack of city services.

Key Vocabulary

equality *n.*, having the same rights as other people

determined *adj.*, working hard to make something happen

civil rights *n.*, basic rights and freedoms

In Other Words

practice and custom people's beliefs and not the law

found themselves trapped were left

movement organized effort for change

Look Into the Text

1. **Cause and Effect** Why were African Americans **determined** to change things?

2. **Author's Point of View** How does the author feel about **segregation**? Support your answer with examples.

The Movement Begins

Thurgood Marshall

One group that fought for equality is the National Association for the Advancement of Colored People (NAACP). The NAACP was founded in 1909. Their goal was to obtain equal rights for all people and to **eliminate** racial hatred and discrimination.

The leader of the NAACP's efforts to end segregation was their top lawyer, Thurgood Marshall. He used the law to fight **injustice** against African Americans. Marshall argued thirty-two cases before the U.S. Supreme Court during his career, and he won twenty-nine of them. Some say that Marshall did more than any other **individual** to win civil rights for African Americans.

Marshall was born in Maryland in 1908. He was raised in a proud middle-class family. Smart and hard working, he was a fine student. Marshall went to college and later attended law school at Howard University in Washington, DC. Marshall graduated in 1933, first in his class.

Most of Marshall's clients were poor. Some couldn't even pay anything, but Marshall worked hard for them anyway. He usually won his cases. He became known as **the "little man's lawyer."** Marshall had a good sense of humor. He enjoyed jokes and often used humor to help him get through **hard times**.

Thurgood Marshall stands in front of the U.S. Supreme Court in 1954. Thirteen years later, he became the nation's first African American Supreme Court justice. ▶

In Other Words

eliminate end
injustice unfair treatment
individual person
the little man's lawyer a lawyer who helped the poor
hard times bad experiences

Government Background

The **U.S. Supreme Court** is the most important court in the nation. It has power over every court in each state. The U.S. Supreme Court is led by the Chief Justice of the United States, or the head of the court, and eight justices.

"Separate But Equal"

Throughout his career, Thurgood Marshall fought the "**separate** but equal" rule. This rule was created in 1896 by the Supreme Court. It said that states could offer separate services to African Americans and whites as long as the services were close to equal, but actually they often were not.

Many states passed laws saying that **local school districts** could decide whether to have separate schools for blacks and whites. The result was that all schools in the South were segregated. And there was nothing "equal" about the education black children were given in their poor, crowded schools.

After World War II, many Southern states tried to improve their blacks-only schools. They wanted to show that these schools were equal, but their efforts were **too little and too late**. By 1952, there were several court cases about segregated schools. The most famous case involved an eight-year-old girl named Linda Brown.

Linda's family lived close to a public school in Topeka, Kansas, but that school accepted only white students. So Linda had to travel by bus to a blacks-only school. To reach their bus stop, she and her sister

▲ Linda Brown (lower right) in a segregated classroom

had to walk through a dangerous railroad yard. Early in 1951, the Browns and some other African American families decided to take the local school district to **court**. In July, the local school board promised they would end segregation "as soon as possible." But that wasn't good enough for the Browns.

Key Vocabulary
  separate *adj.*, apart

In Other Words
  local school districts groups of schools in one area
  too little and too late not enough and happened too slowly
  court a place where a judge would hear their complaint

Historical Background
The U.S. Supreme Court ruled that **separate but equal** services were legal in the 1896 case of *Plessy v. Ferguson.* This decision allowed states and local governments to separate blacks and whites as long as they received similar services.

Brown v. Board of Education

The Browns' case became famous and Thurgood Marshall decided to use it to try to end segregated schools everywhere. He brought the case to the Supreme Court. The court decided to group the Browns' case with four others. Their case is known as *Brown v. Board of Education.*

Marshall argued the case **before** the Supreme Court. He argued that the Fourteenth Amendment of the U.S. Constitution said that states must treat all citizens alike, regardless of race. He said that black children did not receive schooling equal to that given to white children. He also said that black children thought less of themselves because they attended poor schools.

Almost three years after Linda Brown's family started the case, a final decision was reached. On May 17, 1954, the Supreme Court ruled that school segregation went against the Constitution.

After the ruling, the government made many school districts **redraw their borders**. Now white and black students would go to school together. This victory was an important step in the fight for civil rights. Many hoped that **integrating** schools would lead to integrating all of society. But there was still a long struggle ahead.

▲ African American children arrive for class. Segregated schools like this one led to the famous *Brown v. Board of Education* legal case.

Key Vocabulary
integrate *v.*, to bring together

In Other Words
v. (versus) against (in Latin)
before in front of
redraw their borders allow black students to attend

Historical Background
The **Fourteenth Amendment** of the U.S. Constitution was passed in June of 1866. The amendment was designed to grant citizenship for and protect the civil liberties of people who had recently been freed from slavery.

Linda Brown THEN

A young Linda Brown (left) stands with her younger sister Cheryl and her parents. Her father, Reverend Oliver Brown, asked "Why should my child walk four miles when there is a school only four blocks away? Why should I . . . explain to my daughter that she can't attend school with her neighborhood playmates because she is black?"

▲ Linda Brown and her family in the 1950s

Linda Brown TODAY

Today Linda Brown Thompson lives in Topeka, Kansas. She owns an educational consulting firm with her sister. Together, Linda and her sister have spoken about the court case and their experiences across the country. They have also appeared on television and were invited to the White House.

"We lived in the calm of the hurricane's eye, looking out at the storm and wondering how it would end," she recalled on the fiftieth anniversary of the Supreme Court decision to end segregation in public schools.

▲ Linda Brown Thompson, left, signs autographs at the University of Michigan in 2004.

Look Into the Text

1. **Main Idea and Details** Thurgood Marshall fought hard for **civil rights**. Give two examples.
2. **Problem and Solution** Why did the Browns take the school district to court? What was the result?
3. **Conclusions** Why was the Browns' case important? Explain.

▲ National Guard troops stand outside Central High School in 1957.

The Little Rock Nine

Within a year, some school districts desegregated. **Here and there**, African American and white students attended school together. But many school districts, especially in the South, found ways to **resist** and delay the Supreme Court ruling.

Little Rock, Arkansas, became a test case for the new ruling because public schools there were ordered to desegregate in September 1957. The local school board agreed, but the governor of Arkansas, Orval Faubus, refused. He was **facing a tough re-election fight**, and he hoped

In Other Words

Here and there In some places
resist fight against
facing a tough re-election fight trying to become governor again, but had a stong opponent

Historical Background

The **National Guard** is one branch of the U.S. military. Its purpose is to help the nation in times of emergency or war.

to win the support of the many white Arkansas voters who still wanted segregated schools.

When school opened that September, Governor Faubus sent National Guard troops to Central High School. He ordered them to stop nine African American students from entering the newly integrated school. Elizabeth Eckford, one of the **"Little Rock Nine,"** arrived at school alone when **a white mob** began to scream at her.

For three weeks, the **crisis** continued. At this point, President Dwight Eisenhower **stepped in** by placing the Arkansas National Guard under federal control. The nine black students arrived at the school in a U.S. Army car. With soldiers protecting them, the students finally were integrated into the school. Eisenhower had shown that the federal government would protect civil rights.

Later, President Eisenhower wrote a message to parents of the Little Rock Nine. "In the course of our country's progress toward equality of opportunity, you have shown dignity and courage."

▲ Elizabeth Eckford had to walk past a crowd that shouted insults at her.

Look Into the Text

1. **Cause and Effect** What did Governor Faubus do to fight against the Supreme Court ruling?
2. **Problem and Solution** How did President Eisenhower help to **integrate** Central High School?

The Civil Rights Movement **183**

The Struggle Continues

Martin Luther King, Jr.

The legal victory of *Brown v. Board of Education* was just one step in the fight against segregation. It did not change things as quickly as people had hoped. African Americans were ready to do more, and they began to organize. At this moment in history, a new leader arrived. He was a young minister named Martin Luther King, Jr.

King was born in 1929 in Atlanta, Georgia, to a middle class family. He was the son and grandson of Baptist ministers. His mother was a teacher. One of his grandfathers had been a slave. King **excelled at** school. He began college at the age of fifteen in a program for **gifted** students. He went to Morehouse College, a well-known all-black school in Atlanta. By the time King was eighteen, he had decided to **follow in his father's footsteps**.

While at Boston University finishing his studies to be a minister, King met Coretta Scott. She was studying voice and piano. The two were married in 1953 and the following year, Reverend King became pastor of a church in Montgomery, Alabama. He quickly became known for his wisdom and powerful preaching. Then in December 1955, an event **took place** that would make Martin Luther King, Jr., a leader of the Civil Rights Movement.

◀ Dr. Martin Luther King, Jr.

In Other Words
excelled at did really well in
gifted very smart or talented
follow in his father's footsteps
  be a minister like his father
took place happened

Changing the System

Rosa Parks

Montgomery, Alabama, was a segregated city in 1955. African Americans were treated **as second class citizens** there. The public bus system was a constant reminder of this.

As in many Southern cities, more blacks rode the city buses than whites. Even so, the first ten rows of every bus were reserved for white passengers only. If a bus was crowded and a white passenger needed a seat, blacks had to stand. Black passengers had to pay their **fares** at the front of the bus, but then they had to get off the bus and re-board by the back door. At busy times, the bus sometimes left before everyone who had paid got back on.

On December 1, 1955, Rosa Parks was riding the bus home from work. She was a **seamstress**, and she also worked at the local NAACP office. Parks had been on her feet all day, and she was tired. She was sitting in the eleventh row—the first row of seats set aside for African American passengers.

The bus was crowded and some black passengers were standing at the back. When a white man needed a seat, the bus driver ordered Parks and three African Americans in her row to stand. She refused to move and Parks was taken off the bus, arrested, and put in a jail cell.

News of Parks's arrest **shocked** the African American community. Civil rights supporters saw that this was their chance to change the rules. They asked Martin Luther King, Jr., to be their leader. That evening, Dr. King spoke to a cheering crowd of African Americans and he called for them to start a bus boycott, which meant they would not ride the buses.

▲ Rosa Parks is fingerprinted at the police station.

In Other Words

as second class citizens poorly
fares money
seamstress person who sews clothes
shocked surprised

Historical Background

The **bus boycott** led to the formation of the Montgomery Improvement Association, headed by Dr. Martin Luther King, Jr. The boycott lasted 381 days and made news around the world.

Look Into the Text

1. **Sequence** Tell what happened to Rosa Parks on the night of December 1, 1955, and what happened next in the community as a result.
2. **Summarize** Who was Martin Luther King, Jr.? How did he take part in the **Civil Rights** Movement?

◀ Martin Luther King, Jr., inspired people to boycott the public buses in Montgomery.

The Montgomery Bus Boycott

For the next year, very few African Americans rode public buses in Montgomery, Alabama. Most **used car pools** to get to work. The boycott worked. The bus company lost a lot of money. The combination of the city's loss of money and a decision by the Supreme Court forced the Montgomery Bus Company to accept integration.

In June 1956, a federal court ruled that the bus segregation in Alabama was against the Constitution. The city of Montgomery did not **give in** easily. Lawyers for the city took the case to the Supreme Court, but that November, the Supreme Court agreed that segregation on buses was not lawful in the case of *Browder v. Gale*. A little over a year after the day that Rosa Parks refused to move, the Montgomery buses were integrated.

The Montgomery bus boycott was big news. It made Martin Luther King, Jr., famous. *Time* magazine put him on the cover. Requests to speak **poured in** from all over the country, and the **publicity** also led to boycotts in many other parts of the South.

The Protests

In February 1960, four African American college freshmen in Greensboro, North Carolina, decided to take another step toward equality. They sat down at the

In Other Words

used car pools rode together in cars
give in quit
poured in came in
publicity attention

Word History

In Ireland around 1880, landowner Charles Boycott refused to lower his high rents. To protest, renters and others stopped speaking to or working with him. Such planned inaction became known as a *boycott*.

▲ Thousands of African Americans walked to work during the Montgomery bus boycott.

whites-only lunch counter in a Woolworth's store and politely ordered coffee and donuts. The students were **refused service**. At that time, many department stores across the country had lunch counters, but most Southern lunch counters did not serve food to African Americans. Blacks were free to shop at the stores but could not eat there.

To **protest**, the four students sat at the counter for the rest of the afternoon. They returned the next day. This time, twenty more students came with them and each day, more people—both black and white—joined the "sit-in." By Saturday, hundreds **jammed** the lunch counters.

The events in Greensboro became news. At first, white business leaders refused to **bend to** the protest. But then black citizens set up a boycott of local stores. Stores began losing money and finally, on July 25, 1960, the first black person was served lunch at Woolworth's.

During the next eighteen months, thousands of people **staged** sit-ins all over the South. Most of those taking part were black students. Both Martin Luther King, Jr., and Thurgood Marshall supported these nonviolent protests. African Americans had found a new and powerful way to be heard.

In Other Words
refused service not served any food
jammed crowded
bend to change because of
staged held

Look Into the Text

1. **Conclusions** How effective was the bus boycott? Explain your conclusion.
2. **Main Idea and Details** Parks and King set an example for nonviolent **protests**. How did college students follow them?

Achieving the Dream

The Civil Rights Act

In the fall of 1960, John F. Kennedy was elected president of the United States. Kennedy won 70 percent of the **black vote**. He had shown that he would support ending segregation. Kennedy did not make changes quickly, but he did appoint more African Americans to high federal positions than any president before him. Kennedy appointed Thurgood Marshall to be a federal judge.

In June 1963, President Kennedy demanded that Congress pass a strong civil rights bill. In a speech to the nation he asked, "Are we to say to the world—and much more importantly to each other—that this is the land of the free, except for the Negroes?"

To persuade Congress to pass the bill, civil rights leaders A. Philip Randolph and Bayard Rustin organized a huge march on Washington, DC. On August 28, more than 250,000 people—both African Americans and whites—came together in the nation's capital. Labor unions and religious leaders joined the protest.

It was the largest show of support for the Civil Rights Movement so far.

▲ Martin Luther King, Jr., smiles and waves at the huge crowd gathered at the March on Washington.

The march ended at the Lincoln Memorial. For three hours, the crowd listened to a lot of speeches. People were getting sleepy and **restless** when the last speaker, Martin Luther King, Jr., came to the microphone. His famous "I Have a Dream"

In Other Words
black vote votes from African Americans
restless ready to leave

speech **electrified** the crowd.

A few months after the March on Washington, President Kennedy was **assassinated**. His vice-president, Lyndon Johnson, **succeeded him**. President Johnson passed the Civil Rights Act of 1964.

The new law **banned** segregation in public places, and it also banned unfair treatment of workers based on their color, sex, religion, or national origin. ❖

In Other Words

electrified excited
assassinated shot and killed
succeeded him became the
  next president
banned put a stop to

Look Into the Text

1. **Main Idea and Details** How did President Kennedy affect the **Civil Rights** Movement?
2. **Summarize** In the 1960s, how did the Movement move forward?
3. **Judgment** In what ways did the Movement succeed? Explain.

Midway

by Naomi Long Madgett

I've come this far to freedom and I won't turn back.

I'm climbing to the highway from my old dirt track.

    I'm coming and I'm going

    And I'm stretching and I'm growing

5 And I'll reap what I've been sowing or my skin's not black.

I've prayed and slaved and waited and I've sung my song.

You've bled me and you've starved me but I've still grown strong.

    You've lashed me and you've treed me

    And you've everything but freed me

10 But in time you'll know you need me and it won't be long.

I've seen the daylight breaking high above the bough.

I've found my destination and I've made my vow;

    So whether you abhor me

    Or deride me or ignore me,

15 Mighty mountains loom before me and I won't stop now.

In Other Words

reap what I've been sowing get what I deserve

the daylight breaking high above the bough that there is hope

abhor me hate me

Or deride Disrespect

Look Into the Text

1. **Interpret** What does the speaker mean by "I won't turn back"?
2. **Inference** What struggle does the speaker describe?
3. **Symbol** Reread the last line of the poem. What do the mountains symbolize?

Connect Reading and Writing

Vocabulary
Civil Rights
determined
equality
integrate
prejudice
protested
segregation
separate

CRITICAL THINKING

1. **SUM IT UP** Use your Time Line to describe the events in "The Civil Rights Movement." Then summarize the events to a partner.

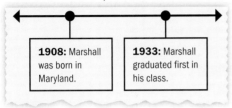

1908: Marshall was born in Maryland.

1933: Marshall graduated first in his class.

Time Line

2. **Compare** Compare the ways **segregation** was different for African Americans in the North and the South during the early 1960s.

3. **Speculate** What do you think life was like for students your age at the time of the **Civil Rights** Movement?

4. **Compare Across Texts** Explain how the poem "Midway" relates to the fight for **equality** in "The **Civil Rights** Movement."

READING FLUENCY

Phrasing Read the passage on page 630 to a partner. Assess your fluency.

1. I did not pause/sometimes paused/ always paused for punctuation.

2. What I did best in my reading was _____.

READING STRATEGY

What strategy helped you understand this selection? Tell a partner about it.

VOCABULARY REVIEW

Oral Review Read the paragraph aloud. Add the vocabulary words.

In 1961, laws in the South enforced _____ that kept blacks and whites _____. Supporters of the _____ Movement were _____ to change this. Black and white students got on buses to _____ public transportation. People who worked for racial _____ were called Freedom Riders. The Freedom Riders _____ unequal treatment and unfair opinions, or _____.

Written Review Imagine you are a reporter during the **Civil Rights** Movement. Report on how one school **integrated** its students. Use five vocabulary words.

WRITE ABOUT THE GUIDING QUESTION

Reflect on Making a Difference
Which person in the selection made the biggest difference during the **Civil Rights** Movement? Support your opinion with examples.

Connect Across the Curriculum

Vocabulary Study

Use Word Parts: Prefixes

Prefix	Meaning
dis-	the opposite of
un-	not
re-	again
non-	not
in-	not
de-	removal, reversal

Academic Vocabulary
- **analyze** (a-nu-līz) *verb*
  When you **analyze**, you separate something into parts and examine, or study, it.

Many English words are made of different word parts. When you **analyze** the parts, you can figure out the meaning of the whole word. For example, the prefix *dis-* in *discomfort* means "the opposite of." Therefore, *discomfort* means "the opposite of comfort."

Find Word Parts Work with a partner. **Analyze** each of these words' parts. Put the meanings together to understand the whole word.

1. unfair   **3.** nonviolent   **5.** re-election

2. injustice   **4.** redraw   **6.** desegregate

Write Sentences Write a sentence for each word. Does the meaning you predicted make sense in the sentence?

Literary Analysis

Evaluate Informational Text

Academic Vocabulary
- **evidence** (e-vu-dents) *noun*
  Evidence can be beliefs, proof, facts, or details that help support a conclusion.

What Makes Evidence Strong? Effective conclusions are supported by **evidence** that is **relevant** and **sufficient**.

NOT OK

> This bus is always slow! I was already running late this morning. I can't believe the bus broke down!

Not Sufficient: This **evidence** is based on one event, so there isn't enough of it.

NOT OK

> This bus is always slow! These bus stops are filthy. Someone really needs to clean them up.

Not Relevant: This **evidence** does not relate to the buses not being on time.

Evaluate Evidence In "The Civil Rights Movement," the author argues that Thurgood Marshall did more than any other individual to win civil rights for African Americans. Decide whether he supported this argument with relevant, sufficient evidence.

Ask for and Give Information

Group Share Tell a small group the information you learned from reading the selection. Ask questions about your classmates' new knowledge. Use present, past, and future tense verbs depending on the time of the action.

> What did you learn about schools during this time period?

> I learned that schools were segregated and that people tried to change them.

Write About a Past Event

Study the Models When you write about an event that happened in the past, you need to be consistent so you don't confuse your readers. Choose verbs that make it clear that the events happened in the past, not in the present.

NOT OK

In the 1950s, Linda Brown **walked** through a dangerous railroad yard on her way to the school bus stop. Then she **travels** by bus to a blacks-only school. Her family **decided** to take the school district to court. Three years later, the Supreme Court **rules** against school segregation.

> The reader thinks: "Did these things all happen a long time ago or right now?" The time is not clear.

OK

In the 1950s, Linda Brown **walked** through a dangerous railroad yard on her way to the school bus stop. Then she **traveled** by bus to a blacks-only school. Her family **decided** to take the school district to court. Three years later, the Supreme Court **ruled** against school segregation.

> This writing is consistent. The time of the events is now clear.

Add Sentences Think of two sentences to add to the OK model above. Be consistent in showing that the events happened in the past.

WRITE ON YOUR OWN Imagine you are one of the "Little Rock Nine" and the year is 1957. Write about what your school day was like yesterday. Use words that make it clear that the events happened in the past.

REMEMBER

Check your past tense verbs for correct spelling.

- If a verb ends in silent **e**, drop the **e** before you add **-ed**.
  rul~~e~~ + -**ed** = rul**ed**

- If the verb has one syllable and ends in one vowel and one consonant, double the consonant.
  stop + p + -**ed** = stop**ped**

- If the verb ends in **y**, change the **y** to **i**. Then add **-ed**.
  tr~~y~~ + -**ed** = tr**ied**

MARTIN'S BIG WORDS

The Life of Dr. Martin Luther King, Jr.

by Doreen Rappaport
illustrated by Bryan Collier

Build Background

Hear Powerful Words

Dr. Martin Luther King, Jr., used the power of language to speak up for civil rights. Forty years after his death, his speeches still inspire people today.

Connect

Quickwrite Words can be powerful. Recall words that have affected you. Perhaps it was advice that helped you, or words from a movie or a song that inspired you. Describe the effect these words had on your life.

Digital Library

myNGconnect.com
◐ View the video.

▲ Dr. Martin Luther King, Jr.

Language & Grammar

Describe an Event

Look at the photograph and listen to the song.
The song is about the March on Washington.

SONG

▲ Dr. Martin Luther King, Jr., gave a powerful speech at the March on Washington in 1963.

We're Marching for Freedom

We're marching for freedom.
Hear us now!
We're marching for freedom.
Hear us now!
We're marching for freedom.
Hear us now!
We want the rights that others have.

We want the right to vote.
Hear us now!
We want the right to vote.
Hear us now!
We want the right to vote.
Hear us now!
We want the rights that others have.

We want our education,
Hear us now!
We want our education,
Hear us now!
We want our education,
Hear us now!
We want the rights that others have.

We want to live in peace.
Hear us now!
We want to live in peace.
Hear us now!
We want to live in peace.
Hear us now!
We want the rights that others have.

Equal rights for all,
Hear us now!
Equal rights for all,
Hear us now!
Equal rights for all,
Hear us now!
We want the rights that others have.

Use Forms of *Be*

The verb **be** is irregular. It has special forms to tell about the present, past, and future.

Action Time Line

Earlier	Now	In the Future
Past Tense	**Present Tense**	**Future Tense**
I **was**	I **am**	I **will be**
you **were**	you **are**	you **will be**
he, she, or it **was**	he, she, or it **is**	he, she, or it **will be**
we **were**	we **are**	we **will be**
they **were**	they **are**	they **will be**

- For the present tense, use **am**, **is**, or **are** to match the subject.
    - EXAMPLES Dr. Martin Luther King, Jr., **is** my hero. (one)
      His ideas **are** still important today. (more than one)

- For the past tense, use **was** or **were**.
    - EXAMPLES Dr. King **was** a great leader. (one)
      His speeches **were** inspiring. (more than one)

- For the future tense, use **will be**.
    - EXAMPLES The assembly about him **will be** next week. (one)
      We **will be** in the third row. (more than one)

Practice Together

Say each sentence with your class. Choose the correct form of **be** in ( ). Then say the sentence again, using the correct form of **be**.

1. A film about Dr. King (was/will be) on TV tomorrow.
2. I (am/are) curious about the film.
3. In 1963, many people in the march (are/were) angry.
4. Dr. King's speech about equality (was/were) inspiring to them.

Try It!

Read each sentence. Write the correct form of **be** in ( ) on a card. Then say the sentence with the correct form of **be**.

1. Dr. King (was/were) a good speaker.
2. One speech (am/will be) part of next week's lesson.
3. His words in 1963 (are/were) about freedom and equality.
4. Dr. King's ideas (is/are) still important today.

▲ Dr. Martin Luther King, Jr., was a famous leader who fought for equal rights.

Tell What Happened

DESCRIBE AN EVENT

We know about things that have happened in the past because people tell and write about the events. Choose an event from history or a past event in the news and describe it in your own words.

Plan what you will say.

Steps	Example
1. Name the event.	Rosa Parks was arrested on a bus in Montgomery, Alabama.
2. Give details about what happened. Tell information that will answer questions that begin with *who, what, where, when, why,* and *how.* Use descriptive words.	She was on her way home after working all day as a seamstress. She was on the bus in the 11th row—the first row of seats set aside for African American passengers.
3. Use sensory words to describe the event. If possible, compare the event to something else.	Rosa's feet ached after standing all day. She was tired, like a runner who had just finished a race.

Now describe the event to a partner. Answer questions that your partner may ask. Trade roles.

HOW TO DESCRIBE AN EVENT

1. Name the event.

2. Give details. Use descriptive words.

3. Use sensory words. Compare people and things to something else.

What happened?

Rosa Parks had no energy after working hard all day. She was like a tired-out runner. She refused to give her bus seat to a white man.

USE FORMS OF *BE* AND PAST TENSE VERBS

To get started with your description, tell what it will be about. Use the future tense of **be**.

EXAMPLE   My description **will be** about the arrest of Rosa Parks.

Then use past tense forms of **be** and other verbs to talk about what happened in the past. Remember:

• The irregular verb **be** has special forms to show the past.

EXAMPLE   Rosa **was** on her way home from work.

• Most other verbs end with **-ed** to tell about the past.

EXAMPLE   She **waited** at the bus stop.

Prepare to Read

Learn Key Vocabulary

Study the Words Use the steps below.

1. Pronounce the word. Say it aloud several times. Spell it.
2. Rate your word knowledge.
3. Study the example. Tell more about the word.
4. Practice it. Make the word your own.

Key Words

admire (ad-mīr) *verb*
▶ page 205

When you **admire** someone, you think highly of them. Many people **admire** Rosa Parks, who worked for civil rights.
Related Word: **admiration**

arrest (u-rest) *noun*
▶ page 204

An **arrest** is when a person is taken by a police officer. Police made many **arrests** of people during the Civil Rights Movement.

convince (kun-vins) *verb*
▶ page 204

When somebody **convinces** you of something, you think it's a good idea. He **convinced** her to agree with him.
Synonym: **persuade**

influence (in-flü-uns) *verb*
▶ page 202

When people **influence** you, they change the way you think. Dr. Martin Luther King, Jr., **influenced** people to work toward equality.
Synonyms: **affect, change**

movement (müv-munt) *noun*
▶ page 204

A **movement** is a group of people working together to make a change. People of all races took part in the Civil Rights **Movement**.

peace (pēs) *noun*
▶ page 202

Peace is freedom from war and fighting. Many people hope for **peace** in the world.
Antonym: **war**

preach (prēch) *verb*
▶ page 202

To **preach** is to tell people what you believe is right. The speaker **preached** the importance of kindness to all.
Related Word: **preacher**

problem (prah-blum) *noun*
▶ page 204

A **problem** is something you have to solve or fix. You can solve a math **problem**.
Synonym: **difficulty**

Practice the Words Work with a partner to write four sentences. Use at least two Key Words in each sentence.

> **EXAMPLE:** My father always preaches to us that peace is better than war.

Text Structure: Chronological Order

How Is Writing Organized? Sometimes, a writer can describe events in time order without including time words. Then, the reader must figure out the order from other clues. For example, "Martin's Big Words" starts without any time words. Later, the writer includes time words. As you read, look for clues to the order of events.

Reading Strategies
- Plan
- Monitor
- **Ask Questions** Think actively by asking and answering questions about the text.
- Make Connections
- Visualise
- Make Inferences
- Determine Importance
- Synthesize

> **Look Into the Text**
>
> Martin grew up. He became a minister like his father. And he used big words he had heard as a child from his parents and from the Bible.
>
> In December 1955 on a cold December day in Montgomery, Alabama, Rosa Parks was coming home from work. A white man told her to get up from her seat on the bus so he could sit. She said No, and was arrested.

ese e order rds show n the t events pened.

"I know that Martin would use big words after he grew up."

Practice Together

Begin a Sequence Chain A Sequence Chain can help you analyze text that is in chronological order. This Sequence Chain shows the first event from the passage above. Each oval shows a different event. Reread the passage, and add to the Sequence Chain.

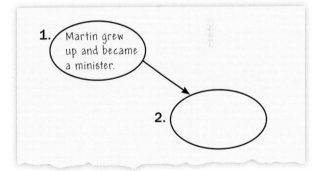

1. Martin grew up and became a minister.

2.

Academic Vocabulary

- **organize** (or-gu-niz) *verb*
  To **organize** means to arrange things in a certain order.

Biography

In a biography, an author tells the story of a real person's life. The events in a biography usually happen in **chronological**, or time, order. Look for **time words** and other clues that show when things happen.

Look Into the Text

In the next ten years, black Americans all over the South protested for equal rights. Martin walked with them and talked with them and sang with them and prayed with them.

As you read, ask yourself questions about why the author included certain quotes or events. Also ask questions about why the author organized the events in the order they appear.

MARTIN'S BIG WORDS

The Life of Dr. Martin Luther King, Jr.

by Doreen Rappaport
illustrated by Bryan Collier

Comprehension Coach

Everywhere in Martin's hometown, he saw the signs, WHITE ONLY. His mother said these signs were in all Southern cities and towns in the United States. Every time Martin read the words, he felt bad, until he remembered what his mother told him: "You are as good as anyone."

In church Martin sang **hymns**. He read from the Bible. He listened to his father **preach**. These words made him feel good.

"When I grow up, I'm going to get big words, too."

Martin grew up. He became a minister like his father. And he used the big words he had heard as a child from his parents and from the Bible.

"Everyone can be great."

He studied the teachings of Mahatma Gandhi. He learned how the Indian nation won freedom using peaceful means. Martin said "love," when others said "hate."

"Hate cannot **drive out** hate. Only love can do that."

He said "together" when others said "separate." He said "**peace**" when others said "war."

"Sooner or later, all the people of the world will have to discover a way to live together."

Key Vocabulary

influence *v.*, to affect what someone thinks or does
preach *v.*, to urge people to believe something
peace *n.*, agreement among people

In Other Words

hymns religious songs
drive out stop

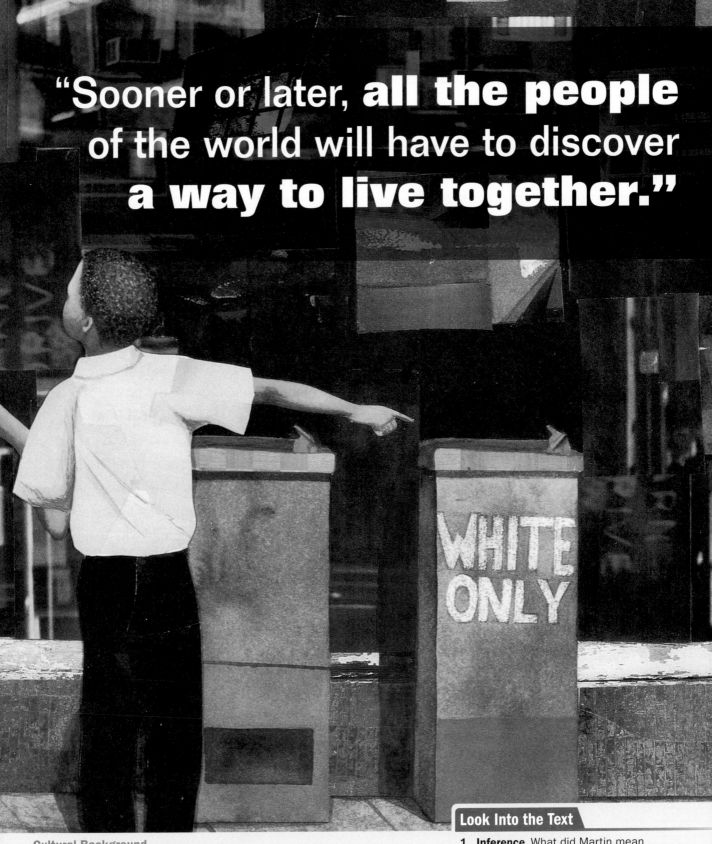

"Sooner or later, **all the people** of the world will have to discover **a way to live together.**"

Look Into the Text

1. **Inference** What did Martin mean when he said he was "going to get big words"?

2. **Summarize** How did words **influence** Martin's beliefs?

3. **Cause and Effect** How did the teachings of Gandhi affect Martin?

In 1955 on a cold December day in Montgomery, Alabama, Rosa Parks was coming home from work. A white man told her to get up from her seat on the bus so he could sit. She said No, and was **arrested**.

Montgomery's black citizens learned of her arrest. It made them angry. They decided not to ride the buses until they could sit anywhere they wanted.

For 381 days they walked to work and school and church. They walked in rain and cold and in **blistering** heat. Martin walked with them and talked with them and sang with them and prayed with them until the white city leaders had to agree they could sit anywhere they wanted.

"When the history books are written, someone will say there lived black people who had the courage to **stand up** for their rights."

In the next ten years, black Americans all over the South protested for equal rights. Martin walked with them and talked with them and sang with them and prayed with them.

White ministers told them to stop. Mayors and governors and police chiefs and judges ordered them to stop. But they kept on marching.

"Wait! For years I have heard the word 'Wait!' We have waited more than three hundred and forty years for our rights."

They were jailed and beaten and murdered. But they kept on marching. Some black Americans wanted to fight back with their fists. Martin **convinced** them not to, by reminding them of the power of love.

"Love is the **key** to the **problems** of the world."

Many white Southerners hated and feared Martin's words. A few threatened to kill him and his family. His house was bombed. His brother's house was bombed. But he refused to stop.

"Remember, if I am stopped, this **movement** will not be stopped, because God is with this movement."

The marches continued. More and more Americans listened to Martin's words. He shared his dreams and **filled them with** hope.

Key Vocabulary

arrest *v.*, to be put under police control
convince *v.*, to make someone believe or agree
problem *n.*, a difficult situation
movement *n.*, an organized effort to reach a goal

In Other Words

blistering very great; extreme
stand up fight
key solution
filled them with gave people

"I have a dream that one day in Alabama little black boys and black girls will join hands with little white boys and white girls as sisters and brothers."

After ten years of protests, the lawmakers in Washington voted to end segregation. The WHITE ONLY signs in the South came down.

Dr. Martin Luther King, Jr., cared about all Americans. He cared about people all over the world. And people all over the world **admired** him.

In 1964, he won the Nobel Peace Prize. He won it because he taught others to fight with words, not fists.

Martin went wherever people needed help. In April 1968 he went to Memphis, Tennessee. He went to help garbage collectors who were on strike. He walked with them and talked with them and sang with them and prayed with them.

On his second day there, he was shot. He died.

His big words are alive for us today. ❖

Cultural Background
The **Nobel Peace Prize** is an international award given by the Nobel Foundation in Sweden. It honors those who work for world peace.

Look Into the Text

1. **Main Idea and Details** What groups of people did Martin speak to? How did his words affect each group?
2. **Paraphrase** In your own words, explain one of Martin's teachings.

▲ Martin Luther King, Jr., with his wife, Coretta, and two of their four children, Marty and Yoki.

The power of Dr. King's words live on in his speeches, letters, and other writing. Here is an excerpt from a famous speech he gave on the steps of the Lincoln Memorial in 1963. Today many consider it to be one of the greatest speeches in human history.

from "I Have a Dream"

. . . I say to you today, my friends, so even though we face the difficulties of today and tomorrow, I still have a dream. It is a dream **deeply rooted in** the American dream.

I have a dream that one day this nation will rise up and **live out the true meaning of its creed**: "We hold these truths to be self-evident; that all men are created equal."

I have a dream that one day, on the red hills of Georgia, sons of former slaves and the sons of former slaveowners will be able to sit down together at the table of brotherhood. . . .

I have a dream that my four little children will one day live in a nation where they will not be judged by the color of their skin but by the content of their character.

In Other Words
deeply rooted in based on the beliefs of
live out the true meaning of its creed follow what is written as our country's beliefs

I have a dream today. . . .

This is our hope. This is the **faith** that I go back to the South with. With this faith we will be able to **hew** out of the mountain of despair a stone of hope. With this faith we will be able to transform the **jangling discords** of our nation into a beautiful **symphony** of brotherhood. With this faith we will be able to work together, to pray together, to struggle together, to stand up for freedom together, knowing that we will be free one day.

And this will be the day. This will be the day when all of God's children will be able to sing with new meaning "My country 'tis of thee, sweet land of liberty, of thee I sing. Land where my fathers died, land of the pilgrim's pride, from every mountainside, let freedom ring."

And if America is to be a great nation this must become true. So let freedom ring from the **prodigious** hilltops of New Hampshire. Let freedom ring from the mighty mountains of New York. Let freedom ring from the heightening **Alleghenies** of Pennsylvania!

Let freedom ring from the snowcapped Rockies of Colorado!

Let freedom ring from the curvaceous slopes of California!

But not only that; let freedom ring from Stone Mountain of Georgia! Let freedom ring from Lookout Mountain of Tennessee.

Let freedom ring from every hill and molehill of Mississippi. From every mountainside, let freedom ring.

And when this happens, and when we allow freedom to ring, when we let it ring from every village and every hamlet, from every state and every city, we will be able to speed up that day when all of God's children, black men and white men, Jews and Gentiles, Protestants and Catholics, will be able to join hands and sing in the words of that old Negro spiritual, "Free at last! Free at last! Thank God Almighty, we are free at last!"

August 28, 1963
Washington, DC

Look Into the Text

1. **Summarize** What was Martin Luther King, Jr's., dream?
2. **Paraphrase** In your own words explain "And if America is to be a great nation this must become true."

About the Author

Doreen Rappaport

In the 1960s, **Doreen Rappaport** was a teacher in Mississippi. Rappaport's students changed her life. She describes them as "extraordinary ordinary people" whose courage inspired her. Her students' heroic struggle for their civil rights encouraged her to write about more "unknown heroes" who helped change history. Rappaport is an award-winning author of several other books, including *Escape from Slavery* and *Freedom River.* Today, she lives in New York and travels across the country to visit schools and talk with young people.

About the Speaker

Martin Luther King, Jr.

Time magazine named **Martin Luther King, Jr.,** (1929–1968) one of the 100 most important people of the twentieth century. "It is a testament to the greatness of Martin Luther King, Jr., that nearly every major city in the U.S. has a street or school named after him," wrote reporter Jack White. Throughout his life, King gave speeches, organized boycotts, and led marches. His birthday is a national holiday celebrated throughout the United States.

Connect Reading and Writing

Vocabulary
admire
arrest
convinced
influenced
movement
peace
preach
problems

CRITICAL THINKING

1. **SUM IT UP** Use your Sequence Chain to describe the events in "Martin's Big Words" and summarize the biography to a partner.

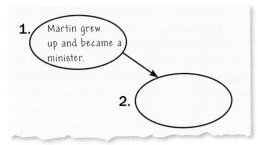

1. Martin grew up and became a minister.
2.

Sequence Chain

2. **Evaluate** Which words from "I Have a Dream" show that Martin got his own "big words"? Tell why you think these powerful words **influenced** his listeners so strongly.

3. **Speculate** Forty years after his death, people still **admire** and learn about Dr. King. Do you predict that in another 40 years children will still learn about him? Explain.

4. **Generalize** Martin said that African American people had the courage to stand up for their rights. Give several examples of this from the selection.

READING FLUENCY

Expression Read the passage on page 631 to a partner. Assess your fluency.

1. My voice never/sometimes/always matched what I read.

2. What I did best in my reading was _____ .

READING STRATEGY

What strategy helped you understand this selection? Tell a partner about it.

VOCABULARY REVIEW

Oral Review Read the paragraph aloud. Add the vocabulary words.

Young Martin Luther King, Jr., _____ people all over the world with his words. He faced risks for his work, including his _____ . But thanks to work like his, African Americans do not live separate lives. King did more than _____ . He started a _____ . He _____ people to solve their _____ with _____ , not violence. Today, people still _____ him.

Written Review Imagine you lived in the 1960s during the Civil Rights **Movement** . Write a letter about your experiences. Use five vocabulary words.

WRITE ABOUT THE **GUIDING QUESTION**

Explore How Words Can Make a Difference

How did Martin Luther King, Jr., use words to **influence** others? Write a paragraph explaining the effect his words had.

Connect Across the Curriculum

Vocabulary Study

Use Word Parts: Suffixes

Suffix	Meaning
-tion	condition or action
-or	one who does an action
-ness	state of
-ly	like; in the manner of
-ic	like; nature of

> **Academic Vocabulary**
> • **individual** (in-de-**vij**-yū-wul) *adjective*
>   Something that is **individual** is separate from other things.

A word has **individual** parts. For example, a **suffix** is a word part added at the end of a base word. When you add a suffix to a base word, you create a new word. For example:

- *Develop* is a verb that means "to grow."
- The suffix *-ment* means "instance or action."
- When you add *-ment* to *develop*, the new word *development* becomes a noun.
- What do you think *development* means?

> The base word is *develop*, which means "to grow." So *development* must mean "the action of growing."

Figure Out Word Meanings Work with a partner to identify the **individual** word parts. Cover the suffix and look at the base word. Then uncover the suffix. How does the suffix affect the base word? Write the meaning of the whole word.

1. movement
2. segregation
3. collectors
4. greatness
5. deeply
6. heroic

Literary Analysis

Analyze Word Choice

Writers or speakers may refer to a familiar person, place, song, story, or other work of art to express their ideas. These references are called *allusions*.

Read this passage from "I Have a Dream." Dr. King quotes lines from a song called "My Country 'Tis of Thee." This allusion creates a vivid image and appeals to people's patriotism.

> And this will be the day. This will be the day when all of God's children will be able to sing with new meaning "My country 'tis of thee, sweet land of liberty, of thee I sing. Land where my fathers died, land of the pilgrim's pride, from every mountainside, let freedom ring."

Identify and Analyze Look back at "I Have a Dream" and find another allusion. Tell what the allusion refers to and what emotion, tone, or image it creates in your mind.

Describe an Event

Quiz Your Partner With a partner, take turns asking and answering questions about events pictured in the selection. Tell your partner what your questions will be about. Then use other forms of *be* and the past tense to ask about and describe what happened at the event.

> Why did the people march instead of fight?

> Dr. King convinced them that peaceful protests were better than violent ones.

Write About the Past

Study the Models When you write about an event that already happened, be consistent and clear about when the events took place. Otherwise, you may confuse your readers.

NOT OK

> Dr. Martin Luther King, Jr., was a great man. He **believed** in peace instead of war. He **has** the courage to stand up for equal rights. He **walked** and **talks** with Americans all over the country. People **listen** to Martin's words.

The reader thinks: "Is the writer describing Dr. King today or in the past? This is confusing."

OK

> Dr. Martin Luther King, Jr., was a great man. He **believed** in peace instead of war. He **had** the courage to stand up for equal rights. He **walked** and **talked** with Americans all over the country. People **listened** to Martin's words.

The reader thinks: "Now I can understand when the events happened."

Add Sentences Think of two more sentences to add to the OK paragraph. Be sure to describe past events consistently.

WRITE ON YOUR OWN Describe an event that you heard or saw on the news recently. Use sentences that make it clear that the event happened in the past. Don't switch back and forth from the past to the present.

REMEMBER

Most **verbs** add **-ed** to make their past tense forms. The irregular verbs *be* and *have* use special forms to show the past tense.

Past Tense of *be*	I **was**	you **were**	he, she, or it **was**	we **were**	they **were**
Past Tense of *have*	I **had**	you **had**	he, she, or it **had**	we **had**	they **had**

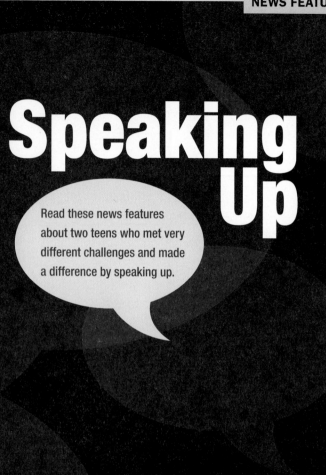

Speaking Up

Read these news features about two teens who met very different challenges and made a difference by speaking up.

Build Background

Connect

Discussion Read the following statements:

1. If an individual wants to achieve his or her dream, he or she must first find others who share that dream.

2. One person, working alone, can achieve more than a group of people.

Which statement do you agree with? In a discussion with your classmates, present arguments to support your opinion.

See Leadership in Action

What does it mean to be a leader? Many teens have made a difference in their communities by speaking up and becoming involved.

Digital Library myNGconnect.com
🌐 View the images.

▲ Teens discover their leadership skills.

Language & Grammar

1 TRY OUT LANGUAGE
2 LEARN GRAMMAR
3 APPLY ON YOUR OWN

Summarize

CD

Look at the photograph and listen to a candidate's campaign speech. He explains why he should be elected class president. Then listen to a summary of the speech.

SUMMARY

Summary of Hector's Speech:

Hector Espinosa wants to be our class president. In his campaign speech, he said that he was honest, fair, loyal, and a good leader.

He also said that he listens when others speak. He knew that we wanted an environmentally friendly, or green, cafeteria. As class president, he will try to make that happen.

Hector also said that he will talk to the teachers about limiting weekend homework and coordinating due dates for projects.

At the end of his speech, he promised to work hard and to make a difference.

Use Verbs in the Past Tense

A **past tense** **verb** shows an action that already happened. For most verbs, add **-ed** to show past tense.

> EXAMPLE   The mayor **talked** about our community. (regular verb)

Use special past tense forms with **irregular verbs.**

> EXAMPLE   He **gave** his speech yesterday. (irregular verb)

Each past tense form of an irregular verb must be memorized.

Examples of Irregular Verbs

Present	Past	Example in the Past
give	gave	I **gave** a letter to the mayor.
get	got	I **got** to see the mayor.
speak	spoke	The mayor **spoke** to us about improving our town.
see	saw	We **saw** photos of places in our community.
feel	felt	Everyone **felt** eager to help.
know	knew	The mayor **knew** my name!
tell	told	I **told** the mayor about some of my ideas.
think	thought	He **thought** my ideas were great.

Practice Together

Say each sentence with your class. Then say the sentence again, using the past tense form of the underlined verb.

1. The students <u>see</u> litter all over the park.
2. They <u>know</u> the problem.
3. They <u>think</u> about what they could do to clean up the area.
4. They <u>get</u> large trash bags.

Try It!

Say each sentence. Write the verb on a card. Then write the past tense form of the verb on the same card. Say the sentence again using the past tense form of the verb.

5. The teacher <u>gives</u> everyone gloves to wear.
6. She <u>tells</u> the students what to do.
7. She <u>speaks</u> to each group about their jobs.
8. Everyone <u>feels</u> good about helping the community.

▲ These students helped their community.

Share How You Have Made a Difference

SUMMARIZE

How have you made a difference in someone's life or in your community? Share what you did with a partner, and summarize your partner's experience.

Follow these steps to create your summary.

1. Take notes as you listen to your partner speak. Decide what information is important to include in your summary and what information can be left out.
2. Just tell the main ideas or most important information. A good summary is shorter than the original telling or text.
3. Use your own words to summarize your partner's experience.

Listen to your partner tell about what he or she did to make a difference. Summarize what your partner said. Trade roles.

HOW TO SUMMARIZE

1. Identify the main ideas or important information.
2. Leave out unimportant or repeated information.
3. Use your own words.

Original telling: Maria gave her neighbor some of the peas, carrots, corn, and broccoli that she grew in her garden.

Summary: Maria gave her neighbor some home-grown vegetables.

USE VERBS IN THE PAST TENSE

The event you summarize happened in the past. You will need to use **past tense verbs** when you talk about it. Remember that most **verbs** add **-ed** to make their past tense forms. **Irregular verbs** use special forms to show the past.

Irregular: Ike **knew** that his elderly neighbor **had** a doctor's appointment.

Regular: Ike **shoveled** the snow off his neighbor's sidewalk. Ike's neighbor **thanked** Ike for his thoughtfulness.

Prepare to Read

Learn Key Vocabulary

Study the Words Use the steps below.

1. Pronounce the word. Say it aloud several times. Spell it.
2. Rate your word knowledge.
3. Study the example. Tell more about the word.
4. Practice it. Make the word your own.

Key Words

challenge (chal-unj) *noun*
▶ page 220

A **challenge** is something that is difficult to do. It is a **challenge** to climb a mountain.

contribute (kun-**trib**-yūt)
verb ▶ page 224

When you **contribute** to something, you give your time or money. The child **contributed** money to help people in need.
Synonyms: **give, provide, donate**

involved (in-**vahlvd**)
adjective ▶ page 220

To get **involved** is to become a part of something. Many people like to be **involved** in improving their communities.
Related Word: **involvement**

leadership (**lēd**-ur-ship)
noun ▶ page 222

Leadership means guiding others in what to do. A person who helps others shows **leadership**.
Related Words: **lead, leader**

negative (**neg**-u-tiv) *adjective*
▶ page 220

If you have a **negative** opinion about something, you don't like it. My sister was **negative** about my idea.
Antonyms: **positive, good**

overcome (ō-vur-**kum**) *verb*
▶ page 225

To **overcome** something is to succeed at something that was difficult. If you used to be afraid of dogs but now you like them, you have **overcome** your fear.

positive (**pahz**-u-tiv) *adjective*
▶ page 221

Positive means good or hopeful. If you have a **positive** attitude, you think things are good.
Antonyms: **negative, bad**

promote (pru-**mōt**) *verb*
▶ page 221

To **promote** something is to tell others that it is a good thing. The firefighters **promote** safety to the students.

Practice the Words Work with a partner to complete an Expanded Meaning Map for each Key Word.

Expanded Meaning Map

Text Structure: Problem and Solution

How Are News Features Organized? Some news features are `organized` around a problem and a solution. A problem is something that needs to be fixed. It might be a personal problem, such as an disagreement with a friend or a community problem, such as pollution or crime.

As you read the passage, identify the problem and the solution.

Look Into the Text

Student Gets Involved to Improve School's Reputation

Arlington had a bad reputation. Students performed low on standardized tests. Many people in the community had a negative image of the school. At first, Eve didn't want to go there. "I hated Arlington until I got involved," she says.

Then, Eve joined the freshman volleyball squad. She got to know some students and teachers. Soon, she saw that Arlington didn't deserve its bad reputation.

Practice Together

Begin a Problem-and-Solution Chain A Problem-and-Solution Chain can help you analyze texts. The first box shows the problem. Reread the passage and fill in the solution.

Problem		Solution
Arlington had a bad reputation.	→	

Reading Strategies
- Plan
- Monitor
- **Ask Questions** Think actively by asking and answering questions about the text.
- Make Connections
- Visualise
- Make Inferences
- Determine Importance
- Synthesize

Academic Vocabulary
- **organize** (or-gu-nīz) *verb*
  To **organize** means to arrange things in a certain order.

News Features

News features give facts about real people and events.

Many news features explain a **problem** and how someone or a group of people worked together to come up with **solutions**. Often headlines and other headings will tell about the problem or the solution.

Look Into the Text

. . . Soon she saw that Arlington didn't deserve its bad reputation.

Sharing Her Pride

Eve set out to change the way people thought of her school.

She and other student leaders gave presentations at nearby middle schools, promoting Arlington. Eve also wrote editorials about Arlington High . . . .

As you read a news article, ask questions to determine the problem and solution. Sometimes, problems and solutions will be stated directly, but other times you will need to make inferences.

Speaking Up

Read these news features about two teens who met very different challenges and made a difference by speaking up.

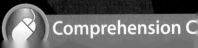

Student Gets Involved to Improve School's Reputation

by Jonathan Blum

What makes a good leader? For Eve Vang, her training started at home. She grew up as the oldest daughter in a large household. "You have to **play second mom** in a big family," says Eve, an 18-year-old student leader at Arlington High School in St. Paul, Minnesota.

Eve's parents expected her to do well in school, plus cook, clean, and help tutor her four younger siblings. It wasn't easy. Sometimes, the family lived on donated canned food and dry milk. "We've come a long, long way," Eve says.

Eve's parents came to Minnesota in the late 1970s from Laos in Southeast Asia. After years of hard work, they own a home and run a small business. Eve's family is Hmong, a **close-knit Asian ethnic minority group**.

Like many Hmong, Eve's parents had to **flee** their homes during the Vietnam War. They survived by living in a refugee camp in Thailand. They often went hungry. Eventually, they came to the United States.

"I hated Arlington until I got involved," recalls Eve Vang.

In junior high, Eve often felt like an outsider. There weren't many other minority students in her classes. Then, in 1999, she started at Arlington High. The school had many other Hmong students, which made her more comfortable. Yet there were new **challenges**.

Arlington had a bad reputation. Students performed low on standardized tests. Many people in the community had a **negative** image of the school. At first, Eve didn't want to go there. "I hated Arlington until I got **involved**," she says.

Then, Eve joined the freshman volleyball squad. She got to know some students and teachers. Soon, she saw that Arlington didn't deserve its bad reputation.

Key Vocabulary

challenge *n.*, a difficult or exciting problem to solve
negative *adj.*, bad, unpleasant
involved *adj.*, a part of something

In Other Words

play second mom be very responsible
close-knit Asian ethnic minority group group of people who share the same cultural background
flee quickly escape

Cultural Background

The Hmong are an ethnic group in China, Vietnam, Laos, and Thailand. Outside of Asia, the United States is home to the largest Hmong population in the world.

Sharing Her Pride

Eve **set out** to change the way people thought of her school.

She and other student leaders gave presentations at nearby middle schools, **promoting** Arlington. Eve also wrote **editorials** about Arlington High, which were published in *The St. Paul Pioneer Press* and the *Hmong Times*. "I wanted to share my pride, and I wanted to share what I love about Arlington High School," Eve says.

Eve also worked to improve the school. She **recruited** a group of student leaders. Together, they formed an organization called VOICE (Voicing Our Intelligence to Challenge Education). They started an annual carnival to promote the **rich mix of** cultures at the school. Eve thinks that cultural diversity is one of the best things about Arlington. Thirty-three different languages are spoken there!

Eve's efforts **sparked** change. In the past two years, **positive** articles on Arlington High School have appeared in the local media. Teachers and staff have started programs that have improved students' academic scores. More freshmen say they are excited to go to Arlington.

Eve Vang speaks to a group of students about school pride.

In Other Words

set out made it her goal
editorials articles in which she gave her opinion
recruited got together
rich mix of large number of different
sparked caused

Look Into the Text

1. **Problem and Solution** Why did Eve get **involved**? What did she discover?

2. **Details** How did Eve **promote** Arlington?

3. **Cause and Effect** What are the results of Eve's efforts? Cite two examples that prove that Arlington's image has changed.

Eve organized a carnival, like this one, at her high school.

The annual carnival Eve helps organize has become a big success. More than 200 people participated last year, along with several area businesses. Other improvements in the school have been rewarded as well. Principal Bill Dunn has been named a Minnesota High School Principal of the Year.

Principal Dunn thinks that Eve's **leadership** skills will **take her far**. "If this young woman **set her mind to** being the mayor, that would happen," he says. "I hope that does happen. She's been a great student leader."

Eve, who stands 4 feet and 11 inches tall, says that it's not always easy being a leader. "People look at me and they **always underestimate me**. They say, 'Oh, this little girl can't do anything,'" Eve explains. "**I feed on that.** When people push you down, you've got to prove them wrong."

Sometimes Eve wants to run away from responsibility. But eventually, she remembers how much she likes making things better for others, especially at her school. ❖

Key Vocabulary
leadership *n.*, the ability to direct or guide other people

In Other Words
take her far help her in the future
set her mind to focused on
always underestimate me don't understand how much I can do
I feed on that. That motivates me.

Eve Vang Today

Today, Eve serves as an advisor to VOICE, the student-led activist group she founded at her high school in 1999. She works with the group to help the community and develop students' leadership skills. She also organized Operation Christmas Child, in which her school sent gifts to developing countries.

A past winner of the 2003 Yoshiyama Award for her service to the community, Eve continues to help others. After graduating from college in 2007, she was awarded a **prestigious** Fulbright U.S. Student Scholarship to teach English as a foreign language in Thailand.

Eve is the first student from her college to participate in the Fulbright program in Thailand. The program is the largest U.S. international exchange program.

Eve will teach English to middle school students outside Bangkok, Thailand. Eve's decision to go to Thailand relates to her own cultural heritage. She says, "Personally, I am taking the journey to Thailand because I want to **immerse** myself back into my Hmong culture—its traditions, language and the people. Culture is a large part of my identity and without it, I could not be me."

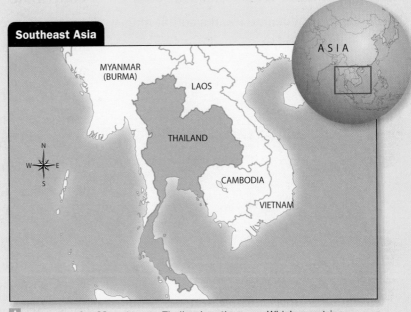

Southeast Asia

MYANMAR (BURMA)
LAOS
THAILAND
CAMBODIA
VIETNAM
ASIA

▲ Interpret the Map Locate Thailand on the map. Which countries border Thailand?

In Other Words
prestigious respected, famous
immerse put

Look Into the Text

1. **Cause and Effect** What **positive** differences has Eve made?
2. **Paraphrase** Explain in your own words what Eve means when she says, "I could not be me" without my culture.
3. **Generalization** What important message can you learn from Eve's story?

Student Works to End Bullying

by Genet Berhane

Matt Cavedon has been busy with a big job over the last few years—making the world a better place. Most recently, that has meant **doing his part** to stop bullying. Matt **witnessed** what it was like for some students to be bullied at his school in Berlin, Connecticut. He decided to take action and do something positive for people because he wanted everyone to be respected.

When national plans for an anti-bullying campaign recently began to **take shape**, Matt saw a cause to which he could **contribute**. While some schools have excellent prevention plans in place, they are often not enough. Even peer mediation systems, where kids meet to work through their problems with other students, do not completely stop the bullying.

One of the biggest problems is that a lot of bullying goes unreported. It's not just about the bullies and the victims, says Matt. Bystanders, the people who see bullying happen, have an important **role to play** in the situation.

"Anyone who sees something should do something," he says. "Don't just be bystanders; get involved."

Matt's contribution to the anti-bullying campaign is something he wanted to do simply because he understands how wrong

Teenager Matt Cavedon believes everyone needs to speak up about bullying.

Key Vocabulary
contribute *v.*, to help

In Other Words
doing his part offering his time and effort
witnessed saw
take shape form; get organized
role to play responsibility

bullying is. He understands that a problem, any problem, deserves attention.

"He wants to be involved," says his mom, Susan Cavedon. "He wants to help the next person."

It's important to remember that you have the power to make a difference, Matt says. Bystanders can get involved by speaking up for victims. He also has some advice for the kids who **have to put up with** bullying.

"No one can make you feel **inferior without your consent**," he says to the victims of bullying. "Keep your **self-esteem** high."

What does he have to say to the bullies?

"Why?" he says. "Why do you do it? Look at others who **overcame** their problems instead of **taking them out on** other people. Have the honor and respect not to take it out on others. You'll be stronger by not bullying."

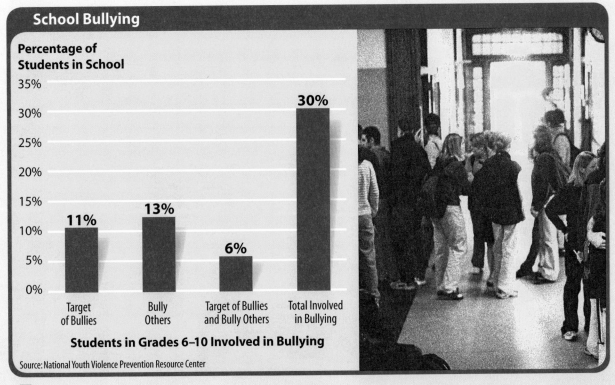

School Bullying

Percentage of Students in School

Target of Bullies	11%
Bully Others	13%
Target of Bullies and Bully Others	6%
Total Involved in Bullying	30%

Students in Grades 6–10 Involved in Bullying

Source: National Youth Violence Prevention Resource Center

▲ **Interpret the Bar Graph** What does the graph reveal about problems of bullying in schools?

Key Vocabulary

overcome *v.*, to succeed at a difficult task

In Other Words

have to put up with experience
inferior without your consent bad unless you let them
self-esteem pride in yourself
taking them out on getting angry at

Making Change Happen

This isn't the first time Matt has done something to make life better for other kids. Even when he was younger, Matt was doing his part to make his community in Berlin, Connecticut, a better place.

"Anyone can make a difference," he says. "Age doesn't matter."

Age certainly never stopped Matt. While in elementary school, he worked with Boundless Playgrounds, an organization that creates play areas **accessible to** kids of all abilities. Matt uses a wheelchair because of a condition that keeps him from **extending his limbs**. He understands the importance of providing play spaces designed to fit everyone.

Matt developed equipment for Boundless Playgrounds and served as a co-chairman of the Jr. Advisory Board for the organization. He is proud of the positive responses his playgrounds have received.

"Everyone seems to love them," he says. ❖

Matt watches children play on equipment that he helped design for Boundless Playgrounds.

In Other Words
accessible to that can be used by
extending his limbs fully moving his arms and legs

Look Into the Text
1. **Vocabulary** How does Matt **contribute** to his community?
2. **Summarize** What is Matt's message to bullies?

Connect Reading and Writing

Vocabulary
challenges
contributes
involved
leadership
negative
overcome
positive
promote

CRITICAL THINKING

1. SUM IT UP Use your Problem-and-Solution Chain to describe the events in "Speaking Up." Then summarize the news feature with a partner.

Problem	Solution
Matt Cavedon saw students in his school being bullied. →	

Problem-and-Solution Chain

2. Interpret Matt asks bullies, "Why do you do it? Look at others who **overcame** their problems instead of taking them out on other people." What does this mean to you? How does the bar graph on page 225 **contribute** support to Matt's ideas?

3. Evaluate Do you agree with Matt that no one can make you feel **negative** about yourself without your consent? Why or why not?

4. Compare Across Texts What **positive** characteristics do Eve Vang and Matt Cavedon have in common with Dr. Martin Luther King, Jr.?

READING FLUENCY

Intonation Read the passage on page 632 to a partner. Assess your fluency.

1. My tone never/sometimes/always matched what I read.

2. What I did best in my reading was _____.

READING STRATEGY

What strategy helped you understand this selection? Tell a partner about it.

VOCABULARY REVIEW

Oral Review Read the paragraph aloud. Add the vocabulary words.

Sometimes in life there are _____. The best way to _____ problems in life is to have a _____ attitude. If a person gives, or _____, very little, then he or she will make situations _____. Even one person can make a difference, and when people work together, they can make life better. Either way, it is important to help, or _____, good _____ by becoming _____ in solving problems.

Written Review Write an e-mail to a friend. Describe a **challenge** you or someone you know faced. Use at least four vocabulary words in the e-mail.

 **WRITE ABOUT THE** GUIDING QUESTION

Explore How Words Can Make a Difference

Think about this question: Why did Eve Vang and Matt Cavedon get **involved** in their communities? What difference did their words and actions make? Show how they **contributed** their ideas to help others.

Connect Across the Curriculum

Vocabulary Study

Use Word Parts

Word Part	Meaning
un-	not; the opposite of
-able	can be or is
re-	again
-ly	in this way; way of being
under-	below; not enough
-tion	the act of

Academic Vocabulary
- **predict** (pri-**dikt**) *verb*
  When you **predict**, you guess about something or tell what will happen.

Many English words are made up of a base word with prefixes and suffixes added. When you know the meaning of the parts, you can figure out the meaning of a whole word.

Figure Out Word Meanings Work with a partner. Break each of these words into word parts. Write the meaning of each word part. Then put the meanings together to **predict** the meaning of the word.

1. uncomfortable
2. uninvolved
3. organization
4. unorganized
5. underestimate
6. untruthfully

Write Sentences Use each word in a sentence. Trade sentences with a partner. Does the meaning you **predicted** make sense?

Listening/Speaking

Deliver a Problem-Solution Presentation

Academic Vocabulary
- **convince** (kun-**vins**) *verb*
  To **convince** means to persuade.

What if you had to **convince** your classmates how to solve a problem at your school? Deliver a presentation to your class about a problem at school and share how you would solve the problem.

1 **Identify a Problem and Determine Solutions** Think about a problem at your school or in your community. Propose a solution. Add evidence to **convince** your listeners that you have a good solution.

2 **Organize Your Presentation** Use a Problem-and-Solution Chain like the one you completed for "Speaking Up" to organize your ideas. Make sure to support your ideas with relevant, sufficient evidence and sound reasoning.

3 **Practice Your Presentation** Work with a partner and practice your presentation.

4 **Give Your Presentation** Share your presentation with the class. Make eye contact and speak clearly and loudly.

Summarize

Pair Share With a partner, summarize either Eve's story or Matt's story. Remember to tell just the main ideas in your summary. Do not include unimportant details. Use past tense verbs in your summary.

> Eve changed the way people thought about her school.

> What were the main things she did to change people's opinions of her school?

Write Consistently About the Past

Study the Models When you write a summary of something that happened in the past, do not switch to the present and then back to the past, or your reader will become confused about when events took place.

NOT OK

Matt **does** many things that made a difference in children's lives. When he was 14, Matt **tells** kids that bullying was wrong. He **spends** a lot of time talking to them. He also worked with an organization and **creates** play areas. He **makes** special playground equipment. Children of all abilities played at Matt's playgrounds.

> It is difficult to understand this writing because the writer switches between past and present.

OK

Matt did many things that made a difference in children's lives. When he was 14, Matt told kids that bullying was wrong. He spent a lot of time talking to them. He also worked with an organization and created play areas. He made special playground equipment. Children of all abilities played at Matt's playgrounds.

> The writer now sticks consistently with the past. The paragraph is much clearer.

WRITE ON YOUR OWN Think of an important or enjoyable event that happened at your school this year. Summarize the key points of the event. Do not switch back and forth between writing in the past and writing in the present.

REMEMBER

Most **verbs** add **-ed** to make their past tense forms. The irregular verbs *be*, *have*, and *do* use special forms to show the past tense.

Past Tense of *be*	I **was**	you **were**	he, she, or it **was**	we **were**	they **were**
Past Tense of *have*	I **had**	you **had**	he, she, or it **had**	we **had**	they **had**
Past Tense of *do*	I **did**	you **did**	he, she, or it **did**	we **did**	they **did**

SPEECHES *on the* LITTLE ROCK NINE

by DWIGHT D. EISENHOWER *&* BILL CLINTON

INTRODUCTION On September 23, 1957, nine African American high school students entered Little Rock's Central High School, ready to learn. Prior to 1957, African American and white students attended separate schools. These nine students were part of an integration plan ordered by the U.S. Supreme Court. Outside the school, a mob of violent protesters gathered, threatening the students' safety. Two days later President Dwight D. Eisenhower sent U.S. Army troops to escort the students to school. To explain his actions to the nation, he gave the following address. Forty years later, the impact of this day is still felt. Bill Clinton tells the nation in 1997 that we've come a long way but still have a long way to go regarding racial harmony.

From President Dwight D. Eisenhower's Radio and TV Address to the Nation, September 24, 1957

2   Good Evening, My Fellow Citizens: For a few minutes this evening I want to speak to you about the serious situation that has arisen in Little Rock. To make this talk I have come to the President's office in the White House. I could have spoken from Rhode Island, where I have been staying recently, but I felt that, in speaking from the house of Lincoln, of Jackson and of Wilson, my words would better convey both the sadness I feel in the action I was compelled today to take and the firmness with which I intend to pursue this course until the orders of the Federal Court at Little Rock can be executed without unlawful interference.

3   In that city, under the **leadership** of **demagogic extremists,** disorderly mobs have **deliberately** prevented the carrying out of proper orders from a Federal Court. Local authorities have not eliminated that violent opposition and, under the law, I yesterday issued a Proclamation calling upon the mob to disperse.

4   This morning the mob again gathered in front of the Central High School of Little Rock, obviously for the purpose of again preventing the carrying out of the Court's order relating to the admission of Negro children to that school.

5   Whenever normal agencies prove inadequate to the task and it becomes necessary for the Executive Branch of the Federal Government to use its powers and

Key Vocabulary
• **leadership** *n.*, the ability to direct or guide other people

In Other Words
demagogic extremists people who use emotion to promote unpopular ideas or actions
deliberately purposefully

authority to uphold Federal Courts, the President's responsibility is inescapable. **In accordance with** that responsibility, I have today issued an Executive Order directing the use of troops under Federal authority to aid in the execution of Federal law at Little Rock, Arkansas. This became necessary when my Proclamation of yesterday was not observed, and the obstruction of justice still continues.

6   It is important that the reasons for my action be understood by all our citizens. As you know, the Supreme Court of the United States has decided that separate public educational **facilities** for the races are inherently unequal and therefore **compulsory** school **segregation** laws are unconstitutional.

7   Our personal opinions about the decision have no bearing on the matter of enforcement; the responsibility and authority of the Supreme Court to interpret the Constitution are very clear. Local Federal Courts were instructed by the Supreme Court to issue such orders and decrees as might be necessary to achieve admission to public schools without regard to race—and with all deliberate speed.

8   During the past several years, many communities in our Southern States have instituted public school plans for gradual progress in the enrollment and attendance of school children of all races in order to bring themselves into compliance with the law of the land.

9   They thus demonstrated to the world that we are a nation in which laws, not men, are supreme. I regret to say that this truth—the cornerstone of our liberties—was not observed in this instance …

10   The interest of the nation in the proper fulfillment of the law's requirements cannot yield to opposition and demonstrations by some few persons. Mob rule cannot be allowed to override the decisions of our courts …

11   And so, with deep confidence, I call upon the citizens of the State of Arkansas to assist in bringing to an immediate end all interference with the law and its processes. If resistance to the Federal Court orders ceases at once, the further presence of Federal troops will be unnecessary and the City of Little Rock will return to its normal habits of **peace** and order and **a blot upon** the fair name and high honor of our nation in the world will be removed.

12   Thus will be restored the image of America and of all its parts as one nation, indivisible, with liberty and justice for all.

> "... *Southern States have instituted public school plans for gradual progress in the enrollment and attendance of school children of all races* ..."

From **President Bill Clinton's Speech at Central High School Little Rock, Arkansas September 25, 1997**

13   On this beautiful, sunshiny day, so many wonderful words have been spoken with so much conviction, I am reluctant to add to them. But I must ask you to remember once more and to ask yourselves, what does what happened here 40 years ago mean today? What does it tell us, most importantly, about our children's tomorrows?

14   On September 4th, 1957, Elizabeth Eckford walked to this door for her first day of school, utterly alone. She was turned away by people who were afraid of change, instructed by ignorance, hating what they simply could not understand. And America saw her, haunted

and taunted for the simple color of her skin, and in the image we caught a very disturbing glimpse of ourselves. We saw not "one Nation under God, indivisible, with liberty and justice for all," but two Americas, divided and unequal …

15 … Imagine, all of you, what it would be like to come to school one day and be shoved against lockers, tripped down stairways, taunted day after day by your classmates, to go all through school with no hope of going to a school play or being on a basketball team or learning in simple peace …

16 Forty years later, what do you young people in this audience believe we have learned? Well, 40 years later, we know that we all benefit—all of us—when we learn together, work together, and come together. That is, after all, what it means to be an American.

17 Forty years later, we know, **notwithstanding some cynics,** that all our children can learn, and this school proves it. Forty years later, we know when the constitutional rights of our citizens are threatened, the National Government must guarantee them. Talk is fine, but when they are threatened, you need strong laws faithfully enforced and upheld by independent courts.

18 Forty years later, we know there are still more doors to be opened, doors to be opened wider, doors we have to keep from being shut again now. Forty years later, we know freedom and **equality** cannot be realized without responsibility for self, family, and the duties of citizenship, or without a commitment to building a community of shared destiny and a genuine sense of belonging.

19 Forty years later, we know the question of race is more complex and more important than ever, embracing no longer just blacks and whites, or blacks and whites and Hispanics and Native Americans, but now people from all parts of the Earth coming here to **redeem** the promise of America.

20 Forty years later, frankly, we know we're bound to come back where we started. After all the weary years and silent tears, after all the stony roads and bitter rides, the question of race is, in the end, still **an affair of the heart.** But if these are our lessons, what do we have to do? First, we must all **reconcile.** Then we must all face the facts of today. And finally we must act.

> *". . . Forty years later, we know there are still more doors to be opened . . ."*

Key Vocabulary
- **equality** *n.*, having the same rights as other people

In Other Words
notwithstanding some cynics even though there are doubters
redeem benefit from
an affair of the heart an emotional issue
reconcile be friends

Compare Writing on the Same Topic

"The Civil Rights Movement" and "Speeches on the Little Rock Nine" both tell about school integration. Compare how the authors approach this topic.

How It Works

Collect and Organize Information To compare the texts, write information about the genre, purpose, and style in a chart like this one.

	"The Civil Rights Movement"	"Speeches on the Little Rock Nine"
Genre	History Article	
Purpose	To describe events and people in the Civil Rights Movement	
Style	Factual	

Comparison Chart

Practice Together

Compare the Information Analyze the chart. Compare how each selection addresses the topic. Notice the **focus** of each selection. Then, begin to compare the selections.

Comparison

> Both selections mention the Little Rock Nine. "The Civil Rights Movement" discusses the Little Rock Nine as one part of the movement, while "Speeches on the Little Rock Nine" focuses only on that event. Also, the authors have different purposes for writing, and they use different genres and styles to convey their ideas.

Try It!

Add answers for "Speeches on the Little Rock Nine" to the chart. Compare and summarize the selections. Use a frame like this one to express your comparison.

Like the author of "_____," the author of "_____" _____. Unlike the author of "_____," the author _____.

Academic Vocabulary
- **focus** (fō-kus) *verb*
  When you **focus** on something, you pay attention to it.

MAKING A
DIFFERENCE

When can one individual make a difference?

Content Library

Leveled Library

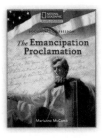

Reflect on Your Reading

Think back on your reading of the unit selections. Discuss what you did to understand what you read.

Focus on Reading **Text Structure: Chronological Order, Problem and Solution**
In this unit, you learned about some ways writers organize ideas: chronological order and problem-and-solution. Draw a diagram that shows the organization of one of the selections from this unit. Use your drawing to explain the organization of the selection to a partner.

Focus Strategy **Ask Questions**
As you read the selections, you learned to ask and answer questions about the text. Explain to a partner how you will use this strategy in the future.

Explore the

Throughout this unit, you have been thinking about when one person can make a difference. Choose one of these ways to explore the Guiding Question:

- **Discuss** With a group, discuss ways an individual can make a difference. Listen to and share examples from life. What challenges may a person have to face to make a positive change?

- **Role-Play** Imagine that you know someone who is being bullied. One person can take that role, and another can offer advice. Be honest about the difficulty the person faces in dealing with the situation.

- **Write** Choose an issue or problem in your community or school that needs to be solved. Write a letter to the editor of a newspaper about the problem.

Book Talk

Which Unit Library book did you choose? Explain to a partner what you learned about individuals making a difference.

At Home in the
World

4

How can your location affect the way you live?

READ MORE!

Content Library
The West Today

Leveled Library
Jane Eyre
by Charlotte Bronte,
adapted by Jane E. Gerver

Knights of the Round Table
by Gwen Gross

The Dragon Prince
by Laurence Yep

Web Links
myNGconnect.com

◀ Boys play in Panama Bay off the coast of
southern Panama, in the shadow of Panama City.

Focus on Reading

Analyze Connections

► Compare and Contrast

Writers organize text by clearly showing how things, ideas, people, and events are connected. When writers use a comparison-and-contrast structure **effectively**, you can easily understand the connections.

How It Works

A **comparison** connects ideas that are similar. A **contrast** connects ideas that are different. Writers use **signal words** to show how ideas are connected. As you read, look for signal words that show similarities and differences.

Words That Signal Similarities	Words That Signal Differences
like	but
both	unlike
also	although
too	different
similarly	in contrast
just as	on the other hand

A Moon and a Planet

Io is a moon that circles the planet Jupiter. Although Io is a moon and Earth is a planet, the two are alike in some ways. For example, Earth's oceans have tides. That is, the level of the ocean water along the shore rises and falls regularly, pulled by the moon's gravity. Like Earth, Io also has tides. But unlike Earth's ocean tides, Io's tides are in its solid surface. Io's solid surface rises and falls, pulled by gravity from the planet Jupiter and two other moons that orbit Jupiter.

While both Earth and Io have active volcanoes, Io has no water and gets no rain. Unlike Earth, Io cannot support life as we know it. In contrast to Io, Earth is a friendly habitat for many kinds of life.

▲ Io (left) has a temperature of −230°F. Earth's most extreme recorded low is −129°F.

> Contrast signal words show how Io and Earth are different.

> Comparison signal words show similarities between Earth and Io.

> Signal words help readers see that the paragraph begins with a comparison, then continues with contrasts.

Academic Vocabulary

• **effectively** (i-**fek**-tiv-lē) *adverb*
Something that is done **effectively** is done in a way that works or gets results.

Practice Together

Read the following passage aloud with your class. As you read, listen for words that help signal connections. What ideas are similar? Which ideas are different?

Kinds of Galaxies

All galaxies are clusters of gases and millions of stars. Earth and its star, the Sun, are part of the Milky Way galaxy. Similar to many galaxies, the Milky Way is a spiral galaxy, which looks like a flat pinwheel of light. In contrast, some other galaxies are elliptical, looking almost like footballs. If a galaxy is neither spiral nor elliptical, it is called irregular.

▲ Milky Way's spiral arms hold billions of stars, just as other spiral galaxies do.

Try It!

Read the following passage. Which ideas are similar and which are different? How do you know?

Star Light, Star Bright

Stars come in many different sizes and colors. The sun's radius, or the distance from its center to its surface, is about 432,000 miles. In contrast, some stars have a radius that is about fifteen times that distance. Unlike those stars, a neutron star may have a radius of only about 6 miles.

Color is also a measure used for stars. Color indicates temperature. Green and blue stars are the hottest. Red stars, on the other hand, are very old and among the coolest. Betelguese and Antares are both red stars. Our sun is a yellow star. It has a temperature in between those of the blue and the red stars.

Focus on Vocabulary

Use Context Clues

When you read, you may come across words you don't know. In many cases, the meaning of an unknown word will become **obvious** if you use **context clues** to figure it out. Common types of context clues include definition, restatement, and examples. Signal words can help you find the clues.

Type of Clue	How It Works	Signal Words	Example Sentences
Definition or Restatement	The context tells the definition of the word or restates the meaning using other words.	*called, which is, or, in other words*	The rocket that lifts the shuttle toward space is *called* a **booster** rocket. The **circumference** of, *or* distance around, Earth is about 25,000 miles.
Examples	The unknown word may be listed as an example of something familiar. Or, you may find familiar examples of the unknown word.	*for example, like, such as, including*	Why are rocks interesting? Gases *such as* **hydrogen** are plentiful in the universe. Oxygen and iron are *examples* of chemical **elements** found in the universe.

How the Strategy Works

Use **context clues** to help make the meaning of new words **obvious** .

1. Use the topic of your reading to narrow down possible meanings for the unfamiliar word.
2. Reread the sentence where the word appears. Look for signal words that point to a definition, a restatement, or an example.
3. Use the sentences around the word to help figure out its meaning.

Use the strategy to figure out the meaning of *moderate*.

> Most life on Earth needs a <u>moderate</u> climate, with temperatures neither too hot nor too cold. These middle temperatures, from around 30 degrees Fahrenheit to about 90 degrees, support life for many species of plants and animals.

Strategy in Action

" This paragraph describes the weather as 'neither too hot nor too cold.' It restates this as 'middle temperatures.' "

☑ **REMEMBER** You can use the context of a passage to figure out the meanings of new or unfamiliar words.

Academic Vocabulary
- **obvious** (ob-vē-us) *adjective*
  Something that is **obvious** is easily seen or understood.

Practice Together

Read the passage aloud with your class. Listen for context clues to help you figure out the meaning of each underlined word. How did context clues help?

Home, Sweet Home

The place where an animal lives, called its <u>habitat</u>, must supply the animal with what it needs to survive. Each habitat must provide <u>necessities</u> such as food, water, and shelter.

▲ Ants make complex tunnels part of their home.

One reason there are so many forms of life on Earth is that it offers so many different habitats. Some habitats are <u>harsh</u>, with difficult living conditions. For example, some animals can live in places with very little water. Others can live at ocean depths where the water pressure would crush even a submarine.

Many living beings <u>adapt</u>, or change and adjust, to the conditions around them. Some plants and animals live in places where most other living beings would not survive. These unusual habitats, or <u>niches</u>, allow creatures to survive in a sometimes dangerous world.

Try It!

Read the following passage. What do the underlined words mean? How do you know?

A Simple Life?

My visit to my grandfather's farm last summer surprised me. I had the idea, or <u>impression</u>, that Granddad led a quiet, simple life in the open air. I soon discovered that life on the farm was not so simple.

I usually think of noisy machinery as something you'd find mostly in the city, but Granddad had a different tool, or <u>implement</u>, for almost everything he did on the farm. He used <u>devices</u> such as an electric saw for cutting wood and a gas-powered machine for digging fence post holes. I expected quiet on a farm, but there was plenty of noise with all the machines.

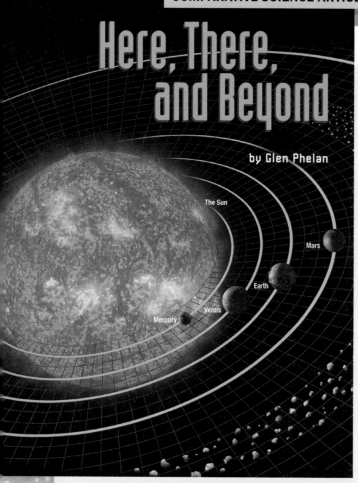

Here, There, and Beyond

by Glen Phelan

The Sun
Mars
Earth
Venus
Mercury

Build Background

Connect

KWL Chart With a partner, create a KWL Chart for the planets in our solar system.

WHAT DO I KNOW?	WHAT DO I WANT TO LEARN?	WHAT DID I LEARN?
The planets in our solar system move around the sun.	Which planet is the biggest?	

KWL Chart

The Solar System

Earth is just one of many objects in our solar system. What else is out there? In addition to eight planets, there are asteroids, comets, and hundreds of moons.

Digital Library

myNGconnect.com
◐ View the video.

◀ There are eight planets in our solar system.

Language & Grammar

Make Comparisons

CD

Study the photographs and listen to the conversation. Listen for a comparison. When people compare things, they tell how they are alike and how they are different.

PICTURE PROMPT

No Place Like Home

Jen: My family has lived in both a big city and a suburb.

Marcus: What were your homes like?

Jen: Well, our home in the suburb was a two-story house. It had a backyard and lots of trees.

Marcus: So you had a lot of space in the suburb.

Jen: Yes. Our home in the city was an apartment. The apartment was smaller than the house. It didn't have a backyard, but there were many parks nearby.

Marcus: So you had less space in the city, but I bet it was more interesting.

Use Nouns in the Subject and Predicate

A complete sentence has two parts: the subject and the predicate. The subject tells whom or what the sentence is about. The predicate often tells what the subject does.

EXAMPLE   **People** **choose different places to live** .

- Nouns can be the **subject** of a sentence.

  EXAMPLE   **People** choose different places to live.
                subject

- Nouns can also be the **object** of an action **verb**. To find the object, turn the verb into a question like: "Choose what?" Your answer is the object.

  EXAMPLE   People **choose** different **places** to live.
                          verb   object

- Many English sentences follow this pattern: subject → verb → object

  EXAMPLES   **People choose** different **places** to live.
                   subject   verb   object

Practice Together

Say each sentence and tell the job of the <u>noun</u>. Is it a subject or an object noun?

1. The <u>man</u> lives in a desert climate.
2. The hot sun warms his <u>home</u> fast.
3. The heat creates a <u>challenge</u>.
4. <u>People</u> wear clothes to protect them from the sun.

Try It!

Say each sentence. Write the job of the <u>noun</u> on a card. Is it a subject or an object noun?

5. Some <u>astronauts</u> live on a space station.
6. They take <u>oxygen</u> with them to breathe.
7. Outer <u>space</u> does not support <u>life</u>.
8. Only <u>Earth</u> supports life.

▲ The man covers his head to protect it from the heat.

Compare Places to Live

MAKE COMPARISONS

What if you could choose any place in the world or universe as your home? What place would you choose? How does your choice compare to those of your classmates?

With a partner, make a list of places where people could live. Take a survey. Ask five other students which place they would choose to live. List their responses in a chart like this one. Then compare the results.

Place	Student 1	Student 2	Student 3	Student 4	Student 5
1. a big city					
2. a suburb					
3. a small town					
4. near an ocean					
5. near the mountains					
6. in a desert					
7. in a space station					
8.					
9.					
10.					

Share the results of your survey with another group. Make comparisons between your survey results and those of another pair of students.

HOW TO MAKE COMPARISONS

1. Tell how things are alike. Use words like *all*, *both*, and *too*.
2. Tell how things are different. Use words like *only* and *but*.

> Both Ana and Jen want to live in a big city, but Katrina prefers a small town.

> Tony prefers a small town, too. Only Jeff wants to live in a space station.

USE NOUNS IN THE SUBJECT AND PREDICATE

When you make comparisons, use **nouns** in the subjects and predicates of your sentences to tell how people, places, and things are alike or different.

In the Subject: Most **people** chose the big city as their favorite place to live.

In the Predicate: Both Rachel and Rosa chose the **mountains** as their favorite place to live.

Prepare to Read

Learn Key Vocabulary

Study the Words Use the steps below.

1. Pronounce the word. Say it aloud several times. Spell it.
2. Rate your word knowledge.
3. Study the example. Tell more about the word.
4. Practice it. Make the word your own.

Key Words

atmosphere (at-mu-sfir) *noun* ▸ page 251

The **atmosphere** is the air that surrounds the Earth. A spaceship can travel outside of Earth's **atmosphere**, but an airplane cannot.

energy (en-ur-jē) *noun* ▸ page 251

Energy is natural power that is used to make things work. We can turn the **energy** of the wind into electricity. *Synonyms: force, power*

feature (fē-chur) *noun* ▸ page 251

Features of something are its parts or details. Some of the **features** of Earth's surface include mountains, lakes, and trees.

measurement (mezh-ur-ment) *noun* ▸ page 256

A **measurement** is the size or quantity of something. I took **measurements** of the rock to find out how long it is.

rotation (rō-tā-shun) *noun* ▸ page 250

Rotation is the spinning of an object, such as a planet. Earth's **rotation** is what gives us night and day. *Related Word: rotate*

solar system (sō-lur sis-tem) *noun* ▸ page 250

Our **solar system** is made up of the sun and the objects that move around it. Earth's **solar system** includes eight planets.

solid (sah-led) *adjective* ▸ page 250

Something that is **solid** is hard or firm. Rocks are **solid** all the way through. *Antonym: soft*

surface (sur-fes) *noun* ▸ page 250

A **surface** is the outside or top layer of an object. The new road has a smoother **surface** than the old road.

Practice the Words Make a Study Card for each Key Word. Then compare your cards with a partner's.

> feature
>
> **What it means:** the details of something
>
> **Example:** My eyes are my best feature.
>
> **Not an example:** I am interested in hockey.

Study Card

Compare and Contrast

How Is Nonfiction Organized? One way that writers organize information is by **comparing** and contrasting ideas.

As you read, look for signal words that help you notice comparisons and contrasting ideas.

Reading Strategies
· Plan and Monitor
· Ask Questions
Make Connections
Combine your knowledge and experiences with the author's ideas and information.
· Visualize
· Make Inferences
· Determine Importance
· Synthesize

Look Into the Text

is a parison. lls about ething that like on the ets—the ace. nmon and are signal ds.

These planets have a lot in common. They are mostly made up of rock and metal, so they all have hard, uneven surfaces.

On the other hand, each planet is also different from the others in its group. For example, each of the four rocky planets has a different kind of atmosphere.

This is a contrast. It tells about something that is different on the planets—the atmosphere. *On the other hand* and *different* are signal words.

Practice Together

Begin a Comparison Chart A Comparison Chart can help you **compare** and contrast information. This Comparison Chart shows how the first passage says the planets are alike. Read the second passage and complete the Comparison Chart.

How the Planets Are Alike	How the Planets Are Different
have similar surfaces	

Academic Vocabulary

● **compare** (**kum**-pair) *verb*
When you **compare**, you look closely at how things are alike or different.

Comparative Science Article

A science article is expository nonfiction that gives information about the natural world.

Science writers often **compare** and **contrast** information about a topic. Thinking about how things are alike or how they are different can help readers better understand and remember the information.

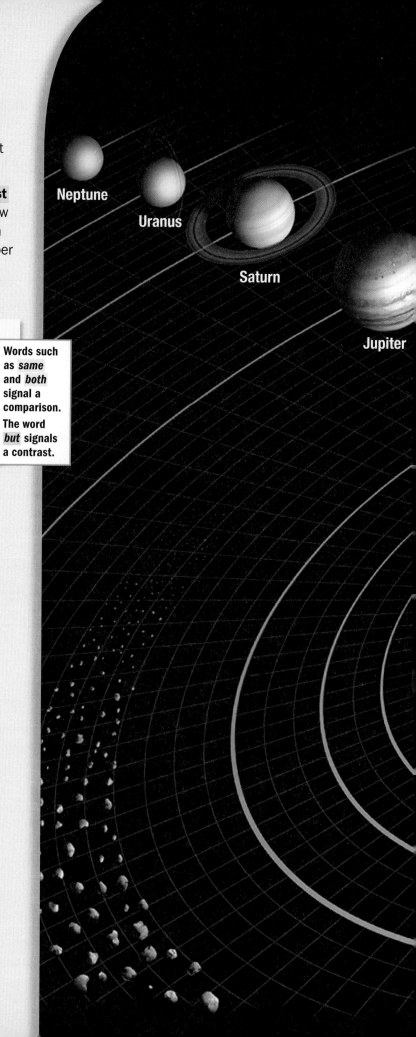

Neptune

Uranus

Saturn

Jupiter

Look Into the Text

. . . In addition, Earth and Mars spin at about the same rate—one rotation every twenty-four hours—but Mercury and Venus both take months to rotate just once.

Words such as *same* and *both* signal a comparison. The word *but* signals a contrast.

As you read combine information in the text with what you already know to make connections.

Here, There, and Beyond

by Glen Phelan

The Sun

Mars

Earth

Venus

Mercury

Comprehension Coach

You probably know your neighborhood well. You know where your school is. You know how to get to the park. You know some nearby stores.

But how well do you know Earth's neighborhood? You can think of Earth's neighbors as all the objects in our **solar system** . These objects include planets. A planet is a large object that moves around a star.

There are eight planets in our solar system. Scientists put these planets into groups. The four planets closest to the sun make up one group.

▲ The Earth

Planets Closest to Our Sun

The four planets closest to the sun are Mercury, Venus, Earth, and Mars. These planets have a lot in common. They are mostly made up of rock and metal, so they all have hard, uneven **surfaces** .

Because of **their content**, the planets closest to the sun have high densities. This means that these planets are made up of condensed, or tightly packed, materials. They also share the qualities of having slow **rotation** and **solid** surfaces.

The rocky planets closest to the sun are also alike in other ways. They are small compared to most of the other planets in our solar system. These planets also do not have many moons, or objects that rotate, or move, around a planet.

▲ The rocky surface of Mars

Key Vocabulary

solar system *n.*, the sun and the objects that move around it

surface *n.*, the outside, or top layer, of an object

rotation *n.*, the movement of one object around another object

solid *adj.*, hard or firm

In Other Words

their content what they have inside

On the other hand, each planet is also different from the others in its group. For example, each of the four rocky planets has a different kind of **atmosphere**. An atmosphere is a blanket of gas that covers a planet.

Different gases trap different amounts of heat from the sun, which means that each planet has a different temperature. For example, Venus is the hottest planet because it has a thick and heavy atmosphere covered with clouds. The clouds let in **energy** from the sun, and this makes Venus's surface temperature hotter than most ovens!

The rocky planets have many other differences. They are each different sizes, and they also have different **features** on their surfaces. In addition, Earth and Mars spin at about the same **rate**—one rotation every twenty-four hours—but Mercury and Venus both take months to rotate just once.

▲ A detailed view of Venus's cloudy atmosphere

THE PLANETS **CLOSEST** TO THE SUN

Mercury   Venus

Earth   Mars

How Are They Similar?

- **Surface** They are rocky and solid.
- **Rings** They do not have planetary rings.
- **Moons** They have few or no moons.
- **Size** They are small compared to other planets—less than 8,000 miles in **diameter**. Even so, Earth is more than 2.5 times bigger than Mercury!

How Are They Different?

- **Planet Life** Earth is the only planet known to have living things.
- **Temperatures** In this group, Venus is the hottest planet (average temperature: 867° F) while Mars is the coldest planet (average temperature: -85° F).
- **Locations** Mercury is closest to the sun, while Mars is farthest from the sun.

Key Vocabulary

atmosphere *n.*, air that surrounds a planet

energy *n.*, a source of usable power

feature *n.*, parts or details

In Other Words

rate time

diameter distance from one end of the planet to another through the center

Look Into the Text

1. **Evidence and Conclusions** Give three details to support this conclusion: The planets closest to the sun have many similarities.
2. **Explain** How is Venus different from the other planets?
3. **Compare and Contrast** How does the rotation of the Earth compare to that of Mars and Mercury?

Planets Farthest from Our Sun

The next four planets are Jupiter, Saturn, Uranus, and Neptune. These planets are huge. Unlike the planets close to the sun, these planets are not **mainly composed** of rock or other solid **matter**. Their atmospheres are mostly made of gases. So, many scientists call these planets "gas giants."

Gas giants have many moons and rings. Their rings are made of dust and rocks. Some gas giants have rings that are hard to see, while others, such as Saturn, have rings that are easy to see from Earth.

Although the gas giants are alike in many ways, each planet is also different. Each gas giant has different features. Some of the gas giants have storms on their surface. For example, the orange-red oval on Jupiter is a storm. This storm has lasted more than 300 years.

Gas giants can also move through space in different ways. For example, Uranus spins differently than other planets. It spins on its side, moving like a rolling ball instead of a spinning top.

THE PLANETS FARTHEST FROM THE SUN

Jupiter

Saturn

Uranus

Neptune

How Are They Similar?

- **Rings** They are surrounded by rings.
- **Atmosphere** They have thick atmospheres made mostly of gases.
- **Movement** They travel around the sun in almost circular paths.
- **Moons** They have many moons.
- **Size** They are large compared to other planets—up to 88,900 miles in diameter.

How Are They Different?

- **Rings** Saturn's rings are the easiest to see from Earth.
- **Storms** Jupiter and Saturn have more storms than Uranus and Neptune.
- **Colors** Jupiter has shades of white, orange, brown, and red while Neptune is blue in color.
- **Temperatures** In this group, Neptune is the coldest planet (average temperature: -328° F) while Jupiter is the warmest planet (average temperature: -166° F).
- **Size** Jupiter is so large that all of the other planets could fit inside of it.

In Other Words
mainly composed made
matter materials

Science Background
Storms on planets are similar to hurricanes, or violent storms, on Earth. Jupiter's storms are twice as big as Earth's storms, and they have strong winds and heavy rain that can last for days.

Saturn's rings

Uranus's rings

The storms of Saturn

Jupiter's rising storm

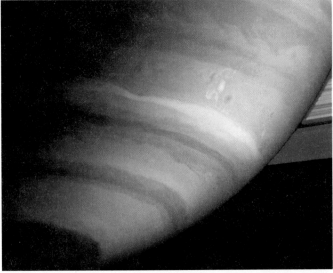

▲ Each gas giant has rings, but only some gas giants have storms on their surfaces.

Look Into the Text

1. **Cause and Effect** Why do scientists call Jupiter, Saturn, Uranus, and Neptune "gas giants"?

2. **Compare** How are the gas giants similar?

3. **Contrast** What are some of the ways that the gas giants differ from the planets closest to the sun?

Asteroids and Meteoroids

Earth has other neighbors in our solar system.
Asteroids are **chunks** of rock and metal.
Like planets, asteroids move around our
sun, and most are found between Mars and
Jupiter. Some asteroids are as small as a
house while others are as big as a city.
One asteroid is the size of Texas!

Meteoroids are chunks of **debris** in
space. They are smaller than asteroids,
and some meteoroids are even smaller
than an ant. Still, others are as big as a
bus. Sometimes a meteoroid falls towards
a planet. A meteoroid that hits a planet is
called a meteorite.

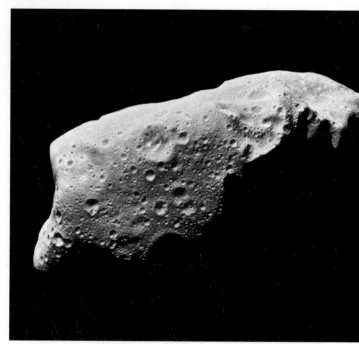

▲ This large asteroid travels around the sun.

This crater, or large hole,
in Arizona was created
by a meteorite.

In Other Words
chunks big pieces
debris pieces of rock

Icy Objects — Dwarf Planets and Comets

Pluto **used to be considered** the ninth planet in our solar system—but this has changed. Scientists have decided that Pluto is not a planet because it is too small. Pluto is now called a dwarf planet.

Pluto is not rocky, like Earth is, and it is not made of gas like Saturn. Pluto has a small, rocky center that is covered with ice. It is like a giant snowball in space. Pluto is farther from the sun than Neptune. It takes Pluto more than 248 years to travel once around the sun.

Pluto is not the only icy object that moves around the sun. Comets do, too. Comets are large chunks of ice, gas, dust, and rock.

Comets are found far from the sun most of the time. When a comet gets close to the sun, the ice on its surface becomes gas. The gas forms an atmosphere, called a coma, around the comet. Some of the gas is pushed from the comet into space, and this gas forms the tail of the comet.

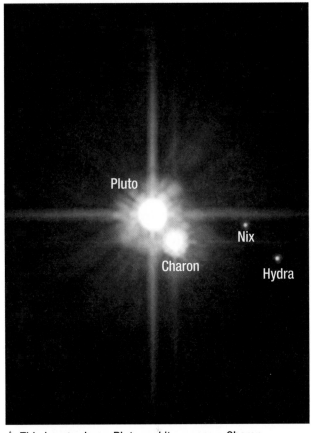

▲ This image shows Pluto and its moons—Charon, Nix, and Hydra.

In Other Words

used to be considered was

Science Background

To be a planet, an object must: orbit around the sun, be large enough to have a round shape, and have an orbit which is free of rocky or icy objects. Pluto is a **dwarf planet** and not a planet, because it travels through an area called the Kuiper Belt, which is full of small icy objects.

Human and Nonhuman Observers

How do we know about objects in our solar system? Scientists use special tools to study them. One tool is the telescope. A telescope makes faraway objects look closer. Telescopes show detailed images of planets and other objects from space. Most telescopes are on Earth; however, some telescopes are in space. Space telescopes are large and can **reveal** important discoveries, such as **the collapse of a comet**.

Spacecraft also help scientists learn about our solar system. Some spacecraft allow scientists to fly into space. These spacecraft let people study the solar system from space. Other spacecraft do not have people on board. They are called probes. Probes take pictures, make **measurements**, and then send the

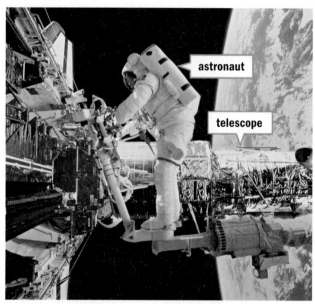

▲ An astronaut checks a telescope in space.

information back to Earth. Spacecraft help us learn more about our neighbors in space. ❖

Spacecraft, like this probe, help scientists learn more about the solar system.

Key Vocabulary
measurement *n.*, the size or quantity of something

In Other Words
reveal show
the collapse of a comet when a comet falls apart
Spacecraft Vehicles designed to travel in space

Look Into the Text

1. **Contrast** How is Pluto different from both the Earth and Saturn?
2. **Summary** What are the main characteristics of asteroids?
3. **Conclusions** Why are telescopes and spacecraft important scientific tools?

Why the Sun and the Moon Live in the Sky

an adaptation of a Nigerian myth

Long before time began, the Sun and the Moon met and got married. They created a home on Land and started their life together. They wanted to tell someone of their happiness, so they invited their friend the Ocean to visit.

"You are very kind to invite me," said the Ocean. "Unfortunately, I cannot accept your invitation."

"Oh dear!" cried the Moon. "You do not like us anymore."

The Ocean replied, "Of course I do. I just don't think I will fit inside your house."

"Aha!" blazed the Sun angrily. "You don't think our home is **fancy enough**."

"I do!" the Ocean insisted. "I'm sure it's **brilliant**, but—."

"Then come in," said the Moon and she opened the doors. The house was huge and stretched as far as the eye could see. The Ocean shyly **inched across the threshold**.

"Come on in, there's lots of space," laughed the Sun. So the Ocean began to flow in more rapidly.

Soon the entire floor was flooded in water. "See? There was nothing to worry about," said the Moon.

"Actually, I have only just begun to enter," said the Ocean and **with that**, a large wave rushed across the room and splashed against the walls. The Sun and the Moon rose higher and higher to avoid getting wet.

In Other Words
fancy enough nice
brilliant beautiful
inched across the
    threshold entered the house
with that after the Ocean spoke

Soon the fish and the other creatures of the sea began to swim around in the house. "I'm so sorry," said the Ocean but the Sun said, "**Think nothing of it**, there is room for all."

As the Ocean continued to pour into the house, the Sun and Moon were forced to rise higher and higher until at last they were up on the roof. "Tell me, Ocean," the Sun called down, "Are you almost in?"

"I am only halfway in," roared the Ocean. "You are so kind to invite me."

The Sun and the Moon knew it would be impolite to take back their invitation so they just rose higher into the sky. Their lovely home floated upside down in the water below.

And that is why the Sun and the Moon **took up permanent residence** in the Sky and found harmony with the Land and the Ocean. To this day, they still watch the Earth and the Ocean with interest, but they have never again touched the ground.

Myths and Storytelling

A myth is a traditional story. Myths usually explain people's beliefs about why something in nature happens. These stories sometimes involve gods, heroes, or animals, and often focus on a life lesson. Myths are sources of how different cultures view the world.

Storytellers and those who pass along myths are known as the keepers of the people's wisdom and beliefs. Nigerian storytelling, for example, requires so much skill that it is considered a form of art. Traditionally, Nigerian storytellers have dramatically entertained their audiences. These storytellers have also tried to teach young people about important customs in Nigerian culture.

In Other Words
Think nothing of it Don't worry
took up permanent residence lived forever

Look Into the Text

1. **Perspectives** Why doesn't the Ocean want to visit the Sun's and the Moon's house? How is this different from what the Sun thinks?
2. **Genre** What are some clues that show this selection is a myth?

Connect Reading and Writing

Vocabulary

atmosphere

energy

features

measurement

rotations

solar system

solid

surface

CRITICAL THINKING

1. **SUM IT UP** Use your Comparison Chart to describe the similarities and differences among planets and other celestial bodies. Summarize the article to a partner. Then complete the KWL chart you began before reading the selection.

What Is Being Compared	How They Are Alike

Comparison Chart

2. **Compare** How do the **features** of asteroids and meteoroids compare with planets?

3. **Interpret** How do the selection and the myth express the idea of being at home in the world?

READING FLUENCY

Phrasing Read the passage on page 633 to a partner. Assess your fluency.

1. I did not pause/sometimes paused/ always paused for punctuation.

2. What I did best in my reading was _____.

READING STRATEGY

What strategy helped you understand this selection? Tell a partner about it.

VOCABULARY REVIEW

Oral Review Read the paragraph aloud. Add the vocabulary words.

Beyond the _____ that surrounds Earth, there are seven other planets. All planets in our _____ revolve, or make _____, around the sun. All the planets get _____ from the sun. The _____ of planets differ in some ways. For example, the _____ of Mars is _____ and rocky, but Saturn is gaseous. There are also differences in size, or _____ .

Written Review Imagine that your mission is to describe one of the planets as you explore its **surface** from a spacecraft. Use five vocabulary words.

 **WRITE ABOUT THE** GUIDING QUESTION

Explore Being at Home in the World

How do planets in the **solar system** compare to communities on Earth? Reread the selection to find **features** that support your ideas.

Connect Across the Curriculum

Use Context Clues: Definition, Example, and Restatement

Academic Vocabulary
- **definition** (de-fu-**ni**-shun) *noun*
  The meaning of a word is its **definition**.

You can use context clues to figure out the meaning of a word or idea.

Type of Clue	Word	Example
A **definition clue** gives the meaning of the word.	atmosphere	An **atmosphere** is a blanket of gas that covers a planet.
A **example** names things that are familiar or like the unknown word.	features	Each gas giant has different **features**. Some of the gas giants have storms on their surfaces.
A **restatement** restates the meaning using other words.	telescope	One tool is the telescope. A **telescope** is a tool that makes faraway objects look closer.

Find Clues Use context clues to explain the underlined words.

These planets also do not have many moons or objects that
rotate, or move, around a planet. . . . Different gases trap
different amounts of heat from the sun, which means that each
planet has a different temperature. For example, Venus is the
hottest planet because it has a thick and heavy atmosphere
covered with clouds.

Analyze Myths

Myths are one of the oldest forms of fiction. Myths can have different themes. Some reflect the values or beliefs of a culture. Others teach life lessons. Many myths explain why things happen.

Read this passage. It shows how a myth can explain a natural event.

A long time ago before the Earth began, Saturn lived next to
Jupiter. One day Jupiter and Saturn bumped into each other.
"Saturn," Jupiter said, "why must you live so close to me? There is
plenty of room in the sky."

Create a Myth Write a myth of your own with a clear theme. Then exchange myths with a partner. Identify the theme of your partner's myth.

Make Comparisons

Group Share Work with a small group. Take turns making comparisons between the planets in our solar system. Use nouns in the subjects and predicates of your sentences.

> Venus is closer to the Sun than Saturn.

> Saturn and Neptune are both gas giants.

Write About Astronomy

Study the Models When you write, you need to use naming words correctly in the different parts of your sentences. The correct use of words makes your writing clear and precise.

NOT OK

My classmates and me visited an observatory. Us used a giant telescope to look at the stars and planets. Some of my classmates saw detailed images of the moon's surface. Them also saw a comet streaking through the sky. This trip inspired we to learn more about the solar system. They also inspired I to become an astronomer.

> This writer uses naming words incorrectly so the ideas are confusing.

OK

My classmates and I visited an observatory. We used a giant telescope to look at the stars and planets. Some of my classmates saw detailed images of the moon's surface. They also saw a comet streaking through the sky. This trip inspired us to learn more about the solar system. It also inspired me to become an astronomer.

> This writer uses naming words correctly. The ideas are clear.

Add Sentences Add two sentences to the OK model above. Be sure to use naming words correctly.

✎ **WRITE ON YOUR OWN** Write about a time you observed the sky at night. What did you see? Use naming words correctly.

Subject Pronouns	I	you	he	she	it	we	you	they
Object Pronouns	me	you	him	her	it	us	you	them

REMEMBER

- A noun or pronoun used as a **subject** tells whom or what the sentence is about.
- A noun or pronoun used as an **object** tells who or what receives the action of the sentence.

Earth (and) Space

by Julie Larson

Build Background

Connect

Question Brainstorm What questions do you have about what it's like to live in space? With a group, list questions you have about each category.

Food in Space Do astronauts have a stove or a refrigerator in space?	Sleep in Space
Gravity in Space	Breathing in Space

Living in Space

What is it like to live far from Earth? Astronauts get to experience life in space.

Digital Library   **myNGconnect.com**
◯ View the video.

▲ Working in space (left) is like and unlike working on Earth.

Language & Grammar

Define and Explain CD

Study the photo and listen to the explanation about gravity. Listen again and chime in.

RAP

A Matter of Gravity

Mass is the measure of matter.
Matter
Is anything you can touch.
The more matter there is
The more mass there is.
That's why matter matters so much.

Gravity is a force.
Its force
Pulls masses of matter together.
The bigger the mass
The stronger the pull.
And the force will continue forever.

Distance is a factor.
It affects gravitational rules.
The longer the distance
Between two masses
The weaker is gravity's pull.

In the universe, gravity rules!
It holds the planets in place
As they orbit the stars
And everything, everything, everything
Continues to travel through space.

Gravity binds us to Earth,
And the Earth to the Sun's galaxy.
As we walk beneath stars,
When we rocket to Mars,
Without gravity, where would we be?

▼ Dr. Mae Jemison floating in Spacelab

▲ Any ship in orbit around the Earth is actually falling slowly toward Earth. It never gets far enough away from Earth to escape Earth's gravitational pull. The astronauts inside the ship are falling at the same speed, so they feel weightless. Their falling motion in orbit creates this effect. It is the same sensation you would have in a free-falling elevator ride.

Language and Grammar, continued

1 TRY OUT LANGUAGE
2 LEARN GRAMMAR
3 APPLY ON YOUR OWN

Use Pronouns in the Subject and Predicate

A **pronoun** refers to a noun. You can use pronouns in the subject or predicate of a sentence.

Subject Pronouns	I	you	he	she	it	we	you	they
Object Pronouns	me	you	him	her	it	us	you	them

- Use a **subject pronoun** as the subject of a sentence.

  EXAMPLE   The **astronauts** floated beside the space shuttle. **They** checked the heat tiles under its wing.

- Use an **object pronoun** as the object of the verb.

  EXAMPLE   The shuttle is equipped with **computers**. The astronauts use **them** to e-mail family members.

- When you talk about yourself, use the pronouns **I** and **me**. Use the pronoun **I** in the subject of a sentence. Use the pronoun **me** as the object in the predicate of a sentence.

  EXAMPLE   **I** wrote to an astronaut. He told **me** about life in the shuttle.

Practice Together

Say each pair of sentences. Add the correct pronoun from the chart and tell what it refers to.

1. Without gravity, objects in the cabin don't stay in place. _____ float everywhere.

2. At meals, plates are tied down. Astronauts secure _____ with straps.

3. If your lunch disappears, look up. You might find _____ on the ceiling!

4. Michael likes the meals in space. _____ thinks the food is tasty.

Try It!

Say each pair of sentences. Write the correct pronoun and what it refers to on a card. Then say the sentence and add the pronoun.

5. The scientists launched the rocket. _____ blasted into outer space.

6. Several astronauts were on board. _____ wore spacesuits.

7. There's no oxygen in space. People need _____ to breathe.

8. Spacesuits supply oxygen. "The suits help _____ survive in space," say the astronauts.

▲ The rocket launched after several delays.

264   Unit 4 At Home in the World

Tell About Your World

DEFINE AND EXPLAIN

Many inventions, such as MP3 players, cell phones, and computers, make our lives easier. It can be hard to remember a time without them.

Work with a small group. Define and explain a gadget or invention you use all the time. Tell why you feel it is important.

First, use a Word Web to collect the important words that go with your invention. Here is a Word Web about a cell phone. Decide which words you may need to define for your group. Use a dictionary if necessary.

Word Web

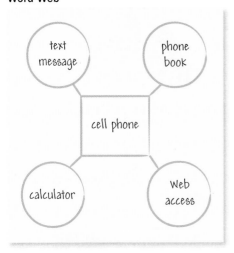

Present your gadget to another group. When you give your explanation, define at least one word. Answer questions they may have. Trade roles.

> A cell phone is a mobile telephone. I can talk to people from wherever I am. This helps me stay in touch with my family and friends.

HOW TO DEFINE AND EXPLAIN

1. **Define:** Tell what the word means.
2. **Explain:** Give details and examples to make the definition more clear.

USE PRONOUNS IN THE SUBJECT AND THE PREDICATE

When you define and explain, you may tell details or give examples to illustrate what you're talking about. If you use pronouns in the subject or predicate of your sentences, remember that the pronoun has to match the subject that it refers to.

In the Subject:	My **laptop** is not heavy. **It** is easy to carry around.
In the Predicate:	I can e-mail my **friends**. I can tell **them** about my life.

Prepare to Read

Learn Key Vocabulary

Study the Words Use the steps below.

1. Pronounce the word. Say it aloud several times. Spell it.
2. Rate your word knowledge.
3. Study the example. Tell more about the word.
4. Practice it. Make the word your own.

Key Words

astronaut (as-tre-not) *noun*
▶ page 270

An **astronaut** is a person trained to travel to space. **Astronauts** need special equipment to travel in space.

element (e-lu-munt) *noun*
▶ page 272

An **element** is something that is part of a whole. Copper is one of the **elements** used to make pennies.
Synonym: **part**

essential (i-sen-shul)
adjective ▶ page 278

Something that is **essential** is needed for survival. Food and water are **essential** for living beings.
Synonym: **necessary**

experience (ik-spir-ē-ens)
verb ▶ page 270

To **experience** something is to go through it yourself. I want to **experience** a ride on a roller coaster.

process (prah-ses) *noun*
▶ page 272

A **process** is a series of actions that lead to a result. The **process** of building the house took a year.

routine (rü-tēn) *noun*
▶ page 280

A **routine** is a normal series of actions that you repeat. As part of my daily morning **routine**, I brush my teeth.
Synonym: **habit**

similarity (si-mu-lair-u-tē)
noun ▶ page 270

A **similarity** is something that makes things alike. The **similarity** between the cars is their color.
Related Word: **similar**
Antonym: **difference**

universe (yu-nu-vers) *noun*
▶ page 270

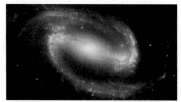

The **universe** is everything that exists, including all of space. Our solar system is just one part of the whole **universe**.
Related Word: **universal**

Practice the Words Make an Expanded Meaning Map for each Key Word. Then compare your maps with a partner.

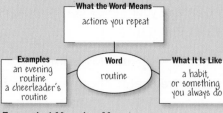

Expanded Meaning Map

Determine Author's Purpose

What is an Author's Purpose? Authors choose to write in different forms, called genres. The genre an author selects depends upon his or her **purpose** for writing.

As you read, think about the author's purpose in each example.

Reading Strategies

- Plan and Monitor
- Ask Questions
- **Make Connections**
  Combine your knowledge and experiences with the author's ideas and information.
- Visualize
- Make Inferences
- Determine Importance
- Synthesize

Look Into the Text

FICTION

Imaginary characters

Once, the Moon and his friend the Sun chased each other in the sky. Then Sun needed to light up the day and could no longer play with the Moon.

> Purpose:
> to entertain

NONFICTION   Fact

By measuring the ages of lunar rocks, we know that the Moon is about 4.6 billion years old.

> Purpose:
> to inform

Look Into the Text

More than fifty years ago in the United States, the National Aeronautics and Space Administration (NASA) began planning the first exploration of space . . . . Today, astronauts from many different countries work together on the International Space Station (ISS).

Purpose:

Fact: More than fifty years ago, NASA began planning the first explorations of space.

Practice Together

Begin an Author's Purpose Chart In an Author's Purpose Chart you can list evidence about the author's purpose, such as facts or imaginary characters. This Author's Purpose Chart provides evidence that shows the author's purpose. Reread the passage above, and add to the Author's Purpose Chart. Use evidence to determine the author's purpose.

Academic Vocabulary

- **purpose** (**pur**-pus) *noun*
  A **purpose** is a reason for doing something.

Science Article and Journal

A science article is nonfiction that gives facts about the natural world. A journal expresses someone's observations and feelings about a topic.

An author writes a science article to inform you about a topic, so you will read a lot of facts. But a journal is written to express, so you will find out what an author was thinking or feeling during an experience.

Look Into the Text

On Earth we experience a force that pulls us to the ground. That force is called gravity. It is probably not something that you think about too much. Yet without gravity, we would all float away into the atmosphere.

> This author uses facts to inform.

"You fly everywhere. You don't walk. That is a lot of fun!"

> This writer describes his experience and feelings about it.

As you read the article and journal entries, think about how the facts and astronaut's feelings connect to what you already know and what you have read about life in space.

Earth (and) Space

by Julie Larson

"Our endeavors in space are so special and essential," says Peggy Whitson. She and other astronauts have compared firsthand the many differences between living on Earth and living in space.

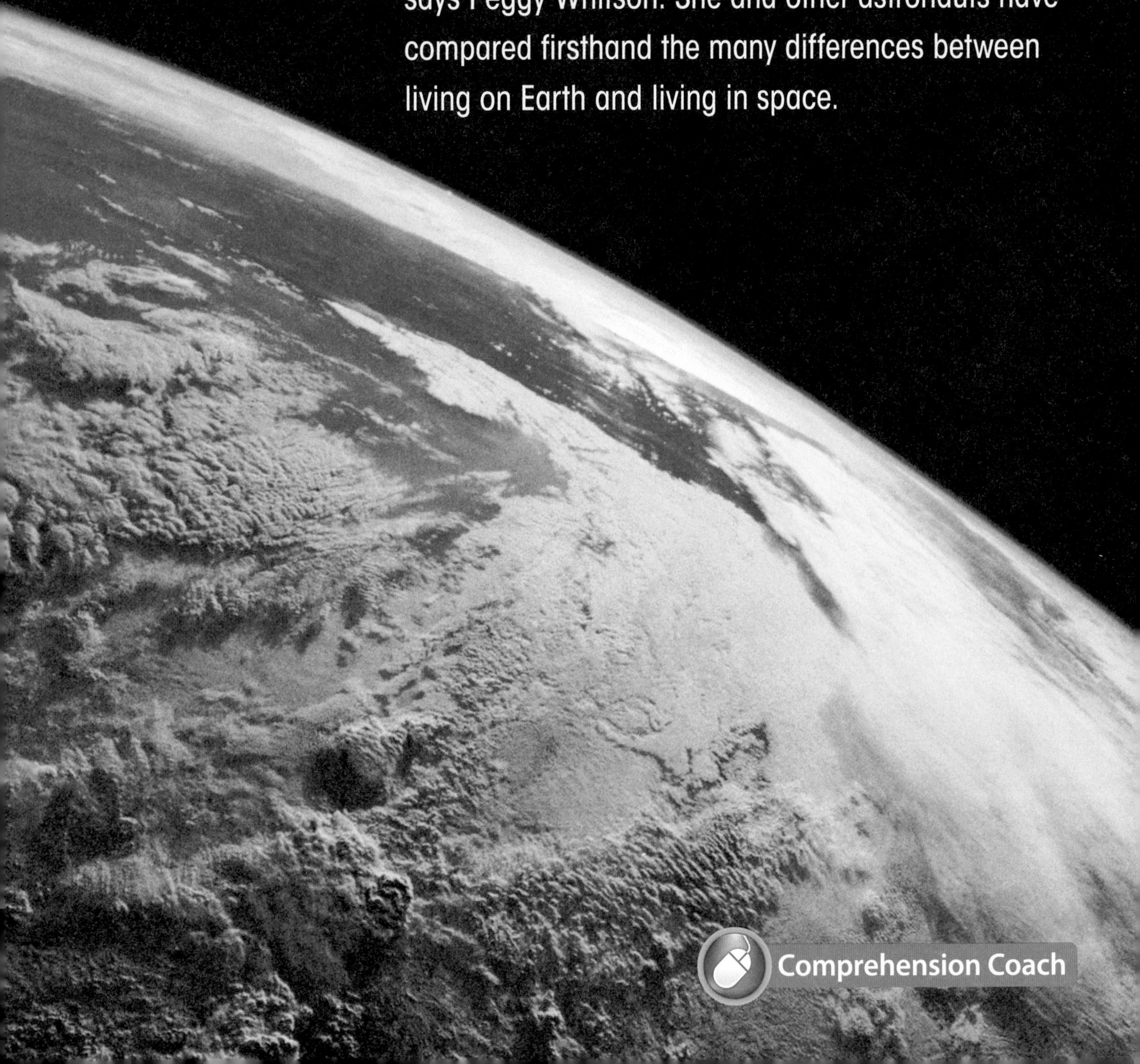

Comprehension Coach

From the beginning of time, humans have been asking questions about our **universe**. For centuries, scientists have wondered how Earth might compare to other planets. More than fifty years ago in the United States, the National Aeronautics and Space Administration (NASA) began planning the first explorations of space.

Today, **astronauts** from many different countries work together on the International Space Station (ISS). It is a huge research facility in space where astronauts work to improve life on Earth and learn about our solar system.

Life in space is very different from life on Earth. Many activities that we **take for granted** on Earth, including eating, sleeping, and even breathing, work differently in space. Some NASA astronauts have written journal entries for their families and friends back home about their life in space. These true **accounts** describe what astronauts **experience** in space.

Compare life in space and on Earth as you get facts and read journal entries from astronauts. You might even discover some **similarities**.

Key Vocabulary
universe *n.*, the world
astronaut *n.*, a person who travels to space
experience *v.*, to live through an event
similarity *n.*, way in which things are alike

On **Earth** and In **Space**

How Strong is the Gravity?

On Earth, we experience a force that pulls us to the ground. That force is called gravity. It is probably not something that you think about too much. Yet without gravity, we would all float away into the atmosphere. Everything from walking, riding a bike, driving a car, or sleeping in a bed is possible because of gravity. Our strong skeletons support our bodies against the pull of Earth's gravity.

In space, the force of gravity is so weak that a feeling of **weightlessness** results. Astronauts use the word *microgravity* to describe this lack of gravity in space. Here's how one NASA astronaut **recounts** the experience.

▶ From the Journal of **Ed Lu**

"You fly everywhere. You don't walk. *That* is a lot of fun! But we do spend a lot of time exercising since microgravity has eliminated the need for crew members to walk. Our muscles and bones would **atrophy** during a six month **tour of duty** because of lack of use. While I am doing all of this exercising, I enjoy listening to music from the space station's large CD collection."

Many different things happen to the human body while in space because of microgravity. Blood shifts from the lower body up to the top. Because of this, astronauts may appear to have **puffy** heads! Fortunately, their heads go back to normal size upon returning to Earth. Astronauts also get a little bit taller during long stays in space. The absence of gravity allows the spine to stretch slightly.

In Other Words

weightlessness weighing nothing
recounts tells about
atrophy lose all of their strength
tour of duty trip to space
puffy large and swollen

Historical Background

The National Aeronautics and Space Administration (NASA) is an organization funded by the United States government. **NASA's** mission is to research and explore space, and to apply this knowledge to improve life on Earth.

Look Into the Text

1. **Cause and Effect** Why do **astronauts** go to space?
2. **Details** What are three things that happen because of microgravity in space?

Where's the Oxygen?

On Earth, our environment is made up of the perfect mixture of **elements** to **sustain** life. Oxygen is one of the most important of those elements. When you take in a breath, what happens? You can feel air going into your body through your nose or mouth. You can't see it, but it's there in the air. We breathe because our bodies need oxygen in the air. Oxygen is like food for our blood. We need it to survive.

In space, there is no oxygen. Because of this, astronauts do not breathe the same as they do on Earth. They have to breathe with the help of a protective spacesuit that supplies them with oxygen. A human being would not survive on a spacewalk for more than a minute or two without a spacesuit.

Compared to getting dressed on Earth, which takes just a few minutes, putting on a spacesuit takes 45 minutes. The astronauts must then spend lots of time breathing only pure oxygen before going outside the space station. This **process** is called prebreathing.

Without a protective space suit, astronauts would not be able to survive on space stations. ▶

Key Vocabulary
element *n.,* something that is part of a whole
process *n.,* a series of actions that lead to a result

In Other Words
sustain support

On Earth as in space, people have oxygen in their blood. People also have another element in their blood called nitrogen. On Earth, nitrogen **takes up** 78 percent of the air we breathe. This gas is harmless when we breathe it on Earth.

In space, however, breathing nitrogen would cause air bubbles in the blood and be very painful. The pure oxygen that astronauts **take in** during prebreathing flushes all of the nitrogen out. Sunita Williams explains this process in her journal.

▶ From the Journal of **Sunita Williams**

"In order to go out the door of the ship safely, we go through a **pretty thorough process** called pre-breathe. In space, if you have nitrogen in your blood, it creates air bubbles. This can cause serious pain. To breathe safely in a spacesuit, there can only be oxygen in the blood. To do this, we spend time breathing in only pure oxygen. We can't get medical care to help us out. So, in this **line of work**, we need to try to eliminate this kind of pain caused by air bubbles in the blood."

In Other Words
takes up is in
take in breathe
pretty thorough process complete set of steps
line of work job

Look Into the Text

1. **Explain** Why is oxygen so important to humans on Earth and in space?

2. **Summarize** Why do **astronauts** go through the process of prebreathing?

What's the Food Like?

Whether in space or on Earth, food is necessary for life—it gives a person's body the nutrients needed to be strong and healthy. The difference between food on Earth and in space is the way it is stored and prepared.

On Earth, food is prepared to be delicious. Think of all of your favorite foods. On Earth we store our food in a freezer, refrigerator, or cupboard. Some foods, such as bowls of fresh fruit, can be set on the counter.

In space, foods are individually packaged for easy handling in microgravity. Most food is **precooked or processed**. It requires no refrigeration and is either ready to eat or can be prepared simply by adding water or by heating it. The only exceptions are the fresh fruit and vegetables **stowed** in the fresh food locker. Without refrigeration, many of these must be eaten within the first two days of the flight or they will **spoil**.

In his journal, astronaut Michael Lopez-Alegria explains more about food in space.

▶ From the Journal of **Michael Lopez-Alegria**

"The food aboard the International Space Station (ISS) is plentiful and tasty, considering the **obstacles in our paths**. We have no refrigerator, we go long periods of time without being able to refill our pantry, and everything we eat is by necessity pre-cooked.

Food comes in a variety of forms. Dehydrated food, or food that is dried out, is packaged in plastic containers or bags. The containers or bags are made so that we can easily add hot or cold water. Once you add the water, you shake up the container. Next thing you know, you have a plate of good food in front of you.

Another form is called thermo-stabilized. This just means that it is packed in a foil pouch. This type of food is like canned food you might find in any grocery store."

In Other Words

precooked or processed already cooked or does not need to be cooked
stowed kept
spoil be ruined
obstacles in our paths challenges

▲ A well-known chef created and packaged these meals for the astronauts. They are shown here next to the same meal freshly prepared to be eaten on Earth.

Science Background

Each meal prepared for space costs an average of $100, mostly due to packaging and testing. It can take six to eight months for food scientists in the lab to develop and test a new food item.

Look Into the Text

1. **Compare and Contrast** What is food like in space compared to on Earth?

2. **Inference** What do you think it is like to prepare a meal in space?

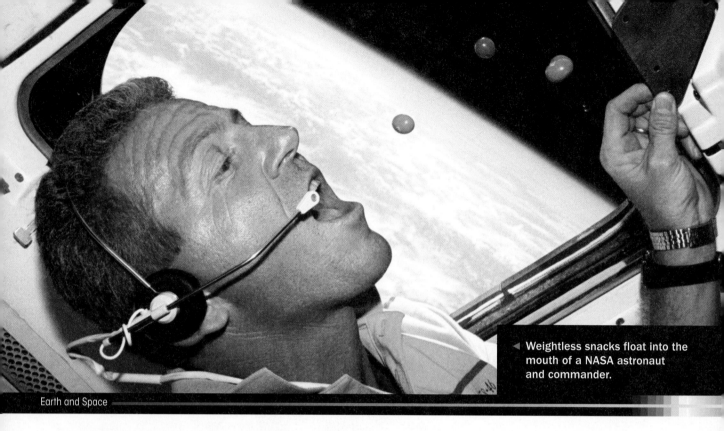

Earth and Space

When is Dinner?

Mealtimes on Earth are often special times. When families or friends gather together to share a meal, they are able to relax, have fun, and share stories about life. Your family might share a holiday dinner, or you might meet your friends in the school cafeteria for lunch. Meals are a great way to **connect** with each other. Here's what Michael Lopez-Alegria writes about mealtimes in space.

▶ From the Journal of **Michael Lopez-Alegria**

"We usually pause for about one hour midday to have our meal together and almost always have dinner together. Meals are our **primary** social time.

One truly **bright spot in** our menu is food that is sent up from our families or friends in **'bonus' containers or care** packages—it's just as you might see it in the store."

In Other Words
connect talk and have fun
primary biggest or main
bright spot in great part about
'bonus' containers or care special

There is one big difference between mealtimes in space and on Earth. On Earth, the plates stay on the table! Compare this to what Ed Lu writes about eating in microgravity.

▶ From the Journal of **Ed Lu**

"We don't have a real kitchen up here, but we do have a kitchen table. You might wonder what use a table is if you can't set anything down on it. But we have **bungee straps and Velcro** on the tabletop so you can keep your food containers, spoon, napkins, **etc.** from floating away."

▲ A family shares a meal on Earth.

▲ Astronauts share a meal on the International Space Station (ISS).

In Other Words

bungee straps and Velcro things to hold down the food
etc. etcetera, also

Look Into the Text

1. **Compare and Contrast** How are mealtimes on Earth and in Space **similar**? How are they different?
2. **Visualize** Describe what you think a typical meal in space would be like. Give details from the text to explain what you imagine.

Time to Sleep!

On Earth, we need to go to sleep every night to rest our bodies and gain energy for a new day. Getting **a good night's** sleep is **essential** to our health and **well being**. On Earth, most people sleep in a bed that is soft and comfortable.

In space, it is still necessary for astronauts to go to sleep every night in order to rest their bodies and stay healthy. Most astronauts even sleep about the same amount of time in space as they do on Earth. But because of microgravity, the way astronauts sleep is very different from the way we sleep on Earth.

There is nothing weighing down the astronauts' bodies in space because there is very little gravity. That's why astronauts have to strap themselves into special sleeping bags that hang from the wall! The sleeping bags have straps that press astronauts to a soft surface and to a pillow. Yet, most astronauts actually like to sleep floating in the air, with only a couple of straps to keep them from bouncing around the cabin. In addition to special sleeping bags, astronauts may need to wear blindfolds to protect them from the strong sunlight that **streams in** the windows during orbit in space.

In her journal, Joan Higginbotham explains how sleeping in space is different from sleeping at home on Earth.

▶ From the Journal of **Joan Higginbotham**

"Everyone thinks that it must be difficult to sleep in space because they imagine there to be a lot of noise. There is a lot of noise on the shuttle, but not so much that it makes it uncomfortable to sleep. You can hear the **fans whirling**—the cabin fans that actually help clean the air. I actually sleep without earplugs. Some of my crewmates did use earplugs. But it wasn't noisy enough that it disturbed their sleep."

Key Vocabulary
essential *adj.*, necessary for success or survival

In Other Words
a good night's enough
well being happiness
streams in comes through
fans whirling loud noise from the fans

On Earth, we sometimes sleep in sleeping bags—but they are always on the ground. ▶

In space, astronauts sleep in sleeping bags, too. The sleeping bags have to be strapped in and attached to the wall so they don't fly away! ▶

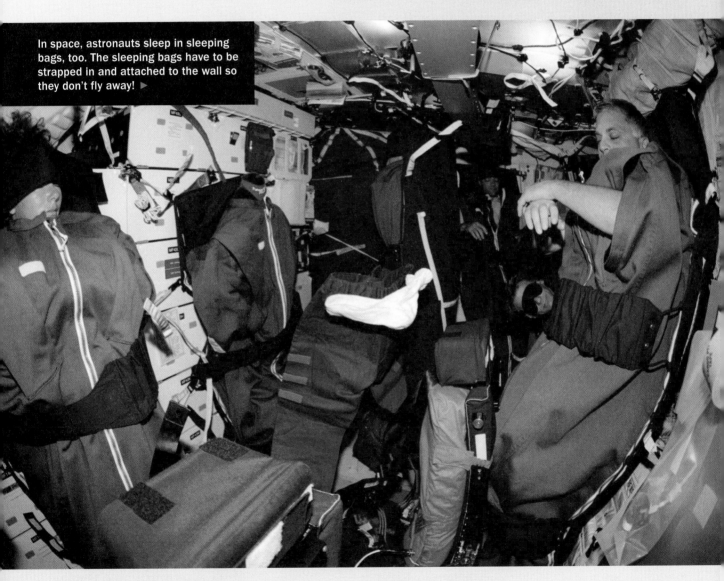

As you can see, astronauts move, breathe, sleep, and eat differently in space than they do on Earth. Astronauts are willing to trade the **routines** they are used to on Earth to travel in space because they have an important job. Astronauts are exploring an unknown world so **future generations** can benefit from what they learn. This special mission outweighs some of the dangers and difficulties astronauts experience in space.

No Place Like Home

Exploring the unknown world of space is an exciting adventure. **On the other hand**, most astronauts will tell you how excited they are to go home to Earth after their mission is over. Clayton Anderson explains.

▶ From the Journal of **Clayton Anderson**

"I am often asked just what it is I miss the most up here. **First and foremost**, of course, is my wonderful family. ... I also miss some significant physical things. ... For example, sometimes as I daydream I **envision** a soft breeze from Galveston Bay and the warm rays of the summer sun, or the smell of freshly cut grass amid the sound of all the neighborhood lawn mowers." ❖

Key Vocabulary
  routine *n.*, a normal process

In Other Words
  future generations people years
    from now
  On the other hand While
    astronauts enjoy being in space
  First and foremost Most
    important
  envision imagine

Look Into the Text

1. **Compare and Contrast** How is sleeping on Earth and in space different?

2. **Interpret** Why are astronauts willing to trade the comforts of home for the dangers of space?

Connect Reading and Writing

Vocabulary

Vocabulary
astronaut
element
essential
experience
process
routine
similarity
universe

CRITICAL THINKING

1. **SUM IT UP** Use your Author's Purpose Chart to gather evidence about the author's purpose throughout. Then use the chart to summarize the article and journal with a partner.

Purpose:
Fact: More than fifty years ago, NASA began planning the first explorations of space.

Author's Purpose Chart

2. **Compare** Compare the **astronauts'** journal entries. Why do you think the entry of Clayton Anderson is included?

3. **Conclusion** **Astronauts** may spend months on a space station. What traits are **essential** to live in space for that long? Review the photos and journal entries for ideas.

4. **Infer** Why is it valuable for **astronauts** to record what they **experience** in journal entries like those in the selection?

READING FLUENCY

Intonation Read the passage on page 634 to a partner. Assess your fluency.

1. My tone never/sometimes/always matched what I read.

2. What I did best in my reading was _____ .

READING STRATEGY

What strategy helped you understand this selection? Tell a partner about it.

VOCABULARY REVIEW

Oral Review Read the paragraph aloud. Add the vocabulary words.

Would you like to explore the _____ as an _____ ? To _____ life in space, it is _____ that you follow a new daily _____ . It may have some _____ to your daily schedule on Earth. However, the _____ by which you eat, sleep, or even breathe, is quite different. For example, you need special equipment to breathe because oxygen, an important _____ of air, is not found in space.

Written Review Imagine you can travel anywhere in the **universe** . Describe what you **experience** . Use four vocabulary words.

WRITE ABOUT THE **GUIDING QUESTION**

Explore Being at Home in the World
Astronauts practice space tasks in an underwater lab. How are the features of living in space **similar** to being in water? Reread the selection to find examples that support your ideas.

Connect Across the Curriculum

Understand Jargon and Specialized Language

Academic Vocabulary
- **unique** (yü-nēk) *adjective*
  Something that is **unique** is different or special.

Language that is **unique** to certain fields of work is called **jargon**. It may not appear in everyday language. Use context to figure out its meaning.

> In space, the force of gravity is so weak that a feeling of weightlessness results. Astronauts use the word *microgravity* to describe this lack of gravity in space.

The context shows that *microgravity* is what astronauts feel in space.

Use Context Clues Discuss the meanings of the underlined jargon.

1. Astronauts must breathe only pure oxygen before going outside. This is called <u>prebreathing</u>.

2. <u>Dehydrated</u> food, or food that is dried out, is packaged in bags.

Choose Media Support

MEDIA & TECHNOLOGY

Academic Vocabulary
- **relate** (ri-lāt) *verb*
  When you **relate** things, you show how they are connected.

How do you select the appropriate media for a presentation? It depends on the purpose and the audience.

1 Learn About Media What is the purpose of your presentation? If it's to inform, you may want to use print media. If it's to entertain, nonprint media may add interest. Be sure your media choices are:

- **Accurate and Reliable** Check the source. Always check facts against a second source, such as an encyclopedia.
- **Appropriate** Use only media that **relate** to the topic.
- **Credited** Identify each reference. For music, identify the composer and performer. For an Internet image, provide the Web site address.

2 Choose Media What media would support a presentation about what it's like to live in space? Share and explain your choices to the class.

Define and Explain

Role-Play With a group, act out a classroom visit by astronauts from the International Space Station. Some of you ask questions. The astronauts answer by defining and explaining their experiences in space. Use pronouns in the subjects and predicates of your sentences as you add details to your questions and answers. Trade roles.

> Does noise on the space shuttle keep you awake?

> Before bed, I put earplugs in my ears. They really help muffle the sound.

Write About an Adventure

Study the Models When you add descriptive details and examples to your sentences, you want to avoid confusing your reader. Be sure to use the correct forms of pronouns to make your writing clear and easy to understand.

NOT OK

Nicole and me remember that there is no gravity in space. Things will float around without them. Nicole hands I the straps. I and she attach the sleeping bags to a wall. That way them won't float. Then she get in.

> The writer confuses the reader by using pronouns incorrectly.

OK

Nicole and I remember that there is no gravity in space. **People and objects** will float around **the cabin** without it. **Before going to bed** , Nicole hands me **some wide straps** . She and I **use the straps** to attach the sleeping bags to a wall. That way they won't float **around the cabin** . Then we **crawl into our bags for a good night's sleep** .

> This writing makes much more sense.

✎ **WRITE ON YOUR OWN** Write about your own adventure. Use descriptive words and phrases to add plenty of details. Be sure to use pronouns correctly.

REMEMBER
• Subject pronouns include: **I, you, he, she, it, we, you, they**
• Object pronouns include: **me, you, him, her, it, us, you, them**

Indian Summer Sun
by Carmen T. Bernier-Grand

Juanita IV, 2004. Lou Wall. Oil on canvas.

Build Background

At Home in the World

"Indian Summer Sun" is about a girl from Puerto Rico who moves to Connecticut. Connecticut is in the northeastern United States near the Atlantic Ocean. Puerto Rico is southeast of the United States near the Caribbean Ocean.

Connect

Quickwrite Have you or someone you know ever moved to a new place? What makes a new place feel like home? Do a Quickwrite of your ideas.

Digital Library

myNGconnect.com
◐ View the images.

▲ There are many places people call home.

Language & Grammar

1 TRY OUT LANGUAGE
3 APPLY ON YOUR OWN

Clarify and Verify

Listen to a conversation between two students. How does the boy make sure he understands what was said? Role-play the conversation.

PICTURE PROMPT

Home Sweet Home

Language & Grammar **285**

Use Verbs in the Active and Passive Voice

The voice of a verb depends on the subject in a sentence.

- In the **active voice**, the subject does, or performs, the action expressed by the verb. The subject is the doer.

  EXAMPLE   The sun **heats** the Earth.

- In the **passive voice**, the subject does not perform the action. The subject is the receiver. The performer then comes after the verb or is omitted. These sentences in the passive voice use a form of **be** (am, is, are, was, were) and the **past participle** of a verb.

  EXAMPLE   The Earth **is warmed** by the sun.
  A heat warning **was given**.

Verb	Past	Past Participle
heat	heated	heated
give	gave	given
warm	warmed	warmed

- Use the active voice to emphasize the subject. Use the passive voice to emphasize the receiver of the action or the action itself.

Practice Together STRUCTURED

Say each sentence with your class. Then change the sentence to the active voice and say it again.

1. The power of the sun was studied by scientists.
2. Earth is given heat by the sun.
3. The planets are affected by its heat, too.
4. The sun's energy is created by exploding gases.

Try It! GUIDED

Say each sentence. Then write who or what performs the action on a card. Use the new subject on the card to say the sentence in the active voice.

5. Long ago, a group of stars was formed by gases and dust.
6. It was called the solar system by scientists.
7. Its center is occupied by the sun.
8. The sun is surrounded by the planets.

▲ The solar system includes the sun and the planets.

Follow the Rules

CLARIFY AND VERIFY

What school or classroom rules are important for new students to know?

With a small group of students, role-play explaining and clarifying a classroom or school rule to a new student. Tell how you could clarify or verify the information.

First, think of some rules and questions about them that a new student might ask. Make a chart like this one.

Classroom/School Rule	Questions the New Student Might Ask
Do not interrupt others while they are speaking.	Could you tell me what "interrupt" means?
	Could you repeat that, please?

Take turns role-playing the new student and the informed student. As the new student, clarify and verify new ideas and information. As the veteran student, clarify and verify the rule.

HOW TO CLARIFY AND VERIFY

1. To get clarification, ask a question about what is unclear.
2. To clarify, restate using new words. Define confusing words. Give examples or compare to something else.
3. To verify, ask for repetition, restate what you heard, or check a trusted source.

> Could you tell me what "interrupt" means?

> When you interrupt, you stop someone from talking. It is considered rude. This rule is posted on the bulletin board in our classroom.

USE VERBS IN THE ACTIVE AND PASSIVE VOICE

When you clarify and verify information, you may need to ask questions or restate information in a way that makes the meaning clear. Use sentences in the active voice to be direct and get to the point quickly. Or use the passive voice to emphasize the receiver of the action.

Active Voice: The hall monitors **give** directions to the classrooms.

Passive Voice: Directions to the classrooms **are given** by the hall monitors.

Prepare to Read

Learn Key Vocabulary

Study the Words Use the steps below.

1. Pronounce the word. Say it aloud several times. Spell it.
2. Rate your word knowledge.
3. Study the example. Tell more about the word.
4. Practice it. Make the word your own.

Rating Scale

1 = I have never seen this word before.

2 = I am not sure of the word's meaning.

3 = I know this word and can teach the word's meaning to someone else.

Key Words

adjustment (u-**just**-ment)
noun ▶ page 292

An **adjustment** is the way you go along with, or get used to a change. It takes a while to make an **adjustment** to moving to a new home.
Related Word: **adjust**

concentrate (**kon**-sen-trāt)
verb ▶ page 296

To **concentrate** means to focus on something. Students have to **concentrate** when studying.
Related Word: **concentration**

couple (**kup**-ul) *noun*
▶ page 293

A **couple** is two people who are together. My grandparents are a happy **couple**.
Synonym: **pair**
Antonym: **single**

ignore (ig-**nor**) *verb*
▶ page 292

To **ignore** means to pay no attention to something. It is best to **ignore** people who are bullies.

opportunity
(op-ur-**tü**-ni-tē) *noun* ▶ page 293

An **opportunity** is a chance to do something. My teacher gave me the **opportunity** to tell my ideas to the other students.

perspective (pur-**spek**-tiv)
noun ▶ page 294

A **perspective** is a way of thinking about something. My teacher's **perspective** on music is that everyone should learn to play.

refuse (ri-**fūz**) *verb*
▶ page 296

To **refuse** means to choose not to do something. The child **refused** to eat any more food.
Antonyms: **agree, obey**

remind (ri-**mīnd**) *verb*
▶ page 294

To **remind** is to help someone remember something or tell them again. As I left for school, my mom **reminded** me to take my lunch.

Practice the Words Make a Definition Map for each Key Word. Then compare your maps with a partner.

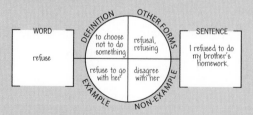

Definition Map

Compare Structures of Texts

How is a Story Structured? Authors of short stories use plot, characters, dialogue, setting, and events to structure their texts.

How is Poetry Structured? Poems often use rhythm to express ideas or emotions. Some poems repeat words and phrases or use similar words for effect. Sometimes poets choose a cadence structure, or a certain number of syllables in each line.

As you read, find examples of how the poetry and short story structures help you understand the theme of how people feel in new places.

Reading Strategies
- Plan and Monitor
- Ask Questions
- **Make Connections**
  Combine your knowledge and experiences with the author's ideas and information.
- Visualize
- Make Inferences
- Determine Importance
- Synthesize

Look Into the Text

Story

Even my friends in Puerto Rico had laughed at my accent and teased me when I spoke English.

There was no way I was going to join Jerry and Kathy and all those other algebra students because they would laugh at my accent, too.

The actions of the Puerto Rican friends help me understand why the narrator is afraid to join Jerry and Kathy.

Poem

I've lost

a land that felt mine

flamboyanes, canarias

going to the bank con papi

learning to cook like mami

The cadence of the last two words in the last two lines help me understand how the poet feels about papi and mami.

Practice Together

Begin a Comparison Chart A Comparison Chart can help you keep track of examples of text structures in the poem and short story. This Comparison Chart shows one element of the text structure of the story. Reread the second passage above and add to the chart.

Genre	Text Structure
Short Story	Characters: laugh at the narrator's accent
Poetry	

Short Story and Poem

A short story is a brief, fictional narrative with characters, a setting, dialogue, and a plot. Poems can take many forms. They often use rhythm, repetition, and cadence to express ideas or emotions.

Short stories and poems are structured differently, but they can express similar ideas. When you know the characteristics of each type of writing and their structures, you'll better understand the writer's message.

Look Into the Text

When I went to the Latino table, Sergio was talking about salsa.

"I bet you're a good dancer," he said.

"I'm not," I answered. "I don't even know how to dance."

"You're Puerto Rican and you don't know how to dance!" That was Norma.

"Exactly," I said . . .

> In the short story, dialogue between characters helps show that being Puerto Rican will be an important part of the story.

My life
almost evenly divided
17 1/2 years Puertorican
20 1/2 years New Yorker

> In the poem, rhythm, repetition, and cadence show the author's feelings about being Puerto Rican.

Making connections between the ideas in a short story and a poem, and to your own life, will help you get the most from your reading.

Indian Summer Sun

by Carmen T. Bernier-Grand

Juanita IV, 2004, Lou Wall. Oil on canvas.

▲ Critical Viewing: Effect What do you notice about the details in this painting? What mood or feeling does this create?

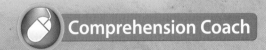

Comprehension Coach

___

The morning wind felt like a sharp knife on my legs, like it was **carving** me. How could it be so cold when the sun was shining?

Would I get used to this and would I ever get to like Connecticut? I doubted it, but here I was, on my first day in an American high school and I had to **make the best of it**.

I went from class to class trying to be **ignored**. I was mostly successful, except for algebra. In that class, I sat in the second row, and, without thinking, rested my feet on the metal basket of the desk in front of me.

This cute guy (Jerry, the teacher later called him) moved the front desk forward and my feet suddenly dropped.

"Oh, I'm sorry," he said and pushed the desk back so I could comfortably rest my feet on the basket again.

The thank-you didn't come out of my mouth and I wondered what he thought of me.

Lunchtime came after algebra class and I sat all by myself at a cafeteria table, looking out the window. Glass windows! This surprised me because there was no glass in the windows in my school in Puerto Rico.

The Connecticut trees were **dressed-up**, as if they were going to the carnival. There were yellow, orange, purple, red, and bright, bright leaves.

I noticed, however, that there were no palm trees anywhere.

I'd made a mistake. Actually, I'd made a huge mistake! I'd left Puerto Rico and my

© Katherine Arion

⚠ **Critical Viewing: Plot** How do the shapes in this image relate to what the narrator describes?

___

Key Vocabulary
adjustment *n.*, a change in situation
ignore *v.*, to give little or no attention to

In Other Words
carving cutting
make the best of it try to like it
dressed-up colorful

father to live with my mother. I missed him but I'd missed her just as much. This was my chance to be with her and it also was an **opportunity** to learn to speak English better. The problem was that all I wanted now was to get out of here.

A group of students I'd seen in algebra came by my table, food trays in hand. "Please, God," I thought in Spanish, "don't let them sit by me."

They sat three tables ahead.

I knew English. My mother is American and she always spoke to me in English. She knew Spanish, but even when she was married to my father and we lived together in Puerto Rico, she'd spoken to me in English. Although I knew English, I always answered in Spanish.

Jerry came in and whispered something to a blonde girl the algebra teacher had called Kathy. I thought that she was probably his girlfriend. They seemed like the perfect **couple** to me and they even looked alike.

Kathy must have noticed my staring because she waved and said, "Come, sit with us."

I looked out the window, pretending I hadn't heard her.

Even my friends in Puerto Rico had laughed at my accent and teased me when I spoke English.

There was no way I was going to join Jerry and Kathy and all those other algebra students because they would laugh at my accent, too.

The guy behind me was wearing earphones, his music was so loud that I could hear it. I recognized that rhythm. Salsa!

Two girls joined him. "Sergio!" one said, *"Baja esa música."*

He obeyed and after turning the music down, he turned it off and took off his earphones.

"¿Hablan español?" This was a stupid question because I'd heard them speaking in Spanish.

"Sí. ¿Y tú?" the other girl asked.

I nodded.

"Pues, siéntate con nosotros," said the girl, her eyes so dark I couldn't even see her pupils.

I sat with them.

Norma was from Cuba, Sergio from the Dominican Republic; Minerva with those beautiful dark eyes was from Mexico. They were not new to the school, but they hung out together. I felt like I had friends! I began to think that I was going to like it here.

Key Vocabulary
  opportunity *n.*, a good chance
  couple *n.*, two people together, a pair

In Other Words (all in Spanish)
Baja esa música Lower the volume of the music
¿Hablan español? Do you all speak Spanish?
Sí. ¿Y tú? Yes, and you?
Pues, siéntate con nosotros Well, sit with us

Look Into the Text

1. **Explain** Why does the narrator experience an **adjustment**?
2. **Contrast** What are some differences between the narrator's experience in Puerto Rico and her experience in Connecticut?
3. **Cause and Effect** Why doesn't the narrator want to sit with the algebra students?

That evening at dinner, when I told my mother about my day, she said, "Cristina, I thought you came to learn English."

The spaghetti I'd rolled around the fork fell off and I didn't want to talk about my English.

"*Vine para estar contigo*," I **reminded** her.

"It is nice that you came to be with me," my mother said. "I love having you here but you also came to **become fluent** in English, or at least that's what you told me before you came. Have you changed your mind?"

I shook my head.

My mother continued. "I'm glad you found somebody to talk to but don't talk just to people who speak Spanish. If that girl from algebra class invites you again, you should join her!"

"*Se van a reír de mi inglés.*"

"So what if they laugh at your English? If I'd worried about Puerto Ricans laughing at my Spanish, would I have learned the language?"

This was easy for her to say. Everybody thought she sounded cute when speaking Spanish but she didn't have to go to a high school where students might have teased her.

The next morning, I prepared myself for the cold. I put on three pairs of socks so that my shoes hardly fit with so many socks. I put on my heavy coat, hat, gloves, and scarf and headed to school. The sun had fooled me the day before, but it wouldn't fool me again.

I was almost at the school entrance when I heard a girl behind me saying, "Johnny, isn't it hot today?"

She and the guy she was with walked by me. He turned and fanned himself. "It sure is," he said.

He was wearing short pants and she had on a short skirt. Other students were wearing tank tops and sandals. I guess I was the only one who was cold.

I went in, opened my locker and threw in my hat, scarf, and gloves and with tears in my eyes, I told Minerva what had happened.

"This is what we call Indian Summer," she explained in Spanish. "It lasts a week or two and then it gets really cold."

Key Vocabulary

perspective *n.*, a way of thinking about something

remind *v.*, to tell someone something again

In Other Words

Vine para estar contigo I came here to be with you (in Spanish)

become fluent learn to speak more

Se van a reír de mi inglés. They are going to laugh at my English. (in Spanish)

Science Background

Indian summer is a brief period of warm, dry weather that occurs late in the season of fall, or autumn. Indian summer is a temporary and warm break from colder temperatures.

Muchacha en la Ventana (Girl in the Window), 2000, Graciela Genoves. Oil on canvas, Zurbaran Gallery, Buenos Aires, Argentina.

▲ Critical Viewing: Character How would you describe the girl's mood in this painting? How might she be similar to Cristina?

You mean it gets really cold? Even colder than this? **No way!**

Everything went wrong that day. The English teacher asked me to read aloud, and I refused . I'd probably flunk the class if I continued doing this.

In algebra Jerry moved his desk toward me so I could rest my feet on the metal basket. That was pretty neat but then I caught Kathy staring at my feet because my socks were **bulging** out of my shoes. How embarrassing!

And then the algebra teacher called on me. "Cristina, could you, please, come up and solve this problem?"

All eyes were on me, but I walked to the board and tried to concentrate on the problem.

$(3x + 5) (2x + 7)$

I remembered what the teacher had said the day before, the word FOIL would help solve this problem.

F for first. Multiply the first two terms.

$(3x) (2x) = 6x^2$

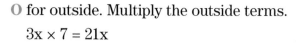

Everything went wrong that day.

O for outside. Multiply the outside terms.

$3x \times 7 = 21x$

I for inside. Multiply the inside terms.

$5 \times 2x = 10x$

L for last. Multiply the last terms.

$5 \times 7 = 35$

So, I came up with: $6x^2 + 21x + 10x + 35$

I almost sat down, but the teacher stopped me. "Wait a minute, Cristina. You need to finish it."

I looked back at the board, and saw what she meant. I needed to add the **common terms** to finish the problem.

$6x^2 + 31x + 35$

"Perfect," the teacher said.

That should have made me feel good, but when I was walking back to my desk, I overheard Jerry whispering to Kathy, "I told you! She understands English."

Kathy didn't answer and instead, she stared at my socks.

When the bell rang, I packed my books in a hurry to go to the bathroom and take off at least one pair of socks.

Key Vocabulary

refuse *v.*, to choose not to do something

concentrate *v.*, to focus on something

In Other Words

No way! I can't believe it!

bulging coming

All eyes were on me Everyone was looking at me

common terms numbers that were similar

Language Background

An acronym (ak-ruh-nim), like **FOIL**, is a word formed from the first letter of each word in a phrase. Acronyms can be helpful in remembering long rules and names.

On my way out, Kathy stopped me and I was sure she'd tell me about my socks—as if I didn't know. But that is not what she did.

Instead, she said, "Tomorrow is a **half-day**. After class a bunch of us are going to my house to eat lunch and party." She paused and looked straight to my eyes. "Do you understand what I'm saying?"

Of course, I did!

I just nodded to show that I understood.

"I hope you can come," she said.

I knew the answer. No, thank you. I just smiled and ran to the bathroom where I took off all of my socks, thinking that I'd rather be cold than look **like an alien**.

Lunch break wasn't much fun either.

When I went to the Latino table, Sergio was talking about salsa.

"I bet you're a good dancer," he said.

"I'm not," I answered. "I don't even know how to dance."

"You're Puerto Rican and you don't know how to dance!" That was Norma.

"Exactly," I said, louder than I had to, because I was feeling as if I didn't **fit in** with this group either.

If I only dared to go to Kathy's party—but what would I do there, just sit and watch? If only she would invite my Latino friends, but they were not in my algebra class.

▲ Critical Viewing: Character How does the girl in this image represent Cristina?

In Other Words
half-day school day that ends early
like an alien different from everyone else
fit in belong

Look Into the Text

1. **Character's Point of View** How is Cristina feeling? Why?
2. **Perspectives** Why does Cristina's mom **remind** her to make friends with people who speak English?
3. **Visualize** How do you imagine that Cristina is dressed in comparison to the other students?

It was an accident, a pure accident. The next day I stood by the door after algebra class, and couldn't go through, too many students in my way and of course, I didn't dare say "Excuse me."

Then I felt a hand on my shoulder. "Cristina, good!" It was Kathy. "Jeremy asked me to make sure you were coming."

Jeremy? Who was that?

Soon I **found myself** walking to Kathy's house with the rest of the class because I just wasn't brave enough to say that I wasn't going to the party.

Mistake, mistake, or so I thought during the first few minutes at Kathy's party. We'd come in and gone straight to the finished basement of the house where there was an entertainment room. I guessed it was an entertainment room because it had a big screen TV and a CD player with speakers almost as tall as I was. I sat on a black leather **recliner** that a guy had moved to a corner so they could have space to dance.

Kathy came down with chips and salsa, put them on the table in front of me and began to dance with the guy who had moved the recliner. How would Jerry feel about this and where was he, anyway?

Everybody joined Kathy, dancing.

Nobody asked me to dance, thank God and nobody made me speak, thank God.

State of My Heart, 2005, Elizabeth Rosen. Mixed media collage, collection of the artist, courtesy of Morgan Gaynin, New York.

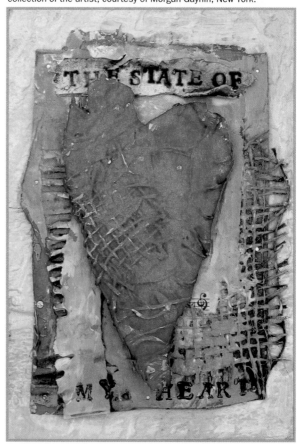

△ **Critical Viewing: Plot** What connection can you make between this image and the story?

In Other Words
found myself was
Mistake, mistake It was not a good idea to go to the party
recliner chair

I felt stupid but then, Jerry came down. He looked like he had just taken a shower. I could tell because his hair was wet. He had on a blue shirt with its long sleeves rolled up to his elbows and he came directly to me and sat by me.

"Hi," he said.

I smiled. "Jerry?" It came out as Yerry, but it was too late to **take it back**.

"My parents and my sister," his chin pointed to Kathy, "call me Jeremy, my real name, but almost everybody else calls me Jerry. You can call me whatever is easier for you."

Jeremy! Kathy's brother— not her boyfriend.

"Why are you always so quiet?" he asked.

"*¿Hablas español?*"

He made a 0 with his fingers. "Zero."

"I have an accent." **That came out** without warning.

"What are you talking about?" he said, almost yelling because the music was loud. "It's cute!"

Why are you always so quiet?

I turned and pretended to be interested in the dancers but all I could feel were his eyes on me. His eyes felt warm and they were full of hazel light as he looked at me. His glance was so powerful that it made my whole inside smile.

"Do you dance?" he asked.

Did a piano fall on me? Not only did I feel weight on my back, but his words **sounded like scratchy music to my ears**.

Why did he have to ask me that?

I had to say the truth, so I shook my head no.

He wiped his forehead with his fingers, and then sighed. "I don't either."

I put my hand on my heart and sighed, too.

We both laughed.

As if we were too shy to look at each other, we turned to watch the dancers.

But a few seconds later, he said, "This music is too loud to talk. Would you like to take a walk?"

In Other Words
take it back change what I had said
That came out I said that
sounded like scratchy music to my ears did not sound good

Spring Thaw, 2005, Elizabeth Rosen. Acrylic on canvas, private collection, courtesy of Morgan Gaynin, New York.

▲ Critical Viewing: Effect How does the mood of the painting compare to Cristina's feelings at the end of the story?

I nodded and stood up.

He held my upper arm and guided me out.

We could still hear the music, but near us the only sound was that of our feet **crunching** leaves.

Was he waiting for me to speak? I had to say something—but what?

A **grove of dark green pines** was before us.

"*¿Cambian de color?*" I thought I could ask but how would it sound?

I practiced it in my head. *Do dose trees . . .* those, *Cristina, like the z in Spanish.*

"Do those trees change color?" I pointed with my chin at the pines.

"No, they're evergreens."

"Like palm trees," I said.

"Do you miss Puerto Rico?" he asked.

"A little," I caught myself saying.

It was then I realized I wasn't cold. And I wasn't wearing a coat. ❖

About the Author

Carmen T. Bernier-Grand

Carmen T. Bernier-Grand (1947–) is the author of many books for young adults. Bernier-Grand writes most of her books in English, her second language. She grew up in Puerto Rico speaking Spanish. Bernier-Grand says that she "thinks, writes, and dreams" in both languages. Her experience of living in different places plays an important part in the creativity of her writing. Today, Bernier-Grand lives in Portland, Oregon.

In Other Words
crunching walking on the
grove of dark green pines group of trees
¿Cambian de color? Do the trees change color? (in Spanish)

Look Into the Text

1. **Confirm Prediction** Was your prediction right? What happened that you didn't expect?
2. **Paraphrase** In your own words, explain what Cristina means when she says, "I realized I wasn't cold."

Almost Evenly Divided
by Emma Suárez-Báez

My life

almost evenly divided

17½ years Puertorican

20½ years New Yorker

5   I've lost

a land that felt mine

flamboyanes, canarias

going to the bank con papi

learning to cook like mami

10 las parrandas

the sun that warms up the chickens

el campo en Lajas

mi prima Adira

la vida lenta

15 ser mujer puertorriqueña

ser mujer puertorriqueña

Almost evenly divided

but half lost

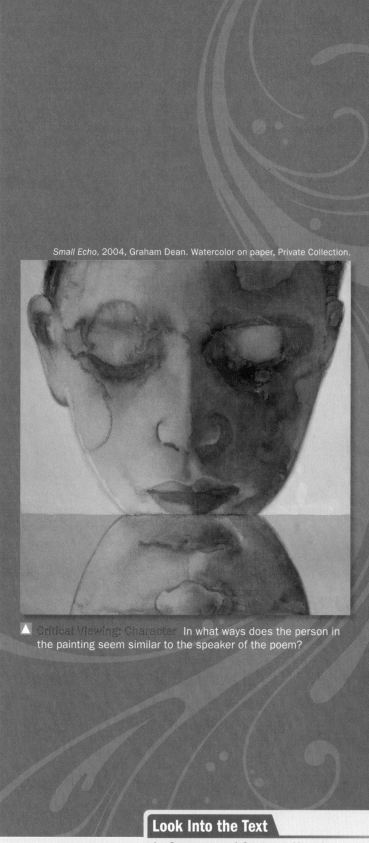

Small Echo, 2004, Graham Dean. Watercolor on paper, Private Collection.

▲ Critical Viewing: Character In what ways does the person in the painting seem similar to the speaker of the poem?

In Other Words (all in Spanish)

flamboyanes, canarias trees and canary birds
con papi with daddy
mami mommy
las parrandas the street celebrations

el campo en Lajas the countryside around Lajas in Puerto Rico
mi prima my cousin
la vida lenta the slow life
ser mujer puertorriqueña being a Puerto Rican woman

Look Into the Text

1. **Compare and Contrast** How does Cristina's experience in "Indian Summer Sun" compare to the experience of the speaker of this poem?

2. **Paraphrase** In your own words, explain what the speaker in the poem means when she says her life is "almost evenly divided".

Connect Reading and Writing

Vocabulary
adjustment
concentrate
couple
ignore
opportunity
perspective
refuse
remind

CRITICAL THINKING

1. **SUM IT UP** Use your Comparison Chart to summarize "Indian Summer Sun" and "Almost Evenly Divided." Discuss how each uses different text structures to show the same theme.

Genre	Text Structure
Short Story "Indian Summer Sun"	Characters: laugh at the narrator's accent
Poetry	

Comparison Chart

2. **Analyze** What is the turning point of the story? Explain how Cristina's **perspective** on her new home changes as a result.

3. **Speculate** What might have happened if Cristina had **refused** to go to the party? Base your answer on events in the story.

4. **Interpret** How are the **perspectives** of the poem and the short story similar and different?

READING FLUENCY

Expression Read the passage on page 635 to a partner. Assess your fluency.

1. My voice never/sometimes/always matched what I read.

READING STRATEGY

What strategy helped you understand this selection? Tell a partner about it.

VOCABULARY REVIEW

Oral Review Read the paragraph aloud. Add the vocabulary words.

Moving to a new place can be a big _____ . You can't simply _____ to change, but you can still be you. Open your mind to the _____ that this is a great _____ to be at home in a new location. _____ on what is positive about the experience and _____ the rest. If you feel alone and everyone seems to be a _____ or in a group, don't worry. _____ yourself that you will soon make new friends.

Written Review Imagine you are Cristina's father. Write a letter to **remind** her how she can make a positive **adjustment** to her new home. Use five vocabulary words.

WRITE ABOUT THE (GUIDING QUESTION)

Explore Being At Home in the World

Choose a character from the story. How did he or she affect Cristina's **adjustment** to her new location? How does this remind you of a situation in your own life? Give examples from the text and your own experience.

Connect Across the Curriculum

Understand Denotation and Connotation

> **Academic Vocabulary**
> • **connotation** (con-ō-tā-shun) *noun*
>   The **connotation** of a word is the set of feelings that is associated with it.

Denotation is the exact dictionary meaning of a word. **Connotation** involves the feelings associated with a word. **Connotations** of words may be positive, negative, or neutral. We usually admire someone who is *determined*. This word has a positive **connotation**. We are less likely to admire someone who is *stubborn*, a word with a negative **connotation**. The synonym *persistent* is neutral in feeling.

Identify Connotation Decide which underlined words have positive, negative, and neutral **connotations**. Use a dictionary to check your ideas.

1. The new student was <u>intelligent</u> and could solve math problems easily.

2. The new student was <u>brilliant</u> and won the school math competition.

3. That car was on sale, so it was <u>inexpensive</u>.

4. The <u>cheap</u> car lost its hubcap after we bought it.

Perform a Poem

> **Academic Vocabulary**
> • **effect** (i-fekt) *noun*
>   An **effect** is the result or an action or cause.

Two elements that make up the rhythm of poetry are **repetition** and **cadence**. **Repetition** refers to repeated words, lines, phrases, and other patterns in writing. **Cadence** refers to the flow of language. It is a mixture of speed, rhythm, and the rise and fall of voice.

1 **Read the Poem** The poem "Almost Evenly Divided" repeats a pattern in lines 3 and 4, using different numbers. What **effect** does the repetition have? What other repetitions can you find? What do you notice about the poem's cadence and rhythm?

2 **Perform the Poem** Present the poem to a partner. Recite the poem in a way that will keep your audience interested. Make eye contact and look at your partner as you speak. Then listen to your partner's performance.

3 **Discuss the Performance** Talk with your partner about your performances. What performance choices did you make? Did your performances add to the poem's meaning? How?

Clarify and Verify

Pair Talk With a partner, talk about things Cristina may have missed after she went to live with her mother. Clarify your ideas by explaining them or comparing them to something else. Verify your ideas with examples from the story. Use sentences in the active voice to emphasize who or what performs the action. Use the passive voice to emphasize the receiver of the action or the action itself.

> Cristina missed palm trees.

> She mentioned them to Jerry when she asked about evergreens.

Write About Fitting In

Study the Models When you write, you want to use a consistent voice so your readers don't get confused. If you use the active voice, for example, change any sentences in the passive voice to the active voice.

NOT OK

> The students at my new school are friendly and helpful. In the lunchroom, Kathy and Jerry are talking and are seen by me. They are interrupted by my entrance, but they wave at me anyway. Then Sergio comes in and is asked by me to sit with him. We are given the same English class by the school. He likes to hear about my old school in Puerto Rico.

> The writer confuses the reader by mixing the active and passive voice in her sentences.

OK

> The students at my new school are friendly and helpful. When I see Kathy and Jerry talking in the lunchroom, they stop and wave at me. Then Sergio comes in and asks me to sit with him. We take the same English class. He likes to hear about my old school in Puerto Rico.

> The writer keeps her sentences in the active voice so the ideas are clear.

Add Sentences Write two more sentences to add to the OK model that add detail and explain more of the events.

WRITE ON YOUR OWN Write about a situation when a friend did not feel comfortable. Tell how that person felt and what happened. Be sure to use correct words in your sentences.

REMEMBER

Keep the voice in your sentences consistent.
- Use the active voice to emphasize who or what performs the action.
- Use the passive voice to emphasize the receiver of the action.

From
So You're Going to MARS

by Arthur C. Clarke

1   So you're going to Mars? That's still quite an adventure—though I suppose that in another ten years no one will think twice about it. Sometimes it's hard to remember that the first ships reached Mars scarcely more than half a century ago and that our colony on the planet is less than thirty years old. (By the way, don't use that word when you get there. Base, settlement, or whatever you like—but not colony, unless you want to hear the ice tinkling all around you.)

2   I suppose you've read all the forms and tourist literature they gave you at the Department of Extraterrestrial Affairs. But there's a lot you won't learn just by reading, so here are some pointers and background information that may make your trip more enjoyable. I won't say it's right up to date—things change so rapidly, and it's a year since I got back from Mars myself but on the whole you'll find it pretty reliable. …

3   If you haven't booked your passage yet, remember that the cost of the ticket varies considerably according to the relative positions of Mars and Earth. That's a complication we don't have to worry about when we're travelling from country to country on our own globe, but Mars can be six times farther away at one time than at another. Oddly enough, the shortest trips are the most expensive since they involve the greatest changes of speed as you hop from one orbit to the other. And in space, speed, not

Science Background

Earth and Mars travel around the sun in different orbital paths. Mars's orbital path is about 1.5 times as long as Earth's, and the two planets will be at different points along their orbital paths at any given time. Therefore, the distance between Earth and Mars is constantly changing.

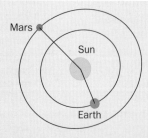

distance, is what costs money. …

4   Now that we've brought up the subject of money, I'd better remind you that the Martian economy is quite different from all those on Earth. Down here, it doesn't cost you anything to breathe, even though you've got to pay to eat. But on Mars the very air has to be synthesized—they break down the **oxides in the ground** to do this—so every time you fill your lungs someone has to **foot the bill**. Food production is planned in the same way—each of the cities, remember, is a carefully balanced ecological system, like a well-organized aquarium. No parasites can be allowed, so everyone has to pay a basic tax which entitles them to air, food and the shelter of the domes.

The tax varies from city to city, but averages about ten Terradollars a day. Since everyone earns at least twenty times as much as this, they can all afford to go on breathing. …

5   You'll land, of course, at Port Lowell: besides being the largest settlement on Mars it's still the only place that has the facilities for handling spaceships. From the air the plastic pressure domes look like a cluster of bubbles—a very pretty sight when the Sun catches them. Don't be alarmed if one of them is deflated. That doesn't mean that there's been an accident. The domes are let down at fairly frequent intervals so that **the envelopes** can be checked for leaks. If you're lucky you may see one being pumped up—it's quite impressive.

In Other Words

oxides in the ground surface materials that contain oxygen
foot the bill pay for it
the envelopes the coverings of the domes

6   After two months in a spaceship, even Port Lowell will seem a mighty metropolis. (Actually, I believe its population is now well over twenty thousand.) You'll find the people energetic, inquisitive, forthright—and very friendly, unless they think you're **trying to be superior**.

7   It's a good working rule never to criticize anything you see on Mars. As I said before, they're very proud of their achievements and after all you are a guest, even if a paying one.

8   Port Lowell has practically everything you'll find in a city on Earth, though of course on a smaller scale. You'll come across many reminders of "home." For example, the main street in the city is Fifth Avenue—but surprisingly enough you'll find Piccadilly Circus where it crosses Broadway.

9   The port, like all the major settlements, lies in the dark belt of **vegetation** that roughly follows the equator and occupies about half the southern hemisphere. The northern hemisphere is almost all desert—the red oxides that give the planet its ruddy color. Some of these desert regions are very beautiful; they're far older than anything on the **surface** of our Earth, because there's been little weathering on Mars to wear down the rocks—at least since the seas dried up, more than 500 million years ago.

10   You shouldn't attempt to leave the city until you've become quite accustomed to living in an oxygen-rich, low-pressure **atmosphere.** You'll have grown **fairly well acclimatized** on the trip, because the air in the spaceship will have been slowly adjusted to conditions on Mars. Outside the domes, the pressure of the natural Martian atmosphere is about equal to that on the top of Mount Everest—and it contains **practically** no oxygen. So when you go out you'll have to wear a helmet, or travel in one of those pressurized jeeps they call "sand fleas."

11   Wearing a helmet, by the way, is nothing like the nuisance you'd expect it to be. The equipment is very light and compact and, as long as you don't do anything silly, is quite foolproof. As it's very unlikely that you'll ever go out without an experienced guide, you'll have no need to worry. Thanks to the low gravity, enough oxygen for twelve hours' normal working can be carried quite easily—and you'll never be away from shelter as long as that.

12   Don't attempt to imitate any of the locals you may see walking around without

---

Key Vocabulary
- **surface** *n.*, the outside, or top layer, of an object
- **atmosphere** *n.*, air that surrounds the Earth

In Other Words
trying to be superior
    acting like you are better than them
vegetation plants
fairly well acclimatized
    ready to enter the atmosphere of Mars
practically almost

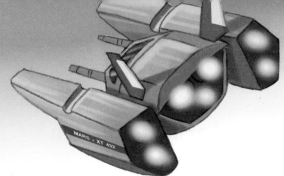

oxygen gear. They're second-generation colonists and are used to the low pressure. They can't breathe the Martian atmosphere any more than you can, but like the old-time native pearl divers they can make one lungful last for several minutes when necessary. Even so, it's a silly sort of trick and they're not supposed to do it.

13 As you know, the other great obstacle to life on Mars is the low temperature. The highest thermometer reading ever recorded is somewhere in the eighties, but that's quite exceptional. In the long winters, and during the night in summer or winter, it never rises above freezing. And I believe the record low is minus one hundred and ninety!

> "... you'll want to see as much of Mars as you can ... "

14 Well, you won't be outdoors at night, and for the sort of **excursions** you'll be doing, all that's needed is a simple thermosuit. It's very light, and traps the body heat so effectively that no other source of warmth is needed.

15 No doubt you'll want to see as much of Mars as you can during your stay. There are only two methods of transport outside the cities—sand fleas for short ranges and aircraft for longer distances. Don't misunderstand me when I say "short ranges"—a sand flea with a full charge of power cells is good for a couple of thousand miles, and it can do eighty miles an hour over good ground. Mars could never have been explored without them. You can survey a planet from space, but in the end someone with **a pick and shovel** has to do the dirty work filling in the map.

16 One thing that few visitors realize is just how big Mars is. Although it seems small beside the Earth, its land area is almost as great because so much of our planet is covered with oceans. So it's hardly surprising that there are vast regions that have never been properly explored, particularly around the **poles**. Those stubborn people who still believe that there was once **an indigenous** Martian civilization pin their hopes on these great blanks. Every so often you hear rumors of some wonderful archaeological discovery in the wastelands, but nothing ever comes of it. …

17 Well, that's all I've got to say, except to wish you a pleasant trip. Oh, there *is* one other thing. My boy collects stamps, and I rather let him down when I was on Mars. If you could drop me a few letters while you're there—there's no need to put anything in them if you're too busy—I'd be much obliged. He's trying to collect a set of space-mail covers postmarked from all the Martian Cities, and if you could help—thanks a lot!

In Other Words
excursions trips
a pick and shovel tools to
    explore land surfaces
poles points on opposite sides of
    the planet
an indigenous a native

Compare Across Texts

Compare and Contrast Forms of Fiction

"Indian Summer Sun," "Why the Sun and the Moon Live in the Sky," and "So You're Going to Mars" are all fiction. But they are different types of fiction. Compare the **characteristics** of these three selections.

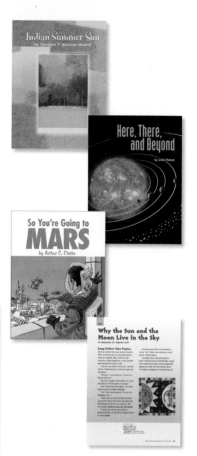

How It Works

Collect and Organize Ideas Use a chart to compare the **characteristics** of three forms of fiction.

Comparison Chart

Comparison Questions	Realistic Fiction such as "Indian Summer Sun"	Myths such as "Why the Sun and the Moon Live in the Sky"	Science Fiction such as "So You're Going to Mars"
1. What things are similar about these forms of fiction?	made up (fiction) has a setting has characters has a theme	made up (fiction) has a setting has characters has a theme	made up (fiction) has a setting has characters has a theme
2. What things are different?			

Practice Together

Compare and Contrast the Ideas To write your comparison, look for how the ideas are alike and explain the connection. Here is a summary for question 1.

Summary

> Realistic fiction, myths, and science fiction are similar because they are all made up from the writers' imagination. They each have characters, settings, and a theme, or message.

Try It!

Make a chart to record your answers to question 2. You may want to use this frame to express your comparison and contrast.

All fiction is made up from a writer's imagination. In realistic fiction, characters _____. Settings in realistic fiction _____. The ideas in realistic fiction show _____. In myths, the settings _____. Characters are _____. Myths show _____. In science fiction, settings _____. Characters are _____. The ideas in science fiction show _____.

Academic Vocabulary
- **characteristic** (kair-ik-tu-**ris**-tik)
  noun
  A **characteristic** is a specific feature or trait that helps you identify something.

At Home in the
World

 GUIDING QUESTION
How can your location affect the way you live?

Content Library

Leveled Library

Reflect on Your Reading

Think back on your reading of the unit selections. Discuss what you did to understand what you read.

Focus on Reading **Analyze Connections**
In this unit, you learned about how a text can make connections among things, ideas, people, and events. Choose two selections from the unit. Explain to a partner one way in which they are connected.

Focus Strategy **Make Connections**
As you read the selections, you learned how making connections helps you understand what you read. Explain to a partner how you will use this strategy in the future.

Explore the GUIDING QUESTION

Throughout this unit, you have been thinking about how people's locations affect the way they live. Choose one of these ways to explore the Guiding Question:

- **Discuss** With a group, discuss the Guiding Question. Listen and learn from your classmates' responses. Discuss examples from the selections that support your ideas.
- **Write** Write a letter to, or as, one of the people in this unit. Compare your location to that of the person you're writing to.
- **Draw** Create a visual response to the Guiding Question. It could be a drawing of your community, state, country, or Earth. Show how this location affects the way you live.

Book Talk

Which Unit Library book did you choose? Explain to a partner what it taught you about feeling at home in the world.

OUR PRECIOUS WORLD

What makes the environment so valuable?

READ MORE!

Content Library
   Ecosystems
   by Nancy Finton

Leveled Library
   The Summer of the Swans
   by Betsy Byars
   And the Earth Did Not Devour Him
   by Tomás Rivera
   Left Behind
   by Velma Wallis

Web Links
   ☐ **myNGconnect.com**

◄ A polar bear looks for the best way to cross the melting ice floes in Norway.

Focus on Reading

Text Features

▶ **Features That Organize**
▶ **Features That Show Information**

Nonfiction text gives information about real events, issues, people, and ideas. Text **features** help readers locate and analyze information.

How It Works

Writers use text **features** to organize information.

- **Headings and subheadings** and **boldface** and **italic type** help you see the organization of a text. These **features** also help you understand which ideas the author thinks are most important. What an author chooses to emphasize is a clue about the author's attitude toward the topic.

Writers also use text **features** to show information.

- **Charts**, **diagrams**, **graphs**, **sidebars**, and **maps**, as well as **illustrations** and **photographs** show specific information visually instead of in words.

Here is an example of how text **features** can help organize and present information in nonfiction.

Forests of the World

> The main heading shows that this topic is important to the author.

Location Matters

> Each subheading names an idea that relates to the main heading.

All forests have trees, but not all forests are alike. Forests can be very different, depending on where they are found in the world.

Central American Tropical Forest　　　　**North American Mountain Forest**

> Labels identify ideas a picture shows.

> Photos show more details than the author can explain in text.

▲ A tropical forest in Central America (left) gets warmer than an evergreen forest in North America (right).

> Captions give more details about photos and other visuals.

Academic Vocabulary

- **feature** (fē-chur) *noun*
  A **feature** is part of something that stands out or is noticeable.

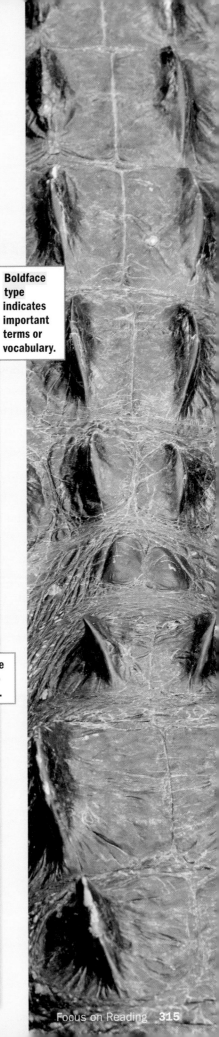

Practice Together

Read the passage below aloud with your class and discuss how the text features help organize the text, provide additional information, and reveal the author's attitude toward the topic.

The American Alligator — [Main heading]

Endangered

People once made shoes and bags from alligator skins. Such fashions and human destruction of alligators' **habitat**, or places to live, were serious threats to these reptiles. In 1967, alligators were listed as **endangered**—that is, in danger of becoming extinct.

[Boldface type indicates important terms or vocabulary.]

Recovered — [Subheading]

By working together, the government and other groups were able to save alligators. The species is now doing well. It was removed from the endangered list in 1987, although the U.S. Fish and Wildlife Service still watches it closely.

Habitat of the American Alligator — [The map title tells what the map shows.]

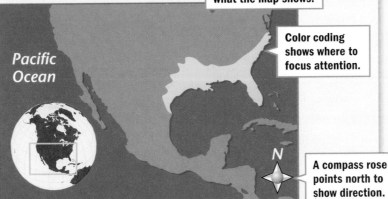

Pacific Ocean

[Color coding shows where to focus attention.]

N

[A compass rose points north to show direction.]

[A caption gives more information about the map.]

▲ As a cold-blooded reptile, the American alligator lives in warm climates, shown here in yellow.

▲ American alligator

Practice Together

Read the passage aloud with your class. What informational text features are here? What does each one do? What do the text features tell you about the author's attitude toward the topic?

Saved from Extinction

The bald eagle is a triumph of wildlife conservation. By the middle of the 1900s, very few bald eagles existed in the United States. Hunting, loss of habitat to humans, and the use of pesticides, or chemicals used to protect crops from insect pests, had nearly wiped out the bald eagle population . . . .

▲ Bald eagles are known for their white heads and tails. Birds are about five years old when their head and tail feathers become white.

National Bird

In 1782, the bald eagle was selected to be the national bird of the new United States. At that time, the bald eagle population was about 100,000 nesting eagles. By 1963, there were only about 400 breeding pairs. Thanks to the work of conservationists, there are now at least 7,500 breeding pairs of bald eagles in most of the United States, not counting Alaska and Hawaii.

Facts About the Bald Eagle	
Food	Fish, small mammals
Life span	Can live about 50 years
Number of eggs	2–3 eggs per year
Wingspan	6–7 ½ feet

BALD EAGLE HABITAT

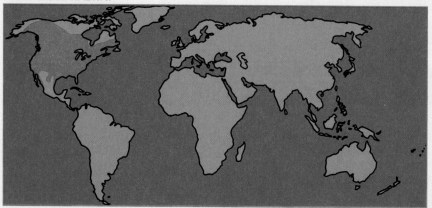

▲ The red area shows the bald eagle's habitat.

Try It!

Read the following passage and text features aloud. What are the text features in this example? How does each one help a reader understand the text and the author's attitude toward the topic?

Falcons Saved Just in Time

Falcon Populations Drop

Peregrine falcons are **raptors**, or birds of prey. They eat smaller animals. The populations of these raptors in the United States dropped dangerously low from the 1940s to the 1970s.

▲ peregrine falcon

Effects of DDT

DDT is a chemical used to control insects. From 1939 to 1972, it was used widely on crops. Then scientists proved it was harmful to wildlife.

Small levels of DDT got into the bodies of small animals. Peregrine falcons ate the animals, and the DDT collected in the falcons' bodies. It caused falcons to lay thin eggs that broke before the babies could hatch.

DDT affected many animals. In 1962, Rachel Carson published *Silent Spring* to make the public aware of the problem. Finally, the Environmental Protection Agency banned the general use of DDT.

Range of the Peregrine Falcon

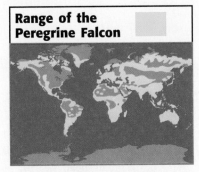

▲ Peregrine falcons are again one of the most common birds of prey, living everywhere but Antarctica.

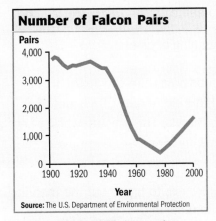

Number of Falcon Pairs

Source: The U.S. Department of Environmental Protection

▲ From 1940–1975 the number of nesting pairs of peregrine falcons dropped from over 3,000 to under 400.

Focus on Vocabulary

Use Context Clues: Multiple-Meaning Words

Some words in English have multiple, or more than one, meaning. For instance, the word *well* has more than one meaning.

> Rosa felt **well** enough to go to the concert. (*well* = not sick)

> My uncle gets water from a **well**. (*well* = a deep hole in the ground)

As you read, if you come to a word you know but that doesn't make sense in the text, the word is probably a multiple-meaning word.

How the Strategy Works

When you come to a word that has more than one meaning, use its **context**, or surrounding text, to figure out which meaning the writer used.

EXAMPLE   Jan is ready to **present** her report.

1. Read the entire sentence or paragraph to find other words that might be clues to the word's meaning.
2. Decide if the word names an action, a thing, or describes something. In this example, Jan is about to do something, so *present* names an action.
3. Try to see how the word affects the rest of the sentence. Jan is ready to do something with her report. What might she do?
4. Restate the sentence. "Jan is ready to *give* her report."
5. Decide the meaning of the word that makes sense. In this example, *present* means "to give or to share."

Use the strategy to figure out the meaning of *close*.

> Are there more kinds of animals now than 100 years ago, or are there fewer? Answering that kind of question is not easy. Scientists spend years of <u>close</u> study to find the answers. They take careful notes and measurements and compare them over time.

 REMEMBER You can often use **context** to figure out the meaning of a word that has more than one meaning.

Academic Vocabulary
- **context** (kon-tekst) *noun*
  Context is the surrounding text near a word or phrase that helps explain the meaning of the word.

Strategy in Action

" The word *close* here describes how scientists study, so it cannot be an action, like closing a book. It might mean 'nearby,' but that doesn't make sense. I think that *close* here means 'careful and exact.' "

Practice Together

Read the passage aloud. As you read, listen for context that helps you figure out the correct meaning of each underlined word.

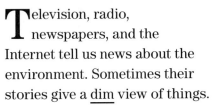

What's the Good News?

Television, radio, newspapers, and the Internet tell us news about the environment. Sometimes their stories give a <u>dim</u> view of things.

Sometimes, however, bad news can lead to action. One good example is California Coastal Cleanup Day.

News reports about the amount of garbage along California's <u>coast</u> caused people to take action. Now more than 50,000 people come together each year on the third Saturday of September to clean up the coast. Since the <u>program</u> began in 1985, more than three <u>quarters</u> of a million volunteers have removed over 12 million pounds of <u>waste</u> and garbage from California shores.

Try It!

Read the following passage. What is the correct meaning of each underlined word? How do you know?

One Person

How can one person help the natural world? Perhaps you don't live in a rain forest or can't do research at the South <u>Pole</u>. But if you <u>long</u> to help the planet, you can make choices that make a difference. Use less water. Use fewer plastics. Recycle whenever it's possible. Keep your home a little cooler in winter and a little warmer in summer. Use batteries that you can recharge. Avoid driving when you can walk. Dispose of trash properly.

None of these <u>tips</u> is new. Think, though, about the difference it would make if the <u>rest</u> of us, all 250 million Americans, followed your <u>lead</u>.

A Natural Balance

based on a book by Nora L. Deans

Build Background

See How Humans Affect the Environment

How do humans affect the environment? Our actions can make the world better or worse. We may not know that some of the things we do harm plants and animals.

Connect

Habitat Drawing Brainstorm what wild animals need to survive. Then draw a habitat, such as the mountains, desert, or forest. What if people built a town on that land? Discuss with a partner how it would affect the animals.

Digital Library

myNGconnect.com
◔ View the video.

▲ Like many plants and animals, gray wolves face danger from humans.

Language & Grammar

Describe Animals and Things

CD

Listen to the rap that describes an animal.
Then listen again and chime in.

RAP

The Okapi

You rarely see an okapi.
She lives quietly and alone
In dense African forests.
For years she was unknown.
Now that we have found her,
She may soon be gone.

She is a funny creature
With a lo-o-ong and clever tongue,
A tongue that is unique among
Her African animal peers.
She uses it to wash her eyelids
And to clean her ears.

She has an awkward body.
It makes you want to laugh.
Her legs are zebra-striped.
That's just her bottom half.
Sitting on her short, thick neck
Is the head of a giraffe.

You may never see an okapi,
And that would be a shame,
Except in a zoo, but you know it's true,
A zoo is not the same
As seeing the okapi
Or any animal you name
Living and free, alive and free
Within its own domain.

▲ The okapi lives in the African rain forest. It is one of the few animals that can lick its own ears with its long tongue. This animal, or species, is in danger of disappearing.

Language and Grammar, continued

Use Adjectives That Describe

You can describe people, places, or things with **adjectives** . They answer the question: *What is the person, place, or thing like?*

> EXAMPLES   The **blue whale** makes **deep sounds**.

Adjectives help the reader imagine people, places, or things.

Use adjectives to describe:	Examples
how something looks	beautiful, huge, long, red, tiny
how something sounds	deep, loud, quiet, rumbling, squeaky
how something feels, tastes, or smells	bitter, cold, salty, slimy, smooth
a person's mood	angry, fearful, helpful, kind, timid
how many	many, plentiful, rare, ten

Often the adjective comes before the **noun** you are describing.

> EXAMPLES   This **large mammal** is a **fast swimmer**.

If your verb is a form of **be**, you can put the adjective after the verb.
The forms of *be* are *am*, *is*, *are*, *was*, and *were*.

> EXAMPLES   The bats' cave **is dark** . Attacks on humans **are rare** .

Practice Together

Say each sentence. Choose an adjective from the box to describe the noun.
Then say the sentence again with the adjective.

| colorful   graceful   loud   slimy   tiny |

1. The bat made a _____ sound as it flew out of the cave.
2. The parrot's feathers are bright and _____.
3. The _____ worm slipped out of my hand.
4. The _____ mouse scampered through the leaves.
5. The _____ eagle soared easily through the air.

Try It!

Say each sentence. Choose an adjective from the box, and
write it on a card. Then say the sentence with the adjective.

| dark   endangered   huge   many   strong |

6. The gray bat lives in _____ caves.
7. The blue whale is _____.
8. Gray wolves travel _____ miles a day to hunt for food.
9. The jaguar is a _____ swimmer.
10. Many animals are _____.

▲ Bats help control insect populations. Some bats are endangered.

Describe an Endangered Animal

DESCRIBE ANIMALS

Many animals are in danger of vanishing from the world. Find out about an endangered animal, and describe what it looks like and where it lives to the class.

Choose an animal from this list or another endangered animal that you know.

Ozark big-eared bat	West Indian manatee	pygmy rabbit
American black bear	Pacific pocket mouse	black rhinoceros
Key deer	ocelot	Hawaiian monk seal
black-footed ferret	northern sea otter	bighorn sheep
jaguar	Florida panther	blue whale

Internet InsideNG.com

Go online to learn what your animal looks like and other interesting information about it. Take notes.

Questions	Answers	Adjectives to Use
What does my animal look like?	glossy fur, black ears	glossy, black
Where does my animal live?		
What does my animal eat?		
What other interesting information do I know?		
Why is my animal endangered?		

Now describe your animal to a group.

> The jaguar is a solitary animal that lives in Central and South America. It has a tan coat with large, black spots. This huge cat is an excellent swimmer, too.

HOW TO DESCRIBE ANIMALS AND THINGS

1. Tell how things look, sound, smell, taste, and feel.

2. Use adjectives to help others picture what you're describing.

USE ADJECTIVES THAT DESCRIBE

Use **adjectives** in your description. Remember that the adjectives you choose should help readers or listeners form pictures in their minds.

Often, the adjective comes before the noun you are describing. If two adjectives both describe the noun, separate them with a comma (,).

EXAMPLES   The **gray** bat has **glossy** fur and **long**, **black** ears. **Gray** bats live in **limestone** caves. Their **summer** caves are **warm**, and their **winter** caves are **cold**.

Prepare to Read

Learn Key Vocabulary

Study the Words Use the steps below.

1. Pronounce the word. Say it aloud several times. Spell it.
2. Rate your word knowledge.
3. Study the example. Tell more about the word.
4. Practice it. Make the word your own.

Key Words

classified (klas-u-fīd) *verb*
▶ page 332

To be **classified** means to be arranged or put into groups. Scientists have **classified** many plants and animals.
Related Word: **classify**

endangered (en-dān-jurd)
adjective ▶ page 330

To be **endangered** means to be at risk of disappearing forever. The ivory-billed woodpecker is an example of an **endangered** animal.

environment
(en-vī-run-ment) *noun* ▶ page 329

The **environment** is all of the living and nonliving things that surround a person, animal, or plant. Every **environment** affects the things that live in it.

extinct (ik-stingt) *adjective*
▶ page 332

Something that is **extinct** is no longer living. The dodo bird became **extinct** because people hunted too many over time.
Related Word: **extinction**

illegal (i-lē-gul) *adjective*
▶ page 332

Something that is **illegal** is against the law. It is **illegal** to park in some areas.
Antonyms: **legal, lawful**

pollution (pul-lü-shun) *noun*
▶ page 330

Pollution is waste, chemicals, and gases that have a harmful effect. Air and water **pollution** hurt living things.

population
(pop-yu-lā-shun) *noun* ▶ page 330

Population is the total number of plants or animals in a group. The human **population** of Earth is more than seven billion.

species (spē-shēz) *noun*
▶ page 330

A **species** is a related group of animals or plants. Lions and tigers are different **species**. African lions and Asian lions are the same **species**.

Practice the Words Work with a partner to complete an Expanded Meaning Map for each Key Word.

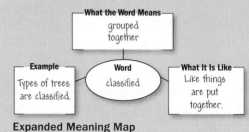

Expanded Meaning Map

Analyze Author's Viewpoint

What is an Author's Viewpoint? An author's viewpoint is the author's attitude toward the topic. Authors often do not state their viewpoints directly, so you must look for clues.

One clue to an author's viewpoint is the purpose for writing. If an author is giving a lot of information about a topic, the author believes that the topic is important. An author's opinions, or statements of belief, also indicate how an author feels about the topic. Strong words that cause clear feelings are also clues. For example, the word *weed* causes a strong negative feeling about a plant.

What clues to author's viewpoint do you see in this passage?

Reading Strategies
- Plan
- Monitor
- Ask Questions
- Make Connections
- **Visualize** Imagine the sights, sounds, smells, tastes, and touch of what the author is describing.
- Make Inferences
- Determine Importance
- Synthesize

Look Into the Text

All across Earth, people are changing the environment in different ways. For example: we cut down trees to build houses, plow fields to grow crops, build roads and parking lots, and empty waste into rivers, lakes, and oceans .... Activities like these greatly affect plants and animals in our environment.

"This opinion statement shows that the author wants to protect the environment."

Practice Together

Begin a Viewpoint Diagram A Viewpoint Diagram can help you analyze an author's viewpoint. This Viewpoint Diagram shows the author's purpose and one opinion from the passage. Reread the passage and add another clue. After you have read the whole selection on pages 327–335, you will add the author's viewpoint.

Author's Purpose: to inform readers about how people endanger the environment

Clues from the Text:
- Opinion: "Activities like these greatly affect plants and animals in our environment."
- _____

Author's Viewpoint:

Environmental Report

An environmental report is expository nonfiction. It gives facts about a topic related to the environment.

A report is written to inform readers about a topic important to the author. While researching the facts, an author often forms an **opinion** about the topic and uses strong words to show those beliefs. Knowing the author's purpose, beliefs, and feelings will help you understand the author's viewpoint.

Look Into the Text

> Think about all of the plants and animals in neighborhood parks. What happens to the population of these plants and animals if the parks turn into apartment buildings? These plants and animals might die or move someplace else because of increased development.

This opinion is a clue to the author's viewpoint.

As you read, also use your experiences to visualize what the author describes.

Green sea turtles swim off the coast of Bora Bora Island. These turtles are endangered in many countries. ▼

A Natural Balance

Balance

based on a book by Nora L. Deans

Comprehension Coach

Boys in Miami Beach, Florida, gather the eggs of sea turtles to protect them from other animals. ▶

Our Effect on the Environment

Beep! Beep! Beep! Your alarm goes off and you hop out of bed. You wash your face, chat with your family, eat your breakfast, and take the bus to school. Even before you go to school, you have connected with many people and things. All of the things you do affect the **environment.**

Your environment is all of the living and nonliving things around you. All across Earth, humans are changing the environment in different ways. For example: we cut down trees to build houses, **plow fields** to grow crops, build roads and parking lots, and empty **waste** into rivers, lakes, and oceans. We also use large nets and boats to catch huge amounts of fish. Activities like these greatly affect plants and animals in our environment.

▲ A kayaker passes by trash along the shore of the Anacostia River.

Are We Helping or Harming?

The way we live our lives can affect our environment in both positive and negative ways. Sometimes our actions **benefit** the environment because we might help a certain plant or animal **population** get larger. For example, imagine that you plant tulips in your neighborhood. This action helps the tulip population grow in your area. Suppose you **put seeds out for** the birds in your area. Then, the bird population might get larger, too.

On the other hand, our activities can also harm plant and animal populations. Think about all of the plants and animals in neighborhood parks. What happens to the population of these plants and animals if the parks turn into apartment buildings? These plants and animals might die or move someplace else because of increased development. As a result, the area's plant and animal population decreases.

Over-hunting, **pollution**, and other activities can also decrease the population of a **species**. The population may become so small that it is in danger of dying out. When a species is in danger of dying out, it is called an **endangered** species.

▲ Florida's black bears need more protection as development moves in.

The Road to Extinction

An easy way to remember the threats facing plants and animals today is HIPPO. It stands for:

- **Habitat loss**—cutting down trees, tearing up the land; such activities often leave plants and animals with no place to live

- **Introduced species**—bringing in new life-forms that crowd out or feed on the ones that were there

- **Pollution**—chemicals and wastes that damage or even kill living things

- **Population growth**—more and more people who need more food and more land

- **Over-consumption**—hunting and fishing and harvesting too many plants or animals

Key Vocabulary
population *n.*, the total number in a group
pollution *n.*, harmful chemicals and waste
species *n.*, a related group
endangered *adj.*, at risk of disappearing

In Other Words
benefit are good for
put seeds out for feed

What's Harming the Habitat?

The way we use or pollute natural resources like water or land affects the environment. Several factors contribute to the loss of habitat, the areas that support plant and animal populations.

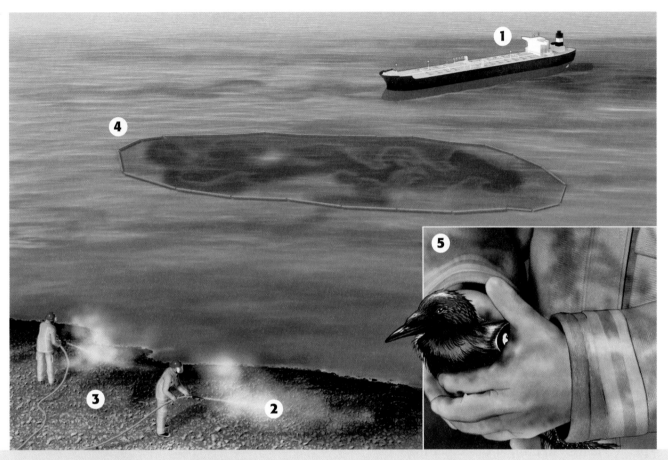

Oil spill emergency

Oil spills are major ocean disasters. An oil spill is what happens when a tanker, or large ship, carrying oil gets a hole in it and leaks the oil.

1 A large tanker gets stuck on shallow land. When crew members start to drive the tanker again, they can put a hole in it, leaking the oil.

2 As part of the clean-up effort, oily shore rocks and sand are rinsed with very hot water.

3 Thousands of workers help clean up the spill.

4 Containment booms surround large areas of oil.

5 Oil-soaked birds are cleaned with absorbent pads. Some survive but hundreds of thousands die. Sea otters, whales, and schools of fish also die.

Look Into the Text

1. **Cause and Effect** What are two details from the text that show how people can help the **environment** in their neighborhood?

2. **Explain** How might buildings that replace parks affect plant and animal **populations**?

3. **Paraphrase** Tell in your own words what threats plants and animals face today.

Are We Solving the Problem?

The problem of the endangered environment is not new, and over time large groups of plants and animals quickly began to disappear. So, people began to look for ways to protect these important species. In the early 1900s, laws were passed to protect certain animals, but the biggest change came many years later. In 1973, the U.S. government passed the Endangered Species Act. This act lists species that are in danger of becoming **extinct**, or lost forever. The act makes it **illegal** to **collect** or harm any of the species on the list and it also protects the areas where the listed species live.

There is only one way that a species can be added to or removed from the list. Congress must agree to the change. In other words, state representatives must meet, vote, and pass a law or an act.

Many species are already on the list and they can be **classified** as either "threatened" or "endangered." A threatened species is less in danger of becoming extinct. An endangered species is most in danger of becoming extinct. A threatened species could, however, become endangered without protection.

Many more plants are endangered than animals. About one out of every ten plants may become extinct.

About 75 percent of the world's bird species are endangered. More than 60 percent of primates, such as apes and monkeys, are also endangered. Some scientists think as many as 100 species become extinct each day.

The Road to Extinction

Going
Threatened

Going
Endangered

Gone
Extinct

▲ A threatened species can become endangered without protection. An endangered species can become extinct.

Key Vocabulary
  extinct *adj.*, no longer living
  illegal *adj.*, against the law
  classified *v.*, placed into groups

In Other Words
  collect take

Science Background
You rely on plants for food, shelter, clothing, medicines, and the air you breathe. Yet, a very large number of plant species are endangered. You can help save these plants by starting your own garden or joining a program in your community.

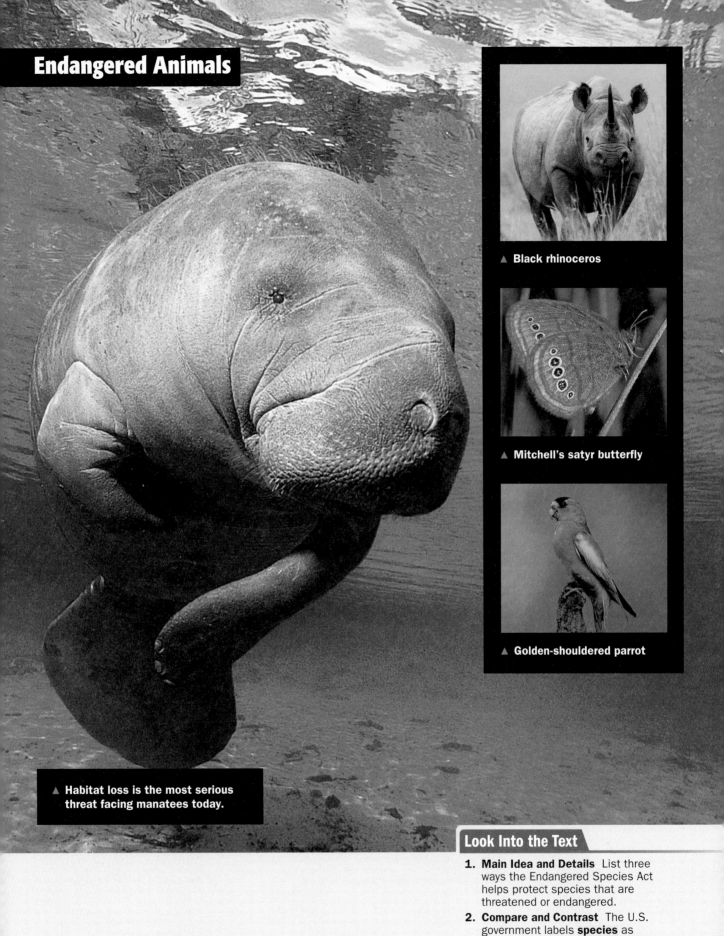

Endangered Animals

▲ Black rhinoceros

▲ Mitchell's satyr butterfly

▲ Golden-shouldered parrot

▲ Habitat loss is the most serious threat facing manatees today.

Look Into the Text

1. **Main Idea and Details** List three ways the Endangered Species Act helps protect species that are threatened or endangered.

2. **Compare and Contrast** The U.S. government labels **species** as either threatened or **endangered**. Explain the difference.

The U.S. Fish and Wildlife Service (FWS) is the government agency **in charge of** enforcing the Endangered Species Act. Many of the scientists at FWS study threatened and endangered plants and animals by **tracking** the populations of the species on the list.

For example, the bald eagle used to be listed as an endangered species. In 1963, there were only 400 pairs left. By 1995, after many **recovery efforts**, the bald eagle population increased enough for the FWS to reclassify the bald eagle from "endangered" to "threatened." Due to government and volunteer efforts, there are about 10,000 pairs today. Thus, the bald eagle has now been removed from the endangered and threatened species list.

The scientists at FWS have a challenging job. They need to protect all the species on the list. Even so, there are always more species in need of protection.

Organizations and individuals try to protect endangered species as well. Zoos and aquariums often work together. They breed and raise rare and endangered animals. Botanical gardens and other groups raise rare and endangered plants. They also save their seeds. In this way, the plants won't disappear.

Not everyone agrees on the best way to help endangered species, especially when people's jobs or way of life may be threatened. Like so many cases involving endangered species, survival means balancing the protection of endangered species with people's way of life. ❖

◀ On June 28, 2007, the bald eagle was taken off the Federal List of Endangered and Threatened Wildlife and Plants. The bald eagle will still be protected by the Bald and Golden Eagle Protection Act.

In Other Words
in charge of responsible for
tracking watching and researching
recovery efforts efforts to save the birds

Endangered Plants

▲ The aloe's habitat is affected by burning and other kinds of habitat destruction.

▲ Orchid smuggling is leading to the loss of many kinds of wild orchids.

▲ The government began protecting the saguaro cactus when it started to disappear. This has prevented it from becoming endangered.

▲ A worker arranges seed plantings in a laboratory in China. These plants will grow fast to create new forests to keep up with China's growing demand for paper, which is made from trees.

Look Into the Text

1. **Sequence** Tell what happened to the bald eagle **population** from 1963 to today.
2. **Author's Viewpoint** According to the author, why is it hard for people to agree on how to protect endangered or threatened species?

In My Dreams

by Francisco X. Alarcón

buffaloes roam
free once again
on the plains

whales become
5   opera singers
of the sea

dolphins are
admired by all for
their smarts and joy

10 in my dreams
there is no word
for "war"

all humans
and all living
15 beings

come together
as one big family
of the Earth

▲ **Critical Viewing: Theme** How does this painting connect to the unit theme "Our Precious World"?

Science Background
A whale song is the sound made by whales to communicate with each other. Sound travels much more quickly under water than above ground.

Look Into the Text

1. **Visualize** Find words and lines that help you see, hear, or feel. How do they help you understand the poem?
2. **Inference** What do you think the speaker dreams will happen? Why is it just a dream?

Connect Reading and Writing

Vocabulary
classified
endangered
environment
extinct
illegal
pollution
population
species

CRITICAL THINKING

1. **SUM IT UP** Use your Viewpoint Diagram to summarize the viewpoint of the author of "A Natural Balance."

> **Author's Purpose:** to inform readers about how people endanger the environment
>
> **Clues from the Text:**
> - Opinion: "Activities like these greatly affect plants and animals in our environment."
> - _____
>
> **Author's Viewpoint:**

Viewpoint Diagram

2. **Speculate** How might the future change if certain plants and animals become **extinct**? Use examples from the text.

3. **Conclusion** **Populations** of wildlife can be **classified** as "**endangered**" or "threatened." Why is the difference important?

4. **Interpret** Are the speaker of the poem "In My Dreams" and the author of "A Natural Balance" hopeful about the **environment**? Explain.

READING FLUENCY

Intonation Read the passage on page 636 to a partner. Assess your fluency.

1. My tone never/sometimes/always matched what I read.

2. What I did best in my reading was _____.

READING STRATEGY

> What strategy helped you understand the selection? Tell a partner about it.

VOCABULARY REVIEW

Oral Review Read the paragraph aloud. Add the vocabulary words.

> In Washington, there are now very few pygmy rabbits, a special type or _____ of rabbit. Once, there were thousands, but now the _____ is decreasing. The U.S. Fish and Wildlife Service has _____ the pygmy rabbit as _____. It is _____ to hunt it. Air and water _____ are not the main problems. Instead, the rabbit is losing its natural _____. This animal is in danger of becoming _____.

Written Review Imagine you are a scientist working to save **endangered** species. Write a brief report to describe the problems and suggest a solution. Use five vocabulary words.

WRITE ABOUT THE **GUIDING QUESTION**

Explore Our Valuable Environment
In your opinion, why is the **environment** so valuable? Reread the selection to find information that supports your ideas.

Connect Across the Curriculum

Use Context Clues: Multiple-Meaning Words

> **Academic Vocabulary**
> • **context** (**kon**-tekst) *noun*
>   Context is the surrounding text near a word
>   that helps explain the meaning of the word.

Many words have more than one meaning. For example, if Eddie lives near a *bank*, do you think he lives near a river or near a business where people keep money? Read on to use **context** to confirm your guess.

EXAMPLES   Eddie lives near a **bank** and enjoys fishing in the river.

Eddie lives near a **bank**, and he keeps his money there.

Think About Multiple Meanings Read these sentences from the selection. Think of two possible meanings for each underlined word. Use **context** to figure out the correct meaning.

1. Imagine that you <u>plant</u> tulips in your neighborhood.

2. Think about all of the animals in neighborhood <u>parks</u>.

3. Scientists <u>track</u> the populations of the endangered species on the list.

Analyze Imagery in Poetry

> **Academic Vocabulary**
> • **image** (**im**-ij) *noun*
>   An **image** is a mental picture of something.

Poets choose words carefully to create **images** in a reader's mind. These "word **images**" are called **imagery**. Do you "see" any special **image** when you read this? *Animals walked on the land again.* Compare that line to these lines from "In My Dreams."

> buffaloes roam
> free once again
> on the plains

Analyze Imagery With a partner, discuss **images** you "see" when you read "In My Dreams." Which examples of imagery are the most powerful? What message is the speaker trying to give?

Describe Animals and Things

Group Game Write names of common objects or familiar animals on index cards. Take turns choosing a card and adding an adjective or two to describe the noun. Then, the group members decide if the adjective accurately describes the noun.

> whale

> enormous whale

> enormous, blue whale

Write About an Animal

Study the Models Descriptive details add a lot of interest to your writing. Words that tell how things look, sound, smell, taste, and feel help readers see and experience what you are writing about.

JUST OK

> Manatees are <u>endangered</u>. These <u>large</u> mammals are related to the elephant. Manatees live in the waters around Florida. Algae often grow on their skin. Manatees use their flippers to steer and their tails to push themselves through water. These animals are <u>playful</u>.

This writer gives few descriptive details.

BETTER

> Manatees are <u>endangered</u>. These <u>large</u>, <u>gentle</u> mammals are related to the elephant. They live in the <u>warm</u>, <u>coastal</u> waters around Florida. Algae often grow on their <u>thick</u>, <u>wrinkled</u> skin. Manatees use their <u>front</u> flippers to steer and their <u>powerful</u>, <u>flat</u> tails to push themselves through <u>shallow</u> water. These <u>slow-moving</u> animals are <u>playful</u>.

This writer adds colorful details. These words help readers picture a manatee more clearly.

Revise It Look back at the JUST OK model above. Work with a partner to improve it. Add different colorful details to help readers see, hear, feel, and smell the things that are described.

✐ **WRITE ON YOUR OWN** Write a descriptive paragraph about an animal you know well. Use colorful adjectives to help the reader imagine the animal's appearance and behavior.

▲ The playful manatee is an endangered species.

Siberian SURVIVORS

by Rene Ebersole

Build Background

See Efforts to Save Our Environment

What is being done to protect wild animals and their habitats? Scientists from many countries are working together to save Siberian tigers.

Connect

Quickwrite What is your favorite animal? Describe it in a Quickwrite. Tell what you know about its appearance, its behavior, and its environment.

Digital Library

myNGconnect.com
◎ View the images.

▲ Tigers are in more danger than other kinds of cats.

Make Comparisons

Study the photographs and listen to this comparison.
How would you compare the two cats? Find one more way.

PICTURE PROMPT

It's All in the Family

The Siberian tiger and the domestic cat are relatives. Both belong to the cat family. However, the tiger lives in the wild and is much larger than the domesticated house cat. Large, wild cats like lions and tigers are often called "big cats."

All cats are natural hunters. They have sharp claws, strong jaws, and thirty sharp teeth. They have powerful bodies with padded feet. The tiger is more powerful and more ferocious than the house cat.

Cats can sneak up and suddenly pounce on their prey. They use their long tails for balance as they jump and leap. They use their rough, moist tongues for cleaning meat from animal bones and for grooming themselves.

All cats have the ability to see well in the dark. They have very good hearing, too. Both big cats and domestic cats mark their territories with their scents. This informs others of their home range. A tiger has a wider home range than a house cat.

▼ Siberian tiger

domestic cat ▶

Use Adjectives That Compare

Use a **comparative adjective** to compare two people, places, or things.

EXAMPLES   The tiger is **fast,** but the cheetah is **faster** .

The tiger is **more powerful than** a house cat.

There are two ways to turn an adjective into a comparative adjective:

1. If the adjective has one syllable, add **-er**.	green cold large heavy green**er** cold**er** larg**er** heavi**er**	
If it ends in silent **e**, drop the **e**. Then add **-er**.	The tiger is **larger than** the house cat.	
If it has two syllables and ends in a consonant plus **y**, change the **y** to **i** before you add **-er**.	The lion is **heavy**, but the tiger is **heavier**.	
2. If the adjective has three or more syllables, use **more** before the adjective.	curious threatening **more** curious **more** threatening	
	Many cats are **curious**, but our cat Fluffy is **more curious than** most.	

If an adjective has two syllables, sometimes you can use either form, but it is safer to use **more**.

EXAMPLES   friendly   fearless
              friendl**ier** or **more** friendly   **more** fearless

Practice Together

Change the adjective in the box to a comparative adjective. Say it. Then say the sentence with the comparative adjective.

1. | colorful | The tiger is colorful, but the parrot is _____ .
2. | heavy | The rhinoceros is _____ than the tiger.
3. | fast | The cheetah is _____ than the tiger.
4. | dangerous | A tiger is _____ than a cheetah.
5. | sensitive | A cat's hearing is _____ than a dog's hearing.

▲ A cheetah is faster than a tiger.

Try It!

Change the adjective in the box to a comparative adjective. Write it on a card. Then say the sentence and add the comparative adjective.

6. | interested | I am _____ in learning about tigers than cows.
7. | cuddly | I think my cat is _____ than your cat.
8. | small | Your cat is small, but my hamster is _____ .
9. | pretty | My cat's eyes are _____ than my dog's eyes.
10. | soft | My cat's fur is _____ than my pillow.

Tell How Animals Are Alike and Different

MAKE COMPARISONS

What is your favorite animal? Return to the Quickwrite you did on page 350. Compare your choice of animal to a partner's choice.

Share what you know about your animal with a partner. Tell your partner what your animal looks like, where it lives, what it eats, and other interesting facts that you know. Then have your partner share information about his or her animal.

	My Animal: Jaguar	My Partner's Animal: Amazon Parrot
Appearance	tan or orange fur with black spots, large paws, sharp claws	green, yellow, and blue feathers, big beak, long claws
Habitat	Central and South America	Central and South America
Diet	eats meat and fish	eats vegetables, fruit, seeds, grains, and nuts
Other facts	strong swimmer, hunter	can talk and sing

Now compare your animal to your partner's animal. Talk about the things that are the same and the things that are different. Trade roles.

HOW TO MAKE COMPARISONS

1. Tell how things are alike.
2. Tell how things are different.
3. Use comparison words to compare details about the two things.

> Both the jaguar and the parrot live in Central and South America. The parrot is more colorful than the jaguar. The jaguar and the parrot have very different diets and abilities.

USE ADJECTIVES THAT COMPARE

When you make comparisons, you describe how things are alike and different. Use **adjectives** that compare details about the two things.

Add **-er** to the end of one-syllable adjectives and two-syllable adjectives that end in a consonant plus **y**.

EXAMPLE   The jaguar is **faster** and **scarier** than the parrot.

For most other two-syllable adjectives, use **more**.

EXAMPLE   The jaguar is a **more skillful** hunter.

If the adjective has three or more syllables, use **more** before the adjective.

EXAMPLE   The parrot is **more colorful** than the jaguar.

Prepare to Read

Learn Key Vocabulary

Study the Words Use the steps below.

1. Pronounce the word. Say it aloud several times. Spell it.
2. Rate your word knowledge.
3. Study the example. Tell more about the word.
4. Practice it. Make the word your own.

Key Words

biologist (bī-ol-u-jist) *noun*
▶ page 348

A **biologist** is a person who studies living things. **Biologists** study how living things grow and where they are found.
Related Word: **biology**

expert (e-kspurt) *noun*
▶ page 350

An **expert** is a person who knows a lot about a subject. A ranger is an **expert** about wildlife in the area.

habitat (hab-i-tat) *noun*
▶ page 350

A **habitat** is the place where a plant or an animal naturally lives. The **habitat** of polar bears is the cold Arctic.

increase (in-krēs) *verb*
▶ page 353

To **increase** means to become larger in number or size. The size of my family **increased** when my brother was born.
Synonym: **grow**

poacher (pō-chur) *noun*
▶ page 350

A **poacher** is a person who hunts plants or animals illegally. The **poacher** saw the "no hunting" sign but hunted animals anyway.

shrink (shringk) *verb*
▶ page 353

To **shrink** means to become smaller. The forests that animals need are **shrinking** as people cut down trees.
Past tense: **shrank**
Past participle: **shrunk**

thrive (thrīv) *verb*
▶ page 353

To **thrive** means to grow strong and healthy. With lots of care, plants can **thrive**.

wildlife (wīld-līf) *noun*
▶ page 350

Wildlife means animals and plants that live freely outdoors without human care. Bears and moose are examples of **wildlife**.

Practice the Words Work with a partner. Write a question using two Key Words. Answer your partner's question. Use at least one Key Word in your answer. Keep going until you have used all the words twice.

> **EXAMPLE:** What is required for wildlife to thrive?
> A safe and healthy habitat.

Compare Viewpoints

What Are Other Viewpoints? In a nonfiction article, the author may explain several different viewpoints and respond to them. Some viewpoints may be similar to the author's own viewpoint. Some viewpoints may be different from the author's viewpoint.

As you read these passages, look for explanations of different viewpoints. Then look for the author's response to each. Does she agree or disagree with each viewpoint?

Reading Strategies
- Plan
- Monitor
- Ask Questions
- Make Connections
- **Visualize** Imagine the sights, sounds, smells, tastes, and touch of what the author is describing.
- Make Inferences
- Determine Importance
- Synthesize

Look Into the Text

> Some people in Asia believe that tiger parts can be used to improve health. Almost every body part is used to make some kind of potion.
>
> Poachers, people who hunt illegally, can make $15,000 from selling just one dead tiger. That's more money than most Asian families make in several years.

"The strong word *potion* shows that the author does not agree with the viewpoint about the value of tiger parts."

Practice Together

Begin a Viewpoints Chart A Viewpoints Chart can help you understand how the author feels about various viewpoints. This Viewpoints Chart shows the viewpoint expressed in the first paragraph above and the author's response to it. Reread the second paragraph and record the viewpoint expressed and the author's response.

Other People's Viewpoint	Author's Response
Some people in Asia believe that tiger parts can be used to improve health. Almost every body part is used to make some kind of potion.	• The word potion causes a negative feeling. • The author disagrees with using tiger parts to improve health.
	• •

Science Feature

A science feature is expository nonfiction about the study of the natural world.

Authors of nonfiction write to inform their audiences. They often present different viewpoints in the same text. As you read, take note of how the author presents and responds to different viewpoints.

Look Into the Text

… by the early 1900s, overhunting had wiped out most of them. Fewer than fifty were left!

By 1947 laws were passed to protect the tigers. The laws have helped a little, but Olga and other tigers still face serious threats.

> In some people's view, the 1947 laws are enough to protect the tigers. But the author uses strong words to show that she disagrees.

To get the clearest picture of the author's ideas, visualize the sights, sounds, smells, tastes, and feelings related to the text.

Siberian SURVIVORS

by Rene Ebersole

Howard Quigley has been stalked by a jaguar, charged by a black bear, and bitten by parasites. But he was most scared when he came face-to-face with Olga, a female Siberian tiger.

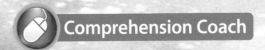
Comprehension Coach

First Meeting

Shivers rolled down Quigley's spine as Olga bellowed a fierce roar. He wasn't sure what the angry cat would do next. Would she stand still? Would she run off? Or would she **pounce**?

The **biologist** remained calm as he carefully aimed his tranquilizer gun at the tiger. Then he squeezed the trigger and a dart soared through the air toward the cat.

Bull's eye! The dart struck Olga in her shoulder. She staggered and slowly slumped to the ground–asleep.

As the cat slept, Quigley and his team of scientists went to work. They had to be careful; a female tiger can weigh 370 pounds. They wanted to finish their work before the cat woke up.

The scientists took blood samples, checked Olga's heartbeat, and measured her body from head to tail.

They also put a radio collar around her neck. The collar sends a radio signal–a series of beeps–that helps scientists track an animal's movements.

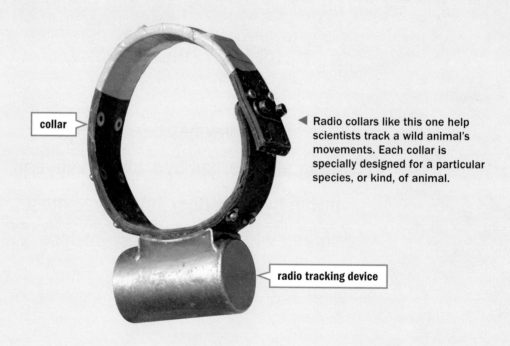

collar

◄ Radio collars like this one help scientists track a wild animal's movements. Each collar is specially designed for a particular species, or kind, of animal.

radio tracking device

Key Vocabulary

biologist *n.*, a scientist who studies living things

In Other Words

Shivers rolled down Quigley's spine Quigley was scared
pounce suddenly jump at him
Bull's eye! Quigley made a good shot.

Science Background

Howard Quigley started and co-directed the Siberian Tiger Project. He is a specialist in the research and protection of carnivores, or meat-eating animals, like tigers.

A scientist places a radio collar on a tiger. Olga was the first tiger to be fitted with a radio collar.

Cat Tracks

Quigley hoped Olga's collar would help him learn more about Siberian tigers. The speed of the beeps from her collar would tell him about the tiger's habits. It would also tell Quigley when she was sleeping, hunting, moving to a new **territory**–or dead.

Quigley needed to learn all he could about Olga's habits. His goal is to keep tigers like her from disappearing from the forest forever, or from becoming extinct.

Quigley wants to protect Siberian tigers because he knows what has happened to other tigers. In the last century, three species, or kinds, of tigers have died out. Only five species, including Siberian tigers, are left.

In Other Words
territory area of land

Look Into the Text

1. **Paraphrase** In your own words, tell how the radio collar works. What information does it provide about Olga?

2. **Problem and Solution** What problem is the **biologist** trying to solve? How is he hoping to accomplish this?

Poaching and Potions

By the time Quigley first saw Olga, many **wildlife experts** worried that Siberian tigers were about to become extinct. Their **habitat**, or home, had almost disappeared.

The big cats once **roamed** the area from eastern Russia to South Korea but by the early 1900s, overhunting had **wiped out** most of them. Fewer than fifty were left!

By 1947 laws were passed to protect the tigers. The laws have helped a little, but Olga and other tigers still face serious threats.

Some people in Asia believe that tiger parts can be used to improve health. Almost every body part is used to make some kind of **potion**. Brains, tails, and whiskers, for instance, are used to treat everything from pimples to toothaches to **paralysis**.

Poachers, people who hunt illegally, can make $15,000 from selling just one dead tiger. That's more money than most Asian families make in several years.

Siberian Tigers' Habitat: Then and Now

SIBERIA
RUSSIA

MONGOLIA

CHINA

NORTH KOREA

SOUTH KOREA

JAPAN

Where Siberian tigers live today

Where Siberian tigers lived 100 years ago

▲ **Interpret the Map** How has the location of Siberian tigers changed over the last 100 years?

Large numbers of trees in the Russian taiga forest are being cut down to make **timber**. This is destroying tiger habitat.

Key Vocabulary

wildlife *n.*, animals living in the wild

expert *n.*, a person who knows a lot about a subject

habitat *n.*, the place where a plant or an animal normally lives

poacher *n.*, a person who hunts animals illegally

In Other Words

roamed lived in
wiped out killed
potion drink used to treat disease
paralysis the inability to move
timber wood used for building

Dangers in the Wild

Poaching isn't the only danger tigers face. The cats are losing their forest habitat.

The Russian taiga is the largest forest on the planet. Scientists say a third of all trees in the world grow there. Many Siberian tigers and their prey–elk, wild boar, and deer–also live there.

But animals aren't alone in the forest. Many people are moving in. They're cutting down trees and tiger habitat.

High climber. Like house cats, Siberian tigers can climb trees.

Look Into the Text

1. **Explain** Laws have been passed to help protect tigers. Why are tigers still in danger?
2. **Cause and Effect** Why do people cut down the trees?

Snow covers the taiga in the harsh winter. Siberian tigers need their thick fur to stay warm in their habitat.

Tiger Protection

Tiger habitat doesn't have to be destroyed. Quigley thinks people can find a way to **balance their needs with those of** the tiger. "It's hard to tell the Russians that they can't sell their natural resources," says Quigley. "It's important to find a way to manage forests so tigers and their prey can continue to have a place to live."

Many experts say we can manage forests **in a cat-friendly way**. Some trees can be cut down, while others are left standing. This could allow people and tigers to use the same forests.

Protecting tiger habitat could even help people who live nearby make money. Tourists could travel there to see tigers. Tourism would create jobs for the local people. People with jobs that pay well are less likely to poach tigers.

In Other Words

balance their needs with those of share the forests with
in a cat-friendly way without disturbing tigers

Tiger Triumph?

Scientists are finding ways to protect Olga and other tigers. So far, they've helped set up anti-poaching **squads** to keep poachers out of the forest.

The squads look for signs that poachers have been in the forest. If they spot gun shells or traps, they know to look for poachers. Their work **is paying off**. They have helped make several arrests.

Some tigers still get poached, and their habitat is still **shrinking** but Siberian tiger numbers are **on the rise**. Nearly 400 may now roam the wild. Some are even moving into areas where they haven't been seen in years.

Four hundred tigers may not sound like a lot. It isn't. But it's a start. There are more tigers today than there were 100 years ago. And their numbers are **increasing**.

In May 2002, Olga gave birth to her sixth litter of cubs. In many ways, she was **thriving** and helping the endangered cats to make an amazing **comeback**. However, Olga's story also shows why poaching remains a serious threat to Siberian tigers.

In January 2005, Olga suddenly disappeared. Officials who were tracking Olga believe she is the victim of poachers. Staff of the Siberian Tiger Project have seen many cases in which poachers first kill the tiger and then destroy its collar. That's why scientists today are more determined than ever to protect endangered tigers, like Olga, from the continued threats to their survival. ❖

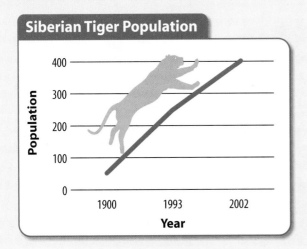

Siberian Tiger Population

Population (y-axis): 0, 100, 200, 300, 400
Year (x-axis): 1900, 1993, 2002

Look Into the Text

1. **Summarize** How can people work together to protect tigers and their **habitats**?
2. **Cause and Effect** Why has the Siberian tiger population **increased**?

Tigers in the Wild

Five species of tigers are still alive today. They live in the wild only in Asia.

Bengal

Population: Scientists believe there are between 3,000-5,000 tigers in the wild.

Indochinese

Population: Scientists believe there are fewer than 2,000 tigers in the wild.

Sumatran

Population: Scientists believe there are about 400 tigers in the wild.

Siberian

Population: Scientists believe there are fewer than 400 tigers in the wild.

South China

Population: Scientists believe there are no tigers left in the wild.

Tiger Facts

- The Siberian tiger is the largest type of tiger. An adult male can grow to be more than 10 feet long and weigh more than 600 pounds.

- Female tigers usually give birth to two or three cubs at a time.

- A newborn cub weighs between two and three pounds.

- Big cats such as tigers can roar, but they can't purr.

- Tigers are one of the few cats that like to swim in water.

Connect Reading and Writing

Vocabulary

biologists

experts

habitats

increase

poachers

shrink

thrive

wildlife

CRITICAL THINKING

1. **SUM IT UP** Use your Viewpoints Chart to summarize the different viewpoints that were presented and how the author responded to them.

Other People's Viewpoint	Author's Response
Some people in Asia believe that tiger parts can be used to improve health. Almost every body part is used to make some kind of potion.	• The word *potion* causes a negative feeling. • The author disagrees with using tiger parts to improve health.
	• •

Viewpoints Chart

2. **Describe and Explain** Tell a partner about the tools and steps that **experts** use to help animals like Olga.

3. **Make Judgments** What has the most harmful effect on tigers and their **habitat**? Give reasons from the text.

4. **Compare** What is the effect of **shrinking habitat** on Bengal tigers compared with Siberian tigers?

READING FLUENCY

Phrasing Read the passage on page 637 to a partner. Assess your fluency.

1. I did not pause/sometimes paused/always paused for punctuation.

2. What I did best in my reading was _____.

READING STRATEGY

What strategy helped you understand this selection? Tell a partner about it.

VOCABULARY REVIEW

Oral Review Read the paragraph aloud. Add the vocabulary words.

_____, scientists who study _____, including tigers, are worried. They want to save endangered animals and give them what they need to _____ so that the animal population will _____. The threats to animals include _____ who illegally hunt them. When people move into new areas, it can hurt the animals' _____. _____ say that if such places _____, some animals will become extinct.

Written Review Imagine you are a **biologist** who protects tigers. Write a journal entry about one day's work. Use five vocabulary words.

WRITE ABOUT THE GUIDING QUESTION

Explore How People Help Animals
How can people everywhere help protect **wildlife**? Reread the selection to find information people should have. Explain which actions have a harmful or helpful effect.

Connect Across the Curriculum

Use Context Clues: Multiple-Meaning Words Across Content Areas

Academic Vocabulary
- **context** (**kon**-tekst) *noun*
  Context is the text near a word or phrase that helps explain its meaning.

Words have different meanings in different subject areas. The word *product* in social science means "something that is made." In math it means "the result of multiplying two numbers."

Think About Context Each of these words has more than one meaning. Guess which meaning the author of the selection used. Then find each word in the selection. Use **context** to determine which meaning makes sense.

1. poach (p. 352)   a. to cook   b. to steal
2. resources (p. 352)   a. a supply   b. money, property, or wealth

---

Give an Informative Report

HEALTH & SCIENCE

Academic Vocabulary
- **research** (**rē**-surch) *noun*
  Research is a collection of information about something.

❶ **Conduct Research** Pick one of the five tigers from "Tigers in the Wild" on page 354. Use resources such as the Internet, books, and magazines to do **research**. Take notes about an aspect of the tiger that interests you and tell why people should work to save that tiger.

> The Sumatran tiger has lived in Sumatra, Indonesia, for over a million years.

❷ **Organize Your Report** Review your notes. Choose the most interesting facts and important details. Give sound reasons for why that species of tiger should be saved.

❸ **Give Your Report** Summarize your findings and tell your classmates what you learned. Remember to speak clearly and make eye contact.

Make Comparisons

Question Quiz Go back to the selection and look for ways to make three comparative statements about the Siberian tiger. Use comparative adjectives in your statements. They may be true or false. Quiz your partner. Trade roles.

> The Siberian tiger population is smaller than it used to be.

> False. The Siberian tiger population is larger than it used to be.

Write to Compare Tigers

Study the Models When you write, you can use comparisons to add details and make your writing more interesting. When you make comparisons, be sure the words show the comparison clearly so your reader can understand them.

NOT OK

The biologist was more fearless than the expedition leader. He bent over the tranquilized Siberian tiger and discovered that it was more large than the one he had examined yesterday. As he ran his hand through the big cat's fur, the biologist realized that its coat was more thicker than any other kind of tiger. The biologist thought that the tiger was beautifuler than any cat he'd seen.

> The reader thinks: "What exactly is 'beautifuler'?"

OK

The biologist was more fearless than the expedition leader. He bent over the tranquilized Siberian tiger and discovered that it was larger than the one he had examined yesterday. As he ran his hand through the big cat's fur, the biologist realized that its coat was thicker than any other kind of tiger. The biologist thought that the tiger was more beautiful than any cat he'd seen.

> The comparisons are now correct and clear.

Add Sentences Think of two sentences to add to the OK model above. Look for more ways that the people or animals are similar or different.

✎ **WRITE ON YOUR OWN** Write to compare the Siberian tigers in Russia with the Bengal tigers in India. Which tigers are larger? Which tigers are safer from poachers? Be sure to use the correct comparison words to make your writing clear.

REMEMBER

- Add **-er** to one-syllable adjectives. A tiger's tail is long**er** than a cat's tail.

- If the adjective ends in **y**, change the **y** to **i**. Then add **-er**. A tiger is heav**ier** than a house cat.

- Add **more** before adjectives with three or more syllables. A tiger's roar is **more ferocious** than a house cat's meow.

- Never use **more** and **-er** together.

Mireya Mayor
Explorer/Correspondent

Build Background

See an Explorer in Action

What does it feel like to explore the world and learn about the environment? Mireya Mayor knows. Her discovery of a tiny animal made a big difference in protecting the environment.

Digital Library

myNGconnect.com
🔘 View the video.

◀ Mireya Mayor travels the world to protect the environment.

Connect

Team Brainstorm Imagine that you are in the rainforest with Mireya Mayor, and you are trying to learn about a tiny animal called a mouse lemur. Brainstorm a list of questions to start your science log.

Questions for Nature Journey
1. What are some facts about the rainforest?
2. What is a mouse lemur?
3. Does it look like a mouse?

Language & Grammar

Elaborate

CD

Study the photos and listen for the differences between the main idea and the elaboration of the main idea. What details do you learn?

Outfoxing a Predator

Main Idea: These scientists are examining a type of fox that is in danger. By capturing and counting the foxes, they are trying to help them survive.

Elaboration: These biologists are examining the island fox, a type of fox that lives on islands near the coast of California. The island fox faces danger from predators that have been introduced to the islands. The biggest threat to the foxes is the golden eagle. It is mostly responsible for the recent decrease in the island fox population.

The island fox is about the size of a house cat. It does not mind being handled by humans. This makes it easier for scientists to capture island foxes, count them, release them, and help them. Scientists hope to increase the number of island foxes by giving them safe places to breed and moving the golden eagle back to its original habitat.

island fox ▶

golden eagle ▶

1 TRY OUT LANGUAGE
2 LEARN GRAMMAR
3 APPLY ON YOUR OWN

Use Adverbs

Adverbs are words that describe verbs, adjectives, or other adverbs. Adverbs can tell *how*, *when*, or *where*.

- Use an adverb to describe a verb. Many adverbs end in **-ly**.

  EXAMPLE   The animal **suddenly makes** a noise. (how)

  verb

Adverbs	
Tell how	The scientist hikes **silently** through the rainforest.
Tell when	She **sometimes** stops to watch and listen.
Tell where	The monkeys look **down** at the scientist.

- Use an adverb to make an adjective or another adverb stronger.

  EXAMPLES   The rainforest is **unusually quiet**.

  adjective

                   The scientist raises the camera **very slowly**.

  adverb

Practice Together

Say each adverb in the box with your class. Then say each sentence. Choose an adverb from the box to describe the underlined word. Say the sentence with the adverb.

again   carefully   peacefully   very

1. Walk _____ through the rainforest.
2. Be _____ respectful of the environment.
3. Look at the monkey sleeping _____ in that tree.
4. We will come _____ to see the monkey.

Try It!

Choose an adverb from the box to describe the underlined word. Then say and write each sentence with the adverb.

loudly   slowly   suddenly   very

5. The scientist _____ sees a snake in a tree.
6. The snake is lying _____ still on a branch.
7. It hisses _____.
8. The scientist moves _____ away.

▲ Scientists study wildlife closely.

Share an Experience

ELABORATE

Tell a partner about a hike or trip that you've taken or would like to take.

Begin by writing down the main points you want to share. Then think of ways you can elaborate on them. Elaborate by adding details, examples, and explanations.

Topic: Trip to Miller's Falls

Main Point	Elaboration
We climbed a hill to get to the waterfall.	We carefully climbed a rocky hill to get to the waterfall. The hill was very steep. We had to hold on tightly to the trees that lined the trail.
The waterfall was powerful.	The waterfall rushed powerfully to the river below. The water crashed down hard. Mist and spray from the waterfall filled the air.

Now share information about your hike or trip with your partner. Add details, examples, and explanations to elaborate. Trade roles.

HOW TO ELABORATE

1. Tell the topic or main point of discussion.
2. Add details. Give background information, examples, or explanations.
3. Tell *when*, *where*, and *how* events happened.

> What was the waterfall like?

> It was absolutely beautiful! The water moved quickly but very gracefully.

USE ADVERBS

When you tell about an experience, add details that tell *when*, *where*, and *how* things happened. Use **adverbs** to add interest and detail.

EXAMPLES We hiked the trail **slowly**. It was **very** steep and rocky. At the top, we **finally** stopped and **gratefully** watched the waterfall plummet **swiftly** to the bottom.

▲ The waterfall rushed swiftly to the river.

Prepare to Read

Learn Key Vocabulary

Study the Words Use the steps below.

1. Pronounce the word. Say it aloud several times. Spell it.
2. Rate your word knowledge.
3. Study the example. Tell more about the word.
4. Practice it. Make the word your own.

Key Words

awareness (u-**wair**-nes)
noun ▸ page 367

Awareness is having knowledge of something. To protect the Earth, it is important to have an **awareness** of things that could harm the planet.
Related Word: **aware**

conservation
(kon-sur-**vā**-shun) *noun* ▸ page 367

Conservation is careful protection of something. **Conservation** efforts protect national parks.

discovery (dis-**kuv**-ur-ē)
noun ▸ page 367

A **discovery** is the act of seeing or finding something for the first time. The hikers made an interesting **discovery** and took a closer look.
Plural: **discoveries**

document (**dok**-yu-ment)
verb ▸ page 368

To **document** something is to provide facts about it. A research study must be **documented** carefully with facts.

ensure (en-**shur**) *verb*
▸ page 366

To **ensure** is to make sure or certain. Humans should **ensure** that rainforests are protected.

establish (i-**stab**-lish) *verb*
▸ page 368

To **establish** something is to start it. My friends and I **established** a yearly food collection for families in need.

expedition
(ek-spu-**di**-shun) *noun* ▸ page 366

An **expedition** is a trip or journey made for a particular purpose. This is an **expedition** through the desert.

explorer (ek-**splor**-ur) *noun*
▸ page 366

An **explorer** goes to a place that is new to him or her to find information about it. Astronauts are **explorers** of our universe.
Related Words: **explore, exploration**

Practice the Words Tell a story that uses the Key Words. Partner 1 uses the first word. Partner 2 uses the next word to continue the story. Continue until you have used all the Key Words.

> **PARTNER 1:** Juana and Hyo have a new <u>awareness</u> of endangered wildlife.
>
> **PARTNER 2:** They want to learn more about <u>conservation</u> of animal habitats.

Analyze Author's Viewpoint

How Authors Express Their Viewpoints Sometimes you can tell an author's viewpoint about a topic by thinking about the decisions the author makes when writing. The author may decide to include certain information or not to include certain information.

As you read, notice what the author decided to include or leave out. What do those decisions tell you about the author's viewpoint?

Reading Strategies
- Plan
- Monitor
- Ask Questions
- Make Connections
- **Visualize** Imagine the sights, sounds, smells, tastes, and touch of what the author is describing.
- Make Inferences
- Determine Importance
- Synthesize

Look Into the Text

It all began in college. [Mireya] Mayor began studying primates. "I was seized by the fact that some of these incredible animals are on the verge of extinction. And they had never been studied. In some cases, not even a mere photograph existed to show their existence. I asked more questions. It became clear to me that much about our natural world still remained a mystery." Mayor decided to dedicate her life to solving that mystery.

Practice Together

Begin an Author's Viewpoint Chart An Author's Viewpoint Chart can help you analyze evidence about the author's viewpoint. This Author's Viewpoint Chart shows evidence from the passage above. Reread the passage above and add to the Author's Viewpoint Chart.

Author's Decision	What the Decision Tells About the Author's Viewpoint
The author decided to tell how Mayor became interested in primates.	This decision shows that the author admires Mayor's work.
The author decided to _____ _____	This decision shows _____ _____

Online Article

Nonfiction online articles are similar to printed articles, though they may have additional text features, such as links or menu items.

Some authors of nonfiction articles may not state a viewpoint, attitude, or position directly. However, they may include certain information and leave out other things. As you read, notice what the author decides to include. This gives a clue about the author's viewpoint.

Look Into the Text

Mireya Mayor has slept in the rainforest among poisonous snakes. She has been chased by gorillas, elephants, and leopards. She even swam with great white sharks!

The author includes these details to show that she believes that Mireya Mayor's job is exciting.

Visualizing the details the author decides to include can also help you understand the author's viewpoint.

Mireya Mayor in Madagascar, where she discovered a rare species of mouse lemur.

Mireya Mayor

Explorer/Correspondent

Emerging Explorers
National Geographic's Next Generation

OUR EXPLORERS	ABOUT THE PROGRAM

MIREYA MAYOR
EXPLORER/CORRESPONDENT

2007	2008	2009

» John Bul Dau
HUMANITARIAN/ SURVIVOR

» David de Rothschild
ENVIRONMENTAL STORYTELLER

» MIREYA MAYOR
EXPLORER/ CORRESPONDENT

» Roshini Thinakaran
FILMMAKER/ GLOBALIST

"The rainforest appears to be a **gigantic, green mishmash** of unknowns. We are still discovering new species and who knows what else might be out there. But we do know that every tree and creature in it plays a vital role in our existence. **Ensuring** their survival helps to ensure ours."

Mireya Mayor has slept in the rainforest among poisonous snakes. She has been chased by gorillas, elephants, and leopards. She even swam with great white sharks! Mayor is a city girl and a former NFL cheerleader. How does she find herself as an **explorer** in situations like this?

It all began in college. Mayor began studying **primates**. "I was **seized by** the fact that some of these incredible animals are **on the verge of** extinction. And they had never been studied. In some cases, not even a mere photograph existed to show their existence. I asked more questions. It became clear to me that much about our natural world still remained a mystery." Mayor decided to dedicate her life to solving that mystery.

Today, Mayor is a Fulbright scholar and a National Science Foundation Fellow. She also appears as a **correspondent** on the National Geographic Ultimate Explorer television series. Each **expedition** allows Mayor to teach viewers about a different species of animal that needs our help.

◀ Page 1 of 5 ▶   Go to page: [   ] Go

Key Vocabulary

ensure *v.*, to make sure that something happens
explorer *n.*, someone who travels around the world to discover new information
expedition *n.*, a trip

In Other Words

gigantic, green mishmash big, green mixture
primates apes, gorillas, and other animals like them
seized by completely focused on
on the verge of close to
correspondent reporter

366 Unit 5 Our Precious World

MIREYA MAYOR
EXPLORER/CORRESPONDENT

Click on map for detail

For example, one of Mayor's Ultimate Explorer TV expeditions allowed her to go to the Gulf of California. Her goal there was to research the powerful six-foot-long Humboldt Squid. It was a time of personal **discovery** that gave Mayor the opportunity to climb rocky cliffs and look at untouched tropical ecosystems.

An expedition led Mayor to Namibia. She went into a veterinarian's haven, or safe place, for leopards. "While caring for the leopards," Mayor explains, "the vet accidentally discovered a cure for fluid in the brain. It is a disease that also occurs in human infants. As a result of our film and the media attention it received, new studies are now taking place in children's hospitals. That is why I consider my television work just as important as my **conservation** field work," she notes. "The TV series sheds light on the **plight** of endangered species and animals around the world. Television has the power to help people know and connect with these animals and habitats that are disappearing. We may be facing the largest mass extinction of our time. **Awareness** is crucial. If we don't act now, it will be too late."

Mayor went to Madagascar on another of her Ultimate Explorer expeditions. On that expedition, she discovered a new species of mouse

◄ Page 2 of 5 ►

Go to page: [ ] Go

Key Vocabulary

discovery *n.*, something that is seen and made known for the first time

conservation *n.*, a careful protection of something

awareness *n.*, having knowledge of

In Other Words

plight difficult situation

Look Into the Text

1. **Fact and Opinion** What is one fact and one opinion that Mayor expresses?
2. **Cause and Effect** What happened as a result of the film that Mayor made at the Leopard haven?

MIREYA MAYOR
EXPLORER/CORRESPONDENT

"I had to get that documentation because only then was I able to lobby to have its (the lemur's) habitat fully protected," said Mayor.

lemur. This discovery brought everyone's attention to Mayor's work. She had to **document** it. Once it was documented, she could try to obtain protection for the animal's habitat. This required **grueling** field work during the **monsoon** season. "There we were, tromping through remote areas of jungle, rain pouring, tents blowing. We were looking for **a nocturnal animal**. One that happens to be the smallest primate in the world," she says. Her careful research and documentation were important. She was able to convince Madagascar's president to declare the species' habitat a national park. He also agreed to triple the number of protected areas in the nation. In addition, he **established** a $50 million conservation fund. As Mayor reports, one tiny discovery became "a huge **ambassador for** all things wild in Madagascar."

Mayor believes that local support for conservation is a key factor in bringing about change.

Mouse lemur

Key Vocabulary
document *v.*, to provide facts
establish *v.*, to create or setup

In Other Words
grueling very hard and tiring
monsoon rainy
a nocturnal animal an animal that stays awake at night and sleeps during the day
ambassador for way to bring attention to

MIREYA MAYOR
EXPLORER/CORRESPONDENT

Related NEWS

» Emerging Explorers News

» Photo Gallery: Best Mountain Photographs of 2008 Announced

» What Triggers Tornadoes? New Season May Hold Answers

"The local people are **the very core** of effective conservation. Without their support, the 'dream' of saving the planet can never become a reality. The rainforest is **literally their backyard**. Yet many Malagasy kids have never even seen a lemur. So I organize lots of field trips into the forest. Only by seeing how amazing these creatures are, will kids want to protect them." Mayor stresses the importance of providing education and opportunities for local communities to learn about the threats to animals and how they can help. She believes it will be critical to protecting the planet.

Healthy Rainforest

Destroyed Rainforest

Mayor's conservation work makes locals aware that the destruction of the rainforest threatens the lives of plants and animals.

◀ Page 4 of 5 ▶   Go to page: [ ] Go

In Other Words

the very core the most important part

literally their backyard so close by

Look Into the Text

1. **Conclusion** Why was it important for Mayor to **document** her **discovery**?

2. **Cause and Effect** Name two things Madagascar's president **established** as a result of Mayor's work.

3. **Paraphrase** Tell in your own words why Mayor organizes field trips.

MIREYA MAYOR
EXPLORER/CORRESPONDENT

Baobab tree in Madagascar

Mayor **circles the globe** on television expeditions, but her heart remains in the rainforests of Madagascar. As she describes it, "This phenomenal natural laboratory could vanish in our lifetime. It could become **the stuff of history books, not science books**. Until I can walk away . . . and know it's going to be okay, I just can't leave." ❖

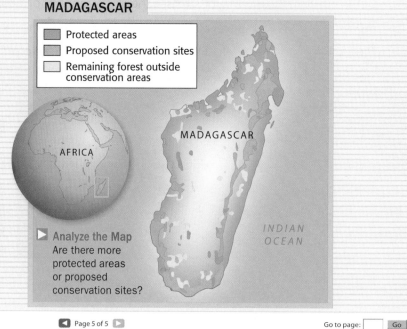

MADAGASCAR

- ▨ Protected areas
- ▨ Proposed conservation sites
- ☐ Remaining forest outside conservation areas

AFRICA

MADAGASCAR

INDIAN OCEAN

▶ Analyze the Map
Are there more protected areas or proposed conservation sites?

In Other Words

circles the globe travels around the world
the stuff of history books, not science books something that is gone forever

Look Into the Text

1. **Conclusion** Why are the **conservation** efforts of people like Mayor important? Support your answer.

2. **Fact and Opinion** State one fact that increased your **awareness** about the environment. Give one opinion of your own about Mayor's work.

Connect Reading and Writing

Vocabulary

awareness

conservation

discovery

document

ensure

establish

expedition

explorer

CRITICAL THINKING

1. **SUM IT UP** Use your Author's Viewpoint Chart to summarize the different decisions the author made and what those decisions tell about the author's viewpoint.

Author's Decision	What the Decision Tells About the Author's Viewpoint
The author decided to tell how Mayor became interested in primates.	This decision shows that the author admires Mayor's work.
The author decided to _____	This decision shows _____

Author's Viewpoint Chart

2. **Classify** Mayor is an **explorer** and a correspondent. First, classify her audience into different groups. Then, classify the different ways she communicates to each group.

3. **Explain** During her Madagascar **expedition**, Mayor had to **document** a **discovery**. Explain this process, using details from the text.

4. **Evaluate** Why is it important to **ensure** that Malagasy kids and other young people develop an **awareness** of animals in their local environment?

READING FLUENCY

Expression Read the passage on page 638 to a partner. Assess your fluency.

1. My voice never/sometimes/always matched what I read.
2. What I did best in my reading was _____.

READING STRATEGY

What strategy helped you understand this selection? Tell a partner about it.

VOCABULARY REVIEW

Oral Review Read the paragraph aloud. Add the vocabulary words.

When an _____ goes on an _____ somewhere, he or she always hopes to make an important _____. To _____ that the facts are correct, this person must _____ what he or she finds. The work of _____ includes developing public _____ of local environments.

Written Review Imagine you are an **explorer** who wants to raise **awareness** about **conservation**. Write a letter to encourage people to learn about their environment. Use five vocabulary words.

 **WRITE ABOUT THE** GUIDING QUESTION

Explore Our Precious World

What traits should an **explorer** who makes **expeditions** around the world have? Reread the selection to find examples that support your ideas.

Connect Across the Curriculum

Use Context Clues: Jargon

> **Academic Vocabulary**
> • **specific** (spi-**sif**-ik) *adjective*
>   When something is **specific**, it is definite or particular.

Words and phrases that have special meanings related to a **specific** subject or job are called **jargon**. You can use **context**, or the words around the jargon, to figure out its meaning.

Use Context Find each of these jargon words in the selection. Use context to figure out the meaning. Use a dictionary if you need more help.

1. haven (p. 367)   **3.** field (p. 367)

2. habitats (p. 367)   **4.** document (p. 368)

How is the **specific** meaning different from other meanings of each word?

Analyze Media: Informational Text

Online articles share some text features with books and magazine articles. Online articles also have unique text features that printed texts do not.

Look at page 369. At the top of the screen is a menu bar. You can click on the buttons there to learn more about explorers and to get information about the explorer program. On the left side of the screen are links. Clicking on these will take you to related articles about explorers.

Analyze and Compare Review "Siberian Survivors" and "Mireya Mayor." Identify the different ways information is presented in each selection. What are the advantages and disadvantages of each type of presentation?

Elaborate

Role-Play With a partner, act out an interview with Mireya Mayor. One partner plays the role of a news reporter and asks questions about Mayor's work and discoveries. The other partner plays Mayor and gives detailed answers. Use adverbs to elaborate. Trade roles.

> What did you recently discover in Madagascar?

> I recently discovered a very small primate. It is the smallest primate in the world!

Write About a Discovery

Study the Models When you write about events, you want to keep your readers interested in your writing. A key way to hold their interest is to elaborate and add colorful details about *when*, *where*, and *how* the events happen. You can provide comparisons to elaborate even more.

NOT OK

Of all endangered species, Mireya studied primates the most serious. She skillful investigated the jungles of Madagascar. The wind blew fierce in her face as she walked deeper into the underbrush. Then she saw it—a new species of mouse lemur. She held the small primate gentle. Then she documented her discovery carefuller than ever before. The expedition was a success.

> **The reader thinks:** "I don't understand the details."

OK

Of all endangered species, Mireya studied primates the most seriously. She skillfully investigated the jungles of Madagascar. The wind blew fiercely in her face as she walked deeper into the underbrush. Then she saw it—a new species of mouse lemur. She held the small primate gently. Then she documented her discovery more carefully than ever before. The expedition was a success.

> **The adverbs are correct, so the details are clear.**

Add Sentences Think of two sentences to add to the OK model above. Look for more ways to add details to your sentences.

WRITE ON YOUR OWN Write a description of a time you discovered something new. Use colorful details that tell *when*, *where*, and *how*. Help the reader see and experience the event you are writing about.

REMEMBER
- Many adverbs end in **-ly**: **slowly, carefully, playfully**

- Use **-er** with one-syllable adverbs to compare two actions: **faster, softer**

- Use **more** with two- or three-syllable adverbs: **more slowly, more carefully, more playfully**

WILDERNESS LETTER

David E. Pesonen   December 3, 1960
Wildland Research Center, Agricultural Experiment Station

Dear Mr. Pesonen:

1   I believe that you are working on the wilderness **portion** of the Outdoor Recreation Resources Review Commission's report. If I may, I should like to **urge** some arguments for wilderness preservation . . . What I want to speak for is not so much the wilderness uses, valuable as those are, but the wilderness idea, which is a resource in itself . . .

2   Something will have gone out of us as a people if we ever let the remaining wilderness be destroyed; if we permit the last **virgin forests** to be turned into comic books and plastic cigarette cases; if we drive the few remaining members of the wild **species** into zoos or to extinction; if we pollute the last clear air and dirty the last clean streams and push our paved roads through the last of the silence, so that never again will Americans be free in their own country from the noise, the exhausts, the stinks of human and automotive waste. And so that never again can we have the chance to see ourselves single, separate, vertical and individual in the world, part of the **environment** of trees and rocks and soil, brother to the other animals, part of the natural world and competent to belong in it. Without any remaining wilderness we are committed wholly, without chance for even momentary reflection and rest, to a **headlong drive** into our technological termite-life, the Brave New World of a completely man-controlled environment. We need wilderness preserved—as much of it as is still left, and as many kinds—because it was the challenge against which our character as a people was formed. The reminder and the reassurance that it is still there is good for our spiritual health even if we never once in ten years set foot in it. It is good for us when we are young, because of the incomparable sanity it can bring briefly, as vacation and rest, into our insane lives. It is important to us when we are old simply because it is there—important, that is, simply as idea.

3   . . . That is the reason we need to put into effect, for its preservation, some other principle than the principles of **exploitation** or "usefulness" or even recreation. We simply need that wild country available to us, even if we never do more than drive to its edge and look in. For it can be a means of reassuring ourselves of our sanity as creatures, a part of the geography of hope.

Very sincerely yours,
Wallace Stegner

"We need wilderness preserved."

Compare Across Texts

Compare Media Treatments

"A Natural Balance," "Siberian Survivors," "Mireya Mayor: Explorer/Correspondent," and "Wilderness Letter" all tell about the **effects** of human activities on the environment. Compare how information was presented in these different types of media.

How It Works

Organize and Compare Ideas Use a chart to compare the ways the four texts use different media treatments to approach the same topic. What are the advantages and disadvantages of each medium?

Comparison Chart

Selection	Media Used	Advantages of the Medium	Disadvantages of the Medium
"A Natural Balance"	Text, photos, diagrams, graphics	Photos clearly show effects, diagram explains oil spills	Too many facts packed into graphics
"Siberian Survivors"	Text, photos, maps	Graphics, maps easy to read	Photos, captions easy to skip
"Mireya Mayor"			
"Wilderness Letter"			

Practice Together

Summarize the Ideas Here is the beginning of a summary comparing the media treatments of the four selections.

Summary

> The four selections use different media to tell about the effects of human activities on the environment. There are advantages and disadvantages to each medium. For example, the photographs and diagrams in "A Natural Balance"...

Try It!

Copy the chart and complete it. Summarize your ideas. You may use this frame to write your summary.

The selections use different media to present information about _____ . There are _____ and _____ to each medium. For example, the _____ and _____ in "_____" _____ . The _____ and _____ in "_____" _____ .

Academic Vocabulary

- **effect** (i-**fekt**) *noun*
  An **effect** is the result of an action or cause.

OUR PRECIOUS WORLD

GUIDING QUESTION

What makes the environment so valuable?

Content Library

Leveled Library

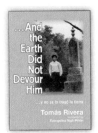
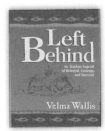

Reflect on Your Reading

Think back on your reading of the unit selections. Discuss what you did to understand what you read.

Focus on Reading **Text Features**

In this unit, you learned how text features, such as charts, graphs, and online links support the author's viewpoint and help you gain information. Choose a feature from one of the selections that was helpful to you. Discuss with a partner why it was useful.

Focus Strategy **Visualize**

As you read the selections, you learned to visualize what you were reading. Explain to a partner how this strategy will help you in the future.

Explore the GUIDING QUESTION

In this unit, you have been reading about our precious world. Choose one of these ways to explore the Guiding Question:

- **Discuss** With a group, discuss the Guiding Question. What makes our environment so valuable? How can we solve its problems? Share your ideas with classmates and give examples from the selections to support them.

- **Role-Play** Imagine that Howard Quigley and Mireya Mayor meet to talk about the Guiding Question. With a partner, role-play their discussion. To help you create the discussion, think of two questions they might ask each other.

- **Draw** Create a drawing to answer to the Guiding Question. Your drawing could be anything that shows your view about the value of our environment.

Book Talk

Which Unit Library book did you choose? Explain to a partner what it taught you about the environment.

CONFLICT AND
RESOLUTION

6

GUIDING
QUESTION
Q

How should people overcome conflict?

READ MORE!

Content Library
    Greek Civilization

Leveled Library
    I Will Paint You a Lilac Tree
    by Laura Hamilton
    The Other Side of the Sky
    by Farrah Ahmedi and Ansary Tamim
    Navajo Code Talkers
    by Andrew Santella

Web Links
    myNGconnect.com

◀ Grape pickers in California march against poor pay and working conditions in January 1966. The farm workers are striking, or refusing to work for, the grape industry until their conditions are met.

Focus on Reading

Determine Author's Purpose

An author's **purpose** is his or her reason for writing. It may be to entertain, inform, express ideas and feelings, or to persuade readers.

How It Works

Recognizing an author's **purpose** for writing can help you understand what the author wants you to know or think. The genre is one clue that can help you figure this out.

Genre	Purposes
Short stories, fables, other fiction	to entertain; to communicate a life lesson
Expository nonfiction	to inform; to express ideas and opinions
Advertisements, other persuasive writing	to convince you to act or think a certain way
Poetry	to express feelings; to entertain

The author's **word choices** also provide clues.

- The words in the title of a text often suggest the genre.
- Words that create a funny, sad, angry, or other kind of mood suggest that the **purpose** is to entertain or persuade.
- Positive words that describe one idea and negative words that describe another idea could show you the author's attitude.
- Words that state facts signal that the **purpose** is to inform.

Study the passage below to discover the author's **purpose**.

The Daydreamer and the Baker

Once there lived a pleasant young man who spent his time daydreaming about the delicious smells from the bakery next door. The stingy baker grew annoyed that the young man enjoyed the aromas but never bought a single thing.

"The title sounds like a folk tale."

Positive words describe the young man.

Negative words describe the baker.

"I think the author's purpose is to communicate a life lesson."

Academic Vocabulary

- **purpose** (**pur**-pus) *noun*
  A **purpose** is a reason for doing something.

Practice Together

Read the following passages aloud with your class. Identify the author's **purpose** in each. How do the word choices provide clues to each **purpose**?

Mistaken Identity

Liza storms into the room. "Dad, my boyfriend is such a jerk! I was at the mall with Shannon, and we saw him there with another girl."

They hear a knock at the door. "Maybe that's Richard now," says Dad.

Richard enters with a girl. "Hi! This is my favorite cousin, Sarah, from Arizona. Sarah, this is Liza, my girlfriend."

Liza blushes. Dad chuckles.

Cesar Chavez

During grape harvest season in 1965, grape growers in the U.S. cut back on how much they paid the farm workers. To fight the pay cut, the farm workers developed a new and effective plan. Under the leadership of Cesar Chavez, the workers went directly to people and asked them to stop buying grapes. Over time, the plan worked. In 1969, the grape growers signed a contract with farm workers promising better pay and fair treatment.

Try It!

Read the following passage aloud. What is the author's **purpose**? How do you know?

Internment in America

In 1942 the United States and Japan were at war. The President of the U.S. issued an Executive Order that said Japanese Americans on the west coast had to leave their homes and live in government camps. Families were forced to move to terrible, overcrowded camps guarded by soldiers. Many of these people were good citizens, and not one had been proved to be a spy.

▲ Thousands of Japanese Americans were forced into internment camps like this one at Gila River, Arizona.

After the war, Japanese Americans spent years working to get an apology from the U.S. government. Finally, Congress passed the Civil Liberties Act of 1988. The Act formally admitted the suffering and losses of the Japanese Americans during World War II. Their honor was properly restored at last.

Focus on Vocabulary

Go Beyond the Literal Meaning

Sometimes writers use words to mean exactly what they say. These exact meanings are called **literal** meanings. **Figurative language** goes beyond the **literal** meanings and creates images in the reader's mind.

Types of Figurative Language

Definitions	Examples	Explanations
A **simile** compares two things, usually using *like*, *as*, or *than*.	A spring breeze arrived **like** a joyful dancer.	The simile compares a spring breeze to a joyful dancer.
A **metaphor** says one thing *is* another.	A spring breeze **was** a gift after the long winter.	This metaphor compares a spring breeze to a gift.
Personification gives human qualities to things that aren't human.	A spring breeze **smiled** on us after the long winter.	A breeze cannot smile; this is a human trait.
In an **idiom**, the words mean something different from their dictionary meanings.	Jon stopped singing when his friends said to **cool it**.	The literal meaning of *cool it* is "to make something colder." The idiom means to stop.
An **analogy** shows how ideas are related to each other.	Stanza **is to** poem **as** verse **is to** song. Stanza : poem :: verse : song	A stanza is related to a poem in the same way as a verse is related to a song.

How the Strategy Works

Use context to help you figure out language that is not **literal**.

1. Decide whether a **literal** meaning could be correct.
2. Look at the figurative language to see what is being compared.
3. Think about what the comparison could mean.
4. Decide what feeling or image the writer is trying to create.

Follow the strategy to figure out the meanings of the underlined phrases.

Marie was new in our school that year. She had lived in many places and was <u>as bright as a new penny</u>. Her mind was <u>a present waiting to be opened</u>. Her stories <u>handed me the world</u>. She was <u>as surprising to me as sunshine is to a dark winter day</u>.

Strategy in Action

" The friend is bright, which also means smart. A new penny is shiny and seems special. The new friend is smart and special. "

☑ **REMEMBER** **Literal** meanings are the exact meanings of words. **Figurative language** extends beyond the exact meanings of words.

Academic Vocabulary

● **literal** (lit-ur-al) *adjective*
The **literal** meaning of a word is its exact meaning.

Practice Together

Read the passage aloud. Figure out the meaning of each underlined phrase.

A Nation Rises

In December of 1941, enemy aircraft attacked the U.S. Naval Base at Pearl Harbor, Hawaii. The attack struck the American people <u>like a thunderbolt</u>. War had been going on in Europe and in Asia for more than two years, but the United States had stayed out.

Many Americans thought war could never reach them. It was <u>a distant buzz</u>, troublesome but far away. That way of thinking soon ended.

Protected by oceans on either side, few Americans imagined the country being attacked. The events of Pearl Harbor <u>were to the nation as shocking as icewater is to an infant</u>.

At first angry, then with determination <u>like steel</u>, <u>America went to work</u>. Millions joined the Army. Factories produced war supplies <u>around the clock</u>. Everyone did what he or she could. A spirit of purpose <u>gripped</u> the nation.

Try It!

Read the following passage. Look at each underlined phrase. What does it mean? How do you know?

GOAL!

<u>The start of a new game was to Tina as exciting as the birth of a new baby is to a mother</u>. She raced <u>like the wind</u> down the sidelines of the soccer field. No defenders were nearby. Looking back up the field, she saw that <u>luck was her friend</u>. Her teammate had broken loose with the ball. Tina cut to the center to get the pass.

She was alone no longer. A <u>hawk of a defender</u> was on her. Tina got the pass and then dribbled left and quickly back right. The defender stayed with her at first, then stumbled and fell back <u>like a confused kitten</u>. With <u>a mind of its own</u>, Tina's <u>foot hammered the ball</u> toward the net. Goal!

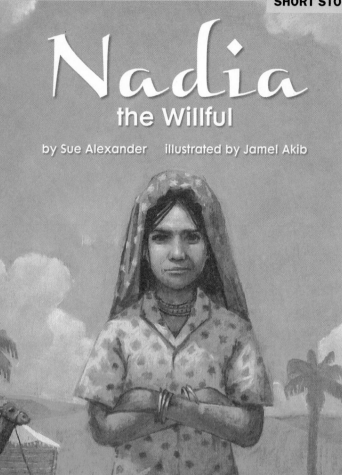

Nadia
the Willful

by Sue Alexander   illustrated by Jamel Akib

Build Background

Connect

Anticipation Guide Conflict is difficult. Read the statements below and tell whether you agree or disagree with them.

	Agree	Disagree
1. You should not talk about problems or feelings.	_____	_____
2. You should never change your mind.	_____	_____
3. If you know something is right, act on your belief.	_____	_____

Anticipation Guide

Bedouin Culture

"Nadia the Willful" takes place in the Bedouin culture of the Arabian Peninsula. Find out more about the lives of Bedouin people today.

Digital Library

myNGconnect.com
◔ View the images.

Bedouin people have their own unique culture. ▶

Express Opinions CD

Listen to the song. What opinion is expressed in this song?
Listen again and sing along.

SONG

I've Been Thinking

Mother, Father, I've been thinking
There are times we don't agree,
Still I think it's good to follow
Family rules and policy.

"Do your schoolwork. Clean your bedroom.
Exercise! Watch less TV."
Such advice is beneficial
Even when I disagree.

But here's a little brief opinion:
We could have more harmony
If you take this small suggestion—
Just a little tip from me.

Doing chores and all my schoolwork
Pleases you and pleases me.
I deserve a small allowance.
That's my view. Do you agree?

Use Compound Sentences

- A **clause** contains a **subject** and a **verb**. An **independent clause** has a subject and verb and can stand alone as a sentence.

    EXAMPLES   My **family** **made** some rules.

independent clause

    We all **follow** them.

independent clause

- A **compound sentence** has at least two independent clauses joined by **and**, **but**, or **or**. The words **and**, **but**, and **or** are **conjunctions**.

- **Conjunctions** join two independent clauses to form a compound sentence. A comma (,) always comes before the conjunction.

    EXAMPLES   My family made some rules, **and** we all follow them.

independent clause   independent clause

Conjunction	Independent Clauses	Compound Sentence
Use **and** to join similar ideas.	Parents make the rules. They believe the rules are fair.	Parents make the rules, **and** they believe the rules are fair.
Use **but** to join different ideas.	Some rules keep people safe. Others promote cooperation.	Some rules keep people safe, **but** others promote cooperation.
Use **or** to show a choice.	A rule can tell you what to do. It can explain what not to do.	A rule can tell you what to do, **or** it can explain what not to do.

Practice Together

Say each pair of sentences. Choose *and*, *but*, or *or* to combine them. Say each new compound sentence and add the correct word.

1. At the Mills home, clothes should be put away. Clothes can be taken to the laundry room.

2. Becca left some jeans in the hallway. Her mom almost tripped over the clothes.

3. Becca used to ignore the rule. Now she picks up her clothes.

Try It!

Say each pair of sentences. Choose *and*, *but*, or *or* to combine them. Write each conjunction on a card. Include the comma. Then use the conjunction to say the compound sentence.

4. Carole thought a rule was unfair. She didn't know what to do about it.

5. She met with her friend. They discussed it.

6. Carole decided to talk to her mom. She might ask her dad to change the rule.

▲ Discussions help people solve conflicts, and they promote understanding.

What Do You Think?

EXPRESS OPINIONS

When you express an opinion, you tell what you think or how you feel about something. Read this story. How do you think Rico should solve his problem?

> Rico looked forward to the football game on Saturday night. The teams were cross-town rivals, and excitement had been building for weeks.
>
> On Saturday morning, Rico's mom told him that she needed him to babysit his five-year-old sister. Their regular sitter had canceled, and Rico's parents had to go to a business dinner.
>
> When Rico protested, his mom told him that there was nothing else they could do.

First, gather your opinions in a list, like this example.

My Opinions:

I think Rico should try to go to the game.

In my opinion, his parents are being unfair.

They could try to find another babysitter.

Then use your list to express your opinions with a group.

HOW TO EXPRESS OPINIONS

1. Tell what you think or believe.

2. Use opinion words like *I think, I don't think, I believe, I don't believe, in my opinion.*

3. Give reasons for your opinions. Then people will take them more seriously.

> I don't think Rico should have to babysit. He's been planning on going to the game for weeks.

USE COMPOUND SENTENCES

When you tell your opinions, use complete sentences to express yourself. When possible, combine your ideas into compound sentences. Make sure to use a **comma** and a **conjunction**.

EXAMPLE   I think Rico's parents are unfair, **and** they should find another sitter.

Prepare to Read

Learn Key Vocabulary

Study the Words Use the steps below.

1. Pronounce the word. Say it aloud several times. Spell it.
2. Rate your word knowledge.
3. Study the example. Tell more about the word.
4. Practice it. Make the word your own.

Key Words

banish (ban-ish) *verb*
▶ page 398

To **banish** means to send away or punish by making someone leave. The referee **banished** the player from the game.

forbid (fur-bid) *verb*
▶ page 398

To **forbid** means to order not to do something. The sign **forbids** anyone to swim in this area.
Related Word: **forbidden**

grief (grēf) *noun*
▶ page 394

To feel **grief** is to feel very sad. My friend felt **grief** when her dog died.
Antonym: **happiness**

memory (me-mu-rē) *noun*
▶ page 394

A **memory** is something remembered. Looking through family photographs can bring back **memories** of good times.

obey (ō-bā) *verb*
▶ page 394

To **obey** is to follow an order. If your parents tell you to clean your room, you must **obey** them.

punishment
(pun-ish-ment) *noun* ▶ page 394

A **punishment** is a penalty for doing something bad. When Dad was a kid, the **punishment** for late homework was to write lines on the chalkboard.
Related Word: **punish**

recall (rē-kawl) *verb*
▶ page 398

To **recall** means to remember. The student tries to **recall** the answer to a test question.
Synonym: **remember**

willful (wil-ful) *adjective*
▶ page 392

Someone who is **willful** refuses to change. A **willful** child only does what he wants, not what others tell him.

Practice the Words Make a Synonym–Antonym Chart for each Key Word.

Word	Synonyms	Antonyms
banish	expel, send away	welcome, invite
forbid		
grief		

Synonym–Antonym Chart

Compare Viewpoints

What is a Reader's Viewpoint? You know that an author's viewpoint is his or her attitude toward a topic. You also know that other people have viewpoints that may differ from the author's. As a reader, you also have a viewpoint. When you read a story, for example, you follow what all of the characters are feeling, doing, and saying. This allows you to view a situation in a different way than a character does.

To identify your viewpoint, put together information that you know and that you learn from the text.

Reading Strategies
- Plan
- Monitor
- Ask Questions
- Visualize
- Make Connections
- **Make Inferences**
  When the author does not say something directly, use what you know to figure out what the author means.
- Determine Importance
- Synthesize

Look Into the Text

Imena gazed lovingly at her new shoes. The shoes gave her the chance to go to school. She could never walk across the desert to the school without those shoes.

"Imena, quit admiring those shoes," said her mother. "Help me clean this house. Fashion is foolish!"

Imena's brother, Nasir, chuckled at his mother's comments.

"I've heard enough from Imena about that school," Nasir thought. "Why does she need an education? I never had the chance to go to school."

Inference Chart

What I Read	What I Already Know
"Fashion is foolish!"	Parents don't always know what their children are thinking.

What I Can Infer: Imena's mother does not understand how important school is to Imena.

Practice Together

Begin a Reader's Viewpoint Chart A Reader's Viewpoint Chart can help you compare your viewpoint with a character's or the author's viewpoint. This Reader's Viewpoint Chart compares one reader's viewpoint with Imena's mother's viewpoint. Reread the passage and add to the chart.

Imena's mother thinks that Imena is admiring how her shoes look.	I know that Imena is thinking about how her shoes help her get an education.	My viewpoint is that Imena's education is more important than a clean house.
Nasir feels	I know that	My viewpoint is that

Short Story

A short story is a short piece of fiction. It has just a few characters and a simple plot.

As with other works of fiction, you can find clues in a short story that tell you what the author thinks or believes about the characters or events. As a reader, when you compare the author's viewpoint to your own viewpoint, you will better understand the story.

Look Into the Text

Nadia's father, the sheik Tarik, whose kindness and graciousness caused his name to be praised in every tent, did not know what to do with his willful daughter.

> **What have you learned about Nadia?**

Only Hamed, the eldest of Nadia's six brothers and Tarik's favorite son, could calm Nadia's temper when it flashed. "Oh, angry one," he would say, "shall we see how long you can stay that way?" And he would laugh and tease and pull at her dark hair until she laughed back. Then she would follow Hamed wherever he led.

As you read, use what you know from your own experiences and what the author says to make inferences.

Nadia
the Willful

by Sue Alexander   illustrated by Jamel Akib

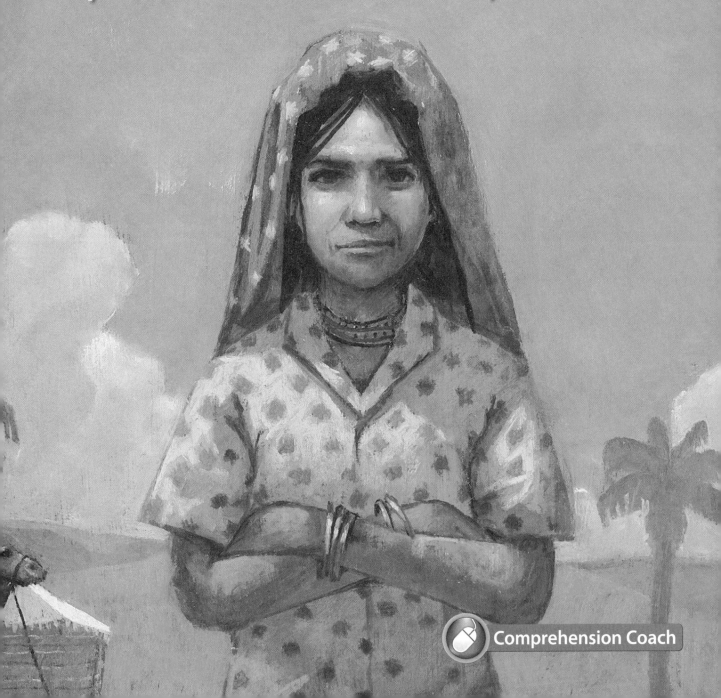

Set a Purpose

Discover why Nadia is called willful.

In the land of the drifting sands where the Bedouin move their tents to **follow the fertile grasses**, there lived a girl whose stubbornness and **flashing temper** caused her to be known throughout the desert as Nadia the **Willful**.

Nadia's father, the **sheik** Tarik, whose kindness and graciousness **caused his name to be praised** in every tent, did not know what to do with his willful daughter.

Only Hamed, the eldest of Nadia's six brothers and Tarik's favorite son, could calm Nadia's temper when it flashed. "Oh, angry one," he would say, "shall we see how long you can stay that way?" And he would laugh and tease and pull at her dark hair until she laughed back. Then she would follow Hamed wherever he led.

⊿ Critical Viewing: Character Which characters does the artist portray in this painting?

Key Vocabulary	In Other Words	Cultural Background
willful *adj.*, doing things your own way	**follow the fertile grasses** find food for their animals **flashing temper** bursts of anger **sheik** old and wise man **caused his name to be praised** made him well-liked	Many **Bedouin** people live in the deserts of the Arabian Peninsula. They move from place to place with their flocks to find food, water, and shelter.

One day before dawn, Hamed mounted his father's great white stallion and rode to the west to seek new grazing ground for the sheep. Nadia stood with her father at the edge of the oasis and watched him go.

Hamed did not return.

Nadia rode behind her father as he traveled across the desert **from oasis to oasis**, seeking Hamed.

Shepherds told them of seeing a great white stallion fleeing before the pillars of wind that stirred the sand. And they said that the horse carried no rider.

Passing merchants, their camels laden with spices and sweets for the **bazaar**, told of the emptiness of the desert they had crossed.

Tribesmen, strangers, everyone whom Tarik asked, sighed and gazed into the desert, saying, "**Such is the will of Allah.**"

At last Tarik knew in his heart that his favorite son, Hamed, had been claimed, as other Bedouin before him, by the drifting sands. And he told Nadia what he knew— that Hamed was dead.

Nadia screamed and wept and stamped the sand, crying, "Not even Allah will take Hamed from me!" until her father could bear no more and **sternly bade her to silence**.

▲ Critical Viewing: Design How does the artist capture the pain of Tarik?

In Other Words
from oasis to oasis stopping at places to get water and shelter
bazaar market
Such is the will of Allah It is meant to be
sternly bade her to silence angrily told her to be quiet

Nadia's **grief knew no bounds**. She walked blindly through the oasis neither seeing nor hearing those who would **console her**. And Tarik was silent. For days he sat inside his tent, speaking not at all and barely tasting the meals set before him.

Then, on the seventh day, Tarik came out of his tent. He called all his people to him, and when they were assembled, he spoke. "From this day forward," he said, "let no one **utter** Hamed's name. **Punishment** shall be swift for those who would remind me of what I have lost."

Hamed's mother wept at the **decree**. The people of the clan looked at one another uneasily. All could see the hardness that had settled on the sheik's face and the coldness in his eyes, and so they said nothing. But they **obeyed**.

Punishment shall be swift.

Nadia, too, did as her father decreed, though each day held something to remind her of Hamed. As she passed her brothers at play, she remembered games Hamed had taught her. As she walked by the women weaving patches for the tents, and heard them talking and laughing, she remembered tales Hamed had told her and how they had made her laugh. And as she watched the shepherds with their flock, she remembered the little black lamb Hamed had loved.

Each **memory** brought Hamed's name to Nadia's lips, but she **stilled the sound**. And each time that she did so, her unhappiness grew until, finally, she could no longer contain it. She wept and raged at anyone and anything that crossed her path. Soon everyone at the oasis fled at her approach. And she was more lonely than she had ever been before.

Key Vocabulary

grief *n.*, great sadness

punishment *n.*, the suffering received for doing wrong

obey *v.*, to do as you are told

memory *n.*, something you remember from the past

In Other Words

knew no bounds did not stop

console her try to make her feel better

utter say

decree order

stilled the sound did not say his name

Look Into the Text

1. **Cause and Effect** What difficulties does Nadia experience? How do they affect her?

2. **Character's Motive** What does Tarik forbid his people to say out loud? Why?

3. **Conflict** How do the people react to Tarik's order? Explain.

One day, as Nadia passed the place where her brothers were playing, she stopped to watch them. They were playing one of the games that Hamed had taught her. But they were playing it wrong.

Without thinking, Nadia called out to them. "That is not the way! Hamed said that first you jump this way and then you jump back!"

Her brothers stopped their game and looked around in fear. Had Tarik heard Nadia say Hamed's name? But the sheik was **nowhere to be seen**.

"Teach us, Nadia, as our brother taught you," said her smallest brother.

And so she did. Then she told them of other games and how Hamed had taught her to play them. And as she spoke of Hamed she felt **an easing of the hurt within her**.

In Other Words
nowhere to be seen not there
**an easing of the hurt within
her** her pain begin to go away

So she went on speaking of him.

She went to where the women sat at their loom and spoke of Hamed. She told them tales that Hamed had told her. And she told how he had made her laugh as he was telling them.

At first the women were afraid to listen to the willful girl and covered their ears, but after a time, they listened and laughed with her.

"Remember your father's promise of punishment!" Nadia's mother warned when she heard Nadia speaking of Hamed. **"Cease, I implore you!"**

Nadia knew that her mother had reason to be afraid, for Tarik, in his grief and **bitterness**, had grown quick-tempered and **sharp of tongue**. But she did not know how to tell her mother that speaking of Hamed eased the pain she felt, and so she said only, "I will speak of my brother! I will!" And she ran away from the sound of her mother's voice. She went to where the shepherds tended the flock and spoke of Hamed. The shepherds ran from her in fear and hid behind the sheep. But Nadia went on speaking. She told of Hamed's love for the little black lamb and how he had taught it to leap at his whistle. Soon the shepherds left off their hiding and came to listen. Then they told their own stories of Hamed and the little black lamb.

The more Nadia spoke of Hamed, **the clearer his face became in her mind**. She could see his smile and the light in his eyes. She could hear his voice. And the clearer Hamed's voice and face became, the less Nadia hurt inside and the less her temper flashed. At last, she was filled with peace.

But her mother was still afraid for her willful daughter. Again and again she sought to quiet Nadia so that Tarik's bitterness would not be turned against her. And again and again Nadia tossed her head and went on speaking of Hamed.

Soon, all who listened could see Hamed's face clearly before them.

The women were afraid to listen.

Look Into the Text

1. **Confirm Prediction** Was your prediction correct? What happens after Nadia begins to talk about Hamed?

2. **Foreshadowing/Prediction** Why does Nadia's mother warn her? What do you think might happen?

One day, the youngest shepherd came to Nadia's tent calling, "Come, Nadia! See Hamed's black lamb, it has grown so big and strong!"

But it was not Nadia who came out of the tent.

It was Tarik.

On the sheik's face was a look **more fierce than that of a desert hawk**, and when he spoke, his words were as **sharp as a scimitar**.

"I have **forbidden** my son's name to be said. And I promised punishment to whoever disobeyed my command. So shall it be. Before the sun sets and the moon casts its first shadow on the sand, you will be gone from this oasis—never to return."

"No!" cried Nadia, hearing her father's words.

"I have spoken!" roared the sheik. "It shall be done!"

Trembling, the shepherd went to gather his possessions. And the rest of the clan looked at one another uneasily and muttered among themselves.

In the hours that followed, fear of being **banished** to the desert made everyone turn away from Nadia as she tried to tell them of Hamed and the things he had done and said.

And the less she was listened to, the less she was able to **recall** Hamed's face and voice. And the less she recalled, the more her temper raged within her, destroying the peace she had found.

By evening, she could stand it no longer. She went to where her father sat, staring into the desert, and stood before him.

"You will not **rob me** of my brother Hamed!" she cried, stamping her foot. "I will not let you!"

Tarik looked at her, his eyes colder than the desert night.

But before he could utter a word, Nadia spoke again. "Can you recall Hamed's face? Can you still hear his voice?"

Tarik started in surprise, and his answer seemed to come **unbidden to his lips**. "No, I cannot! Day after day I have sat in this spot where I last saw Hamed, trying to remember the look, the sound, the happiness that was my beloved son—but I cannot."

Key Vocabulary
forbid *v.*, to not allow
banish *v.*, to send away
recall *v.*, to remember

In Other Words
more fierce than that of a desert hawk that was extremely scary
sharp as a scimitar painful as a sword
rob me take away the memory
unbidden to his lips without thinking

▲ Critical Viewing: Character What does this girl's expression convey? How does this relate to Nadia's feelings in the story?

And he wept.

Nadia's **tone** became gentle. "There is a way, honored father," she said. "Listen."

And she began to speak of Hamed. She told of walks she and Hamed had taken, and of talks they had had. She told how he had taught her games, told her tales and calmed her when she was angry. She told many things that she remembered, some happy and some sad.

And when she was done with the telling, she said gently, "Can you not recall him now, Father? Can you not see his face? Can you not hear his voice?"

Tarik nodded through his tears, and for the first time since Hamed had been gone, he smiled.

"Now you see," Nadia said, her tone more gentle than the softest of the desert breezes, "there is a way that Hamed can be with us still."

The sheik **pondered** what Nadia had said. After a long time, he spoke, and the sharpness was gone from his voice.

"Tell my people to come before me,

In Other Words
tone voice
pondered thought about

Nadia," he said. "I have something to say to them."

When all were assembled, Tarik said, "From this day forward, let my daughter Nadia be known not as Willful, but as Wise. And let her name be praised in every tent, for she has given me back my beloved son."

And so it was. The shepherd returned to his flock, kindness and graciousness returned to the oasis, and Nadia's name was praised in every tent. And Hamed lived again—in the hearts of all who remembered him. ❖

About the Author

Sue Alexander

Sue Alexander (1933–) loves to write stories and is the author of more than twenty books for young people. Alexander wrote *Nadia the Willful* because she had a similar experience. When her brother died, her father found it painful to talk about him. Alexander needed to talk about her brother and did not know how to explain this to her father. She decided to write a story about it. Because Alexander had always had an interest in the Bedouin culture, she set her story in the desert.

About the Illustrator

Jamel Akib

Jamel Akib (1965–) is an award-winning illustrator of English and Malaysian ancestry. His work has been shown in museums and galleries. Akib's style includes both chalk pastels and digital artwork. Akib lives in Essex, England with his family.

Look Into the Text

1. **Confirm Prediction** Was your prediction correct? What **punishment** does Tarik give to the shepherd? How does Nadia change his mind?

2. **Theme** How does Nadia's behavior reflect the theme of conflict and resolution?

Quilt

by Janet S. Wong

Our family
is a quilt

of odd **remnants**
patched together

5 in a strange
pattern,

threads fraying, fabric
wearing thin—

but made to keep
10 its warmth

even in bitter
cold.

▲ Critical Viewing: Design How does this image show that a quilt
or other object can also be art?

In Other Words
remnants unused pieces of cloth
wearing thin old, used

Look Into the Text

1. **Paraphrase** Using your own
   words explain what "Our family
   is a quilt" means.
2. **Compare and Contrast** How
   does Nadia's family compare
   to the family in "Quilt"?

Chief Koruinka's Song

a traditional poem from Chile

Face in Landscape, John Martin.

The entire earth is one soul
to which we belong.
Our souls will not die.
Change they might,
5 go out they will not.
We are one soul,
there is just one world.

▲ Critical Viewing: Design How does the artist create more
than one image?

Look Into the Text

1. **Mood** What is the mood or feeling
of this poem? What words or lines
give it this feeling?

2. **Perspectives** The message of this
poem is that we are all connected.
Would Nadia in "Nadia the Willful"
agree or disagree? Why do you
think so?

Connect Reading and Writing

Vocabulary
banish
forbidden
grief
memory
obey
punishment
recall
willful

CRITICAL THINKING

1. SUM IT UP How would you describe Nadia? Use your Reader's Viewpoint Chart to put together the information you learned from different viewpoints, including your own. Describe to a partner what you think Nadia is really like, then use the chart to summarize the story.

What Nadia's father thinks:	What I know:	My viewpoint:

Reader's Viewpoint Chart

2. Infer Why might Tarik have **forbidden** people to talk about Hamed?

3. Compare Use a line in "Quilt" or "Chief Koruinka's Song" to express an idea about Nadia's family.

4. Analyze Look again at the Anticipation Guide on page 384. Do you want to change any responses? With a group, discuss when you should or should not change your mind in a conflict.

READING FLUENCY

Phrasing Read the passage on page 639 to a partner. Assess your fluency.

1. I did not pause/sometimes paused/ always paused for punctuation.

2. What I did best in my reading was _____.

READING STRATEGY

What strategy helped you understand the selection? Tell a partner about it.

VOCABULARY REVIEW

Oral Review Read the paragraph aloud. Add the vocabulary words.

The mayor said she will _____ people from the park if they do not _____ the rules. I _____ what happened last year when my brother tried to climb the tallest tree. The sign said, "Climbing is _____." But he is _____ and never fears _____. He almost got hurt. My family would have felt such _____. That awful event is just a _____ now, but one that we will never forget.

Written Review Imagine you are Tarik. Write a journal entry to tell how your feelings have changed about **forbidding** people's actions. Use four vocabulary words.

WRITE ABOUT THE GUIDING QUESTION

Explore Conflict and Understanding
Tell how conflict can hurt or help a family. Can it ever do both? Reread "Nadia the Willful" to find examples that support your opinion.

Connect Across the Curriculum

Identify Similes, Metaphors, Personification, and Analogies

> **Academic Vocabulary**
> - **compare** (kum-**pair**) *verb*
>   When you **compare**, you look closely at how things are alike or different.

Review Figurative Language Writers use figurative language to create mental images and express ideas beyond the literal meaning of the words.

- A **simile** uses comparison words to compare things or ideas.
- A **metaphor** compares things or ideas without using comparison words.
- **Personification** gives human qualities to non-human things.
- An **analogy** shows how ideas are related to each other.

Analyze Figurative Language Work with a partner to identify the type of figurative language and the meaning of these phrases.

1. Nadia's grief knew no bounds. . .
2. . . . a look more fierce than that of a desert hawk . . .
3. She could see his smile and the light in his eyes.
4. Books are as necessary for him as water is for a fish.

Interpret Metaphor

Sometimes a metaphor makes a comparison by saying that one thing is another thing. It does not use comparison words, such as *like, as,* or *than.* For example: *The desert sun is a ball of fire.*

"Quilt" and "Chief Koruinka's Song" are poems that use **metaphors** to express ideas. When you interpret the metaphors, you can better understand the meanings of the poems.

With the class, reread the poem "Quilt" aloud. Follow these steps to interpret the metaphor and better understand the meaning of the poem:

- Identify the two things being compared. (The speaker's *family* is a *quilt.*)
- Ask questions about what is compared. (*How is a family like a quilt?*)
- Look closely at each line and word to answer your questions.
- To interpret the poem's meaning, examine the effect of the comparison.

Analyze a Metaphor With a partner, reread "Chief Koruinka's Song." Follow the steps to interpret the metaphor. How does the metaphor help you understand the poem?

Express Opinions

Group Share With a group, express your opinions about the decree, or order, that Tarik made. Give reasons for your opinions. Use complete sentences and combine ideas into compound sentences when you can.

> In my opinion, Tarik's decree was too harsh, and his daughter suffered because of it.

Write About Conflicts

Study the Models When you write about real and fictional conflicts, you want readers to understand. Use complete sentences to show what the conflict is and how it affects people.

NOT OK

The **people** in front of Tarik's tent. They looked at one another uneasily. Some trembled. They saw the hardness. **Tarik** his people to speak Hamed's name. **Wept** at the decree. **Walked** blindly through the oasis. Thought about Hamed. **Brought** Hamed's name to her lips.

> **The reader thinks:** "**What is this story about? I don't understand!**"

OK

The **people** **assembled** in front of Tarik's tent. They looked at one another uneasily, or they trembled when they saw the hardness **on the sheik's face**. **Tarik** **forbade** his people to speak Hamed's name. **Hamed's mother** **wept** at the decree. **Nadia** **walked** blindly through the oasis, and she thought only of Hamed. Each **memory** **brought** Hamed's name to her lips.

> **This writer uses complete sentences, combines ideas into compound sentences, and adds detail to the paragraph.**

Add Sentences Think of three sentences to add to the OK model above. Try to use some compound sentences and be sure all your sentences are complete.

✎ **WRITE ON YOUR OWN** Write about a time when someone you know did not want to follow a rule. Did he or she think the rule was unfair or unreasonable? Why? Check your sentences to be sure they are complete.

> **REMEMBER**
>
> When you combine ideas, use the conjunction that shows what you mean.
> - Use **and** to join like ideas.
> - Use **but** to join different ideas.
> - Use **or** to show a choice. Don't put too many ideas together with commas or **and**. If your sentences are too long, your reader can't understand them.

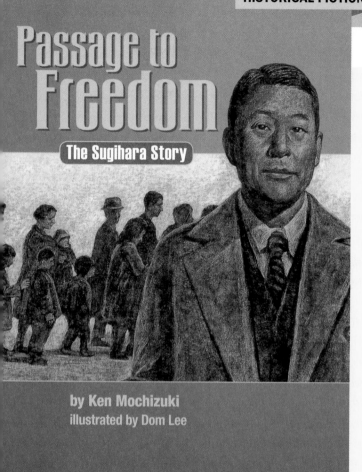

Passage to Freedom
The Sugihara Story

by Ken Mochizuki
illustrated by Dom Lee

Build Background

Overcoming Conflict

How do people overcome a conflict that affects thousands of people? Meet Chiune Sugihara of Japan who faced a life and death conflict in 1940.

Connect

Brainstorm Make a list of people who have risked their lives to save others. Think of movies you have seen, books you have read, or other sources. Describe what one person on your list did to save others.

Digital Library

myNGconnect.com
🔍 View the video.

▲ Chiune Sugihara (top left) and his family helped thousands of Jews escape the Nazis during World War II.

Engage in Discussion

CD

Look at the photo and listen to the discussion.
Do you agree with Daniel?

What Would You Do?

Daniel: My history teacher says that wherever there are people, there will be conflicts.

Martina: Why can't people get along?

Fred: That's a good question, but I don't have the answer. People don't get along for a lot of reasons. There are disagreements between friends or neighbors, and there are disagreements between countries. Some are little problems, and some are huge issues.

Daniel: Sometimes people are afraid to speak up. Everyone should be willing to say what they think is right, wouldn't you agree?

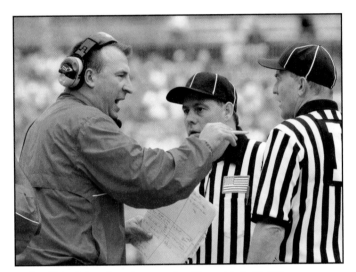

▲ Conflicts take place in everyday life, even in sports.

Fred: True, but I would not risk my life needlessly.

Martina: No, but you probably would be willing to take a risk if it was important to your life or a loved one's life.

Daniel: Lots of people risk their lives defending their countries and helping people. I'm sure most of them don't even think about the risks because it's their job. Wouldn't it be easier if people everywhere just got along?

Fred: It sure would!

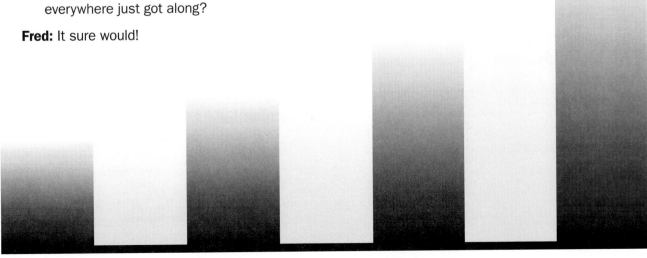

1 TRY OUT LANGUAGE
2 LEARN GRAMMAR
3 APPLY ON YOUR OWN

Use Complex Sentences

A **complex sentence** is a sentence with two kinds of clauses—an independent clause and a dependent clause.

- A clause has a **subject** and a **verb**. An independent clause can stand alone as a sentence.

    EXAMPLE   Some **people** **risk** their lives.
    independent clause

- A dependent clause also has a subject and a verb. However, it cannot stand alone because it begins with a conjunction like **when**.

    EXAMPLE   when **they** **aid** others
    dependent clause

- You can use the conjunction to "hook" the dependent clause to an independent clause. The new sentence is complete, and it is called a complex sentence.

    EXAMPLE   Some people risk their lives when they aid others.
    independent clause   *dependent clause*

> Some **conjunctions** that can connect dependent clauses to independent clauses include:
>
> | | |
> |---|---|
> | after | since |
> | although | unless |
> | as | until |
> | before | when |
> | even though | whenever |
> | if | wherever |
> | only if | while |

Practice Together

Match each independent clause on the left to a dependent clause on the right. Add punctuation. Say the new complex sentence.

1. Rescue workers rush to help others
2. Floods often occur
3. Many people become stranded
4. Victims wait nervously

a. because they can't reach dry ground
b. until they can be rescued
c. after heavy rains
d. when there is a natural disaster

Try It!

Match each independent clause on the left to a dependent clause on the right. Write the complex sentence on a card. Say the new sentence.

5. A house fire is very dangerous
6. Firefighters risk their lives
7. They can get burned
8. Everything will burn

a. even if they wear safety gear
b. whenever they go to a fire
c. unless firefighters arrive in time
d. because it is unpredictable

▲ He chose a career in medicine because he wants to help others stay healthy.

Share Your Ideas About Heroes

ENGAGE IN DISCUSSION

Look at the photo. What do you think is happening? What makes a person a hero? Does a person have to save lives to be a hero, or can a person be heroic in an everyday situation?

Discuss the questions above in a small group. Ask questions to help clarify ideas that might seem confusing. Express your opinions and listen to others' opinions.

Take turns talking. Make sure everyone in the group has the chance to speak.

HOW TO ENGAGE IN DISCUSSION

1. Focus on the discussion topic. Listen for key ideas. Summarize for yourself what others are saying.
2. Ask and answer questions.
3. Tell your point of view or opinion.
4. Respect others' ideas.

> What do you think makes someone a hero? In my opinion, a hero saves someone's life and risks his or her own life to do so.

> That's an interesting idea, but I don't really agree. I think a person can be a hero without risking his or her life.

USE COMPLEX SENTENCES

In your discussion, ask questions and use a variety of sentences. When possible, combine your ideas into complex sentences.

Simple Sentences: Heroes are brave. Heroes think about others' safety first.

Complex Sentence: Heroes are brave because they think about others' safety first.

Prepare to Read

Learn Key Vocabulary

Study the Words Use the steps below.

1. Pronounce the word. Say it aloud several times. Spell it.
2. Rate your word knowledge.
3. Study the example. Tell more about the word.
4. Practice it. Make the word your own.

Key Words

agreement (a-grē-ment) *noun* ▸ page 422

To have an **agreement** is to have an understanding with people about something. My aunt signed an **agreement** to buy a car.
Related Word: **agree**

approach (u-prōch) *verb* ▸ page 423

To **approach** means to come closer or near. The diver **approached** the dolphin.

diplomat (dip-lō-mat) *noun* ▸ page 414

A **diplomat** is a person who represents his or her government. To do his or her job, a **diplomat** lives in another country.
Related Word: **diplomatic**

insist (in-sist) *verb* ▸ page 422

To **insist** means to demand or to keep saying. The child **insisted** on walking the other direction.

issue (i-shü) *verb* ▸ page 418

To **issue** means to give or hand out. The agent **issued** tickets to the passengers.
Antonym: **take**

permission (pur-mish-un) *noun* ▸ page 418

When you have **permission**, you are allowed to do something. You must ask **permission** to go onto private property.
Related Word: **permit**

refugee (ref-yu-jē) *noun* ▸ page 418

A person who must leave his or her home or country to be safe is a **refugee**. A **refugee** may have to live with just a few belongings.
Related Word: **refuge**

translate (trans-lāt) *verb* ▸ page 416

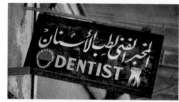

To **translate** means to explain in another language. The sign **translates** information into English.
Related Word: **translation**

Practice the Words Make an Expanded Meaning Map for each Key Word. Compare with a partner.

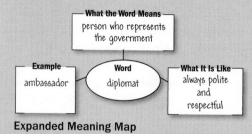

Expanded Meaning Map

Evaluate Historical Fiction

What is Historical Fiction? Historical fiction, like "Passage to Freedom," is made up, but based on true events.

To **evaluate** historical fiction, ask:

- **Setting** Are the places real or made up?
- **Characters** Is the story about a real person? Who is telling the story?
- **Events** Did the story events actually happen? What details tell if events are fact or fiction?

Reading Strategies

- Plan
- Monitor
- Ask Questions
- Make Connections
- Visualize
- **Make Inferences**
  When the author does not say something directly, use what you know to figure out what the author means.
- Determine Importance
- Synthesize

Look Into the Text

Akiko and her family traveled from Japan to America. It was 1910, and many Japanese immigrants came to America in search of better jobs.

The immigration process was long and complicated. Families often waited for weeks or months in an immigration station before they could enter the United States. Akiko often wept with frustration. They were so close to their dream but sometimes it seemed so far away!

Practice Together

Begin a T Chart A T Chart can help you analyze the credibility of a text. This T Chart shows one fact and one fictional detail in the passage. Reread the second paragraph of the passage above and add to the T Chart.

Fact	Fiction
In 1910, many Japanese immigrants came to America.	Akiko and her family are imaginary characters.

Academic Vocabulary

- **evaluate** (i-**val**-yu-wāt) *verb*
  To **evaluate** is to decide on the quality of something.

Historical Fiction

Historical fiction is based on real historical events or on real historical people, or on both. The author's purpose is to both inform and entertain.

The author may create dialogue and tell the story from the point of view of a real person or a fictional character.

Look Into the Text

> In 1940, my father was a diplomat, representing the country of Japan.
> Our family lived in a small town in the small country called Lithuania. . . .
> Then one early morning in late July, my life changed forever.

As you read historical fiction, you may have to make inferences about whether characters or events are made-up or based on fact.

Passage to Freedom

The Sugihara Story

by Ken Mochizuki

illustrated by Dom Lee

Comprehension Coach

Set a Purpose

*A young boy's life changes forever.
Find out what changes it.*

There is a **saying that the eyes tell** everything about a person.

At a store, my father saw a young Jewish boy who didn't have enough money to buy what he wanted. So my father gave the boy some of his. That boy looked into my father's eyes and, to thank him, invited my father to his home.

That is when my family and I went to a Hanukkah celebration for the first time. I was five years old.

In 1940, my father was a **diplomat**, representing the country of Japan. Our family lived in a small town in the small country called Lithuania. There was my father and mother, my Auntie Setsuko, my younger brother Chiaki, and my three-month-old baby brother, Haruki. My father worked in his office downstairs.

In the mornings, birds sang in the trees. We played with girls and boys from the neighborhood at a huge park near our home. Houses and churches around us were hundreds of years old. In our room, Chiaki and I played with toy German soldiers, tanks, and planes. **Little did we** know that the real soldiers were coming our way.

Then one early morning in late July, my life changed forever.

My mother and Auntie Setsuko woke Chiaki and me up, telling us to get dressed quickly. My father ran upstairs from his office.

"There are a lot of people outside," my mother said. "We don't know what is going to happen."

In the living room, my parents told my brother and me not to let anybody see us looking through the window. So, I **parted** the curtains a tiny bit. Outside, I saw hundreds of people **crowded around the gate** in front of our house.

{ My life changed forever. }

Key Vocabulary
diplomat *n.*, a person who represents his or her government

In Other Words
saying that the eyes tell belief that a person's eyes show
Little did we We did not
parted opened
crowded around the gate waiting closely together

Cultural Background
Hanukkah is an eight-day Jewish holiday, also called the Festival of Lights. People eat special foods, light candles, and play games to celebrate the miracle of freedom.

▲ Critical Viewing: Effect What part of the selection goes with this image? Why did the artist place the boy's eyes in the center?

The grown-ups shouted in Polish, a language I did not understand. Then I saw the children. They stared at our house through the iron bars of the gate. Some of them were my age. Like the grown-ups, their eyes were red from not having slept for days. They wore heavy winter coats—some wore more than one coat, even though it was

Language Background
Here is how to pronounce the names of family members in the selection:
   Setsuko (set-sü-kō)
   Chiaki (chē-ah-kē)
   Haruki (hah-ru-kē)
   Sugihara (sü-gē-hah-rah)

warm outside. These children looked as though they had dressed in a hurry. But if they came from somewhere else, where were their suitcases?

"What do they want?" I asked my mother.

"They have come to ask for your father's help," she replied. "**Unless we** help, they may be killed or taken away by some bad men."

Some of the children held on tightly to the hands of their fathers, some **clung** to their mothers. One little girl sat on the ground, crying.

I felt like crying, too. "Father," I said, "please help them."

My father stood quietly next to me, but I knew he saw the children. Then some of the men in the crowd began climbing over the fence. Borislav and Gudje, two young men who worked for my father, tried to keep the crowd calm.

My father walked outside. **Peering** through the curtains, I saw him standing on the steps. Borislav **translated** what my father said: He asked the crowd to choose five people to come inside and talk.

▶ Critical Viewing: Effect How do you think the people in this image feel? How does the artist create this mood?

Key Vocabulary
translate *v.*, to explain in another language

In Other Words
Unless we If we do not
clung stayed very close
Peering Looking secretly

My father met downstairs with the five men. My father could speak Japanese, Chinese, Russian, German, French, and English. At this meeting, everyone spoke Russian.

I couldn't help but stare out the window and watch the crowd, while downstairs, for two hours, my father listened to frightening stories. These people were **refugees** —people who ran away from their homes because, if they stayed, they would be killed. They were Jews from Poland, escaping from the Nazi soldiers who had taken over their country.

The five men had heard my father could give them visas— **official** written **permission** to travel through another country. The hundreds of Jewish refugees outside hoped to travel east through the Soviet Union and end up in Japan. Once in Japan, they could go to another country. Was it true? the men asked.

{ Would he put our family in danger? }

Could my father **issue** these visas? If he did not, the Nazis would soon **catch up with** them.

My father answered that he could issue a few, but not hundreds. To do that, he would have to ask for permission from his government in Japan.

That night, the crowd stayed outside our house. Exhausted from the day's excitement, I slept soundly. But it was one of the worst nights of my father's life. He had to make a decision. If he helped these people, would he put our family in danger? If the Nazis found out, what would they do?

But if he did not help these people, they could all die.

My mother listened to the bed squeak as my father **tossed and turned** all night.

The next day, my father said he was going to ask his government about the visas. My mother agreed it was the right thing to do.

Key Vocabulary

refugee *n.*, someone who must leave his or her country for safety

permission *n.*, allowing something to happen

issue *v.*, to give or hand out

In Other Words

official the government's
catch up with find
tossed and turned moved and did not sleep

▲ Critical Viewing: Design Describe this image. What details does the artist use to show emotion?

My father sent his message by **cable**. Gudje took my father's written message down to the telegraph office.

I watched the crowd as they waited for the Japanese government's reply. The five representatives came into our house several times that day to ask if an answer had been received. Any time the gate opened, the crowd tried to **charge** inside.

Finally, the answer came from the Japanese government. It was "no." My father could not issue that many visas to Japan. For the next two days, he thought about what to do.

Hundreds more Jewish refugees joined the crowd. My father sent a second message to his government, and again the answer was "no." We still couldn't go outside. My little brother Haruki cried often because we **were running out of** milk.

I grew tired of staying indoors. I asked my father **constantly**, "Why are these people

{ **The refugees needed his help.** }

here? What do they want? Why do they have to be here? Who are they?"

My father always took the time to explain everything to me. He said the refugees needed his help, that they needed permission from him to go to another part of the world where they would be safe.

"I cannot help these people yet," he calmly told me. "But when the time comes, I will help them all that I can."

My father **cabled his superiors yet a third time**, and I knew the answer by the look in his eyes. That night, he said to my mother, "I have to do something. I may have to disobey my government, but if I don't, I will be disobeying God."

In Other Words
charge run
were running out of did not have enough
constantly all the time
cabled his superiors yet a third time sent another message to his bosses

Look Into the Text

1. **Summarize** Tell what the **refugees** want from the **diplomat** and why.
2. **Conclusion** Why is the **diplomat's** decision so difficult?

Predict
The diplomat faces a hard choice.
What will he decide to do?

The next morning, he brought the family together and asked what he should do. This was the first time he ever asked all of us to help him with anything.

My mother and Auntie Setsuko **had already made up their minds**. They said we had to think about the people outside before we thought about ourselves. And that is what my parents had always told me—that I must think as if I were in someone else's place. If I were one of those children out there, what would I want someone to do for me?

In Other Words
had already made up their minds knew what they wanted

I said to my father, "If we don't help them, won't they die?"

With the entire family in **agreement**, I could tell **a huge weight was lifted off my father's shoulders**. His voice was firm as he told us, "I will start helping these people."

Outside, the crowd went quiet as my father spoke, with Borislav translating.

"I will issue visas to **each and every one of you to the last**. So, please wait patiently."

The crowd **stood frozen** for a second. Then the refugees burst into cheers. Grown-ups embraced each other, and some reached to the sky. Fathers and mothers hugged their children. I was especially glad for the children.

My father opened the garage door and the crowd tried to rush in. To keep order, Borislav handed out cards with numbers. My father wrote out each visa by hand. After he finished each one, he looked into the eyes of the person receiving the visa and said, "Good luck."

Refugees **camped out** at our favorite park, waiting to see my father. I was finally able to go outside.

Chiaki and I played with the other children in our toy car. They pushed as we rode, and they rode as we pushed.

We chased each other around the big trees. We did not speak the same language, but that didn't stop us.

For about a month, there was always a line leading to the garage. Every day, from early in the morning till late at night, my father tried to write three hundred visas. He **watered down** the ink to make it last. Gudje and a young Jewish man helped out by stamping my father's name on the visas.

My mother offered to help write the visas, but my father **insisted** he be the only

Key Vocabulary

agreement *n.*, an understanding between people
insist *v.*, to keep saying or repeating something

In Other Words

a huge weight was lifted off my father's shoulders my father felt better
each and every one of you to the last everyone

stood frozen stopped moving
camped out waited
watered down mixed water with

422 Unit 6 Conflict and Resolution

⚠ **Critical Viewing: Effect** How do the facial expressions in the image relate to the text?

one, so no one else could get into trouble. So my mother watched the crowd and told my father how many were still in line.

One day, my father pressed down so hard on his fountain pen, the tip broke off. During that month, I only saw him late at night. His eyes were always red and he could hardly talk. While he slept, my mother massaged his arm, **stiff and cramped** from writing all day.

Soon my father grew so tired, he wanted to quit writing the visas. But my mother encouraged him to continue. "Many people are still waiting," she said. "Let's issue some more visas and save as many lives as we can."

While the Germans **approached** from the west, the Soviets came from the east and took over Lithuania. They ordered my father to leave. So did the Japanese government, which **reassigned him** to Germany. Still, my father wrote the visas until we **absolutely**

Key Vocabulary
approach *v.*, to come closer

In Other Words
stiff and cramped hurt
reassigned him moved his work
absolutely finally

Government Background
In order to enter some countries, visitors from other countries must have a **visa** stamped in or attached to their passports. Today, Japan has seven types of visa, and the time it takes to get a visa depends on the person's reason for travel to Japan.

had to move out of our home. We stayed at a hotel for two days, where my father still wrote visas for the many refugees who followed him there.

Then it was time to leave Lithuania. Refugees who had slept at the train station crowded around my father. Some refugee men surrounded my father to protect him. He now just issued permission papers— blank pieces of paper with his signature.

As the train pulled away, refugees ran alongside. My father still handed permission papers out the window. As the train **picked up speed**, he threw them out to waiting hands. The people in the front of the crowd looked into my father's eyes and cried, "We will never forget you! We will see you again!"

I **gazed** out the train window, watching Lithuania and the crowd of refugees **fade away**. I wondered if we would ever see them again.

"Where are we going?" I asked my father.

"We are going to Berlin," he replied.

Chiaki and I became very excited about going to the big city. I had so many questions for my father. But he fell asleep as soon as he settled into his seat. My mother and Auntie Setsuko looked really tired, too.

Back then, I did not fully understand what the three of them had done, or why it was so important.

I do now. ❖

In Other Words
picked up speed went faster
gazed looked
fade away appear smaller as we rode away

Look Into the Text

1. **Confirm Predictions** Was your prediction correct? What happened that you didn't expect?
2. **Inference** How does the boy's father feel when his family decides that he should help the people? How can you tell?
3. **Paraphrase** Tell in your own words what happened to the family at the train station.

A Message from Hiroki Sugihara

Each time that I think about what my father did at Kaunas, Lithuania, in 1940, my appreciation and understanding of the incident continues to grow. In fact, it makes me very emotional to realize that his deed saved thousands of lives, and that I had the opportunity to be a part of it.

I am proud that my father had the courage to do the right thing. Yet, his superiors in the Japanese government did not agree. The years after my family left Kaunas were difficult ones. We were imprisoned for eighteen months in a Soviet internment camp; and when we finally returned to Japan, my father was asked to resign from diplomatic service. After holding several different jobs, my father joined an export company, where he worked until his retirement in 1976.

My father remained concerned about the fate of the refugees, and at one point left his address at the Israeli Embassy in Japan. Finally, in the 1960s, he started hearing from "Sugihara survivors," many of whom had kept their visas, and considered the worn pieces of paper to be family treasures.

▲ Japanese Emperor Akihito visits a monument dedicated to Chiune Sugihara in Vilnius, Lithuania. Several monuments around the world honor Sugihara.

In 1969, my father was invited to Israel, where he was taken to the famous Holocaust memorial, Yad Vashem. In 1985, he was chosen to receive the "Righteous Among Nations" Award from Yad Vashem. He was the first and only Asian to have been given this great honor.

Historical Background
The **Holocaust** (1933-1945) was the organized mass murder of millions of European Jews and other groups viewed as inferior, or of less worth, by Germany's Nazi party.

In 1992, six years after his death, a monument to my father was dedicated in his birthplace of Yaotsu, Japan, on a hill that is now known as the Hill of Humanity.

In 1994, a group of Sugihara survivors traveled to Japan to re-dedicate the monument in a ceremony that was attended by several high officials of the Japanese government.

The story of what my father and my family experienced in 1940 is an important one for young people today. It is a story that I believe will inspire you to care for all people and to respect life. It is a story that proves that one person can make a difference.

About the Author

Ken Mochizuki

To write *Passage to Freedom*, **Ken Mochizuki** had to gather as much factual information as possible. To do this, he worked closely with the Sugihara family. He also decided to write the account in the first person, as if he was Hiroki, the son of Sugihara. Mochizuki wrote the book in honor of those who have put the safety of others before themselves.

About the Author

Hiroki Sugihara

Hiroki Sugihara has honored his father's memory in many ways. He donated hundreds of family photos to the Bay Area Holocaust Oral History Project. This helped create "Visas for Life," a photo exhibit that appeared in over 100 museums worldwide. Sugihara has helped to honor diplomats like his father who helped save the lives of Jewish people during World War II.

Look Into the Text

1. **Determine Importance** What important information does the Afterword add?
2. **Inference** Why do you think the government's treatment of Sugihara's father changed? Cite evidence from the text.

Connect Reading and Writing

CRITICAL THINKING

1. SUM IT UP What was it like to live in Lithuania in 1940? Use your T Chart to summarize to a partner what it might have been like, paying attention to the facts and fiction that shaped your summary.

Facts	Fiction

T Chart

2. Speculate Many **refugees approached** Mr. Sugihara for visas. Why do countries have to give people **permission** to enter?

3. Infer Why did Mr. Sugihara ask his family if he should act without his government's **permission**?

4. Evaluate Reread the last paragraph of the Afterword on page 426. Hiroki Sugihara **insists** that his father's story will inspire young people. Do you agree with him? Explain.

READING FLUENCY

Intonation Read the passage on page 640 to a partner. Assess your fluency.

1. My tone never/sometimes/always matched what I read.

2. What I did best in my reading was _____.

READING STRATEGY

What strategy helped you understand the selection? Tell a partner about it.

Vocabulary
agreement
approached
diplomats
insist
issue
permission
refugees
translate

VOCABULARY REVIEW

Oral Review Read the paragraph aloud. Add the vocabulary words.

_____, or people who represent a country, usually speak two or more languages. This helps them _____ communications between countries. They also make an _____ to follow certain rules. To do otherwise, they must ask the government for _____. Even then, the government may _____ that they follow the rule. Sometimes, they are asked to _____ visas. For example, they may be _____ by _____ who ask for their government's protection.

Written Review Write a news report about Mr. Sugihara and the Lithuanian **refugees**. Use five vocabulary words.

WRITE ABOUT THE GUIDING QUESTION

Explore Conflict and Bravery
If Mr. Sugihara had known what would happen, would he have made the same decision? Read the selection again to find support for your opinion.

Connect Across the Curriculum

Interpret Idioms

Academic Vocabulary
- **literal** (lit-ur-al) *adjective*
  The **literal** meaning of a word is its exact meaning.

An **idiom** is a group of words that together mean something different than their **literal** meaning. "It's raining cats and dogs" does not mean that animals are falling from the sky. This idiom means "It is raining hard."

Interpret Idioms With a partner, interpret these idioms.

1. My father *tossed and turned* all night.
2. We *were running out* of milk.
3. The crowd *stood frozen* for a second.

Writing/Speaking

Deliver an Oral Response to Literature

DRAMA

Academic Vocabulary
- **response** (ri-**spons**) *noun*
  A **response** is an answer or reply to something that has happened or has been said.

How did the Sugiharas deal with a difficult situation? Tell your class what you think and why. Give your **response** to the story.

1 **Plan** Follow these steps:
- Read the story and think about your reaction to the story.
- Look at the different elements of the story—plot, characters, setting, and theme. Use them to support your **response**.
- Make notes about your response to the story.

2 **Practice** Review your notes and practice with a partner.
- Give a short summary of the main events and details in the story.
- Tell what you learned from the story and what you think it means.
- Include several examples from the text to support your ideas.

3 **Present** Follow these steps to keep your **response** focused and clear:
- Let your feelings about the story show in your words, tone of voice, facial expressions, and gestures.
- Make eye contact with your audience, and speak clearly.

Unsupported response

> Even though a problem might seem big, one person can solve it. The father did a lot to help others.

Supported response

> After reading "Passage to Freedom," I learned that one person can make a difference. The father issued visas to help refugees travel to a safe country. He saved many lives.

Engage in Discussion

Group Talk With a small group, discuss what Chiune Sugihara did and the risks he took. Was he wise to do what he did? Listen attentively to others' opinions. Use complex sentences to present some of your ideas.

> Mr. Sugihara was a hero, but he took some big risks.

> Many people were helped by Mr. Sugihara because he wasn't afraid of the consequences.

Write About a Heroic Action

Study the Models You can make your writing more interesting by using a variety of sentences. You can also make your writing easier to read by combining your ideas into longer, more interesting sentences. Longer sentences show how ideas relate to each other.

NOT OK

My father looked out the window. He saw many people. They were crowded around the gate in front of the house. My father read the government's answer. He knew in his heart it was wrong. He could obey the government. He could do what he thought was right. It was a difficult decision. It was worth it.

The reader thinks: "This writing does not flow. It's hard to see how the ideas relate."

OK

When my father looked out the window, he saw many people crowded around the gate in front of the house. My father read the government's answer, and he knew in his heart it was wrong. The people would be in danger if he didn't help them. He could obey the government, or he could do what he thought was right. It was a difficult decision, but it was worth it.

This writing combines some ideas into smoother, more connected sentences.

WRITE ON YOUR OWN Write a paragraph about a time when you helped someone. What did you have to risk or give up? Use a variety of sentences in your writing.

REMEMBER

Don't string together too many ideas in one sentence. It can confuse the reader.

Zlata's Diary
by Zlata Filipović

Build Background

Connect

Word Webs What comes to mind when you think of the words *peace* and *war*? Create a web for each word to show your ideas.

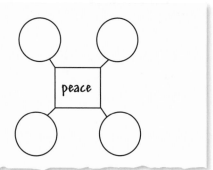

Word Web

The Effects of War

Zlata Filipović lived through a war. When she decided to keep a personal diary about the conflict, she had no idea that it would become famous around the world.

Digital Library
myNGconnect.com
View the video.

Zlata Filipović ▶

Justify

Look at the photo and listen to the discussion. Think about the reason Laila gives to justify, or explain, her view.

A Little Effort **Goes a Long Way**

Laila: Did you read this article about refugees in some parts of Africa?

Tony: No, what does it say?

Laila: Daily life is getting worse for people who have lost their homes because of war and other conflicts. Not only are people losing their homes and towns, but now food is in short supply. In addition, there isn't enough clean water for people to drink. If these people need food, then I'm going to help!

Tony: How? What could you do to help?

Laila: I could start a food drive to donate food. It will take some work, but it will be worth it because this is an important cause.

1 TRY OUT LANGUAGE
2 LEARN GRAMMAR
3 APPLY ON YOUR OWN

Combine Sentences

Combine sentences to make them more interesting and easier to read.

- Use a **coordinating conjunction** to join ideas of equal importance into a **compound sentence**. Always use a **comma** before the conjunction.

    EXAMPLE   Sometimes reporters share news about other countries. Other times, they describe local events.

    Reporters share news about other countries, **or** they describe local events.
    <u>independent clause</u>   <u>independent clause</u>

> **Some Coordinating Conjunctions**
> | | |
> |---|---|
> | and | or |
> | but | so |
> | for | yet |

- Use a **subordinating conjunction** to join ideas of unequal importance into a **complex sentence**. If the dependent clause comes first, separate it from the independent clause with a **comma**.

    EXAMPLE   My family watches the 6 o'clock news. Then we discuss the events.

    After we watch the 6 o'clock news, my family discusses the events.
    <u>dependent clause</u>   <u>independent clause</u>

    If the dependent clause comes last, do <u>not</u> use a comma.

    EXAMPLE   It is important to follow the news. It can affect your opinion.

    It is important to follow the news **because** it can affect your opinion.
    <u>independent clause</u>   <u>dependent clause</u>

> **Some Subordinating Conjunctions**
> | | |
> |---|---|
> | after | since |
> | although | when |
> | because | while |

Practice Together

Use the conjunction to combine each pair of sentences. Say the new compound or complex sentence.

1. while   Dad listens to the news on the radio. He drives to work.
2. so   Mom likes the evening news. She turns it on every night at 6 p.m.
3. but   The world news is on Channel 5. The local news is on Channel 8.
4. or   Ted wants to be a news reporter. He can be a weather forecaster.

Try It!

Use the conjunction to combine each pair of sentences. Write the new sentence on a card. Use a comma if needed. Then say the sentence.

5. when   We read the news. We learn about current events.
6. but   Some news makes you smile. Other news makes you worry.
7. because   Some countries fight. They disagree about government.
8. and   Other communities work together. They solve their problems.

▲ News reporters cover world eve
wherever they happen.

What's Your Position?

JUSTIFY

There are at least two sides or approaches to every issue. Read the following statements. Choose one and justify your thoughts in a group.

First, choose a statement.

1. There will always be conflict in the world.
2. Peace is possible in our lifetime.

Then organize your thoughts in a T Chart like this one:

T Chart

Opinion	Reason
I think there will always be conflict in the world.	People don't always agree with each other.
I believe that conflicting ideas can be good.	Different ideas can lead to new solutions.

Now justify your opinions to a group. Listen to the positions of other group members.

HOW TO JUSTIFY

1. State an opinion or idea.
2. Give logical reasons for it.
3. Combine your ideas to make the logic clear.

A little conflict can be good because it leads to new ideas.

Peace is possible if we respect others' ideas.

COMBINE SENTENCES

When you justify your position, use compound and complex sentences to express your ideas. For your complex sentences, choose words like *if* or *because* to show a condition or logical reason for your idea. Such words will "hook" the condition or reason to your idea or opinion.

Condition Words	Reason Words
if, if only as long as unless, until	because since therefore

Simple Sentences: Peace is possible. People listen to each other.

Compound Sentence: Peace is what most people want, and it is possible.

Complex Sentence: Peace is possible **if** people listen to each other.

Prepare to Read

Learn Key Vocabulary

Study the Words Use the steps below.

1. Pronounce the word. Say it aloud several times. Spell it.
2. Rate your word knowledge.
3. Study the example. Tell more about the word.
4. Practice it. Make the word your own.

Key Words

conflict (kon-flikt) *noun*
▶ page 438

A **conflict** is a fight between two people or groups of people. My friend and I got into a **conflict** over a book she borrowed from me.

desperate (des-pu-rit)
adjective ▶ page 439

Someone who is **desperate** has lost hope. The **desperate** team tried hard but lost.
Related Word: **desperation**

destroy (di-**stroi**) *verb*
▶ page 439

To **destroy** means to completely ruin. The house was **destroyed** by a fire.
Antonym: **create**

humanity (hū-man-i-tē)
noun ▶ page 440

Humanity is kindness and caring about the suffering of others. Firefighters show **humanity** by doing what they must to save others.
Related Word: **human**

impact (im-pakt) *verb*
▶ page 443

To **impact** means to have an effect. The new sales people will continue to **impact** the sales numbers, pushing them up.

innocent (in-u-sent)
adjective ▶ page 441

Someone who is **innocent** is without guilt. The puppy looks **innocent** and sweet.
Related Words: **innocence, innocently**

politics (pol-i-tiks) *noun*
▶ page 442

Politics are people's beliefs about government and its plans. People with similar **politics** came to the convention.
Related Words: **political, politician**

reality (rē-a-lu-tē) *noun*
▶ page 442

Reality is what people actually experience in life. I wish I could have whatever I liked, but the **reality** is that I must work to pay for things.

Practice the Words Make a Study Card for each Key Word.

> politics
>
> **What it means:** a person's feelings about how government should be run
>
> **Example:** My family often talks about politics.
>
> **Not an example:** We discussed which movie to watch.

Study Card

Analyze Author's Viewpoint

What is an Author's Viewpoint? Remember that an author always writes from a specific viewpoint. Figuring out an author's purpose for writing a text can help you determine the viewpoint.

A diary is a genre people write to express their private thoughts, feelings, and opinions that show their viewpoints. Because a diary is private, some authors consider it a trusted friend, sometimes even giving it a pet name.

Reading Strategies

- Plan
- Monitor
- Ask Questions
- Make Connections
- Visualize
- **Make Inferences**
  When the author does not say something directly, use what you know to figure out what the author means.
- Determine Importance
- Synthesize

Look Into the Text

Sunday, April 5, 1992
Dear Mimmy,

   I'm trying to concentrate so I can do my homework (reading), but I simply can't. Something is going on in this town. You can hear gunfire from the hills. Columns of people are spreading out from Dobrinja. They're trying to stop something, but they themselves don't know what.....

   Mimmy, I'm afraid of WAR!!!

   -Zlata

Practice Together

Begin a Mind Map A Mind Map can help you analyze an author's viewpoint. This Mind Map shows one clue to the author's viewpoint. Reread the passage above and add more clues to the Mind Map. After you have read the entire diary on pages 439–442, you will fill in the author's viewpoint.

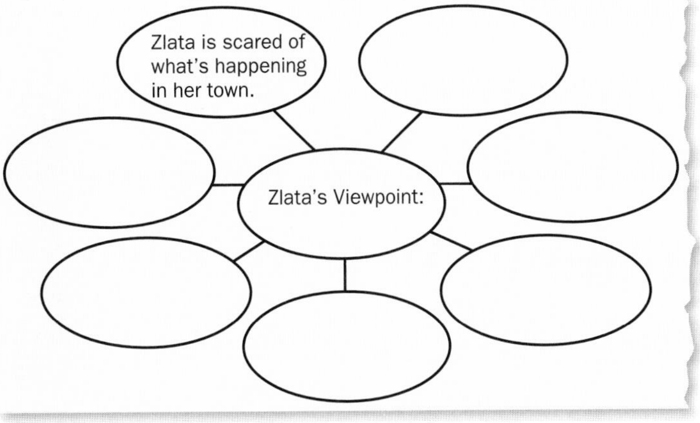

Zlata is scared of what's happening in her town.

Zlata's Viewpoint:

Diary

A diary is a daily account of the events, thoughts, and feelings in a person's life. Most diaries are kept private.

Some writers, however, will publish their diaries to share important experiences with others. Knowing an author's purpose for writing can help you figure out the author's viewpoint about an event or experience.

Look Into the Text

Tuesday, September 15, 1992
Dear Mimmy,

    I have another sad piece of news for you. A boy from my drama club got KILLED! . . . A shell fell in front of the community center and a horrible piece of shrapnel killed him.

To figure out the author's viewpoint, think about the author's purpose and make inferences as you read.

Zlata's Diary

by Zlata Filipović

War has many effects that go beyond the battlefield. In 1992, the city of Sarajevo was attacked. What was this experience like for a young person who lived through it?

Comprehension Coach

In 1992, **shells rocked** the city of Sarajevo in the former republic of Yugoslavia. The cause of this attack was a `conflict` among the three main ethnic groups who lived in the area—the Serbs, the Croats, and the Muslims.

Eleven-year-old Zlata Filipović and her parents were witnesses to the **destruction** of Sarajevo. Zlata wrote about the effects of the war in her diary until her family was able to escape to Paris, France, in 1993. When her diary was **published** it became **an international bestseller** and was translated into thirty-six languages.

The following is a brief excerpt from her diary, which she called "Mimmy."

▼ This is a view of downtown Sarajevo through a shattered window, in 1994.

Key Vocabulary
conflict *n.*, a fight or disagreement

In Other Words
shells rocked bullets and explosives damaged
destruction damage, ruin
published made into a book
an international bestseller popular all over the world

from *Zlata's Diary*

Sunday, April 5, 1992
Dear Mimmy,

I'm trying to concentrate so I can do my homework (reading), but I simply can't. Something is going on in town. You can hear gunfire from the hills. **Columns** of people are spreading out from **Dobrinja**. They're trying to stop something, but they themselves don't know what. You can simply feel that something is coming, something very bad. On TV I see people in front of the B-H parliament building. The radio keeps playing the same song: "Sarajevo, My Love." That's all very nice, but **my stomach is still in knots** and I can't concentrate on my homework anymore.

Mimmy, I'm afraid of WAR!!!

~Zlata

Monday, April 6, 1992
Dear Mimmy,

Yesterday the people in front of the parliament tried peacefully to cross the Vrbanja bridge. But they were shot at. Who? How? Why? A girl, a medical student from Dubrovnik, was KILLED. Her blood spilled onto the bridge. In her final moments all she said was: "Is this Sarajevo?" HORRIBLE, HORRIBLE HORRIBLE!

NO ONE AND NOTHING HERE IS NORMAL!

The **Baščaršija** has been **destroyed**! Those "fine gentlemen" from Pale fired on Baščaršija!

Since yesterday people have been inside the B-H parliament. Some of them are standing outside, in front of it. We've moved my television set into the living room, so I watch Channel 1 on one TV and "Good Vibrations" on the other. Now they're shooting from the Holiday Inn, killing people in front of the parliament. And Bokica is there with Vanja and Andrej. Oh, God!

Maybe we'll go to the **cellar**. You, Mimmy, will go with me, of course. I'm **desperate**. The people in front of the parliament are desperate too. Mimmy, war is here. PEACE, NOW!

They say they're going to attack RTV Sarajevo [radio and TV center]. But they haven't. They've stopped shooting in our neighborhood. KNOCK! KNOCK! (I'm knocking on wood for good luck.)

WHEW! It was tough. Oh, God! They're shooting again!!!

~Zlata

Key Vocabulary
destroy *v.*, to ruin or to damage
desperate *adj.*, loss of hope

In Other Words
Columns Groups
Dobrinja a nearby part of town
my stomach is still in knots I am so nervous
Baščaršija main street
cellar basement

Look Into the Text

1. **Paraphrase** Tell in your own words how the war is affecting Zlata. Why is she **desperate**?

2. **Inference** What did the medical student mean when she said, "Is this Sarajevo?"

Sunday, April 12, 1992

Dear Mimmy,

The new sections of town—Dobrinja, Mojmilo, Vojničko polje—are being badly shelled. Everything is being destroyed, burned, the people are in **shelters**. Here in the middle of town, where we live, it's different. It's quiet. People go out. It was a nice warm spring day today. We went out too. Vaso Miškin Street was full of people, children. It looked like a peace march. People came out to be together, they don't want war. They want to live and enjoy themselves the way they used to. That's only **natural**, isn't it? Who likes or wants war, when it's the worst thing in the world?

I keep thinking about the march I joined today. It's bigger and stronger than war. That's why it will win. The people must be the ones to win, not the war, because war has nothing to do with **humanity**. War is something inhuman.

~Zlata

▼ **Sarajevo in peacetime** Several bridges were destroyed during the war.

Key Vocabulary

humanity *n.*, kindness and compassion for others

In Other Words

shelters temporary homes
natural normal

440 Unit 6 Conflict and Resolution

Tuesday, September 15, 1992
Dear Mimmy,

    I have another sad piece of news for you. A boy from my drama club got KILLED! . . . A shell fell in front of the community center and a horrible piece of **shrapnel** killed him. His name was Eldin and he was a **refugee** from Grbavica.

    Another **innocent** victim of this disgusting war, another child among the thousands of other children killed in Sarajevo. I feel so sorry, he was a sweet, good boy. Oh, God, what is happening here? Hasn't there been enough!?

    ~Zlata

Thursday, September 17, 1992
Dear Mimmy,

    Today is Alma's birthday. We gave her two herbal shampoos. We had a super time, but . . . I looked out the window and saw a flash. I thought it was somebody signaling, that's not unusual in war time. But . . . BOOM!! Shattered glass, falling plaster. A shell fell in front of the shop next door and I saw it all from the fourth floor. We rushed over to Nedo's apartment and watched TV.

    The birthday party wasn't bad, but it would have been even better if that shell hadn't spoiled it.

    ~Your Zlata

▲ A building in Sarajevo burns after being hit by shells.

Thursday, November 19, 1992
Dear Mimmy,

    Nothing new on the political front. **They are adopting some resolutions, the "kids" are negotiating**, and we are dying, freezing, starving, crying, parting with our friends, leaving our loved ones.

Look Into the Text

1. **Compare and Contrast** Describe how the new sections of town are different from where Zlata lives.
2. **Details** What happened at the community center and next door to Zlata's house?

I keep wanting to explain these stupid **politics** to myself, because it seems to me that politics caused this war, making it our everyday **reality**. War has crossed out the day and replaced it with horror, and now horrors are unfolding instead of days. It looks to me as though these politics mean Serbs, Croats and Muslims. But they are all people. They are all the same. They all look like people, there's no difference. They all have arms, legs and heads, they walk and talk, but now there's "something" that wants to make them different.

Among my girlfriends, among our friends, in our family, there are Serbs and Croats and Muslims. It's a mixed group and I never knew who was a Serb, a Croat or a Muslim. Now politics has started **meddling around**. It has put an "S" on Serbs, an "M" on Muslims and a "C" on Croats, it wants to separate them. And to do so it has chosen the worst, blackest pencil of all—the pencil of war which spells only misery and death.

Why is politics making us unhappy, separating us, when we ourselves know who is good and who isn't? We mix with the good, not with the bad. And among the good there are Serbs and Croats and Muslims, just as there are among the bad. I simply don't understand it. Of course, I'm "young," and politics are **conducted** by "grown-ups." But I think we "young" would do it better. We certainly wouldn't have chosen war.

The "kids" really are playing, which is why us kids are not playing, we are living in fear, we are suffering, we are not enjoying the sun and flowers, we are not enjoying our childhood, WE ARE CRYING.

A bit of philosophizing on my part, but I was alone and felt I could write this to you, Mimmy. You understand me. Fortunately, I've got you to talk to.

And now,

Love,

Zlata ❖

Zlata Filipović Today

As a twelve-year-old girl, Zlata Filipović never knew how much her diary would **impact** her life. Her diary not only helped her get through the emotional pain of war, it also helped her escape.

Many people were interested in publishing Filipović's diary. Her family chose a French publisher with connections to the French government. In exchange, the publisher promised to help Filipović and her parents escape the fighting.

In 1993, the publisher kept the promise and Filipović and her family were flown to Paris in safety. After years of living without electricity, not going to school, and not having enough to eat, Zlata was finally free. To her great surprise, she was also famous.

"I had no idea of the impact the diary had, because we had no TV, no newspapers, no way to see what all these journalists coming to interview me had done," she says. "We thought we'd come to France and be regular refugees, start our life again, but coming out of the plane there were cameras, photographers . . . people who could pronounce my name and had a sense of who I was based on the **scribbles** I'd done for myself as a twelve-year-old girl."

For the next four months, Filipović shared her book and met with students around the world. Sometimes she felt guilty because she was one of the few people to get out of Sarajevo.

"There was a level of guilt because my best friend stayed behind. Why was I different from another thirteen-year-old girl in Bosnia?" she remembers asking herself. "My responsibility was to use this in some kind of way for all those who remained. If people were willing to listen, I'd tell them about it."

Today, in her twenties, Filipović is still sharing her voice and experiences. She lives in Ireland and has a college degree in International Peace Studies. Filipović teamed up with another writer to edit a book titled *Stolen Voices*, a collection of young people's diaries written during wars—from World War I to the Iraq War. As she explains, when you study history there are "all the names and dates that you forget . . . but with a diary or an individual story . . . you connect."

Look Into the Text

1. **Summarize** Describe what Zlata could not understand about war.
2. **Explain** How did Zlata's diary help her escape?
3. **Cause and Effect** Why was Zlata surprised when she saw all the people waiting for her at the plane in France?

Last Night I Had the Strangest Dream

by Ed McCurdy

Chorus

Last night I had the strangest dream,
I'd ever dreamed before,
I dreamed the world had all agreed
To put an end to war.

I dreamed I saw a mighty room,
Filled with women and men
And the paper they were signing said
They'd never fight again.

And when the paper was all signed,
And a million copies made,
They all joined hands and bowed their heads
And grateful pray'rs were prayed.

And the people in the streets below
Were dancing 'round and 'round,
And swords and guns and uniforms
Were scattered on the ground.

Chorus

Last night I had the strangest dream,
I'd ever dreamed before,
I dreamed the world had all agreed
To put an end to war.

©Joel Nakamura, 2001.

▲ **Critical Viewing: Design** What details do you see in this image? How do they relate to the song's message?

Words and Music by Ed McCurdy. TRO–© Copyright 1950 (Renewed), 1951 (Renewed), 1955 (Renewed) Folkways Music Publishers, Inc., New York, NY. Used by Permission.

Historical Background

Ed McCurdy (1919-2000) wrote this famous song in 1950 when he wished for peace in the world. The song has been recorded in many different languages and covered by well-known singers, including Simon and Garfunkel.

Look Into the Text

1. **Explain** What is the singer's dream?
2. **Interpret** Why were swords, guns, and uniforms scattered on the ground in the dream?

Connect Reading and Writing

Vocabulary
conflict
desperate
destroy
humanity
impacted
innocent
politics
reality

CRITICAL THINKING

1. **SUM IT UP** Using your Mind Map, discuss with a partner how Zlata's experience with war **impacted** her **reality**. Then summarize the selection.

Zlata is scared of what's happening in her town.

Zlata's Viewpoint:

Mind Map

2. **Interpret** Zlata writes that people feel **desperate**. What does she mean? Give an example from the text.

3. **Infer** Do you think that Zlata feels **desperate** or hopeful about **humanity** today? Support your inference with examples from the text.

4. **Speculate** If Zlata could read "Last Night I Had the Strangest Dream," which stanza would most remind her of her diary? Why?

READING FLUENCY

Expression Read the passage on page 641 to a partner. Assess your fluency.

1. My voice never/sometimes/always matched what I read.

2. What I did best in my reading was _____.

READING STRATEGY

What strategy helped you understand this selection? Tell a partner about it.

VOCABULARY REVIEW

Oral Review Read the paragraph aloud. Add the vocabulary words.

Throughout history, war has _____ people's lives. Today, TV news lets us see the harsh _____ of war. It has the power to _____ buildings, countries, and, worst of all, _____ children and adults. The _____ behind war can be confusing. War makes people feel _____. To end such a terrible _____, we must respect all of _____ around the world.

Written Review Write an ad for "Zlata's Diary." Why is it important for people to read about the terrible **reality** that Zlata experienced? Use four vocabulary words.

WRITE ABOUT THE GUIDING QUESTION

Explore Living with Conflict
How does writing about **conflict** help a person live with it? Reread "Zlata's Diary" and look for details that support your ideas.

Connect Across the Curriculum

Vocabulary Study

Shades of Meaning and Word Choice

> **Academic Vocabulary**
> • **scale** (skāl) *noun*
> A **scale** is a graphic organizer that shows how a series of items are related.

Even among words that mean the same thing there are **shades of meaning,** or slightly different meanings.

Analyze a Scale of Meaning You can arrange synonyms on a **scale** to examine their different meanings.

Zlata thinks war is bad. She also thinks it is "disgusting" and "horrible." This is how those shades of meaning might look on a **scale** :

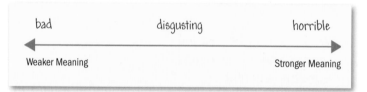

bad   disgusting   horrible

Weaker Meaning   Stronger Meaning

Make Word Choices Find each word in the selection. See how it is used. Create a **scale** for each word. Use a thesaurus or dictionary to help.

1. nice (p. 439)   **2.** tough (p. 439)   **3.** freezing (p. 441)

Literary Analysis

Evaluate Literature: Word Choice

Writers carefully choose words to convey specific meanings or feelings. In her diary, Zlata uses specific words that let you feel her emotions. This is the tone, or the feelings you get from reading her diary.

A word's **connotation** is the feeling or idea that the word suggests. One word might have a stronger effect than another. In "Zlata's Diary," she calls the attackers "fine gentlemen." Would you feel the same way if she had called them "soldiers?" Which word choices create a stronger effect? Why?

Analyze Word Choice Reread "Zlata's Diary" to find examples of thoughtful word choices. Tell the **connotation** of the words. Then discuss how the words make you feel, and how they help to create the tone.

Justify

Group Talk With a group, take turns talking about what you would and would not write about in a diary. Justify your opinions and ideas. Use compound and complex sentences to give reasons and conditions for your ideas.

> I would write about my family because they are important to me.

> A diary is private, but I would trust my best friend to read my words.

Write About Your Opinion

Study the Models When you write, use a variety of sentences to make your writing more interesting. Use longer sentences with connecting words that show reasons, conditions, and other explanations for your ideas and opinions. Then your reader will understand why you believe something.

JUST OK

I ate lunch with the new student today and he told me what life was like in his homeland it was scary to hear about the danger his family was in. Don't blame him for wanting a better life. If I had to decide whether to stay or leave, I'd leave. Because living in a place where everyone is fighting is not good. Even if you have to leave your friends and neighbors behind.

> The reader thinks: "This writer just rambles on. The ideas don't connect very well."

BETTER

I ate lunch with the new student today, and he told me what life was like in his homeland. It was scary to hear about the danger his family was in. Who could blame him for wanting a better life? If I had to decide whether to stay or leave, I'd leave. Living surrounded by fighting is not good, even if you must leave friends and neighbors behind.

> This writer uses sentences that are varied and more smoothly connected.

WRITE ON YOUR OWN Write about a current event in the news. Tell what you think of the event. Give reasons for your thinking. Use a variety of sentences, and combine ideas smoothly to explain your opinions. Then read what you wrote aloud. Make sure it makes sense to your reader.

REMEMBER
Don't string together too many ideas in one sentence. It can confuse the reader.

▲ People have many different opinions of current events.

PROTECTING HUMAN RIGHTS

by Marty Schmitt and the United Nations

1   Nesse Godin was 13 years old when the Nazis occupied her town in Lithuania during World War II. Because she and her family were Jewish, they were sent to a concentration camp. By the end of the war, over 6 million people would die in similar camps. Once the stories of Holocaust survivors like Nesse Godin were made public, world leaders vowed to never let something like this happen again. The United Nations, an organization of 51 nations, established a Commission on Human Rights to decide which rights all people should have.

THE UNIVERSAL DECLARATION OF HUMAN RIGHTS

2   The members of this commission came from different cultural backgrounds, but they worked together to create a "common standard of achievement for all people and all nations." On December 10, 1948, the UN General Assembly approved the commission's Universal Declaration of Human Rights.

3   The Declaration is organized into 30 articles, each of which addresses a different type of right. Together, the articles describe everyday rights such as the right to life, work, travel, education, medical care, self-expression, participation in government, and many others.

THE IMPACT OF HUMAN RIGHTS

4   The declaration has had an impact on people and governments. For example, during the 1960s–1980s, countries around the world pressured the Republic of South Africa to grant human rights to its non-white population. Many countries refused to trade with South Africa, and the country was barred from participating in the Olympic Games from 1964–1990.

5   In 1994, South Africa finally gave in to the pressure and held elections in which all people could vote. The people elected Nelson Mandela, a leader of the African population, as president. This action showed the power of human rights.

6   The declaration is part of the International Bill of Rights, **a legally binding agreement** signed by the majority of the world's countries. It has also inspired more than 80 other international human rights treaties and declarations. According to the United Nations, the declaration remains "the first **pillar** of twentieth-century human rights law and the **cornerstone** of the universal human rights movement." This will continue to be a pillar of law in the twenty-first century.

Historical Background

From 1939 to 1945, Germany, Italy, and Japan formed the Axis Powers of World War II. Dictator Adolph Hitler led Nazis, also known as the National Socialist German Workers' Party. They were responsible for the Holocaust during which they set up camps to imprison and kill approximately six million Jewish people.

In Other Words

a legally binding agreement an agreement that can be enforced by a court of law
pillar building block
cornerstone foundation

Universal Declaration of Human Rights: The First Five Articles

7 **ARTICLE 1.**

All human beings are born free and equal in dignity and rights. They are **endowed with reason and conscience** and should act towards one another in a spirit of brotherhood.

8 **ARTICLE 2.**

Everyone is entitled to all the rights and freedoms set forth in this Declaration, without distinction of any kind, such as race, color, sex, language, religion, political or other opinion, national or social origin, property, birth or other status. Furthermore, no distinction shall be made on the basis of the political, jurisdictional or international status of the country or territory to which a person belongs, whether it be independent, trust, non-self-governing or under any other limitation of **sovereignty**.

9 **ARTICLE 3.**

Everyone has the right to life, liberty and **security of person**.

10 **ARTICLE 4.**

No one shall be held in slavery or servitude; slavery and the slave trade shall be prohibited in all their forms.

11 **ARTICLE 5.**

No one shall be subjected to torture or to cruel, inhuman or degrading treatment or punishment.

In Other Words

endowed with reason and conscience able to think and to make good choices

sovereignty independence of its citizens

security of person personal safety

Compare Across Texts

Compare Themes

"Nadia the Willful," "Passage to Freedom," "Zlata's Diary," and "Protecting Human Rights" all have similar themes. They focus on people facing problems in different time periods.

How It Works

Collect and Organize Ideas To compare themes across selections, ask questions that help you **identify** ideas that are similar and different.

Comparison Chart

Questions	"Nadia the Willful"	"Passage to Freedom"	"Zlata's Diary"	"Protecting Human Rights"
1. What are the setting and the conflict?	desert; Nadia's brother dies	Lithuania, 1940; father helps Jews escape	Sarajevo, 1992; war	1948, human rights violations
2. What does the story say about difficult times?				

Practice Together

Compare Ideas Compare the answers for question 1, and then summarize. Show how the ideas are similar and different.

Summary

> The texts are set in different times and places but all deal with fear and loss. Nadia loses her brother. The Sugiharas face danger as the Nazis approach. Zlata sees war and destruction all around her. The UN General Assembly knows about horrible things in the world.

Try It!

Make a chart to answer question 2. Compare and contrast ideas and explain their **connection** to the unit theme. Use this frame.

"Nadia the Willful," "Passage to Freedom," "Zlata's Diary," and "Protecting Human Rights" all show people dealing with _____. However, _____. Nadia teaches _____. Mr. Sugihara faces _____. Zlata expresses _____. The UN General Assembly sees _____. All four selections show that _____.

Academic Vocabulary

- **identify** (ĭ-**den**-tu-fī) *verb*
  When you **identify** something, you name it or tell what it is.
- **connection** (ku-**nek**-shun) *noun*
  The **connection** between two things is something they have in common.

CONFLICT AND RESOLUTION

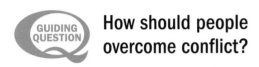

 GUIDING QUESTION
How should people overcome conflict?

Content Library

Leveled Library

Reflect on Your Reading

Think back on your reading of the unit selections. Discuss what you did to understand what you read.

Focus on Reading **Determine Author's Purpose**
In this unit, you learned that authors have many different purposes for writing. They use word choice to support their purpose for writing. Choose a selection from the unit. Then, list words and phrases that show why the author wrote that selection. Trade lists with a partner, and explain how each word choice supports the author's purpose.

Focus Strategy **Make Inferences**
As you read the selections, you made inferences based on the text and your own experiences. Explain to a partner how you will use this strategy in the future.

Explore the

Throughout this unit, you have considered how people overcome conflict. Choose one of these ways to explore the Guiding Question:

- **Discuss** With a group, discuss the Guiding Question. Use quotations, dialogue, photographs, and events from the selections to support your answer.
- **Write** Imagine that one of the characters or people in the selections wrote you a letter about his or her conflict. Write a letter back to offer advice.
- **Reflect** Think about a conflict that people often face in real life. With a partner, brainstorm the best ways to overcome the conflict, using an example from one of the selections during discussion.

Book Talk

Which Unit Library book did you choose? Discuss with a partner what you learned about people in conflict.

FAIR IS FAIR

7

What should you do when life is unfair?

◀ Leaders of the 1963 Civil Rights March on Washington, D.C., lock arms to show that they are united in their purpose.

Focus on Reading

Compare Text Structures

The structure of a text is the **logical** way ideas are organized. An author chooses a text structure that fits his or her viewpoint. For example, an author might use a chronological order text structure to show the importance of the sequence, or time order, of events. Another author might use a cause-and-effect text structure to show the importance of how events affect each other.

How It Works

If the order of events is most important, an author might use time order clue words, such as dates and times, *before, later, soon, when, during, by the time...,* or *finally.* If how events affect each other is most important, an author might use clue words like *because, since, so, due to, as a result,* or *the outcome.*

Read each passage and look for clue words.

These clue words reveal a chronological order text structure. This shows that the sequence of events is most important to the author.

The Underground Railroad

Before 1863, slavery was legal in southern states. During those years many enslaved people ran away from their "masters." They had to travel hundreds of miles to reach freedom. Soon many began to use a network called the Underground Railroad.

The Underground Railroad did not have trains. It was a group of free people who shared their homes with people who were escaping slavery. When the runaways moved from one home to another, a "conductor" made sure they arrived safely. At the end of their journey, the runaways were able to start new lives as free people.

The Underground Railroad

For many years slavery was legal in southern states. So, many enslaved people ran away from their "masters." Because they often traveled hundreds of miles to reach freedom, many used a network called the Underground Railroad.

The Underground Railroad did not have trains. It was a group of free people who shared their homes with people who were escaping slavery. Since the runaways moved from one home to another, a "conductor" made sure they arrived safely. As an outcome of the help from this network, the runaways were able to start new lives as free people.

These clue words reveal a cause-and-effect structure. This shows that how events affect each other is most important to the author.

Academic Vocabulary

- **logical** (lah-ji-kul) *adjective*
  When something is **logical**, it makes sense or is reasonable.

Practice Together

Two students wrote stories about events that happened in their town. As you read their stories, look for clues to text structures.

Mayor and Councilor Clash

On Monday morning, the peace of the city was shattered by a noisy confrontation.

At 7:28 Councilor Ortiz parked her car in the spot closest to the city offices. Just a moment later, Mayor Chu arrived. By the time he entered the parking lot, however, the best spot was taken.

When the mayor finally found a spot, he was late for his meeting with the city council. Soon the paths of the mayor and the councilor crossed and bystanders were shocked to hear harsh words exchanged by the two leaders.

Luckily, by the time the meeting concluded, the peaceful relationship between the mayor and the councilor was restored.

Unprofessional Leaders

The recent altercation between two city leaders was unnecessary and unprofessional.

The situation began in the city parking lot. The councilor arrived first, so she parked her car in a convenient spot closest to the city offices. The only remaining parking spot was a considerable distance away. Due to this situation, the mayor was late to the city council meeting.

The outcome of this circumstance was an embarrassing argument between the mayor and the councilor on the way to the meeting. Fortunately, since both leaders are mature adults, the meeting proceeded as planned.

How are the passages alike? How are they different? What is most important to each author?

Try It!

Read the following passages aloud. How is each passage organized? How do you know? What does the text structure tell you about each author's viewpoint?

A Model Plan

Because the United States declared its independence from Britain, it needed a new government. So the new leaders wrote a plan. Due to the fact that the plan did not work well, Americans wrote a second plan. Because this plan worked well, it became a model for governments around the world.

A Model Plan

The United States declared its independence from Britain in 1776. Soon it needed a new government. First, the new leaders wrote a plan that did not work well. Next, they wrote another plan. It worked very well. Later, the second plan became a model for governments around the world.

Focus on Vocabulary

Use Word Origins

Many English words have their **origins** in other languages, like Greek and Latin. Certain roots, or word parts, help form many words.

Some Common Roots for English Words

Root	Source and Meaning	Example
bio-	Greek, *bios* (life), of or about living things	biology—study of life
cred-	Latin, *credere* (to believe), about beliefs	incredible—unbelievable
divi-	Latin, *dividere* (to separate), in parts or disconnected	divide—to separate
leg-	Latin, *lex* (law), of or about the law	legal—according to law
-ology	Greek, *logos* (word), the study or science of	geology—study of Earth
psych-	Greek, *psyche* (spirit), of or about the mind or emotions	psychology—study of the mind
posi-	Latin, *positus* (place), put in place or set down	deposit—to put down
uni-	Latin, *unus* (one), one, or singular	unite—to bring together

How the Strategy Works

Use **origins** to figure out the meanings of unfamiliar words.

> EXAMPLE   We don't give much **credence** to her statement.

1. Study the word. Look for a root. (*cred-*)
2. Think of a word you know that has a similar root. (in*cred*ible)
3. Use this similarity to figure out the meaning of the unfamiliar word. (*cred-* means "*believe*")

Follow the strategy to figure out the meanings of the underlined words:

> What causes conflict between people? Psychologists and biologists have studied the role of conflict in human life. Out of their many different questions and ideas, scientists hope to find a universal answer.

Strategy in Action

" I know *bio* means life and *–ology* means the study of something. A *biologist* must study life. "

☑ **REMEMBER** You can use roots to figure out many new words.

Academic Vocabulary
- **origin** (or-u-jin) *noun*
  The **origin** of something is its source or beginning.

Practice Together

Read the passage aloud with your class. Find the root in each underlined word. Use it to help you figure out the meaning of the underlined word.

A House Divided

The future of the <u>United</u> States was in question in 1861. As President Abraham Lincoln took office, some southern states were thinking of <u>dividing</u> the <u>Union</u>. Leaders of those states were unhappy with the U.S. government.

They wanted to quit the nation and start a new one. Lincoln's view was clear. The United States was <u>indivisible</u>. Every action Lincoln took as president was meant to end <u>division</u> and <u>unify</u> the country.

▲ Our sixteenth president struggled to save the Union.

Try It!

Read the following passage. What does each underlined word mean? How do you know?

The Voice of the People

You don't need to be elected to office to take part in government. In many states, people can take <u>legislative</u> action in other ways. In California, citizens can suggest ideas for new laws, taxes, and other state changes. They state their ideas in a <u>proposition</u> for voters to decide on. If enough voters <u>unite</u> to pass the proposition, it can become law.

The Clever Magistrate

by Linda Fang
illustrated by Marilee Heyer

Build Background

Connect

Quickwrite What's the best way to settle an argument? Write down your thoughts in a Quickwrite. Share your ideas with classmates.

See Fairness in Action

How do you decide what is fair? What is the best way to decide what is fair?

myNGconnect.com
🔊 View the images.

▲ In a trial, a judge listens to an argument and decides what is fair.

Language & Grammar

1 TRY OUT LANGUAGE
2 LEARN GRAMMAR
3 APPLY ON YOUR OWN

Tell an Original Story

CD

Look at the pictures and listen to the story.

STORY

It was time to rake the leaves. The boys' mother was working inside the house while they worked outside.

The older brother relaxed while the younger brother was busy raking.

The mother gave each son a small payment for a job well done.

The older son knew he did not do his share of the work. Later, he felt guilty, and gave most of his payment to the real worker, his younger brother.

1 TRY OUT LANGUAGE
2 LEARN GRAMMAR
3 APPLY ON YOUR OWN

Use Participles as Adjectives

Verbs have four **principal parts**. For example:

Present	Present Participle	Past	Past Participle
write	writing	wrote	written
smile	smiling	smiled	smiled

- Sometimes a **participle** is part of a verb phrase. A verb phrase contains a **helping verb** and a **participle**.

  Present Participle:　He was **writing** a folktale about a fox.

  Past Participle:　He had **written** folktales about foxes before.

- Sometimes a **participle** acts as an adjective to describe a **noun** or **pronoun**. If the participle starts the sentence, use a comma after it.

  EXAMPLES　**Writing**, he worked hard for weeks.

  His **written** tale is ready for us to read.

- Sometimes you can combine sentences using participles.

  EXAMPLE　The writer looked for two pages. Two pages were **missing**.

  The writer looked for two **missing** pages.

Practice Together

Combine each pair of sentences. Move the <u>participle</u> to tell about a noun or a pronoun in the first sentence. Say the new sentence.

1. The fox looked up at the crow. He was <u>smiling</u>.
2. The crow held some cheese in her beak. She was <u>resting</u>.
3. The fox had a plan to trick the crow. He was <u>skilled</u>.

Try It!

Combine each pair of sentences. Move the <u>participle</u> to tell about the noun in the first sentence. Write the new sentence on a card. Say it.

4. The fox's words were nice. He had <u>spoken</u> the words.
5. The crow didn't drop the cheese. The crow was <u>surprised</u>.
6. The fox wandered away. He was <u>disappointed</u>.

▲ The grinning fox tried to trick the crow.

Create a Story

TELL AN ORIGINAL STORY

A good story holds people's attention. It makes them want to hear more. What story do you want to tell? To whom will you tell it? With a group, discuss your ideas for a story to tell a small child.

With your group, think about the characters and the setting. Discuss a conflict or problem and its complications. Decide how it will be resolved. Fill out a chart like this one to help your group plan its story.

Story Element	Group Choice
Characters (who is in the story)	a polar bear and a seal
Setting (where and when the story happens)	an icy island in the Arctic Ocean
Conflict (the problem and complications the characters face)	
Plot (the events that happen as the characters try to solve the conflict)	
Resolution (how the conflict is solved)	

Work with your group to improve the story. Add details. Tell the new story to another group.

HOW TO TELL AN ORIGINAL STORY

1. Introduce the characters and setting.
2. Tell about the problem.
3. Describe how characters try to solve the problem.
4. Tell how the story ends.

> Once upon a time, a hungry polar bear sat on the tip of a huge iceberg in the Arctic Ocean. The iceberg was his home.

USE PARTICIPLES AS ADJECTIVES

When you tell a story, use **participles** as adjectives to describe the characters and events.

EXAMPLES   The polar bear's **rumbling** stomach gave away his problem.
The **worried** seal had to stay far away from him.

Prepare to Read

Learn Key Vocabulary

Study the Words Use the steps below.

1. Pronounce the word. Say it aloud several times. Spell it.
2. Rate your word knowledge.
3. Study the example. Tell more about the word.
4. Practice it. Make the word your own.

Key Words

argument (ar-gyu-munt)
noun ▶ page 467

An **argument** is a strong disagreement. My friend and I got into an **argument** because he was late.
Related Word: **argue**

complaint (kum-plānt) *noun*
▶ page 468

> YOUR VIEWS ■ LETTERS TO THE EDITOR
>
> To the Editor:
> I have a complaint. Elm Park is not big enough for our town. It gets crowded. We need another park so all kids have room to play.

To give a **complaint** is to tell others that you are unhappy about something. I sent my **complaint** in a letter to the editor.
Antonym: **praise**

damage (dam-ij) *noun*
▶ page 466

Damage means harm that is done. I threw a baseball, which caused **damage** to the window.
Antonym: **repair**

furious (fyur-ē-us) *adjective*
▶ page 466

Someone who is **furious** is very angry. The man was **furious** when his car was hit.
Related Word: **fury**
Synonym: **angry**

inevitable (i-nev-i-tu-bul)
adjective ▶ page 470

Something that is **inevitable** will happen no matter what. If you throw a ball up, it is **inevitable** that it will come down.

mercy (mur-sē) *noun*
▶ page 468

Mercy is kindness to someone in trouble. My mom showed **mercy** when I spilled food on the floor.
Related Word: **merciful**

plead (plēd) *verb*
▶ page 467

To **plead** means to strongly ask for something. Children might **plead** for a larger allowance.

relent (ri-lent) *verb*
▶ page 467

To **relent** means to stop. After flooding the town, the rain finally **relented**.

Practice the Words Make a Word Map for each Key Word. Then compare your maps with a partner.

Definition	Characteristics
to stop trying	after strong effort / after many tries / after pushing hard
My cousin wanted to borrow money from me, but he finally relented.	to question / to insist / to remind
Example	Non-examples

Word: relent

Word Map

Determine Theme

What Is a Folk Tale About? A folk tale is a simple story that has been shared for many years by a **culture**. Understanding the purpose of a text can help you determine its theme. The purpose of a folk tale is to share an important life lesson. So, the theme of a folk tale is usually a lesson that applies to people anywhere and at any time.

Look for clues to theme in the title, setting, thoughts and actions of the characters, and plot. You learn more about the theme from how the characters' thoughts and actions change throughout the story.

Reading Strategies
- Plan
- Monitor
- Ask Questions
- Make Connections
- Visualize
- Make Inferences
- **Determine Importance**
  Focus your attention on the author's most significant ideas and information.
- Synthesize

Look Into the Text

The Clever Wish

Long ago, an old woman was granted a wish. She decided to ask her daughter and her daughter's husband to tell her their wishes.

"I wish to be rich," said the daughter.

"I wish to be in the king's court," said the husband.

The old woman had never wanted wealth or power. What she wanted was a grandchild.

To make her wish, the old woman said: "I wish for a grandson who is a rich prince." When that clever wish was granted, everyone was happy!

Practice Together

Begin a Theme Chart A Theme Chart can help you understand the theme of a text. This Theme Chart shows two clues to the theme of the folk tale. Reread "The Clever Wish" and add clues and the theme to the chart.

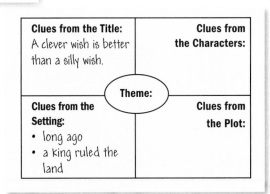

Clues from the Title:
A clever wish is better than a silly wish.

Clues from the Characters:

Theme:

Clues from the Setting:
- long ago
- a king ruled the land

Clues from the Plot:

Academic Vocabulary
- **culture** (**kul**-chur) *noun*
  Culture includes the beliefs, attitudes, and behaviors shared by a group of people.

Folk Tale

A folk tale is a story that has been shared for many years by a **culture**. Because a folk tale is meant to share a life lesson, its theme is often something that applies to everyone.

Like other fictional narratives, a folk tale is told in time order and the characters' dialogue helps move the story along.

Look Into the Text

One cold winter day, a farmer was carrying two buckets of spoiled food from a restaurant to his pigsty. As he was passing a coat shop, he accidentally spilled some of the slop on the ground. Ugh! Ugh! What a smell!

As you read a folk tale, use the most important information about the characters, setting, and plot to figure out its theme.

The Clever Magistrate

by Linda Fang
illustrated by Marilee Heyer

Set a Purpose
Find out what happens to a farmer and a shopkeeper.

One cold winter day, a farmer was carrying two buckets of **spoiled** food from a restaurant to **his pigsty**. As he was passing a coat shop, he accidentally spilled some of the slop on the ground. Sour cabbage, rotten eggs, and fish bones scattered all over the ground. Ugh! Ugh! What a smell!

The shopkeeper, who happened to be standing inside the door, saw this and was **furious**. He rushed out, grabbed the man, and shouted, "You dirty beggar! Look what you've done in front of my shop! It will be impossible to get rid of the smell! How are you going to pay for the **damage**?"

"I am so sorry," said the farmer. "I will clean it up right away. As for the damage, all I have is this coin." He took out a coin and handed it to the shopkeeper.

The shopkeeper snatched the coin,

Key Vocabulary
furious *adj.*, extremely angry
damage *n.*, the result of an accident

In Other Words
spoiled rotten
his pigsty where he kept his pigs

Science Background
Silver and gold are very soft metals. In the past, it was common for people to bite into coins to find out if they were made from real silver or gold. If the coins were real, the bite would leave tooth marks.

put it between his teeth, and bit down on it. The metal was soft, which proved that it contained silver. He thrust it into his pocket and said, "All right, I will take it. But you still need to clean up the mess."

"Let me go and get some rags and a mop," said the farmer. "I will be right back."

"No," said the shopkeeper. "I want you to clean it up right away. It smells so bad that I am going to be sick. Take off your coat and wipe up the mess."

"Please don't ask me to do that!" cried the farmer. "This is the only **quilted** coat I have, and if I use it to wipe up the mess, it will be ruined. I won't be able to wear it anymore."

"That's your problem, not mine!" said the shopkeeper. "In fact, the coat you are wearing is no better than rags. If you don't do what I say, I am going to take you to court."

The farmer **pleaded** with him to reconsider, but the shopkeeper would not **relent**.

Just then they heard, "**Make way for the magistrate**! Make way for the magistrate!"

Key Vocabulary
plead v., to ask for something in an emotional way
relent v., to stop trying
argument n., disagreement, fight

In Other Words
quilted padded and warm
Make way for the magistrate! The judge is coming!

Look Into the Text

1. **Summarize** What is the **argument** about? Explain.
2. **Details** How does the farmer offer to repay the shopkeeper for the **damage**?
3. **Judgment** Is the shopkeeper's reaction fair? Why or why not?

The county magistrate was coming down the road in his sedan chair. When he saw the **commotion**, he ordered his guards to put down the chair and bring the two men before him.

"What is the matter?" he asked.

The shopkeeper quickly replied, *"Ta-jen*, this man made a mess in front of my shop. He gave me a coin to pay for the damage, but when I asked him to wipe up the mess, he wouldn't do it."

The magistrate stepped down from his chair and went over to look at the mess. Sour cabbage, rotten eggs, and fish bones were scattered all over the place. Ugh! Ugh! What a smell!

"Why don't you clean up the mess?" asked the magistrate.

"He wants me to wipe up the mess with my coat," said the farmer. "It will be ruined if I do so. And this is the only coat I have."

"Is that what you want?" the magistrate asked the shopkeeper.

"Yes, that is exactly what I want."

"And you will not **settle for less**?"

"No, I will not settle for anything less."

"Well," said the magistrate to the farmer, "if that is what he wants, you'd better do it."

"Ta-jen, have **mercy**! I can't do that!" cried the farmer. "Without the coat I will **freeze to death**."

"I am sorry," said the magistrate. "But that doesn't change anything. If you don't do it, I will have to put you in jail."

"That is not **just**!" cried the farmer.

"Hmm…" said the magistrate. He looked angry.

"*Ouh! Ouh! Ouh!*" cried the guards. "*Ouh! Ouh! Ouh!*" They looked threatening.

The farmer realized that there was no way out. **Reluctantly, he used** his coat to clean up the mess. Sour cabbage, rotten eggs, and fish bones. Ugh! Ugh! What a smell! He threw the coat into one of his buckets and stood shivering in front of the magistrate.

The shopkeeper laughed. "Ha, ha, ha!"

"Well," said the magistrate to the shopkeeper, "are you satisfied now?"

"Yes, *Ta-jen*, I am completely satisfied."

"No more **complaints**?"

Key Vocabulary

mercy *n.*, kindness shown to someone in trouble

complaint *n.*, an expression of unhappiness about something

In Other Words

commotion confusion, excitement
Ta-jen Your Excellency (in Chinese)
settle for less agree to anything else
freeze to death be too cold
just fair
Reluctantly, he used He had no choice but to use

"No more complaints!" said the shopkeeper.

"**Case closed**," said the magistrate.

"Case closed."

"But his case against you is now open."

"What!" said the shopkeeper, stunned.

"Well, you see, he is now freezing without a coat. In such weather he could catch a cold. Is that not possible?" asked the magistrate.

"Yes, *Ta-jen*."

"His cold could develop into pneumonia. Is that not possible?"

"Yes, *Ta-jen*."

Cultural Background

A **magistrate** is a person elected to enforce laws. In the past, a magistrate might have traveled in a **sedan chair**— a covered chair that is carried on poles by two people. This showed power and authority.

"Then he could die. His family could sue you for murder, and if **you are convicted**, you would be put to death. Isn't that almost **inevitable**?"

"Yes, *Ta-jen*."

"Well, I don't think you can **afford** that, can you?"

"Oh, no, *Ta-jen*. I cannot afford that. What shall I do?"

"Well, it would be better to settle this out of court."

"Yes, yes, we'd better settle this out of court. But how?"

"We should get him a coat so he won't catch a cold."

"But where can we get one?"

"Right here, from your coat shop."

The shopkeeper looked **as if he had swallowed a fly alive**. He yelled at the farmer, "Go get a coat and be gone!"

The farmer went into the shop, picked out a very cheap coat, and came out. The magistrate stopped him.

He looked as if he had swallowed a fly.

"You poor thing!" he said. "Look at the coat you've got. It is so thin. You could still catch a cold, isn't that so?"

"Yes, *Ta-jen*."

"You might get pneumonia, isn't that so?"

"Yes, *Ta-jen*."

"You might even die, isn't that so?"

"Yes, *Ta-jen*."

"And then your family could come and **harass** this nice gentleman. I know all your tricks!" The magistrate turned to one of his guards. "Go into the shop and get him the warmest coat you can find."

So the guard went into the shop and picked out the warmest coat he could find for the farmer. As you might guess, the warmest coat happened to be the most expensive.

When the farmer left, the magistrate smiled at the shopkeeper. "Well, what do you think about the way I settled this case? Didn't I handle it very well?"

Key Vocabulary
inevitable *adj.*, not possible to avoid

In Other Words
you are convicted it is decided that his death is your fault
afford risk
as if he had swallowed a fly alive scared, horrified
harass bother

"Yes, *Ta-jen*," the shopkeeper said **glumly**. "There is no question about that."

"I am glad I was able to take care of this case," said the magistrate. "You have to watch out for these troublemakers. Next time, if you have a case like this, don't try to settle it yourself. Be sure to let me handle it for you." ❖

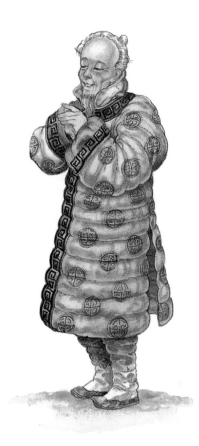

About the Author

Linda Fang

Linda Fang grew up in Shanghai, China. As a child, Fang was extremely shy. A teacher who wanted to help her overcome her shyness gave Fang a special assignment. The teacher gave her a book to read at home and said, "Come back tomorrow and see if you can tell it to me." This helped Fang discover her talent for storytelling. Fang went on to win storytelling competitions and became a professional storyteller whose tales delight both children and adults.

In Other Words
glumly sadly, unhappily

Look Into the Text

1. **Confirm Predictions** Was your prediction correct? If so, what evidence did you use? If not, what happened that you did not expect?
2. **Explain** Why does the magistrate say, "his case against you is now open"?
3. **Problem and Solution** How does the magistrate solve the farmer's problem?

The Clever Old Woman

In ancient days, a farmer and his clever old mother lived in a village ruled by an **ignorant** young chief. The chief believed that old people were useless, so he ordered that everyone over seventy be taken to the mountains and **abandoned**. Away went the clever old judges, the knowledgeable old doctors, and the wise old teachers, up to the mountains.

The good farmer could not bear to do such a **heartless** thing. Instead, he hid his mother in a cave that he dug under his house.

One day, powerful Lord Higa and his warriors rode into the village and threatened to conquer it. The ignorant chief begged for mercy, although he himself had never shown mercy to others. "Set us any task," he pleaded, "and it shall be done."

"Any task?" said Lord Higa. "I am fair and I do admire cleverness, so let's see if there is any cleverness in this village."

He ordered the villagers to complete three impossible tasks.

"But no one can do what is impossible!" protested the chief.

"Fair is fair," replied Lord Higa. "You did say 'any task.' Now then, first you must make a rope out of ashes. Next, run a thread through a crooked log. Lastly, make a drum that plays without being tapped on top." With that, Lord Higa and his warriors galloped away, vowing to come back before it was fully dark. Already the light was fading from the sky.

With no time to lose, the chief asked all the people in the village for their advice, but they didn't **have a clue**. "If only the elders were still living among us!" they all cried. "Think of how clever they were and all that they had learned over the years."

When the clever old woman heard the chatter of confusion above her, she

In Other Words
ignorant uncaring
abandoned left alone
heartless mean
have a clue know what to do

Language Background
Lord and **Chief** are titles for leaders who have control, or authority, over others.

couldn't take it any longer and dared to step out among them.

"How dare you!" **bellowed** the ignorant chief, but the clever old woman ignored him and quickly set to work. First, she soaked rope in salt water and then dried it. When the villagers set the rope on fire, it burned away, but the ash remained in the shape of a rope. Next, she put honey at one end of a log and an ant tied with silk thread at the other end. The ant raced through the log, pulling the thread behind it. Lastly, she opened one side of a drum and **sealed** a bumblebee inside. As the bee beat against the sides of the drum to escape, the drum played without being tapped on top.

When the ignorant chief saw how clever the old woman was, he hung his head in shame for having treated old people so unfairly. By then, darkness had fallen and Lord Higa and his warriors returned, ready to destroy the village. But when they saw that all three impossible tasks had been completed, they were **astonished**.

How dare you!

"Fair is fair," said Lord Higa. "Clearly everyone in this village deserves to be treated with respect."

"Yes, everyone deserves to be treated with respect," said the clever old woman **firmly**, as she stared **intently** at the chief.

So Lord Higa left and never again bothered the village, the ignorant chief changed his ways, and the old people came back down from the mountain. As for the clever old woman, she went on being clever for many, many years.

In Other Words
bellowed shouted
sealed put
astonished amazed
firmly strongly
intently closely

Look Into the Text

1. **Compare** How are "The Clever Old Woman" and "The Clever Magistrate" alike and different?

2. **Speculate** How would the story change if the farmer had not helped his mother?

3. **Judgment** Which characters in the two stories are the most fair? Why do you think so?

Argument

by Eve Merriam

Good morning.
  Hmm.
Nice day.
  Dim.
5 Sorry.
  Glad.

Hadn't.
  Had.
Go.
10   Stay.
  Work.
Play.
Pro.
  Con.
15 Off.
  On.
Front.
  Back.
  Taut.
20 Slack.
Open.
  Shut.
And.
  But.
25 Over.
  Under.
Cloudless.
  Thunder.
Detour.
30   Highway.
New way.
  Thruway.
Byway...?
  MY WAY!

Connect Reading and Writing

Vocabulary

- **argument**
- **complaint**
- **damage**
- **furious**
- **inevitable**
- **mercy**
- **pleaded**
- **relented**

CRITICAL THINKING

1. SUM IT UP Review the Theme Chart you completed as you read. Use it to summarize the selection.

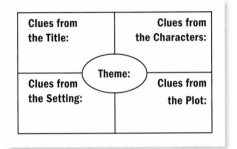

Clues from the Title:	Clues from the Characters:
Clues from the Setting:	Clues from the Plot:

(Theme:)

Theme Chart

2. Explain Why does the shopkeeper **relent** and give the farmer what is fair?

3. Compare How are characters in "The Clever Magistrate" like those in "The Clever Old Woman"?

4. Generalize In both the folk tales and the poem, **arguments** take place. Are arguments an **inevitable** part of people's lives? Explain.

READING FLUENCY

Expression Read the passage on page 642 to a partner. Assess your fluency.

1. My voice never/sometimes/always matched what I read.

2. What I did best in my reading was _____.

READING STRATEGY

What strategy helped you understand this selection? Tell a partner about it.

VOCABULARY REVIEW

Oral Review Read the paragraph aloud. Add the vocabulary words.

> My older sister and I got into an _____ when she accidentally drove over my bike. When I saw the _____ this caused, I felt _____. She _____ with me to be fair. After all, I had left the bike lying in the garage, hidden behind the car. So it was _____ that someone would drive over it. I felt sorry about making a _____, so I _____. Out of kindness and _____, my sister replaced the wheel.

Written Review Write a diary entry to tell how you feel about **arguments**. Use four vocabulary words.

WRITE ABOUT THE (GUIDING QUESTION)

Explore Fairness

Write as the shopkeeper or the farmer in "The Clever Magistrate." Judge if the magistrate was fair when he settled each **complaint**. Support your judgment with examples from the text.

Connect Across the Curriculum

Vocabulary Study

Use Word Origins: Borrowed Words

> **Academic Vocabulary**
> • **definition** (de-fu-**ni**-shun) *noun*
>   The meaning of a word is its **definition**.

Borrowed words are words taken from another language. They keep their original **definitions** . Read the dictionary entry below. The history of the word is in brackets.

> **coat** (kōt) [from Old French *cote*, meaning "robe, coat"]
> **1** *n.* an outer garment with sleeves.
> **2** *n.* the natural outer covering of an animal.
> **3** *n.* a layer covering a surface.

Dictionary Entry

Identify Word Origins Read the following borrowed words. Use a dictionary to find each word's **definition** and language it came from.

   1. banana   **2.** parka   **3.** canyon   **4.** sofa

Listening/Speaking

DRAMA

Read a Poem Aloud

> **Academic Vocabulary**
> • **structure** (struk-chur) *noun*
>   A **structure** is how parts are arranged or organized.

The **structure** of the poem "Argument" expresses ideas and creates a mood. You can use the **structure** to plan a read-aloud of the poem.

1 **Find Clues in the Poem** Reread "Argument." Note clues in the **structure** that tell you how to read the poem.
- The lines are staggered. Some start to the left. Some start to the right. I think this means _____.
- The lines are really short. I think I should read them _____.
- Most lines end with a period, but the last two lines _____.
- The mood of the poem is _____.

2 **Do a Poetry Reading** Work with a partner. Decide who will read which lines. Practice reading with facial expression. Vary your pace and volume. Present your best reading to your classmates.

Tell an Original Story

Group Tale With a group, create a new story to tell. First, brainstorm the topic of the story. Then, one person starts the story with a sentence or two. When that person stops, the next person continues the story to tell what happens next. Continue around the group several times until you create an end to the story. Use participles in your story.

> One day a shopkeeper stepped out of his store. Surprised, he saw a mess at his door.

> The shopkeeper shouted, "Who left this at my door?"

Write to Add Details to Sentences

Study the Models When you describe an event, add descriptive details and combine ideas to create smoother, richer sentences.

OK

> The writer looked at the tip of his quill pen. It was broken. He had been writing all night. He rubbed his eyes. He was tired. Then he listened to the rain hitting the roof. The rain was pouring. He realized the importance of his work. He was smiling. He grabbed a new quill pen and continued to write. The words were powerful. They were written.

This writing is choppy and does not add descriptive details smoothly to the sentences.

BETTER

> The writer looked at the tip of his <u>broken</u> quill pen. He had been writing all night. <u>Tired</u>, he rubbed his eyes. Then he listened to the <u>pouring</u> rain hitting the roof. <u>Smiling</u>, he realized the importance of his work. He grabbed a new quill pen and continued to write. The <u>written</u> words were powerful.

This writer adds descriptive details and combines ideas to make sentences less choppy.

WRITE ON YOUR OWN Rewrite the description. Describe the event as if it happened yesterday. Add details and avoid choppy sentences by using participles as adjectives.

REMEMBER

Verb forms change depending on how they are used.

Present	Present Participle	Past	Past Participle
impress	impressing	impressed	impressed
write	writing	wrote	written

THE CONSTITUTION
by Paul Finkelman

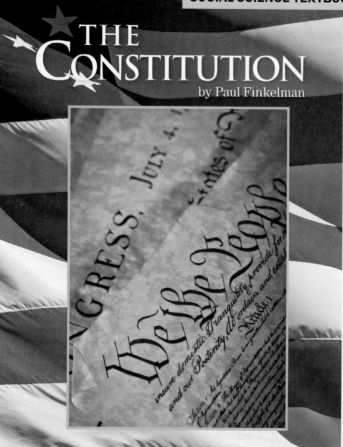

SELECTION 2 OVERVIEW

▶ **Build Background**

▶ **Language & Grammar**
Summarize
Use Participial Phrases to Combine Sentences

▶ **Prepare to Read**
Learn Key Vocabulary
Analyze Main Idea and Details

▶ **Read and Write**
Introduce the Genre
Social Science Textbook
Focus on Reading
Analyze Main Idea and Details
Apply the Focus Strategy
Determine Importance
Critical Thinking
Reading Fluency
Read with Phrasing
Vocabulary Review
Write About the Guiding Question

▶ **Connect Across the Curriculum**
Vocabulary Study
Use Word Origins: Greek, Latin, and Anglo-Saxon Roots
Literary Analysis
Analyze Poetry: Symbol
Language and Grammar
Summarize
Writing and Grammar
Write to Elaborate

Build Background

Connect

KWL Chart Create a KWL Chart about the Constitution. After you read the selection, you will record what you have learned.

WHAT I KNOW	WHAT I WANT TO KNOW	WHAT I LEARNED
Sets up branches of government	Which branch of government is most important?	

KWL Chart

Explore the Constitution

How did our nation create a system of fairness for all? In 1787, 55 people met in Philadelphia to write a plan of government.

Digital Library

myNGconnect.com
↻ View the video.

◀ Benjamin Franklin is one of the best known signers of the U.S. Constitution.

Language & Grammar

Summarize

CD

Look at the picture and listen to the speech. Then listen to a summary of the speech. A summary contains only the most important ideas and details of a longer work.

PICTURE PROMPT

Washington as Statesman at the Constitutional Convention, 1856, Junius Brutus Stearns.
Oil on canvas, Virginia Museum of Fine Arts, Richmond, Virginia.

Summary

Benjamin Franklin wanted to persuade delegates at the Convention to sign the completed Constitution. Even though Franklin didn't agree with everything in the document, he believed that having a central government for the United States was necessary. He felt that the Constitution they wrote was as good as possible.

He urged the delegates to talk positively about the Constitution when they presented it to the voters in their states. He also urged those delegates who were unsure about the document to support it for the good of the country.

1 TRY OUT LANGUAGE
2 LEARN GRAMMAR
3 APPLY ON YOUR OWN

Use Participial Phrases to Combine Sentences

A **participle** is a verb form that sometimes acts as an adjective.
A **participial phrase** begins with a participle. Participles and participial phrases describe nouns and pronouns.

- A participle ends in **-ing** or **-ed**, or it has a special form. It can stand alone, or it can come at the start of a group of words called a **participial phrase**.

    EXAMPLES   **Caring** delegates wrote laws for the new country.
    Writing for months, they created an impressive document.
    Often exhausted, the writers kept going.
    Written carefully, the document defined the new government.

- You can use participial phrases to combine or expand sentences. Use a comma after a participial phrase that starts a sentence.

    EXAMPLE   The document was very important. It was **protecting all Americans**.

    Protecting all Americans, the document was very important.

Practice Together

Use a participial phrase to combine each pair of sentences. Say each new sentence.

1. The colonists drafted a document. They were choosing the best ideas.
2. New laws were added. They were written carefully.
3. The writers asked for approval. They were satisfied with the results.

Try It!

Use a participial phrase to combine each pair of sentences. Write each new sentence on a card. Then say each new sentence.

4. A man said the document was done. He was speaking from the podium.
5. The delegates signed their names. They were pleased with their efforts.
6. The men shook hands. They were congratulating each other.

▲ **Written in Philadelphia, the Constitution describes our government.**

Tell About Ben

SUMMARIZE

You are exposed to lots of information every day. It's impossible to remember everything you read and hear. How do you share what's important with others? Summarize! You don't need to remember everything. Many details are fun and interesting but not all that important.

With a partner, read this passage about Benjamin Franklin.

> Benjamin Franklin once said, "If you would not be forgotten as soon as you are dead and rotten, either write things worth reading, or do things worth the writing." He followed his own advice and did both. Today, Ben Franklin is remembered as one of our Founding Fathers. He helped write both the Declaration of Independence and the Constitution of the United States. He is also remembered as an inventor. Some of his inventions include bifocal glasses, the lightning rod, and the Franklin stove. Franklin was also a skilled printer. He printed paper money and helped begin our paper currency system. Did you know that his face appears on a hundred-dollar bill?

Now decide with your partner what information is important to remember. List just the most important or main ideas. Create a summary of the passage in your own words.

Main Ideas
Franklin was a Founding Father of the U.S.
He was an inventor.

Read your summary to a small group.

HOW TO SUMMARIZE

1. Identify the main ideas and important information.
2. Leave out less important information and most details and examples that are used to illustrate the main ideas.
3. Use your own words to tell about what you heard or read.

> Franklin was a Founding Father of this country. He helped write the Constitution. He was also an inventor.

USE PARTICIPLES TO COMBINE SENTENCES

When you write a summary, you may want to use **participles** to combine sentences and **participial phrases** to add details. If the participial phrase starts the sentence, use a comma after it.

EXAMPLES   **Known** as a statesman, Franklin was also a printer.
His **smiling face** appears on paper money.

Prepare to Read

Learn Key Vocabulary

Study the Words Use the steps below.

1. Pronounce the word. Say it aloud several times. Spell it.
2. Rate your word knowledge.
3. Study the example. Tell more about the word.
4. Practice it. Make the word your own.

Key Words

amend (u-mend) *verb*
▶ page 491

To **amend** means to change or to improve. I **amended** the sentence to make it complete.
Related Word: **amendment**
Synonym: **improve**

delegate (del-i-get) *noun*
▶ page 492

A **delegate** is a person who has the power to act and speak for others. The **delegates** met to talk about laws that would help people.

democracy (di-**mok**-ru-sē) *noun* ▶ page 499

In a **democracy**, people have the power to vote for what they believe. The United States is a **democracy**.
Related Word: **democratic**

government (**guv**-urn-ment) *noun* ▶ page 486

A **government** is a group of people who are in charge of a country, state, or city. The U.S. **government** is run by many people.

independence (in-di-**pen**-duns) *noun* ▶ page 487

Independence means freedom from control by others. The U.S. celebrates its **independence** with fireworks on the Fourth of July.
Related Word: **independent**

interpret (in-**tur**-prut) *verb* ▶ page 494

To **interpret** means to explain the meaning of something. A judge **interprets** the meanings of laws.

justice (**jus**-tis) *noun* ▶ page 486

Justice means fairness. Our court system is set up to give everyone an opportunity for **justice**.
Related Word: **just**

represent (rep-ri-zent) *verb* ▶ page 492

To **represent** means to speak or act for a person or group. The president **represents** all of the people of his or her country.
Related Word: **representative**

Practice the Words Make an Expanded Meaning Map for each Key Word. Then compare your maps with a partner.

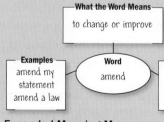

Expanded Meaning Map

Analyze Main Idea and Details

How is Writing Organized? Nonfiction texts are often organized in sections of text with headings. In this way, the text is divided into its most important, or main, ideas. Sometimes the author states the main idea of a section directly. Sometimes you must figure it out from the details.

As you read each section, look for clues about its main idea.

Reading Strategies

- Plan
- Monitor
- Ask Questions
- Make Connections
- Visualize
- Make Inferences
- **Determine Importance**
  Focus your attention on the author's most significant ideas and information.
- Synthesize

Look Into the Text

Introduction

What would it be like if our government had no president or one top leader? What if the government could not collect taxes to pay its bills? What if each state had its own kind of money? You would have to change your Pennsylvania money into Virginia money as you traveled south. What if a criminal only had to slip out of state to escape justice? That is what the United States was like before the Constitution was written.

"Every detail seems to lead up to the last sentence."

"The main idea was not stated directly. I used details to determine it."

Practice Together

Begin a Main-Idea Diagram A Main-Idea Diagram can help you analyze text that is organized by main ideas. This Main-Idea Diagram shows the first detail from the passage above. Reread the passage and add the other details. Then use the details to determine the main idea of the passage.

Main Idea:
Detail: Before the Constitution, there was no president or leader.
Detail:
Detail:
Detail:

Social Science Textbook

A social science textbook presents information about real people, real events, and real conditions in the world. The information in the textbook is usually organized into sections with each section having its own main idea and details.

Textbooks often contain a lot of facts, explanations, and details. Remembering all that information can difficult. But when you figure out the main ideas, you only have to remember those ideas that are the most important.

Look Into the Text

Introduction

A new nation needs a written plan of government. When the United States declared its independence from Britain, it needed a new government. Its first plan created a weak national government that did not work well. So, Americans wrote a second plan, the U.S. Constitution. This new plan worked, and it has become a model for governments around the world!

As you read each section of a textbook, look for important details that give clues to its main idea.

THE CONSTITUTION

by Paul Finkelman

 Comprehension Coach

Introduction

What would it be like if our **government** had no president or any one leader? What if the government could not collect taxes to pay its bills? What if each state had its own kind of money? You would have to change your Pennsylvania money into Virginia money as you traveled south. What if a criminal only had to **slip out of** state to escape **justice**? That is what the United States was like before the Constitution was written.

Key Vocabulary
government *n.*, people who rule a country or state
justice *n.*, equality or fairness

In Other Words
slip out of leave a

A new nation needs a written plan of government. When the United States declared its **independence** from Britain, it needed a new government. Its first plan created a weak national government that did not work well. So, Americans wrote a second plan, the U.S. Constitution. This new plan worked, and it has become a model for governments around the world! What does the U.S. Constitution say and what does it mean in our lives? Let's find out.

The Constitution is at work when a President makes the annual State of the Union Address to the three branches of government.

Key Vocabulary
independence *n.*, freedom from the control of others

Look Into the Text

1. **Explain** What is the Constitution? Why does a new nation need one?
2. **Inference** Describe what life in the United States would be like without the U.S. Constitution.

On Display

The original Constitution was written in 1787 on four sheets of parchment, a heavy kind of paper. It was kept in various cities until 1952, when it was placed in the National Archives Building in Washington, D.C. In 2003, a major **renovation** of the National Archives was completed. The entire Constitution is now on display.

First of Its Kind

The U.S. Constitution has about 4,500 words. It is the oldest and the shortest written constitution of any government in the world today.

Who Signed It?

Thirty-nine men signed the Constitution. The oldest was 81-year-old Benjamin Franklin of Pennsylvania. The youngest was Jonathan Dayton of New Jersey, who was 26.

The Clerk's Fee

The clerk who wrote out the Constitution was paid $30 for the job. That is worth about $575 today.

Visitors look at the original Constitution at the National Archives Building in Washington, DC.

In Other Words
renovation repair and update

Historical Background
The **National Archives Building** holds our nation's most important documents including the Bill of Rights and The Declaration of Independence. The building looks like a temple and covers two city blocks.

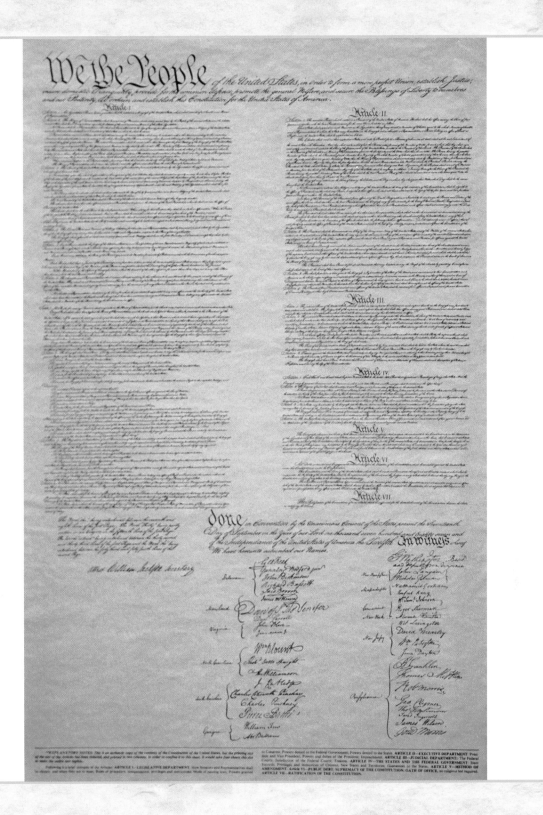

Look Into the Text

1. **Details** Describe the Constitution.
2. **Compare and Contrast** How is the Constitution different from other countries' constitutions?

A Closer Look

The Constitution has three parts. There is an introduction called the Preamble, seven articles that describe the plan of the national government, and the amendments, or changes to the Constitution.

The Preamble

The first paragraph of the Constitution states the basic purposes of the new plan of government: (1) to create a union where the states work together; (2) to create a system of laws that are fair; (3) to keep peace within the country; (4) to protect the nation from **outside attack**; (5) to improve the lives of all Americans; and (6) to make sure that **our free society survives in the future**.

Preamble

We the people of the United States, in order to form a more perfect union, establish justice, insure domestic tranquility, provide for the common defense, promote the general welfare, and secure the blessings of liberty to ourselves and our posterity, do ordain and establish this Constitution for the United States of America.

In Other Words

outside attack an attack by another country

our free society survives in the future we always have freedom

The Articles

The seven articles **set out** the powers of Congress, the President, and the federal courts. The articles also explain how the states are to relate to the national government and how the Constitution can be **amended**, or changed. Most importantly, the articles declare that the Constitution and all laws made by Congress will be the "supreme law of the land." All states must obey the national laws and follow the Constitution.

The Amendments

The amendments, or changes to the Constitution, were not written at the Constitutional Convention. They were added later, when changing conditions showed a need for a change to our plan of government. Changing the Constitution is not easy. There have been only twenty-seven amendments in more than 200 years.

"We the people"

The Constitution begins with the famous words, "We the people of the United States." This means that the government is our government. It is established by "the people," not by a king or any other authority.

The Constitutional Convention took place in Philadelphia in 1787 and lasted four months. During this time, fifty-five delegates met to create the Constitution of the United States.

Key Vocabulary
amend *v.*, to make changes or improvements

In Other Words
set out describe

Look Into the Text

1. **Paraphrase** In your own words, tell one purpose of the Preamble.
2. **Cause and Effect** Why are amendments necessary?

Three Branches of Government

The Constitution created a government with three separate branches, or divisions. They are the legislative, executive, and judicial branches.

Legislative Branch

- ★ called Congress
- ★ includes the House of Representatives and the Senate
- ★ makes our laws

Executive Branch

- ★ includes the President, government agencies, and the military
- ★ carries out our laws

Judicial Branch

- ★ includes the Supreme Court and other federal courts
- ★ hears cases and interprets our laws

The Legislative Branch

The Constitution begins with the Congress. The **delegates** started here because this branch passes the laws. It is the most important branch. It is also the part of government that is closest to the people. This branch **represents** the people of each state. Article I sets up the House of Representatives and the Senate. It says how the members of **each body** will be chosen, who can be a member, and how many members each body will have. The most important part of Article I tells what kinds of laws Congress can pass and what kinds it cannot pass. Among other things, Congress can enact taxes, borrow money, and declare war.

The New York Times.
LATE CITY EDITION
U. S. DECLARES WAR, PACIFIC BATTLE WIDENS; MANILA AREA BOMBED; 1,500 DEAD IN HAWAII; HOSTILE PLANES SIGHTED AT SAN FRANCISCO

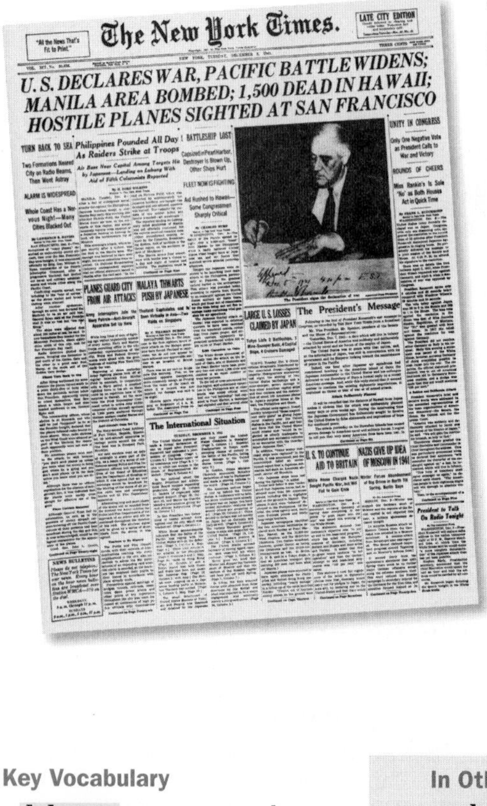

A serious responsibility of Congress is to declare war at the request of the President.

Key Vocabulary

delegate *n.*, a person chosen to speak for U.S. citizens

represent *v.*, to serve a group and present their beliefs

In Other Words

each body the House of Representatives and the Senate

Congress cannot favor one state over another or grant titles of nobility, such as duke or earl. Finally, Article I says Congress also can make any laws "necessary and proper" to carrying out its powers. This **elastic** clause was a way for future Americans to expand the meaning of the Constitution.

The Executive Branch

Article II describes the office of the President and who can **fill the office**. It also tells what powers and duties that person has. The President serves as commander-in-chief of the military. With Senate approval, the President also makes treaties and **appoints** ambassadors and judges. One of the President's most important duties is to give Congress information about the State of the Union. This means the President reports on how the United States is doing and urges Congress to pass laws that the country needs.

Today, the executive branch of government is huge. It employs millions of people. The delegates never imagined how our government would grow. They gave the President enough power, however, to carry out Congress's laws. As our society **grew and became more complex**, so did our government.

The President leads the government from his office in the White House.

In Other Words

elastic changing, flexible
fill the office become the President
appoints decides who will be
grew and became more complex became larger and more difficult to manage

Look Into the Text

1. **Summarize** How does the Legislative Branch **represent** the people?
2. **Details** What are the duties of the Executive Branch?

The Judicial Branch

This branch consists of the Supreme Court and other federal courts. This branch **interprets** the law. That means these courts hear cases to decide how the Constitution and other national laws apply to them. Article III creates the office of Chief Justice of the United States and tells Congress to create a Supreme Court. The Constitution also allows Congress to create other federal courts. Today, we have federal courts for trials, appeals, and special areas of the law, such as immigration. An appeal means a transfer of a legal case from a lower to a higher court for a new hearing.

The Supreme Court building

Justices of the U.S. Supreme Court in 2007

Checks and Balances

Government needs to have power to do its job. However, it may use this power to do wrong. Governments have used the police to take away the rights of the people. Officials have used tax money to make themselves rich. Governments have gone to war when many citizens believed it was wrong.

The delegates wanted to control the power they gave to our government. To do this, they built into the Constitution a system of **checks and balances.** They created three separate branches of government. They wanted each branch to help control the power of the others.

To take one example, Congress passes laws, but the President signs the laws. The President can veto, or reject, a law. However, if two-thirds of the members of the House and the Senate then vote for the law, **they can override** the President's veto. Later, if a legal case results from the law, the Supreme Court can decide whether the law is unconstitutional. In this way, all three branches of government have a role in seeing that our laws are fair.

If Congress believes a President has seriously misused power, it can impeach, or formally charge, him or her with misconduct. The Senate puts the President on trial. If found guilty, the President can be removed from office. In U.S. history, two Presidents, Andrew Johnson and William Jefferson Clinton, have been impeached and brought to trial. Neither was found guilty.

A political cartoon in 1833 portrays President Andrew Jackson as a king stepping on the Constitution. Critics felt he wanted too much power.

In Other Words

checks and balances fairness
they can override their vote will be used instead of

Look Into the Text

1. **Vocabulary** How does the Judicial Branch **interpret** the law?
2. **Explain** Tell how the system of checks and balances works.

The Amendments

The delegates in Philadelphia knew that they were not perfect. They understood that the Constitution might have to be changed.

The delegates wanted the Constitution changed only when it was very important and when most of the people in the country agreed. So, they made changing the Constitution a difficult process. Two-thirds of each house of Congress must vote for an amendment. After that, three-quarters of the states must **ratify** the amendment. Only then does the amendment become part of the Constitution.

Americans celebrate the passage of the 13th Amendment, which ended slavery in 1865.

In Other Words
ratify approve

The Bill of Rights

At first, the Constitution did not include a bill of rights. Many people thought it was a mistake that the Constitution did not have one. That problem was fixed by the first ten amendments, our Bill of Rights. The amendments of the Bill of Rights protect the basic freedoms of individuals. These include freedom of religion, freedom of speech, freedom to protest government actions peacefully, and the right to a fair trial.

These amendments guarantee that people accused of crimes will have a lawyer. They are guaranteed that they will be given a trial held in the open—not in secret. People convicted of a crime are guaranteed they will not receive "cruel and unusual punishment." These amendments also guarantee a free government and an open society. Sometimes we may have to listen to people whose ideas we do not share. This is part of living in a free country. Freedom, as protected by the Bill of Rights, means we must **tolerate** those who disagree with us. It also means we respect those who have a different religion from ours or no religion at all.

The Bill of Rights allows people to peacefully fight for what they think is fair.

In Other Words
tolerate respect

Look Into the Text

1. **Describe** What process is used to **amend** the Constitution?
2. **Main Idea and Details** What is the Bill of Rights, and what four basic freedoms does it protect?

Later Changes

After the Bill of Rights was ratified, the Constitution was still not perfect. So, we have added another seventeen amendments since 1791. Some amendments were needed to fix things that did not work well. Here is an example. At first, a new President was elected in November, but did not **take office** until March. This made sense in an age of horses and sailing ships. It took time to get the news from one place to the other. It took time for people to get to the national capital. Now, in an age of trains, cars, and planes, this no longer makes sense. In 1933, the 20th Amendment changed the date the new President takes office to January 20.

Women celebrate passage of the 19th Amendment in 1920.

In Other Words

take office begin the job as President

Some of the most important amendments have created more freedom, liberty, and political opportunity for all Americans. The Constitution could not solve the problem of slavery. In the end, a very bloody Civil War was needed to end slavery. After the war, we added the 13th, 14th, and 15th amendments to end all slavery and make the former slaves full citizens of the United States.

Other amendments have **expanded** American **democracy**. The 15th Amendment allowed all adult men, including former slaves, to vote. The 19th Amendment allowed women to vote. The 24th Amendment says states cannot discriminate against poor people by making people pay a tax if they want to vote. The 26th Amendment allowed 18-year-olds to vote.

In 1987, people celebrate the 200th anniversary of the signing of the Constitution at Independence Hall, in Philadelphia.

Key Vocabulary
  democracy *n.*, a system where the people have the power to vote for what they believe

In Other Words
  expanded increased

200 Years Old—and Still Working

Our Constitution has been **in operation** for more than 200 years. It is the oldest working constitution in the world. It is not perfect. We have changed it twenty-seven times. Yet, for all its faults and problems, it has brought more **liberty** to more people than any other system of government in the history of the world. Over the years, millions of immigrants have come to the United States. One reason they came was because they understood that this nation had a strong Constitution. It guaranteed them a voice to say what they want, and the right to vote for their leaders.

The delegates in Philadelphia said in the Preamble that they wanted to create "a more perfect Union." They wanted to "establish Justice" and "secure the Blessings of Liberty" to the American people. They succeeded remarkably well. ❖

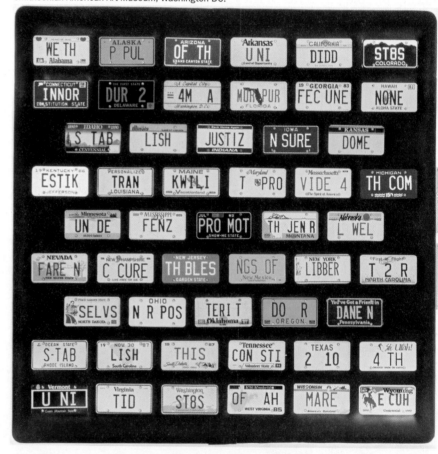

Preamble, 1987, Mike Wilkins. Painted metal on vinyl and wood, Smithsonian American Art Museum, Washington DC.

This 1987 work by American sculptor Mike Wilkins uses license plates to celebrate the U.S. Constitution on its 200th birthday. What do the words on the plates spell out?

In Other Words

in operation used
liberty freedom

Look Into the Text

1. **Cause and Effect** Describe two improvements that have resulted from amendments.
2. **Main Idea and Details** How does the Constitution make people's lives better? Give an example.

The Star-Spangled Banner

by Francis Scott Key

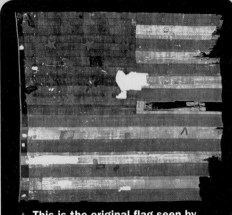

▲ This is the original flag seen by Francis Scott Key flying over Fort McHenry, in Maryland.

O! say, can you see by the dawn's early light,

What so proudly we **hail'd** at the twilight's last gleaming;

Whose broad stripes and bright stars through the **perilous** fight

O'er the ramparts we watched were so gallantly streaming;

And the rocket's red glare, the bombs bursting in air,

Gave proof through the night that our flag was still there;

O! say, does the star-spangled banner yet wave,

O'er the land of the free and the home of the brave!

In Other Words
hail'd saw
perilous dangerous
O'er the ramparts we watched The stars and stripes waving over the fort

Historical Background
The British attacked Fort McHenry on September 13, 1814. The next morning, Francis Scott Key saw that the flag was still flying above the fort. This inspired him to write "The Star-Spangled Banner," the national anthem, or song of the U.S.

Look Into the Text

1. **Conclusion** What does the flag represent in this song?

The Flag We Love
by Pam Muñoz Ryan

When people come to our great country
Aboard ships that cross the sea
They are welcomed to our harbors
By the flags of liberty.

5   Citizens march for freedom
With action, faith, and **word**.
A righteous banner guarantees
Their voices will be heard.

Celebrate the flag we love
10   **A majesty** in the sky
And feel the pride that swells inside
As our banner goes streaming by.

In Other Words
Aboard On
word through the words they speak
A majesty Greatness

Look Into the Text

1. **Paraphrase** In your own words, explain what "A righteous banner guarantees their voices will be heard" means.
2. **Theme** How do *The Star-Spangled Banner* and the poem relate to this unit's theme?

Connect Reading and Writing

Vocabulary
amend
delegates
democracy
government
independence
interpret
justice
represent

CRITICAL THINKING

1. **SUM IT UP** Review the Main-Idea Diagram you started on page 483. Use it to summarize the article. Then complete the KWL Chart you started on page 478.

Main Idea:
Detail 1:
Detail 2:
Detail 3:

Main-Idea Diagram

2. **Analyze** Use examples in the selection to explain what **independence** meant to the **delegates**.

3. **Evaluate** In a **democracy** how important is one branch of **government** compared to the other two branches? Give examples from the text.

4. **Compare** Use details from the poems and the selection to tell how the Constitution and the U.S. flag are alike and how they are different.

READING FLUENCY

Phrasing Read the passage on page 643 to a partner. Assess your fluency.

1. I did not pause/sometimes paused/ always paused for punctuation.

2. What I did best in my reading was _____.

READING STRATEGY

What strategy helped you understand this selection? Tell a partner about it.

VOCABULARY REVIEW

Oral Review Read the paragraph aloud. Add the vocabulary words.

> When the United States declared _____ from Britain and became a _____, it needed a new plan of _____. Without the Constitution, who would _____ the laws and _____ the people? The _____ who wrote the Constitution could not think of everything. Over time, it became necessary to change, or _____ the Constitution. These changes helped bring liberty and _____ to all.

Written Review Imagine that you view the original Constitution. Write a brief message about what it **represents** to you. Use four vocabulary words.

WRITE ABOUT THE GUIDING QUESTION

Explore Fairness for All

The Constitution was written more than 200 years ago. Why do you think people still follow this plan of **government** today? Read the selection to find information that supports your ideas.

Connect Across the Curriculum

Vocabulary Study

Use Word Origins: Greek, Latin, and Anglo-Saxon Roots

Academic Vocabulary
- **origin** (or-u-jin) *noun*
  The **origin** of something is its source or beginning.

Many English words have their **origins** in ancient languages.

Root	Meaning	Related English Word
dem, Greek	people	democracy
riht, Anglo-Saxon	straight	direct
popul, Latin	people	population

Identify Word Origins Match each word from the selection with its correct **origin**. Then work with a partner to say a sentence using each word.

1. legislative
2. judicial
3. constitution
4. twilight

A. *constitu*, Latin; to set up
B. *twi*, Anglo-Saxon; two, twice, double
C. *jud*, Latin; judge
D. *leg*, Latin; law

Literary Analysis

Analyze Poetry: Symbols

Academic Vocabulary
- **symbol** (sim-bul) *noun*
  A **symbol** is an object or idea that represents something else.

Symbol is an element of poetry that writers use to express their ideas. A **symbol** is something that represents something other than itself. **Poets** use symbols to help structure their ideas.

In the two poems "The Star-Spangled Banner" and "The Flag We Love," the flag is a **symbol**. What is it a **symbol** of? Both poems use the flag to convey a universal theme, or message.

Practice Together

Compare Poems Reread "The Star-Spangled Banner" and "The Flag We Love." One way to identify the meaning of the **symbol** is to look at the writer's word choice and descriptive language. Notice how both writers use words that appeal to your senses. Compare the words and phrases used in both poems. Do they tell you what the flag symbolizes?

Summarize

Group Share Work in a group. Take turns summarizing different sections of the selection. Identify and tell just the main ideas and important information, using your own words. Use participial phrases to combine some of your sentences.

> Written concisely, the U.S. Constitution is the shortest constitution of any government in the world today. A few chosen people wrote the Constitution.

Write to Elaborate

Study the Models When you write, use plenty of details to elaborate on your ideas. Use participial phrases to elaborate and combine ideas so that your sentences flow.

NOT OK

> The teens wanted a skateboard park. They exercised their right to free speech. They talked with the mayor. They knew she supported their idea. Now they needed the City Council to approve the plan. They met first with local business people **seeking approval for the park** . Then they wrote letters. They asked for money to help build the skateboard park. Many businesses gave money to the project. They wanted to show their support. Next, the teens got the support of the local homeowners. They were ready to present their plan to the City Council.

The reader thinks: "**This is confusing. I don't know who is seeking approval for the park.**"

OK

> The teens wanted a skateboard park. **Exercising their right to free speech** , they talked to the mayor who supported the idea. Now they needed the City Council to approve the plan. **Seeking approval for the park** , they met first with local business people. Then they wrote letters and asked for money to help build the skateboard park. **Showing their support** , many businesses gave money to the project. **Getting local homeowners' support next** , the teens were ready to present their plan to the City Council.

This writer moved the misplaced words to correctly describe the teens. The writer combined some ideas, too.

✎ **WRITE ON YOUR OWN** Describe how you would use your right to free speech. Combine ideas so your writing flows.

REMEMBER

Use participial phrases to add detail to your sentences or to combine ideas. For example:
- **Showing interest in their community**, the teens took action.
- **Forming a committee**, they made a plan.
- **Working together**, they reached their goal.

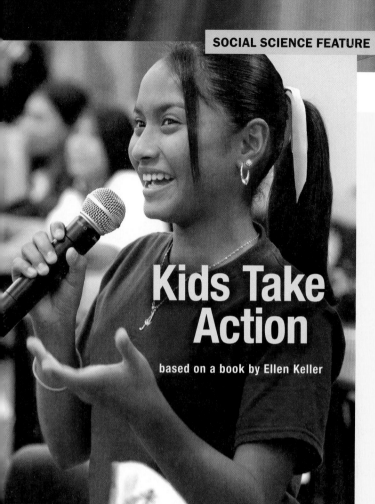

Kids Take Action

based on a book by Ellen Keller

Build Background

Connect

Anticipation Guide Tell whether you agree or disagree with these statements.

	Agree	Disagree
1. It is important to speak out against unfairness.	_____	_____
2. Not everyone should get involved in their community.	_____	_____
3. There is no way for students to make their voices heard.	_____	_____

Anticipation Guide

See a Campaign in Action

What is it like to get involved in a campaign? These students know. We can all create positive change in our communities.

Digital Library   myNGconnect.com
◆ View the video.

◀ Kids can help in their communities.

Language & Grammar

1 TRY OUT LANGUAGE
2 LEARN GRAMMAR
3 APPLY ON YOUR OWN

Give and Follow Directions

Look at the photograph and listen to the directions.
Follow along carefully to understand each step.

PICTURE PROMPT

How to Use a Voting Machine

1. First, enter the voting machine booth.

2. Then, read each item that you are voting on.

3. Next, press the X next to the candidate or item you wish to select. The X will light up.

4. To change a selection, press the button next to the X that is lighted. The light will go out. Then make another selection.

5. To write in a candidate's name, press the WRITE–IN button. Then use the keypad at the bottom of the machine to enter the person's name, one letter at a time.

6. Review all your selections after you make your choices. Changes can only be made before you press the large VOTE button.

7. Finally, press the large VOTE button to cast your ballot.

8. Exit the voting machine booth.

Use Gerunds and Infinitives

- The present participle of a verb, its **-ing** form, can be used as a noun. When it acts likes a noun, it is called a **gerund** . A gerund can be the **subject** of a sentence. When a gerund is used as a subject, the verb is always singular.

  EXAMPLES   **Campaigning** is how candidates advertise their qualities.
            gerund   verb

             Watching a candidate helps citizens decide who to vote for.
            gerund phrase   verb

- A **gerund** can also be the **object of a verb** or the **object of a preposition**.

  EXAMPLES   Ruth Zeller likes **campaigning** .
                   verb   object

             She is very good at **stating her position**.
                      preposition   object

- The word **to** plus a main verb forms an **infinitive** . Like a noun, you can use an infinitive as the **object of a verb**.

  EXAMPLES   Ruth Zeller likes **to campaign** .
                  verb   infinitive

             She offers **to discuss issues with the voters**.
            verb   infinitive phrase

Practice Together

Turn the verb into a gerund or an infinitive to complete the sentence. Say the new sentence.

1. travel   _____ is on most candidates' schedules.

2. speak   Many like _____ at rallies.

3. ask   _____ questions is how voters find out the candidate's beliefs.

4. give   Voters applaud candidates for _____ honest answers.

Try It!

Turn the verb into a gerund or an infinitive to complete the sentence. Write the sentence on a card. Then say the sentence.

5. debate   Some candidates agree _____ the issues.

6. televise   _____ a debate allows many people to see the candidates.

7. respond   A moderator explains the rules for _____.

8. shout   _____ is not allowed.

▲ The candidate likes to speak about the issues.

Make a Campaign Sign

GIVE AND FOLLOW DIRECTIONS

Campaign signs are everywhere before an election. Candidates use them to advertise their names and the offices they seek. Signs come in all sizes and colors, with different wording. How would you make a campaign sign?

With a partner, create step-by-step directions for making a campaign sign. Use words that tell the sequence, or the order, of the steps.

▲ Campaign signs help candidates get votes.

How to Make a Campaign Sign

1. First, find your materials: poster board, markers, etc.
2. Next, decide what information to put on the sign.
3. Then,
4. After that,
5. Finally,

Read your directions to another group. Have them repeat your directions to make sure they are clear. If they are not, make changes.

HOW TO GIVE AND FOLLOW DIRECTIONS

1. Give directions in steps. Use sequence words.
2. Use simple vocabulary and speak clearly and concisely. Use gestures when appropriate.
3. Ask the people receiving the directions to repeat them back to you in their own words.

Next, plan the information you will include on the sign. Then, make sure the words are printed clearly.

OK. The next thing I should do is plan what to put on the sign. Then, I need to make sure the words are easy to read.

USE GERUNDS AND INFINITIVES

When you give directions, you can use **gerunds** and **infinitives** to combine sentences and avoid unnecessary words. Using gerunds and infinitives can also help you vary your sentences and make them more interesting.

EXAMPLES   **Printing neatly** makes the letters on the sign readable.
The campaign sign says **to vote for your candidate**.

Prepare to Read

Learn Key Vocabulary

Study the Words Use the steps below.

1. Pronounce the word. Say it aloud several times. Spell it.
2. Rate your word knowledge.
3. Study the example. Tell more about the word.
4. Practice it. Make the word your own.

Key Words

campaign (kam-pān) *noun*
► page 514

A **campaign** is a series of actions by an individual or a group working toward a goal. John F. Kennedy led a **campaign** to become president in 1960.

citizen (sit-u-zen) *noun*
► page 519

A **citizen** is a person who was born in a country or becomes a member of a country. All American **citizens** share the same rights.
Related Word: **citizenship**

debate (di-bāt) *verb*
► page 519

To **debate** means to discuss different views of something. In a **debate**, two or more people tell why they have different opinions or ideas.

informed (in-formd)
adjective ► page 516

To be **informed** is to have knowledge. It is our duty to be **informed** about issues.
Related Word: **information**
Synonym: **aware**

persuade (pur-swād) *verb*
► page 518

To **persuade** means to try to make others agree. The student **persuaded** us by giving a strong speech with good ideas.
Synonym: **convince**

petition (pu-tish-un) *noun*
► page 514

A **petition** is a written request for a government or leader to take action. If enough people sign our **petition**, it may convince the mayor to do what we ask.

support (su-pōrt) *noun*
► page 514

To have **support** means that people help you. Students need the **support** of their teachers.
Related Word: **supportive**
Synonym: **help**

volunteer (vol-en-tēr) *verb*
► page 515

To **volunteer** means to work without pay. One way I can help others is to **volunteer** at the soup kitchen.

Practice the Words Work with a partner to write four sentences. Use at least two Key Words in each sentence.

> **EXAMPLE:** I volunteer at a park after school to support the community soccer program.

Relate Cause and Effect

How Are Events Related? As you read, think about how some events relate to other events in the text. When writers want to explain how one thing affects another, they often use a cause-and-effect structure to organize their writing.

- A cause is *why* something happens. An effect is *what* happens.
- Sometimes a cause has more than one effect, or an effect has more than one cause.
- Sometimes one effect can be the cause of another effect.

As you read, take note of clue words that reveal a cause-and-effect text structure.

Reading Strategies

- Plan
- Monitor
- Ask Questions
- Make Connections
- Visualize
- Make Inferences
- **Determine Importance**
  Focus your attention on the author's most significant ideas and information.
- Synthesize

Look Into the Text

> The teens in Burnsville, Minnesota, had no place to skateboard. They were getting in trouble for skateboarding in public places. So they met with the mayor and suggested that the city build a skateboarding park. Because the mayor liked the idea, she told the teens they needed to… get it approved and funded.

Practice Together

Begin a Cause-and-Effect Chain

A Cause-and-Effect Chain can help you analyze the cause-and-effect structure of a text. This Cause-and-Effect Chain shows the original cause and the first effect that resulted from it. Reread the passage above and add to the Cause-and-Effect Chain.

	First Effect	Second Effect
The teens in Burnsville, Minnesota, had no place to skateboard.	They got in trouble for skateboarding in public places.	
Original Cause	Second Cause	Third Cause

Academic Vocabulary

- **relate** (ri-lāt) *verb*
  When you **relate** things, you show how they are connected.

Social Science Feature

Social science features often tell about people getting involved in the world around them.

Many articles use a **cause-and-effect organization** to show why people get involved and the results of their actions.

Persuading the City Council

The teens worked on a speech to give before the City Council. . . . They got people to agree with their point of view and to volunteer to talk for them before the City Council. The mayor also said she would support them. . . .

All the hard work paid off— the City Council voted in favor of the park. The teens' reward for all their effort was a brand-new skateboarding park.

As you read feature articles, take notes of ideas that are personally important to you.

A student expresses her opinion about an after-school program at her school. ▶

Kids Take
Action

based on a book by Ellen Keller

 Comprehension Coach

The teens in Burnsville, Minnesota, had no place to skateboard. They were getting in trouble for skateboarding in public places, and they thought that was unfair. So they met with the mayor and suggested that the city build a skateboarding park. Because the mayor liked the idea, she told the teens they needed to go to the City Council to get it approved and **funded**. She advised them on what steps they should take.

▲ Students in Burnsville, Minnesota helped construct a public skateboard park.

Campaign Skateboard Park

The teens started a **campaign** to get **support** for a skateboarding park. First, they contacted local business people, met with them in person, and explained what they were trying to do.

Then, they wrote letters to the business people asking for money to help build their skateboarding park. They pointed out that the park would help them by **eliminating** skateboarding in front of their buildings and by offering advertising space. Everyone would gain something. Many businesses gave money to show their support.

Getting Local Support

In the next step, the teens met with the people who lived in the area. They explained how the skateboarding park would help the residents: there would no longer be skateboarding on sidewalks or in public places. The local people were convinced to sign **petitions** showing their support for the park.

Now the teens had local support and some of the money to build the park. However, they still had one more step to take: they had to present their plan to the City Council. The City Council would

---

Key Vocabulary

campaign *n.*, an organized effort by people working towards the same goal
support *n.*, help or funding
petition *n.*, a formal written request

In Other Words

funded paid for
eliminating stopping

then vote on whether or not to support the skateboarding park and to give the rest of the money needed to build the park.

Persuading the City Council

The teens worked on a speech to give before the City Council. They practiced it until they knew it **by heart**. They got people to agree with their point of view and to **volunteer** to talk for them before the City Council. The mayor also said she would support them.

In their speech, the teens explained why the skateboarding park was important to them. They described the benefits, or good things, that a park would create and used examples from their own lives to personalize the speech.

Finally, it was time for the City Council to vote. All the hard work **paid off**—the City Council voted **in favor of** the park. The teens' reward for all their effort was a brand-new skateboarding park.

Key Vocabulary
  volunteer *v.*, to perform a
    service without getting paid

In Other Words
  by heart perfectly
  paid off was worth it
  in favor of for

Look Into the Text

1. **Sequence** What did the teens want to accomplish? What steps did they take?
2. **Judgment** Which part of the process got the most **support**? Explain your answer.

Making Your Voice Heard

The students in Burnsville, Minnesota, **made their voices heard**. They had an opinion, and then made sure it was an **informed** opinion. An informed opinion is based on facts that can be checked. It reflects careful thinking about all sides of an issue. There are millions of people in this country with their own **points of view on** issues. Expressing your own point of view can seem like a Herculean effort.

Even if you yelled very loudly, would the government hear you and listen to your point of view?

Making your voice heard does not mean speaking loudly. It means getting others to listen to you and getting **a majority of** people to agree with what you're saying.

How do you make your voice heard? How do you get the government and other people to hear you?

◄ A member of the Chicago Bulls raised his voice to encourage people to volunteer in a Hurricane Relief event. Many students responded.

Key Vocabulary

informed *adj.*, having information and knowledge

In Other Words

made their voices heard expressed their beliefs
points of view on beliefs about
a majority of most

Language Background

Hercules is a hero from Greek mythology. He is known for his strength, courage, and kindness. To say that something is **"Herculean"** means that it is a big job that requires a lot of strength or work.

Writing Letters

One way to express your beliefs is to write a letter. If you write it to the editor of your local newspaper it might be published. Then everyone in your community can read it.

Carl Franklin wrote this letter to his local paper after deciding that his school needed a new community teen center.

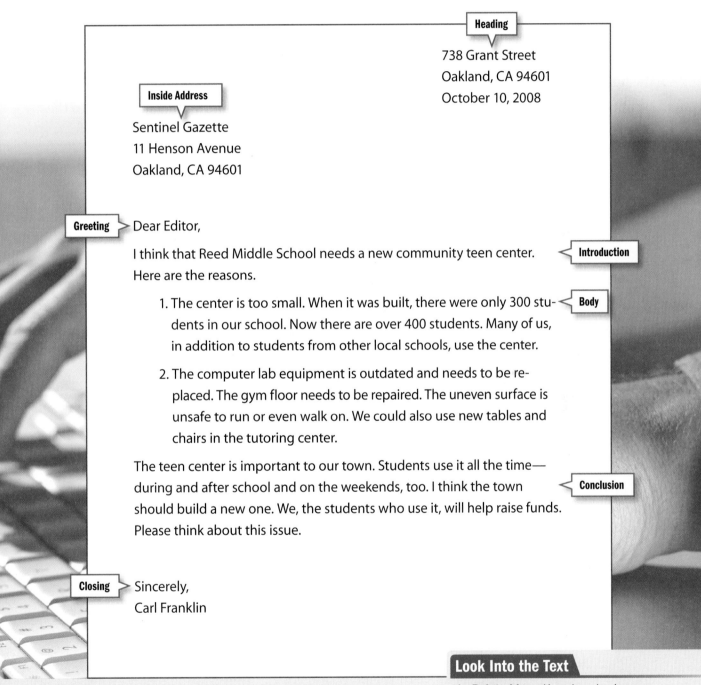

Heading

738 Grant Street
Oakland, CA 94601
October 10, 2008

Inside Address

Sentinel Gazette
11 Henson Avenue
Oakland, CA 94601

Greeting

Dear Editor,

Introduction

I think that Reed Middle School needs a new community teen center. Here are the reasons.

Body

1. The center is too small. When it was built, there were only 300 students in our school. Now there are over 400 students. Many of us, in addition to students from other local schools, use the center.

2. The computer lab equipment is outdated and needs to be replaced. The gym floor needs to be repaired. The uneven surface is unsafe to run or even walk on. We could also use new tables and chairs in the tutoring center.

Conclusion

The teen center is important to our town. Students use it all the time—during and after school and on the weekends, too. I think the town should build a new one. We, the students who use it, will help raise funds. Please think about this issue.

Closing

Sincerely,
Carl Franklin

Look Into the Text

1. **Relate Ideas** How does having an informed opinion help make your voice heard?
2. **Evaluate Argument** What details in the letter might help **persuade** others?

Starting a Petition

Another way that you can make your voice heard is to start a petition. A petition is a formal document, or paper, that tells what you want. People who agree with your request sign your petition. The signed petition is presented to an official, a person who makes decisions. A petition with a lot of signatures might **persuade** that official to support what you want.

Let's say that you think that your community should have an arts center. You and your friends see that the library has a room that is often empty so you talk with the librarian who agrees that the room could be turned into an arts center. How can you get the town to support your idea?

You and your friends decide to start a petition. With the help of others, you collect as many signatures as possible. Soon the town is talking about what a good idea it would be to have an arts center.

Finally, you present your petition to the local government. The town council reads the petition and **acts on it**. A few months later, the arts center opens!

◄ Students urge people to protect the environment by adding their signatures to a petition.

Key Vocabulary
persuade *v.*, to try to make others agree

In Other Words
acts on it decides to do something

Creating a Campaign

A campaign, or series of planned actions, is another way to call attention to a problem or **issue**. In a campaign, you use the tools you just read about to make your voice heard. For example, in a presidential election, candidates start a campaign to get people to vote for them. The candidates write letters, make speeches, and work with others to win the election. Another example of a campaign is the Civil Rights Movement, which focused on ending racial segregation. Dr. Martin Luther King, Jr., helped lead the campaign by giving speeches, writing letters, and working with others.

Giving a Speech

Freedom of speech is an important right that you have as a **citizen** of the United States. You have the right to say what you want as long as it doesn't harm another person. Giving a speech is one way you can share your point of view and try to persuade others to agree with you.

During an election, candidates **running for office** give speeches and **debate** each other. In their speeches and debates, they tell how they feel about issues and try to get people to vote for them.

Many famous people have used speeches to make their points heard and understood.

A good speech stays in people's minds and can even earn a place in history. For example, here are memorable lines from speeches given by famous leaders.

Memorable Voices

"The only thing we have to fear is fear itself."

–Franklin D. Roosevelt

"Government of the people, by the people, for the people, shall not perish from the earth."

–Abraham Lincoln

"My fellow Americans, ask not what your country can do for you. Ask what you can do for your country."

–John F. Kennedy

Key Vocabulary

citizen *n.*, a person who lives in a country and has certain rights and duties

debate *v.*, to discuss different views about an issue

In Other Words

issue a topic of strong interest to people

running for office who are trying to get elected

Staying Involved

Good citizens are involved in their communities. They care about what happens and take action to change things that need changing. Sometimes they work with others and sometimes they work alone. But they make their voices heard. ❖

▶ People gather in support of a campaign.

> **Write a leTTer!**
>
> Dear Senator Graham,
> I am a student learning about the need to protect my health. I will do my part by not smoking and staying away from drugs. Please do your part by keeping our air safe to breathe. Vote for the Clean Power Act! Kids need clean air for healthy lungs!
>
> Sincerely,
> Your name
> Your School

Look Into the Text

1. **Steps in a Process** Describe the process of starting a **petition**.
2. **Paraphrase** In your own words, describe what a campaign is.

Connect Reading and Writing

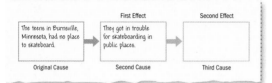

Vocabulary

campaign

citizen

debate

informed

persuade

petition

support

volunteers

CRITICAL THINKING

1. SUM IT UP Review the Cause-and-Effect Chain you completed as you read. Use it to summarize the selection.

First Effect

Second Effect

The teens in Burnsville, Minnesota, had no place to skateboard.	They got in trouble for skateboarding in public places.	
Original Cause	Second Cause	Third Cause

Cause-and-Effect Chain

2. Paraphrase In your own words, tell how skateboarders took action to **persuade** their city to build a park.

3. Make Judgments In your judgment, which of the skateboarders' actions would help win the most **support** for an issue? Why?

4. Evaluate Review the Anticipation Guide on page 506. Now that you are more **informed** about the way kids take action, do you want to change your responses? **Persuade** a partner to agree with you.

READING FLUENCY

Intonation Read the passage on page 644 to a partner. Assess your fluency.

1. My tone never/sometimes/always matched what I read.

2. What I did best in my reading was _____.

READING STRATEGY

What strategy helped you understand this selection? Tell a partner about it.

VOCABULARY REVIEW

Oral Review Read the paragraph aloud. Add the vocabulary words.

Suppose you want to change something in your state. What actions can you take to _____ the public to agree with you? First, create a _____ to bring attention to the issue. Ask _____ to sign a _____ to show their _____. If people disagree with you, invite them to _____ the issue. The more you share facts and opinions, the more it will help every _____ make an _____ decision.

Written Review Create a **petition** for an issue you would like changed at school. Describe the purpose. Use four vocabulary words.

WRITE ABOUT THE (GUIDING QUESTION)

Explore Taking Action

How important is it for people to **volunteer** in their communities? Why? Support your opinion with examples from the selections.

Connect Across the Curriculum

Use Word Origins: Greek and Latin Mythology

An allusion is a reference to a familiar person, place, or work of art. Some words can make allusions to characters or events in myths. Look at the sentence below.

> Changing your community can take a **Herculean** effort.

Herculean refers to Hercules, a hero in a Greek myth, who performed twelve difficult tasks. To make a *Herculean effort* is to try extremely hard.

Use Word Origins Use the chart to determine the meanings of these sentences.

Mentor	a trustworthy and wise character in ancient Greek myth
Vulcan	ancient Roman god of fire
Achilles	Greek soldier whose only weak spot was his heel

1. Ms. Alvarez is a great teacher who has been a **mentor** to me.
2. There are still active **volcanoes** in Hawaii.
3. Not doing her homework has been her **Achilles heel**.

Give an Informative Speech

SOCIAL SCIENCE

Academic Vocabulary
- **organize** (or-gu-nīz) *verb*
  To **organize** means to arrange things in a certain order.

Think of something that has changed for the better in your community. Write and deliver a speech to explain how the change came about.

❶ **Organize Information** To **organize** your speech, use a cause-and-effect structure to explain what happened. To research your topic, interview people in the community or read local newspaper articles. Take notes.

❷ **Prepare Your Speech** Write a strong introduction that makes your subject clear. As you conclude, restate your topic. Practice your speech.

❸ **Present Your Speech** Make eye contact with your audience. Speak clearly and loudly. Refer to your notes if you need to, but try to use them as little as possible.

Give and Follow Directions

Pair Share Work with a partner. Give directions to your partner on how to write a letter to the editor to change the name of a street in your town. Tell about the parts of a letter, where in the letter the parts are placed, and any special punctuation that is needed. Use gerunds and infinitives to combine some of the sentences in your directions. Have your partner repeat your directions in his or her own words. Trade roles.

> You want to write the closing and then sign your name.

> OK. The closing is the last thing I write before I sign my name.

Write to Be Concise

Study the Models You can keep your writing interesting by varying your sentences and keeping the relationships among ideas clear and sharp. You can use gerunds and infinitives to combine sentences and avoid too many unnecessary words.

OK

I believe more of us should visit the elderly in retirement homes. Many don't get visitors. They spend too much time alone. They don't deserve it. Many of the residents have cards. If you ask them they might play. They also tell stories. The stories are about their past. Sometimes they ask for my dog. That's so they can pet her which makes them smile. I'd like a group of us to visit the retirement home together. Won't you join me?

> **This writing has a lot of short, choppy sentences and unnecessary words.**

BETTER

I think more of us should visit the elderly in retirement homes. Many don't get visitors; they don't deserve **to spend so much time alone**. Many residents like **to play cards**. **Telling stories about their past** is something else they enjoy. Sometimes they ask **to see my dog**. **Petting her** makes them smile. I'd like a group of us to visit the retirement home together. Won't you join me?

> **The writer uses gerunds and infinitives to combine some ideas and avoid unnecessary words. The writing is concise.**

WRITE ON YOUR OWN Write about an issue you feel strongly about. Combine ideas to avoid unnecessary words and to make your writing concise.

> **REMEMBER**
> Use gerunds and infinitives like nouns to combine ideas and avoid unnecessary words.

from
The Words We Live By
by Linda R. Monk

WE THE PEOPLE . . .

1   These first three words of the Constitution are the most important. They clearly state that the people—not the king, not the legislature, not the courts—are the true rulers in American **government**. This principle is known as popular sovereignty.

2   But who are "We the People"? This question troubled the nation for centuries. As Lucy Stone, one of America's first **advocates** for women's rights, asked in 1853: "'We the People'? Which 'We the People'? The women were not included." Neither were white males who did not own property, Native Americans, or African Americans—slave or free.

Justice Thurgood Marshall, the first African American on the Supreme Court, described the limitation:

3   *For a sense of **the evolving nature of the Constitution**, we need look no further than the first three words of the document's preamble: 'We the people.' When the founding fathers used this phrase in 1787, they did not have in mind the majority of America's **citizens** . . .*

4   *The men who gathered in Philadelphia in 1787 could not . . . have imagined, nor would they have accepted, that the document they were drafting would one day be construed by a Supreme Court **to which had been appointed** a woman and the descendant of an African slave.*

Marshall was not the first African American to speak out about the phrase.

Key Vocabulary
- **government** *n.*, people who rule a country or state
- **citizen** *n.*, a person who lives in a country and has certain rights and duties

In Other Words
advocates supporters
the evolving nature of the Constitution the way the meaning of the Constitution can change
to which had been appointed that included

DOUGLASS
1818-1895

ANTHONY
1820-1906

GINSBURG
BORN 1933

NOT WE, THE WHITE PEOPLE
FREDERICK DOUGLASS

5 *We, the people—not we, the white people—not we, the citizens, or the legal voters—not we, the privileged class, and excluding all other classes but we, the people; not we, the horses and cattle, but we the people—the men and women, the human inhabitants of the United States, do **ordain** and establish this Constitution.*

WE, THE WHOLE PEOPLE
SUSAN B. ANTHONY

6 *It was we, the people; not we, the white male citizens; not yet we, the male citizens; but we, the whole people, who formed the Union. And we formed it, not to give the blessings of liberty, but to secure them; not to the half of ourselves and the half of our **posterity**, but to the whole people—women as well as men. And it is a downright mockery to talk to women of their enjoyment of the blessings of liberty while they are denied the use of the only means of securing them provided by this democratic-republican government—the ballot.*

GENTLEMEN OF THEIR TIME
JUSTICE RUTH BADER GINSBURG

7 *It **manifests** no disrespect for the Constitution to note that the **framers** were gentlemen of their time, and therefore had a distinctly limited vision of those who counted among "We the People." Not until the adoption of the post-Civil War Fourteenth Amendment did the word "equal," in relation to the stature of individuals, even make an appearance in the Constitution. But the equal dignity of all persons is nonetheless a vital part of our constitutional **legacy**, even if the culture of the framers held them back from perceiving that universal ideal. We can best celebrate that legacy by striving to form a "more perfect Union" for ourselves and the generations to come.*

8 Through the amendment process, more and more Americans were eventually included in the Constitution's definition of "We the People." After the Civil War, the Thirteenth Amendment ended slavery, the Fourteenth Amendment gave African Americans citizenship, and the Fifteenth Amendment gave black men the right to vote. In 1920, the Nineteenth Amendment gave women the right to vote nationwide.

In Other Words
ordain choose; demand
posterity future generations
manifests shows
framers creators of the Constitution
legacy history

Compare Across Texts

Compare Text Structures

The selections in this unit all have messages about fairness, but they are organized differently. Compare the text structures and **analyze** what the authors wanted to show by using those structures.

How It Works

Collect and Organize Ideas To compare text structures in more than one selection, record the genres and structures in a chart like this one.

Comparison Chart

Selection	Genre	Text Structure
"The Clever Magistrate"/ "The Clever Old Woman"	folk tales	chronological, cause-and-effect
"The Constitution"	social science textbook	main idea and details
"Kids Take Action"		
"The Words We Live By"		

Practice Together

Analyze and Compare Ideas Compare the information you collected. Then summarize how the structures are useful for the selections.

Summary

"The Clever Magistrate" and "The Clever Old Woman" are stories so chronological order works well to tell when things happen. When the author uses cause-and-effect, it helps you figure out why the characters act the way they do. The author of "The Constitution" organizes the text using . . .

Try It!

Compare how the text structures of the selections help express similar ideas. You may want to use this frame.

For "The Clever Magistrate" and "The Clever Old Woman," the _____ and _____ structures lead you to understand that it's important to _____ and _____. Both "The Constitution" and "The Words We Live By" use the _____ structure to explain _____. The _____ structure in "Kids Take Action," helps you know _____ and _____.

Academic Vocabulary

● **analyze** (a-nu-līz) *verb*
When you **analyze**, you separate something into parts and examine, or study, it.

FAIR IS FAIR

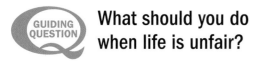

 What should you do when life is unfair?

GUIDING QUESTION

Content Library

Leveled Library

Reflect on Your Reading

Think back on your reading of the unit selections. Discuss what you did to understand what you read.

Focus on Reading **Compare Text Structures**

In this unit, you learned about some ways writers organize ideas using different text structures. Choose two selections from the unit with different genres. Draw a chart that compares the two text structures. Use your drawing to explain how the text structures are different to a partner.

Focus Strategy **Determine Importance**

As you read the selections, you learned how to determine importance. Explain to a partner how you will use this strategy in the future.

Explore the **GUIDING QUESTION**

Throughout this unit, you have been thinking about fairness. Choose one of these ways to explore the Guiding Question:

- **Discuss** With a group, discuss the Guiding Question. Give details from the selections that support your ideas.
- **Plan** With a group, brainstorm examples of unfairness. Recall what people in the selections did when life was unfair. Make a plan to show actions they might take to improve one situation.
- **Illustrate** Show fairness in action in a collage. Use ideas from the selections and your experience.

Book Talk

Which Unit Library book did you choose? Explain to a partner what it taught you about fairness.

Food for Thought

8

How can we provide for our communities?

◄ A child carries maize, or corn, harvested in Madagascar.

Focus on Reading

Evaluate Argument

In persuasive writing, an author tries to convince the reader to agree with his or her **position**, or viewpoint, on an issue. Persuasive writing includes essays, speeches, newspaper editorials, and advertisements.

How It Works

A writer's statement of his or her viewpoint is called the **claim**. Statements to convince the reader to agree with the claim are called the **argument**. Writers use several kinds of **appeals**, or ways of persuading readers.

- **Appeals to logic,** also called evidence, make sense, are relevant or relate to the claim, and include support that can be proved. Such evidence includes facts, statistics, opinions of experts, and details from personal experience.
- **Appeals to ethics** speak to the reader's sense of right and wrong.
- **Appeals to emotions** focus on readers' feelings.

Study this passage to learn more about persuasive writing.

Inappropriate Argument Techniques
Unsupported Inferences: conclusions that aren't supported by the evidence
Fallacious Reasoning: an argument based on a **fallacy**—that is, an idea that is misleading or false
Propaganda: an argument based on unsound reasoning and emotional appeals
Irrelevant Information: support for an argument that is not related to the claim

Nutrition First

Teens need nutritious diets, but vending machines tempt them to make bad food choices. Our schools should get rid of their vending machines.

> Claim: the writer's viewpoint

The typical vending machine offers too much of a bad thing. Most snacks offered are high in sugar and fats. Candy bars, chips, and cookies make up 80% of the snack choices. Vending machines cause crowding in school hallways as students stand in line to grab snacks.

> Facts as evidence

> Information that is not relevant

According to Lee Oto, Nutrition Director, "School meals help meet the required daily servings of fruits and vegetables, but students don't choose the school meal if they pass a vending machine."

> Opinion of a reliable expert as evidence

Isn't the health of our children more important than profit? We need to do the right thing. Remove the machines!

> Propaganda: an appeal to ethics

Academic Vocabulary
- **appeal** (a-pēl) *noun*
An **appeal** is a request for a response.

Practice Together

Read the following passage aloud with your class. As you read, identify the claims and argument, the type of evidence, and the **appeals** the author uses. Determine whether the argument techniques are appropriate.

Food Fight

Vending machines help students get through the long day, so they must stay. It takes too long to stand in the cafeteria line during our short lunch periods, and grabbing something from a vending machine is quicker. We need vending machines for after-school events like sports practices, too. Without them we would starve! Coach Mathis agrees. "Many of our sports activities are funded by vending machine profits." We students want vending machines to stay. They fill a gap in our need for nutrition during the day.

Try It!

Read the following passage. What are the writer's viewpoint and argument? What types of evidence and **appeals** does the writer use? Are the argument techniques appropriate?

Change for Vending Machines

Schools depend on profits from vending machines, but poor food quality is a health problem. Students cannot learn properly with only junk food in their systems. The School Board, therefore, demands more nutritious foods in vending machines rather than removing the machines.

Superintendent Kacy Miles states, "Student success depends on good health." We don't want students relying on high-fat snacks and sugary beverages. We'll require more drinks and snacks like milk, vegetable juices, water, fruits, salads, yogurt, and granola bars. If necessary, we'll insist on newer models of vending machines to handle these foods. Students can still use vending machines but will have healthier choices. "We know our responsible students will appreciate and grow to love the new vending machines," Miles states. "They won't even miss the junk food."

Focus on Vocabulary

Use Context Clues and References: Specialized Language and Vocabulary

Specialized language and vocabulary includes **technical** terms, jargon, and special cultural references. Like other words in English, some specialized words have more than one meaning. Using the context and a dictionary, you can figure out which meaning is used.

How the Strategy Works

When you come to a specialized word you don't know, use the context along with a dictionary to confirm the meaning.

1. Think about the topic of the piece and the subject area it covers.
2. See how the word fits into the sentence. Does the word seem like jargon or a **technical** term?
3. Make a guess about the meaning of the word.
4. Use the context and information about the word in a dictionary to figure out its meaning.

Use the strategy to figure out the meaning of the underlined words.

Almost all of the drinking water in rural areas comes from <u>aquifers</u>. However, some areas may be losing their ground water. Many places report that their aquifers are drier than in the past. In other areas, well diggers must drill much deeper to reach water. Protecting water <u>reserves</u> is increasingly important, now and into the future.

Dictionary Entries

entry word   **pronunciation**

aquifer (ak'wə-fər) *n.* underground layer of rock or sand —**definition**
that can absorb and hold water

reserve (rĭ-zurv′) 1 *v.* to save for future use. 2 *v.* to secure
for oneself; retain. 3 *n.* something kept or stored for future use.
4 *n.* the act of making an arrangement in advance

part of speech

☑ **REMEMBER** You can use context and a dictionary to help you figure out the meaning of specialized language.

Academic Vocabulary

- **technical** (**tek-ni-kul**) *adjective*
  Something that is **technical** is based on scientific knowledge.

Strategy in Action

" If an *aquifer* can get 'drier' it must be something that gets wet. Yes, its definition is 'an underground layer of rock or sand that holds water.' "

Strategy in Action

" The text says water is stored in aqui[fers] some of which are drying up. But if the water *reserves* are protected, we have water for the future. That make[s] me think that *reserves* are also place[s] where water is stored. Yes, the third meaning in the dictionary is the only one that makes sense. "

Practice Together

Read the passage aloud with your class. Listen to each underlined word.
Use the context and a dictionary to figure out its meaning in the passage.

The Changing Farm

Farming has changed with the rest of the world. The simple image of a farmer in a field is outdated. Farming is a business, and <u>agribusiness</u> is a huge industry. It takes complicated equipment and larger and larger <u>acreages</u> to farm today.

The tools of farming have changed, too. Almost all farms today use computers to plan and keep records. The Internet is also important because farmers check markets, weather, and crop conditions <u>online</u>.

▲ Farming equipment is changing with the times.

Some tractor models include air-conditioned <u>operator stations</u>, self-steering ability, and a <u>global positioning</u> satellite system (GPS) to guide the machines.

Try It!

Read the passage. What do the underlined words mean? How did you figure out the meanings?

The Price of Change

Probably the biggest change in society in the last 25 years has been the growth of the personal computer. <u>PCs</u> were once not much more than toys. Now they help us do everything. <u>Networks</u> link computers to other computers and help people share information freely.

Technology can come with a price, though. All that information is stored on other computers. Anything you enter on a <u>search engine</u>, any <u>Web site</u> you visit on the Internet, or any <u>data</u> about you creates a record somewhere. If someone uses a computer to <u>hack</u> into a <u>database</u>, your personal information could be stolen. Although technology can solve problems, it also creates new ones.

Feeding the World

by Peter Winkler

Build Background

Connect

Quickwrite In your opinion, why is there hunger in the world? Do a Quickwrite about two possible causes of this problem.

Explore an Issue

Some people argue that we should use science to improve the foods people eat. Others say that such changes could be unsafe. People on both sides of the issue agree that world hunger is a problem. Now find out why they disagree about how to solve it.

Digital Library

myNGconnect.com
◗ View the video.

▲ Is it helpful or harmful to make scientific changes to food?

Language & Grammar

1 TRY OUT LANGUAGE
2 LEARN GRAMMAR
3 APPLY ON YOUR OWN

Persuade

Study the photo, and listen to the conversation. Listen to how one friend persuades another friend to volunteer. When you persuade someone, you convince that person to do something.

PICTURE PROMPT

Help End Hunger

Emilio: I can't help out today because I planned to see a movie.

Sarah: I think you should volunteer today instead. I volunteer because many people in our community do not have enough food to feed their families. We can help.

Emilio: That is a good reason.

Sarah: In fact, about 25,000 people in the *world* are in great danger every day because of hunger! It is very important that we give some of our time to do something.

Emilio: Well, you convinced me! I can see a movie anytime. I want to volunteer today, too. How can I help?

Sarah: We are collecting canned food for a food drive at school. You can help collect canned food.

1 TRY OUT LANGUAGE
2 LEARN GRAMMAR
3 APPLY ON YOUR OWN

Use Verbs in the Present Perfect Tense

- If you know when an action happened in the past, use a **past tense** verb.

  EXAMPLE   I **helped** last week.

- If you're not sure when a past action happened, use a **verb** in the **present perfect tense** .

  EXAMPLE   Volunteers **have helped** people in the past.

- You can also use the present perfect tense to show that an action began in the past and may still be happening now.

  EXAMPLES   Mrs. Park and other volunteers **have served** many meals to people in poor countries. (And they are probably still serving meals.)

  Mrs. Park **has served** meals to hungry children every Saturday. (And she is probably still serving meals on Saturdays.)

- To form the present perfect, use the helping verb **have** or **has** plus the **past participle** of the main verb. For regular verbs, the past participle ends in -**ed**.

Verb	Past Tense	Past Participle
help	helped	helped
serve	served	served
try	tried	tried

Practice Together

Say each sentence. Choose the correct form of the verb.

1. Last year, Mr. Lopez (joined/has joined) a relief organization.
2. He (tried/has tried) joining the group for a long time.
3. People in the organization (wanted/have wanted) to help hungry families for a while.

Try It!

Say each sentence. Write the correct form of the verb on a card. Then say the sentence with the correct verb.

4. Last night, a new shipment of supplies (arrived/has arrived).
5. Truck drivers (delivered/have delivered) supplies here for months.
6. Volunteers (unload/have unloaded) the boxes from the trucks each time.

Feed the World

PERSUADE

World hunger is a serious problem. What is the best way to help feed the world?

Work with a group to write three ways to help feed the world. Use persuasive language to make your argument more convincing.

Proposition: We should volunteer our time.

Support
1. If we collect food, we can do our part to help people locally.
2.
3.

Present your proposition and support to another group. Then listen to their arguments. Which group was more persuasive? Why?

HOW TO PERSUADE

1. Tell your opinion, or proposition.

2. Give support for your opinion.

3. Use persuasive language and emotional words, or appeals.

> We should help feed the world. We can do our part by starting locally. We help many people when we collect food.

USE VERBS IN THE PRESENT PERFECT TENSE

When you make persuasive arguments, you may need to change the tense of the verb to tell about an action that started in the past and is still going on. If so, use the **present perfect tense** when you talk about these actions.

Our class **has worried** about hungry families for a long time. We **have thought** about ways to help them for weeks.

▲ People have given food to help the hungry for a long time.

Prepare to Read

Learn Key Vocabulary

Study the Words Use the steps below.

1. Pronounce the word. Say it aloud several times. Spell it.
2. Rate your word knowledge.
3. Study the example. Tell more about the word.
4. Practice it. Make the word your own.

Key Words

agricultural

(ag-ri-**kul**-chur-ul) *adjective* ▶ page 545

Something that is **agricultural** is related to farms or farming. Growing vegetables to sell as food is one kind of **agricultural** business.

gene (jēn) *noun*

▶ page 542

A **gene** is a physical unit that controls what a living cell is like. The color of your hair depends on your **genes**. *Related Word:* **genetics**

mission (mish-un) *noun*

▶ page 544

A **mission** is the goal of someone's work. An astronaut's **mission** is to explore space. *Synonyms:* **aim, purpose**

modified (mod-u-fīd)

adjective ▶ page 543

```
5 Minute Chili Con Queso Dip
Ingredients:                    or without
   1 can (15.5 ounces) chili with beans
2 bags  jar (15.5 ounces) processed cheese
   1 bag of tortilla or corn chips
Directions:
In microwavable bowl, mix chili and cheese. Heat 2 or 3
minutes, or until cheese melts. Stir. Serve with chips.
```

Something that has been **modified** has been changed. We **modified** the recipe to feed more people.

technique (tek-**nēk**) *noun*

▶ page 543

Technique is a skilled way of doing something. My serving **technique** improved after taking tennis lessons.

technology (tek-**nol**-u-jē)

noun ▶ page 543

Technology is the use of knowledge to do a task or to improve how the task is done. Because of new **technology**, computers are faster and smaller than they once were.

viewpoint (vyü-point) *noun*

▶ page 543

A **viewpoint** is the way a person thinks about things. My friends and I had different **viewpoints** about which way to go.

virus (vī-rus) *noun*

▶ page 542

A **virus** is a tiny particle that can cause disease in people, plants, and animals. My brother had a **virus** so he couldn't go to school.

Practice the Words Make a Study Card for each Key Word. Then compare your cards with a partner's.

agricultural

What it means: related to farming

Example: California has large areas of agricultural land.

Not an example: the beach

Study Card

Analyze Argument and Support

What are Pro and Con Arguments? Text that states a claim and tries to convince the reader is called persuasive text. An argument in favor of a persuasive claim is called a pro argument. An argument against a claim is called a con argument. Authors of persuasive texts use different kinds of **evidence** to support both pro and con arguments:

- **Facts:** Dates, names, and statements that can be proved
- **Expert Opinions:** Ideas from people who know the topic
- **Personal Experience:** Details about the author's experience

As you read persuasive texts, look for pro or con arguments and the **evidence** that supports them.

Reading Strategies
- Plan
- Monitor
- Ask Questions
- Make Connections
- Visualize
- Make Inferences
- Determine Importance

> **Synthesize** Bring together ideas gained from texts and blend them into a new understanding.

Look Into the Text

Supporters of genetic engineering argue that high-tech foods are a safe way to improve farming. *[Claim]* They point to the fact that genetically modified corn and soybeans have been used … since 1966 and … no one has suffered … *[argument]*

African growers desperately need access to the best management practices and fertilizer. They need better seeds and biotechnology to help improve crop production. Crop production is currently the lowest in the world …

Practice Together

Begin a Pro Arguments Chart A Pro Arguments Chart can help you understand arguments in favor of a claim. This Pro Arguments Chart shows an argument in favor of the claim in the first passage. Read the second passage and add to the chart.

Pro Arguments	Support	Type of Evidence
High-tech foods are a safe way to improve farming.	Genetically modified corn and soybeans have been used … since 1996 and … no one has suffered.	Fact

Academic Vocabulary

- **evidence** (e-vu-dents) *noun*
  Evidence can be beliefs, proof, facts, or details that help support a conclusion.

Persuasive Article

In a persuasive article, a writer makes a claim about an issue and tries to persuade readers to agree. The writer presents an argument either in favor of or against an issue and supports that viewpoint with evidence. It's always a good idea to evaluate the information to decide if the writer's reasoning is sound.

Look Into the Text

Yes, new technology can help protect against hunger.

> The argument gives the writer's opinion.

. . . I learned firsthand about the enormous challenge of breaking the cycle of poverty and hunger in rural Africa. . . .

> Personal experience is one type of evidence.

   African growers desperately need access to the best management practices . . .

> Emotional appeals are common.

As you read, synthesize the information. Then you can form your own opinion about the ideas.

Feeding the World

by Peter Winkler

Scientist Florence Wambugu wants to help farmers grow more food.

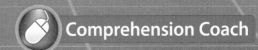
Comprehension Coach

How much food do people need?

The average adult needs between 2,200 and 2,900 calories each day, and also requires a variety of vitamins, minerals, and other nutrients to stay healthy. For many people, having enough food to meet these requirements isn't a problem; for others it is.

Poverty, war, and poor farming practices are among the reasons that people go hungry. In some parts of the world there are millions of hungry people. According to the United Nations, Asia has the largest number of underfed people—about half a billion. Africa comes next with about 200,000,000 hungry people.

Scientists, politicians, and citizens around the world disagree about how to solve the problem of world hunger. Scientists have discovered new technology to create more food, but many people disagree that it's a good method. The one thing everyone agrees on is that no one in the world should have to go hungry.

The Need for Food

Scientist Florence Wambugu works with farmers in Kenya. Kenya is a country in East Africa. She helps farmers grow bigger and better crops. Wambugu is interested in finding simple ways to **raise** more food. In the past ten years, Wambugu has spent a lot of time studying sweet potatoes. Sweet potatoes are an important food in her part of Kenya. A **virus** kept attacking the plants. It stopped the sweet potatoes from growing properly. Some farmers, says Wambugu, lost three-quarters of their crops because of the virus.

Wambugu **went to war against** the virus. Her search for a **weapon that could** save the sweet potatoes led to a **laboratory** in St. Louis, Missouri. Scientists there are studying new ways to create better plants.

The lab's work focuses on genes. **Genes** are the chemical "computer programs" found

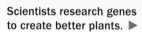
Scientists research genes to create better plants. ▶

in the cells of living things. Genes tell a plant to produce pink flowers. Genes tell an animal to grow black hair. Now scientists move genes from one living thing to another. That process is called genetic engineering.

Wambugu spent three years at the lab. She created a sweet potato plant using the **techniques** of genetic engineering. This sweet potato plant could actually fight off the virus. Wambugu tested her research in Kenya. Her plants produced magnificent sweet potatoes.

Wambugu believes that's just the beginning. Genetically **modified** foods, she argues, could help farmers in poor countries grow desperately needed crops. "What farmers need," Wambugu says, "is **technology** that is **packaged in** the seed." She believes expensive chemicals and machines aren't needed. Further, she argues that by creating strong plants that farmers can raise simply, fewer people will go hungry.

Scientists disagree about genetically modified food and the question of how to feed the world is widely debated. Now read different **viewpoints**—one pro and one con—about this new technology.

▲ A worker checks genetically modified rice in Africa.

Key Vocabulary
technique *n.*, a skilled way of doing something
modified *adj.*, changed
technology *n.*, a process or invention based on scientific knowledge
viewpoint *n.*, a way of thinking about something

In Other Words
packaged in inside

Look Into the Text

1. **Cause and Effect** Why did Wambugu spend three years working at a lab in St. Louis? What **techniques** did she learn?

2. **Problem and Solution** What does Wambugu think will help farmers in poor countries grow crops?

PRO

Supporters of genetic engineering argue that high-tech foods are a safe way to improve farming. They point to the fact that genetically modified corn and soybeans have been used in the United States since 1996 and say that no one has suffered as a result. Florence Wambugu supports this view on the issue in the following editorial.

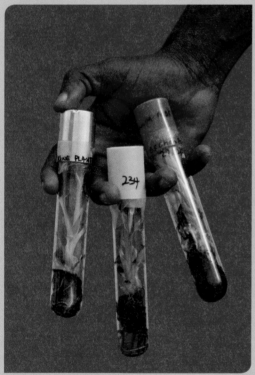

▲ Biotechnology is used to create important crops in Ibaden, Nigeria. Scientists store the plants in test tubes to keep them strong and free of pests.

Is genetically modified food a good way to feed the world?

Yes, new technology can help protect against hunger.

Florence Wambugu, *The Washington Post*

I was one in a family of nine children growing up on a small farm in Kenya's **highlands**. I learned firsthand about the enormous challenge of **breaking the cycle of** poverty and hunger in rural Africa. In fact, the reason I became a plant scientist was to help farmers like my mother. My mother sold the only cow our family owned to pay for my secondary education. This was a **sacrifice** because I, like most children in Kenya, was needed on the farm.

I have since made it my **mission** to alert others to the urgent need for new technology in Africa. New technology can help protect against hunger, environmental damage, and poverty. African growers desperately need access to the best **management practices and fertilizer**. They need better seeds and biotechnology to help improve crop production. Crop production is currently the lowest in the world per unit area of land.

Key Vocabulary
mission *n.*, the goal of someone's work

In Other Words
highlands mountains
breaking the cycle of ending
sacrifice loss
management practices and fertilizer ways to plant the land and enrich the soil

Science Background
Biotechnology is a specific kind of science. Scientists who study biotechnology change the genetic materials of living organisms. They make different products, such as crops that cannot be damaged by pests.

▲ A farmer plows a field in Kenya.

Traditional **agricultural** practices continue to produce only **low yields** and poor people. These practices will not be **sufficient** to feed the additional millions of people who will live on the continent fifty years from now. So the question becomes, why aren't these types of biotechnology applications more readily available to African farmers?

The priority of Africa must be to feed its people and to **sustain** agricultural production and the environment.

The people of Africa cannot wait for others to debate the **merits of** biotechnology. America and other developed nations must act now to **allocate** technologies that can prevent suffering and starvation.

Look Into the Text

1. **Fact and Opinion** Find two facts and one opinion in Wambugu's article. Why do you think she includes her opinions?

2. **Summarize** According to Wambugu, why do African growers need new **technology**?

Key Vocabulary
  agricultural *adj.*, farming

In Other Words
  low yields small amounts of food
  sufficient enough
  sustain support
  merits of good and bad points about
  allocate give other countries

CON

Some scientists and other critics of genetic engineering argue that we do not know the effects of this technology. We do not know how mixing genes will affect plants and animals in the future. Michael Bloch supports this view in the following editorial.

▲ Activists unite in Greece to protest against genetically modified food.

Is genetically modified food a good way to feed the world?

No, genetically modified food is a risky form of technology.

Michael Bloch, *Oak High School Gazette*

Genetically modified (GM) food is not the best way to feed the world. In my opinion, genetically modified food is a harmful and risky form of technology.

I do not think we should genetically modify our food because it harms plant and animal life. GM plants can accidentally mix with wild plants. When this happens, superweeds, or giant weeds, grow. Farmers need to use stronger forms of **pesticide** to kill superweeds. Stronger pesticides are bad for other plants and for the air we breathe.

Animals are also affected by GM foods. Some GM corn crops are a major health risk to animals that eat them. A **study** done in the U.S. showed that 44% of caterpillars of the monarch butterfly died when fed large amounts of pollen, or powder, from GM corn.

We know that GM foods negatively affect plant and animal life. It is important to think

In Other Words
pesticide chemicals
study reseach project

Science Background
The **monarch butterfly** is a flying insect, with vivid orange and black markings, commonly found in North America. Caterpillars transform into adult butterflies in about two weeks.

about the risks GM foods pose to humans as well. Many experts caution against GM foods. Ronnie Cummins of the Organic Consumers Association warns, "We are rushing **headlong** into a new technology. **We are courting disaster if we don't look before we leap.**" Furthermore, Dr. Mae-Wan Ho, a geneticist and physicist, cautions that, "Genetic engineering is **inherently** dangerous."

Since nearly half the U.S. corn and soybean crops are now genetically modified, we must act now. We do not know the health effects of these foods. Until we do, it is in everyone's interest to find better ways of feeding the world.

▼ Protesters fight for labels on genetically modified foods.

In Other Words

headlong too fast
We are courting disaster if we don't look before we leap. We should think more about the risks of GM food.
inherently basically

Look Into the Text

1. **Evaluating Sources** How do the experts quoted support Bloch's arguments?

2. **Compare and Contrast** How are Wambugu's and Bloch's calls to action similar and different?

3. **Cause and Effect** In a U.S. study, what caused a large number of monarch caterpillars to die?

Market Women

by Daisy Myrie

Down from the hills, they come
With swinging hips and steady **stride**
To feed the hungry Town
They **stirred the steep dark land**
5   To place within the growing seed.
And in the rain and sunshine
Tended the young green plants,
They **bred, and dug and reaped.**
And now, as Heaven has blessed their **toil,**
10 They come, bearing the fruits,
These **hand-maids** of the Soil,
Who bring full baskets down,
To feed the hungry Town.

The Marketplace, 1988, Carlton Murrell. Oil on canvas, private collection.

▲ **Critical Viewing: Design** What details in the artwork remind you of details in the poem?

In Other Words
stride walk
stirred the steep dark farmed the
bred, and dug and reaped cared
   for the plants and harvested them
toil work
hand-maids women

Look Into the Text

1. **Inference** Do the farmers in the poem care about the food they grow? How do you know?
2. **Mood** What is the feeling at the end of the poem? Which words or phrases help create this feeling?

Connect Reading and Writing

agricultural

genes

mission

modified

techniques

technology

viewpoint

viruses

CRITICAL THINKING

1. SUM IT UP Use your Pro Arguments Chart and Con Arguments Chart to summarize each writer's **viewpoint** on **modified** food.

Pro Arguments	Support	Type of Evidence
1. High-tech foods are a safe way to improve farming.	1. Genetically modified corn and soybeans have been used ... since 1996 and...no one has suffered.	1. Fact

Pro Arguments Chart

2. Interpret Why does Wambugu say, "Africa cannot wait for others to debate the merits of biotechnology"?

3. Infer Soybeans and corn have had **modified genes** since 1996. Why do you think Bloch says "We do not know the health effects of these foods"?

4. Compare Compare the feelings of the speaker in "Market Women" with each writer's **viewpoint** in "Feeding the World."

READING FLUENCY

Intonation Read the passage on page 645 to a partner. Assess your fluency.

1. My tone never/sometimes/always matched what I read.

2. What I did best in my reading was _____ .

READING STRATEGY

What strategy helped you understand this selection? Tell a partner about it.

VOCABULARY REVIEW

Oral Review Read the paragraph aloud. Add the vocabulary words.

Modern _____ can protect crops from harmful _____ . For example, the _____ in the plant cells can be _____ in a lab. Some people who do _____ work say this is helpful. But other people look at the issue from a different _____ . Although people disagree on which _____ to use in growing food, everyone agrees that feeding the world is an important _____ .

Written Review Write a paragraph to describe **techniques** people might use to feed the world. Use five vocabulary words.

 **WRITE ABOUT THE** GUIDING QUESTION

Explore Feeding the World

Which writer makes the stronger argument about the best way to feed the world? Support your **viewpoint** with examples from the selection.

Connect Across the Curriculum

Use Context Clues: Technical Vocabulary

Recognize Technical Terms Technical terms are words used in different ways for particular subjects. You can use context clues to help understand their meanings. Reread "The Need for Food" on pages 542–543. Answer the questions, using context clues to understand the term *genetic engineering*.

1. What is a gene?

2. What do genes do in living things?

3. What can scientists now do with genes?

Identify Propaganda

Academic Vocabulary

- **propaganda** (prop-u-**gan**-da) *noun*
  Propaganda is the use of faulty methods to persuade an audience.

Sometimes writers use misleading persuasive techniques. They may introduce irrelevant evidence, use unsound reasoning, or make emotional claims that are unsupported by facts. This is called **propaganda**.

Here are three common types of **propaganda**:

Propaganda Type	Example
Glittering generality uses impressive words that may skip past the truth.	"Try the **new** and **improved** Sudso, a more **modern** way to clean your floors."
Bandwagon appeals claim that everyone else is doing something, so you should, too.	"The Guzzler is the **number one selling SUV** in the country. It must be the best for you."
Name calling makes negative claims or attacks on a person or product.	"My opponent in this election is **just a rich city boy.** Who wants **that kind of person** for this office?"

Identify Propaganda
Collect examples of ads that use **propaganda** techniques from newspapers, radio, and television. Discuss whether they are effective. Explain.

Persuade

Group Debate Work in a group. Divide into two teams. Take turns debating the pros and cons of genetically modified food. Use past tense and present perfect tense verbs in your arguments, depending on the time of the action.

> I think the idea of genetically modified food has given some countries hope for solving their hunger problem.

> I think genetically modified food may be dangerous. We don't know the effects of eating some of these foods.

Write Effectively About Events

Study the Models When you write, make sure your readers can understand what you want to say. Choose verbs carefully to make it clear when events happen.

NOT OK

> Zack has wanted to help people for a long time, so yesterday he **has gone** to a volunteer agency. There he **has heard** stories about how volunteers **have helped** farmers around the world produce healthy fish to eat. For years, they **taught** farmers how to build ponds and increase fish production. Zack knew a lot about fish, so that very day he **has volunteered**.

This writer uses the present perfect tense to tell about something that happened yesterday. The reader is confused.

OK

> Zack **has wanted** to help people for a long time, so yesterday he **went** to a volunteer agency. There he **heard** stories about how volunteers **have helped** farmers around the world produce healthy fish to eat. For years, they **have taught** farmers how to build ponds and increase fish production. Zack knew a lot about fish, so that very day he **volunteered**.

This writer makes it easier to follow the action.

Add Sentences Think of two sentences to add to the OK model above. Be sure to use words correctly as you tell when events occur.

✎ **WRITE ON YOUR OWN** Think about a time when you heard something that inspired you. Describe the event. Be careful to choose words that make it clear when the action happened.

REMEMBER

- **Past tense** verbs tell about an action that already happened.
- **Present perfect tense** verbs tell about past actions that may still be going on.

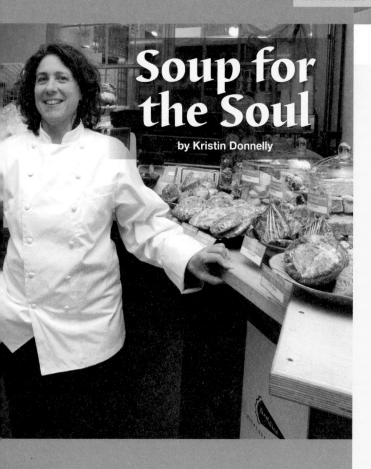

INTERVIEW

Soup for the Soul

by Kristin Donnelly

Build Background

Providing for the Community

How can one person help provide for her community? Mary Ellen Diaz decided to cook delicious, healthy food for the homeless.

Digital Library

myNGconnect.com
🌐 View the video.

▲ Everyone needs to eat healthy foods.

Connect

Anticipation Guide Tell whether you agree or disagree with these statements.

	Agree	Disagree
1. One person can't help feed a community.	_____	_____
2. It doesn't matter to hungry people what they eat.	_____	_____
3. Sharing good meals can change people's lives.	_____	_____

Anticipation Guide

Language & Grammar

Negotiate

CD

Study the photo. Listen to the conversation as a teenager negotiates with her parents. When people negotiate, they try to reach an agreement with each other.

PICTURE PROMPT

Work for Change

Alexis: Mom, Mrs. Park needs a babysitter so she can volunteer at the soup kitchen. You know Mrs. Park. She lives on the corner. She has a little girl and needs a sitter on Tuesdays after school and on Saturday mornings. Babysitting would be a great job for me.

Mother: Yes, babysitting can be good experience, Alexis, but it is also hard work and a big responsibility. I don't think it's a good idea because you won't have time for your homework.

Alexis: I understand what you're saying, Mom, but I really want this job. I can do my homework in study hall.

Father: I have an idea. How about if you babysit just on Saturday morning? If you help Mrs. Park one morning a week, it will give you valuable experience and leave enough time for homework, chores, and other activities.

Alexis: That sounds like a great idea, Dad. I'll get experience and make a little spending money, and I won't have a conflict with school work.

Use Verbs in the Past Perfect Tense

The **past perfect tense** of a verb shows that one action in the past happened before another past action.

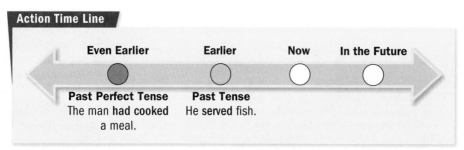

Action Time Line

| Even Earlier | Earlier | Now | In the Future |

Past Perfect Tense
The man **had cooked** a meal.

Past Tense
He served fish.

- Use the **past tense** of a verb to tell about an action that was completed in the past.

  EXAMPLE   Yesterday, Mr. Park **came** to the shelter.

- If you want to show that one past action happened before another, use the **past perfect tense** for the action that happened first.

  EXAMPLE   Mr. Park **had read** about the shelter before he volunteered.

- To form the past perfect tense, use **had** plus the **past participle** of the main verb.

  EXAMPLES   Mr. Park **had worked** at a restaurant before he started at the shelter.
  He **had waited** on tables before he retired.

Practice Together

Change the verb in the box to the past perfect tense. Say it. Then say the sentence and add the past perfect tense verb.

1. | arrive | The homeless people _____ at the shelter at 5 p.m.
2. | greet | Mr. Park _____ them before he filled their plates.
3. | eat | After they _____, the people thanked Mr. Park.

Try It!

Change the verb in the box to the past perfect tense. Write the past perfect tense verb on a card. Then say the sentence and add the past perfect tense verb.

4. | set | Before the people arrived, the volunteers _____ the tables.

5. | see | The volunteers placed extra napkins on the table because they _____ how full the soup bowls were.

6. | warm | Before dinner was over, the people agreed that the food _____ them up.

▲ The man had been a chef before he volunteered at the homeless shelter.

Reach an Agreement

NEGOTIATE

People negotiate when they try to reach an agreement with each other. When they negotiate, they often compromise, or agree to a type of change.

Work with a partner to role-play a teen and his or her parent negotiating one of these issues: getting an after-school job, an increase in allowance, or extending a weekend curfew. Use calm and polite language when you negotiate.

Polite Words and Phrases		
please	I understand	let's try
may I	I guess	how about if we
can I	could you	why don't we

One important word in negotiations is *but*. When you use it, it means there is a certain condition to remember.

EXAMPLE   You can get an allowance, but you must earn it.

Negotiate an issue with your partner, then act out your negotiation in front of a small group. Talk about the compromise that you reached. Identify strengths and weaknesses in the negotiation. Then listen to another pair negotiate.

HOW TO NEGOTIATE

1. State the issue and your opinion in a calm and polite way.
2. Listen respectfully to other ideas. Calmly state your side.
3. Make a compromise.

> I really want to buy that hat. Can I babysit to earn money?

> You can babysit, but only on the weekend.

USE VERBS IN THE PAST PERFECT TENSE

When you negotiate, you may want to show that one action happened before another action in the past. If so, use the **past perfect tense** for the action that happened first.

EXAMPLES   Before I asked for an allowance, I **had listed** all the things I could do to earn it.

After they **had read** the list, Mom and Dad discussed my request.

Prepare to Read

Learn Key Vocabulary

Study the Words Use the steps below.

1. Pronounce the word. Say it aloud several times. Spell it.
2. Rate your word knowledge.
3. Study the example. Tell more about the word.
4. Practice it. Make the word your own.

Key Words

benefit (ben-e-fit) *noun*
▶ page 564

A **benefit** is something that is good for people, places, or things. One **benefit** of exercise is that it makes you strong.
Antonyms: **damage, hurt**

career (ku-rear) *noun*
▶ page 561

A **career** is a job that someone does for a long time. For 20 years, my aunt has had a **career** as a doctor.
Synonyms: **job, work**

donate (dō-nāt) *verb*
▶ page 563

To **donate** means to give to people in need. I always try to **donate** some of my spending money to help others.
Related Word: **donation**

founder (fown-der) *noun*
▶ page 560

A **founder** is a person who starts something. My uncle is the **founder** of his own company.

ingredient (in-grē-dē-unt)
noun ▶ page 560

An **ingredient** is something that is part of a mixture. These **ingredients** are used to make cookies.
Synonyms: **part, piece**

inspiration
(in-spu-rā-shun) *noun* ▶ page 561

An **inspiration** is a reason for doing or creating something. Artists often find their **inspiration** in the beauty of nature.

organic (or-gan-ik) *adjective*
▶ page 560

Organic refers to a type of food that is all natural. **Organic** fruits and vegetables are grown without chemicals.

organization
(or-gu-nu-zā-shun) *noun* ▶ page 560

An **organization** is a group of people who work toward a common goal. The Red Cross is an **organization**.
Related Word: **organize**

Practice the Words Make an Example Web for each Key Word. Then compare your webs with a partner's.

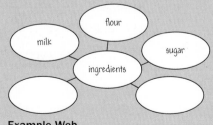

Example Web

Compare Writing About the Same Topic

How Do Texts Differ? Writers can approach topics in different ways, even using various genres to express their thoughts.

As you read, first identify the topic of the text. Then take note of the different kinds of information provided about the topic.

Reading Strategies

- Plan
- Monitor
- Ask Questions
- Make Connections
- Visualize
- Make Inferences
- Determine Importance
- **Synthesize** Bring together ideas gained from texts and blend them into a new understanding.

Look Into the Text

"Leftovers" by Kevin Hall

When I worked in a restaurant, I was surprised at how much food I saw people waste. Many diners would pick at their food and, instead of asking for bags to take the leftovers home, they would send back almost-full plates.

"Wasted Food" by Carolyn Lincoln

Something must be done about food waste! Every day, restaurants throw away thousands of pounds of food. Some of the garbage is remnants from diners' plates. The rest is food that is no longer fresh enough to serve customers.

Practice Together

Begin a Venn Diagram A Venn Diagram can help you compare texts about the same topic. This Venn Diagram shows the topic of both texts and some of the information provided in the first text. Reread the second text and complete the Venn Diagram.

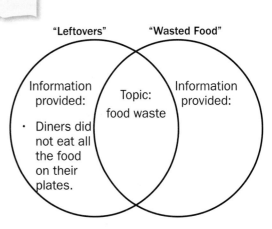

"Leftovers"   "Wasted Food"

Information provided:
- Diners did not eat all the food on their plates.

Topic: food waste

Information provided:

Interview and Persuasive Essay

Different texts, such as an interview and a persuasive essay, can address the same topic. An interview is a series of questions and answers. The **interviewer** asks the questions, and the **interviewee** answers. Listen to each voice in this interview about starting a soup kitchen.

Look Into the Text

Q: *What's the biggest lesson you've learned since starting First Slice?*

A: The smallest things can help change somebody's life. Saying hello to a homeless person instead of looking away.

In a persuasive essay, a writer gives an opinion about a topic and presents arguments and evidence to get readers to agree.

Look Into the Text

Do you want to feel stress and pressure every day at your job? Of course not! If you don't want a stressful job, you probably should not work in a restaurant.

> The writer wants to convince readers that working at a restaurant is stressful.

As you read the interview and persuasive essays about restaurant work, pull together details from all three texts. Add your own knowledge to draw conclusions about the topic.

Chef Mary Ellen Diaz prepares food in the First Slice kitchen. ▶

Soup for the Soul

by Kristin Donnelly

Mary Ellen Diaz's food is good enough for Chicago's best restaurants. Instead, she gives meals away to people in need.

▲ Mary Ellen Diaz uses her skills as a chef to help people.

"Pie is a symbol of community, and giving the first slice is like giving the best," says Mary Ellen Diaz.

Diaz is the **founder** of **an innovative** Chicago soup kitchen called First Slice. "This **organization** gives the first slice to people who rarely get anything special." A former chef at Chicago's **acclaimed** North Pond restaurant, Diaz feeds 400 homeless people each week, preparing delicious meals with fresh, locally grown, mostly **organic ingredients** —dishes like butternut squash soup or spicy multigrain-vegetable soup.

First Slice soup kitchen is successful partly because of generous people who work as volunteers, donate money, or become customers. Diaz opened a restaurant called First Slice Pie Café. It serves a seasonal menu including **made-from-scratch** pies. Diaz also started a program that allows busy families to help the hungry. At the same time, they are making their own schedule a little bit easier. Families may sign up to receive three gourmet meals a week. Every meal is nourishing, balanced, and prepared from local organic ingredients. Profits from both the private chef service and the café go toward the soup kitchen.

Key Vocabulary

founder *n.*, a person who forms an organization or group
organization *n.*, a group of people working toward a common goal
organic *adj.*, naturally grown
ingredient *n.*, a part of a mixture

In Other Words

an innovative a new and creative
acclaimed award-winning, famous
made-from-scratch fresh, homemade

Q: *What inspired you to leave your job as a chef and launch First Slice?*

A: I had a great restaurant **career**, but I felt like I had to make a choice about whether or not to stay. I wanted to be home at night reading books to my little girl instead of **slaving away** in the kitchen. I was also reading a lot about Jane Addams. She ran her own community kitchen that served food to people living on the street. She also helped women who were trying to **enter the workforce**. Jane Addams is still very much the **inspiration** for First Slice. I also started volunteering in soup kitchens, and I realized feeding forty to fifty people takes talent. I never thought of using my skills that way until then.

Q: *What kind of food do you cook at First Slice?*

A: Last year we made a lot of Cajun food to feed **displaced victims** of Hurricane Katrina. We also get a lot of requests for food with Latin flavors, dishes that might use tortillas. Smothered pork chops are really popular. A pot of greens is definitely a big thing, because most people on the street don't have access to farm-fresh produce. It's interesting: A lot of **our clientele** grew up in rural communities, and they know more about growing fruit and vegetables than I do. They ask really specific questions about the soil and the farming methods. It's wonderful that we can make that fresh-from-the-farm connection.

▲ A student volunteer helps prepare a meal at First Slice.

Key Vocabulary
career *n.*, a job that you do for a long time
inspiration *n.*, reason for doing something

In Other Words
slaving away working too much
enter the workforce get jobs
displaced victims the people who had to leave their homes because
our clientele the people we cook for

Look Into the Text

1. **Problem and Solution** How does Diaz's **organization** help feed the homeless?

2. **Cause and Effect** What **inspired** Diaz to start First Slice?

3. **Recall and Interpret** Think about the food served at First Slice. What is important to Diaz? Explain.

Q: *Where do most of your ingredients come from?*

A: I use a lot of the same local suppliers that I did when I was a restaurant chef. The farmers I work with are community-based and **a bit quirky and anti-establishment**, like me.

Q: *Is soup a big part of your program?*

A: Definitely. In the fall and winter we serve soup on a street corner every Tuesday night to homeless youth. We probably have thirty different recipes. We hide a lot of vegetables in our soups—I **play the same game** with the kids on the streets that I do with my own two kids. They might think they're eating just cheddar cheese soup but it's been thickened with vegetables like butternut squash.

Q: *What's the biggest lesson you've learned since starting First Slice?*

A: The smallest things can help change somebody's life. Saying hello to a homeless person instead of looking away. Or cooking something really simple and giving it to a homeless person so she feels good.

Q: *How do you work with volunteers?*

A: There's a food writer who comes in four hours a week and all she does is roll pie dough for us. She just loves pie dough. We serve a lot of pie, and making pie dough is really **therapeutic**. There's a man who comes in and just wants to chop onions. He recently applied for a job at a new **gourmet** store. He didn't get it, but I was thrilled that chopping onions gave him the confidence to start looking for a job; he's been out of work for so many years.

In Other Words

a bit quirky and anti-establishment
 like to do things differently
play the same game do the
 same thing
therapeutic relaxing
gourmet high-quality food

Q: *What's the best way for people to help feed the homeless?*

A: Make a connection with a **food pantry** and find a way to **donate** nutritious food. Fresh fruit and vegetables are always appreciated. Canned beans are always great to have around. Rice, dried grains, canned tomatoes and jarred salsa are also good to have. I have issues with the fact that the first thing I see in most food pantries are overstarched, oversugared things. Homeless people need nutritious food as much as anyone, even more.

Q: *What do you eat to stay healthy?*

A: A lot of salads, like one with carrots from the farm, radishes, organic greens, blue cheese, spiced pecans and pepitas [pumpkin seeds]—with bacon on the side.

Q: *How do you find balance in your life between work and family?*

▲ Mary Ellen Diaz encourages students of all ages to get involved with feeding the world.

A: What's neat is that I can bring my kids to anything we do at First Slice; they love what I do and they love to come with me. The people **get a kick out of** them, and **vice versa**. My daughter mentioned to me this morning that when it's her birthday, she is going to have a party and ask people to bring her a toy that she can donate to kids in need. How great is that? ❖

Key Vocabulary
donate *v.*, to give something to a person in need

In Other Words
food pantry place that collects food for the homeless
get a kick out of enjoy
vice versa they enjoy the people

Look Into the Text

1. **Problem and Solution** How does Diaz make sure that the kids she serves get enough vegetables?
2. **Explain** Who else does Diaz help besides the homeless?

Would it be fun to run a restaurant?

Running a restaurant is a lot of fun.

YES!

Wouldn't it be great to have a job that you really like? My aunt does. She runs a restaurant.

I think working in a restaurant is a lot of fun. For **one thing**, you get to be creative. According to the National Restaurant Association, culinary creativity plays a key role in the restaurant business. When I help out my aunt in her restaurant, we create many recipes for each night's menu. The menu creativity and effort inspires restaurant employees and makes customers feel special.

A second **benefit** of running a restaurant is that you get to make other people happy. According to the National Restaurant Association, four out of five people think going out to a restaurant is a better use of their time than cooking and cleaning up. I know that my aunt feels good about making the quality of people's lives better.

Finally, the most important reason that running a restaurant is an enjoyable job is because you get to be a part of the community. My aunt is involved in many community groups and a lot of meetings are held at her restaurant. The restaurant is a great space to relax and **socialize**.

If you want a great job, I urge you to consider working in a restaurant. You can develop important skills, be creative, and meet many different people.

Key Vocabulary
benefit *n.*, positive result, advantage

In Other Words
one thing example
socialize talk with other people

Would it be fun to run a restaurant?

Running a restaurant is no fun.

Do you want to feel stress and pressure every day at your job? Of course not! If you don't want a stressful job, you probably should not work in a restaurant.

Running a restaurant can be a very tiring job because it is so much work. My cousin, Steve, is the manager of a large restaurant. Steve often has to work up to fourteen hours per day! A recent article in the *San Francisco Chronicle* supports Steve's experience by stating that, "restaurants **are among the most labor-intensive of businesses**." Furthermore, having this much responsibility at work means you don't have much free time to do the other things you like to do.

Another problem with running a restaurant is the possibility of losing your job. Everyone knows that the restaurant business is very risky. According to a study by Cornell University and Michigan State, a quarter of all new restaurants in the U.S. go out of business in the first year. That number rises to 50 percent after three years and 70 percent after ten years. That risk puts pressure and stress on workers who may have to worry about losing their jobs.

For all these reasons, I strongly believe that running a restaurant is not much fun. If you want to enjoy your free time, avoid stress, and have greater security, you may want to consider another job.

In Other Words

are among the most labor-intensive of businesses require a lot of hard work

Look Into the Text

1. **Compare and Contrast** What are the **benefits** of and problems with running a restaurant?
2. **Fact and Opinion** What facts are given to support the opinion that running a restaurant is risky?

Holding Up the Sky
a tale from China

One day an elephant saw a hummingbird lying on the ground with its tiny feet up in the air. "Why are you doing that?" the elephant asked.

"I heard that the sky might fall today," the hummingbird replied. "I am going to help hold it up."

The mighty elephant made fun of the little bird. "Do you think," he **sneered**, "that those tiny feet could hold up the sky?"

The hummingbird kept his feet up in the air as he replied, "Not alone. But everyone must do whatever he can. And this is what I can do."

Science Background
Hummingbirds are very small birds. They are named for the hum, or sound, that their wings make when they move.

In Other Words
sneered said meanly

Look Into the Text

1. **Conclusions** What is the message of this folk tale?
2. **Compare** How are the actions of the hummingbird and Mary Ellen Diaz similar?

Connect Reading and Writing

Vocabulary
benefits
career
donate
founder
ingredients
inspiration
organic
organization

CRITICAL THINKING

1. **SUM IT UP** Review the Venn Diagram you completed as you read. Use the diagram to summarize the interview and persuasive essays.

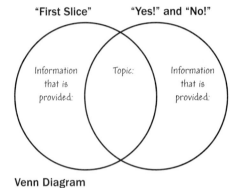

"First Slice"   "Yes!" and "No!"

Information that is provided: Topic: Information that is provided:

Venn Diagram

2. **Analyze** Review the Anticipation Guide on page 552. Do you have new ideas? With a group, discuss the **benefits** of an **organization** like First Slice.

3. **Draw Conclusions** Why does Diaz put so much thought into choosing **ingredients**? Support your conclusion with evidence from the text.

4. **Speculate** If Diaz read the essays and the poem, which might give her **inspiration**? Explain.

READING FLUENCY

Phrasing Read the passage on page 646 to a partner. Assess your fluency.

1. I did not pause/sometimes paused/ always paused for punctuation.

2. What I did best in my reading was _____ .

READING STRATEGY

What strategy helped you understand this selection? Tell a partner about it.

VOCABULARY REVIEW

Oral Review Read the paragraph aloud. Add the vocabulary words.

One way to help your community is to support an _____ that feeds the hungry. Meet with the _____ who started it, or share ideas with its members. You could cook, buy, or even grow _____ vegetables and other healthy _____ . If you have a busy job or _____ , you can _____ money instead. The _____ of helping include new friendships, and more hope and _____ for everyone.

Written Review Imagine you had an **organic** garden. Write a diary entry to tell how you would use it to provide food for your community. Use five vocabulary words.

WRITE ABOUT THE GUIDING QUESTION

Explore Feeding Our Communities

What advice would you give to the **founder** of an **organization** to feed people in need? Use examples from the selections to support your advice.

Connect Across the Curriculum

Vocabulary Study

Use Context Clues: Jargon

Academic Vocabulary

- **technical** (tek-ni-kal) *adjective*
  Something that is **technical** is based on scientific knowledge.

> The server is saying that three tables of four people just sat down.

Do you know what a server means when he or she says: *I just got three four-tops down*? This is an example of **jargon**, a specialized language used in certain tasks or settings. Jargon may consist of **technical** terms or slang.

Use Context Clues Read each sentence. Discuss with a partner how context helps you understand each term.

1. Rather than just buying desserts for First Slice, Diaz spends hours preparing made-from-scratch pies.

2. Many homeless people would have a hard time feeding themselves if they could not get supplies that are donated to local food pantries.

Literary Analysis

Analyze Persuasive Language

Some persuasive writing is more effective than others.

- **Details** Good writers use details to make appeals easier to understand:

  > A. Leaking faucets waste lots of water.
  > B. That little drip, drip, drip sends hundreds of gallons down the drain.

Specific details bring the second sentence to life.

- **Word Choice** Choosing the right words can make a difference:

  > A. Our school is too warm. We are hot in our classroom.
  > B. Our school is overheated. We roast in our classroom.

Different words have shades of meaning that can strengthen or weaken an argument.

Analyze and Compare With a partner, read the essays on pages 564 and 565. Identify the persuasive language in each. Then discuss how word choice and details affect the essays' meaning and tone.

Negotiate

Role-Play With a group, act out a negotiation between volunteers at a soup kitchen and local farmers. Use present perfect and past perfect tense verbs as you negotiate and make compromises.

> We had needed more tomatoes, but now we need more beans.

> We have given you extra beans for over a month.

Write About Helping Others

Study the Models When you write, make sure your readers can follow the action without confusion. Use the correct verbs depending on when the action happens.

NOT OK

Raul **wanted** to do something for others before he volunteered at the shelter. After he and the shelter's director **discussed** what he could do, Raul decided to collect food donations. Before he left to pick up the food, he **received** directions to the donation sites. After he had loaded his truck with canned goods, bread, and other foods, he **had driven** back to the shelter.

> This writing is confusing because the reader can't tell which action happened first.

OK

Raul **had wanted** to do something for others before he volunteered at the shelter. After he and the shelter's director **had discussed** how he could help, Raul decided to collect food donations. Before he left to pick up the food, he **had received** directions to the donation sites. After he had loaded his truck with canned goods and bread, he **drove** back to the shelter.

> This writing clearly shows when the actions happened.

Add Sentences Think of two sentences to add to the OK model above. Be sure to make it clear which action happened first.

WRITE ON YOUR OWN Write about something you have done in the past to help someone. Be sure to use words correctly to show when the action happened. Make sure your reader can follow the action without confusion.

REMEMBER

- Use the **past tense** to tell about a completed past action.
- Use the **past perfect tense** to show that one past action happened before another.

THE GIRL AND THE CHENOO
by Joseph Bruchac

Wounded Sleep, 2005, Gouache and ink, Durga Bernhard, collection of the artist.

Build Background

Learn About the Abenaki

"The Girl and the Chenoo" is a Native American play in the Abenaki tradition. It takes place in the northeast of what is now the United States. The Chenoo is a legendary monster who appears in the stories of many Native American cultures.

Connect

Brainstorm and Role-Play How does food connect people? With a group, brainstorm ways that people have found, prepared, and shared food throughout time. Choose one idea to role-play for the class.

Digital Library

myNGconnect.com
◐ View the images.

▲ Abenaki people today

Language & Grammar

Use Appropriate Language

Listen to the two raps. Then listen again and chime in. How do the words in each rap fit with the place and the occasion?

RAP

Dinner at a Fancy Restaurant

Good evening.
Welcome to the *Tropical Bay*.
My name is Robert,
And I'll be your server today.
I'll leave while you look at the menu,
But first allow me to say,
We have some very nice specials,
Which I'll tell you about if I may.

Pizza Lunch

Hi! What can I get you?
Do you need more time to decide?
OK, I hear you.
One pepperoni pizza
With a salad on the side.
Right! One pizza coming up!
It'll be ready in a little bit.
In the meantime, while you are waiting,
Why don't you just sit?

1 TRY OUT LANGUAGE
2 LEARN GRAMMAR
3 APPLY ON YOUR OWN

Use Conditionals

A **conditional sentence** tells how one action depends upon another.

- A conditional sentence has a dependent clause beginning with **if** or **when** that states a condition and an independent clause that states the result.

    EXAMPLE **If** the restaurant is open, we will stop to eat.

    dependent clause   independent clause

- To tell about a result that is always true, use the **present tense** in both clauses. To tell about a real possibility in the future, use the **present tense** in the **if**-clause and **will** plus a main verb in the independent clause.

    EXAMPLES If you **heat** ice, it **melts**. (This is a fact.)

    He **will feel** better all day if he **eats** breakfast.
    (This happens all the time.)

- Sometimes a conditional expresses an unlikely or impossible event in the present or future. An unreal conditional uses a **past tense verb** in the **if**-clause and **would** (**could** or **might**) plus a main verb in the independent clause.

    EXAMPLE If Ted **had** time, he **would go** with them.

    past   would + main verb

    (Ted doesn't have time, so he can't go with them.)

Practice Together

Choose a verb from the box to complete the sentence. Say the sentence and add the verb.

goes	will	would

1. If the café has pizza, I _____ go with them.

2. If Sarah _____ with me, I will be happy.

3. If I knew the answer, I _____ tell you.

Try It!

Choose a verb from the box to complete the sentence. Write the sentence on a card. Then say the sentence.

order	will	would

4. If he is hungry enough, he will _____ two meals.

5. If I asked him, Justin _____ take me home.

6. If it is sunny, we _____ eat outside.

▲ If the tables are set, the waiters will serve the food.

Place an Order

USE APPROPRIATE LANGUAGE

Our body language and the language, tone, and volume of our voices all change depending on the social situation. For example, formal language is appropriate to use in presentations, interviews, and other formal or academic settings. Informal, or relaxed, language is appropriate to use when talking with friends and family.

With a partner, role-play how you would order from a waiter at a fancy restaurant. Then role-play how you would order from a neighbor who works at a casual restaurant. Use verb tenses correctly. Trade roles.

Language Type	Formal	Informal
Body Language	make eye contact, stand or sit up straight	relaxed
Tone	serious	relaxed
Volume	loud, clear	varies with the situation (can range from a whisper to a shout)
Example	I would like to order the steak, please.	How's it going? I'll have a slice of pepperoni, please.

Have other students listen to your role-play and note what they think is appropriate in each situation, such as the words you use or the tone of your voice.

HOW TO USE APPROPRIATE LANGUAGE

1. Use words that match the audience and the occasion.
2. Use appropriate tone, volume, and body language.

> Formal:
> I'd like to order a salad, please.

> Informal:
> Hey, Miguel, can I get a slice of cheese pizza?

USE CONDITIONALS

If you are speaking about possibilities, you can use conditionals. Use **if**-clauses to state the condition and **will plus a main verb** to state the result.

EXAMPLES **If you have pizza** on the menu, **I will order** a few slices.
If the service is good, I will leave a tip.

Prepare to Read

Learn Key Vocabulary

Study the Words Use the steps below.

1. Pronounce the word. Say it aloud several times. Spell it.
2. Rate your word knowledge.
3. Study the example. Tell more about the word.
4. Practice it. Make the word your own.

Key Words

brag (brag) *verb*
▶ page 579

To **brag** means to show too much pride about doing something well. The fisherman **bragged** that he caught more fish than anyone else.

confident (kon-fi-dent)
adjective ▶ page 579

A **confident** person is someone who is sure of his or her abilities. You have to be **confident** to succeed.

engage (en-gāj) *verb*
▶ page 579

To **engage** means to take part or get involved in an activity. She **engaged** her friends in a conversation.

hesitant (hez-i-tent) *adjective*
▶ page 580

A **hesitant** person feels unsure, or not ready to do something. The boy is **hesitant** to pet the rabbit.
Related Word: **hesitate**

modest (mod-ist) *adjective*
▶ page 580

A **modest** person does not act overly proud of an accomplishment or success. The girl was **modest** about winning first prize.

react (rē-akt) *verb*
▶ page 590

To **react** means to show your feelings about something. A person may **react** in fear to a scary movie.
Related Word: **reaction**
Synonym: **respond**

relative (rel-u-tiv) *noun*
▶ page 591

A **relative** is a family member. I love my **relatives**, and I am especially close with my grandmother.
Synonym: **family**

talented (tal-en-tid) *adjective*
▶ page 578

A **talented** person is good at doing one or more activities. They are very **talented** musicians.
Base Word: **talent**

Practice the Words Work with a partner. Write a question using one Key Word. Answer your partner's question. Use at least one Key Word in your answer. Keep going until you have used all of the words twice.

EXAMPLE: Are you hesitant to run in the race?

No, I feel confident I will win!

Analyze Drama

How is Drama Organized? An important <mark>characteristic</mark> of drama is its use of dialogue to tell the story. Plays are mostly dialogue, or conversations between characters. Dialogue, not description, reveals many of the events. The writer does not use "he said" or "she said," but presents all dialogue in a script for actors to say aloud.

As you read drama, look for clues about events from the dialogue.

Reading Strategies

- Plan
- Monitor
- Ask Questions
- Make Connections
- Visualize
- Make Inferences
- Determine Importance
- **Synthesize** Bring together ideas gained from texts and blend them into a new understanding.

Look Into the Text

UNCLE MUSKRAT. Where are my nephews? Have they not come back from their hunt?

LITTLE LISTENER. No, uncle. My brothers have not yet returned. I am sure they will arrive soon and tell us of their adventures.

SECOND BROTHER. ...today was fine for me...I shot two deer.

WILLOW WOMAN. And where are those two big deer?

SECOND BROTHER. I didn't bring them back with me.

UNCLE MUSKRAT. I can see that. But why?

SECOND BROTHER. ...there was this mountain lion, actually, two mountain lions. Yes! They grabbed my two deer and carried them off...I did bring this. This very fat rabbit.

Practice Together

Begin a Dialogue-and-Events Chart. A Dialogue-and-Events Chart can help you see how dialogue reveals events in a play. This Dialogue-and-Events Chart shows one piece of dialogue and the event it reveals. Read the second piece of dialogue and add to the Dialogue-and-Events Chart.

Dialogue	Events the Dialogue Reveal
LITTLE LISTENER. No, uncle. My brothers have not yet returned...	The nephews have gone on a hunt but have not returned.
SECOND BROTHER. ...two mountain lions...grabbed my two deer and carried them off...I did bring this. This very fat rabbit.	

Academic Vocabulary

- **characteristic** (kair-ik-tu-**ris**-tik)
  noun
  A **characteristic** is a specific feature or trait that helps you identify something.

Play

A play is a story written to be performed by actors for an audience. Most plays are divided into sections called **acts**. Acts are divided into **scenes**. Each scene is a change in time or place.

The **lines**, or words characters speak, are arranged in sequence and signaled by the **character's name** in bold type. The characters' lines give clues to what is going on in a play. Pay attention to how characters' conversations reveal important events.

Look Into the Text

MOOSBAS. [*snatching food from a young child*] Give me some of that.
[*The young child looks upset but does not say anything.*]
LITTLE LISTENER. Moosbas, there's enough food for everyone.

Stage directions in italics tell actors how to move and talk.

As you read, combine details from the text with examples from your own experience to understand the text better.

THE GIRL AND THE CHENOO

by Joseph Bruchac

▲ **Critical Viewing: Effect** What feeling or mood does the painting create? What details help the artist create that mood?

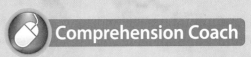
Comprehension Coach

Characters

LITTLE LISTENER— *a girl of the Abenaki people long ago. Bright, alert, helpful, a very good cook and* **talented** *at many other things especially listening to stories. Twelve* **winters of age**.

UNCLE MUSKRAT— *LITTLE LISTENER'S uncle*

WILLOW WOMAN— *LITTLE LISTENER'S aunt*

OLDEST BROTHER— *LITTLE LISTENER'S oldest brother, seventeen winters of age*

SECOND BROTHER— *the middle brother, fifteen winters of age*

THIRD BROTHER— *the youngest brother, fourteen winters of age*

MOOSBAS— *a young boy or girl from the village*

THE CHENOO— *a giant, greedy monster*

OTHER CHILDREN AND VILLAGERS— *other people in LITTLE LISTENER'S village*

Key Vocabulary
talented *adj.*, good at doing things

In Other Words
winters of age years old

ACT 1: **In The Village**

SETTING. *Several wigwams are in the background. Wigwams are dome shaped and covered with birch bark. Villagers are* **engaged** *in various activities. Two wigwams are set to the front. Between them* LITTLE LISTENER *stirs a pot over the cooking fire.* WILLOW WOMAN *adds wood to the fire.*

ACT 1, SCENE 1 UNCLE MUSKRAT *comes in carrying a string of fish.*

WILLOW WOMAN. Husband, you've done well!

UNCLE MUSKRAT. My fish trap was **good to us** today, my wife. There's more than enough for us and our niece and our three hungry nephews. With these fish and your big stew of vegetables, we can feed the whole village. Where are my nephews? Have they not come back from their hunt?

LITTLE LISTENER. No, uncle. My brothers have not yet returned. I am sure they will arrive soon and tell us of their adventures.

UNCLE MUSKRAT. Adventures? Well, adventures won't feed our village, so I hope they come back with more than stories!

LITTLE LISTENER. My brothers are great hunters. Don't worry, uncle. I am sure they will bring us more food.

WILLOW WOMAN. And even more stories! [*She and the uncle look at each other and* **chuckle**.] Look, here they are now.

[*The three brothers of* LITTLE LISTENER *enter, each holding a small bag. First, there is* OLDEST BROTHER *who is seventeen winters of age. Then* SECOND BROTHER *enters. He is fifteen winters of age. The* THIRD BROTHER *is fourteen winters of age. They are good hunters, but their imagination is greater than their hunting skills. They walk over to the fire, looking* **confident** *and proud. As they walk over, they are talking among themselves and* **bragging** *about their day of hunting.*]

Key Vocabulary
engage *v.*, to be involved in an activity
confident *adj.*, sure of oneself
brag *v.*, to express too much pride

In Other Words
good to us successful
chuckle laugh

ALL THREE BROTHERS. [*talking **in unison***] What a great day of hunting we had. Yes, probably the best day ever!

OLDEST BROTHER. Is the food ready?

SECOND BROTHER. It smells good.

THIRD BROTHER. Oooh, oooh! Fish stew! I can't wait!

UNCLE MUSKRAT. How was your hunting? I see you brought something back. What did you bring? [*He looks over at his wife and* LITTLE LISTENER *and winks.*]

[*The three brothers stop what they are doing and act **hesitant**. Not wanting to appear as if they are bragging, they act **modest** and wait for encouragement to share their stories.*]

LITTLE LISTENER. Yes, brothers. How was the hunting? Please tell us your stories.

OLDEST BROTHER. Ah, I had a very good day hunting.

UNCLE MUSKRAT. Really?

OLDEST BROTHER. Today I shot a very big deer.

WILLOW WOMAN. Where is it?

OLDEST BROTHER. Ah, it fell into the river and was swept away. [*He reaches into his **game bag**.*] But I did catch this squirrel.

SECOND BROTHER. And today was a fine day for me, too. I shot two deer. [*He **mimes** pulling a bow and arrow.*]

UNCLE MUSKRAT. Two deer?

SECOND BROTHER. Believe me uncle. And these were really big ones. Bigger than the one that Oldest Brother shot.

WILLOW WOMAN. [*aside to the uncle*] Any deer is bigger than no deer! [*She turns to* SECOND BROTHER.] And where are those two big deer?

SECOND BROTHER. I didn't bring them back with me.

UNCLE MUSKRAT. I can see that. But why?

SECOND BROTHER. [*hesitating*] Why?

LITTLE LISTENER. Yes, brother. Why did you not bring back those two deer?

SECOND BROTHER. Because there was this mountain lion, actually, two mountain lions. Yes! They grabbed my two deer and carried them off before I could stop them. Two mountain lions. **Imagine that!**

Key Vocabulary

hesitant *adj.*, feeling unsure, or not ready to do something
modest *adj.*, quiet and selfless, or shy

In Other Words

in unison at the same time
game bag bag that holds the animals he hunted
mimes acts like he is
Imagine that! Can you believe it?

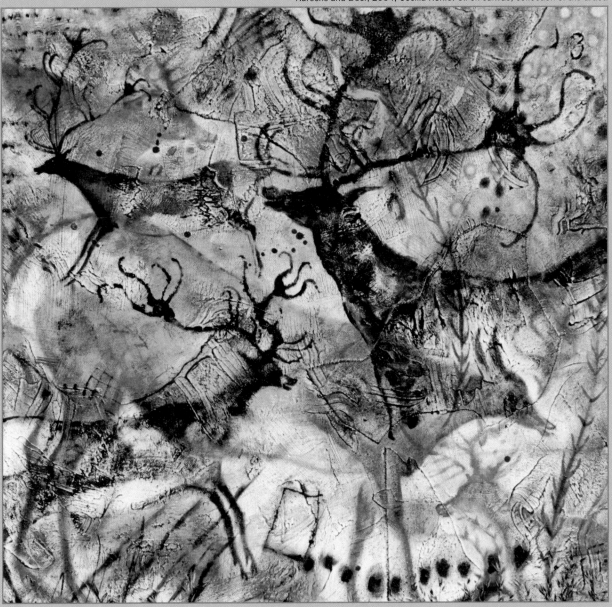

Aurochs and Deer, 2004, Cecilia Henle. Oil on canvas, collection of the artist.

▲ Critical Viewing: Effect Describe the shapes you see in this image. What effect does the artist create by overlapping these shapes?

UNCLE MUSKRAT. Yes, indeed.

SECOND BROTHER. But I did bring this. [*He reaches into his game bag.*] This very fat rabbit.

UNCLE MUSKRAT. [*to* THIRD BROTHER, *who is leaning over the cooking pot and reaching in to pull out a bit of fish*] And what about you, nephew?

THIRD BROTHER. What?

WILLOW WOMAN. How was your hunting today?

THIRD BROTHER. Today was a good day. It was very good indeed, better than my brothers. I shot three moose!

UNCLE MUSKRAT. [*holding out his hands and looking up at the sky*] Three moose!

THIRD BROTHER. With one arrow.

WILLOW WOMAN. One arrow?

THIRD BROTHER. I waited till they were all lined up so that my arrow went through them one after another.

UNCLE MUSKRAT. Of course. Why waste arrows?

WILLOW WOMAN. I hate to ask this.

THIRD BROTHER. Ask what?

WILLOW WOMAN. Those three moose. Where are they?

THIRD BROTHER. Oh, right. Well, what happened was that . . .

LITTLE LISTENER. Go on, brother. I am listening.

THIRD BROTHER. I went to try to find my brothers so they could help me skin those moose and bring the meat back to camp. But while I was gone a group of bears came and they dragged all three moose away. [*He reaches into his game bag.*] But I did get this fat **pheasant**.

LITTLE LISTENER. Brothers, you did well. We can add the game you brought back to what we have. We will share our **feast** with the whole village.

END OF ACT 1, SCENE 1

In Other Words
pheasant wild bird
feast food

ACT 1, SCENE 2 *The people of the village are all sitting around eating. They are talking happily, sharing food with each other. But one child in a circle of children around* LITTLE LISTENER *does not want to share.*

MOOSBAS. [*snatching food from a young child*] Give me some of that.

[*The young child looks upset but does not say anything.*]

LITTLE LISTENER. Moosbas, there's enough food for everyone.

MOOSBAS. But I wanted that piece of fish. It was a very good piece of fish.

LITTLE LISTENER. That's all the more reason to share. You know, if you are too greedy and selfish, you might turn into a Chenoo.

MOOSBAS. What is a Chenoo?

LITTLE LISTENER. Are you sure you want to know? It's getting dark and this is a scary story.

MOOSBAS. Tell me. I won't be afraid.

OTHER CHILDREN. Tell us. Please, please.

LITTLE LISTENER. I can see that you are all brave, so I'll tell you. A Chenoo is a huge monster whose hunger is never satisfied.

Its stomach hurts all the time because it is so hungry. And do you know what a Chenoo looks like?

MOOSBAS. [*hesitating before he speaks*] No.

OTHER CHILDREN. Tell us, tell us.

LITTLE LISTENER. It looks like a giant person, but it is covered with **shaggy** hair like a great bear. It has sharp teeth like those of the wolf. It has long claws like a mountain lion and red, **piercing** eyes. Long ago, it was once a human being. But it was a greedy, selfish human being who would never share his food.

OTHER CHILDREN. Didn't he remember to give thanks to the plants and animals for **providing food for** him? Didn't he help to provide for his village?

LITTLE LISTENER. No, he forgot to give thanks. He kept everything for himself. He forgot everything except for satisfying his own hunger. He became so greedy and selfish that one day his human heart

In Other Words
snatching taking
shaggy lots of
piercing scary, frightening
providing food for feeding

froze into ice and he turned into a horrible monster. Now the Chenoo wanders through the forest always looking for food. It eats anything it finds, even human beings! And if the Chenoo sees you, you cannot escape. It has a terrible cry, so loud and piercing that anything close to it that hears the cry will drop dead! Soooo . . . unless you want to become a Chenoo, too, you must always share your food with others.

UNCLE MUSKRAT. [*leaning over* MOOSBAS *from behind*] ARRRGGHH!

MOOSBAS. [*falling over in fright*] EEEEEYYY!

LITTLE LISTENER. [*helping* MOOSBAS *sit back up*] It's all right. It's only my uncle being silly.

MOOSBAS. I wasn't really scared.

LITTLE LISTENER. I can see that.

MOOSBAS. [*looking down at his bowl and then turning to the younger child*] Red Bird, would you like some more of this fish? This is the best part.

[LITTLE LISTENER'S *three brothers have entered from stage left while this is going on. They've been engaging in* conversation with each other and now come over to LITTLE LISTENER.]

OLDEST BROTHER. Sister, the three of us have come to a decision.

SECOND BROTHER. The hunting is no longer good around here.

THIRD BROTHER. We need to travel to the north where the hunting is much better. We will go far into the forest and camp. Because you love to hear our stories, we would be happy to have you come along.

OLDEST BROTHER. If you choose to come along, as the youngest, you will need to stay behind and take care of our camp. While we are out **on the game trails**, you will need to repair the bark-covered lodge, gather plants for food, and dry wood for the fire. Then, near the end of the day, you will need to cook our meal in the big pot.

SECOND BROTHER. Will you come with us on our hunting trip?

LITTLE LISTENER. [*She looks thoughtfully at the three of them.*] Thank you, my brothers. I will travel with you.

END OF ACT 1, SCENE 2

In Other Words
on the game trails hunting

Look Into the Text

1. **Recall and Interpret** What kind of stories do the brothers tell? Why do they decide to travel?
2. **Explain** What is a Chenoo? Describe how a person could become a Chenoo.
3. **Inference** Why do the brothers ask Little Listener to go with them?

ACT 2: **In The Forest to The North**

SCENE 1 *A hunting camp deep in the forest with a river nearby. Show trees around a single wigwam covered with birchbark.* LITTLE LISTENER *sits by the fire outside the wigwam stirring a cooking pot. Each night, when her three brothers return from their hunting, they all sit around the fire and speak of what happened to them that day. On this day, her three brothers came back from hunting, entering from stage left, with even more exciting stories to tell.*

LITTLE LISTENER. Welcome back, brothers. How was your day?

ALL THREE BROTHERS. [*talking at once and over each other*] Good. Very good. A great day. I have a great story to tell. Me, too. As do I.

LITTLE LISTENER. And how did your hunting go?

OLDEST BROTHER. Today, I found the tracks of a great moose and followed them across the hills. At last I caught up with the moose **by the fork in the crooked stream**. But when I saw how big it was, I knew that if I killed it, it would be hard to carry it back to our camp. And I already had caught enough game for the day. So I let it go.

SECOND BROTHER. Today, I found the den of a big bear. Just as I looked inside for it, I heard a sound behind me. There was that bear! But when I saw it was a mother with cubs, I knew it would not be right to kill it. I had to run for my life to escape.

THIRD BROTHER. Today, I was on the track of two deer. I had one arrow, so I waited until they were standing right next to each other. When I shot, my arrow went through the first deer and also killed the second one. Why have I brought home only one deer? After I put down my bow, a great mountain lion dropped from a tree branch. I picked up a stick and fought for a long time. See the scratch here on my hand? When it saw it could **now defeat me**, it grabbed the bigger deer and ran off.

In Other Words
by the fork in the crooked stream where the stream went in two directions
now defeat me win

[*The three brothers continue to brag about their day and their "great" deeds as hunters. After much laughing and sharing, they turn their attention to their sister.*]

OLDEST BROTHER. How was your day, sister?

SECOND BROTHER. Yes, tell us about your day, sister. What did you do?

LITTLE LISTENER. My day was quiet. I gathered wood, food, and plants. I made a fire and cooked our meal. Now let us eat.

END OF ACT 2, SCENE 1

Indian Camp, Eanger Irving Couse (1866–1936), oil on canvas.

⚠ **Critical Viewing: Setting** How does the setting of this painting compare to how you imagine the setting of the play?

ACT 2, SCENE 2 *At the hunting camp the following day.* LITTLE LISTENER *is waiting as always for her brothers.*

[*The three brothers come running on from stage right,* **stumbling**, *looking back over their shoulders, breathing hard from running. All three of them seem to be badly frightened and* **shaken up**.]

LITTLE LISTENER. What is wrong?

OLDEST BROTHER. I have seen strange tracks to the north, like those of a man but much larger.

SECOND BROTHER. I have also seen those tracks, but I saw them to the west.

THIRD BROTHER. I have seen such tracks, too. I found those tracks to the south.

LITTLE LISTENER. I have gathered berries and firewood, and I have made our meal. Now let us eat.

[*The three brothers dish out food for themselves and start eating. They all sit quietly around the fire. Finally the oldest brother speaks.*]

OLDEST BROTHER. Brothers, I think we were mistaken. I think those were only the tracks of bears.

SECOND BROTHER. Yes, I think you are right, Oldest Brother.

THIRD BROTHER. Ooh, ooh! I am sure you are right. Those footprints I saw were just bear prints that looked bigger than usual because they were in such soft earth.

[*The brothers* **gradually act relieved**. *They laugh and joke about being frightened by mere bear tracks.* LITTLE LISTENER *continues to eat her dinner and doesn't say anything. She is* **deep in thought**.]

LITTLE LISTENER. [*out loud but to herself; her brothers continue eating, laughing, and talking, and they don't hear what she says*] I, too, have seen those tracks. They were very close to the edge of the hill by our camp. And I know that those were not bear tracks. There is only one creature that could make such tracks. But I mustn't speak the name out loud, or I will invite it into our camp. I will remain quiet, but I must make a plan.

END OF ACT 2, SCENE 2

In Other Words
stumbling almost falling down
shaken up upset
gradually act relieved slowly start
 to relax
deep in thought thinking about
 something

ACT 2, SCENE 3 *In the forest. Actor dressed as* DEER ***grazes*** *peacefully in the foreground. All seems peaceful and quiet.*

DEER. [*quietly grazing on some leaves*] Munch, chew, swallow. Munch, chew, swallow. Munch, chew, chew, chew.

[*The* Chenoo *enters from stage left.*]

CHENOO. [*making grunting and grumbling sounds*] Garrnh. Garg. Arrk. Grrr.

[*The* Chenoo *then sees* DEER, *but* DEER *is looking in the other direction. The* Chenoo ***creeps up on*** DEER, *raises his big hands high in the air.*]

CHENOO. [*heads toward deer and lets out a loud howling sound*] YAAAAAAAAARRRRRRRHHHHHH.

[*This loud howl could be done by the actor or come from an amplified sound source. It should be very loud and piercing.*]

DEER. Yeeep!

[DEER *falls over dead. Other small animals, such as birds and squirrels, drop onto the stage as if falling out of the air and treetops. The* Chenoo *gathers up the birds and animals.*]

END OF ACT 2, SCENE 3

In Other Words

grazes eats
creeps up on slowly moves
    towards

Look Into the Text

1. **Confirm Prediction** Was your prediction correct? What did the brothers encounter on their trip?
2. **Character** Describe Little Listener. How do you know that she loves her brothers?
3. **Character's Motive** Why does Little Listener stay quiet about the bear tracks?

Mountain Buck, 2000, Durga Bernhard. Gouache on paper collage, Michael Densmore collection.

▲ **Critical Viewing: Effect** How does the artist create a sense of motion and other effects in this image?

ACT 3: **At The Camp**

SCENE 1 *The next morning the three brothers set out to hunt as usual, leaving their sister behind to care for the camp. LITTLE LISTENER is cooking by the fire. But this time she has a much larger cooking pot than usual. She does not do her usual chores. Instead she cooks up a big batch of stew. She gathers bearskin robes and spreads them out behind the lodge to make a* **place of honor** *as if for an expected guest.*

LITTLE LISTENER. I think this may be enough food. [*She gets up and looks behind the wigwam.*] And I have spread out all of our blankets to make a resting place back here. Yes, I think everything is ready. [*She looks toward stage left and cups her hand over her ear to listen. LITTLE LISTENER sits down with her back toward stage left.*]

[*Boom, boom. BOOM, BOOM. The sound comes closer until the Chenoo appears at stage left, walking heavily. It* **stalks** *forward slowly, lifting a foot and* **thudding** *it down. LITTLE LISTENER does not seem to hear it or move. The Chenoo seems* *puzzled by that, lifts another foot and thuds it down. Still, LITTLE LISTENER doesn't* **react** *.*]

CHENOO. Garrnh. Garg. Arrk. Grrr?

[*The Chenoo stalks closer until he is standing right over LITTLE LISTENER. He raises his arms up as if to grab her. Suddenly LITTLE LISTENER turns around and smiles up at the Chenoo in delight.*]

LITTLE LISTENER. Grandfather! I am glad you have come to visit me. [*She stands up and wraps her arms around the monster in a big hug.*] Oh, grandfather!

CHENOO. [*snarls*] Garrh! Garg! Grrrrrannnndfatherrrr?

Key Vocabulary

react *v.*, to show your feelings about something

In Other Words

place of honor special place to sleep
stalks moves
thudding loudly putting
puzzled confused

LITTLE LISTENER. Yes, grandfather. Welcome to our camp. [*She takes the* Chenoo *by the hand.*] Come over here, sit down, grandfather. I have cooked a special meal for you.

[*The* Chenoo *looks confused but takes her hand and follows her. They sit by the fire.*]

CHENOO. [*in a **rumbling** voice*] Grrrrranddaughter, I accept your invitation.

LITTLE LISTENER. Here, grandfather, you must be hungry. Have some of this stew. This food is for you to eat.

[Chenoo *takes some of the stew, eats it, likes it. Then picks up the pot and swallows down all of the rest of the stew.*]

CHENOO. Gooood [*he rumbles*]. Granddaughterrrrrr, I am glad you **greeted** me and invited me to your camp. I was about to eat you. But now that I have learned you are my **relative**, I will not hurt you or the others who live at this camp. Tell me what I can do to help you.

LITTLE LISTENER. Grandfather, I am glad you have recognized me. There may indeed be some things that you can do to help. Now, though, all I want you to do is rest. I know you must be tired, grandfather. [*She takes him by the hand and leads him behind the wigwam.*] I have made a place for you to sleep with these bear robes. You can rest until your grandsons come back.

CHENOO. Grrr. Grrrranndsons? I have grrrrrrandsons?

LITTLE LISTENER. Shhh, grandfather. Go to sleep.

CHENOO. Granddaughter, I am tired indeed. I will do as you say, and I will rest. [*She covers him with blankets and soon the* Chenoo *is asleep.*]

[LITTLE LISTENER *goes back to the fire and sits in front of the wigwam with a smile on her face. The three brothers enter from stage right, excited and happy, carrying what they have caught. They are eager to share their stories.*]

OLDEST BROTHER. Today, I have hunted well. Look at these rabbits I have brought back.

SECOND BROTHER. Today, I, too, have hunted well. See the fine goose I have here.

THIRD BROTHER. Ah, brothers, I have also had a successful day. I have brought home this fine deer that I killed with one arrow.

[LITTLE LISTENER *sits smiling in front of the wigwam, saying nothing.*

Key Vocabulary
relative *n.*, a family member

In Other Words
rumbling loud
greeted said hello to; welcomed

The brothers pause, surprised that she is not more excited. They notice the empty stew pot and that there is no food cooking. They look at each other, puzzled.]

THIRD BROTHER. Tell us about your day, sister. What did you do?

LITTLE LISTENER. My day was quiet. I gathered berries and firewood. I made a big stew and invited our grandfather into our camp.

OLDEST BROTHER. Grandfather? Our grandfather is here?

SECOND BROTHER. What grandfather?

THIRD BROTHER. Do we have a grandfather?

LITTLE LISTENER. Indeed. He is sleeping now. I will wake him, but you must promise me to greet him as your relative when he comes outside.

OLDEST BROTHER. Of course we will greet him. Wake him up.

[*LITTLE LISTENER stands up and taps on the side of the lodge.*]

LITTLE LISTENER. Grandfather, your three grandsons are here. They wish to greet you.

[Chenoo *sits up and then stands, looming over the three brothers who are **paralyzed with terror**. They stare at the* Chenoo, *so frightened that they cannot speak.*]

CHENOO. Garrrh?

LITTLE LISTENER. [*nudges* OLDEST BROTHER] Greet our grandfather.

OLDEST BROTHER, SECOND BROTHER, and THIRD BROTHER. [*together in shaking voices*] Welcome, grandfather.

CHENOO. Grrrranndsooons?

OLDEST BROTHER. [*still shaking but steps forward to greet the* Chenoo] We are glad to see you. It has been so long since we have seen you that you appear new to us.

SECOND BROTHER and THIRD BROTHER. [*standing behind* OLDEST BROTHER, *nodding their heads in unison*] Unh-hunnh.

CHENOO. Grrr, grandsons, I am glad you have greeted me as a relative. I see you have gotten food for my dinner.

[*The* Chenoo *reaches out to take the rabbit, goose, and deer from the three brothers, and stuffs the food into his mouth.*]

In Other Words
paralyzed with terror very afraid

LITTLE LISTENER. Grandfather, now that you have eaten, we have nothing for our own meal. Can you bring us some food?

CHENOO. Grrr? Yes, whatever you ask, I will do. [*The* Chenoo *goes off stage.*]

LITTLE LISTENER. Brothers, try to remember to be more friendly to our grandfather when he returns.

[***No sooner has she finished speaking than** the* Chenoo *comes **striding** back, **dragging** several large animals.*]

CHENOO. Here is a herd of moose. Is that gooood?

END OF ACT 3, SCENE 1

Teepees in the Moonlight, Ralph Albert Blakelock (1847–1919), oil on canvas.

⚠ **Critical Viewing: Setting** Describe how this image suggests peace.

In Other Words

No sooner has she finished speaking than Just when she finished speaking
striding walking
dragging carrying

ACT 3, SCENE 2 *The camp in the forest. Now, though, there are piles of tanned skins and much meat hanging on the drying racks. Another wigwam, this one shaped like a dome and covered with blankets, has been built to stage left of the fire.* LITTLE LISTENER, *her brothers, and the* Chenoo *are all sitting together around the fire.*

LITTLE LISTENER. Grandfather, you have helped my brothers with their hunting. We now have many skins **for trade** and have dried much meat to share with our people in the village. It is time for us to say good-bye. We must go back to our village now. Thank you for working so hard with us to provide for our village.

CHENOO. Granddaughter, I wish to come with you.

OLDEST BROTHER. Grandfather, you have been good to us and . . .

SECOND BROTHER. Grandfather, we have enjoyed being with you, but . . .

THIRD BROTHER. Grandfather, you will scare the other people in our village.

CHENOO. Grrrr, I fear you are right. I do not wish to frighten the people. Although I may not appear fearsome to you, my grandchildren, some people may be afraid of the way I look. Will you help me?

LITTLE LISTENER. Yes, grandfather. Tell me what we must do.

CHENOO. Make for me a sweat lodge and make it very hot.

[LITTLE LISTENER *and her three brothers make a big sweat lodge.*]

[*When it is ready, the* Chenoo *goes inside by himself and closes the door of the lodge. The three brothers use forked branches to lift the heated stones from the fire and hand them in through the door of the lodge.*]

CHENOO. Now pour the waterrrrr.

[LITTLE LISTENER *hands him a big pot of water.*]

CHENOO. Close the dooorrrr.

[*They cover the opening with blankets. Some time passes.*]

CHENOO. [*from inside the lodge*] Not hot enough.

In Other Words
for trade to exchange for other goods

[LITTLE LISTENER *opens the door, and her brothers pass along more hot stones. They repeat this three more times. During this time, inside the lodge, the* Chenoo *begins to sing.*]

CHENOO. GRRR-AH, WAY YA, GRRR-AH WAY YAH.

[*The hissing sound of water poured over hot rocks follows his chant.*]

CHENOO. RRR-AH, WAY YA! RRR-AH WAY YAH! [*His voice is loud, but not as loud as before. Hissing sound of steam again.*]

CHENOO. Rah-way yah, rah way yah. [*Now his voice is almost normal. Steam sound.*]

CHENOO. Ah way yah, ah way yah. [*His voice is very different now, like that of an old man. Suddenly it is very quiet and a long time seems to pass.*]

LITTLE LISTENER. Grandfather, are you all right?

CHENOO. [*in a small, weak voice*] Open the door. I am ready.

[*They open the door of the lodge and out steps not the giant* Chenoo *but an old man, no larger than any other* **elderly** *man. His hair is long and white. He holds his hands out to show them something.*]

CHENOO (NOW GRANDFATHER). Granddaughter, that is the icy heart of a greedy monster. Throw it into the fire, and I will be able to remain a human being as you see me now.

In Depth, 2006, Carmen Hathaway.
Acrylic on canvas, collection of the artist.

🔺 **Critical Viewing: Plot** How does this image relate to the Chenoo changing?

In Other Words
elderly old

Cultural Background
Sweat lodges are used during traditional Native American rituals. Sweat lodges are small structures heated with hot rocks and water to create a warm, steamy room. The lodges are seen as a place that gives healing and life.

[*The brothers are too afraid to touch it but* LITTLE LISTENER *uses two sticks to pick up the ice heart and throws it into the fire. From offstage the scream of the* Chenoo *is heard—but at a much lower volume than before.*]

CHENOO (NOW GRANDFATHER). Thank you, granddaughter. Now I can go with you and truly be your grandfather.

LITTLE LISTENER AND BROTHERS. Grandfather!

[LITTLE LISTENER *and her three brothers all join together in a big hug with their grandfather who had been a* Chenoo.]

CURTAIN ❖

About the Author

Joseph Bruchac

Joseph Bruchac (1942–) grew up listening to customers' stories in his grandparents' general store. Bruchac's grandparents raised him, and they were important influences in his life. His grandfather was an Abenaki Indian. His grandmother was an avid reader. Most of Bruchac's writing is about his childhood and his Abenaki ancestry. "I wanted to share those stories with my sons," he says, "so I started to write them down." Bruchac became the storyteller instead of the listener. He has written more than seventy books, hundreds of poems and articles, and several plays. He has been honored with the Lifetime Achievement Award from the Native Writers Circle of the Americas.

Look Into the Text

1. **Confirm Prediction** Was your prediction correct? What happened that you didn't expect?

2. **Characters' Viewpoint** How do the brothers feel when they first meet their "grandfather"? How do they act toward him?

3. **Symbolism** What does Grandfather have in his hands when he comes out of the sweat lodge? What does it symbolize?

Connect Reading and Writing

Vocabulary
brag
confident
engages
hesitant
modest
react
relative
talented

CRITICAL THINKING

1. **SUM IT UP** Review the Dialogue-and-Events Chart you completed as you read. Use it to summarize the play.

Dialogue	Events the Dialogue Reveal
LITTLE LISTENER. No, uncle. My brothers have not yet returned...	The nephews have gone on a hunt but have not returned.

Dialogue-and-Events Chart

2. **Describe** Describe the Chenoo before and after he becomes a **relative**. What does his appearance represent?

3. **Generalize** Recall how Little Listener **engages** Chenoo and how he **reacts**. Add examples of your own to form a generalization.

4. **Interpret** Explain the real **talents** of **modest** Little Listener and her **bragging** brothers.

READING FLUENCY

Expression Read the passage on page 647 to a partner. Assess your fluency.

1. My voice never/sometimes/always matched what I read.

2. What I did best in my reading was _____.

READING STRATEGY

What strategy helped you understand this selection? Tell a partner about it.

VOCABULARY REVIEW

Oral Review Read the paragraph aloud. Add the vocabulary words.

> Everyone is gifted, or _____, in some way. For example, you might be good at cooking or singing. Perhaps your parents or another _____ taught you how to fish or draw. It's good to feel _____ about your skills, but don't _____ about them. Likewise, don't be so shy and _____ that you are _____ to say anything. If an activity _____ your interest, say so. Others will _____ to that with interest, too.

Written Review Write a brief comparison of two **relatives** in the play. Use five vocabulary words.

 **WRITE ABOUT THE** (GUIDING QUESTION)

Consider How People Provide Food

In "The Girl and the Chenoo" who is the most **talented** at providing food for the community? Use examples from the selection to support your opinion.

Connect Across the Curriculum

Vocabulary Study

Use Context Clues: Specialized Language

Specialized language consists of words or phrases used in a certain place or situation. In some cases, specialized language may be related to a particular setting or culture, as it is in "The Girl and the Chenoo."

> [*He reaches into his game bag.*] But I did catch this squirrel.

The context shows that a *game bag* is a place to keep things caught on a hunt.

Use Context Clues First, without looking at the selection, guess the meanings of the words below. Then, look at the selection and check your guesses by using context clues.

1. wigwam (page 579, top)
2. game trails (page 584, col. 2)
3. bearskin robes (page 590, top)
4. sweat lodge (page 594, col. 2)

Listening/Speaking

Analyze Live Performance

Good actors visualize their lines and make performance choices that create strong, memorable characters. Their gestures, intonation, and phrasing can help bring their characters to life.

Sometimes actors will slightly change the script, adding or leaving out words. Actors may also give the audience a different impression of their characters than the one intended by the writer. For example, an actor might make a villain more sympathetic by speaking softly and hesitating before saying important lines.

Every actor's performance of a role is different.

Analyze and Discuss Pick one of the group performances of "The Girl and the Chenoo" you watched. Look at your notes and re-read Act I Scene 1. Work with a partner and discuss how closely the group's performances matched your own visualization of the scene. What elements of the group's performance were effective? What elements didn't fit your understanding of the script?

Use Appropriate Language

Act It Out With a partner, role-play Little Listener talking with another young girl in the tribe. Then role-play Little Listener talking to the Chenoo. Use appropriate language in each situation. Use conditionals to show how one event depends on another. Trade roles.

> If I collect berries, we will have something for dinner.

> Grandfather, I was happy that you had come to our camp.

Write About a Memory

Study the Models Sometimes when you write you want your readers to understand how one event depends on another. Use words correctly to describe a condition and its result.

NOT OK

Yesterday I picked berries in the forest. As I worked, I thought about how hungry everyone was. "If I **picked** enough berries, we will have something to eat. And, if my brothers **did** well hunting, we will make stew with the meat." Soon, I carried the berries back to camp. "If the cooking pot is full," I thought, "I **might** be thankful." As I entered camp, the smell of stew filled my nostrils.

> This writer confuses the reader by using the incorrect verbs to express real possibilities.

OK

Yesterday I picked berries in the forest. As I worked, I thought about how hungry everyone was. "If I **pick** enough berries, we will have something to eat. And, if my brothers **do** well hunting, we will make stew with the meat." Soon, I carried the berries back to camp. "If the cooking pot is full," I thought, "I **will** be thankful." As I entered camp, the smell of stew filled my nostrils.

> This writer uses verbs correctly to describe conditions and real possibilities for the future.

Add Sentences Think of two sentences to add to the OK model above. Be sure to use the correct verbs to show how one event depends on another.

WRITE ON YOUR OWN Write a paragraph about a memory you have of your family working together. Use correct verbs to show the relationship of events and their possible or imaginary results.

from The Omnivore's Dilemma

by Michael Pollan

VIEWPOINT #1

There Goes the Sun

1   Like most factories, **the industrial farm** is powered with fossil fuels. There's the natural gas in the fertilizer and the fossil fuel energy it takes to make the **pesticides**, the diesel used by the tractors, and the fuel needed to harvest, dry, and transport the corn. Add it all up and you find that every bushel of corn from an industrial farm requires about half a gallon of oil to grow. That's around seventy-five gallons of oil per acre of corn.

2   Here's another way to look at it. Calories, like the calories in food, are units of energy. On the industrial farm, it takes about ten calories of fossil fuel energy to produce one calorie of food energy. That means the industrial farm is using up more energy than it is producing. This is the opposite of what happened before chemical fertilizers. Back then, the Naylor farm produced more than two calories of food energy for every calorie of fossil fuel energy invested. In terms of energy, the modern farm is a **losing proposition.** It's too bad we can't simply drink the **petroleum** directly—it would be more efficient.

3   The factory farm produces more food much faster than the old solar-based farm. But the system only works as long as fossil fuel energy is cheap.

Eating Oil

4   My industrial **organic** meal is nearly as drenched in fossil fuel as a non-organic meal. Asparagus traveling in a **747** from Argentina; blackberries trucked up from Mexico; a salad chilled to thirty-six degrees from the moment it was picked to the moment I walk it out the doors of my supermarket. That takes a lot of energy and a lot of fossil fuel. Organic farmers

---

Key Vocabulary
- **viewpoint** *n.*, a way of thinking about something
- **organic** *adj.*, naturally grown

In Other Words
the industrial farm a farm that is run with machinery and technology
pesticides chemicals that kill unwanted plants and animals
losing proposition plan that won't work
petroleum fuel
747 jet plane

generally use less fuel to grow their crops. Yet most of the fuel burned by the food industry isn't used to grow food. Almost 80 percent of the fuel burned is used to process food and move it around. This is just as true for an organic bag of lettuce as a non-organic one.

5   The original organic food movement thought organic farming should be sustainable. That means it should be, as much as possible, a closed loop, recycling fertility and using renewable energy. The industrial organic food chain is anything but a closed, renewable loop. The food in our organic meal had floated to us on a sea of petroleum just as surely as the corn-based meal we'd had from McDonald's.

6   Well, at least we didn't eat it in the car.

"... the industrial farm is using up more energy than it is producing."

Food Miles and Jet-Setting Carrots

7   The term "food miles" tells you how far your food has traveled from where it was originally grown to your supermarket. In the U.S., that's usually about 1,500 miles—or 27 times farther than it would travel to a local market. For example, while carrots at the farmers' market are likely grown within 50 miles of your house, the carrots you find at the grocery store traveled around 1,800 miles (or about the distance between New York City and Denver). Many of our fruits, vegetables, and meat also come from foreign countries—and in a typical TV dinner, at least five of the **ingredients** are shipped in from abroad.

Key Vocabulary
• **ingredient** *n.*, a part of a mixture

Math for Locavores

by Stephen Budiansky

1   The local food movement now threatens to devolve into another one of those self-indulgent—and self-defeating—do-gooder **dogmas**. Words like "sustainability" and "food miles" are thrown around without any clear understanding of the larger picture of energy and land use. For instance, it is sinful in New York City to buy a tomato grown in a California field because of the energy spent to truck it across the country; it is virtuous to buy one grown in a lavishly heated greenhouse in, say, **the Hudson Valley**.

2   One popular and oft-repeated statistic is that is takes 36 (sometimes it's 97) calories of fossil fuel energy to bring one calorie of iceberg lettuce from California to the East Coast. That's an **apples and oranges** comparison to begin with, because you can't eat petroleum or burn iceberg lettuce.

3   It is also an almost complete misrepresentation of reality, as those numbers reflect the entire energy cost of producing lettuce from seed to dinner table, not just transportation. Studies have shown that whether it's grown in California or Maine, or whether it's organic or conventional, about 5,000 calories of energy go into one pound of lettuce. Given how efficient trains and tractor-trailers are, shipping a head of lettuce across the country actually adds next to nothing to the total energy bill. Overall, transportation accounts for about 14 percent of the total energy consumed by the American food system.

4   Other favorite targets of **sustainability advocates** include the fertilizers and chemicals used in modern farming. But their share of the food system's energy use is even lower, about 8 percent.

Key Vocabulary
- **viewpoint** *n.*, a way of thinking about something

In Other Words
dogmas beliefs
the Hudson Valley a place about an hour from New York City
apples and oranges unequal
sustainability advocates people who encourage farming practices that don't destroy resources

5 The real energy hog, it turns out, is not industrial agriculture at all, but you and me. Home preparation and storage account for 32 percent of all energy use in our food system, the largest component by far.

6 A single 10-mile round-trip by car to the grocery store or the farmers' market will easily eat up about 14,000 calories of fossil fuel energy. Just running your refrigerator for a week consumes 9,000 calories of energy. That assumes it's one of the latest high-efficiency models; otherwise, you can double that figure. Cooking and running dishwashers, freezers, and second or third refrigerators (more than 25 percent of American households have more than one) all add major hits. Indeed, households make up for 22 percent of all the energy **expenditures** in the United States.

"The real energy hog . . . is you and me."

7 Agriculture, on the other hand, accounts for just 2 percent of our nation's energy usage; that energy is mainly devoted to running farm machinery and manufacturing fertilizer. In return for that quite modest energy investment, we have fed hundreds of millions of people, liberated tens of millions from backbreaking **manual labor** and spared hundreds of millions of acres for nature preserve forests and parks that otherwise would have come under the plow.

8 Eating locally grown produce is a fine thing in many ways. But it is not an end in itself, nor is it a virtue in itself. The **relative pittance** of our energy budget that we spend on modern farming is one of the wisest energy investments we can make, when we honestly look at what it returns to our land, our economy, our environment and our well-being.

In Other Words
expenditures spending
manual labor work done by hand
relative pittance very small
  amount in comparison to another
  amount

Compare Across Texts

Compare Persuasive Texts

The Pro/Con essays in "Feeding the World," the Yes!/No! essays in "Would It Be Fun to Run a Restaurant?," and the essays from *Omnivore's Dilemma* and "Math for Locavores" are persuasive texts. Compare their persuasive techniques. Then **evaluate** how effective the texts are.

How It Works

Collect and Organize Ideas Make a chart like this one. List each selection on your chart. **Evaluate** the writers' arguments, support, and word choice. Do they **convince** you? Under *Is It Effective?*, write "Yes" or "No," and then give reasons for your opinion.

Comparison Chart

Title	Argument and Support	Persuasive Language	Is It Effective?
Genetically Modified Food: Pro	GM food is a good way to feed the world. New technology improves crops so there is more food.	"I learned firsthand about. . .poverty and hunger" "urgent need for new technology"	

Practice Together

Compare Ideas Identify the persuasive elements in each essay. Note each argument and its support. Then compare the two essays. Tell which essay **convinced** you. Explain.

Try It!

Complete the chart, then summarize. Which essay persuaded you? Why? You may want to use a frame like this one to help you express your comparison.

In "_____," the writer argues that _____. The writer supports the argument by saying _____. In "_____," the writer argues that _____. The writer supports the argument by saying _____. The more persuasive of these two essays is _____ because _____.

Academic Vocabulary

- **convince** (kun-**vins**) *verb*
  To **convince** means to persuade.
- **evaluate** (i-**val**-yu-wāt) *verb*
  To **evaluate** is to decide on the quality of something.

Food for Thought

GUIDING QUESTION

How can we provide for our communities?

Content Library

Leveled Library

Reflect on Your Reading

Think back on your reading of the unit selections. Discuss what you did to understand what you read.

Focus on Reading   **Evaluate Argument**

In this unit, you learned how to evaluate arguments made by writers. Choose a selection from the unit that you thought included valid arguments with sound reasoning and relevant evidence. List reasons that support your opinion. Trade lists with a partner.

Focus Strategy   **Synthesize**

As you read the selections, you learned to synthesize. Explain to a partner how this skill could be useful in the future.

Explore the GUIDING QUESTION

Throughout this unit, you have explored how people provide food for their communities. Choose one of these ways to explore the Guiding Question:

- **Discuss** With a group, discuss the Guiding Question. Remember, there can be many answers. Use details from the selections to support your ideas.
- **Interview** Conduct an interview with a partner. Take turns role-playing a character or person in one of the selections. Ask questions to find out the best ways to help end hunger.
- **Dramatize** With a group, create a skit about a community that faces a conflict in providing food for people. Act out your skit for other groups.

Book Talk

Which Unit Library book did you choose? Explain to a partner what it taught you about the ways people provide for or help their communities.

Resources

Reading Handbook

Reading Strategies

What Are Reading Strategies?

Reading strategies are hints or techniques you can use to help you become a better reader. They help you interact with the text and take control of your own reading comprehension. Reading strategies can be used before, during, and after you read.

Plan and Monitor

Before you read, plan how to approach the selection by using prereading strategies. **Preview** the selection to see what it is about and try to make a prediction about its content. Keep in mind that English is read from left to right, and that text moves from the top of the page to the bottom. **Set a purpose** for reading, or decide why you will read the selection. You might want or need to adjust your purpose for reading as you read. Monitor your reading to check how well you understand and remember what you read.

How to Select and Use Prereading Strategies	
Title:	Surfing the Pipeline
Author:	Christina Rodriguez
Preview the Text	• Look at the title: Surfing the Pipeline. • Look at the organization of the text, including any chapter titles, heads, and subheads. • Look at any photos and captions. • Think about what the selection is about.
Activate Prior Knowledge	• I know many people surf in the ocean on surfboards. • I've seen a film about people trying to surf on huge waves in California.
Ask Questions	• What is the pipeline? • Where is the pipeline? • Who surfs the pipeline? • Why do people try to surf the pipeline?
Set a Purpose for Reading	• I want to read to find out how people surf the pipeline.

How to Make and Confirm Predictions

Making **predictions** about a selection will help you understand and remember what you read. As you preview a selection, **ask questions** and think about any **prior knowledge** you have about the subject. If you do not learn enough additional information from these steps, read the first few paragraphs of the selection.

Think about the events taking place, and then predict what will happen next. If you are reading fiction or drama, you can use what you know about common plot patterns to help you predict what may happen in the story. After you read each section, confirm your predictions, or see if they were correct. Sometimes you will need to revise your predictions for the next section based on what you read.

Preview to Anticipate Read the title. Think about what the selection will be about as you read the first few paragraphs. Look for clues about the selection's content.

Make and Confirm Predictions As you read, predict what will happen next in the selection based on text evidence or personal experience. Take notes while you are reading, and use a **Prediction Chart** to record your ideas. As you continue to read the selection, confirm your predictions. If a prediction is incorrect, revise it.

Surfing the Pipeline

There Uli was, standing on the white, sandy shores of Oahu, Hawaii. Right in front of her was the famous Banzai Pipeline—one of the most difficult and dangerous places to surf in the world. Uli looked out and saw twelve-foot waves crashing toward her.

Uli had been waiting for this day for a long time. She was ready.

Uli grabbed her surfboard and entered the water. The waves were fierce and strong that morning. It took all of Uli's energy to swim out to the surfing location. Uli could see rocks sticking up through the water. She finally found the perfect starting point and waited anxiously to begin surfing.

Prediction Chart

Prediction	Did It Happen?	Evidence
Uli is going to surf at the Banzai Pipeline.	Not yet, but she will soon.	She is at the starting point to begin surfing. (text evidence)
Surfing the Banzai Pipeline will be hard for Uli.	Not yet, but it will soon.	New activities are always hard when I try them for the first time. (personal experience)

How to Monitor Your Reading

When you **monitor your reading**, you are checking to make sure you understand the information you read. You can check your understanding by keeping track of your thinking while reading. Pause while reading to think about images you may be creating in your mind, connections you are making between words or topics within the text, or problems you are having with understanding the text. When you read something that doesn't make sense to you, use these monitoring strategies to help you.

Strategy	How to Use It	Example Text
Reread to Clarify Ideas	Reread silently the passage you do not understand. Then reread the passage aloud. Continue rereading until you feel more confident about your understanding of the passage.	I will silently reread the first paragraph. Then I will read it aloud. The paragraph is more understandable now.
Use Resources to Clarify Vocabulary	Look up confusing words in a dictionary or thesaurus, or ask a classmate for help.	"... dangerous places to surf ..." I'm not sure what "surf" means. I'll look it up.
Read On and Use Context Clues to Clarify Ideas and Vocabulary	Read past the part of the text where you are confused. What does the rest of the information tell you? Are there nearby words or phrases, context clues or visuals that help you understand?	"... looked out and saw twelve-foot waves ..." Maybe "surf" means riding ocean waves.
Adjust Your Reading Rate	Read slowly when something is confusing or difficult. Keep in mind that English is read from left to right and that text runs down the page from the top. If you are having a difficult time understanding what you're reading, first make sure that you're reading it in the right order.	"Right in front of her was the famous Banzai Pipeline ..." I've never heard of the Banzai Pipeline. I'll read slower to find out what it is.
Adjust Your Purpose for Reading	Think of the purpose you set for reading before you started to read. Have you found a new purpose, or reason to read? If so, adjust your purpose and read on.	I originally wanted to read to find out how people surf the pipeline. Now I want to read to see if Uli actually does it.

How to Use Graphic Organizers

Before you read, you can use graphic organizers to prepare for better comprehension. For example, use a **KWL Chart** to record your prior knowledge about the topic.

KWL Chart

WHAT I <u>K</u>NOW	WHAT I <u>WANT</u> TO KNOW	WHAT I <u>L</u>EARNED

As you read, use a variety of graphic organizers such as diagrams and charts to help keep track of your thinking. Take notes about any ideas or vocabulary that confuse you. Writing down ideas keeps you actively involved in your reading. It also can help clear up any confusion you may have about information in a selection.

Use graphic organizers to capture your thoughts and to help you remember information based on how it was described in the text or based on the text structure. Here are some more examples of graphic organizers:

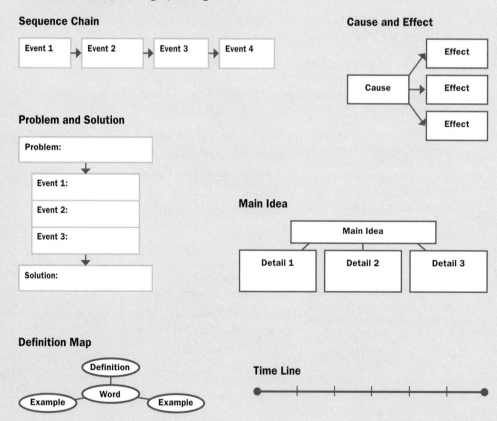

Sequence Chain

Event 1 → Event 2 → Event 3 → Event 4

Cause and Effect

Cause → Effect, Effect, Effect

Problem and Solution

Problem:
Event 1:
Event 2:
Event 3:
Solution:

Main Idea

Main Idea
Detail 1 | Detail 2 | Detail 3

Definition Map

Definition
Example — Word — Example

Time Line

Determine Importance

Determining importance is a reading strategy you can use to find the most important details or ideas in a selection. A good way to think about what is important in the selections you read is to **summarize**. When you summarize, you state the main idea and only the most important details in a selection, usually in a sentence or two. To summarize, identify the topic of a paragraph or selection, find the main idea and the most important details, and put them in your own words.

Stated Main Ideas

The main idea of a selection is the most important point a writer wants to relate to readers. Writers often state the main idea in a topic sentence near the beginning of a selection.

What's in a Name?

All college sports teams have special names. Many of these names are common, such as the Bears or the Tigers. However, more teams should have names that are unique and express the school's individuality. The University of Arkansas team names are Razorbacks and Lady Razorbacks. Virginia Tech athletes are called Hokies. Purdue has the Boilermakers. My favorite is the University of California at Santa Cruz's Banana Slugs and Lady Slugs. Slugs are unusual creatures. They have soft, slimy bodies and enjoy moist environments. These unique names make the college sports world a more interesting and fun place.

How to Identify Stated Main Ideas	
What is the paragraph about?	• names of college teams
Look for supporting details.	• Some teams have unique names like Razorbacks, Hokies, Boilermakers, and Lady Slugs. • The author feels these names make the college sports world more fun.
Eliminate unnecessary information or details.	• Slugs are slimy and enjoy moist environments.
Summarize the main idea.	• Unique sports team names are better and more fun than common names.

Implied Main Ideas

Sometimes a main idea is implied, or not directly stated. Readers have to figure out the main idea by studying all of the details in a selection.

The Future of Humankind

Many people agree that space exploration is important. However, when government spending is discussed, many people insist there are problems on Earth that need attention and money first. Don't they realize that the future of the human race depends on space exploration? Someday, the Earth's resources may run out. Paying for more exploration will allow us to learn more about space and how we can better care for our planet.

How to Identify Implied Main Ideas	
What is the paragraph about?	• space exploration
Find and list details.	• Many people feel other issues are more important than space exploration. • Our future depends on exploration.
What message is the author trying to convey?	• If we explore space now, we can better take care of ourselves and Earth.
Summarize the implied main idea.	• Space exploration should be paid for because it is just as important as any other issue. We could die without it.

Personal Relevance

An additional way to determine importance while reading a selection is to look for details that have personal relevance to you. These details may be important to you because they remind you of someone or something in your own life. For example, you might relate to "What's in a Name?" because you have a favorite sports team name. You might understand the main point that the writer is trying to make because you might agree that sports team names should be unique.

Make Connections

Making connections is a reading strategy you can use to better understand or enjoy the information presented in a selection.

As you read, think about what the information reminds you of. Have you seen or heard something like this before? Have you read or experienced something like this? Thinking about what you already know helps you make a connection to the new information.

Type of Connection	Description	Example
Text to Self	A connection between the text you are reading and something that has happened in your own life. A text-to-self connection can also be a feeling, such as happiness or excitement, that you feel as you are reading.	This part of the story reminds me of the first time I drove a car. My dad showed me how to turn and stop. I remember how scared I was. Thinking about this memory helps me better understand how the character is feeling as he learns how to drive.
Text to Text	A connection between the text you are reading and another selection you have read, a film you have seen, or a song you have heard. Sometimes the text you are reading might have a similar theme, or message, to something you've read, seen, or heard before. A text may also belong to a genre, such as mystery or biography, that you are familiar with.	This part of the news article reminds me of a movie I saw about space. Astronauts were taking a trip to the moon, but their spaceship lost all power. I can think about the movie as I read about the most recent space shuttle mission.
Text to World	A connection between something you read in the text and something that is happening or has happened in the world. You might also make a connection with the time period or era that a selection takes place in, such as the Great Depression or the 1980s. The setting may also be familiar.	This part of the text reminds me of presidential elections. I remember candidates giving speeches to tell why they should be president. Thinking about this helps me understand why the characters in the selection give speeches.

Use a chart like the one below to help make and record text-to-self, text-to-text, or text-to-world connections as you read.

Make Connections Chart

The text says ...	This reminds me of ...	This helps me because ...

Make Inferences

Making inferences is a reading strategy in which you make educated guesses about the text's content based on experiences that you've had in everyday life or on facts or details that you read.

Sometimes people call making inferences "reading between the lines." This means looking at *how* the text was written along with what is being discussed. When you "read between the lines," you pay attention to the writer's tone, voice, use of punctuation, or emphasis on certain words. Writers can also use irony, dialogue, or descriptions to infer messages.

When you add your prior knowledge or personal experiences to what you are reading, you can make inferences by reading all the clues and making your best guesses.

How to Make Inferences Using Your Own Experience

Read the following paragraph and chart to learn how to make an inference using your own experiences.

The Waiting

Rain pounded against the windows as Sarah stomped up and down the stairs. She only stopped going up and down to check the time on the clock downstairs every five minutes. She had been dressed and ready to go for more than an hour! Sarah had spent weeks picking out her dress and shoes, and she had even paid $50 to have her hair styled. She threw the flower she had so excitedly bought yesterday in the corner beside the camera. Sarah wondered, "Where is he? Will I have to go alone tonight?"

Inferences Based on Your Own Experience	
You read	Sarah had been dressed and ready to go somewhere for more than an hour. She spent a lot of time selecting her dress and shoes. She threw her flower in the corner by the camera.
You know	I know that people spend a lot of time choosing special outfits for events like dances, weddings, or parties. I know that my parents took a photo of me and my date for the prom last year. My date and I both had flowers for our outfits that night.
You infer	Sarah had a date to a special event that night. She was upset because she cared a lot about the event she was going to and didn't want to be late or go alone.

How to Make Inferences Using Text Evidence

Read the following paragraph and chart to learn how to make an inference by using clues that appear in the text.

The Waiting

Rain pounded against the windows as Sarah stomped up and down the stairs. She only stopped going up and down to check the time on the clock downstairs every five minutes. She had been dressed and ready to go for more than an hour! Sarah had spent weeks picking out her dress and shoes, and she had even paid $50 to have her hair styled. She threw the flower she had so excitedly bought yesterday in the corner beside the camera. Sarah wondered, "Where is he? Will I have to go alone tonight?"

Inferences Based on Text Evidence	
You read	Sarah had been dressed and ready to go somewhere for more than an hour. She spent a lot of time selecting her dress and shoes. She threw her flower in the corner by the camera.
You infer	Sarah had plans to go somewhere special that evening and was waiting for her date. She cared a lot about the event she was going to. Someone is late, and she is angry at him.

Ask Questions

You can **ask questions** to learn new information, to clarify, and to understand or figure out what is important in a selection. Asking questions of yourself and the author while reading can help you locate information you might otherwise miss.

How to Self-Question

Ask yourself questions to understand something that is confusing, keep track of what is happening, or think about what you know.

Ask and Write Questions Use a question word such as *Who, What, When, Where, Why,* or *How* to write your questions.

Examples: How can I figure out what this word means? What are the characters doing? Why is this important? Do I agree with this?

Answer the Questions and Follow Up Use the text, photographs, or other visuals to answer your questions. Write your answer next to the question. Include the page number where you found the answer.

How to Question the Author

Sometimes, you may have questions about what the author is trying to tell you in a selection. Write these types of questions, and then try to answer them by reading the text. The answers to these questions are known as "author and you" answers.

Questions to Ask the Author

- What is the author trying to say here?
- Does the author explain his or her ideas clearly?
- What is the author talking about?
- Does the author support his or her ideas or opinions with facts?

How to Find Question-Answer Relationships

Where you find the answers to your questions is very important. Sometimes the answers are located right in the text. Other times, your questions require you to use ideas and information that are not in the text. Some questions can be answered by using your background knowledge on a topic. Read the chart to learn about question-answer relationships.

Type of Answer	How to Find the Answers
"Right There"	Sometimes you can simply point to the text and say that an answer to one of your questions is "right there."
"Think and Search"	Look back at the selection. Find the information the question is asking about. Think about how the information fits together to answer the question.
"Author and You"	Use ideas and information that are not stated directly in the text. Think about what you have read, and create your own ideas or opinions based on what you know about the author.
"On Your Own"	Use your feelings, what you already know, and your own experiences to find these answers.

Synthesize

When you **synthesize**, you gather your thoughts about what you have read to draw conclusions, make generalizations, and compare the information to information you've read in other texts. You form new overall understandings by putting together ideas and events.

How to Draw Conclusions

Reading is like putting a puzzle together. There are many different parts that come together to make up the whole selection. Synthesizing is the process of putting the pieces together while we read. We combine new information with what we already know to create an original idea or to form new understandings.

Read this passage and the text that follows to help you understand how to synthesize what you read.

Distracted Drivers

Cell phone use in cars has steadily risen in the past decade. Studies from the Departments of Highway Safety show that the more distracted drivers are, the more likely they are to be in an accident. Lawmakers in some states have successfully passed laws requiring drivers to use hands-free accessories while a vehicle is moving. This means they may use an earpiece or a speaker-phone device but not hold the phone in their hands. Many people feel that talking on cell phones is not the only distracting activity that should be illegal for drivers.

Use text evidence from the selection and your own experience to draw conclusions as you read.

Drawing Conclusions	
Look for Details	The more distracted a driver is, the more likely he or she is to be involved in an accident. Cell phones are distracting.
Think About What You Know	I know people who have been in car accidents while talking on their cell phones.
Decide What You Believe	Lawmakers should continue to work on laws to stop drivers from being distracted.

How to Make Generalizations

Generalizations are broad statements that apply to a group of people, a set of ideas, or the way things happen. You can make generalizations as you read, using experience and text evidence from a selection to help you.

- **Take notes about the facts or opinions** Look for the overall theme or message of the selection.
- **Add examples** Think about what you know about the topic from your own knowledge and experience.
- **Construct a generalization** Write a statement that combines the author's statements and your own.

  Example: Using a cell phone while driving can make you have an accident.

How to Compare Across Texts

Comparing two or more texts helps you combine ideas, develop judgments, and draw conclusions. Read the following paragraph, and think about how it connects to the paragraph on page 617.

Graduated Driver's License Programs

More and more states are creating graduated driver's license (GDL) laws. Studies show that these programs help teen driver accidents and deaths to decline. The programs differ from state to state, but most GDL programs require an adult with a valid driver's license to be present when a teen is driving, and a teen driver must enroll in a certified driver's education and training course. Each state has various restrictions for teen drivers and punishments for when those restrictions are ignored.

Think About Something You Have Already Read In "Distracted Drivers," you read that cell phones are distracting to drivers and that many people feel it should be illegal to use one while driving.

Think About What You Are Reading Right Now Many states have graduated driver's license programs. Accidents involving teen drivers have declined.

Compare Across Texts and Draw Conclusions Both articles are about laws related to driving. Lawmakers hope that all of the laws they pass related to driving will create safer driving conditions for everyone.

Comparing across texts can help you foster an argument or advance an opinion. Having multiple opinions and facts from different sources makes your argument or opinion more credible.

Visualize

When you **visualize**, you use your imagination to better understand what the author is describing. While reading, create an image or picture in your mind that represents what you are reading about. Look for words that tell how things look, sound, smell, taste, and feel.

My Favorite Car Is a Truck

My name is Stephen, and today was a magical day. I've been working hard and saving money all summer. I finally have enough money for a down payment on a new car. Today my father took me to a car dealership to pick out my car. I immediately found my favorite vehicle. It was a red, shiny pickup truck with gleaming wheels. I climbed inside and looked around. The brown seats were sparkling clean, and the truck still had that new car smell inside the cab. I put the key in the ignition and turned it on. The quiet hum of the engine made me so happy. After a long test-drive, my father and I agreed this was the truck for me.

How to Visualize Using Sketches

- **Read the Text** Look for words that help create pictures in your mind about the characters, setting, and events.
- **Picture the Information in Your Mind** Stop and focus on the descriptive words. Create pictures in your mind using these words.
- **Draw the Events** Sketch pictures to show what is happening. You could draw Stephen climbing inside the pickup truck.

How to Visualize Using Senses

- **Look for Words** Find adjectives and sensory words: smell, look, sound, taste, and feel. Stephen uses the words *red*, *shiny*, *with gleaming wheels*; *brown seats*, *sparkling clean*; *new car smell*; and *quiet hum of the engine* to talk about the truck.
- **Create a Picture in Your Mind of the Scene** What do you hear, feel, see, smell, and taste? Examine how these details improve your understanding.

  I smell: new car smell   **I hear**: engine humming
  I see: red, shiny truck   **I feel**: texture of the seats, the key

How to Recognize Emotional Responses

Do any of the words in the selection make you feel certain emotions? Asking yourself how you feel when you read can help you remember the information.

Example: I feel excited for the main character because I know what it's like to pick out something new.

What Is Reading Fluency?

Reading fluency is the ability to read smoothly and expressively with clear understanding. Fluent readers are able to better understand and enjoy what they read. Use the strategies that follow to build your fluency in these four key areas:

- accuracy and rate
- phrasing
- intonation
- expression

How to Improve Accuracy and Rate

Accuracy is the correctness of your reading. Rate is the speed of your reading.

How to read accurately:

- Use correct pronunciation.
- Emphasize correct syllables.
- Recognize most words.

How to read with proper rate:

- Match your reading speed to what you are reading. For example, if you are reading an exciting story, read slightly faster. If you are reading a sad story, read slightly slower.
- Recognize and use punctuation.

Test your accuracy and rate:

- Choose a text you are familiar with, and practice reading it aloud or silently multiple times.
- Keep a dictionary with you while you read, and look up words you do not recognize.
- Use a watch or clock to time yourself while you read a passage.
- Ask a friend or family member to read a passage for you, so you know what it should sound like.

Use the formula below to measure a reader's accuracy and rate while reading aloud. For passages to practice with, see **Reading Fluency Practice**, pp. 624–647.

Accuracy and Rate Formula

_____	−	_____	=	_____
words attempted in one minute		number of errors		words correct per minute (wcpm)

How to Improve Intonation

Intonation is the rise and fall in the pitch or tone of your voice as you read aloud. Pitch and tone both mean the highness or lowness of the sound.

How to read with proper intonation:

- Change the sound of your voice to match what you are reading.
- Make your voice flow, or sound smooth while you read.
- Make sure you are pronouncing words correctly.
- Raise the sound of your voice for words that should be stressed, or emphasized.
- Use proper rhythm and meter.
- Use visual clues. (see box below)

Visual Clue and Meaning	Example	How to Read It
Italics: draw attention to a word to show special importance	She is *smart*.	Emphasize "smart."
Dash: shows a quick break in a sentence	She is—smart.	Pause before saying "smart."
Exclamation: can represent energy, excitement, or anger	She is smart!	Make your voice louder at the end of the sentence.
All capital letters: can represent strong emphasis, or yelling	SHE IS SMART.	Emphasize the whole sentence.
Bold facing: draws attention to a word to show importance	She is **smart**.	Emphasize "smart."
Question mark: shows curiosity or confusion	She is smart?	Raise the pitch of your voice slightly at the end of the sentence.

Use the rubric below to measure how well a reader uses intonation while reading aloud. For intonation passages, see **Reading Fluency Practice**, pp. 624–647.

Intonation Rubric		
1	**2**	**3**
The reader's tone does not change. The reading all sounds the same.	The reader's tone changes sometimes to match what is being read.	The reader's tone always changes to match what is being read.

How to Improve Phrasing

Phrasing is how you use your voice to group words together.

How to read with proper phrasing:

- Use correct rhythm and meter by not reading too fast or too slow.
- Pause for key words within the text.
- Make sure your sentences have proper flow and meter, so they sound smooth instead of choppy.
- Make sure you sound like you are reading a sentence instead of a list.
- Use punctuation to tell you when to stop, pause, or emphasize. (see box below)

Punctuation	How to Use It
. period	stop at the end of the sentence
, comma	pause within the sentence
! exclamation point	emphasize the sentence and pause at the end
? question mark	emphasize the end of the sentence and pause at the end
; semicolon	pause within the sentence between two related thoughts
: colon	pause within the sentence before giving an example or explanation

One way to practice phrasing is to copy a passage, then place a slash (/), or pause mark, within a sentence where there should be a pause. One slash (/) means a short pause. Two slashes (//) mean a longer pause, such as a pause at the end of a sentence.

Read aloud the passage below, pausing at each pause mark. Then try reading the passage again without any pauses. Compare how you sound each time.

There are many ways / to get involved in your school / and community. // Joining a club / or trying out for a sports team/ are a few of the options. // Volunteer work can also be very rewarding. // You can volunteer at community centers, / nursing homes, / or animal shelters. //

Use the rubric below to measure how well a reader uses phrasing while reading aloud. For phrasing passages, see **Reading Fluency Practice**, pp. 624–647.

Phrasing Rubric		
1	**2**	**3**
Reading is choppy. There are usually no pauses for punctuation.	Reading is mostly smooth. There are some pauses for punctuation.	Reading is very smooth. Punctuation is being used properly.

How to Improve Expression

Expression in reading is how you use your voice to express feeling.

How to read with proper expression:

- Match the sound of your voice to what you are reading. For example, read louder and faster to show strong feeling. Read slower and quieter to show sadness or seriousness.
- Match the sound of your voice to the genre. For example, read a fun, fictional story using a fun, friendly voice. Read an informative, nonfiction article using an even tone and a more serious voice.
- Avoid speaking in monotone, which is using only one tone in your voice.
- Pause for emphasis and exaggerate letter sounds to match the mood or theme of what you are reading.

Practice incorrect expression by reading this sentence without changing the tone of your voice: *I am so excited!*

Now read the sentence again with proper expression: *I am so excited!* The way you use your voice while reading can help you to better understand what is happening in the text.

For additional practice, read the sentences below aloud with and without changing your expression. Compare how you sound each time.

- I am very sad.
- That was the most *boring* movie I have ever seen.
- We won the game!

Use the rubric below to measure how well a reader uses expression while reading aloud. For expression passages, see **Reading Fluency Practice**, pp. 624–647.

Expression Rubric		
1	**2**	**3**
The reader sounds monotone. The reader's voice does not match the subject of what is being read.	The reader is making some tone changes. Sometimes, the reader's voice matches what is being read.	The reader is using proper tones and pauses. The reader's voice matches what is being read.

Practice Intonation: "American Names"

Intonation is the rise and fall in the pitch or tone of your voice as you read aloud. Use this passage to practice reading with proper intonation. Print a copy of this passage from myNGconnect.com to help you monitor your progress.

My name's Arturo, "Turo" for short. For my father, and my grandfather, and *his* father, back and back. Arturos—like stacks of strong adobe bricks, forever, my grandmother says.

Really, my name *was* Arturo. Here's why: Three years ago our family came up from Mexico to L.A. From stories they'd heard, my parents were worried for our safety in "that hard-as-a-fist Los Angeles." But Papi needed better work.

Rosa, my little sister, wailed, "'Nighted States, no! Too dark!" My brother, Luis, and I pretty much clammed up. I guess numbed by the thought of leaving our home, and a little scared, too, about the tough barrio.

Like some random, windblown weeds, we landed in L.A., home to movie stars and crazies and crazy movie stars.

From "American Names," page 16

Practice Expression: "A Lion Hunt"

Expression in reading is how you use your voice to express feeling. Use this passage to practice reading with proper expression. Print a copy of this passage from myNGconnect.com to help you monitor your progress.

Everyone was in a trance.

I felt that something inside me was about to burst, that my heart was about to come out. I was ready. Then we came face-to-face with the lions. The female lion walked away, but the male stayed. We formed a little semicircle around the male, with our long spears raised. We didn't move. The lion had stopped eating and was now looking at us. It felt like he was looking right at me. He was big, really big. His tail was thumping the ground.

He gave one loud roar to warn us. Everything shook. The ground where I was standing started to tremble. I could see right into his throat, that's how close we were. His mouth was huge and full of gore from the cow. I could count his teeth. His face and mane were red with blood. Blood was everywhere.

From "A Lion Hunt," page 38

Practice Phrasing: *"from* The House on Mango Street"

Phrasing is how you use your voice to group words together. Use this passage to practice reading with proper phrasing. Print a copy of this passage from myNGconnect.com to help you monitor your progress.

We didn't always live on Mango Street. Before that we lived on Loomis on the third floor, and before that we lived on Keeler. Before Keeler it was Paulina, and before that I can't remember. But what I remember most is moving a lot. Each time it seemed there'd be one more of us. By the time we got to Mango Street we were six—Mama, Papa, Carlos, Kiki, my sister Nenny and me.

The house on Mango Street is ours, and we don't have to pay rent to anybody, or share the yard with the people downstairs, or be careful not to make too much noise, and there isn't a landlord banging on the ceiling with a broom. But even so, it's not the house we'd thought we'd get.

From *"from* The House on Mango Street" page 60

Practice Phrasing: "On the Menu"

Phrasing is how you use your voice to group words together. Use this passage to practice reading with proper phrasing. Print a copy of this passage from myNGconnect.com to help you monitor your progress.

Cats arch their backs to look big and scary. Green grasshoppers blend into grass. Claws and teeth help animals fight.

These adaptations, or useful traits, are quite different. Yet they share one purpose. They all keep an animal from landing on the menu.

Camouflage helps animals hide from hungry predators. Did you know that it also helps predators hide from their prey? Why would predators need to hide? Sometimes they need help finding—and catching—dinner.

Some predators are awfully slow, and they can't run as fast as their prey. Camouflage lets them sneak up at their own pace.

Other predators are quick but sneaky. Clever coloring helps them hide from view. They lie in wait, hoping a meal will wander by. Surprise! The predator snaps up its prey.

From "On the Menu," page 92

Practice Intonation: "The Three Chicharrones"

Intonation is the rise and fall in the pitch or tone of your voice as you read aloud. Use this passage to practice reading with proper intonation. Print a copy of this passage from myNGconnect.com to help you monitor your progress.

"Pereza, Gordo, and Astuto, it's time for you to go into the world and make your fortunes."

He handed them each little bags. "You'll receive the same number of *pesos* I received from my *papá* when I was your age."

They opened their bags and found two hundred coins.

"Can't we stay here a little longer, *Papá*?" drawled Pereza, yawning, for he was lazy.

"This is impossible. How can we make our way in the world like this?" whined Gordo, who always looked for the quickest way to everything.

"I'll do my best, *Papá*," said Astuto, who always worked hard.

"With two hundred *pesos* and a lot of work, I did well for myself." Their father spread his arms out, indicating his large house. "Now, get packed, *hijos*."

From "The Three Chicharrones," page 114

Practice Expression: "Dragon, Dragon"

Expression in reading is how you use your voice to express feeling. Use this passage to practice reading with proper expression. Print a copy of this passage from myNGconnect.com to help you monitor your progress.

"Ladies and gentlemen," said the king when everyone was present, "I've put up with that dragon as long as I can. He has got to be stopped."

All the people whispered amongst themselves. The king smiled, pleased with the impression he had made.

But the wise cobbler said gloomily, "It's all very well to talk about it—but how are you going to do it?"

And now all the people smiled and winked as if to say, "Well, King, he's got you there!"

The king frowned.

"It's not that His Majesty hasn't tried," the queen spoke up loyally.

"Yes," said the king. "I've told my knights again and again that they ought to slay that dragon. But I can't *force* them to go. I'm not a tyrant."

From "Dragon, Dragon," page 136

Practice Phrasing: "The Civil Rights Movement"

Phrasing is how you use your voice to group words together. Use this passage to practice reading with proper phrasing. Print a copy of this passage from myNGconnect.com to help you monitor your progress.

In the South, segregation was enforced by Jim Crow laws. These laws had controlled the lives of Southern blacks since the late 1800s. Jim Crow laws said that blacks and whites must use different schools, restaurants, hotels, theaters, parks, sections of trains and buses, and so on. Even funeral homes and cemeteries were segregated! In the few places where blacks and whites shared public services—such as post offices and banks—African Americans had to wait for all whites to be served first.

In the North, segregation happened by practice and custom. Many African Americans moved to Northern cities during the 1940s, and whites responded by moving to the suburbs. African Americans found themselves trapped in city slums—poor neighborhoods where housing and schools were bad and where there were few jobs.

From "The Civil Rights Movement," page 174

Practice Expression: "Martin's Big Words"

Expression in reading is how you use your voice to express feeling. Use this passage to practice reading with proper expression. Print a copy of this passage from myNGconnect.com to help you monitor your progress.

After ten years of protests, the lawmakers in Washington voted to end segregation. The WHITE ONLY signs in the South came down.

Dr. Martin Luther King, Jr., cared about all Americans. He cared about people all over the world. And people all over the world admired him.

In 1964, he won the Nobel Peace Prize. He won it because he taught others to fight with words, not fists.

Martin went wherever people needed help. In April 1968 he went to Memphis, Tennessee. He went to help garbage collectors who were on strike. He walked with them and talked with them and sang with them and prayed with them.

On his second day there, he was shot.

He died.

His big words are alive for us today.

From "Martin's Big Words," page 200

Practice Intonation: "Speaking Up"

Intonation is the rise and fall in the pitch or tone of your voice as you read aloud. Use this passage to practice reading with proper intonation. Print a copy of this passage from myNGconnect.com to help you monitor your progress.

Principal Dunn thinks that Eve's leadership skills will take her far. "If this young woman set her mind to being the mayor, that would happen," he says. "I hope that does happen. She's been a great student leader."

Eve, who stands 4 feet and 11 inches tall, says that it's not always easy being a leader. "People look at me and they always underestimate me. They say 'Oh, this little girl can't do anything,'" Eve explains. "I feed on that. When people push you down, you've got to prove them wrong."

Sometimes Eve wants to run away from responsibility. But eventually, she remembers how much she likes making things better for others, especially at her school.

From "Speaking Up," page 218

Practice Phrasing: "Here, There, and Beyond"

Phrasing is how you use your voice to group words together. Use this passage to practice reading with proper phrasing. Print a copy of this passage from myNGconnect.com to help you monitor your progress.

The four planets closest to the sun are Mercury, Venus, Earth, and Mars. These planets have a lot in common. They are mostly made up of rock and metal, so they all have hard, uneven surfaces.

Because of their content, the planets closest to the sun have high densities. This means that these planets are made up of condensed, or tightly packed, materials. They also share the qualities of having slow rotation and solid surfaces.

The rocky planets closest to the sun are also alike in other ways. They are small compared to most of the other planets in our solar system. These planets also do not have many moons, or objects that rotate, or move, around a planet.

From "Here, There, and Beyond," page 248

Practice Intonation: "Earth and Space"

Intonation is the rise and fall in the pitch or tone of your voice as you read aloud. Use this passage to practice reading with proper intonation. Print a copy of this passage from myNGconnect.com to help you monitor your progress.

We breathe because our bodies need oxygen in the air. Oxygen is like food for our blood. We need it to survive.

In space, there is no oxygen. Because of this, astronauts do not breathe the same as they do on Earth. They have to breathe with the help of a protective spacesuit that supplies them with oxygen. A human being would not survive on a spacewalk for more than a minute or two without a spacesuit.

Compared to getting dressed on Earth, which takes just a few minutes, putting on a spacesuit takes 45 minutes. The astronauts must then spend lots of time breathing only pure oxygen before going outside the space station. This process is called prebreathing.

From "Earth and Space," page 268

Practice Expression: "Indian Summer Sun"

Expression in reading is how you use your voice to express feeling. Use this passage to practice reading with proper expression. Print a copy of this passage from myNGconnect.com to help you monitor your progress.

"Hi," he said.

I smiled. "Jerry?" It came out as Yerry, but it was too late to take it back.

"My parents and my sister," his chin pointed to Kathy, "call me Jeremy, my real name, but almost everybody else calls me Jerry. You can call me whatever is easier for you."

Jeremy! Kathy's brother—not her boyfriend.

"Why are you always so quiet?" he asked.

"*¿Hablas español?*"

He made a 0 with his fingers. "Zero."

"I have an accent." That came out without warning.

"What are you talking about?" he said, almost yelling because the music was loud. "It's cute!"

From "Indian Summer Sun," page 290

Practice Intonation: "A Natural Balance"

Intonation is the rise and fall in the pitch or tone of your voice as you read aloud. Use this passage to practice reading with proper intonation. Print a copy of this passage from myNGconnect.com to help you monitor your progress.

Beep! Beep! Beep! Your alarm goes off and you hop out of bed. You wash your face, chat with your family, eat your breakfast, and take the bus to school. Even before you go to school, you have connected with many people and things. All of the things you do affect the environment.

Your environment is all of the living and nonliving things around you. All across Earth, humans are changing the environment in different ways. For example: we cut down trees to build houses, plow fields to grow crops, build roads and parking lots, and empty waste into rivers, lakes, and oceans. We also use large nets and boats to catch huge amounts of fish. Activities like these greatly affect plants and animals in our environment.

From "A Natural Balance," page 326

Practice Phrasing: "Siberian Survivors"

Phrasing is how you use your voice to group words together. Use this passage to practice reading with proper phrasing. Print a copy of this passage from myNGconnect.com to help you monitor your progress.

The biologist remained calm as he carefully aimed his tranquilizer gun at the tiger. Then he squeezed the trigger and a dart soared through the air toward the cat.

Bull's eye! The dart struck Olga in her shoulder. She staggered and slowly slumped to the ground—asleep.

As the cat slept, Quigley and his team of scientists went to work. They had to be careful; a female tiger can weigh 370 pounds. They wanted to finish their work before the cat woke up.

The scientists took blood samples, checked Olga's heartbeat, and measured her body from head to tail.

They also put a radio collar around her neck. The collar sends a radio signal—a series of beeps—that helps scientists track an animal's movements.

From "Siberian Survivors," page 346

Practice Expression: "Mireya Mayor Explorer/Correspondent"

Expression in reading is how you use your voice to express feeling. Use this passage to practice reading with proper expression. Print a copy of this passage from myNGconnect.com to help you monitor your progress.

Mayor believes that local support for conservation is a key factor in bringing about change. "The local people are the very core of effective conservation. Without their support, the 'dream' of saving the planet can never become a reality. The rainforest is literally their backyard. Yet many Malagasy kids have never even seen a lemur. So I organize lots of field trips into the forest. Only by seeing how amazing these creatures are, will kids want to protect them." Mayor stresses the importance of providing education and opportunities for local communities to learn about the threats to animals and how they can help. She believes it will be critical to protecting the planet.

From "Mireya Mayor Explorer/Correspondent," page 364

Practice Phrasing: "Nadia the Willful"

Phrasing is how you use your voice to group words together. Use this passage
to practice reading with proper phrasing. Print a copy of this passage from
<u>myNGconnect.com</u> to help you monitor your progress.

Nadia rode behind her father as he traveled across the desert
from oasis to oasis, seeking Hamed.

Shepherds told them of seeing a great white stallion fleeing
before the pillars of wind that stirred the sand. And they said that
the horse carried no rider.

Passing merchants, their camels laden with spices and sweets
for the bazaar, told of the emptiness of the desert they had
crossed.

Tribesmen, strangers, everyone whom Tarik asked, sighed and
gazed into the desert, saying, "Such is the will of Allah."

At last Tarik knew in his heart that his favorite son, Hamed, had
been claimed, as other Bedouin before him, by the drifting sands.
And he told Nadia what he knew—that Hamed was dead.

From "Nadia the Willful," page 390

Practice Intonation: "Passage to Freedom"

Intonation is the rise and fall in the pitch or tone of your voice as you read aloud. Use this passage to practice reading with proper intonation. Print a copy of this passage from myNGconnect.com to help you monitor your progress.

I said to my father, "If we don't help them, won't they die?"

With the entire family in agreement, I could tell a huge weight was lifted off my father's shoulders. His voice was firm as he told us, "I will start helping these people."

Outside, the crowd went quiet as my father spoke, with Borislav translating.

"I will issue visas to each and every one of you to the last. So, please wait patiently."

The crowd stood frozen for a second. Then the refugees burst into cheers. Grown-ups embraced each other, and some reached to the sky. Fathers and mothers hugged their children. I was especially glad for the children.

From "Passage to Freedom," page 412

Practice Expression: "Zlata's Diary"

Expression in reading is how you use your voice to express feeling. Use this passage to practice reading with proper expression. Print a copy of this passage from myNGconnect.com to help you monitor your progress.

Thursday, September 17, 1992

Dear Mimmy,

Today is Alma's birthday. We gave her two herbal shampoos. We had a super time, but . . . I looked out the window and saw a flash. I thought it was somebody signaling, that's not unusual in war time. But . . . BOOM!! Shattered glass, falling plaster. A shell fell in front of the shop next door and I saw it all from the fourth floor. We rushed over to Nedo's apartment and watched TV.

The birthday party wasn't bad, but it would have been even better if that shell hadn't spoiled it.

–Your Zlata

From "Zlata's Diary," page 436

Practice Expression: "The Clever Magistrate"

Expression in reading is how you use your voice to express feeling. Use this passage to practice reading with proper expression. Print a copy of this passage from myNGconnect.com to help you monitor your progress.

One cold winter day, a farmer was carrying two buckets of spoiled food from a restaurant to his pigsty. As he was passing a coat shop, he accidentally spilled some of the slop on the ground. Sour cabbage, rotten eggs, and fish bones scattered all over the ground. Ugh! Ugh! What a smell!

The shopkeeper, who happened to be standing inside the door, saw this and was furious. He rushed out, grabbed the man, and shouted, "You dirty beggar! Look what you've done in front of my shop! It will be impossible to get rid of the smell! How are you going to pay for the damage?"

"I am so sorry," said the farmer. "I will clean it up right away. As for the damage, all I have is this coin."

From "The Clever Magistrate," page 464

Practice Phrasing: "The Constitution"

Phrasing is how you use your voice to group words together. Use this passage to practice reading with proper phrasing. Print a copy of this passage from <u>myNGconnect.com</u> to help you monitor your progress.

The Constitution has three parts. There is an introduction called the Preamble, seven articles that describe the plan of the national government, and the amendments, or changes to the Constitution.

The first paragraph of the Constitution states the basic purposes of the new plan of government: (1) to create a union where the states work together; (2) to create a system of laws that are fair; (3) to keep peace within the country; (4) to protect the nation from outside attack; (5) to improve the lives of all Americans; and (6) to make sure that our free society survives in the future.

From "The Constitution," page 484

Practice Intonation: "Kids Take Action"

Intonation is the rise and fall in the pitch or tone of your voice as you read aloud. Use this passage to practice reading with proper intonation. Print a copy of this passage from myNGconnect.com to help you monitor your progress.

Freedom of speech is an important right that you have as a citizen of the United States. You have the right to say what you want as long as it doesn't harm another person. Giving a speech is one way you can share your point of view and try to persuade others to agree with you.

During an election, candidates running for office give speeches and debate each other. In their speeches and debates, they tell how they feel about issues and try to get people to vote for them.

Many famous people have used speeches to make their points heard and understood.

A good speech stays in people's minds and can even earn a place in history.

From "Kids Take Action," page 512

Practice Intonation: "Feeding the World"

Intonation is the rise and fall in the pitch or tone of your voice as you read aloud. Use this passage to practice reading with proper intonation. Print a copy of this passage from myNGconnect.com to help you monitor your progress.

I was one in a family of nine children growing up on a small farm in Kenya's highlands. I learned firsthand about the enormous challenge of breaking the cycle of poverty and hunger in rural Africa. In fact, the reason I became a plant scientist was to help farmers like my mother. My mother sold the only cow our family owned to pay for my secondary education. This was a sacrifice because I, like most children in Kenya, was needed on the farm.

I have since made it my mission to alert others to the urgent need for new technology in Africa. New technology can help protect against hunger, environmental damage, and poverty.

From "Feeding the World," page 540

Practice Phrasing: "Soup for the Soul"

Phrasing is how you use your voice to group words together. Use this passage to practice reading with proper phrasing. Print a copy of this passage from myNGconnect.com to help you monitor your progress.

Q: *What kind of food do you cook at First Slice?*

A: Last year we made a lot of Cajun food to feed displaced victims of Hurricane Katrina. We also get a lot of requests for food with Latin flavors, dishes that might use tortillas. Smothered pork chops are really popular. A pot of greens is definitely a big thing, because most people on the street don't have access to farm-fresh produce. It's interesting: A lot of our clientele grew up in rural communities, and they know more about growing fruit and vegetables than I do. They ask really specific questions about the soil and the farming methods. It's wonderful that we can make that fresh-from-the-farm connection.

From "Soup for the Soul," page 558

Practice Expression: "The Girl and the Chenoo"

Expression in reading is how you use your voice to express feeling. Use this passage to practice reading with proper expression. Print a copy of this passage from myNGconnect.com to help you monitor your progress.

MOOSBAS. [*snatching food from a young child*] Give me some of that.

[*The young child looks upset but does not say anything.*]

LITTLE LISTENER. Moosbas, there's enough food for everyone.

MOOSBAS. But I wanted that piece of fish. It was a very good piece of fish.

LITTLE LISTENER. That's all the more reason to share. You know, if you are too greedy and selfish, you might turn into a Chenoo.

MOOSBAS. What is a Chenoo?

LITTLE LISTENER. Are you sure you want to know? It's getting dark and this is a scary story.

MOOSBAS. Tell me. I won't be afraid.

OTHER CHILDREN. Tell us. Please, please.

LITTLE LISTENER. I can see that you are all brave, so I'll tell you. A Chenoo is a huge monster whose hunger is never satisfied. Its stomach hurts all the time because it is so hungry. And do you know what a Chenoo looks like?

MOOSBAS. [*hesitating before he speaks*] No.

From "The Girl and the Chenoo," page 576

Glossary

The definitions in this glossary are for words as they are used in the selections in this book. Use the Pronunciation Key below to help you use each word's pronunciation. Then read about the parts of an entry.

Pronunciation Key

Symbols for Consonant Sounds				Symbols for Short Vowel Sounds		Symbols for R-controlled Sounds		Symbols for Variant Vowel Sounds	
b	box	p	pan						
ch	chick	r	ring	a	hat	ar	barn	ah	father
d	dog	s	bus	e	bell	air	chair	aw	ball
f	fish	sh	fish	i	chick	ear	ear	oi	boy
g	girl	t	hat	o	box	ir	fire	ow	mouse
h	hat	th	earth	u	bus	or	corn	oo	book
j	jar	th	father			ur	girl	ü	fruit
k	cake	v	vase	**Symbols for Long Vowel Sounds**					
ks	box	w	window					**Miscellaneous Symbols**	
kw	queen	wh	whale	ā	cake				
l	bell	y	yarn	ē	key			shun	fraction
m	mouse	z	zipper	ī	bike			chun	question
n	pan	zh	treasure	ō	goat			zhun	division
ng	ring			yū	mule				

• Academic Vocabulary

Certain words in this glossary have a red dot indicating that they are academic vocabulary words. These are the words that you will use as you study many different subjects in school.

Parts of an Entry

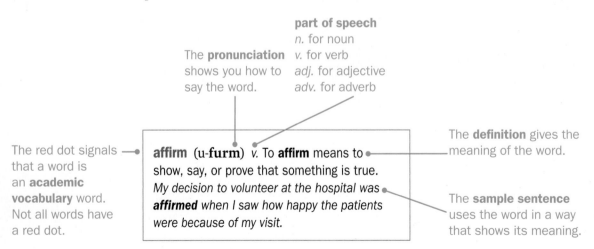

part of speech
n. for noun
v. for verb
adj. for adjective
adv. for adverb

The **pronunciation** shows you how to say the word.

The **definition** gives the meaning of the word.

The red dot signals that a word is an **academic vocabulary** word. Not all words have a red dot.

affirm (u-**furm**) *v.* To **affirm** means to show, say, or prove that something is true. *My decision to volunteer at the hospital was affirmed when I saw how happy the patients were because of my visit.*

The **sample sentence** uses the word in a way that shows its meaning.

A

- **adaptation** (a-dap-tā-shun) *n.* An **adaptation** is a feature or behavior that helps animals survive. *The cat's arched back is an adaptation that protects it.*

- **adjustment** (u-**just**-ment) *n.* An **adjustment** is the way you go along with or get used to a change. *It takes a while to make an adjustment to a new home.*

admire (ad-**mīr**) *v.* When you **admire** someone, you think highly of them. *Many people admire Rosa Parks, who worked for civil rights.*

advantage (ad-**van**-tij) *n.* When you have an **advantage**, you have a better chance to succeed than others. *If you are stronger or faster, it is an advantage.*

advice (ad-**vīs**) *n.* To give **advice** means to share wise words. *Parents give advice to their children.*

- **affect** (u-**fekt**) *v.* When you **affect** something, you change it in some way. *The rain will affect the water level in the lake.*

agreement (a-**grē**-ment) *n.* To have an **agreement** is to have an understanding with people about something. *We made an agreement to follow the rules of the school.*

agricultural (ag-ri-**kul**-chur-ul) *adj.* Something that is **agricultural** is related to farms or farming. *Growing vegetables to sell as food is one kind of agricultural business.*

- **amend** (u-**mend**) *v.* To **amend** means to change or to improve. *I amended the sentence to make it complete.*

- **analyze** (a-nu-**līz**) *v.* When you **analyze**, you separate something into parts and examine, or study, it. *Rey has to analyze the stem of the flower.*

- **appeal** (u-**pēl**) *n.* An **appeal** is a request for a response. *The school made an appeal to the community for more textbooks.*

- **appreciate** (u-**prē**-shē-āt) *v.* When you **appreciate** something, you understand its importance. *You appreciate an umbrella when it rains.*

- **approach** (u-**prōch**) *v.* To **approach** means to come closer or near. *The diver approached the dolphin.*

argument (**ar**-gyū-ment) *n.* An **argument** is a strong disagreement. *My friend and I got into an argument because he was late.*

arrest (u-**rest**) *n.* An **arrest** is when a person is taken by a police officer. *Police made many arrests of people during the Civil Rights Movement.*

astronaut (**as**-tre-not) *n.* An **astronaut** is a person trained to travel to space. *Astronauts need special equipment to travel in space.*

atmosphere (**at**-mu-sfir) *n.* The **atmosphere** is the air that surrounds Earth. *A spaceship can travel outside of Earth's atmosphere, but an airplane cannot.*

- **awareness** (u-**wair**-nes) *n.* **Awareness** is having knowledge of something. *To protect Earth, it is important to have an awareness of things that could harm the planet.*

B

banish (**ban**-ish) *v.* To **banish** means to send away or punish by making someone leave. *The referee banished the player from the game.*

bargain (**bar**-gen) *n.* A **bargain** is an agreement between people about what each person gives and receives. *He made a bargain with the salesperson for the car.*

- **benefit** (**ben**-e-fit) *n.* A **benefit** is something that is good for people, places, or things. *One benefit of exercise is that it makes you strong.*

biologist (bī-**ol**-u-jist) *n.* A **biologist** is a person who studies living things. *Biologists study how living things grow and where they are found.*

brag (**brag**) *v.* To **brag** means to show too much pride about doing something well. *The fisherman bragged that he caught more fish than anyone else.*

bravery (**brā**-vu-rē) *n.* **Bravery** means courage, or not being afraid. *Firefighters show bravery when they put out fires.*

brotherhood (**bruth**-ur-hood) *n.* A **brotherhood** is a close group of people. *A sports team can be a brotherhood.*

business (**biz**-nis) *n.* A **business** is where you do work for money. *Some people's place of business is in an office.*

C

camouflage (**kam**-a-flazh) *n.* **Camouflage** is a color or pattern that helps people or animals hide. *People use camouflage to help them hide when they hunt.*

- Academic Vocabulary

Glossary

campaign (kam-**pān**) *n.* A **campaign** is a series of actions by an individual or a group working toward a goal. *John F. Kennedy led a **campaign** to become President in 1960.*

career (ku-**rear**) *n.* A **career** is a job that someone does for a long time. *For twenty years, my aunt has made a **career** as a doctor.*

• **challenge** (**chal**-unj) *n.* A **challenge** is something that is difficult to do. *It is a **challenge** to climb a mountain.*

• **characteristic** (kair-ik-tu-**ris**-tik) *n.* A **characteristic** is a specific feature or trait that helps you identify something. *A loud roar is one **characteristic** of a lion.*

cheat (**chēt**) *v.* When you **cheat**, you act unfairly. *It is wrong to **cheat** on a test.*

citizen (**sit**-i-zun) *n.* A **citizen** is a person who was born in a country or becomes a member of a country. *All American **citizens** share the same rights.*

civil rights (**siv**-ul **rīts**) *n.* Your **civil rights** are the rights you have as a member of society. *Many people marched to gain **civil rights** for all.*

classified (**klas**-u-fīd) *v.* To be **classified** means to be arranged or put into groups. *Scientists have **classified** many plants and animals.*

• **community** (ku-**myū**-nu-tē) *n.* A **community** is a group of people in a specific area. *Our **community** started a recycling program.*

• **compare** (kum-**pair**) *v.* When you **compare**, you look closely at how things are alike. *We have to **compare** the two houses.*

complaint (kum-**plānt**) *n.* To give a **complaint** is to tell others that you are unhappy about something. *I sent my **complaint** in a letter to the editor.*

• **compound** (**kahm**-pownd) *adj.* Something that is **compound** is made up of two or more parts. *The x-ray showed a **compound** fracture in her arm.*

• **concentrate** (**kon**-sen-trāt) *v.* To **concentrate** means to focus on something. *Students have to **concentrate** when studying.*

confident (**kahn**-fi-dent) *adj.* A **confident** person is someone who is sure of his or her abilities. *You have to be **confident** to succeed.*

• **conflict** (**kahn**-flikt) *n.* A **conflict** is a fight between two people or groups of people. *My friend and I got into a **conflict** over a book she borrowed from me.*

• **connection** (ku-**nek**-shun) *n.* The **connection** between two things is something they have in common.

• **connotation** (con-ō-**tā**-shun) *n.* The **connotation** of a word is the set of feelings that is associated with it. *One **connotation** of the word "waterfall" can be "peaceful".*

conservation (kon-sur-**vā**-shun) *n.* **Conservation** is careful protection of something. ***Conservation** efforts protect national parks.*

• **context** (**kon**-tekst) *n.* **Context** is the surrounding text near a word or phrase that helps explain the meaning of the word. *The **context** of the sentence helps you understand what a new word means.*

contribute (kun-**trib**-yūt) *v.* When you **contribute** to something, you give your time or money. *The child **contributed** money to help people in need.*

• **convince** (kun-**vints**) *v.* When somebody **convinces** you of something, you think it's a good idea. *He **convinced** her to agree with him.*

• **couple** (**kup**-ul) *n.* A **couple** is two people who are together. *My grandparents are a happy **couple**.*

• **culture** (**kul**-chur) *n.* A **culture** is a set of beliefs and customs that a group of people share. *Dancing is a custom found in many **cultures**.*

D

damage (**dam**-ij) *n.* **Damage** means harm that is done. *I threw a baseball, which caused **damage** to the window.*

deal (**dēl**) *n.* A **deal** is an agreement. *If you agree to mow your neighbor's lawn for money, you have made a **deal** with your neighbor.*

• **debate** (di-**bāt**) *v.* To **debate** means to discuss different views of something. *In a **debate**, two or more people tell why they have different opinions or ideas.*

decent (**dē**-sent) *adj.* When you are **decent**, you are good and kind. *A **decent** person welcomes a new neighbor.*

• **Academic Vocabulary**

- **decision** (dē-**si**-zhun) *n.* A **decision** is a choice. *You make a **decision** when you choose clothes to wear each day.*

defend (dē-**fend**) *v.* When you **defend** something, you protect it. *A mother animal **defends** its young.*

- **definition** (de-fu-**ni**-shun) *n.* The meaning of a word is its **definition**. *Please look up the **definition** of five new words in the dictionary.*

delegate (**del**-i-get) *n.* A **delegate** is a person who has the power to act and speak for others. *The **delegates** met to talk about laws that would help people.*

democracy (di-**mok**-ru-sē) *n.* In a **democracy**, people have the power to vote for what they believe. *The United States is a **democracy**.*

deserve (di-**zurv**) *v.* When you **deserve** something it means you have worked hard to earn it. *If you study hard for a test, you **deserve** a good grade.*

desperate (**des**-pu-rit) *adj.* Someone who is **desperate** has lost hope. *The **desperate** team tried hard but lost.*

- **despite** (di-**spīt**) *prep.* **Despite** means even though or without regard to. *The man felt cold, **despite** his warm jacket.*

destroy (di-**stroi**) *v.* To **destroy** means to completely ruin. *The house was **destroyed** by a fire.*

determined (dē-**tur**-mind) *adj.* When you are **determined** to do something, you work hard at it. *The football team was **determined** to win.*

diplomat (**dip**-lō-mat) *n.* A **diplomat** is a person who represents his or her government. *To do his or her job, a **diplomat** lives in another country.*

discovery (dis-**kuv**-ur-ē) *n.* A **discovery** is the act of seeing or finding something for the first time. *The teen made an interesting **discovery** and took a closer look.*

disfavor (dis-**fā**-vor) *n.* When you show **disfavor**, you show that you don't like something. *A thumbs down is one way to show **disfavor** about something.*

disguise (dis-**gīz**) *n.* When you wear a **disguise**, you try to look different from what you normally look like. *A **disguise** can help people or animals hide.*

disgusted (di-**skus**-tid) *adj.* To be **disgusted** means that you dislike something. *Some people are **disgusted** by frogs.*

document (**dok**-yu-ment) *v.* To **document** something is to provide facts about it. *A research study must be **documented** carefully with facts.*

donate (**dō**-nāt) *v.* To **donate** means to give to people in need. *I always try to **donate** some of my money to help others.*

doubt (**dowt**) *n.* When you feel **doubt**, you are not sure. *The girl had **doubts** about the food after she saw how it was cooked.*

E

- **effect** (e-**fekt**) *n.* An **effect** is the result of an action or cause. *The coach's positive attitude has had a good **effect** on the team.*

- **effectively** (i-**fek**-tiv-lē) *adv.* Something that is done **effectively** is done in a way that works or gets results. *The teacher **effectively** taught us how to add and subtract.*

- **element** (**e**-lu-munt) *n.* An **element** is something that is part of a whole. *Copper is one of the **elements** use to make pennies.*

endangered (en-**dān**-jurd) *adj.* To be **endangered** means to be at risk of disappearing forever. *The ivory-billed woodpecker is an example of an **endangered** animal.*

- **energy** (**en**-ur-jē) *n.* **Energy** is natural power that is used to make things work. *We can turn the **energy** of the wind into electricity.*

engage (en-**gāj**) *v.* To **engage** means to take part or get involved in an activity. *She **engaged** her friends in a conversation.*

- **ensure** (en-**shur**) *v.* To **ensure** is to make sure or certain. *Humans should **ensure** that rainforests are protected.*

- **environment** (en-**vī**-run-ment) *n.* The **environment** is all of the living and nonliving things that surround a person, animal, or plant. *People plant trees to improve the **environment**.*

equality (ē-**kwal**-i-tē) *n.* When you have the same rights as other people, you have **equality**. ***Equality** is important within any group of people.*

erase (e-**rās**) *v.* When you **erase** something, you make it go away. *We can **erase** mistakes when we write.*

- **Academic Vocabulary**

Glossary

essential (e-**sen**-shul) *adj.* Something that is **essential** is needed for survival. *Food and water are essential for living beings.*

• **establish** (es-**tab**-lish) *v.* To **establish** something is to start it. *My friends and I established a yearly food collection for families in need.*

• **evaluate** (i-**val**-yū-wāt) *v.* To **evaluate** is to decide on the quality of something. *The test will evaluate how well the students are doing.*

• **evidence** (**e**-vi-dents) *n.* **Evidence** can be beliefs, proof, facts, or details that help support a conclusion. *The police need evidence to solve the crime.*

excessive (ik-**ses**-iv) *adj.* When something is **excessive**, it is too much. *That is an excessive number of pancakes for one person.*

expectation (eks-pek-**tā**-shun) *n.* An **expectation** is something you look forward to or have ideas about. *We had great expectations about our project.*

expedition (eks-pe-**dish**-un) *n.* An **expedition** is a trip or journey made for a particular purpose. *The explorer led an expedition through the desert.*

experience (eks-**pēr**-ē-ens) *v.* To **experience** something is to go through it yourself. *My first experience on a roller coaster was scary but fun.*

• **expert** (**eks**-purt) *n.* An **expert** is a person who knows a lot about a subject. *A ranger is an expert about wildlife in the area.*

explorer (eks-**plor**-er) *n.* An **explorer** goes to a place that is new to him or her to find information about it. *Astronauts are explorers of our universe.*

extinct (eks-**stingt**) *adj.* Something that is **extinct** is no longer living. *The dodo bird became extinct because people hunted too many over time.*

F

• **feature** (**fē**-chur) *n.* **Features** of something are its parts or details. *Some of the features of Earth's surface include mountains, lakes, and trees.*

• **focus** (**fō**-kus) *v.* When you **focus** on something, you pay attention to it. *You must focus all your attention to hear what the speaker is saying.*

forbid (for-**bid**) *v.* To **forbid** means to order not to do something. *The sign forbids anyone to swim in this area.*

fortune (**for**-chun) *n.* A **fortune** is a large amount of money or a lot of good things. *The woman worked hard to earn her fortune.*

founder (**fown**-der) *n.* A **founder** is a person who starts something. *My uncle is the founder of his own company.*

frustration (frus-**trā**-shun) *n.* When you feel **frustration**, you feel angry because you cannot do something. *If you do not understand your homework, you may feel frustration.*

furious (**fyur**-ē-us) *adj.* Someone who is **furious** is very angry. *The man was furious when his car was hit.*

G

gene (jēn) *n.* A **gene** is a physical unit that controls what a living cell is like. *The color of your hair depends on your genes.*

government (**guv**-urn-ment) *n.* A **government** is a group of people who are in charge of a country, state, or city. *The U.S. government is run by many people.*

grief (grēf) *n.* To feel **grief** is to feel very sad. *My friend felt grief when her dog died.*

H

habitat (**hab**-i-tat) *n.* A **habitat** is the place where a plant or an animal naturally lives. *The habitat of polar bears is the cold Arctic.*

hesitant (**hez**-i-tunt) *adj.* A **hesitant** person feels unsure, or not ready to do something. *The boy was hesitant to pet the rabbit for fear that it would bite.*

humanity (hū-**man**-i-tē) *n.* **Humanity** is kindness and caring about the suffering of others. *Firefighters show humanity by doing what they must to save others.*

I

• **identify** (ī-**den**-ti-fī) *v.* When you **identify** something, you name it or tell what it is. *Can you identify which jacket is yours?*

ignore (ig-**nor**) *v.* To **ignore** means to pay no attention to something. *It is best to ignore people who are bullies.*

• Academic Vocabulary

illegal (i-**lē**-gul) *adj.* Something that is **illegal** is against the law. *It is **illegal** to hunt in some areas.*

• **image** (**im**-ij) *n.* An **image** is a mental picture of something. *Moira has a mental **image** of her grandmother baking cookies.*

• **impact** (**im**-pakt) *v.* To **impact** means to have an effect. *The new salespeople will continue to **impact** the sales numbers, pushing them up.*

increase (in-**krēs**) *v.* To **increase** means to become larger in number or size. *The size of my family **increased** when my brother was born.*

independence (in-di-**pen**-duns) *n.* **Independence** means freedom from control by others. *The U.S. celebrates its **independence** with fireworks on the Fourth of July.*

• **individual** (in-de-**vij**-yū-wul) **1** *adj.* Something that is individual is separate from other things. *Most students like to receive **individual** attention from their teacher.* **2** *n.* An **individual** is one person. *Only one **individual** can sit on the chair.*

• **inevitable** (i-**nev**-i-tu-bul) *adj.* Something that is **inevitable** will happen no matter what. *If you throw a ball up, it is **inevitable** that it will come down.*

influence (**in**-flü-uns) *v.* When people **influence** you, they change the way you think. *Martin Luther King, Jr. **influenced** people to work toward equality.*

informed (in-**formd**) *adj.* To be **informed** is to have knowledge. *It is our duty to be **informed** about issues.*

ingredient (in-**grē**-dē-unt) *n.* An **ingredient** is something that is part of a mixture. *Flour, sugar, and butter are **ingredients** used to make cookies.*

innocent (**in**-u-sent) *adj.* Someone who is **innocent** is without guilt. *The puppy looks **innocent** and sweet.*

insist (in-**sist**) *v.* To **insist** means to demand or to keep saying. *The child **insisted** on walking the other direction.*

inspiration (in-spu-**rā**-shun) *n.* An **inspiration** is a reason for doing or creating something. *Artists often find their **inspiration** in the beauty of nature.*

• **integrate** (**in**-te-grāt) *v.* When you **integrate** groups, you bring them together. *Martin Luther King, Jr. worked to **integrate** schools.*

• **involved** (in-**vahlvd**) *adj.* To get **involved** is to become a part of something. *Many people are **involved** in improving their communities.*

J

• **judgment** (**juj**-ment) *n.* **Judgment** is the ability to make good decisions. *He used good **judgment** by coming home before it started to rain.*

justice (**jus**-tis) *n.* **Justice** means fairness. *Our court system is set up to give everyone an opportunity for **justice**.*

K

kingdom (**king**-dum) *n.* A **kingdom** is a land or area ruled by a king or a queen. *The **kingdom** was made up of three countries.*

L

landlord (**land**-lawrd) *n.* A **landlord** is a person who owns land or buildings. *My **landlord** always makes sure the building is clean.*

leadership (**lēd**-ur-ship) *n.* **Leadership** means guiding others in what to do. *A person who helps others shows **leadership**.*

• **literal** (**lit**-ur-al) *adj.* The **literal** meaning of a word is its exact meaning. *Always use **literal** words when explaining things to children.*

• **location** (lō-**kā**-shun) *n.* The **location** is the site or place where a person lives. *She lives in a **location** close to the beach.*

• **logical** (**lah**-ji-kul) *adj.* When something is **logical**, it makes sense or is reasonable. *It is **logical** to close the windows when it rains.*

M

measurement (**mezh**-ur-ment) *n.* A **measurement** is the size or quantity of something. *I took **measurements** of the rock to find out how long it is.*

memory (**mem**-e-rī) *n.* A **memory** is something remembered. *Looking through family photographs can bring back **memories** of good times.*

Glossary

mercy (**mur**-sē) *n.* **Mercy** is kindness to someone in trouble. *My mom showed* ***mercy*** *when I spilled food all over the floor.*

mission (**mish**-un) *n.* A **mission** is the goal of someone's work. *An astronaut's* ***mission*** *is to explore space.*

modest (**mod**-ist) *adj.* A **modest** person does not act overly proud of an accomplishment or success. *The girl was* ***modest*** *about winning first prize.*

• **modified** (**mod**-i-fīd) *adj.* Something that has been **modified** has been changed. *We* ***modified*** *the recipe to feed more people.*

movement (**müv**-ment) *n.* A **movement** is a group of people working together to make a change. *People of all races took part in the Civil Rights* ***Movement***.

N

• **negative** (**neg**-u-tiv) *adj.* If you have a **negative** opinion about something, you don't like it. *My sister was* ***negative*** *about my idea.*

nervous (**ner**-vus) *adj.* When you are **nervous**, you feel worried. *The basketball player felt* ***nervous*** *before the game.*

O

obey (ō-**bā**) *v.* To **obey** is to follow an order. *If your parents tell you to clean your room, you must* ***obey*** *them.*

• **obvious** (**ob**-vē-us) *adj.* Something that is **obvious** is easily seen or understood. *It was* ***obvious*** *he was sick because he had a fever.*

opinion (ō-**pin**-yun) *n.* An **opinion** is a belief about something. *Reporters ask people for their* ***opinions*** *about events in the news.*

opportunity (op-ur-**tü**-ni-tē) *n.* An **opportunity** is a chance to do something. *My teacher gave me the* ***opportunity*** *to tell my ideas to the other students.*

organic (or-**gan**-ik) *adj.* **Organic** refers to a type of food that is all natural. ***Organic*** *fruits and vegetables are grown without chemicals.*

organization (or-ge-nī-**zā**-shun) *n.* An **organization** is a group of people who work toward a common goal. *The Red Cross is an* ***organization***.

• **organize** (**or**-ge-nīz) *v.* To **organize** means to arrange things in a certain order. *Please* ***organize*** *the students by height.*

• **origin** (**or**-u-jin) *n.* The **origin** of something is its source or beginning. *The map shows the* ***origin*** *of the river.*

overcome (ō-vur-**kum**) *v.* To **overcome** something is to succeed at something that is difficult. *If you used to be afraid of dogs but now you like them, you have* ***overcome*** *your fear.*

P

pact (pakt) *n.* A **pact** is a promise between people. *Friends might make a* ***pact*** *to always help each other.*

peace (pēs) *n.* **Peace** is freedom from war and fighting. *Many people hope for* ***peace*** *in the world.*

permission (pur-**mish**-un) *n.* When you have **permission**, you are allowed to do something. *You must ask* ***permission*** *to go onto private property.*

• **perspective** (pur-**spek**-tiv) *n.* A **perspective** is a way of thinking about something. *My teacher's* ***perspective*** *on music is that everyone should learn to play.*

persuade (pur-**swād**) *v.* To **persuade** means to try to make others agree. *The student* ***persuaded*** *us by giving a strong speech with good ideas.*

petition (pe-**tish**-un) *n.* A **petition** is a written request for a government or leader to take action. *If enough people sign our* ***petition***, *it may convince the mayor to do what we ask.*

plague (plāg) *v.* When something really bothers you, it **plagues** you. *The thought of the Monday morning math test* ***plagued*** *her all weekend.*

plead (plēd) *v.* To **plead** means to strongly ask for something. *A student might* ***plead*** *for a larger allowance.*

poacher (**pō**-chur) *n.* A **poacher** is a person who hunts plants or animals illegally. ***Poachers*** *are a problem to endangered wildlife.*

politics (**pol**-i-tiks) *n.* **Politics** are people's beliefs about government and its plans. *People with similar* ***politics*** *came to the convention.*

pollution (pul-lü-shun) *n.* **Pollution** is waste, chemicals, and gases that have a harmful effect. *Air and water **pollution** hurt living things.*

population (pop-yū-lā-shun) *n.* **Population** is the number of plants or animals in a group. *The human **population** of Earth is more than six billion.*

• **positive** (pahz-u-tiv) *adj.* **Positive** means good or hopeful. *If you have a **positive** attitude, you think things are good.*

preach (prēch) *v.* To **preach** is to tell people what you believe is right. *The speaker **preached** the importance of kindness to all.*

predator (pre-duh-tur) *n.* A **predator** is an animal that eats other animals for food. *Lions and tigers are **predators**.*

• **predict** (prē-dikt) *v.* When you **predict**, you guess about something or tell what will happen. *We will **predict** what happens next in the story.*

prejudice (prej-ū-dis) *n.* If you have **prejudice**, you judge things and people before you know about them. *Many people fought to end **prejudice**.*

prey (prā) *n.* **Prey** is an animal that other animals eat. *A mouse is **prey** for a snake.*

pride (prīd) *n.* When you feel **pride**, you feel good about something you or someone else does. *The boy felt **pride** when he graduated from high school.*

problem (prahb-lum) *n.* A **problem** is something you have to solve or fix. *You can solve a math **problem**.*

• **process** (präs-es) *n.* A **process** is a series of actions that lead to a result. *The **process** of building the house took a year.*

• **promote** (prō-mōt) *v.* To **promote** something is to tell others that it is a good thing. *The firemen **promote** safety to the students.*

• **propaganda** (prop-u-gan-da) *n.* **Propaganda** is the use of faulty methods to persuade an audience. *The report was **propaganda** and not based on facts.*

property (prop-er-tē) *n.* **Property** is what someone owns, like a house or land. *People can sell their **property** to someone else.*

protest (prō-test) *v.* To **protest** something means to show you are against it. *Americans **protested** unfair treatment of African Americans.*

punishment (pun-ish-ment) *n.* A **punishment** is a penalty caused by doing something bad. *We were noisy during class, so as **punishment** we had to stay after school.*

• **purpose** (pur-pus) *n.* A **purpose** is a reason for doing something. *His **purpose** for going to the store was to buy milk.*

Q

quest (kwest) *n.* A **quest** is a journey or trip to find something. *The knight is on a **quest** to find the dragon's cave.*

R

• **react** (rē-akt) *v.* To **react** means to show your feelings about something. *A person may **react** in fear to a scary movie.*

reality (rē-al-it-ē) *n.* **Reality** is what people actually experience in life. *I wish I could have whatever I liked, but the **reality** is that I must work to pay for things.*

recall (rē-kawl) *v.* To **recall** means to remember. *The student tried to **recall** the answer to a test question.*

recite (ri-sīt) *v.* When you **recite** something, you are speaking or reading something aloud in public. *Every morning before class, we **recite** the Pledge of Allegiance.*

refugee (ref-yu-jē) *n.* A person who must leave his or her home or country to be safe is a **refugee**. *A **refugee** may have to live with just a few belongings.*

refuse (ri-fūz) *v.* To **refuse** means to choose not to do something. *The child **refused** to eat any more food.*

• **relate** (ri-lāt) *v.* When you **relate** things, you show how they are connected. *The report should **relate** how ice and water are alike.*

relative (rel-u-tiv) *n.* A **relative** is a family member. *I love my **relatives**, but I am especially close with my grandmother.*

relent (ri-lent) *v.* To **relent** means to stop. *After flooding the town, the rain finally **relented**.*

remind (ri-**mīnd**) v. To **remind** is to help someone remember something or tell them again. *As I left for school, my mom **reminded** me to take my lunch.*

rent (**rent**) n. When you pay **rent**, you pay money to the owner of a property to live there. *The mother paid **rent** for the family's apartment every month.*

represent (**rep**-ri-zent) v. To **represent** means to speak or act for a person or group. *The president **represents** all of the people of his or her country.*

• **research** (**rē**-surch) n. **Research** is a collection of information about something. *There is a lot of **research** on the solar system.*

• **response** (ri-**spons**) n. A **response** is an answer or reply to something that has happened or has been said. *The fireman had a quick **response** to the alarm bell.*

rotation (rō-**tā**-shun) n. **Rotation** is the spinning of an object, such as a planet. *Earth's **rotation** is what gives us night and day.*

routine (rü-**tēn**) n. A **routine** is a normal series of actions that you repeat. *As part of my daily morning **routine**, I brush my teeth.*

S

• **scale** (**skāl**) n. A **scale** is a graphic organizer that shows how a series of items are related. *The **scale** on the map measures distance in miles.*

scrape (**skrāp**) v. When you **scrape** something, you damage it. *Did you **scrape** your knee when you fell?*

segregation (seg-ri-**gā**-shun) n. **Segregation** is when people are kept apart. *The **segregation** of African American people in the 1950s was wrong.*

separate (**sep**-u-rut) adj. If you are **separate** from other people, you are not with them. *It is not fun to feel **separate** from the group.*

shame (**shām**) n. When you feel **shame**, you feel badly about something you did. *She felt **shame** about the mistake she made.*

shrink (**shringk**) v. To **shrink** means to become smaller. *The forests that animals need are **shrinking** as people cut down trees.*

• **similar** (**si**-mu-lur) adj. Things that are nearly alike are **similar**. *The brothers are very **similar** in appearance.*

similarity (sim-e-**lār**-et-ē) n. A **similarity** is something that makes things alike. *The **similarity** between the cars is their color.*

society (so-**sī**-e-tē) n. A **society** is a group of people who share beliefs and goals. *The historical **society** met to find out about our town's history.*

solar system (**sō**-lur **sis**-tem) n. Our **solar system** is made up of the sun and the objects that move around it. *Earth's **solar system** includes eight planets.*

solid (**säl**-ed) adj. Something that is **solid** is hard or firm. *Rocks are **solid** all the way through.*

species (**spē**-shēz) n. A **species** is a related group of animals or plants. *Lions and tigers are different **species**. African lions and Asian lions are the same **species**.*

• **specific** (spe-**sif**-ik) adj. When something is **specific**, it is definite or particular. *Follow the **specific** directions to do the experiment correctly.*

strength (**strength**) n. **Strength** is the quality of being powerful. *The **strength** of the storm destroyed many homes.*

• **structure** (**struk**-chur) n. A **structure** is how parts are arranged or organized. *The **structure** of the bridge is very solid.*

support (su-**pōrt**) n. To have **support** means that people help you. *Students need the **support** of their teachers.*

surface (**sur**-fes) n. A **surface** is the outside or top layer of an object. *The new road has a smoother **surface** than the old road.*

• **survive** (sur-**vīv**) v. When you **survive**, you stay alive. *In cold weather, you need warm clothes to **survive**.*

• **symbol** (**sim**-bul) n. A **symbol** is an object that stands for something else. *In the U.S., the Bald Eagle is a **symbol** of power.*

T

talented (**tal**-en-tid) adj. A **talented** person is good at doing one or more activities. *They are very **talented** musicians.*

• **technical** (**tek**-nih-kal) adj. Something that is **technical** is based on scientific knowledge. *The science textbook is written in **technical** terms.*

• **Academic Vocabulary**

- **technique** (tek-**nēk**) *n.* **Technique** is a skilled way of doing something. *My serving **technique** improved after taking tennis lessons.*

- **technology** (tek-**nol**-uj-ē) *n.* **Technology** is the use of knowledge to do a task or to improve how the task is done. *Because of new **technology**, computers are faster and smaller than they once were.*

- **temporary** (**tem**-pō-rair-ē) *adj.* When something is **temporary**, it lasts only a short time. *They had **temporary** housing.*

threat (**thret**) *n.* A **threat** is a danger. *Clouds show the **threat** of a storm.*

thrive (**thrīv**) *v.* To **thrive** means to grow strong and healthy. *With lots of care, plants can **thrive**.*

translate (**trans**-lāt) *v.* To **translate** means to explain in another language. *The sign **translates** information into English.*

U

- **unique** (yū-**nēk**) *adj.* Something that is **unique** is different or special. *The giraffe has a **unique** neck.*

universe (**yu**-nu-vers) *n.* The **universe** is everything that exists, including all of space. *Our solar system is just one part of the whole **universe**.*

V

viewpoint (**vyū**-point) *n.* A **viewpoint** is the way a person thinks about things. *My friends and I had different **viewpoints** about which way to go.*

virus (**vī**-rus) *n.* A **virus** is a tiny particle that can cause disease in people, plants, and animals. *My brother had a **virus** so he couldn't go to school.*

volunteer (vol-en-**tēr**) *v.* To **volunteer** means to work without pay. *One way I can help others is to **volunteer** at the soup kitchen.*

W

warrior (**wor**-ē-yur) *n.* A **warrior** is someone who protects his people. *Some **warriors** hunt animals for food.*

wildlife (**wīld**-līf) *n.* **Wildlife** means animals and plants that live freely outdoors without human care. *Bears and moose are examples of **wildlife**.*

willful (**wil**-ful) *adj.* Someone who is **willful** refuses to change. *A **willful** child only does what he wants, not what others tell him.*

• **Academic Vocabulary**

• Academic Vocabulary Master Word List

adaptation	couple	identify	**resource**
adjust	**create**	**illustrate**	response
adjustment	**credit**	image	**result**
affect	culture	**immigrant**	**role**
aid	**data**	impact	**route**
amend	debate	individual	scale
analyze	decision	inevitable	**section**
appeal	**define**	integrate	**select**
apply	definition	**interview**	**sequence**
appreciate	**demonstrate**	involve	**series**
approach	**describe**	**job**	similar
appropriate	**design**	judgment	**situation**
area	despite	literal	**solve**
arrange	**device**	**locate**	**source**
assignment	**discover**	location	**space**
assist	**discuss**	logical	specific
associate	**distinguish**	**migrate**	structure
assume	effect	**model**	**style**
attach	effectively	modify	**support**
available	element	negative	survive
awareness	**emerge**	obvious	symbol
belief	**encounter**	organize	**team**
benefit	energy	origin	technical
bond	ensure	**original**	technique
capable	environment	**outcome**	technology
category	**equipment**	perspective	temporary
challenge	establish	positive	**theme**
chapter	evaluate	predict	**topic**
characteristic	evidence	**presentation**	**tradition**
classic	**exact**	process	**trait**
collapse	**experiment**	**professional**	unique
collect	expert	promote	**vary**
communicate	**explain**	propaganda	
community	**explanation**	purpose	
compare	**express**	react	
compound	**fact**	**record**	
concentrate	feature	**refer**	
conflict	focus	**reflect**	
connect	**force**	**region**	
connotation	**freedom**	relate	
context	**goal**	**release**	
contrast	**generate**	**report**	
convince	**globe**	research	

• Words in red appear in Level C.

Literary Terms

A

Alliteration The repetition of the same sounds (usually consonants) at the beginning of words that are close together. **Example:** Molly makes magnificent mousse, though Pablo prefers pecan pie.

See also **Repetition**

Allusion A key form of literary language, in which one text makes the reader think about another text that was written before it. Allusion can also mean a reference to a person, place, thing, or event that is not specifically named. **Example:** When Hannah wrote in her short story that vanity was the talented main character's "Achilles heel," her teacher understood that Hannah was referring to a character in a Greek myth. So, she suspected that the vanity of the main character in Hannah's short story would prove to be the character's greatest weakness.

See also **Connotation; Literature; Poetry**

Argument A type of writing or speaking that supports a position or attempts to convince the reader or listener. Arguments include a claim that is supported by reasons and evidence.

See also **Claim; Reason; Evidence**

Article A short piece of nonfiction writing on a specific topic. Articles appear in newspapers and magazines.

See also **Expository nonfiction; Nonfiction**

Autobiography The story of a person's life, written by that person. **Example:** Mahatma Gandhi wrote an autobiography titled *Gandhi: An Autobiography: The Story of My Experiments With Truth*.

See also **Diary; Journal; Personal narrative**

B

Biographical fiction A fictional story that is based on real events in the life of a real person. **Example:** Although the book *Farmer Boy* by Laura Ingalls Wilder is about her husband's childhood, the conversations between characters are from the author's imagination. They are based on what she thought the characters might have said at the time.

See also **Biography; Fiction**

Biography The story of a person's life, written by another person.

See also **Autobiography; Biographical fiction**

C

Character A person, an animal, or an imaginary creature in a work of fiction.

See also **Characterization; Character traits**

Characterization The way a writer creates and develops a character. Writers use a variety of ways to bring a character to life: through descriptions of the character's appearance, thoughts, feelings, and actions; through the character's words; and through the words or thoughts of other characters.

See also **Character; Character traits; Motive**

Character traits The special qualities of personality that writers give their characters.

See also **Character; Characterization**

Claim A statement that clearly identifies an author's ideas or opinion.

See also **Argument; Reason; Evidence**

Climax The turning point or most important event in a plot.

See also **Falling action; Plot; Rising action**

Complication *See* **Rising action**

Conflict The main problem faced by a character in a story or play. The character may be involved in a struggle against nature, another character, or society. The struggle may also be between two elements in the character's mind.

See also **Plot**

Connotation The feelings suggested by a word or phrase, apart from its dictionary meaning. **Example:** The terms "used car" and "previously owned vehicle" have different connotations. To most people, the phrase "previously owned vehicle" sounds better than "used car."

See also **Denotation; Poetry**

D

Denotation The dictionary meaning of a word or phrase. Denotation is especially important in functional texts and other types of nonfiction used to communicate information precisely.

See also **Connotation; Functional text; Nonfiction**

Descriptive language Language that creates a "picture" of a person, place, or thing—often using words that appeal to the five senses: sight, hearing, touch, smell, and taste. **Example:** The bright, hot sun beat down on Earth's surface. Where once a vibrant lake cooled the skin of hippos and zebras, only thin, dry cracks remained, reaching across the land like an old man's fingers, as far as the eye could see. The smell of herds was gone, and only silence filled the space.

See also **Imagery**

Dialogue What characters say to each other. Writers use dialogue to develop characters, move the plot forward, and add interest. In most writing, dialogue is set off by quotation marks; in play scripts, however, dialogue appears without quotation marks.

Diary A book written by a person about his or her own life as it is happening. Unlike an autobiography, a diary is not usually meant to be published. It is made up of entries that are written shortly after events occur. The person writing a diary often expresses feelings and opinions about what has happened.

See also **Autobiography; Journal**

Drama A kind of writing in which a plot unfolds in the words and actions of characters performed by actors.

See also **Genre; Play; Plot**

E

Essay A short piece of nonfiction, normally in prose, that discusses a single topic without claiming to do so thoroughly. Its purpose may be to inform, entertain, or persuade.

See also **Nonfiction; Photo-essay; Topic**

Evidence Information provided to support a claim.

See also **Argument; Claim; Reasons**

Exaggeration Figurative language that makes things seem bigger than they really are in order to create a funny image in the reader's mind. **Example:** My eyes are so big they pop out of my face when I get surprised or angry.

See also **Figurative language; Hyperbole**

Exposition The rising action of a story in which characters and the problems they face are introduced.

See also **Rising action**

Expository nonfiction Writing that gives information and facts. It is usually divided into sections that give information about subtopics of a larger topic.

See also **Article; News feature; Nonfiction; Report; Textbook; Topic**

F

Fable A brief fictional narrative that teaches a lesson about life. Many fables have animals instead of humans as characters. Fables often end with a short, witty statement of their lesson. **Example:** "The Tortoise and the Hare" is a famous fable in which a boastful, quick-moving hare challenges a slow-moving tortoise to a race. Because the overconfident hare takes a nap during the race, the tortoise wins. The moral of the fable is that slow and steady wins the race.

See also **Fiction; Folk tale;**

Fairy tale See **Fantasy; Folk tale**

Falling action The actions and events in a plot that happen after the climax. Usually, the major problem is solved in some way, so the remaining events serve to bring the story to an end.

See also **Climax; Conflict; Plot, Rising action**

Fantasy Fiction in which imaginary worlds differ from the "real" world outside the text. Fairy tales, science fiction, and fables are examples of fantasy.

See also **Fable; Fiction**

Fiction Narrative writing about imaginary people, places, things, or events.

See also **Biographical fiction; Fable; Fantasy; Folk tale; Historical fiction; Myth; Novel; Realistic fiction; Short story**

Figurative language The use of a word or phrase to say one thing and mean another. Figurative language is especially important in literature and poetry because it gives writers a more effective way of expressing what they mean than using direct, literal language. **Example:** Upon receiving her monthly bills, Victoria complained that she was "drowning in debt."

See also **Exaggeration; Hyperbole; Idiom; Imagery; Literature; Metaphor; Personification; Poetry; Simile; Symbol**

Folk tale A short, fictional narrative shared orally rather than in writing, and thus partly changed through its retellings before being written down. Folk tales include myths, legends, fables, ghost stories, and fairy tales.

See also **Fable; Legend; Myth**

Folklore The collection of a people's beliefs, customs, rituals, spells, songs, sayings, and stories as shared mainly orally rather than in writing.

See also **Folk tale; Legend; Myth**

Functional text Writing in which the main purpose is to communicate the information people need to accomplish tasks in everyday life. **Examples:** résumés, business letters, technical manuals, and the help systems of word-processing programs.

G

Genre A type or class of literary works grouped according to form, style, and/or topic. Major genres include fictional narrative prose (such as short stories and most novels), nonfiction narrative prose (such as autobiographies, diaries, and journals), drama, poetry, and the essay.

See also **Essay; Fiction; Literature; Nonfiction; Poetry; Prose; Style; Topic**

H

Hero or **Heroine** In myths and legends, a man or woman of great courage and strength who is celebrated for his or her daring feats.

See also **Legend; Myth**

Historical fiction Fiction based on events that actually happened or on people who actually lived. It may be written from the point of view of a "real" or an imaginary character, and it usually includes invented dialogue.

See also **Fiction**

Hyperbole Figurative language that exaggerates, often to the point of being funny, to emphasize something. **Example:** When his mother asked how long he had waited for the school bus that morning, Jeremy grinned and said, "Oh, not long. Only about a million years."

See also **Exaggeration; Figurative language**

I

Idiom A phrase or expression that means something different from the word or words' dictionary meanings. Idioms cannot be translated word for word into another language because an idiom's meaning is not the same as that of the individual words that make it up. **Example:** "Mind your p's and q's" in English means to be careful, thoughtful, and behave properly.

Imagery Figurative language that communicates sensory experience. Imagery can help the reader imagine how people, places, and things look, sound, taste, smell, and feel. It can also make the reader think about emotions and ideas that commonly go with certain sensations. Because imagery appeals to the senses, it is sometimes called *sensory language*.

See also **Descriptive language; Figurative language; Symbol**

Interview A discussion between two or more people in which questions are asked and answered so that the interviewer can get information. The record of such a discussion is also called an interview.

J

Jargon Specialized language used by people to describe things that are specific to their group or subject. **Example:** *Mouse* in a computer class means "part of a computer system," not "a rodent."

Journal A personal record, similar to a diary. It may include accounts of actual events, stories, poems, sketches, thoughts, essays, a collection of interesting information, or just about anything the writer wishes to include.

See also **Diary**

L

Legend A very old story, usually written about a hero or heroine or to explain something in nature. Legends are mostly fiction, but some details may be true.

See also **Folk tale; Hero or Heroine; Myth**

Literature Works written as prose or poetry.

See also **Poetry; Prose**

M

Metaphor A type of figurative language that compares two unlike things by saying that one thing is the other thing. **Example:** Dhara says her grandfather can be a real mule when he doesn't get enough sleep.

See also **Figurative language; Simile; Symbol**

Meter The patterning of language into regularly repeating units of rhythm. Language patterned in this way is called *verse*. By varying the rhythm within a meter, the writer can heighten the reader's attention to what is going on in the verse and reinforce meaning.

See also **Poetry; Rhythm**

Mood The overall feeling or atmosphere a writer creates in a piece of writing.

See also **Tone**

Motive The reason a character has for his or her thoughts, feelings, actions, or words. **Example:** Maria's motive for bringing cookies to her new neighbors was to learn what they were like.

See also **Characterization**

Myth A fictional narrative, often a folk tale, that tells of supernatural events as a way of explaining natural events and their relation to human life. Myths commonly involve gods, goddesses, monsters, and superhuman heroes or heroines.

See also **Folk tale; Hero** or **Heroine; Legend**

N

Narrative writing Writing that gives an account of a set of real or imaginary events (the story), which the writer selects and arranges in a particular order (the plot). Narrative writing includes nonfiction works such as news articles, autobiographies, and journals, as well as fictional works such as short stories, novels, and plays.

See also **Autobiography; Fiction; Journal; Narrator; Nonfiction; Plot; Story**

Narrator Someone who gives an account of events. In fiction, the narrator is the teller of a story (as opposed to the real author, who invented the narrator as well as the story). Narrators differ in how much they participate in a story's events. In a first-person narrative, the narrator is the "I" telling the story. In a third-person narrative, the narrator is not directly involved in the events and refers to characters by name or as *he*, *she*, *it*, or *they*. Narrators also differ in how much they know and how much they can be trusted by the reader.

See also **Character; Point of view**

News feature A nonfiction article that gives facts about real people and events.

See also **Article; Expository nonfiction; Nonfiction**

Nonfiction Written works about events or things that are not imaginary; writing other than fiction.

See also **Autobiography; Biography; Diary; Essay; Fiction; Journal; Personal narrative; Photo-essay; Report; Textbook**

Novel A long, fictional narrative, usually in prose. Its length enables it to have more characters, a more complicated plot, and a more fully developed setting than shorter works of fiction.

See also **Character; Fiction; Plot; Prose; Setting; Short story**

Literary Terms

O

Onomatopoeia The use of words that imitate the sounds they refer to. **Examples:** *buzz*, *slam*, *hiss*

P

Personal narrative An account of a certain event or set of events in a person's life, written by that person.
> See also **Autobiography; Diary; Journal**

Personification Figurative language that describes animals, things, or ideas as having human traits. **Examples:** In the movie *Babe* and in the book *Charlotte's Web*, the animals are all personified.
> See also **Figurative language**

Persuasive writing Writing that attempts to get someone to do or agree to something by appealing to logic or emotion. Persuasive writing is used in advertisements, editorials, and political speeches.

Photo-essay A short nonfiction piece made up of photographs and captions. The photographs are as important as the words in presenting information.
> See also **Essay; Nonfiction**

Play A work of drama, especially one written to be performed on a stage. **Example:** Lorraine Hansberry's *A Raisin in the Sun* was first performed in 1959.
> See also **Drama**

Plot The pattern of events and situations in a story or play. Plot is usually divided into four main parts: *conflict* (or *problem*), *rising action* (or *exposition* or *complication*), *climax*, and *falling action* (or *resolution*).
> See also **Climax; Conflict; Drama; Falling action; Fiction; Rising action; Story**

Poetry A form of literary expression that uses line breaks for emphasis. Poems often use connotation, imagery, metaphor, symbol, allusion, repetition, and rhythm. Word patterns in poetry include rhythm or meter, and often rhyme and alliteration.
> See also **Alliteration; Connotation; Figurative language; Meter; Repetition; Rhyme; Rhythm**

Point of view The position from which the events of a story seem to be observed and told. A first-person point of view tells the story through what the narrator knows, experiences, concludes, or can find out by talking to other characters. A third-person point of view may be *omniscient*, giving the narrator unlimited knowledge of things, events, and characters, including characters' hidden thoughts and feelings. Or it may be *limited* to what one or a few characters know and experience. **Example** of First-Person Point of View: I'm really hungry right now, and I can't wait to eat my lunch. **Example** of Third-Person Limited Point of View: Olivia is really hungry right now and she wants to eat her lunch. **Example** of Third-Person Omniscient Point of View: Olivia is really hungry right now and she wants to eat her lunch. The other students are thinking about their weekend plans.

The teacher is wondering how she will finish the lesson before the bell rings.
> See also **Character; Fiction; Narrator**

Propaganda A type of persuasion that twists or doesn't tell the whole truth. Types of propaganda include *glittering generalities* (using impressive words to skip past the truth), *transfers* (using appealing ideas or symbols that aren't directly related to the topic), *testimonials* (using the words of famous people), *plain folks* (showing that a product or idea has the same values as the audience), *bandwagon* (claiming that everyone else is doing it), and *name calling*.
> See also **Persuasive writing**

Prose A form of writing in which the rhythm is less regular than that of verse and more like that of ordinary speech.
> See also **Poetry; Rhythm**

Proverb A short saying that expresses a general truth. Proverbs are found in many different languages and cultures. **Example:** An apple a day keeps the doctor away.

Purpose An author's reason for writing. Most authors write to entertain, inform, or persuade. **Example:** An author's purpose in an editorial is to persuade the reader to think or do something.
> See also **Expository nonfiction; Narrative writing; Persuasive writing**

R

Realistic fiction Fiction in which detailed handling of imaginary settings, characters, and events produces a lifelike illusion of a "real" world. **Example:** Although Upton Sinclair's *The Jungle* is a work of fiction, the author's graphic, detailed descriptions of the slaughterhouse workers' daily lives led to real changes in the meatpacking industry.
> See also **Fiction**

Reason A logical explanation that connects a piece of evidence to a writer or speaker's claim.
> See also **Argument; Claim; Evidence**

Repetition The repeating of individual vowels and consonants, syllables, words, phrases, lines, or groups of lines. Repetition can be used because it sounds pleasant, to emphasize the words in which it occurs, or to help tie the parts of a text into one structure. It is especially important in creating the musical quality of poetry, where it can take such forms as alliteration and rhyme.
> See also **Alliteration; Poetry; Rhyme**

Report A usually short piece of nonfiction writing on a particular topic. It differs from an essay in that it normally states only facts and does not directly express the writer's opinions.
> See also **Essay; Nonfiction; Topic**

Resolution *See* **Falling action**

Rhyme The repetition of ending sounds in different words. Rhymes usually come at the end of lines of verse, but they may also occur within a line. **Examples:** *look, brook, shook*

    See also **Poetry; Repetition; Rhyme scheme**

Rhyme scheme The pattern of rhymed line endings in a work of poetry or a stanza. It can be represented by giving a certain letter of the alphabet to each line ending on the same rhyme. **Example:** Because the end word of every other line rhymes in the following poem, the rhyme scheme is *abab*:

Winter night falls quick (a)
The pink sky gone, blackness overhead (b)
Looks like the snow will stick (a)
Down the street and up the hill I tread (b)

    See also **Poetry; Rhyme; Stanza**

Rhythm The natural rise and fall, or "beat," of language. Rhythm is present in all language, including speech and prose, but it is most obvious in poetry.

    See also **Meter; Poetry; Prose**

Rising action The part of a plot that presents actions or events that lead to the climax.

    See also **Climax; Conflict; Exposition; Falling action; Plot**

S

Setting The time and place in which the events of a story occur.

Short story A brief, fictional narrative. Like the novel, it organizes the action, thought, and dialogue of its characters into a plot. But it tends to focus on fewer characters and to center on a single event.

    See also **Character; Fiction; Novel; Plot; Story**

Simile A type of figurative language that compares two unlike things by using a word or phrase such as *like, as, than, similar to, resembles,* or *seems.* **Examples:** The tall, slim man had arms as willowy as a tree's branches. The woman's temper is like an unpredictable volcano.

    See also **Figurative language; Metaphor**

Song lyrics Words meant to be sung. Lyrics have been created for many types of songs, including love songs, religious songs, work songs, sea chanties, and children's game songs. Lyrics for many songs were shared orally for generations before being written down. Not all song lyrics are lyrical like poems; some are the words to songs that tell a story. Not all poems called songs were written to be sung.

    See also **Folk literature; Poetry**

Speech A message on a specific topic, spoken before an audience; also, spoken (not written) language.

Stanza A group of lines that forms a section of a poem and has the same pattern (including line lengths, meter, and usually rhyme scheme) as other sections of the same poem. In printed poems, stanzas are separated from each other by a space.

    See also **Meter; Poetry; Rhyme scheme**

Story A series of events (actual or imaginary) that can be selected and arranged in a certain order to form a narrative or dramatic plot. It is the raw material from which the finished plot is built. Although there are technical differences, the word *story* is sometimes used in place of *narrative.*

    See also **Drama; Plot**

Style The way a writer uses language to express the feelings or thoughts he or she wants to convey. Just as no two people are alike, no two styles are exactly alike. A writer's style results from his or her choices of vocabulary, sentence structure and variety, imagery, figurative language, rhythm, repetition, and other resources.

    See also **Figurative language; Genre; Imagery; Repetition; Rhythm**

Symbol A word or phrase that serves as an image of some person, place, thing, or action but that also calls to mind some other, usually broader, idea or range of ideas. **Example:** An author might describe doves flying high in the sky to symbolize peace.

    See also **Figurative language; Imagery**

T

Textbook A book prepared for use in schools for the study of a subject.

Theme The underlying message or main idea of a piece of writing. It expresses a broader meaning than the topic of the piece.

    See also **Topic**

Tone A writer's or speaker's attitude toward his or her topic or audience or toward him- or herself. A writer's tone may be positive, negative, or neutral. The words the writer chooses, the sentence structure, and the overall pattern of words convey the intended tone.

    See also **Connotation; Figurative language; Literature; Mood; Rhythm; Topic**

Topic What or who is being discussed in a piece of writing; the subject of the piece.

    See also **Theme**

Index of Skills

Index of Authors and Titles

Index of Art and Artists

Acknowledgments, continued from page ii

Grateful acknowledgement is also given for permission to provide audio recordings of literature and informational text *selections* included in this book.

Almanac Music, Inc., c/o The Richmond Organization: "Last Night I Had the Strangest Dream," words and music by Ed McCurdy. TRO. Copyright © 1950 (Renewed), 1951 (Renewed), 1955 (Renewed) Folkways Music Publishers, Inc., New York, NY. Used by Permission.

American Express Publishing Corporation: "Soup for the Soul" by Kristin Donnelly is comprised of excerpts from "Soul-Soothing Soups" from *Food & Wine*, November 2006. Text copyright © by Kristin Donnelly. Reprinted by permission of Food and Wine, a publication of American Express Publishing Corporation.

Carmen T. Bernier-Grand: "Indian Summer Sun" by Carmen T. Grand from *Once Upon a Cuento*, edited by Lyn Miller-Lachmann, published by Curbstone Press. Used by permission of the author.

Georges Borchardt, Inc.: "Dragon, Dragon" by John Gardner from *Dragon, Dragon and Other Tales*. Copyright © 1975 by Boskydell Artists, Ltd. Reprinted by permission of Georges Borchardt, Inc., for the Estate of John Gardner.

Diana Chang: "Saying Yes" by Diana Chang. Copyright © Diana Chang. Used by permission of the author.

Charlesbridge Publishing: "The Flag We Love" by Pam Muñoz Ryan. Text copyright © 1996 by Pam Muñoz Ryan. Illustrations copyright © 1996 by Ralph Masiello. Used with permission by Charlesbridge Publishing, Inc. All rights reserved.

Counterpoint Press: Excerpt from *The Selected Letters of Wallace Stegner* by Wallace Stegner, edited by Page Stegner. Copyright © 2007 by Page Stegner. Reprinted by permission of Counterpoint.

Curtis Brown, LTD.: Excerpt from *Nadia the Wilful*, by Sue Alexander, published by Alfred A. Knopf, Inc. Copyright © 1983 by Sue Alexander. Reprinted by permission of Curtis Brown, LTD.

Estate of Dr. Martin Luther King, Jr.: Excerpt from "I Have a Dream" by Martin Luther King, Jr. Copyright 1963; copyright renewed 1991 Coretta Scott King. Reprinted by arrangement with the Heirs of the Estate of Martin Luther King Jr., c/o Writers House as agent for the proprietor New York, NY.

Farrar, Straus and Giroux, LLC: "The Clever Magistrate" from The *Ch'i-Lin Purse* by Linda Fang, illustrations by Jeanne Lee. Text copyright © 1995 by Linda Fang. Illustrations copyright © 1995 by Jeanne Lee. Reprinted by permissions of Farrar, Straus and Giroux, LLC.

"The Three Chicharrones" from *Red Ridin' In the Hood and Other Cuentos* by Patricia Marcantonio. Copyright © 2005 by Patricia Marcantonio. Reprinted by permissions of Farrar, Straus and Giroux, LLC.

Groundwood Books: "Chief Koruinka's Song" from *Messengers of Rain and Other Poems* from Latin America, compilation edited by Claudia M. Lee. Copyright © 2002 by Groundwood Books. First published in Canada by Groundwood Books Ltd. Reprinted by permission of the publisher.

Hyperion Books for Children: Excerpt from *Martin's Big Words* by Doreen Rappaport. Copyright © 2001 by Doreen Rappaport, Illustrations copyright © 2001 by Bryan Collier. Reprinted by permission of Hyperion Books for Children. All rights reserved.

Hyperion: Excerpt from *The Words We Live By: Your Annotated Guide to the Constitution* by Linda R. Monk. Copyright © 2003 by Linda R. Monk and Stonesong Press, Inc. Used by permission of Hyperion. All rights reserved.

Lee and Low Books, Inc.: "In My Dreams" by Francisco X. Alarcón from *Poems to Dream Together: Poems Para Soñar Juntos*. Text © 2005 by Francisco X. Alarcón, illustrations copyright © 2005 by Paula Barrgán. Permission arranged with Lee & Low Books, Inc., New York, NY 10016.

Excerpt from *Passage to Freedom: The Sugihara Story* by Ken Mochizuki. Text copyright © 1997 by Ken Mochizuki; illustrations copyright © 1997 by Dom Lee. Permission arranged with Lee & Low Books, Inc., New York, NY 10016.

Naomi Long Madgett: "Midway" by Naomi Long Madgett from *Star by Star*. Copyright © 1965, 70 by Naomi Long Madgett. Reprinted in *Connected Islands: New and Selected Poems* by Naomi Long Madgett. By permission of the author.

Daisy Myrie: "Market Women" by Daisy Myrie from *New Ships: An Anthology of West Indian Poems*, edited by Donald G. Wilson, Savacou Publications Ltd.

NASA: "Between Earth and Space" astronaut journal excerpts are from the journal entries of the Johnson Space Center astronauts, which can be found online at www.nasa.gov/centers/johnson/journals_astronauts.html.

National Geographic Society: "A Lion Hunt," from *Facing the Lion* by Joseph Lemasolai Lekuton, with Herman Viola. Copyright © 2003 Joseph Lemasolai Lekuton and Herman Viola. Reprinted with permission of the National Geographic Society. All rights reserved.

"Mireya Mayor: Ultimate Explorer" is adapted from "Mireya Mayor: Primatologist/Conservationist" from NationalGeographic.com. Used by permission of National Geographic Society. All rights reserved.

New York Times: Excerpt from "Math Lessons for Locavores" by Stephen Budiansky from the *New York Times*, August 20, 2010. Copyright © the New York Times. Reprinted by permission of the New York Times.

Penguin Books Ltd: Excerpt from *Zlata's Diary: A Child's Life in Sarajevo* by Zlata Filipovic, translated by Christina Pribichevich-Zoric. Copyright © Fixot et editions Robert Laffont, 1993. First published in France as 'Le Journal de Zlata' by Fixot et editions Robert Laffont, 1993. Reproduced by permission of Penguin Books Ltd.

Penguin Group (USA) Inc.: "Diary Entries", from ZLATA'S DIARY by Zlata Filipovic, translated by Christina Pribichevich-Zoric, copyright © 1994 Editions Robert Laffont/Fixot. Used by permission of Viking Penguin, a division of Penguin Group (USA) Inc.

Excerpt from The *Omnivores Dilemma: Young Readers Edition* by Michael Pollan. Copyright © 2009 by Michael Pollan. Used by permission of Dial Books for Young Readers, a division of Penguin Group (USA) Inc.

Marian Reiner: "Argument" by Eve Merriam from *Out Loud*. Copyright © 1973 by Eve Merriam. Used by permission of Marian Reiner.

Scholastic, Inc.: "Getting Involved" by Jonathan Blum. From "School Spirit" by Jonathan Blum, from *Scholastic Action*, May 8, 2003. Copyright © 2003 by Scholastic Inc. Reprinted by permission.

"Taking Action" by Genet Berhane from "Matt Cavedon Says Enough is Enough!" from *Scholastic News Online*. Copyright © 2007 by Scholastic, Inc. Reprinted by permission.

Excerpt from *Any Small Goodness: A Novel of the Barrio* by Tony Johnston. Copyright © 2001 by Roger D. Johnston and Susan T. Johnston as Trustees of the Johnston Family Trust. Published by Scholastic Inc./The Blue Sky Press. Reprinted by permission.

Emma Suárez-Báez: "Almost Evenly Divided" by Emma Suárez-Báez. Copyright © 1999 by Emma Suárez-Báez. Used by permission of the author.

Susan Bergholz Literary Services: Excerpt from *The House on Mango* Street by Sandra Cisneros. Copyright © 1984 by Sandra Cisneros, published by Vintage Books, a division of Random House, Inc., and in hardcover by Alfred A. Knopf in 1994. Reprinted by permission of Susan Bergholz Literary Services, New York, NY and Lamy, NM. All rights reserved.

W. W. Norton & Company and David Higham Associates: Excerpt from "So You're Going to Mars" by Arthur C. Clarke from *The Snows of Olympus: A Garden on Mars*. Copyright © 1994 by Arthur C. Clarke. Used by permission of W. W. Norton & Company, Inc. and David Higham Associates.

Dr. Florence Wambugu: "Is genetically modified food a good way to feed the world?" is from "Taking the Food Out of Our Mouths" by Florence Wambugu, published in the *Washington Post*, August 26, 2001. Dr. Florence Wambugu was the CEO of Africa Harvest, whose vision is "An Africa free of hunger, poverty and malnutrition". The Foundation's vision is to use science and technology - especially biotechnology - to help the poor in Africa achieve food security, economic well-being and sustainable rural development.

Janet Wong: "Quilt" by Janet S. Wong from *A Suitcase of Seaweed and Other Poems*. Copyright © 1996 by Janet S. Wong. Reprinted with the permission of the author.

Photography

Cover ©JH Pete Carmichael/Riser/Getty Images. **Back cover** ©Loeiza JACQ/Gamma-Rapho via Getty Images. **iii** ©J. Helgason/Shutterstock.com. **iii** ©Mark Thiessen/National Geographic Image Collection. **iii** ©Randy Wells/Stone/Getty Images. **iii** ©Lou Wall/Corbis. **1** ©2011 Randy Olson/National Geographic Image Collection. **3** ©George Doyle/Stockbyte/Getty Images. **4** ©Premier Edition Image Library/Superstock. **6** ©PhotoDisc/Getty Images. **7** ©Koji Aoki/Aflo Foto Agency/Alamy. **9** ©Visual Mozart/ImageZoo/Corbis. **9** ©Visuals Unlimited/Corbis. **10** ©Morgan Gaynin. **10** ©Rick Gayle Studio/Corbis. **11** ©Sara-Jane Cleland/Lonely Planet Images/Getty Images. **12** ©Oberhuser/Caro/Alamy. **12** ©Milk Photographie/Corbis. **14** ©Image Source/Corbis. **14** ©Brian Drouin/National Geographic Image Collection. **14** ©Burazin/Photographer's Choice/Getty Images. **14** ©Jodi Cobb/National Geographic Stock. **14** ©PM Images/Iconica/Getty Images. **14** ©Stockbyte/Getty Images. **14** ©Stockbyte/Getty Images. **14** ©Urs Kuester/Photodisc/Getty Images. **17** ©Morgan Gaynin. **18** ©Jose Ramirez. **21** ©Fotosearch. **23** ©Frank Romero. **28** ©Richard Nowitz/National Geographic Stock. **31** ©SW Productions/Photodisc/Getty Images. **31** ©Paul Souders/WorldFoto/Alamy. **31** ©WorldFoto/Alamy. **32** ©Richard Du Toit/Minden Pictures/Getty Images. **32** ©Linda Holthaus Crumpecker. **32** ©Carl & Ann Purcell/Corbis. **34** ©Julie Harris/Alamy. **35** ©Rob C. Nunnington. Gallo Images/Corbis. **36** ©MEDFORD TAYLOR/National Geographic. **36** ©AP Photo/Gerry Broome. **36** ©Jeff Foott/Discovery Channel Images/Getty Images. **36** ©JOHN EASTCOTT AND YVA MOMATIUK/National Geographic Stock. **36**

671

672

Illustration

50 Mapping Specialists. **60–63, 65–66, 68–69, 76** Rafael Lopez. **109** Meilo So. **154** Mapping Specialists. **285** Ben Shannon. **350, 370** Mapping Specialists. **385** Steve Bjorkman. **384, 390–393, 395–396, 399–400** Jamel Akib. **412–413, 415–417, 419, 421–424** Dom Lee. **458, 526** Marilee Heyer. **459** Ben Shannon. **464–467, 470–471, 472–473** Marilee Heyer.

Fine Art

20 *El Lonche*, ©1993 Simon Silva. Oils, used with permission of the illustrator and Bookstop Literary Agency, Orinda, California. **26** *Santa Fe Roadside Prickly Pear*, ©2007, Claudette Moe. Acrylic on canvas, collection of the artist. **55** ©Peter Horree/ Alamy/Salvador Dalí, Fundació Gala-Salvador Dalí, Artists Rights Society (ARS). **158** ©Easton Press/MBI Inc./Image from Norman Rockwell Museum. **302** *Small Echo* ©2004 (water color on handmade Indian paper) Dean Graham. Private Collection, The Bridgeman Art Library. **324** *Study of a Dodo*, Hart F (19th Century). Oil on canvas, Royal Albert Memorial Museum, Exeter, Devon UK/©The Bridgeman Art Library. **491** *The Signing of the Constitution of the United States in 1787*, 1940, Christy Howard Chandler (1873–1952). Oil on canvas, Hall of Representatives, Washington D.C., USA/©The Bridgeman Art Library. **548** *The Marketplace*, 1988, Murrell Carlton. Oil on canvas, Private Collection/©The Bridgeman Art Library. **570, 577** *Wounded Sleep* ©2006, Durga Bernhard. Gouache and ink, collection of the artist. **581** *Aurochs and Deer*, ©2004 Cecilia Henle. Oil on canvas, collection of the artist. **589** *Mountain Buck*, ©2000 Durga Bernhard. Gouache on paper collage, Michael Densmore collection. **595** *In Depth*, ©2006 Carmen Hathaway. Acrylic on canvas, collection of the artist.

Common Core State Standards

Common Core State Standards, continued

Selection 1 American Names, continued

Pages	Lesson	Code	Standards Text
11–13	**Language & Grammar** Ask and Answer Questions	SL.8.1	Engage effectively in a range of collaborative discussions (one-on-one, in groups, and teacher-led) with diverse partners on grade 8 topics, texts, and issues, building on others' ideas and expressing their own clearly.
		L.8.1.c	Demonstrate command of the conventions of standard English grammar and usage when writing or speaking. Form and use verbs in the indicative, imperative, interrogative, conditional, and subjunctive moods.
	Use Complete Sentences	L.8.1.c	Demonstrate command of the conventions of standard English grammar and usage when writing or speaking. Form and use verbs in the indicative, imperative, interrogative, conditional, and subjunctive moods.
14	**Key Vocabulary**	RL.8.4	Determine the meaning of words and phrases as they are used in a text, including figurative and connotative meanings; analyze the impact of specific word choices on meaning and tone, including analogies or allusions to other texts.
		L.8.4	Determine or clarify the meaning of unknown and multiple-meaning words or phrases based on grade 8 reading and content, choosing flexibly from a range of strategies.
15	**Reading Strategy** Plan, Monitor, and Ask Questions	RL.8.4	Determine the meaning of words and phrases as they are used in a text, including figurative and connotative meanings; analyze the impact of specific word choices on meaning and tone, including analogies or allusions to other texts.
	Literary Analysis Use Text Evidence	RL.8.10	By the end of the year, read and comprehend literature, including stories, dramas, and poems, at the high end of grades 6–8 text complexity band independently and proficiently.
		RL.8.1	Cite the textual evidence that most strongly supports an analysis of what the text says explicitly as well as inferences drawn from the text.
16–28	**Reading Selection**	RL.8.1	Cite the textual evidence that most strongly supports an analysis of what the text says explicitly as well as inferences drawn from the text.
		RL.8.3	Analyze how particular lines of dialogue or incidents in a story or drama propel the action, reveal aspects of a character, or provoke a decision.
		RL.8.4	Determine the meaning of words and phrases as they are used in a text, including figurative and connotative meanings; analyze the impact of specific word choices on meaning and tone, including analogies or allusions to other texts.
		RL.8.10	By the end of the year, read and comprehend literature, including stories, dramas, and poems, at the high end of the grades 6–8 text complexity band independently and proficiently.
29	**Connect Reading and Writing** Critical Thinking	RL.8.2	Determine a theme or central idea of a text and analyze its development over the course of the text, including its relationship to the characters, setting, and plot; provide an objective summary of the text.
	Vocabulary Review	L.8.6	Acquire and use accurately grade-appropriate general academic and domain-specific words and phrases; gather vocabulary knowledge when considering a word or phrase important to comprehension or expression.
	Write About the GQ	W.8.9	Draw evidence from literary or informational texts to support analysis, reflection, and research.
		W.8.10	Write routinely over extended time frames (time for research, reflection, and revision) and shorter time frames (a single sitting or a day or two) for a range of discipline-specific tasks, purposes, and audiences.

Selection 1 American Names, continued

Pages	Lesson	Code	Standards Text
30	**Vocabulary Study** Use Compound Words	L.8.4	Determine or clarify the meaning of unknown and multiple-meaning words or phrases based on grade 8 reading and content, choosing flexibly from a range of strategies.
		L.8.6	Acquire and use accurately grade-appropriate general academic and domain-specific words and phrases; gather vocabulary knowledge when considering a word or phrase important to comprehension or expression.
30	**Research/Speaking** Research Healthy Foods	SL.8.1.a	Engage effectively in a range of collaborative discussions (one-on-one, in groups, and teacher-led) with diverse partners on grade 8 topics, texts, and issues, building on others' ideas and expressing their own clearly. Come to discussions prepared, having read or researched material under study; explicitly draw on that preparation by referring to evidence on the topic, text, or issue to probe and reflect on ideas under discussion.
		SL.8.4	Present claims and findings, emphasizing salient points in a focused, coherent manner with relevant evidence, sound valid reasoning, and well-chosen details; use appropriate eye contact, adequate volume, and clear pronunciation.
		SL.8.6	Adapt speech to a variety of contexts and tasks, demonstrating command of formal English when indicated or appropriate.
31	**Language and Grammar** Ask and Answer Questions	SL.8.1	Engage effectively in a range of collaborative discussions (one-on-one, in groups, and teacher-led) with diverse partners on grade 8 topics, texts, and issues, building on others' ideas and expressing their own clearly.
		L.8.1.c	Demonstrate command of the conventions of standard English grammar and usage when writing or speaking. Form and use verbs in the indicative, imperative, interrogative, conditional, and subjunctive moods.
31	**Writing and Grammar** Write About Your Name	W.8.3.d	Write narratives to develop real or imagined experiences or events using effective technique, relevant descriptive details, and well-structured event sequences. Use precise words and phrases, relevant descriptive details, and sensory language to capture the action and convey experiences and events.
		L.8.1.c	Demonstrate command of the conventions of standard English grammar and usage when writing or speaking. Form and use verbs in the indicative, imperative, interrogative, conditional, and subjunctive moods.

Selection 2 A Lion Hunt

Pages	Lesson	Code	Standards Text
32	**Connect**	SL.8.1	Engage effectively in a range of collaborative discussions (one-on-one, in groups, and teacher-led) with diverse partners on grade 8 topics, texts, and issues, building on others' ideas and expressing their own clearly.
		SL.8.2	Analyze the purpose of information presented in diverse media and formats (e.g., visually, quantitatively, orally) and evaluate the motives (e.g., social, commercial, political) behind its presentation.

Common Core State Standards, continued

Selection 2 A Lion Hunt, continued

Pages	Lesson	Code	Standards Text
33–35	**Language & Grammar** Give Information	SL.8.4	Present claims and findings, emphasizing salient points in a focused, coherent manner with relevant evidence sound valid reasoning, and well-chosen details; use appropriate eye contact, adequate volume, and clear pronunciation.
		L.8.1	Demonstrate command of the conventions of standard English grammar and usage when writing or speaking.
	Use Nouns in Sentences	L.8.1	Demonstrate command of the conventions of standard English grammar and usage when writing or speaking.
		L.8.2.c	Demonstrate command of the conventions of standard English capitalization, punctuation, and spelling when writing. Spell correctly.
36	**Key Vocabulary**	RI.8.4	Determine the meaning of words and phrases as they are used in a text, including figurative, connotative, and technical meanings; analyze the impact of specific word choices on meaning and tone, including analogies or allusions to other texts.
		L.8.4	Determine or clarify the meaning of unknown and multiple-meaning words or phrases based on grade 8 reading and content, choosing flexibly from a range of strategies.
37	**Reading Strategy** Make Inferences, Determine Importance, and Synthesize	RI.8.1	Cite the textual evidence that most strongly supports an analysis of what the text says explicitly as well as inferences drawn from text.
	Literary Analysis: Use Text Evidence and Determine Main Idea	RI.8.2	Determine a central idea of a text and analyze its development over the course of the text, including its relationship to supporting ideas; provide an objective summary of the text.
38–50	**Reading Selection**	RI.8.1	Cite the textual evidence that most strongly supports an analysis of what the text says explicitly as well as inferences drawn from text.
		RI.8.2	Determine a central idea of a text and analyze its development over the course of the text, including its relationship to supporting ideas; provide an objective summary of the text.
		RI.8.4	Determine the meaning of words and phrases as they are used in a text, including figurative, connotative, and technical meanings; analyze the impact of specific word choices on meaning and tone, including analogies or allusions to other texts.
		RI.8.10	By the end of the year, read and comprehend literary nonfiction at the high end of the grades 6–8 text complexity band independently and proficiently.
51	**Connect Reading and Writing** Critical Thinking	RI.8.2	Determine a central idea of a text and analyze its development over the course of the text, including its relationship to supporting ideas; provide an objective summary of the text.
	Vocabulary Review	L.8.6	Acquire and use accurately grade-appropriate general academic and domain-specific words and phrases; gather vocabulary knowledge when considering a word or phrase important to comprehension or expression.
	Write About the GQ	W.8.9	Draw evidence from literary or informational texts to support analysis, reflection, and research.
		W.8.10	Write routinely over extended time frames (time for research, reflection, and revision) and shorter time frames (a single sitting or a day or two) for a range of discipline-specific tasks, purposes, and audiences.
52	**Vocabulary Study** Use Suffixes	L.8.4.b	Determine or clarify the meaning of unknown and multiple-meaning words or phrases based on grade 8 reading and content, choosing flexibly from a range of strategies. Use common, grade-appropriate Greek or Latin affixes and roots as clues to the meaning of a word (e.g., *precede, recede, secede*).
		L.8.6	Adapt speech to a variety of contexts and tasks, demonstrating command of formal English when indicated or appropriate.

Selection 2 A Lion Hunt, continued

Pages	Lesson	Code	Standards Text
52	**Listening/Speaking** Discuss Different Viewpoints	SL.8.1.a	Engage effectively in a range of collaborative discussions (one-on-one, in groups, and teacher-led) with diverse partners on grade 8 topics, texts, and issues, building on others' ideas and expressing their own clearly. Come to discussions prepared, having read or researched material under study; explicitly draw on that preparation by referring to evidence on the topic, text, or issue to probe and reflect on ideas under discussion.
		SL.8.1.c	Engage effectively in a range of collaborative discussions (one-on-one, in groups, and teacher-led) with diverse partners on grade 8 topics, texts, and issues, building on others' ideas and expressing their own clearly. Pose questions that connect the ideas of several speakers and respond to others' questions and comments with relevant evidence, observations, and ideas.
		SL.8.1.d	Engage effectively in a range of collaborative discussions (one-on-one, in groups, and teacher-led) with diverse partners on grade 8 topics, texts, and issues, building on others' ideas and expressing their own clearly. Acknowledge new information expressed by others, and, when warranted, qualify or justify their own views in light of the evidence presented.
		SL.8.3	Delineate a speaker's argument and specific claims, evaluating the soundness of the reasoning and relevance and sufficiency of the evidence and identifying when irrelevant evidence is introduced.
		SL.8.4	Present claims and findings, emphasizing salient points in a focused, coherent manner with relevant evidence, sound valid reasoning, and well-chosen details; use appropriate eye contact, adequate volume, and clear pronunciation.
53	**Language and Grammar** Give Information	SL.8.4	Present claims and findings, emphasizing salient points in a focused, coherent manner with relevant evidence, sound valid reasoning, and well-chosen details; use appropriate eye contact, adequate volume, and clear pronunciation.
		L.8.1	Demonstrate command of the conventions of standard English grammar and usage when writing or speaking.
53	**Writing and Grammar** Write About Bravery	W.8.3.d	Write narratives to develop real or imagined experiences or events using effective technique, relevant descriptive details, and well-structured event sequences. Use precise words and phrases, relevant descriptive details, and sensory language to capture the action and convey experiences and events.
		L.8.1	Demonstrate command of the conventions of standard English grammar and usage when writing or speaking.
		L.8.2.c	Demonstrate command of the conventions of standard English capitalization, punctuation, and spelling when writing. Spell correctly.

Selection 3 from The House on Mango Street

Pages	Lesson	Code	Standards Text
54	**Connect**	SL.8.1	Engage effectively in a range of collaborative discussions (one-on-one, in groups, and teacher-led) with diverse partners on grade 8 topics, texts, and issues, building on others' ideas and expressing their own clearly.
		SL.8.2	Analyze the purpose of information presented in diverse media and formats (e.g., visually, quantitatively, orally) and evaluate the motives (e.g., social, commercial, political) behind its presentation.

Common Core State Standards, continued

Selection 3 from The House on Mango Street, continued

Pages	Lesson	Code	Standards Text
55–57	**Language & Grammar** Express Ideas and Opinions	SL.8.1	Engage effectively in a range of collaborative discussions (one-on-one, in groups, and teacher-led) with diverse partners on grade 8 topics, texts, and issues, building on others' ideas and expressing their own clearly.
		L.8.1.c	Demonstrate command of the conventions of standard English grammar and usage when writing or speaking. Form and use verbs in the indicative, imperative, interrogative, conditional, and subjunctive moods.
		L.8.3.a	Use knowledge of language and its conventions when writing, speaking, reading, or listening. Use verbs in the active and passive voice and in the conditional and subjunctive mood to achieve particular effects (e.g., emphasizing the actor or the action; expressing uncertainty, or describing a state contrary to fact).
	Use Action Verbs	L.8.1.c	Demonstrate command of the conventions of standard English grammar and usage when writing or speaking. Form and use verbs in the indicative, imperative, interrogative, conditional, and subjunctive moods.
58	**Key Vocabulary**	RL.8.4	Determine the meaning of words and phrases as they are used in a text, including figurative and connotative meanings; analyze the impact of specific word choices on meaning and tone, including analogies or allusions to other texts.
		L.8.4	Determine or clarify the meaning of unknown and multiple-meaning words or phrases based on grade 8 reading and content, choosing flexibly from a range of strategies.
59	**Reading Strategy** Make Connections and Visualize	RL.8.1	Cite the textual evidence that most strongly supports an analysis of what the text says explicitly as well as inferences drawn from the text.
	Literary Analysis Use Text Evidence	RL.8.4	Determine the meaning of words and phrases as they are used in a text, including figurative and connotative meanings; analyze the impact of specific word choices on meaning and tone, including analogies or allusions to other texts.
60–70	**Reading Selection**	RL.8.1	Cite the textual evidence that most strongly supports an analysis of what the text says explicitly as well as inferences drawn from the text.
		RL.8.10	By the end of the year, read and comprehend literature, including stories, dramas, and poems, at the high end of grades 6–8 text complexity band independently and proficiently.
71	**Connect Reading and Writing** Critical Thinking	RL.8.2	Determine a theme or central idea of a text and analyze its development over the course of the text, including its relationship to the characters, setting, and plot; provide an objective summary of the text.
	Vocabulary Review	L.8.6	Acquire and use accurately grade-appropriate general academic and domain-specific words and phrases; gather vocabulary knowledge when considering a word or phrase important to comprehension or expression.
	Write About the GQ	W.8.9	Draw evidence from literary or informational texts to support analysis, reflection, and research.
		W.8.10	Write routinely over extended time frames (time for research, reflection, and revision) and shorter time frames (a single sitting or a day or two) for a range of discipline-specific tasks, purposes, and audiences.

Selection 3 from The House on Mango Street, continued

Pages	Lesson	Code	Standards Text
72	**Vocabulary Study** Use Word Parts	L.8.4.b	Determine or clarify the meaning of unknown and multiple-meaning words or phrases based on grade 8 reading and content, choosing flexibly from a range of strategies. Use common, grade-appropriate Greek or Latin affixes and roots as clues to the meaning of a word (e.g., *precede, recede, secede*).
72	**Literary Analysis** Analyze Theme	RL.8.2	Determine a theme or central idea of a text and analyze its development over the course of the text, including its relationship to the characters, setting, and plot; provide an objective summary of the text.
73	**Language and Grammar** Express Ideas and Opinions	SL.8.1	Engage effectively in a range of collaborative discussions (one-on-one, in groups, and teacher-led) with diverse partners on grade 8 topics, texts, and issues, building on others' ideas and expressing their own clearly.
		L.8.1.c	Demonstrate command of the conventions of standard English grammar and usage when writing or speaking. Form and use verbs in the indicative, imperative, interrogative, conditional, and subjunctive moods.
73	**Writing and Grammar** Write with Colorful Action Words	W.8.3.d	Write narratives to develop real or imagined experiences or events using effective technique, relevant descriptive details, and well-structured event sequences. Use precise words and phrases, relevant descriptive details, and sensory language to capture the action and convey experiences and events.
		L.8.1.c	Demonstrate command of the conventions of standard English grammar and usage when writing or speaking. Form and use verbs in the indicative, imperative, interrogative, conditional, and subjunctive moods.
74–75	**Close Reading**	RL.8.10	By the end of the year, read and comprehend literature, including stories, dramas, and poems, at the high end of grades 6–8 text complexity band independently and proficiently.

Compare Across Texts

Pages	Lesson	Code	Standards Text
76	**Compare Universal Themes**	SL.8.1	Engage effectively in a range of collaborative discussions (one-on-one, in groups, and teacher-led) with diverse partners on grade 8 topics, texts, and issues, building on others' ideas and expressing their own clearly.
		SL.8.1.b	Engage effectively in a range of collaborative discussions (one-on-one, in groups, and teacher-led) with diverse partners on grade 8 topics, texts, and issues, building on others' ideas and expressing their own clearly. Follow rules for collegial discussions and decision- making, track progress toward specific goals and deadlines, and define individual roles as needed.

Common Core State Standards, continued

Unit Wrap-Up

Pages	Lesson	Code	Standards Text
77	**Reflect on Your Reading**	RL.8.1	Cite the textual evidence that most strongly supports an analysis of what the text says explicitly as well as inferences drawn from the text.
		RL.8.2	Determine a theme or central idea of a text and analyze its development over the course of the text, including its relationship to the characters, setting, and plot; provide an objective summary of the text.
		RL.8.4	Determine the meaning of words and phrases as they are used in a text, including figurative and connotative meanings; analyze the impact of specific word choices on meaning and tone, including analogies or allusions to other texts.
		RL.8.10	By the end of the year, read and comprehend literature, including stories, dramas, and poems, at the high end of grades 6-8 text complexity band independently and proficiently.
		RI.8.1	Cite the textual evidence that most strongly supports an analysis of what the text says explicitly as well as inferences drawn from the text.
		RI.8.2	Cite the textual evidence that most strongly supports an analysis of what the text says explicitly as well as inferences drawn from the text. RI.8.2 Determine a central idea of a text and analyze its development over the course of the text, including its relationship to supporting ideas; provide an objective summary of the text.
		RI.8.4	Determine the meaning of words and phrases as they are used in a text, including figurative, connotative, and technical meanings; analyze the impact of specific word choices on meaning and tone, including analogies or allusions to other texts.
		RI.8.10	By the end of the year, read and comprehend literary nonfiction at the high end of the grades 6-8 text complexity band independently and proficiently.
	Explore the GQ/Book Talk	W.8.10	Write routinely over extended time frames (time for research, reflection, and revision) and shorter time frames (a single sitting or a day or two) for a range of discipline-specific tasks, purposes, and audiences.
		SL.8.1	Engage effectively in a range of collaborative discussions (one-on-one, in groups, and teacher-led) with diverse partners on grade 8 topics, texts, and issues, building on others' ideas and expressing their own clearly.

Unit 2 Stand or Fall

Unit Launch

Pages	Lesson	Code	Standards Text
78–79	**Unit Opener**	SL.8.1	Engage effectively in a range of collaborative discussions (one-on-one, in groups, and teacher-led) with diverse partners on grade 8 topics, texts, and issues, building on others' ideas and expressing their own clearly.
80–83	**Focus on Reading** Analyze Elements of Fiction: Plot, Character, Setting	RL.8.3	Analyze how particular lines of dialogue or incidents in a story or drama propel the action, reveal aspects of a character, or provoke a decision.

Pages	Lesson	Code	Standards Text
84–85	**Focus on Vocabulary** Relate Words	RL.8.4	Determine the meaning of words and phrases as they are used in a text, including figurative and connotative meanings; analyze the impact of specific word choice on meaning and tone, including analogies or allusions to other texts.
		RI.8.4	Determine the meaning of words and phrases as they are used in a text, including figurative, connotative, and technical meanings; analyze the impact of specific word choices on meaning and tone, including analogies or allusions to other texts.
		L.8.5	Demonstrate understanding of figurative language, word relationships, and nuances in word meanings.
		L.8.5.b	Demonstrate understanding of figurative language, word relationships, and nuances in word meanings. Use the relationship between particular words to better understand each of the words.
		L.8.5.c	Demonstrate understanding of figurative language, word relationships, and nuances in word meanings. Distinguish among the connotations (associations) of words with similar denotations (definitions) (e.g., *bullheaded, willful, firm, persistent, resolute.*)

Selection 1 On the Menu

Pages	Lesson	Code	Standards Text
86	**Connect**	SL.8.1	Engage effectively in a range of collaborative discussions (one-on-one, in groups, and teacher-led) with diverse partners on grade 8 topics, texts, and issues, building on others' ideas and expressing their own clearly.
		SL.8.2	Analyze the purpose of information presented in diverse media and formats (e.g., visually, quantitatively, orally) and evaluate the motives (e.g., social, commercial, political) behind its presentation.
87–89	**Language & Grammar** Define and Explain	SL.8.1	Engage effectively in a range of collaborative discussions (one-on-one, in groups, and teacher-led) with diverse partners on grade 8 topics, texts, and issues, building on others' ideas and expressing their own clearly.
	Use Pronouns as Subjects	L.8.1	Demonstrate command of the conventions of standard English grammar and usage when writing or speaking.
90	**Key Vocabulary**	RI.8.4	Determine the meaning of words and phrases as they are used in a text, including figurative, connotative, and technical meanings; analyze the impact of specific word choices on meaning and tone, including analogies or allusions to other texts.
		L.8.4	Determine or clarify the meaning of unknown and multiple-meaning words or phrases based on grade 8 reading and content, choosing flexibly from a range of strategies.
91	**Academic Vocabulary**	RI.8.1	Cite the textual evidence that most strongly supports an analysis of what the text says explicitly as well as inferences drawn from the text.
	Reading Strategy Monitor	RI.8.3	Analyze how a text makes connections among and distinctions between individuals, ideas, or events (e.g., through comparisons, analogies, or categories).
	Literary Analysis Relate Cause and Effect	L.8.6	Acquire and use accurately grade-appropriate general academic and domain-specific words and phrases; gather vocabulary knowledge when considering a word or phrase important to comprehension or expression.

Common Core State Standards, continued

Selection 1 On the Menu, continued

Pages	Lesson	Code	Standards Text
92–104	**Reading Selection**	RI.8.3	Analyze how a text makes connections among and distinctions between individuals, ideas, or events (e.g., through comparisons, analogies, or categories).
		RI.8.10	By the end of the year, read and comprehend literary nonfiction at the high end of the grades 6-8 text complexity band independently and proficiently.
105	**Connect Reading and Writing** Critical Thinking	RI.8.2	Determine a central idea of a text and analyze its development over the course of the text, including its relationship to supporting ideas; provide an objective summary of the text.
	Vocabulary Review	L.8.6	Acquire and use accurately grade-appropriate general academic and domain-specific words and phrases; gather vocabulary knowledge when considering a word or phrase important to comprehension or expression.
	Write About the GQ	W.8.9	Draw evidence from literary or informational texts to support analysis, reflection, and research.
		W.8.10	Write routinely over extended time frames (time for research, reflection, and revision) and shorter time frames (a single sitting or a day or two) for a range of discipline-specific tasks, purposes, and audiences.
106	**Vocabulary Study** Relate Words: Synonyms	L.8.4	Determine or clarify the meaning of unknown and multiple-meaning words or phrases based on grade 8 reading and content, choosing flexibly from a range of strategies.
		L.8.5	Demonstrate understanding of figurative language, word relationships, and nuances in word meanings.
		L.8.5.b	Demonstrate understanding of figurative language, word relationships, and nuances in word meanings. Use the relationship between particular words to better understand each of the words.
		L.8.5.c	Demonstrate understanding of figurative language, word relationships, and nuances in word meanings. Distinguish among the connotations (associations) of words with similar denotations (definitions) (e.g., *bullheaded, willful, firm, persistent, resolute*).
		L.8.6	Acquire and use accurately grade-appropriate general academic and domain-specific words and phrases; gather vocabulary knowledge when considering a word or phrase important to comprehension or expression.
106	**Literary Analysis** Analyze Cause and Effect	RI.8.3	Analyze how a text makes connections among and distinctions between individuals, ideas, or events (e.g., through comparisons, analogies, or categories).
107	**Language and Grammar** Define and Explain	SL.8.1	Engage effectively in a range of collaborative discussions (one-on-one, in groups, and teacher-led) with diverse partners on grade 8 topics, texts, and issues, building on others' ideas and expressing their own clearly.
		L.8.1	Demonstrate command of the conventions of standard English grammar and usage when writing or speaking.
107	**Writing and Grammar** Write About an Animal	W.8.3.d	Write narratives to develop real or imagined experiences or events using effective technique, relevant descriptive details, and well-structured event sequences. Use precise words and phrases, relevant descriptive details, and sensory language to capture the action and convey experiences and events.
		L.8.1	Demonstrate command of the conventions of standard English grammar and usage when writing or speaking.

Selection 2 The Three Chicharrones

Pages	Lesson	Code	Standards Text
108	**Connect**	SL.8.1	Engage effectively in a range of collaborative discussions (one-on-one, in groups, and teacher-led) with diverse partners on grade 8 topics, texts, and issues, building on others' ideas and expressing their own clearly.
		SL.8.2	Analyze the purpose of information presented in diverse media and formats (e.g., visually, quantitatively, orally) and evaluate the motives (e.g., social, commercial, political) behind its presentation.
109–111	**Language & Grammar** Retell a Story	SL.8.1	Engage effectively in a range of collaborative discussions (one-on-one, in groups, and teacher-led) with diverse partners on grade 8 topics, texts, and issues, building on others' ideas and expressing their own clearly.
		L.8.1.c	Demonstrate command of the conventions of standard English grammar and usage when writing or speaking. Form and use verbs in the indicative, imperative, interrogative, conditional, and subjunctive moods.
	Use Forms of the Verbs *Be* and *Have*	L.8.1.c	Demonstrate command of the conventions of standard English grammar and usage when writing or speaking. Form and use verbs in the indicative, imperative, interrogative, conditional, and subjunctive moods.
112	**Key Vocabulary**	RL.8.4	Determine the meaning of words and phrases as they are used in a text, including figurative and connotative meanings; analyze the impact of specific word choices on meaning and tone, including analogies or allusions to other texts.
		L.8.4	Determine or clarify the meaning of unknown and multiple-meaning words or phrases based on grade 8 reading and content, choosing flexibly from a range of strategies.
113	**Reading Strategy** Monitor	RL.8.1	Cite the textual evidence that most strongly supports an analysis of what the text says explicitly as well as inferences drawn from the text.
	Literary Analysis Analyze Modern Fiction	RL.8.9	Analyze how a modern work of fiction draws on themes, patterns of events, or character types from myths, traditional stories, or religious works such as the Bible, including describing how the material is rendered new.
114–126	**Reading Selection**	RL.8.2	Determine a theme or central idea of a text and analyze its development over the course of the text, including its relationship to the characters, setting, and plot; provide an objective summary of the text.
		RL.8.10	By the end of the year, read and comprehend literature, including stories, dramas, and poems, at the high end of grades 6–8 text complexity band independently and proficiently.
127	**Connect Reading and Writing** Critical Thinking	RL.8.2	Determine a theme or central idea of a text and analyze its development over the course of the text, including its relationship to the characters, setting, and plot; provide an objective summary of the text.
	Vocabulary Review	L.8.6	Acquire and use accurately grade-appropriate general academic and domain-specific words and phrases; gather vocabulary knowledge when considering a word or phrase important to comprehension or expression.
	Write About the GQ	W.8.9	Draw evidence from literary or informational texts to support analysis, reflection, and research.
		W.8.10	Write routinely over extended time frames (time for research, reflection, and revision) and shorter time frames (a single sitting or a day or two) for a range of discipline-specific tasks, purposes, and audiences.
128	**Vocabulary Study** Relate Words: Cognates	L.8.5.b	Demonstrate understanding of figurative language, word relationships, and nuances in word meanings. Use the relationship between particular words to better understand each of the words.

Common Core State Standards, continued

Selection 2 The Three Chicharrones, continued

Pages	Lesson	Code	Standards Text
128	**Literary Analysis** Analyze Character Traits	RL.8.3	Analyze how particular lines of dialogue or incidents in a story or drama propel the action, reveal aspects of a character, or provoke a decision.
129	**Language and Grammar** Retell a Story	SL.8.1	Engage effectively in a range of collaborative discussions (one-on-one, in groups, and teacher-led) with diverse partners on grade 8 topics, texts, and issues, building on others' ideas and expressing their own clearly.
		L.8.1.c	Demonstrate command of the conventions of standard English grammar and usage when writing or speaking. Form and use verbs in the indicative, imperative, interrogative, conditional, and subjunctive moods.
129	**Writing and Grammar** Write About a Folk Tale	W.8.3.d	Write narratives to develop real or imagined experiences or events using effective technique, relevant descriptive details, and well-structured event sequences. Use precise words and phrases, relevant descriptive details, and sensory language to capture the action and convey experiences and events.
		L.8.1.c	Demonstrate command of the conventions of standard English grammar and usage when writing or speaking. Form and use verbs in the indicative, imperative, interrogative, conditional, and subjunctive moods.

Selection 3 Dragon, Dragon

Pages	Lesson	Code	Standards Text
130	**Connect**	SL.8.1	Engage effectively in a range of collaborative discussions (one-on-one, in groups, and teacher-led) with diverse partners on grade 8 topics, texts, and issues, building on others' ideas and expressing their own clearly.
		SL.8.2	Analyze the purpose of information presented in diverse media and formats (e.g., visually, quantitatively, orally) and evaluate the motives (e.g., social, commercial, political) behind its presentation.
131–133	**Language & Grammar** Engage in Conversations	SL.8.1	Engage effectively in a range of collaborative discussions (one-on-one, in groups, and teacher-led) with diverse partners on grade 8 topics, texts, and issues, building on others' ideas and expressing their own clearly.
		SL.8.1.b	Engage effectively in a range of collaborative discussions (one-on-one, in groups, and teacher-led) with diverse partners on grade 8 topics, texts, and issues, building on others' ideas and expressing their own clearly. Follow rules for collegial discussions and decision-making, track progress toward specific goals and deadlines, and define individual roles as needed.
	Use Indefinite Pronouns	L.8.1	Demonstrate command of the conventions of standard English grammar and usage when writing or speaking.
134	**Key Vocabulary**	RL.8.4	Determine the meaning of words and phrases as they are used in a text, including figurative and connotative meanings; analyze the impact of specific word choices on meaning and tone, including analogies or allusions to other texts.
		L.8.4	Determine or clarify the meaning of unknown and multiple-meaning words or phrases based on grade 8 reading and content, choosing flexibly from a range of strategies.
135	**Reading Strategy** Monitor	RL.8.1	Cite the textual evidence that most strongly supports an analysis of what the text says explicitly as well as inferences drawn from the text.
	Literary Analysis Analyze Plot	RL.8.3	Analyze how particular lines of dialogue or incidents in a story or drama propel the action, reveal aspects of a character, or provoke a decision.
	Academic Vocabulary	L.8.6	Acquire and use accurately grade-appropriate general academic and domain-specific words and phrases; gather vocabulary knowledge when considering a word or phrase important to comprehension or expression.

Selection 3 Dragon, Dragon, continued

Pages	Lesson	Code	Standards Text
136–154	**Reading Selection**	RL.8.3	Analyze how particular lines of dialogue or incidents in a story or drama propel the action, reveal aspects of a character, or provoke a decision.
		RL.8.10	By the end of the year, read and comprehend literature, including stories, dramas, and poems, at the high end of grades 6-8 text complexity band independently and proficiently.
		RI.8.10	By the end of the year, read and comprehend literary nonfiction at the high end of the grades 6–8 text complexity band independently and proficiently.
155	**Connect Reading and Writing** Critical Thinking	RL.8.2	Determine a theme or central idea of a text and analyze its development over the course of the text, including its relationship to the characters, setting, and plot; provide an objective summary of the text.
	Vocabulary Review	L.8.6	Acquire and use accurately grade-appropriate general academic and domain-specific words and phrases; gather vocabulary knowledge when considering a word or phrase important to comprehension or expression.
	Write About the GQ	W.8.9	Draw evidence from literary or informational texts to support analysis, reflection, and research.
		W.8.10	Write routinely over extended time frames (time for research, reflection, and revision) and shorter time frames (a single sitting or a day or two) for a range of discipline-specific tasks, purposes, and audiences.
156	**Vocabulary Study** Relate Words	L.8.4	Determine or clarify the meaning of unknown and multiple-meaning words or phrases based on grade 8 reading and content, choosing flexibly from a range of strategies.
		L.8.5	Demonstrate understanding of figurative language, word relationships, and nuances in word meaning.
		L.8.5.b	Demonstrate understanding of figurative language, word relationships, and nuances in word meaning. Use the relationship between particular words to better understand each of the words.
		L.8.5.c	Demonstrate understanding of figurative language, word relationships, and nuances in word meaning. Distinguish among the connotations (associations) or words with similar denotations (definitions) (e.g., *bullheaded, willful, firm, persistent, resolute*).
		L.8.6	Adapt speech to a variety of contexts and tasks, demonstrating command of formal English when indicated or appropriate.
156	**Literary Analysis** Analyze Dialogue	RL.8.3	Analyze how particular lines of dialogue or incidents in a story or drama propel the action, reveal aspects of a character, or provoke a decision.
157	**Language and Grammar** Engage in Conversation	SL.8.1	Engage effectively in a range of collaborative discussions (one-on-one, in groups, and teacher-led) with diverse partners on grade 8 topics, texts, and issues, building on others' ideas and expressing their own clearly.
		SL.8.1.b	Engage effectively in a range of collaborative discussions (one-on-one, in groups, and teacher-led) with diverse partners on grade 8 topics, texts, and issues, building on others' ideas and expressing their own clearly. Follow rules for collegial discussions and decision-making, track progress toward specific goals and deadlines, and define individual roles as needed.
		L.8.1	Demonstrate command of the conventions of standard English grammar and usage when writing or speaking.

Common Core State Standards, continued

Selection 3 Dragon, Dragon, continued

Pages	Lesson	Code	Standards Text
157	**Writing and Grammar** Write About a Character in the Story	L.8.1	Demonstrate command of the conventions of standard English grammar and usage when writing or speaking.
		W.8.3.d	Write narratives to develop real or imagined experiences or events using effective technique, relevant descriptive details, and well-structured event sequences. Use precise words and phrases, relevant descriptive details, and sensory language to capture the action and convey experiences and events.
158–159	**Close Reading**	RL.8.10	By the end of the year, read and comprehend literature, including stories, dramas, and poems, at the high end of grades 6–8 text complexity band independently and proficiently.

Compare Across Texts

Pages	Lesson	Code	Standards Text
160	**Compare Characters, Settings, and Problems**	SL.8.1	Engage effectively in a range of collaborative discussions (one-on-one, in groups, and teacher-led) with diverse partners on grade 8 topics, texts, and issues, building on others' ideas and expressing their own clearly.

Unit Wrap-Up

Pages	Lesson	Code	Standards Text
161	**Reflect on Your Reading**	RL.8.1	Cite the textual evidence that most strongly supports an analysis of what the text says explicitly as well as inferences drawn from the text.
		RL.8.3	Analyze how particular lines of dialogue or incidents in a story or drama propel the action, reveal aspects of a character, or provoke a decision.
	Explore the GQ/Book Talk	W.8.10	Write routinely over extended time frames (time for research, reflection, and revision) and shorter time frames (a single sitting or a day or two) for a range of discipline-specific tasks, purposes, and audiences.
		SL.8.1	Engage effectively in a range of collaborative discussions (one-on-one, in groups, and teacher-led) with diverse partners on grade 8 topics, texts, and issues, building on others' ideas and expressing their own clearly.
		SL.8.5	Integrate multimedia and visual displays into presentations to clarify information, strengthen claims and evidence, and add interest.

Unit 3 Making a Difference
Unit Launch

Pages	Lesson	Code	Standards Text
162–163	**Unit Opener**	SL.8.1	Engage effectively in a range of collaborative discussions (one-on-one, in groups, and teacher-led) with diverse partners on grade 8 topics, texts, and issues, building on othersí ideas and expressing their own clearly.
164–165	**Focus on Reading** Text Structure	RI.8.5	Analyze in detail the structure of a specific paragraph in a text, including the role of particular sentences in developing and refining a key concept.
166–167	**Focus on Vocabulary** Use Word Parts	RI.8.4	Determine the meaning of words and phrases as they are used in a text, including figurative, connotative, and technical meanings; analyze the impact of specific word choices on meaning and tone, including analogies or allusions to other texts.
		L.8.4.b	Determine or clarify the meaning of unknown and multiple-meaning words or phrases based on grade 8 reading and content, choosing flexibly from a range of strategies. Use common, grade-appropriate Greek or Latin affixes and roots as clues to the meaning of a word (e.g., *precede, recede, secede*).
		L.8.6	Acquire and use accurately grade-appropriate general academic and doman-specific words and phrases; gather vocabulary knowledge when considering a word or phrase important to comprehension or expression.

Selection 1 The Civil Rights Movement

Pages	Lesson	Code	Standards Text
168	**Connect**	SL.8.1	Engage effectively in a range of collaborative discussions (one-on-one, in groups, and teacher-led) with diverse partners on grade 8 topics, texts, and issues, building on others' ideas and expressing their own clearly.
		SL.8.1.a	Engage effectively in a range of collaborative discussions (one-on-one, in groups, and teacher-led) with diverse partners on grade 8 topics, texts, and issues, building on others' ideas and expressing their own clearly.
			Come to discussions prepared, having read or researched material under study; explicitly draw on that preparation by referring to evidence on the topic, text, or issue to probe and reflect on ideas under discussion.
		SL.8.2	Analyze the purpose of information presented in diverse media and formats (e.g., visually, quantitatively, orally) and evaluate the motives (e.g., social, commercial, political) behind its presentation.
169–171	**Language & Grammar** Ask for and Give Information Use Present, Past, and Future Tense Verbs	L.8.1.c	Demonstrate command of the conventions of standard English grammar and usage when writing or speaking.
			Form and use verbs in the indicative, imperative, interrogative, conditional, and subjunctive moods.
		L.8.3	Use knowledge of language and its conventions when writing, speaking, reading, or listening.
172	**Key Vocabulary**	RI.8.4	Determine the meaning of words and phrases as they are used in a text, including figurative, connotative, and technical meanings; analyze the impact of specific word choices on meaning and tone, including analogies or allusions to other texts.
		L.8.4	Determine or clarify the meaning of unknown and multiple-meaning words or phrases based on grade 8 reading and content, choosing flexibly from a range of strategies.
173	**Reading Strategy** Ask Questions: Self-Question	RI.8.1	Cite the textual evidence that most strongly supports an analysis of what the text says explicitly as well as inferences drawn from text.
	Literary Analysis Analyze Text Structure: Chronological Order	RI.8.5	Analyze in detail the structure of a specific paragraph in a text, including the role of particular sentences in developing and refining a key concept.
174–190	**Reading Selection**	RI.8.1	Cite the textual evidence that most strongly supports an analysis of what the text says explicitly as well as inferences drawn from the text.
		RI.8.2	Determine a central idea of a text and analyze its development over the course of the text, including its relationship to supporting ideas; provide an objective summary of the text.
		RI.8.3	Analyze how a text makes connections among and distinctions between individuals, ideas, or events (e.g., through comparisons, analogies, or categories).
		RI.8.6	Determine an author's point of view or purpose in a text and analyze how the author acknowledges and responds to conflicting evidence or viewpoints.
		RI.8.10	By the end of the year, read and comprehend literary nonfiction at the high end of the grades 6–8 text complexity band independently and proficiently.

Common Core State Standards, continued

Selection 1 The Civil Rights Movement, continued

Pages	Lesson	Code	Standards Text
191	**Connect Reading and Writing** Critical Thinking	RI.8.2	Determine a central idea of a text and analyze its development over the course of the text, including its relationship to supporting ideas; provide an objective summary of the text.
	Vocabulary Review	L.8.6	Acquire and use accurately grade-appropriate general academic and domain-specific words and phrases; gather vocabulary knowledge when considering a word or phrase important to comprehension or expression.
	Write About the GQ	W.8.9	Draw evidence from literary or informational texts to support analysis, reflection, and research.
		W.8.10	Write routinely over extended time frames (time for research, reflection, and revision) and shorter time frames (a single sitting or a day or two) for a range of discipline-specific tasks, purposes, and audiences.
192	**Vocabulary Study** Use Word Parts: Prefixes	L.8.4	Determine or clarify the meaning of unknown and multiple-meaning words or phrases based on grade 8 reading and content, choosing flexibly from a range of strategies.
		L.8.4.b	Determine or clarify the meaning of unknown and multiple-meaning words or phrases based on grade 8 reading and content, choosing flexibly from a range of strategies. Use common, grade-appropriate Greek or Latin affixes and roots as clues to the meaning of a word (.e.g, *precede, recede, secede*)..
		L.8.6	Acquire and use accurately grade-appropriate general academic and domain-specific words and phrases; gather vocabulary knowledge when considering a word or phrase important to comprehension or expression.
192	**Literary Analysis** Evaluate Informational Text	RI.8.8	Delineate and evaluate the argument and specific claims in a text, assessing whether the reasoning is sound and the evidence is relevant and sufficient; recognize when irrelevant evidence is introduced.
193	**Language and Grammar** Ask for and Give Information	SL.8.1.c	Engage effectively in a range of collaborative discussions (one-on-one, in groups, and teacher-led) with diverse partners on grade 8 topics, texts, and issues, building on others' ideas and expressing their own clearly. Pose questions that connect the ideas of several speakers and respond to others' questions and comments with relevant evidence, observations, and ideas.
		L.8.1.c	Demonstrate command of the conventions of standard English grammar and usage when writing or speaking. Form and use verbs in the indicative, imperative, interrogative, conditional, and subjunctive moods.
193	**Writing and Grammar** Write About a Past Event	W.8.3.d	Write narratives to develop real or imagined experiences or events using effective technique, relevant descriptive details, and well-structured event sequences. Use precise words and phrases, relevant descriptive details, and sensory language to capture the action and convey experiences and events.
		L.8.1.c	Demonstrate command of the conventions of standard English grammar and usage when writing or speaking. Form and use verbs in the indicative, imperative, interrogative, conditional, and subjunctive moods.
		L.8.3	Use knowledge of language and its conventions when writing, speaking, reading, or listening.

Selection 2 Martin's Big Words

Pages	Lesson	Code	Standards Text
194	**Connect**	SL.8.1	Engage effectively in a range of collaborative discussions (one-on-one, in groups, and teacher-led) with diverse partners on grade 8 topics, texts, and issues, building on others' ideas and expressing their own clearly.
		SL.8.2	Analyze the purpose of information presented in diverse media and formats (e.g., visually, quantitatively, orally) and evaluate the motives (e.g., social, commercial, political) behind its presentation.

Selection 2 Martin's Big Words Movement, continued

Pages	Lesson	Code	Standards Text
195–197	**Language & Grammar** Describe an Event	SL.8.1.c	Engage effectively in a range of collaborative discussions (one-on-one, in groups, and teacher-led) with diverse partners on grade 8 topics, texts, and issues, building on others' ideas and expressing their own clearly. Pose questions that elicit elaboration and respond to others' questions and comments with relevant observations and ideas that bring the discussion back on topic as needed.
	Use Forms of *Be*	L.8.1.c	Demonstrate command of the conventions of standard English grammar and usage when writing or speaking. Form and use verbs in the indicative, imperative, interrogative, conditional, and subjunctive moods.
198	**Key Vocabulary**	RI.8.4	Determine the meaning or words and phrases as they are used in a text, including figurative, connotative, and technical meanings; analyze the impact of specific word choices on meaning and tone, including analogies or allusions to other texts.
		L.8.4	Determine or clarify the meaning of unknown and multiple-meaning words or phrases based on grade 8 reading and content, choosing flexibly from a range of strategies.
199	**Reading Strategy** Ask Questions	RI.8.1	Cite the textual evidence that most strongly supports an analysis of what the text says explicitly as well as inferences drawn from the text.
	Literary Analysis Analyze Text Structure: Chronological Order	RI.8.5	Analyze in detail the structure of a specific paragraph in a text, including the role of particular sentences in developing and refining a key concept.
200–208	**Reading Selection**	RI.8.1	Cite textual evidence that most strongly supports an analysis of what the text says explicitly as well as inferences drawn from the text.
		RI.8.10	By the end of the year, read and comprehend literary nonfiction at the high end of the grades 6–8 text complexity band independently and proficiently.
209	**Connect Reading and Writing** Critical Thinking	RI.8.2	Determine a central idea of a text and analyze its relationship to supporting ideas; provide an objective summary of the text.
	Vocabulary Review	L.8.6	Acquire and use accurately grade-appropriate general academic and domain-specific words and phrases; gather vocabulary knowledge when considering a word or phrase important to comprehension or expression.
	Write About the GQ	W.8.9	Draw evidence from literary or informational texts to support analysis, reflection, and research.
		W.8.10	Write routinely over extended time frames (time for research, reflection, and revision) and shorter time frames (a single sitting or a day or two) for a range of discipline-specific tasks, purposes, and audiences.
210	**Vocabulary Study** Use Word Parts: Suffixes	L.8.6	Acquire and use accurately grade-appropriate general academic and domain-specific words and phrases; gather vocabulary knowledge when considering a word or phrase important to comprehension or expression.
210	**Literary Analysis** Analyze Word Choice	RI.8.4	Determine the meaning of words and phrases as they are used in a text, including figurative, connotative, and technical meanings; analyze the impact of specific word choices on meaning and tone, including analogies or allusions to other texts.

Common Core State Standards, continued

Selection 2 Martin's Big Words Movement, continued

Pages	Lesson	Code	Standards Text
211	**Language and Grammar** Describe an Event	SL.8.1.a	Engage effectively in a range of collaborative discussions (one-on-one, in groups, and teacher-led) with diverse partners on grade 8 topics, texts, and issues, building on others' ideas and expressing their own clearly. Come to discussions prepared, having read or researched material under study; explicitly draw on that preparation by referring to evidence on the topic, text, or issue to probe and reflect on ideas under discussion.
		L.8.1.c	Demonstrate command of the conventions of standard English grammar and usage when writing or speaking. Form and use verbs in the indicative, imperative, interrogative, conditional, and subjunctive moods.
211	**Writing and Grammar** Write About the Past	W.8.3.d	Write narratives to develop real or imagined experiences or events using effective technique, relevant descriptive details, and well-structured event sequences. Use precise words and phrases, relevant descriptive details, and sensory language to capture the action and convey experiences and events.
		L.8.1.c	Demonstrate command of the conventions of standard English grammar and usage when writing or speaking. Form and use verbs in the indicative, imperative, interrogative, conditional, and subjunctive moods.

Selection 3 Water at Work

Pages	Lesson	Code	Standards Text
212	**Connect**	SL.8.1	Engage effectively in a range of collaborative discussions (one-on-one, in groups, and teacher-led) with diverse partners on grade 8 topics, texts, and issues, building on others' ideas and expressing their own clearly.
		SL.8.1.a	Engage effectively in a range of collaborative discussions (one-on-one, in groups, and teacher-led) with diverse partners on grade 8 topics, texts, and issues, building on others' ideas and expressing their own clearly. Come to discussions prepared, having read or researched material under study; explicitly draw on that preparation by referring to evidence on the topic, text, or issue to probe and reflect on ideas under discussion.
		SL.8.2	Analyze the purpose of information presented in diverse media and formats (e.g., visually, quantitatively, orally) and evaluate the motives (e.g., social, commercial, political) behind its presentation.
213–215	**Language & Grammar** Summarize	RI.8.2	Determine a central idea of a text and analyze its development over the course of the text, including its relationship to supporting ideas; provide an objective summary of the text.
		SL.8.4	Present claims and findings, emphasizing salient points in a focused, coherent manner with relevant evidence, sound valid reasoning, and well-chosen details; use appropriate eye contact, adequate volume, and clear pronunciation.
		SL.8.5	Integrate multimedia and visual displays into presentations to clarify information, strengthen claims and evidence, and add interest.
	Use Verbs in the Past Tense	L.8.1.c	Demonstrate command of the conventions of standard English grammar and usage when writing or speaking. Form and use verbs in the indicative, imperative, interrogative, conditional, and subjunctive moods.
		L.8.2.c	Demonstrate command of the conventions of standard English capitalization, punctuation, and spelling when writing. Spell correctly.

Selection 3 Water at Work, continued

Pages	Lesson	Code	Standards Text
216	**Key Vocabulary**	RL.8.4	Determine the meaning of words and phrases as they are used in a text, including figurative and connotative meanings; analyze the impact of specific word choices on meaning and tone, including analogies or allusions to other texts.
		L.8.4	Determine or clarify the meaning of unknown and multiple-meaning words or phrases based on grade 8 reading and content, choosing flexibly from a range of strategies.
217	**Reading Strategy** Ask Questions	RI.8.1	Cite the textual evidence that most strongly supports an analysis of what the text says explicitly as well as inferences drawn from the text.
	Literary Analysis Analyze Text Structure: Problem and Solution	RI.8.5	Analyze in detail the structure of a specific paragraph in a text, including the role of particular sentences in developing and refining a key concept.
218–226	**Reading Selection**	RI.8.10	By the end of the year, read and comprehend literary nonfiction at the high end of the grades 6–8 text complexity band independently and proficiently.
227	**Connect Reading and Writing** Critical Thinking	RI.8.2	Determine a central idea of a text and analyze its relationship to supporting ideas; provide an objective summary of the text.
	Vocabulary Review	L.8.6	Acquire and use accurately grade-appropriate general academic and domain-specific words and phrases; gather vocabulary knowledge when considering a word or phrase important to comprehension or expression.
	Write About the GQ	W.8.9	Draw evidence from literary or informational texts to support analysis, reflection, and research.
		W.8.10	Write routinely over extended time frames (time for research, reflection, and revision) and shorter time frames (a single sitting or a day or two) for a range of discipline-specific tasks, purposes, and audiences.
228	**Vocabulary Study** Use Word Parts	L.8.6	Acquire and use accurately grade-appropriate general academic and domain-specific words and phrases; gather vocabulary knowledge when considering a word or phrase important to comprehension or expression.
228	**Listening/Speaking** Deliver a Problem-Solution Presentation	SL.8.4	Present claims and findings, emphasizing salient points in a focused, coherent manner with relevant evidence, sound valid reasoning, and well-chosen details; use appropriate eye contact, adequate volume, and clear pronunciations.
		SL.8.6	Adapt speech to a variety of contexts and tasks, demonstrating command of formal English when indicated or appropriate.
229	**Language and Grammar** Summarize	RI.8.2	Determine a central idea of a text and analyze its development over the course of the text, including its relationship to supporting ideas; provide an objective summary of the text.
		SL.8.4	Present claims and findings, emphasizing salient points in a focused, coherent manner with relevant evidence, sound valid reasoning, and well-chosen details; use appropriate eye contact, adequate volume, and clear pronunciation.
		L.8.1.c	Demonstrate command of the conventions of standard English grammar and usage when writing or speaking. Form and use verbs in the indicative, imperative, interrogative, conditional, and subjunctive moods.

Common Core State Standards, continued

Selection 3 Water at Work, continued

Pages	Lesson	Code	Standards Text
229	**Writing and Grammar** Write Consistently About the Past	W.8.3.d	Write narratives to develop real or imagined experiences or events using effective technique, relevant descriptive details, and well-structured event sequences. Use precise words and phrases, relevant descriptive details, and sensory language to capture the action and convey experiences and events.
		SL.8.4	Present claims and findings, emphasizing salient points in a focused, coherent manner with relevant evidence, sound valid reasoning, and well-chosen details; use appropriate eye contact, adequate volume, and clear pronunciation. volume, and clear pronunciation.
		L.8.1.c	Demonstrate command of the conventions of standard English grammar and usage when writing or speaking. Form and use verbs in the indicative, imperative, interrogative, conditional, and subjunctive moods.
		L.8.2.c	Demonstrate command of the conventions of standard English capitalization, punctuation, and spelling when writing. Spell correctly.
230–233	**Close Reading**	RI.8.10	By the end of the year, read and comprehend literary nonfiction at the high end of the grades 6–8 text complexity band independently and proficiently.

Compare Across Texts

Pages	Lesson	Code	Standards Text
234	**Compare Writing on the Same Topic**	SL.8.1	Engage effectively in a range of collaborative discussions (one-on-one, in groups, and teacher-led) with diverse partners on grade 8 topics, texts, and issues, building on others' ideas and expressing their own clearly.
235	**Reflect on Your Reading**	RI.8.1	Cite the textual evidence that most strongly supports an analysis of what the text says explicitly as well as inferences drawn from the text.
		RI.8.5	Analyze in detail the structure of a specific paragraph in a text, including the role of particular sentences in developing and refining a key concept.
	Explore the GQ/Book Talk	W.8.10	Write routinely over extended time frames (time for research, reflection, and revision) and shorter time frames (a single sitting or a day or two) for a range of discipline-specific tasks, purposes, and audiences.
		SL.8.1	Engage effectively in a range of collaborative discussions (one-on-one, in groups, and teacher-led) with diverse partners on grade 8 topics, texts, and issues, building on others' ideas and expressing their own clearly.

Unit 4   At Home in the World

Unit Launch

Pages	Lesson	Code	Standards Text
236–237	**Unit Opener**	SL.8.1	Engage effectively in a range of collaborative discussions (one-on-one, in groups, and teacher-led) with diverse partners on grade 8 topics, texts, and issues, building on others' ideas and expressing their own clearly.
238–239	**Focus on Reading** Analyze Connections	RI.8.3	Analyze how a text makes connections among and distinctions between individuals, ideas, or events (e.g., through comparisons, analogies, or categories).

Unit Launch, continued

Pages	Lesson	Code	Standards Text
240–241	**Focus on Vocabulary** Use Context Clues	RL.8.4	Determine the meaning of words and phrases as they are used in a text, including figurative and connotative meanings; analyze the impact of specific word choices on meaning and tone, including analogies or allusions to other texts.
		RI.8.4	Determine the meaning of words and phrases as they are used in a text, including figurative, connotative, and technical meanings; analyze the impact of specific word choices on meaning and tone, including analogies or allusions to other texts.
		L.8.4	Determine or clarify the meaning of unknown and multiple-meaning words or phrases based on grade 8 reading and content, choosing flexibly from a range of strategies.
		L.8.4.a	Determine or clarify the meaning of unknown and multiple-meaning words or phrases based on grade 8 reading and content, choosing flexibly from a range of strategies. Use context (e.g., the overall meaning of a sentence or paragraph; a word's position or function in a sentence) as a clue to the meaning of a word or phrase.
		L.8.6	Acquire and use accurately grade-appropriate general academic and domain-specific words and phrases; gather vocabulary knowledge when considering a word or phrase important to comprehension or expression.

Selection 1 Here, There, and Beyond

Pages	Lesson	Code	Standards Text
242	**Connect**	SL.8.1	Engage effectively in a range of collaborative discussions (one-on-one, in groups, and teacher-led) with diverse partners on grade 8 topics, texts, and issues, building on others' ideas and expressing their own clearly.
		SL.8.2	Analyze the purpose of information presented in diverse media and formats (e.g., visually, quantitatively, orally) and evaluate the motives (e.g., social, commercial, political) behind its presentation.
243–245	**Language & Grammar** Make Comparisons	SL.8.1	Engage effectively in a range of collaborative discussions (one-on-one, in groups, and teacher-led) with diverse partners on grade 8 topics, texts, and issues, building on others' ideas and expressing their own clearly.
	Use Nouns in the Subject and Predicate	L.8.1	Demonstrate command of the conventions of standard English grammar and usage when writing or speaking.
246	**Key Vocabulary**	RI.8.4	Determine the meaning of words and phrases as they are used in a text, including figurative, connotative, and technical meanings; analyze the impact of specific word choices on meaning and tone, including analogies or allusions to other texts.
		L.8.4	Determine or clarify the meaning of unknown and multiple-meaning words or phrases based on grade 8 reading and content, choosing flexibly from a range of strategies.
247	**Reading Strategy** Make Connections	RI.8.1	Cite the textual evidence that most strongly supports an analysis of what the text says explicitly as well as inferences drawn from the text.
	Literary Analysis Compare and Contrast	RI.8.3	Analyze how a text makes connections among and distinctions between individuals, ideas, or events (e.g., through comparisons, analogies, or categories).

Common Core State Standards, continued

Selection 1 Here, There, and Beyond, continued

Pages	Lesson	Code	Standards Text
248–258	**Reading Selection**	RL.8.1	Cite the textual evidence that most strongly supports an analysis of what the text says explicitly as well as inferences drawn from the text.
		RL.8.10	By the end of the year, read and comprehend literature, including stories, dramas, and poems, at the high end of grades 6–8 text complexity band independently and proficiently.
		RI.8.1	Cite the textual evidence that most strongly supports an analysis of what the text says explicitly as well as inferences drawn from the text.
		RI.8.3	Analyze how a text makes connections among and distinctions between individuals, ideas, or events (e.g., through comparisons, analogies, or categories).
		RI.8.10	By the end of the year, read and comprehend literary nonfiction at the high end of the grades 6–8 text complexity band independently and proficiently.
259	**Connect Reading and Writing** Critical Thinking	RI.8.2	Determine a central idea of a text and analyze its development over the course of the text, including its relationship to supporting ideas; provide an objective summary of the text.
	Vocabulary Review	L.8.6	Acquire and use accurately grade-appropriate general academic and domain-specific words and phrases; gather vocabulary knowledge when considering a word or phrase important to comprehension or expression.
	Write About the GQ	W.8.9	Draw evidence from literary or informational texts to support analysis, reflection, and research.
		W.8.10	Write routinely over extended time frames (time for research, reflection, and revision) and shorter time frames (a single sitting or a day or two) for a range of discipline-specific tasks, purposes, and audiences.
260	**Vocabulary Study** Use Context Clues: Definition, Example, and Restatement	L.8.4	Determine or clarify the meaning of unknown and multiple-meaning words or phrases based on grade 8 reading and content, choosing flexibly from a range of strategies.
		L.8.4.a	Determine or clarify the meaning of unknown and multiple-meaning words or phrases based on grade 8 reading and content, choosing flexibly from a range of strategies. Use context (e.g., the overall meaning of a sentence or paragraph; a word's position or function in a sentence) as a clue to the meaning of a word or phrase.
		L.8.6	Acquire and use accurately grade-appropriate general academic and domain-specific words and phrases; gather vocabulary knowledge when considering a word or phrase important to comprehension or expression.
260	**Literary Analysis** Analyze Myths	RL.8.2	Determine a theme or central idea of a text and analyze its development over the course of the text, including its relationship to the characters, setting, and plot; provide an objective summary of the text.
261	**Language and Grammar** Make Comparisons	SL.8.1	Engage effectively in a range of collaborative discussions (one-on-one, in groups, and teacher-led) with diverse partners on grade 8 topics, texts, and issues, building on others' ideas and expressing their own clearly.
		L.8.1	Demonstrate command of the conventions of standard English grammar and usage when writing or speaking.
261	**Writing and Grammar** Write About Astronomy	W.8.3.d	Write narratives to develop real or imagined experiences or events using effective technique, relevant descriptive details, and well-structured event sequences. Use precise words and phrases, relevant descriptive details, and sensory language to capture the action and convey experiences and events.
		L.8.1	Demonstrate command of the conventions of standard English grammar and usage when writing or speaking.

Selection 2 Earth and Space

Pages	Lesson	Code	Standards Text
262	**Connect**	SL.8.1	Engage effectively in a range of collaborative discussions (one-on-one, in groups, and teacher-led) with diverse partners on grade 8 topics, texts, and issues, building on others' ideas and expressing their own clearly.
		SL.8.2	Analyze the purpose of information presented in diverse media and formats (e.g., visually, quantitatively, orally) and evaluate the motives (e.g., social, commercial, political) behind its presentation.
263–265	**Language & Grammar** Define and Explain	SL.8.1	Engage effectively in a range of collaborative discussions (one-on-one, in groups, and teacher-led) with diverse partners on grade 8 topics, texts, and issues, building on others' ideas and expressing their own clearly.
	Use Pronouns in the Subject and Predicate	L.8.1	Demonstrate command of the conventions of standard English grammar and usage when writing or speaking.
266	**Key Vocabulary**	RI.8.4	Determine the meaning of words and phrases as they are used in a text, including figurative, connotative, and technical meanings; analyze the impact of specific word choices on meaning and tone, including analogies or allusions to other texts.
		L.8.4	Determine or clarify the meaning of unknown and multiple-meaning words or phrases based on grade 8 reading and content, choosing flexibly from a range of strategies.
267	**Reading Strategy** Make Connections	RI.8.1	Cite the textual evidence that most strongly supports an analysis of what the text says explicitly as well as inferences drawn from the text.
	Literary Analysis Determine Author's Purpose	RI.8.6	Determine an author's point of view or purpose in a text and analyze how the author acknowledges and responds to conflicting evidence or viewpoints.
268–280	**Reading Selection**	RI.8.1	Cite the textual evidence that most strongly supports an analysis of what the text says explicitly as well as inferences drawn from the text.
		RI.8.3	Analyze how a text makes connections among and distinctions between individuals, ideas, or events (e.g., through comparisons, analogies, or categories).
		RI.8.10	By the end of the year, read and comprehend literary nonfiction at the high end of the grades 6–8 text complexity band independently and proficiently.
281	**Connect Reading and Writing** Critical Thinking	RI.8.1	Cite the textual evidence that most strongly supports an analysis of what the text says explicitly as well as inferences drawn from the text.
		RI.8.2	Determine a central idea of a text and analyze its development over the course of the text, including its relationship to supporting ideas; provide an objective summary of the text.
	Vocabulary Review	L.8.6	Acquire and use accurately grade-appropriate general academic and domain-specific words and phrases; gather vocabulary knowledge when considering a word or phrase important to comprehension or expression.
	Write About the GQ	W.8.9	Draw evidence from literary or informational texts to support analysis, reflection, and research.
		W.8.10	Write routinely over extended time frames (time for research, reflection, and revision) and shorter time frames (a single sitting or a day or two) for a range of discipline-specific tasks, purposes, and audiences.

Common Core State Standards, continued

Selection 2 Earth and Space, continued

Pages	Lesson	Code	Standards Text
282	**Vocabulary Study** Understand Jargon and Specialized Language	RI.8.4	Determine the meaning of words and phrases as they are used in a text including figurative, connotative, and technical meanings; analyze the impact of specific word choices on meaning and tone, including analogies or allusions to other texts.
		L.8.4	Determine or clarify the meaning of unknown and multiple-meaning words or phrases based on grade 8 reading and content, choosing flexibly from a range of strategies.
		L.8.4.a	Determine or clarify the meaning of unknown and multiple-meaning words or phrases based on grade 8 reading and content, choosing flexibly from a range of strategies. Use context (e.g., the overall meaning of a sentence or paragraph; a word's position or function in a sentence) as a clue to the meaning of a word or phrase.
		L.8.4.d	Determine or clarify the meaning of unknown and multiple-meaning words or phrases based on grade 8 reading and content, choosing flexibly from a range of strategies. Verify the preliminary determination of the meaning of a word or phrase (e.g., by checking the inferred meaning in context or in a dictionary).
		L.8.6	Acquire and use accurately grade-appropriate general academic and domain-specific words and phrases; gather vocabulary knowledge when considering a word or phrase important to comprehension or expression.
282	**Media/Speaking** Choose Media Support	SL.8.1.a	Engage effectively in a range of collaborative discussions (one-on-one, in groups, and teacher-led) with diverse partners on grade 8 topics, texts, and issues, building on others' ideas and expressing their own clearly. Come to discussions prepared, having read or researched material under study; explicitly draw on that preparation by referring to evidence on the topic, text, or issue to probe and reflect on ideas under discussion.
		SL.8.2	Analyze the purpose of information presented in diverse media and formats (e.g., visually, quantitatively, orally) and evaluate the motives (e.g., social, commercial, political) behind its presentation.
		SL.8.5	Integrate multimedia and visual displays into presentations to clarify information, strengthen claims and evidence, and add interest.
283	**Language and Grammar** Define and Explain	SL.8.1	Engage effectively in a range of collaborative discussions (one-on-one, in groups, and teacher-led) with diverse partners on grade 8 topics, texts, and issues, building on others' ideas and expressing their own clearly.
		L.8.1	Demonstrate command of the conventions of standard English grammar and usage when writing or speaking.
283	**Writing and Grammar** Write About An Adventure	W.8.3.d	Write narratives to develop real or imagined experiences or events using effective technique, relevant descriptive details, and well-structured event sequences. Use precise words and phrases, relevant descriptive details, and sensory language to capture the action and convey experiences and events.
		L.8.1	Demonstrate command of the conventions of standard English grammar and usage when writing or speaking.

Selection 3 Indian Summer Sun

Pages	Lesson	Code	Standards Text
284	**Connect**	SL.8.1	Engage effectively in a range of collaborative discussions (one-on-one, in groups, and teacher-led) with diverse partners on grade 8 topics, texts, and issues, building on others' ideas and expressing their own clearly.
		SL.8.2	Analyze the purpose of information presented in diverse media and formats (e.g., visually, quantitatively, orally) and evaluate the motives (e.g., social, commercial, political) behind its presentation.

Selection 3 Indian Summer Sun, continued

Pages	Lesson	Code	Standards Text
285–287	**Language & Grammar** Clarify and Verify	SL.8.1.c	Engage effectively in a range of collaborative discussions (one-on-one, in groups, and teacher-led) with diverse partners on grade 8 topics, texts, and issues, building on others' ideas and expressing their own clearly. Pose questions that connect the ideas of several speakers and respond to others' questions and comments with relevant evidence, observations, and ideas.
	Use Verbs in the Active and Passive Voice	L.8.1.b	Demonstrate command of the conventions of standard English grammar and usage when writing or speaking. Form and use verbs in the active and passive voice.
		L.8.3.a	Use knowledge of language and its conventions when writing, speaking, reading, or listening. Use verbs in the active and passive voice and in the conditional and subjunctive mood to achieve particular effects (e.g., emphasizing the actor or the action; expressing uncertainty, or describing a state contrary to fact.
288	**Key Vocabulary**	RL.8.4	Determine the meaning or words and phrases as they are used in a text, including figurative and connotative meanings; analyze the impact of specific word choices on meaning and tone, including analogies or allusions to other texts.
		L.8.4	Determine or clarify the meaning of unknown and multiple-meaning words or phrases based on grade 8 reading and content, choosing flexibly from a range of strategies.
289	**Reading Strategy** Make Connections	RL.8.1	Cite the textual evidence that most strongly supports an analysis of what the text says explicitly as well as inferences drawn from the text.
	Literary Analysis Compare Structures of Texts	RL.8.5	Compare and contrast the structure of two or more texts and analyze how the differing structure of each text contributes to its meaning and style.
290–302	**Reading Selection**	RL.8.1	Cite the textual evidence that most strongly supports an analysis of what the text says explicitly as well as inferences drawn from the text.
		RL.8.10	By the end of the year, read and comprehend literature, including stories, dramas, and poems, at the high end of grades 6–8 text complexity band independently and proficiently.
303	**Connect Reading and Writing** Critical Thinking	RL.8.2	Determine a theme or central idea of a text and analyze its development over the course of the text, including its relationship to the characters, setting, and plot; provide an objective summary of the text.
	Vocabulary Review	L.8.6	Acquire and use accurately grade-appropriate general academic and domain-specific words and phrases; gather vocabulary knowledge when considering a word or phrase important to comprehension or expression.
	Write About the GQ	W.8.9	Draw evidence from literary or informational texts to support analysis, reflection, and research.
		W.8.10	Write routinely over extended time frames (time for research, reflection, and revision) and shorter time frames (a single sitting or a day or two) for a range of discipline-specific tasks, purposes, and audiences.

Common Core State Standards, continued

Pages	Lesson	Code	Standards Text
304	**Vocabulary Study** Understanding Denotation and Connotation	RL.8.4	Determine the meaning of words and phrases as they are used in a text, including figurative and connotative meanings; analyze the impact of specific word choices on meaning and tone, including analogies or allusions to other texts.
		RI.8.4	Determine the meaning of words and phrases as they are used in a text, including figurative, connotative, and technical meanings; analyze the impact of specific word choices on meaning and tone, including analogies or allusions to other texts.
		L.8.4	Determine or clarify the meaning of unknown and multiple-meaning words or phrases based on grade 8 reading and content, choosing flexibly from a range of strategies.
		L.8.5.c	Demonstrate understanding of figurative language, word relationships, and nuances in word meanings. Distinguish among the connotations (associations) or words with similar denotations (definitions) (e.g., *bullheaded, willful, firm, persistent, resolute*).
		L.8.6	Acquire and use accurately grade-appropriate general academic and domain-specific words and phrases; gather vocabulary knowledge when considering a word or phrase important to comprehension or expression.
304	**Listening/Speaking** Perform a Poem	RL.8.7	Analyze the extent to which a filmed or live production of a story or drama stays faithful to or departs from the text or script, evaluating the choices made by the director or actors.
		SL.8.4	Present claims and findings, emphasizing salient points in a focused, coherent manner with relevant evidence, sound valid reasoning, and well-chosen details; use appropriate eye contact, adequate volume, and clear pronunciation.
		SL.8.6	Adapt speech to a variety of contexts and tasks, demonstrating command of formal English when indicated or appropriate.
305	**Language and Grammar** Clarify and Verify	SL.8.1.c	Engage effectively in a range of collaborative discussions (one-on-one, in groups, and teacher-led) with diverse partners on grade 8 topics, texts, and issues, building on others' ideas and expressing their own clearly. Pose questions that connect the ideas of several speakers and respond to others' questions and comments with relevant evidence, observations, and ideas.
		L.8.1.b	Demonstrate command of the conventions of standard English grammar and usage when writing or speaking. Form and use verbs in the active and passive voice.
		L.8.3.a	Use knowledge of language and its conventions when writing, speaking, reading, or listening. Use verbs in the active and passive voice and in the conditional and subjunctive mood to achieve particular effects (e.g. emphasizing the actor or the action; expressing uncertainty, or describing a state contrary to fact.)
305	**Writing and Grammar** Write About Fitting In	W.8.3.d	Write narratives to develop real or imagined experiences or events using effective technique, relevant descriptive details, and well-structured event sequences. Use precise words and phrases, relevant descriptive details, and sensory language to capture the action and convey experiences and events.
		L.8.1.b	Demonstrate command of the conventions of standard English grammar and usage when writing or speaking. Form and use verbs in the active and passive voice.
		L.8.3.a	Use knowledge of language and its conventions when writing, speaking, reading, or listening. Use verbs in the active and passive voice and in the conditional and subjunctive mood to achieve particular effects (e.g., emphasizing the actor or action; expressing uncertainty, or describing a state contrary to fact).

Selection 3 Indian Summer Sun, continued

Pages	Lesson	Code	Standards Text
306–309	Close Reading	RL.8.10	By the end of the year, read and comprehend literature, including stories, dramas, and poems, at the high end of grades 6–8 text complexity band independently and proficiently.

Compare Across Texts

Pages	Lesson	Code	Standards Text
310	Compare and Contrast Forms of Fiction	RL.8.5	Compare and contrast the structure of two or more texts and analyze how the differing structure of each text contributes to its meaning and style.

Unit Wrap-Up

Pages	Lesson	Code	Standards Text
311	Reflect on Your Reading	RL.8.1	Cite the textual evidence that most strongly supports an analysis of what the text says explicitly as well as inferences drawn from the text.
		RI.8.1	Cite the textual evidence that most strongly supports an analysis of what the text says explicitly as well as inferences drawn from the text.
		RI.8.3	Analyze how a text makes connections among and distinctions between individuals, ideas, or events (e.g., through comparisons, analogies, or categories).
	Explore the GQ/Book Talk	W.8.10	Write routinely over extended time frames (time for research, reflection, and revision) and shorter time frames (a single sitting or a day or two).
		SL.8.1	Engage effectively in a range of collaborative discussions (one-on-one, in groups, and teacher-led) with diverse partners on grade 8 topics, texts, and issues, building on others' ideas and expressing their own clearly.
		SL.8.5	Integrate multimedia and visual displays into presentations to clarify information, strengthen claims and evidence, and add interest.

Unit 5   Our Precious World

Unit Launch

Pages	Lesson	Code	Standards Text
312–313	Unit Opener	SL.8.1	Engage effectively in a range of collaborative discussions (one-on-one, in groups, and teacher-led) with diverse partners on grade 8 topics, texts, and issues, building on others' ideas and expressing their own clearly.
314–317	Focus on Reading Text Features	RI.8.6	Determine an author's point of view or purpose in a text and analyze how the author acknowledges and responds to conflicting evidence or viewpoints.
318–319	Focus on Vocabulary Use Context Clues: Multiple-Meaning Words	RI.8.4	Determine the meaning of words and phrases as they are used in a text, including figurative, connotative, and technical meanings; analyze the impact of specific word choices on meaning and tone, including analogies or allusions to other texts.
		L.8.4	Determine or clarify the meaning of unknown and multiple-meaning words or phrases based on grade 8 reading and content, choosing flexibly from a range of strategies.
		L.8.4.a	Determine or clarify the meaning of unknown and multiple-meaning words or phrases based on grade 8 reading and content, choosing flexibly from a range of strategies. Use context (e.g., the overall meaning of a sentence or paragraph; a word's position or function in a sentence) as a clue to the meaning of a word or phrase.

Selection 1 A Natural Balance

Pages	Lesson	Code	Standards Text
320	Connect	SL.8.2	Analyze the purpose of information presented in diverse media and formats (e.g., visually, quantitatively, orally) and evaluate the motives (e.g., social, commercial, political) behind its presentation.

Common Core State Standards, continued

Selection 1 A Natural Balance, continued

Pages	Lesson	Code	Standards Text
321–323	**Language & Grammar** Describe Animals and Things	SL.8.1	Engage effectively in a range of collaborative discussions (one-on-one, in groups, and teacher-led) with diverse partners on grade 8 topics, texts, and issues, building on others' ideas and expressing their own clearly.
	Adjectives That Describe	L.8.1	Demonstrate command of the conventions of standard English grammar and usage when writing or speaking.
324	**Key Vocabulary**	RI.8.4	Determine the meaning of words and phrases as they are used in a text, including figurative, connotative, and technical meanings; analyze the impact of specific word choices on meaning and tone, including analogies or allusions to other texts.
		L.8.4	Determine or clarify the meaning of unknown and multiple-meaning words or phrases based on grade 8 reading and content, choosing flexibly from a range of strategies.
325	**Literary Analysis** Analyze Author's Viewpoint	RI.8.4	Determine the meaning of words and phrases as they are used in a text, including figurative, connotative, and technical meanings; analyze the impact of specific word choices on meaning and tone, including analogies or allusions to other texts.
		RI.8.6	Determine an author's point of view or purpose in a text and analyze how the author acknowledges and responds to conflicting evidence or viewpoints.
326–336	**Reading Selection**	RL.8.1	Cite the textual evidence that most strongly supports an analysis of what the text says explicitly as well as inferences drawn from the text.
		RI.8.1	Cite the textual evidence that most strongly supports an analysis of what the text says explicitly as well as inferences drawn from the text.
		RI.8.2	Determine a central idea of a text and analyze its development over the course of the text, including its relationship to supporting ideas; provide an objective summary of the text.
		RI.8.3	Analyze how a text makes connections among and distinctions between individuals, ideas, or events (e.g., through comparisons, analogies, or categories).
		RI.8.6	Determine an author's point of view or purpose in a text and analyze how the author acknowledges and responds to conflicting evidence or viewpoints.
		RI.8.10	By the end of the year, read and comprehend literary nonfiction at the high end of the grades 6–8 text complexity band independently and proficiently.
337	**Connect Reading and Writing** Critical Thinking	RI.8.2	Determine a central idea of a text and analyze its development over the course of the text, including its relationship to supporting ideas: provide an objective summary of the text.
	Vocabulary Review	L.8.6	Acquire and use accurately grade-appropriate general academic and domain- specific words and phrases; gather vocabulary knowledge when considering a word or phrase important to comprehension or expression.
	Write About the GQ	W.8.9	Draw evidence from literary or informational texts to support analysis, reflection, and research.
		W.8.10	Write routinely over extended time frames (time for research, reflection, and revision) and shorter time frames (a single sitting or a day or two) for a range of discipline-specific tasks, purposes, and audiences.

Selection 1 A Natural Balance, continued

Pages	Lesson	Code	Standards Text
338	**Vocabulary Study** Use Context Clues: Multiple-Meaning Words	RI.8.4	Determine the meaning of words and phrases as they are used in a text, including figurative, connotative, and technical meanings; analyze the impact of specific word choices on meaning and tone, including analogies or allusions to other texts.
		L.8.4	Determine or clarify the meaning of unknown and multiple-meaning words or phrases based on grade 8 reading and content, choosing flexibly from a range of strategies.
		L.8.4.a	Determine or clarify the meaning of unknown and multiple-meaning words or phrases based on grade 8 reading and content, choosing flexibly from a range of strategies. Use context (e.g., the overall meaning of a sentence or paragraph; a word's position or function in a sentence) as a clue to the meaning of a word or phrase.
		L.8.4.d	Determine or clarify the meaning of unknown and multiple-meaning words or phrases based on grade 8 reading and content, choosing flexibly from a range of strategies. Verify the preliminary determination of the meaning of a word or phrase (e.g., by checking the inferred meaning in context or in a dictionary).
		L.8.6	Acquire and use accurately grade-appropriate general academic and domain-specific words and phrases; gather vocabulary knowledge when considering a word or phrase important to comprehension or expression.
339	**Language and Grammar** Describe Animals and Things	SL.8.1	Engage effectively in a range of collaborative discussions (one-on-one, in groups, and teacher-led) with diverse partners on grade 8 topics, texts, and issues, building on others' ideas and expressing their own clearly.
339	**Writing and Grammar** Write About an Animal	W.8.3.d	Write narratives to develop real or imagined experiences or events using effective technique, relevant descriptive details, and well-structured event sequences. Use precise words and phrases, relevant descriptive details, and sensory language to capture the action and convey experiences and events.
		L.8.1	Demonstrate command of the conventions of standard English grammar and usage when writing or speaking.

Selection 2 Siberian Survivors

Pages	Lesson	Code	Standards Text
340	**Connect**	SL.8.2	Analyze the purpose of information presented in diverse media and formats (e.g., visually, quantitatively, orally) and evaluate the motives (e.g., social, commercial, political) behind its presentation.
341–343	**Language & Grammar** Make Comparisons	SL.8.1	Engage effectively in a range of collaborative discussions (one-on-one, in groups, and teacher-led) with diverse partners on grade 8 topics, texts, and issues, building on others' ideas and expressing their own clearly
	Use Adjectives That Compare	L.8.1	Demonstrate command of the conventions of standard English grammar and usage when writing or speaking.
344	**Key Vocabulary**	RI.8.4	Determine the meaning or words and phrases as they are used in a text, including figurative, connotative, and technical meanings; analyze the impact of specific word choices on meaning and tone, including analogies or allusions to other texts.
		L.8.4	Determine or clarify the meaning of unknown and multiple-meaning words or phrases based on grade 8 reading and content, choosing flexibly from a range of strategies.
345	**Literary Analysis** Compare Viewpoints	RI.8.6	Determine an author's point of view or purpose in a text and analyze how the author acknowledges and responds to conflicting evidence or viewpoints.
346–354	**Reading Selection**	RI.8.10	By the end of the year, read and comprehend literary nonfiction at the high end of the grades 6–8 text complexity band independently and proficiently.

Common Core State Standards, continued

Selection 2 Siberian Survivors, continued

Pages	Lesson	Code	Standards Text
355 **Connect Reading and Writing** Critical Thinking		RI.8.2	Determine a central idea of a text and analyze its development over the course of the text, including its relationship to supporting ideas; provide an objective summary of the text.
	Vocabulary Review	L.8.6	Acquire and use accurately grade-appropriate general academic and domain-specific words and phrases; gather vocabulary knowledge when considering a word or phrase important to comprehension or expression.
	Write About the GQ	W.8.9	Draw evidence from literary or informational texts to support analysis, reflection, and research.
		W.8.10	Write routinely over extended time frames (time for research, reflection, and revision) and shorter time frames (a single sitting or a day or two) for a range of discipline-specific tasks, purposes, and audiences.
356 **Vocabulary Study** Use Context Clues: Multiple-Meaning Words Across Content Areas		L.8.4	Determine or clarify the meaning of unknown and multiple-meaning words or phrases based on grade 8 reading and content, choosing flexibly from a range of strategies.
		L.8.4.a	Determine or clarify the meaning of unknown and multiple-meaning words or phrases based on grade 8 reading and content, choosing flexibly from a range of strategies. Use context (e.g., the overall meaning of a sentence or paragraph; a word's position or function in a sentence) as a clue to the meaning of a word or phrase.
		L.8.4.d	Determine or clarify the meaning of unknown and multiple-meaning words or phrases based on grade 8 reading and content, choosing flexibly from a range of strategies. Verify the preliminary determination of the meaning of a word or phrase (e.g., by checking the inferred meaning in context or in a dictionary).
		L.8.6	Acquire and use accurately grade-appropriate general academic and domain-specific words and phrases; gather vocabulary knowledge when considering a word or phrase important to comprehension or expression.
356 **Research/Speaking** Give an Informative Report		SL.8.4	Present claims and findings, emphasizing salient points in a focused, coherent manner with relevant evidence, sound valid reasoning, and well-chosen details; use appropriate eye contact, adequate volume, and clear pronunciation.
357 **Language and Grammar** Make Comparisons		SL.8.1	Engage effectively in a range of collaborative discussions (one-on-one, in groups, and teacher-led) with diverse partners on grade 8 topics, texts, and issues, building on others' ideas and expressing their own clearly.
357 **Writing and Grammar** Use Adjectives That Compare		W.8.3.d	Write narratives to develop real or imagined experiences or events using effective technique, relevant descriptive details, and well-structured event sequences. Use precise words and phrases, relevant descriptive details, and sensory language to capture the action and convey experiences and events.
		L.8.1	Demonstrate command of the conventions of standard English grammar and usage when writing or speaking.
		L.8.2.c	Demonstrate command of the conventions of standard English capitalization, punctuation, and spelling when writing. Spell correctly.

Selection 3 Mireya Mayor

Pages	Lesson	Code	Standards Text
358	Connect	SL.8.2	Analyze the purpose of information presented in diverse media and formats (e.g., visually, quantitatively, orally) and evaluate the motives (e.g., social, commercial, political) behind its presentation.

Selection 3 Mireya Mayor, continued

Pages	Lesson	Code	Standards Text
359–361	**Language & Grammar** Elaborate	SL.8.1.a	Engage effectively in a range of collaborative discussions (one-on-one, in groups, and teacher-led) with diverse partners on grade 8 topics, texts, and issues, building on others' ideas and expressing their own clearly. Come to discussions prepared, having read or researched material under study; explicitly draw on that preparation by referring to evidence on the topic, text, or issue to probe and reflect on ideas under discussion.
	Use Adverbs	L.8.1	Demonstrate command of the conventions of standard English grammar and usage when writing or speaking.
362	**Key Vocabulary**	RI.8.4	Determine the meaning of words and phrases as they are used in a text, including figurative, connotative, and technical meanings; analyze the impact of specific word choices on meaning and tone, including analogies or allusions to other texts.
		L.8.4	Determine or clarify the meaning of unknown and multiple-meaning words or phrases based on grade 8 reading and content, choosing flexibly from a range of strategies.
363	**Literary Analysis** Analyze Author's Viewpoint	RI.8.6	Determine an author's point of view or purpose in a text and analyze how the author acknowledges and responds to conflicting evidence or viewpoints.
364–370	**Reading Selection**	RI.8.10	By the end of the year, read and comprehend literary nonfiction at the high end of the grades 6–8 text complexity band independently and proficiently.
371	**Connect Reading and Writing** Critical Thinking	RI.8.2	Determine a central idea of a text and analyze its development over the course of the text, including its relationship to supporting ideas; provide an objective summary of the text.
	Vocabulary Review	L.8.6	Acquire and use accurately grade-appropriate general academic and domain-specific words and phrases; gather vocabulary knowledge when considering a word or phrase important to comprehension or expression.
	Write About the GQ	W.8.9	Draw evidence from literary or informational texts to support analysis, reflection, and research.
		W.8.10	Write routinely over extended time frames (time for research, reflection, and revision) and shorter time frames (a single sitting or a day or two) for a range of discipline-specific tasks, purposes, and audiences.
372	**Vocabulary Study** Use Context Clues: Jargon	L.8.4	Determine or clarify the meaning of unknown and multiple-meaning words or phrases based on grade 8 reading and content, choosing flexibly from a range of strategies.
		L.8.4.a	Determine or clarify the meaning of unknown and multiple-meaning words or phrases based on grade 8 reading and content, choosing flexibly from a range of strategies. Use context (e.g., the overall meaning of a sentence or paragraph; a word's position or function in a sentence) as a clue to the meaning of a word or phrase.
		L.8.6	Acquire and use accurately grade-appropriate general academic and domain-specific words and phrases; gather vocabulary knowledge when considering a word or phrase important to comprehension or expression.
372	**Literary Analysis** Analyze Media: Informational Text	RI.8.7	Evaluate the advantages and disadvantages of using different mediums (e.g., print or digital text, video, multimedia) to present a particular topic or idea.
373	**Language and Grammar** Elaborate	SL.8.1.a	Engage effectively in a range of collaborative discussions (one-on-one, in groups, and teacher-led) with diverse partners on grade 8 topics, texts, and issues, building on others' ideas and expressing their own clearly. Come to discussions prepared, having read or researched material under study; explicitly draw on that preparation by referring to evidence on the topic, text, or issue to probe and reflect on ideas under discussion.
		L.8.1	Demonstrate command of the conventions of standard English grammar and usage when writing or speaking.

Common Core State Standards, continued

Unit 5 Our Precious World continued

Selection 3 Mireya Mayor, continued

Pages	Lesson	Code	Standards Text
373	**Writing and Grammar** Write About a Discovery	W.8.3.d	Write narratives to develop real or imagined experiences or events using effective technique, relevant descriptive details, and well-structured event sequences. Use precise words and phrases, relevant descriptive details, and sensory language to capture the action and convey experiences and events.
		L.8.1	Demonstrate command of the conventions of standard English grammar and usage when writing or speaking.
		L.8.2	Demonstrate command of the conventions of standard English capitalization, punctuation, and spelling when writing.
374–375	**Close Reading**	RI.8.10	By the end of the year, read and comprehend literary nonfiction at the high end of the grades 6–8 text complexity band independently and proficiently.

Compare Across Texts

376	**Compare Media Treatments**	RI.8.7	Evaluate the advantages and disadvantages of using different mediums (e.g., print or digital text, video, multimedia) to present a particular topic or idea.

Unit Wrap-Up

377	**Reflect on Your Reading**	RI.8.4	Determine the meaning of words and phrases as they are used in a text, including figurative, connotative, and technical meanings; analyze the impact of specific word choices on meaning and tone, including analogies or allusions to other texts.
		RI.8.6	Determine an author's point of view or purpose in a text and analyze how the author acknowledges and responds to conflicting evidence or viewpoints.
	Explore the GQ/Book Talk	W.8.10	Write routinely over extended time frames (time for research, reflection, and revision) and shorter time frames (a single sitting or a day or two) for a range of discipline-specific tasks, purposes, and audiences.
		SL.8.1	Engage effectively in a range of collaborative discussions (one-on-one, in groups, and teacher-led) with diverse partners on grade 8 topics, texts, and issues, building on others' ideas and expressing their own clearly.
		SL.8.1.a	Engage effectively in a range of collaborative discussions (one-on-one, in groups, and teacher-led) with diverse partners on grade 8 topics, texts, and issues, building on others' ideas and expressing their own clearly. Come to discussions prepared, having read or researched material under study; explicitly draw on that preparation by referring to evidence on the topic, text, or issue to probe and reflect on ideas under discussion.
		SL.8.5	Integrate multimedia and visual displays into presentations to clarify information, strengthen claims and evidence, and add interest.

Unit 6 Conflict and Resolution

Unit Launch

378–379	**Unit Opener**	SL.8.1	Engage effectively in a range of collaborative discussions (one-on-one, in groups, and teacher-led) with diverse partners on grade 8 topics, texts, and issues, building on others' ideas and expressing their own clearly.
380–381	**Focus on Reading** Determine Author's Purpose	RL.8.6	Analyze how differences in the points of view of the characters and the audience or reader (e.g., created through the use of dramatic irony) create such effects as suspense or humor.
		RI.8.6	Determine an author's point of view or purpose in a text and analyze how the author acknowledges and responds to conflicting evidence or viewpoints.

Unit Launch, continued

Pages	Lesson	Code	Standards Text
382–383	**Focus on Vocabulary** Interpret Figurative Language	RL.8.4	Determine the meaning of words and phrases as they are used in a text, including figurative and connotative meanings; analyze the impact of specific word choices on meaning and tone, including analogies or allusions to other texts.
		L.8.4.a	Determine or clarify the meaning of unknown and multiple-meaning words or phrases based on grade 8 reading and content, choosing flexibly from a range of strategies. Use context (e.g., the overall meaning of a sentence or paragraph; a word's position or function in a sentence) as a clue to the meaning of a word or phrase.
		L.8.5	Demonstrate understanding of figurative language, word relationships, and nuances in word meanings.
		L.8.5.a	Demonstrate understanding of figurative language, word relationships, and nuances in word meanings. Interpret figures of speech (e.g. verbal irony, puns) in context.
		L.8.6	Acquire and use accurately grade-appropriate general academic and domain-specific words and phrases; gather vocabulary knowledge when considering a word or phrase important to comprehension or expression.

Selection 1 Nadia The Willful

Pages	Lesson	Code	Standards Text
384	**Connect**	SL.8.1	Engage effectively in a range of collaborative discussions (one-on-one, in groups, and teacher-led) with diverse partners on grade 8 topics, texts, and issues, building on others' ideas and expressing their own clearly.
		SL.8.2	Analyze the purpose of information presented in diverse media and formats (e.g., visually, quantitatively, orally) and evaluate the motives (e.g., social, commercial, political) behind its presentation.
385–387	**Language & Grammar** Express Opinions	SL.8.1	Engage effectively in a range of collaborative discussions (one-on-one, in groups, and teacher-led) with diverse partners on grade 8 topics, texts, and issues, building on others' ideas and expressing their own clearly.
	Use Compound Sentences	L.8.1.c	Demonstrate command of the conventions of standard English grammar and usage when writing or speaking. Form and use verbs in the indicative, imperative, interrogative, conditional, and subjunctive moods.
		L.8.2.a	Demonstrate command of the conventions of standard English capitalization, punctuation, and spelling when writing. Use punctuation (comma, ellipsis, and dash) to indicate a pause or break.
388	**Key Vocabulary**	RL.8.4	Determine the meaning of words and phrases as they are used in a text, including figurative and connotative meanings; analyze the impact of specific word choices on meaning and tone, including analogies or allusions to other texts.
		L.8.4	Determine or clarify the meaning of unknown and multiple-meaning words or phrases based on grade 8 reading and content, choosing flexibly from a range of strategies.
389	**Reading Strategy** Make Inferences	RL.8.1	Cite the textual evidence that most strongly supports an analysis of what the text says explicitly as well as inferences drawn from the text.
	Literary Analysis Compare Viewpoints	RL.8.6	Analyze how differences in the points of view of the characters and the audience or reader (e.g., created through the use of dramatic irony) create such effects as suspense or humor.

Common Core State Standards, continued

Selection 1 Nadia The Willful, continued

Pages	Lesson	Code	Standards Text
390–402	**Reading Selection**	RL.8.1	Cite the textual evidence that most strongly supports an analysis of what the text says explicitly as well as inferences drawn from the text.
		RL.8.2	Determine a theme or central idea of a text and analyze its development over the course of the text, including its relationship to the characters, setting, and plot; provide an objective summary of the text.
		RL.8.10	By the end of the year, read and comprehend literature, including stories, dramas, and poems, at the high end of the grades 6–8 text complexity band independently and proficiently.
		L.8.5	Demonstrate understanding of figurative language, word relationships, and nuances in word meanings.
403	**Connect Reading and Writing** Critical Thinking	RL.8.1	Cite the textual evidence that most strongly supports an analysis of what the text says explicitly as well as inferences drawn from the text.
		RL.8.2	Determine a theme or central idea of a text and analyze its development over the course of the text, including its relationship to the characters, setting, and plot; provide an objective summary of the text.
	Vocabulary Review	L.8.6	Acquire and use accurately grade-appropriate general academic and domain-specific words and phrases; gather vocabulary knowledge when considering a word or phrase important to comprehension or expression.
	Write About the GQ	W.8.9	Draw evidence from literary or informational texts to support analysis, reflection, and research.
		W.8.10	Write routinely over extended time frames (time for research, reflection, and revision) and shorter time frames (a single sitting or a day or two) for a range of discipline-specific tasks, purposes, and audiences.
404	**Vocabulary Study** Identify Similes, Metaphors, Personification, and Analogies	RL.8.4	Determine the meaning of words and phrases as they are used in a text, including figurative and connotative meanings; analyze the impact of specific word choices on meaning and tone, including analogies or allusions to other texts.
		L.8.5	Demonstrate understanding of figurative language, word relationships, and nuances in word meanings.
		L.8.5.a	Demonstrate understanding of figurative language, word relationships, and nuances in word meanings. Interpret figures of speech (e.g. verbal irony, puns) in context.
		L.8.6	Acquire and use accurately grade-appropriate general academic and domain-specific words and phrases; gather vocabulary knowledge when considering a word or phrase important to comprehension or expression.
404	**Literary Analysis** Interpret Metaphor	RL.8.4	Determine the meaning of words and phrases as they are used in a text, including figurative and connotative meanings; analyze the impact of specific word choices on meaning and tone, including analogies or allusions to other texts.
		L.8.5	Demonstrate understanding of figurative language, word relationships, and nuances in word meanings.
		L.8.5.a	Demonstrate understanding of figurative language, word relationships, and nuances in word meanings. Interpret figures of speech (e.g. verbal irony, puns) in context.

Selection 1 Nadia The Willful, continued

Pages	Lesson	Code	Standards Text
405	**Language and Grammar** Express Opinions	SL.8.1	Engage effectively in a range of collaborative discussions (one-on-one, in groups, and teacher-led) with diverse partners on grade 8 topics, texts, and issues, building on others' ideas and expressing their own clearly.
		L.8.1.c	Demonstrate command of the conventions of standard English grammar and usage when writing or speaking. Form and use verbs in the indicative, imperative, interrogative, conditional, and subjunctive moods.
405	**Writing and Grammar** Write About Conflicts	W.8.3.d	Write narratives to develop real or imagined experiences or events using effective technique, relevant descriptive details, and well-structured event sequences. Use precise words and phrases, relevant descriptive details, and sensory language to capture the action and convey experiences and events.
		L.8.1.c	Demonstrate command of the conventions of standard English grammar and usage when writing or speaking. Form and use verbs in the indicative, imperative, interrogative, conditional, and subjunctive moods.
		L.8.2.a	Demonstrate command of the conventions of standard English capitalization, punctuation, and spelling when writing. Use punctuation (comma, ellipsis, dash) to indicate a pause or break.

Selection 2 Passage to Freedom

Pages	Lesson	Code	Standards Text
406	**Connect**	SL.8.1	Engage effectively in a range of collaborative discussions (one-on-one, in groups, and teacher-led) with diverse partners on grade 8 topics, texts, and issues, building on others' ideas and expressing their own clearly.
		SL.8.2	Analyze the purpose of information presented in diverse media and formats (e.g., visually, quantitatively, orally) and evaluate the motives (e.g., social, commercial, political) behind its presentation.
407–409	**Language & Grammar** Engage in Discussion	SL.8.1.b	Engage effectively in a range of collaborative discussions (one-on-one, in groups, and teacher-led) with diverse partners on grade 8 topics, texts, and issues, building on others' ideas and expressing their own clearly. Follow rules for collegial discussions and decision-making, track progress toward specific goals and deadlines, and define individual roles as needed.
		SL.8.1.c	Engage effectively in a range of collaborative discussions (one-on-one, in groups, and teacher-led) with diverse partners on grade 8 topics, texts, and issues, building on others' ideas and expressing their own clearly. Pose questions that connect the ideas of several speakers and respond to others' questions and comments with relevant evidence, observations, and ideas.
		SL.8.1.d	Engage effectively in a range of collaborative discussions (one-on-one, in groups, and teacher-led) with diverse partners on grade 8 topics, texts, and issues, building on others' ideas and expressing their own clearly. Acknowledge new information expressed by others, and, when warranted, qualify or justify their own views in light of the evidence presented.
	Use Complex Sentences	L.8.1.c	Demonstrate command of the conventions of standard English grammar and usage when writing or speaking. Form and use verbs in the indicative, imperative, interrogative, conditional, and subjunctive moods.
		L.8.2.a	Demonstrate command of the conventions of standard English capitalization, punctuation, and spelling when writing. Use punctuation (comma, ellipsis, and dash) to indicate a pause or break.

Common Core State Standards, continued

Selection 2 Passage to Freedom, continued

Pages	Lesson	Code	Standards Text
410	**Key Vocabulary**	RL.8.4	Determine the meaning of words and phrases as they are used in a text, including figurative and connotative meanings; analyze the impact of specific word choices on meaning and tone, including analogies or allusions to other texts.
		L.8.4	Determine or clarify the meaning of unknown and multiple-meaning words or phrases based on grade 8 reading and content, choosing flexibly from a range of strategies.
411	**Reading Strategy** Make Inferences **Literary Analysis** Evaluate Historical Fiction	RL.8.1	Cite the textual evidence that most strongly supports an analysis of what the text says explicitly as well as inferences drawn from the text.
412–426	**Reading Selection**	RL.8.1	Cite the textual evidence that most strongly supports an analysis of what the text says explicitly as well as inferences drawn from the text.
		RL.8.10	By the end of the year, read and comprehend literature, including stories, dramas, and poems, at the high end of grades 6–8 text complexity band independently and proficiently.
427	**Connect Reading and Writing** Critical Thinking	RL.8.1	Cite the textual evidence that most strongly supports an analysis of what the text says explicitly as well as inferences drawn from the text.
		RL.8.2	Determine a theme or central idea of a text and analyze its development over the course of the text, including its relationship to the characters, setting and plot; provide an objective summary of the text.
	Vocabulary Review	L.8.6	Acquire and use accurately grade-appropriate general academic and domain-specific words and phrases; gather vocabulary knowledge when considering a word or phrase important to comprehension or expression.
	Write About the GQ	W.8.9	Draw evidence from literary or informational texts to support analysis, reflection, and research.
		W.8.10	Write routinely over extended time frames (time for research, reflection, and revision) and shorter time frames (a single sitting or a day or two) for a range of discipline-specific tasks, purposes, and audiences.
428	**Vocabulary Study** Interpret Idioms	RI.8.4	Determine the meaning of words and phrases as they are used in a text, including figurative, connotative, and technical meanings; analyze the impact of specific word choices on meaning and tone, including analogies or allusions to other texts.
		L.8.5	Demonstrate understanding of figurative language, word relationships, and nuances in word meanings.
		L.8.5.a	Demonstrate understanding of figurative language, word relationships, and nuances in word meanings. Interpret figures of speech (e.g. verbal irony, puns) in context.
		L.8.6	Acquire and use accurately grade-appropriate general academic and domain-specific words and phrases; gather vocabulary knowledge when considering a word or phrase important to comprehension or expression.
428	**Writing/Speaking** Deliver an Oral Response to Literature	SL.8.1.a	Engage effectively in a range of collaborative discussions (one-on-one, in groups, and teacher-led) with diverse partners on grade 8 topics, texts, and issues, building on others' ideas and expressing their own clearly. Come to discussions prepared, having read or researched material under study; explicitly draw on that preparation by referring to evidence on the topic, text, or issue to probe and reflect on ideas under discussion.
		SL.8.4	Present claims and findings, emphasizing salient points in a focused, coherent manner with relevant evidence, sound valid reasoning, and well-chosen details; use appropriate eye contact, adequate volume, and clear pronunciation.

Selection 2 Passage to Freedom, continued

Pages	Lesson	Code	Standards Text
429	**Language and Grammar** Engage in Discussion	SL.8.1.b	Engage effectively in a range of collaborative discussions (one-on-one, in groups, and teacher-led) with diverse partners on grade 8 topics, texts, and issues, building on others' ideas and expressing their own clearly. Follow rules for collegial discussions and decision-making, track progress toward specific goals and deadlines, and define individual roles as needed.
		SL.8.1.c	Engage effectively in a range of collaborative discussions (one-on-one, in groups, and teacher-led) with diverse partners on grade 8 topics, texts, and issues, building on others' ideas and expressing their own clearly. Pose questions that connect the ideas of several speakers and respond to others' questions and comments with relevant evidence, observations, and ideas.
		SL.8.1.d	Engage effectively in a range of collaborative discussions (one-on-one, in groups, and teacher-led) with diverse partners on grade 8 topics, texts, and issues, building on others' ideas and expressing their own clearly. Acknowledge new information expressed by others, and, when warranted, qualify or justify their own views in light of the evidence presented.
		L.8.1.c	Demonstrate command of the conventions of standard English grammar and usage when writing or speaking. Form and use verbs in the indicative, imperative, interrogative, conditional, and subjunctive moods.
429	**Writing and Grammar** Write About a Heroic Action	W.8.3.d	Write narratives to develop real or imagined experiences or events using effective technique, relevant descriptive details, and well-structured event sequences. Use precise words and phrases, relevant descriptive details, and sensory language to capture the action and convey experiences and events.
		L.8.1.c	Demonstrate command of the conventions of standard English grammar and usage when writing or speaking. Form and use verbs in the indicative, imperative, interrogative, conditional, and subjunctive moods.
		L.8.2.a	Demonstrate command of the conventions of standard English capitalization, punctuation, and spelling when writing. Use punctuation (comma, ellipsis, and dash) to indicate a pause or break.

Selection 3 Zlata's Diary

Pages	Lesson	Code	Standards Text
430	**Connect**	SL.8.1	Engage effectively in a range of collaborative discussions (one-on-one, in groups, and teacher-led) with diverse partners on grade 8 topics, texts, and issues, building on others' ideas and expressing their own clearly.
		SL.8.2	Analyze the purpose of information presented in diverse media and formats (e.g., visually, quantitatively, orally) and evaluate the motives (e.g., social, commercial, political) behind its presentation.
431–433	**Language & Grammar** Justify	SL.8.4	Present claims and findings, emphasizing salient points in a focused, coherent manner with relevant evidence, sound valid reasoning, and well-chosen details; use appropriate eye contact, adequate volume, and clear pronunciation.
	Combine Sentences	L.8.1.c	Demonstrate command of the conventions of standard English grammar and usage when writing or speaking. Form and use verbs in the indicative, imperative, interrogative, conditional, and subjunctive moods.
		L.8.2.a	Demonstrate command of the conventions of standard English capitalization, punctuation, and spelling when writing. Use punctuation (comma, ellipsis, and dash) to indicate a pause or break.

Common Core State Standards, continued

Selection 3 Zlata's Diary, continued

Pages	Lesson	Code	Standards Text
434	**Key Vocabulary**	RI.8.4	Determine the meaning of words and phrases as they are used in a text, including figurative, connotative, and technical meanings; analyze the impact of specific word choices on meaning and tone, including analogies or allusions to other texts
		L.8.4	Determine or clarify the meaning of unknown and multiple-meaning words or phrases based on grade 8 reading and content, choosing flexibly from a range of strategies.
435	**Reading Strategy** Make Inferences	RI.8.1	Cite the textual evidence that most strongly supports an analysis of what the text says explicitly as well as inferences drawn from the text.
	Literary Analysis Analyze Author's Viewpoint	RI.8.6	Determine an author's point of view or purpose in a text and analyze how the author acknowledges and responds to conflicting evidence or viewpoints.
436–444	**Reading Selection**	RI.8.10	By the end of the year, read and comprehend literary nonfiction at the high end of the grades 6–8 text complexity band independently and proficiently.
		SL.8.2	Analyze the purpose of information presented in diverse media and formats (e.g., visually, quantitatively, orally) and evaluate the motives (e.g., social, commercial, political) behind its presentation.
445	**Connect Reading and Writing** Critical Thinking	RI.8.1	Cite the textual evidence that most strongly supports an analysis of what the text says explicitly as well as inferences drawn from the text.
		RI.8.2	Determine a central idea of a text and analyze its development over the course of the text, including its relationship to supporting ideas; provide an objective summary of the text.
	Vocabulary Review	L.8.6	Acquire and use accurately grade-appropriate general academic and domain-specific words and phrases; gather vocabulary knowledge when considering a word or phrase important to comprehension or expression.
	Write About the GQ	W.8.9	Draw evidence from literary or informational texts to support analysis, reflection, and research.
		W.8.10	Write routinely over extended time frames (time for research, reflection, and revision) and shorter time frames (a single sitting or a day or two) for a range of discipline-specific tasks, purposes, and audiences.
446	**Vocabulary Study** Shades of Meaning and Word Choice	RI.8.4	Determine the meaning of words and phrases as they are used in a text, including figurative, connotative, and technical meanings; analyze the impact of specific word choices on meaning and tone, including analogies or allusions to other texts.
		L.8.4	Determine or clarify the meaning of unknown and multiple-meaning words or phrases based on grade 8 reading and content, choosing flexibly from a range of strategies.
		L.8.5.c	Demonstrate understanding of figurative language, word relationships, and nuances in word meanings. Distinguish among the connotations (associations) of words with similar denotations (definitions) (e.g., *bullheaded, willful, firm, persistent, resolute*).
446	**Literary Analysis** Evaluate Literature: Word Choice	RI.8.4	Determine the meaning of words and phrases as they are used in a text, including figurative, connotative, and technical meanings; analyze the impact of specific word choices on meaning and tone, including analogies or allusions to other texts

Selection 3 Zlata's Diary, continued

Pages	Lesson	Code	Standards Text
447	**Language and Grammar** Justify	SL.8.4	Present claims and findings, emphasizing salient points in a focused, coherent manner with relevant evidence, sound valid reasoning, and well-chosen details; use appropriate eye contact, adequate volume, and clear pronunciation.
		L.8.1.c	Demonstrate command of the conventions of standard English grammar and usage when writing or speaking. Form and use verbs in the indicative, imperative, interrogative, conditional, and subjunctive moods.
447	**Writing and Grammar** Write About Your Opinion	L.8.1.c	Demonstrate command of the conventions of standard English grammar and usage when writing or speaking. Form and use verbs in the indicative, imperative, interrogative, conditional, and subjunctive moods.
		L.8.2.a	Demonstrate command of the conventions of standard English capitalization, punctuation, and spelling when writing. Use punctuation (comma, ellipsis, dash) to indicate a pause or break.
		W.8.3.d	Write narratives to develop real or imagined experiences or events using effective technique, relevant descriptive details, and well-structured event sequences. Use precise words and phrases, relevant descriptive details, and sensory language to capture the action and convey experiences and events.
448–449	**Close Reading**	RI.8.10	By the end of the year, read and comprehend literary nonfiction at the high end of the grades 6–8 text complexity band independently and proficiently.

Compare Across Texts

Pages	Lesson	Code	Standards Text
450	**Compare Themes**	SL.8.1	Engage effectively in a range of collaborative discussions (one-on-one, in groups, and teacher-led) with diverse partners on grade 8 topics, texts, and issues, building on others' ideas and expressing their own clearly.
		SL.8.1.b	Engage effectively in a range of collaborative discussions (one-on-one, in groups, and teacher-led) with diverse partners on grade 8 topics, texts, and issues, building on others' ideas and expressing their own clearly. Follow rules for collegial discussions and decision- making, track progress toward specific goals and deadlines, and define individual roles as needed.

Unit Wrap-Up

Pages	Lesson	Code	Standards Text
451	**Reflect on Your Reading**	RL.8.1	Cite the textual evidence that most strongly supports an analysis of what the text says explicitly as well as inferences drawn from the text.
		RL.8.6	Analyze how differences in the points of view of the characters and the audience or reader (e.g., created through the use of dramatic irony) create such effects as suspense or humor.
		RI.8.1	Cite the textual evidence that most strongly supports an analysis of what the text says explicitly as well as inferences drawn from the text.
		RI.8.6	Determine an author's point of view or purpose in a text and analyze how the author acknowledges and responds to conflicting evidence or viewpoints.
	Explore the GQ/Book Talk	W.8.10	Write routinely over extended time frames (time for research, reflection, and revision) and shorter time frames (a single sitting or a day or two) for a range of discipline-specific tasks, purposes, and audiences.
		SL.8.1	Engage effectively in a range of collaborative discussions (one-on-one, in groups, and teacher-led) with diverse partners on grade 8 topics, texts, and issues, building on others' ideas and expressing their own clearly.

Common Core State Standards, continued

Unit Launch

Pages	Lesson	Code	Standards Text
452–453	**Unit Opener**	SL.8.1	Engage effectively in a range of collaborative discussions (one-on-one, in groups, and teacher-led) with diverse partners on grade 8 topics, texts, and issues, building on others' ideas and expressing their own clearly.
454–455	**Focus on Reading** Compare Text Structures	RL.8.5	Compare and contrast the structure of two or more texts and analyze how the differing structure of each text contributes to its meaning and style.
456–457	**Focus on Vocabulary** Use Word Origins	RL.8.4	Determine the meaning of words and phrases as they are used in a text, including figurative and connotative meanings; analyze the impact of specific word choices on meaning and tone, including analogies or allusions to other texts.
		RI.8.4	Determine the meaning of words and phrases as they are used in a text, including figurative, connotative, and technical meanings; analyze the impact of specific word choices on meaning and tone, including analogies or allusions to other texts.
		L.8.4.b	Determine or clarify the meaning of unknown and multiple-meaning words or phrases based on grade 8 reading and content, choosing flexibly from a range of strategies. Use common, grade-appropriate Greek or Latin affixes and roots as clues to the meaning of a word (e.g., *precede, recede, secede*).
		L.8.6	Acquire and use accurately grade-appropriate general academic and domain-specific words and phrases; gather vocabulary knowledge when considering a word or phrase important to comprehension or expression of a word.

Selection 1 The Clever Magistrate

Pages	Lesson	Code	Standards Text
458	**Connect**	SL.8.1	Engage effectively in a range of collaborative discussions (one-on-one, in groups, and teacher-led) with diverse partners on grade 8 topics, texts, and issues, building on others' ideas and expressing their own clearly.
		SL.8.2	Analyze the purpose of information presented in diverse media and formats (e.g., visually, quantitatively, orally) and evaluate the motives (e.g., social, commercial, political) behind its presentation.
459–461	**Language & Grammar** Tell an Original Story	SL.8.1	Engage effectively in a range of collaborative discussions (one-on-one, in groups, and teacher-led) with diverse partners on grade 8 topics, texts, and issues, building on others' ideas and expressing their own clearly.
	Use Participles as Adjectives	L.8.1.a	Demonstrate command of the conventions of standard English grammar and usage when writing or speaking. Explain the function of verbals (gerunds, participles, infinitives) in general and their function in particular sentences.
		L.8.2.a	Demonstrate command of the conventions of standard English capitalization, punctuation, and spelling when writing. Use punctuation (comma, ellipsis, dash) to indicate a pause or break.
462	**Key Vocabulary**	RL.8.4	Determine the meaning of words and phrases as they are used in a text, including figurative and connotative meanings; analyze the impact of specific word choices on meaning and tone, inciuding analogies or allusions to other texts.
		L.8.4	Determine or clarify the meaning of unknown and multiple-meaning words or phrases based on grade 8 reading and content, choosing flexibly from a range of strategies.
463	**Reading Strategy** Determine Importance **Literary Analysis** Determine Theme	RL.8.2	Determine a theme or central idea of a text and analyze its development over the course of the text, including its relationship to the characters, setting, and plot; provide an objective summary of the text.

Selection 1 The Clever Magistrate, continued

Pages	Lesson	Code	Standards Text
464–474	**Reading Selection**	RL.8.1	Cite the textual evidence that most strongly supports an analysis of what the text says explicitly as well as inferences drawn from the text.
		RL.8.10	By the end of the year, read and comprehend literature, including stories, dramas, and poems, at the high end of grades 6-8 text complexity band independently ad proficiently.
475	**Connect Reading and Writing** Critical Thinking	RL.8.2	Determine a theme or central idea of a text and analyze its development over the course of the text, including its relationship to the characters, setting, and plot; provide an objective summary of the text.
	Vocabulary Review	L.8.6	Acquire and use accurately grade-appropriate general academic and domain-specific words and phrases; gather vocabulary knowledge when considering a word or phrase important to comprehension or expression.
		W.8.9	Draw evidence from literary or informational texts to support analysis, reflection, and research.
	Write About the GQ	W.8.10	Write routinely over extended time frames (time for research, reflection, and revision) and shorter time frames (a single sitting or a day or two) for a range of discipline-specific tasks, purposes, and audiences.
476	**Vocabulary Study** Use Word Origins: Borrowed Words	L.8.4	Determine or clarify the meaning of unknown and multiple-meaning words or phrases based on grade 8 reading and content, choosing flexibly from a range of strategies.
		L.8.4.c	Determine or clarify the meaning of unknown and multiple-meaning words or phrases based on grade 8 reading and content, choosing flexibly from a range of strategies. Consult general and specialized reference materials (e.g., dictionaries, glossaries, thesauruses), both print and digital, to find the pronunciation of a word or determine or clarify its precise meaning or its part of speech.
		L.8.6	Acquire and use accurately grade-appropriate general academic and domain-specific words and phrases; gather vocabulary knowledge when considering a word or phrase important to comprehension or expression.
476	**Listening and Speaking** Read a Poem Aloud	SL.8.6	Adapt speech to a variety of contexts and tasks, demonstrating command of formal English when indicated or appropriate.
477	**Language and Grammar** Tell an Original Story	SL.8.1	Engage effectively in a range of collaborative discussions (one-on-one, in groups, and teacher-led) with diverse partners on grade 8 topics, texts, and issues, building on others' ideas and expressing their own clearly.
		L.8.1.a	Demonstrate command of the conventions of standard English grammar and usage when writing or speaking. Explain the function of verbals (gerunds, participles, infinitives) in general and their function in particular sentences.
477	**Writing and Grammar** Write to Add Details to Sentences	W.8.3.d	Write narratives to develop real or imagined experiences or events using effective technique, relevant descriptive details, and well-structured event sequences. Use precise words and phrases, relevant descriptive details, and sensory language to capture the action and convey experiences and events.
		L.8.1.a	Demonstrate command of the conventions of standard English grammar and usage when writing or speaking. Explain the function of verbals (gerunds, participles, infinitives) in general and their function in particular sentences.
		L.8.2.a	Demonstrate command of the conventions of standard English capitalization, punctuation, and spelling when writing. Use punctuation (comma, ellipsis, dash) to indicate a pause or break.

Common Core State Standards, continued

Selection 2 The Constitution

Pages	Lesson	Code	Standards Text
478	**Connect**	SL.8.1	Engage effectively in a range of collaborative discussions (one-on-one, in groups, and teacher-led) with diverse partners on grade 8 topics, texts, and issues, building on others' ideas and expressing their own clearly.
		SL.8.2	Analyze the purpose of information presented in diverse media and formats (e.g., visually, quantitatively, orally) and evaluate the motives (e.g., social, commercial, political) behind its presentation.
479–481	**Language & Grammar** Summarize	RI.8.2	Determine a central idea of a text and analyze its development over the course of the text, including its relationship to supporting ideas; provide an objective summary of the text.
		SL.8.4	Present claims and findings, emphasizing salient points in a focused, coherent manner with relevant evidence, sound valid reasoning, and well-chosen details; use appropriate eye contact, adequate volume, and clear pronunciation.
	Use Participial Phrases to Combine Sentences	L.8.1.a	Demonstrate command of the conventions of standard English grammar and usage when writing or speaking. Explain the function of verbals (gerunds, participles, infinitives) in general and their function in particular sentences.
482	**Key Vocabulary**	RI.8.4	Determine the meaning of words and phrases as they are used in a text , including figurative, connotative, and technical meanings; analyze the impact of specific word choices on meaning and tone, including analogies or allusions to other texts.
		L.8.4	Determine or clarify the meaning of un-known and multiple-meaning words or phrases based on grade 8 reading and content, choosing flexibly from a range of strategies.
483	**Reading Strategy** Determine Importance **Literary Analysis** Analyze Main Idea and Details	RI.8.2	Determine a central idea of a text and analyze its development over the course of the text, including its relationship to supporting ideas; provide an objective summary of the text.
484–502	**Reading Selection**	RI.8.2	Determine a central idea of a text and analyze its development over the course of the text, including its relationship to supporting ideas; provide an objective summary of the text.
		RI.8.10	By the end of the year, read and comprehend literary nonfiction at the high end of the grades 6–8 text complexity band independently and proficiently.
503	**Connect Reading and Writing** Critical Thinking	RI.8.2	Determine a central idea of a text and analyze its development over the course of a text, including its relationship to supporting ideas; provide an objective summary of the text.
	Vocabulary Review	L.8.6	Acquire and use accurately grade-appropriate general academic and domain- specific words and phrases; gather vocabulary knowledge when considering a word or phrase important to comprehension or expression.
	Write About the GQ	W.8.9	Draw evidence from literary or informational texts to support analysis, reflection, and research.
		W.8.10	Write routinely over extended time frames (time for research, reflection, and revision) and shorter time frames (a single sitting or a day or two) for a range of discipline-specific tasks, purposes, and audiences.

Selection 2 The Constitution, continued

Pages	Lesson	Code	Standards Text
504	**Vocabulary Study** Use Word Origins: Greek, Latin, Anglo-Saxon Roots	L.8.4	Determine or clarify the meaning of unknown and multiple-meaning words or phrases based on grade 8 reading and content, choosing flexibly from a range of strategies.
		L.8.4.b	Determine or clarify the meaning of unknown and multiple-meaning words or phrases based on grade 8 reading and content, choosing flexibly from a range of strategies. Use common, grade- appropriate Greek or Latin affixes and roots as clues to the meaning of a word (e.g., *precede, recede, secede*).
		L.8.6	Acquire and use accurately grade-appropriate general academic and domain-specific words and phrases; gather vocabulary knowledge when considering a word or phrase important to comprehension or expression.
504	**Literary Analysis** Analyze Poetry: Symbols	RL.8.5	Compare and contrast the structure of two or more texts and analyze how the differing structures of each text contribute to its meaning and depth.
505	**Language and Grammar** Summarize	RI.8.2	Determine a central idea of a text and analyze its development over the course of the text, including its relationship to supporting ideas; provide an objective summary of the text.
		SL.8.4	Present claims and findings, emphasizing salient points in a focused, coherent manner with relevant evidence, sound valid reasoning, and well-chosen details; use appropriate eye contact, adequate volume, and clear pronunciation.
		L.8.1.a	Demonstrate command of the conventions of standard English grammar and usage when writing or speaking. Explain the function of verbals (gerunds, participles, infinitives) in general and their function in particular sentences.
505	**Writing and Grammar** Write to Elaborate	W.8.3.d	Write narratives to develop real or imagined experiences or events using effective technique, relevant descriptive details, and well-structured event sequences. Use precise words and phrases, relevant descriptive details, and sensory language to capture the action and convey experiences and events.
		L.8.1.a	Demonstrate command of the conventions of standard English grammar and usage when writing or speaking. Explain the function of verbals (gerunds, participles, infinitives) in general and their function in particular sentences.
		L.8.2.a	Demonstrate command of the conventions of standard English capitalization, punctuation, and spelling when writing. Use punctuation (comma, ellipsis, dash) to indicate a pause or break.

Selection 3 Kids Take Action

Pages	Lesson	Code	Standards Text
506	**Connect**	SL.8.1	Engage effectively in a range of collaborative discussions (one-on-one, in groups, and teacher-led) with diverse partners on grade 8 topics, texts, and issues, building on others' ideas and expressing their own clearly.
		SL.8.2	Analyze the purpose of information presented in diverse media and formats (e.g., visually, quantitatively, orally) and evaluate the motives (e.g., social, commercial, political) behind its presentation.
507–509	**Language & Grammar** Give and Follow Directions	SL.8.1	Engage effectively in a range of collaborative discussions (one-on-one, in groups, and teacher-led) with diverse partners on grade 8 topics, texts, and issues, building on others' ideas and expressing their own clearly.
	Use Gerunds and Infinitives	L.8.1.a	Demonstrate command of the conventions of standard English grammar and usage when writing or speaking. Explain the function of verbals (gerunds, participles, infinitives) in general and their function in particular sentences.

Common Core State Standards, continued

Selection 3 Kids Take Action, continued

Pages	Lesson	Code	Standards Text
510	**Key Vocabulary**	RI.8.4	Determine the meaning of words and phrases as they are used in a text, including figurative, connotative, and technical meanings; analyze the impact of specific word choices on meaning and tone, including analogies or allusions to other texts.
		L.8.4	Determine or clarify the meaning of un- known and multiple-meaning words or phrases based on grade 8 reading and content, choosing flexibly from a range of strategies.
511	**Reading Strategy** Determine Importance **Literary Analysis** Relate Cause and Effect	RI.8.3	Analyze how a text makes connections among and distinctions between individuals, ideas, or events (e.g., through comparisons, analogies, or categories).
512–520	**Reading Selection**	RI.8.10	By the end of the year, read and comprehend literary nonfiction at the high end of the grades 6–8 text complexity band independently and proficiently.
521	**Connect Reading and Writing** Critical Thinking	RI.8.2	Determine a central idea of a text and analyze its development over the course of the text, including its relationship to supporting ideas; provide an objective summary of the text.
	Vocabulary Review	L.8.6	Acquire and use accurately grade-appropriate general academic and domain-specific words and phrases; gather vocabulary knowledge when considering a word or phrase important to comprehension or expression.
	Write About the GQ	W.8.9	Draw evidence from literary or informational texts to support analysis, reflection, and research.
		W.8.10	Write routinely over extended time frames (time for research, reflection, and revision) and shorter time frames (a single sitting or a day or two) for a range of discipline-specific tasks, purposes, and audiences.
522	**Vocabulary Study** Use Word Origins: Greek and Latin Mythology	RI.8.4	Determine the meaning of words and phrases as they are used in a text, including figurative, connotative, and technical meanings; analyze the impact of specific word choices on meaning and tone, including analogies or allusions to other texts.
522	**Writing/Speaking** Give an Informative Speech	SL.8.4	Present claims and findings, emphasizing salient points in a focused, coherent manner with relevant evidence, sound valid reasoning, and well-chosen details; use appropriate eye contact, adequate volume, and clear pronunciation.
523	**Language and Grammar** Give and Follow Directions	SL.8.1	Engage effectively in a range of collaborative discussions (one-on-one, in groups, and teacher-led) with diverse partners on grade 8 topics, texts, and issues, building on others' ideas and expressing their own clearly.
		L.8.1.a	Demonstrate command of the conventions of standard English grammar and usage when writing or speaking. Explain the function of verbals (gerunds, participles, infinitives) in general and their function in particular sentences.
523	**Writing and Grammar** Write to Be Concise	W.8.3.d	Write narratives to develop real or imagined experiences or events using effective technique, relevant descriptive details, and well-structured event sequences. Use precise words and phrases, relevant descriptive details, and sensory language to capture the action and convey experiences and events.
		L.8.1.a	Demonstrate command of the conventions of standard English grammar and usage when writing or speaking. Explain the function of verbals (gerunds, participles, infinitives) in general and their function in particular sentences.
524–525	**Close Reading**	RI.8.10	By the end of the year, read and comprehend literary nonfiction at the high end of the grades 6–8 text complexity band independently and proficiently.

Compare Across Texts

Pages	Lesson	Code	Standards Text
526	Compare Text Structures	RL.8.5	Compare and contrast the structure of two or more texts and analyze how the differing structure of each text contributes to its meaning and style.
		SL.8.1	Engage effectively in a range of collaborative discussions (one-on-one, in groups, and teacher-led) with diverse partners on grade 8 topics, texts, and issues, building on others' ideas and expressing their own clearly

Unit Wrap-Up

Pages	Lesson	Code	Standards Text
527	Reflect on Your Reading	RL.8.2	Determine a theme or central idea of a text and analyze its development over the course of a text, including its relationship to the characters, setting and plot; provide an objective summary of the text.
		RL.8.5	Compare and contrast the structure of two or more texts and analyze how the differing structure of each text contributes to its meaning and style.
		RI.8.2	Determine a central idea of a text and analyze its development over the course of a text, including its relationship to supporting ideas; provide an objective summary of the text.
	Explore the GQ/Book Talk	W.8.10	Write routinely over extended time frames (time for research, reflection, and revision) and shorter time frames (a single sitting or a day or two) for a range of discipline-specific tasks, purposes, and audiences.
		SL.8.1	Engage effectively in a range of collaborative discussions (one-on-one, in groups, and teacher-led) with diverse partners on grade 8 topics, texts, and issues, building on others' ideas and expressing their own clearly.
		SL.8.1.a	Engage effectively in a range of collaborative discussions (one-on-one, in groups, and teacher-led) with diverse partners on grade 8 topics, texts, and issues, building on others' ideas and expressing their own clearly.
			Come to discussions prepared, having read or researched material under study; explicitly draw on that preparation by referring to evidence on a topic, text, or issue to probe and reflect on ideas under discussion.
		SL.8.5	Integrate multimedia and visual displays into presentations to clarify information, strengthen claims and evidence, and add interest.

Unit 8   Food for Thought

Unit Launch

Pages	Lesson	Code	Standards Text
528–529	Unit Opener	SL.8.1	Engage effectively in a range of collaborative discussions (one-on-one, in groups, and teacher-led) with diverse partners on grade 8 topics, texts, and issues, building on others' ideas and expressing their own clearly.
530–531	Focus on Reading Evaluate Argument	RI.8.8	Delineate and evaluate the argument and specific claims in a text, assessing whether the reasoning is sound and the evidence is relevant and sufficient; recognize when irrelevant evidence is introduced.

Common Core State Standards, continued

Unit Launch, continued

Pages	Lesson	Code	Standards Text
532–533 **Focus on Vocabulary** Use Context Clues and References		RI.8.4	Determine the meaning of words and phrases as they are used in a text, including figurative, connotative, and technical meanings; analyze the impact of specific word choices on meaning and tone, including analogies or allusions to other texts.
		L.8.4.a	Determine or clarify the meaning of unknown and multiple-meaning words or phrases based on grade 8 reading and content, choosing flexibly from a range of strategies. Use context (e.g., the overall meaning of a sentence or paragraph; a word's position or function in a sentence) as a clue to the meaning of a word or phrase.
		L.8.4.c	Determine or clarify the meaning of unknown and multiple-meaning words or phrases based on grade 8 reading and content, choosing flexibly from a range of strategies. Consult general and specialized reference materials (e.g., dictionaries, glossaries, thesauruses), both print and digital, to find the pronunciation of a word or determine or clarify its precise meaning or its part of speech.
		L.8.4.d	Determine or clarify the meaning of unknown and multiple-meaning words or phrases based on grade 8 reading and content, choosing flexibly from a range of strategies. Verify the preliminary determination of the meaning of a word or phrase (e.g., by checking the inferred meaning in context or in a dictionary).
		L.8.6	Acquire and use accurately grade-appropriate general academic and domain-specific words and phrases; gather vocabulary knowledge when considering a word or phrase important to comprehension or expression.

Selection 1 Feeding the World

Pages	Lesson	Code	Standards Text
534 **Connect**		SL.8.1	Engage effectively in a range of collaborative discussions (one-on-one, in groups, and teacher-led) with diverse partners on grade 8 topics, texts, and issues, building on others' ideas and expressing their own clearly.
		SL.8.2	Analyze the purpose of information presented in diverse media and formats (e.g., visually, quantitatively, orally) and evaluate the motives (e.g., social, commercial, political) behind its presentation.
535–537 **Language & Grammar** Persuade		SL.8.3	Delineate a speaker's argument and specific claims, evaluating the soundness of the reasoning and relevance and sufficiency of the evidence and identifying when irrelevant evidence is introduced.
		SL.8.4	Present claims and findings, emphasizing salient points in a focused, coherent manner with relevant evidence, sound valid reasoning, and well-chosen details; use appropriate eye contact, adequate volume, and clear pronunciation.
Use Verbs in the Present, Perfect Tense		L.8.1.c	Demonstrate command of the conventions of standard English grammar and usage when writing or speaking. Form and use verbs in the indicative, imperative, interrogative, conditional, and subjunctive moods.
538 **Key Vocabulary**		RI.8.4	Determine the meaning of words and phrases as they are used in a text, including figurative, connotative, and technical meanings; analyze the impact of specific word choices on meaning and tone, including analogies or allusions to other texts.
		L.8.4	Determine or clarify the meaning of unknown and multiple-meaning words or phrases based on grade 8 reading and content, choosing flexibly from a range of strategies.
539 **Reading Strategy** Synthesize **Literary Analysis** Analyze Argument and Support		RI.8.8	Delineate and evaluate the argument and specific claims in a text, assessing whether the reasoning is sound and the evidence is relevant and sufficient; recognize when irrelevant evidence is introduced.

Selection 1 Feeding the World, continued

Pages	Lesson	Code	Standards Text
540–548	**Reading Selection**	RL.8.1	Cite the textual evidence that most strongly supports an analysis of what the text says explicitly as well as inferences drawn from the text.
		RI.8.1	Cite the textual evidence that most strongly supports an analysis of what the text says explicitly as well as inferences drawn from the text.
		RI.8.10	By the end of the year, read and comprehend literary nonfiction at the high end of the grades 6–8 text complexity band independently and proficiently.
549	**Connect Reading and Writing** Critical Thinking	RI.8.1	Cite the textual evidence that most strongly supports an analysis of what the text says explicitly as well as inferences drawn from the text.
		RI.8.2	Determine a central idea of a text and analyze its development over the course of the text, including its relationship to supporting ideas; provide an objective summary of the text.
	Vocabulary Review	L.8.6	Acquire and use accurately grade-appropriate general academic and domain- specific words and phrases; gather vocabulary knowledge when considering a word or phrase important to comprehension or expression.
	Write About the GQ	W.8.9	Draw evidence from literary or informational texts to support analysis, reflection, and research.
		W.8.10	Write routinely over extended time frames (time for research, reflection, and revision) and shorter time frames (a single sitting or a day or two) for a range of discipline-specific tasks, purposes, and audiences.
550	**Vocabulary Study** Use Context Clues: Technical Vocabulary	RI.8.4	Determine the meaning of words and phrases as they are used in a text, including figurative, connotative, and technical meanings; analyze the impact of specific word choices on meaning and tone, including analogies or allusions to other texts.
		L.8.4	Determine or clarify the meaning of unknown and multiple-meaning words or phrases based on grade 8 reading and content, choosing flexibly from a range of strategies.
		L.8.4.a	Determine or clarify the meaning of unknown and multiple-meaning words or phrases based on grade 8 reading and content, choosing flexibly from a range of strategies. Use context (e.g., the overall meaning of a sentence or paragraph; a word's position or function in a sentence) as a clue to the meaning of a word or phrase.
		L.8.6	Acquire and use accurately grade-appropriate general academic and domain-specific words and phrases; gather vocabulary knowledge when considering a word or phrase important to comprehension or expression.
550	**Literary Analysis** Identify Propaganda	RI.8.8	Delineate and evaluate the argument and specific claims in a text, assessing whether the reasoning is sound and the evidence is relevant and sufficient; recognize when irrelevant evidence is introduced.
		SL.8.2	Analyze the purpose of information presented in diverse media and formats (e.g., visually, quantitatively, orally) and evaluate the motives (e.g., social, commercial, political) behind its presentation.

Common Core State Standards, continued

Selection 1 Feeding the World, continued

Pages	Lesson	Code	Standards Text
551	**Language and Grammar** Persuade	SL.8.3	Delineate a speaker's argument and specific claims, evaluating the soundness of the reasoning and relevance and sufficiency of the evidence and identifying when irrelevant evidence is introduced.
		SL.8.4	Present claims and findings, emphasizing salient points in a focused, coherent manner with relevant evidence, sound valid reasoning, and well-chosen details; use appropriate eye contact, adequate volume, and clear pronunciation.
		L.8.1.c	Demonstrate command of the conventions of standard English grammar and usage when writing or speaking. Form and use verbs in the indicative, imperative, interrogative, conditional, and subjunctive moods.
551	**Writing and Grammar** Write Effectively About Events	W.8.3.d	Write narratives to develop real or imagined experiences or events using effective technique, relevant descriptive details, and well-structured event sequences. Use precise words and phrases, relevant descriptive details, and sensory language to capture the action and convey experiences and events.
		L.8.1.c	Demonstrate command of the conventions of standard English grammar and usage when writing or speaking. Form and use verbs in the indicative, imperative, interrogative, conditional, and subjunctive moods.

Selection 2 Soup for the Soul

Pages	Lesson	Code	Standards Text
552	**Connect**	SL.8.1	Engage effectively in a range of collaborative discussions (one-on-one, in groups, and teacher-led) with diverse partners on grade 8 topics, texts, and issues, building on others' ideas and expressing their own clearly.
		SL.8.2	Analyze the purpose of information presented in diverse media and formats (e.g., visually, quantitatively, orally) and evaluate the motives (e.g., social, commercial, political) behind its presentation.
553–555	**Language & Grammar** Negotiate	SL.8.1.d	Engage effectively in a range of collaborative discussions (one-on-one, in groups, and teacher-led) with diverse partners on grade 8 topics, texts, and issues, building on others' ideas and expressing their own clearly. Acknowledge new information expressed by others, and, when warranted, qualify or justify their own views in light of the evidence presented.
		SL.8.4	Present claims and findings, emphasizing salient points in a focused, coherent manner with relevant details; use appropriate eye contact, adequate volume, and clear pronunciation.
		SL.8.6	Adapt speech to a variety of contexts and tasks, demonstrating command of formal English when indicated or appropriate.
	Use Verbs in the Past Perfect Tense	L.8.1.c	Demonstrate command of the conventions of standard English grammar and usage when writing or speaking. Form and use verbs in the indicative, imperative, interrogative, conditional, and subjunctive moods.
556	**Key Vocabulary**	RI.8.4	Determine the meaning of words and phrases as they are used in a text, including figurative, connotative, and technical meanings; analyze the impact of specific word choices on meaning and tone, including analogies and allusions to other texts.
		L.8.4	Determine or clarify the meaning of unknown and multiple-meaning words or phrases based on grade 8 reading and content, choosing flexibly from a range of strategies.

Selection 2 Soup for the Soul, continued

Pages	Lesson	Code	Standards Text
557	**Reading Strategy** Synthesize **Literary Analysis** Compare Writing About the Same Topic	RI.8.9	Analyze a case in which two or more texts provide conflicting information on the same topic and identify where the texts disagree on matters of fact or interpretation.
558–566	**Reading Selection**	RI.8.1	Cite the textual evidence that most strongly supports an analysis of what the text says explicitly as well as inferences drawn from the text.
		RI.8.3	Analyze how a text makes connections among and distinctions between individuals, ideas, or events (e.g., through comparisons, analogies, or categories
		RI.8.10	By the end of the year, read and comprehend literary nonfiction at the high end of the grades 6–8 text complexity band independently and proficiently.
567	**Connect Reading and Writing** Critical Thinking	RI.8.2	Determine a central idea of a text and analyze its development over the course of a text, including its relationship to supporting ideas; provide an objective summary of the text.
	Vocabulary Review	L.8.6	Acquire and use accurately grade-appropriate general academic and domain-specific words and phrases; gather vocabulary knowledge when considering a word or phrase important to comprehension or expression.
	Write About the GQ	W.8.9	Draw evidence from literary or informational texts to support analysis, reflection, and research.
		W.8.10	Write routinely over extended time frames (time for research, reflection, and revision) and shorter time frames (a single sitting or a day or two) for a range of discipline-specific tasks, purposes, and audiences.
568	**Vocabulary Study** Use Context Clues: Jargon	RI.8.4	Determine the meaning of words or phrases as they are used in a text, including figurative, connotative, and technical meanings; analyze the impact of specific word choices on meaning and tone, including analogies or allusions to other texts.
		L.8.4	Determine or clarify the meaning of unknown and multiple-meaning words or phrases based on grade 8 reading and content, choosing flexibly from a range of strategies.
		L.8.4.a	Determine or clarify the meaning of unknown and multiple-meaning words or phrases based on grade 8 reading and content, choosing flexibly from a range of strategies. Use context (e.g., the overall meaning of a sentence or paragraph; a word's position or function in a sentence) as a clue to the meaning of a word or phrase.
		L.8.6	Acquire and use accurately grade-appropriate general academic and domain-specific words and phrases; gather vocabulary knowledge when considering a word or phrase important to comprehension or expression.
568	**Literary Analysis** Analyze Persuasive Language	RI.8.4	Determine the meaning of words or phrases as they are used in a text, including figurative, connotative, and technical meanings; analyze the impact of specific word choices on meaning and tone, including analogies or allusions to other texts.

Common Core State Standards, continued

Selection 2 Soup for the Soul, continued

Pages	Lesson	Code	Standards Text
569	**Language and Grammar** Negotiate	SL.8.1.d	Engage effectively in a range of collaborative discussions (one-on-one, in groups, and teacher-led) with diverse partners on grade 8 topics, texts, and issues, building on others' ideas and expressing their own clearly. Acknowledge new information expressed by others, and, when warranted, qualify or justify their own views in light of the evidence presented.
		SL.8.4	Present claims and findings, emphasizing salient points in a focused, coherent manner with relevant details; use appropriate eye contact, adequate volume, and clear pronunciation.
		SL.8.6	Adapt speech to a variety of contexts and tasks, demonstrating command of formal English when indicated or appropriate.
		L.8.1.c	Demonstrate command of the conventions of standard English grammar and usage when writing or speaking. Form and use verbs in the indicative, imperative, interrogative, conditional, and subjunctive moods.
569	**Writing and Grammar** Write About Helping Others	W.8.3.d	Write narratives to develop real or imagined experiences or events using effective technique, relevant descriptive details, and well-structured event sequences. Use precise words and phrases, relevant descriptive details, and sensory language to capture the action and convey experiences and events.
		L.8.1.c	Demonstrate command of the conventions of standard English grammar and usage when writing or speaking. Form and use verbs in the indicative, imperative, interrogative, conditional, and subjunctive moods.

Selection 3 The Girl and the Chenoo

Pages	Lesson	Code	Standards Text
570	**Connect**	SL.8.1	Engage effectively in a range of collaborative discussions (one-on-one, in groups, and teacher-led) with diverse partners on grade 8 topics, texts, and issues, building on others' ideas and expressing their own clearly.
		SL.8.2	Analyze the purpose of information presented in diverse media and formats (e.g., visually, quantitatively, orally) and evaluate the motives (e.g., social, commercial, political) behind its presentation.
571–573	**Language & Grammar** Use Appropriate Language Use Conditionals	SL.8.6	Adapt speech to a variety of contexts and tasks, demonstrating command of formal English when indicated or appropriate.
		L.8.1.c	Demonstrate command of the conventions of standard English grammar and usage when writing or speaking. Form and use verbs in the indicative, imperative, interrogative, conditional, and subjunctive moods.
		L.8.2.a	Demonstrate command of the conventions of standard English capitalization, punctuation, and spelling when writing. Use punctuation (comma, ellipsis, dash) to indicate a pause or break.
		L.8.3.a	Use knowledge of language and its conventions when writing, speaking, reading, or listening. Use verbs in the active and passive voice and in the conditional and subjunctive mood to achieve particular effects (e.g., emphasizing the actor or the action; expressing uncertainly, or describing a state contrary to fact).

Selection 3 The Girl and the Chenoo, continued

Pages	Lesson	Code	Standards Text
574	**Key Vocabulary**	RL.8.4	Determine the meaning of words and phrases as they are used in a text, including figurative and connotative meanings; analyze the impact of specific word choices on meaning and tone, including analogies or allusions to other texts.
		L.8.4	Determine or clarify the meaning of unknown and multiple-meaning words or phrases based on grade 8 reading and content, choosing flexibly from a range of strategies.
575	**Reading Strategy** Synthesize **Literary Analysis** Analyze Drama	RL.8.1	Cite the textual evidence that most strongly supports an analysis of what the text says explicitly as well as inferences drawn from the text.
576–596	**Reading Selection**	RL.8.10	By the end of the year, read and comprehend literature, including stories, dramas, and poems, at the high end of grades 6–8 text complexity band independently and proficiently.
597	**Connect Reading and Writing** Critical Thinking	RL.8.2	Determine a theme or central idea of a text and analyze its development over the course of the text, including its relationship to the characters, setting and plot; provide an objective summary of the text.
	Vocabulary Review	L.8.6	Acquire and use accurately grade-appropriate general academic and domain-specific words and phrases; gather vocabulary knowledge when considering a word or phrase important to comprehension or expression.
	Write About the GQ	W.8.9	Draw evidence from literary or informational texts to support analysis, reflection, and research.
		W.8.10	Write routinely over extended time frames (time for research, reflection, and revision) and shorter time frames (a single sitting or a day or two) for a range of discipline-specific tasks, purposes, and audiences.
598	**Vocabulary Study** Use Context Clues: Specialized Language	L.8.4	Determine or clarify the meaning of unknown and multiple-meaning words or phrases based on grade 8 reading and content, choosing flexibly from a range of strategies.
		L.8.4.a	Determine or clarify the meaning of unknown and multiple-meaning words or phrases based on grade 8 reading and content, choosing flexibly from a range of strategies. Use context (e.g., the overall meaning of a sentence or paragraph; a word's position or function in a sentence) as a clue to the meaning of a word or phrase.
		L.8.4.d	Determine or clarify the meaning of unknown and multiple-meaning words or phrases based on grade 8 reading and content, choosing flexibly from a range of strategies. Verify the preliminary determination of the meaning of a word or phrase (e.g., by checking the inferred meaning in context or in a dictionary).
		L.8.6	Acquire and use accurately grade-appropriate general academic and domain-specific words and phrases; gather vocabulary knowledge when considering a word or phrase important to comprehension or expression.
598	**Listening/Speaking** Analyze Live Performance	RL.8.7	Analyze the extent to which a filmed or live production of a story or drama stays faithful to or departs from the text or script, evaluating the choices made by the director or actors.
		SL.8.1.a	Engage effectively in a range of collaborative discussions (one-on-one, in groups, and teacher-led) with diverse partners on grade 8 topics, texts, and issues, building on others' ideas and expressing their own clearly. Come to discussions prepared, having read or researched material under study; explicitly draw on that preparation by referring to evidence on the topic, text, or issue to probe and reflect on ideas under discussion.

Common Core State Standards, continued

Selection 3 The Girl and the Chenoo, continued

Pages	Lesson	Code	Standards Text
599	**Language and Grammar** Use Appropriate Language	SL.8.6	Adapt speech to a variety of contexts and tasks, demonstrating command of formal English when indicated or appropriate.
		L.8.1.c	Demonstrate command of the conventions of standard English grammar and usage when writing or speaking. Form and use verbs in the indicative, imperative, interrogative, conditional, and subjunctive moods.
		L.8.3.a	Use knowledge of language and its conventions when writing, speaking, reading, or listening. Use verbs in the active and passive voice and in the conditional and subjunctive mood to achieve particular effects (e.g., emphasizing the actor or the action; expressing uncertainty, or describing a state contrary to fact.
599	**Writing and Grammar** Write About a Memory	W.8.3.d	Write narratives to develop real or imagined experiences or events using effective technique, relevant descriptive details, and well-structured event sequences. Use precise words and phrases, relevant descriptive details, and sensory language to capture the action and convey experiences and events.
		L.8.1.c	Demonstrate command of the conventions of standard English grammar and usage when writing or speaking. Form and use verbs in the indicative, imperative, interrogative, conditional, and subjunctive moods.
		L.8.3.a	Use knowledge of language and its conventions when writing, speaking, reading, or listening. Use verbs in the active and passive voice and in the conditional and subjunctive mood to achieve particular effects (e.g., emphasizing the actor or the action; expressing uncertainty, or describing a state contrary to fact.
600–603	**Close Reading**	RI.8.10	By the end of the year, read and comprehend literary nonfiction at the high end of the grades 6–8 text complexity band independently and proficiently.

Compare Across Texts

Pages	Lesson	Code	Standards Text
604	**Compare Persuasive Texts**	RI.8.9	Analyze a case in which two or more texts provide conflicting information on the same topic and identify where the texts disagree on matters of fact or interpretation.
		SL.8.1	Engage effectively in a range of collaborative discussions (one-on-one, in groups, and teacher-led) with diverse partners on grade 8 topics, texts, and issues, building on others' ideas and expressing their own clearly.

Unit Wrap-Up

Pages	Lesson	Code	Standards Text
605	Reflect on Your Reading	RL.8.10	By end of the year, read and comprehend literature, including stories, dramas, and poems, at the high end of grades 6-8 text complexity band independently and proficiently.
		RI.8.8	Delineate and evaluate the argument and specific claims in a text, assessing whether the reasoning is sound and the evidence is relevant and sufficient; recognize when irrelevant evidence is introduced.
		RI.8.9	Analyze a case in which two or more texts provide conflicting information on the same topic and identify where the texts disagree on matters of fact or interpretation.
		RI.8.10	By end of the year, read and comprehend literary nonfiction at the high end of the grades 6-8 text complexity band independently and proficiently.
		L.8.4	Determine or clarify the meaning of unknown and multiple-meaning words or phrases based on grade 8 reading and content, choosing flexibly from a range of strategies.
	Explore the GQ/Book Talk	W.8.10	Write routinely over extended time frames (time for research, reflection, and revision) and shorter time frames (a single sitting or a day or two) for a range of discipline- specific tasks, purposes, and audiences.
		SL.8.1	Engage effectively in a range of collaborative discussions (one-on-one, in groups, and teacher-led) with diverse partners on grade 8 topics, texts, and issues, building on others' ideas and expressing their own clearly.
		SL.8.1.a	Engage effectively in a range of collaborative discussions (one-on-one, in groups, and teacher-led) with diverse partners on grade 8 topics, texts, and issues, building on others' ideas and expressing their own clearly. Come to discussions prepared, having read or researched material under study; explicitly draw on that preparation by referring to evidence on the topic, text, or issue to probe and reflect on ideas under discussion.

Reading Handbook

Pages	Lesson	Code	Standards Text
607–610	Plan and Monitor	RL.8.1	Cite the textual evidence that most strongly supports an analysis of what the text says explicitly as well as inferences drawn from the text.
		RL.8.10	By the end of the year, read and comprehend literature, including stories, dramas, and poems, at the high end of grades 6-8 text complexity band independently and proficiently.
		RI.8.1	Cite the textual evidence that most strongly supports an analysis of what the text says explicitly as well as inferences drawn from text.
		RI.8.10	By the end of the year, read and comprehend literary nonfiction at the high end of the grades 6-8 text complexity band independently and proficiently.
611–612	Determine Importance	RI.8.1	Cite the textual evidence that most strongly supports an analysis of what the text says explicitly as well as inferences drawn from text.
		RI.8.2	Determine a central idea of a text and analyze its development over the course of the text, including its relationship to supporting ideas; provide an objective summary of the text.
613	Make Connections	RL.8.1	Cite the textual evidence that most strongly supports an analysis of what the text says explicitly as well as inferences drawn from the text.
		RI.8.1	Cite the textual evidence that most strongly supports an analysis of what the text says explicitly as well as inferences drawn from text.
614–615	Make Inferences	RL.8.1	Cite the textual evidence that most strongly supports an analysis of what the text says explicitly as well as inferences drawn from the text.

Common Core State Standards, continued